Entrepreneurship and Small Business

Start-up, growth and maturity

Fourth edition

PAUL BURNS

Emeritus Professor of Entrepreneurship,
University of Bedfordshire, UK

palgrave

First edition 2001
Reprinted 8 times
Second edition 2007
Reprinted 4 times
Third edition 2011
Reprinted 9 times
This edition 2016

Published by
PALGRAVE

Palgrave in the UK is an imprint of Macmillan Publishers Limited, registered in England, company number 785998, of 4 Crinan Street, London, N1 9XW.

Palgrave Macmillan in the US is a division of St Martin's Press LLC, 175 Fifth Avenue, New York, NY 10010.

Palgrave is a global imprint of the above companies and is represented throughout the world.

Palgrave® and Macmillan® are registered trademarks in the United States, the United Kingdom, Europe and other countries.

ISBN 978–1–137–43035–9

This book is printed on paper suitable for recycling and made from fully managed and sustained forest sources. Logging, pulping and manufacturing processes are expected to conform to the environmental regulations of the country of origin.

A catalogue record for this book is available from the British Library.

Library of Congress Cataloging-in-Publication Data

Names: Burns, Paul, 1949- author.
Title: Entrepreneurship and small business : start-up, growth and maturity / Paul Burns.
Description: Fourth edition. | New York : Palgrave Macmillan, 2016. | Revised edition of the author's Entrepreneurship and small business, 2011. | Includes index.
Identifiers: LCCN 2015044424 | ISBN 9781137430359 (paperback)
Subjects: LCSH: Entrepreneurship—Study and teaching. | Business education. | Small business—Case studies. | Entrepreneurship—Case studies. | BISAC: BUSINESS & ECONOMICS / Entrepreneurship. | BUSINESS & ECONOMICS / Management. | BUSINESS & ECONOMICS / Small Business.
Classification: LCC HD2341 .B873 2016 | DDC 658.02/2—dc23
LC record available at http://lccn.loc.gov/2015044424

Printed in China

"This text is well structured, following the life cycle of small business start-up, growth and maturity. It is highly engaging and has a comprehensive coverage of key topics in start-up entrepreneurship. Its practical approach provides useful guidance to students, and the cases and videos are valuable resources for lecturers."

—Catherine Wang, Royal Holloway, University of London, UK

"Yet another masterpiece by Paul Burns. The book touches on contemporary issues in the field of entrepreneurship and it does so by bringing in the contexts of both advanced and developing economies. It covers key concepts from business idea, start-up to growth and maturity in a unique fashion. The cases it uses to illustrate this will make it easier for students to assimilate entrepreneurship-related concepts while stimulating debate."

—Amon Simba, Nottingham Trent University, UK

"After nearly 25 years in business and almost 16 years teaching the subject, this must rank as one of the most comprehensive books in the area of entrepreneurship and small business management that I have come across. It covers a wide array of very pertinent topics and should leave the reader with a thorough understanding as well as a useful set of tools and techniques to succeed in modern day business."

—Shafeek Sha, Rhodes University, South Africa

"*Entrepreneurship and Small Business* is yet another superb book authored by Professor Paul Burns. I hesitate to refer to this as a "textbook" as I believe one of its great strengths lies in its utility to a variety of audiences including students, aspiring entrepreneurs and those already immersed in start-ups and new ventures. The text is structured perfectly insofar as it seeks to progress the reader from an understanding of entrepreneurship and its role as an engine of economic growth, through to ideation, start-up, growth and maturity. Far too many texts focus on the very earliest stages of entrepreneurial ventures and ignore the pitfalls of developing a *sustainable* small business. Professor Burns has again brought to bear an inimitable writing style that effectively conveys vital information in a highly readable format. Case insights and practice insights are summarized appropriately for ease of reference and are used to illustrate and clarify key points in the preceding content, with focused accompanying questions which serve to reinforce imortant learning objectives. Clearly, acknowledging the international nature of entrepreneurship, Professor Burns draws on exemplars from around the globe and includes a variety of industry sectors to illustrate specific and important issues that entrepreneurs are confronted with as their businesses are born, develop, thrive and, unfortunately sometimes fail.

It is an exceptional treatise that I fully expect to use in my teaching, not only for undergraduate and graduate level students, but also as I mentor those involved in development stage small businesses."

—Zahed Subhan, Drexel University, USA

"A very relevant and practical handbook to inspire students in their entrepreneurial journey. Explanation on entrepreneurship theories is clear and thought provoking, to encourage discussions among the students and instructors. The best part is that it has many cases and insights from all over the world; I will enjoy sharing these stories with my students!"

—Poh Yen Ng, Dubai Men's College, United Arab Emirates

To Jean
My love and my inspiration

Contents overview

Contents

Index of case insights

List of figures and tables

TABLES

ABOUT THE AUTHOR

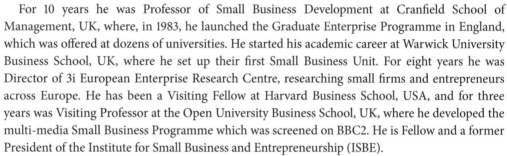

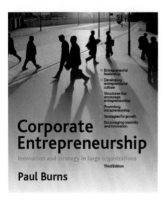

Paul Burns is Emeritus Professor of Entrepreneurship at the University of Bedfordshire Business School, UK. He has been Pro Vice Chancellor and for 10 years was Dean of the Business School, stepping down in 2011. Over his 40-year career he has been an academic, an accountant and an entrepreneur – giving him unrivalled academic and practical insight into the entrepreneurial process. As well as launching and running his own business, he has helped develop hundreds of business plans and has worked with entrepreneurs, small firms and their advisors, helping launch successful businesses.

For 10 years he was Professor of Small Business Development at Cranfield School of Management, UK, where, in 1983, he launched the Graduate Enterprise Programme in England, which was offered at dozens of universities. He started his academic career at Warwick University Business School, UK, where he set up their first Small Business Unit. For eight years he was Director of 3i European Enterprise Research Centre, researching small firms and entrepreneurs across Europe. He has been a Visiting Fellow at Harvard Business School, USA, and for three years was Visiting Professor at the Open University Business School, UK, where he developed the multi-media Small Business Programme which was screened on BBC2. He is Fellow and a former President of the Institute for Small Business and Entrepreneurship (ISBE).

Paul qualified as a Chartered Accountant with Arthur Andersen & Co., where he worked with many growing businesses. He launched and ran his own business, Design for Learning Ltd., advising and training on entrepreneurship and growing firms where he worked with organizations such as the accounting firms Grant Thornton and BDO Stoy Hayward, venture capitalists 3i, and banks such as the Royal Bank of Scotland, Barclays and Lloyds. He has advised and consulted at various levels of government in the UK and overseas, and Margaret Thatcher wrote the forward to one of his books, *Entrepreneur: Eight British success stories of the eighties* (Macmillan, 1988).

He has authored dozens of books and hundreds of journal articles and research reports. His last textbook, *New Venture Creation: A framework for entrepreneurial start-ups* (Palgrave Macmillan) was published in 2014. This sets out a comprehensive framework to help students through the whole process of new venture creation, including finding a business idea, developing a value proposition for customers and refining a business model that can be developed into a professional business plan. It has been praised as 'the go-to-guide when it comes to new venture creation' that is 'bound to ensure that this book becomes a core text for new venture creation modules'.

Corporate Entrepreneurship: Innovation and strategy in large organizations (Palgrave Macmillan) was first published in 2005. The third edition, published in 2013, was praised as a 'definitive guide' that 'combines a profound understanding of theory with practical guidance'. It shows how strategies for encouraging entrepreneurship and innovation might be embedded in larger organizations through the concept of 'architecture' – leadership, culture and structure.

ACKNOWLEDGEMENTS

Author's acknowledgements

I would like to thank all those who have helped me with this book, including the students and staff who inspired me to write it. Particular thanks go to Niki Jayatunga at Palgrave, and the (anonymous) reviewers from around the world for their pertinent comments and suggestions.

My thanks go to Rachel Taylor for permission to use her business plan for One Day, and to Tahseen Arshi at Majan College, Oman, for permission to use his two Case insights: Sadaf Gallery and Ice Cream Mama.

My wife, Jean, helps me with all my books, providing inspiration and insights. She is an invaluable sounding board for new ideas and is my rock when things go wrong. She also patiently helps with much-needed proofreading. Any errors or omissions, however, remain my own.

The publisher and author are grateful to all those who have provided third-party material for this book. All credit lines appear on the page next to the material in question.

PREFACE TO THE FOURTH EDITION

Entrepreneurship and Small Business has been the market-leading textbook on entrepreneurship in the UK for over a decade. Its strength comes from its ability to blend the theory and practice of entrepreneurship, reflecting the background of the author as entrepreneur, advisor and academic. The major strengths of the book have been retained in the fourth edition:

> The unique breadth of coverage which allows a holistic approach to the issues facing the entrepreneurial organization as it grows;
> The way it synthesizes theory and research with practice, using Case insights and quotes from entrepreneurs in the real world;
> The engaging style that makes the book so accessible and easily understood by students, without sacrificing its academic content.

This fourth edition has been completely rewritten and updated. It has grown in size – again. New features include:

> More *Case insights* with a broader international coverage – over 150 Case insights into organizations from 17 countries around the world, including the UK, USA, India, China as well as Europe, Asia and the Gulf;
> New *Practice insights* that provide tips on how to get things done or access additional resources;

> New chapters on the economics of entrepreneurship and public policy as well as operations and risk;
> Integration of social and civic entrepreneurship with the main body of the book, so that it is no longer treated as an entirely separate organizational form;
> Extended coverage of values and ethics, corporate social responsibility, sustainable entrepreneurship and entrepreneurial philanthropy;
> Greater focus on internet and e-commerce businesses both in the text and the Case insights;
> Improved coverage of lean start-ups and the opportunities provided for this by the internet;
> Improved online learning resources that include an instructors' manual, PowerPoint slides and 'Meet the Entrepreneur' video case studies as well as an interactive ebook format of the book.

Keeping up to date is a challenge in any text that sets out to be practical and current. This is achieved by the extensive signposting to websites that offer up-to-date information about organizations that feature in the Case insights as well as those offering practical help and advice.

I would like to thank all those academic colleagues who continue to recommend the book and those who have suggested improvements. I hope I have met your expectations with this fourth edition.

Meet the author and hear about his own experiences as both an academic and entrepreneur by clicking on the play button in your ebook.

HOW TO USE THE BOOK

This book is written for a range of undergraduate and postgraduate courses, with the aim of developing an understanding of entrepreneurship as well as fostering entrepreneurial talent and developing entrepreneurial skills. It is supported by an interactive ebook and further online teaching and learning resources.

What the book aims to do

The book blends the practice and the theory of entrepreneurship with up-to-date research. It looks at many different forms of entrepreneurship, including social, civic, sustainable and philanthropic. It covers the process of entrepreneurship from start-up, growth and through to maturity. It looks at the links with innovation and economic growth as well as public policy towards entrepreneurship. Concepts and theories do not have to be complicated, and the engaging, accessible style of the book makes it easy to understand.

The book is also practical. It contains Practice insights – tips and advice about how to do things as well as signposts to where resources can be found. Entrepreneurship is a risky activity and anything you can do to reduce the risk of failure must be good. So, students can learn from the successes and mistakes of other entrepreneurs. This book contains over 150 Case insights into organizations from 17 countries around the world. There are also numerous quotes from entrepreneurs, reinforcing the theory and research. The research outlined in the book tells students which tips have the best chance of working (and which do not) and theory tells them why they might work. The Case insights show them how they work.

Who the book is aimed at

The book can be used as a specialist text on entrepreneurship for both undergraduate and postgraduate courses such as a MBA. While entrepreneurship is recognized as a topic in its own right, for students who have previously studied business and management, an entrepreneurship course typically aims to integrate and apply most of the functional areas they have previously studied and give it a creative and practical focus. This helps them better see the interconnections in the topics they have already studied and realize that the solutions to real business problems require the application of all the areas they have studied. For these students, the case studies are particularly important, while some of the chapters that cover the 'basics' of business can be skimmed over.

The book can also be used as a comprehensive core text for an 'introduction to business' course, albeit with an entrepreneurial focus. It covers core areas such as management, strategy, marketing, accounting and finance. However, rather than teach the subject in subject-based compartments, relevant chapters are designed to act as a holistic introduction to the topic of business studies in the practical context of a business start-up and growth. Again, students can better see the interconnections and realize that solutions to real business problems require the application of a wide range of business subjects. Relevance and practicality can also aid motivation.

Learning style and resources

Each chapter starts with the learning outcomes that identify the key concepts to be covered and the key knowledge and skills that are gained by reading the chapter and undertaking the activities. At the end of each chapter there is a chapter summary that provides an overview of the main points covered.

For all students, the practical focus of what is needed to start up and grow your own business is both motivating and practical. But, while I do believe that you can enhance entrepreneurial skills through education, I also believe that you really learn these skills by 'doing' rather than by just reading a book. This is why the learning resources contained in the book and on the supporting website are important. They are an integral part of the 'learning'.

Case insights

Embedded in each chapter are Cases insights – each with questions. These are designed to make students think about and apply the concepts being explained and discussed in that chapter. Case notes are available on the lecturers' password-protected part of the supporting website.

 Social enterprise cases

Many insights are on issues affecting social enterprise and these are denoted by an additional symbol.

 Practice insights

These provide a range of practical tips and advice on how to get things done or access additional resources, replicating some the characteristics of more 'how-to-do-it' texts.

 Activities

Activities at the end of each chapter involve doing something, in the main further research. This research is often desk-based – including visits to information or organization websites – but some of the most popular assignments, in my experience, involve students going out to do things – such as interviewing entrepreneurs.

Group discussion topics

Each chapter has topics for group discussion. These can be used as a basis for tutorials. They are designed to make students think about the text material and develop their critical and reflective understanding of it and what it means in the real world.

References

Each chapter has full journal and book references so that students can follow up on the details of any research cited. There are also selected further textbooks, organized by topic, and selected journals on the supporting website.

 Meet the Entrepreneurs video case studies

At the end of each Part of the book there are installments of seven video case studies featuring real-life entrepreneurs who share their stories and experiences, highlighting key themes and topics discussed in the chapters.

In the final analysis, any course on entrepreneurship must challenge students to think entrepreneurially. It must make them aware of opportunities in the marketplace and generate a 'can-do' mentality. It must empower them and convince them that they can shape their own destinies. It must make them realize how important the entrepreneur is to the small firm and to society as a whole. It must make them realize how business problems do not come in neatly labelled boxes reflecting the way the subject is taught. But, most of all, it must be interesting and fun.

Learning outcomes

The major challenge facing business schools today is how to encourage and develop the entrepreneurial skills of students. This book is designed to address this issue. It is written to motivate students to become more entrepreneurial at the same time as providing frameworks to nurture these precious skills in a systematic way. At its core is creativity and innovation – invaluable skills in today's competitive markets. Its holistic nature crosses artificial subject boundaries and integrates traditional disciplines. Its practical focus means that skills have to be applied.

The book will help students:

> Critically analyse and understand the process of entrepreneurship from start-up through growth to maturity;
> Develop a holistic range of applied business and management skills to enable them to start up a new venture and understand how it might grow to achieve its full potential;
> Critically assess and reflect on whether they have the character traits of an entrepreneur;
> Critically analyse what is needed to become an entrepreneurial leader and how to structure an organization so as to maintain its entrepreneurial character;
> Write a professional business plan.

It will help them develop cognitive skills in the following areas:

> Data and information interpretation, critical analysis and evaluation;
> Problem identification and solving;
> ICT, in particular the use of the internet;
> The ability to use research and link theory with practice;
> Writing and presentation.

GUIDED TOUR OF THE BOOK

Click on the play button in the ebook to watch a video interview of Paul Burns on the subject of entrepreneurship.

Author video interviews open each part of the book, introducing some of the key questions and issues to be discussed.

Learning outcomes identify the key concepts to be covered in the chapter and the key knowledge and skills you will acquire by reading it and undertaking the related activities.

Learning outcomes

When you have read this chapter and undertaken the related activities you will be able to:

> Critically analyse the changing commercial environment and how it impacts on entrepreneurship;
> Explain how the approach entrepreneurs take to management in a risky, uncertain environment differs from 'traditional' management;
> Define an entrepreneur and understand the different forms entrepreneurship might take;
> Define small firms and understand their characteristics;
> Explain why entrepreneurs and small firms are so important to the economies of modern countries;
> Understand the role of social and civic entrepreneurs and the issues they face;
> Understand the meaning of sustainable entrepreneurship.

Practice insights give tips on how to get things done or access additional resources.

(◉) Practice insight   Measuring your entrepreneurial tendency

The General Enterprise Tendency (GET) test provides you with the opportunity to reflect on whether you have an entrepreneurial character. It is a 54-question instrument that measures your personal character traits in five dimensions of entrepreneurial character – need for independence, need for achievement, internal locus of control, acceptance of measured risk and uncertainty, and creativity and innovation. It can be taken free online in about five minutes on www.GET2test.net.

The results are automatically analysed and a personal report on your character traits can then be printed out. It provides an indicative, although not a definitive, measure of your entrepreneurial tendency. The test was developed by Caird and Johnson at Durham University Business School over a number of years. Caird (1991a, 1991b) established the construct validity and reliability of the test by testing it

on entrepreneurs and comparing it to occupational groups including teachers, nurses, civil servants, clerical workers and lecturers and trainers. Overall, entrepreneurs were found to be significantly more enterprising than the other groups, however they were not the only group to score highly on *individual* measures. Stormer et al. (1999) applied the test to 128 owners of new (75) and successful (53) small firms. They concluded that the test was acceptable for research purposes, particularly for identifying owner-managers, but it was poor at predicting business success. Either the test scales need to be refined for this purpose or the test did not include sufficient indicators of success such as antecedent influences on the individual or other factors related to the business rather than the individual setting it up. So, the GET scores need to be looked at overall rather than individually, and the test does not predict business success.

Quotes from entrepreneurs give their views and insights into entrepreneurship.

> Sometimes people imagine that going into business is a smooth trajectory from struggling start-up to fully-fledged global brand. But that's never really the case. Growing a company is all about overcoming endless challenges, big and small. This is also what makes starting a business the most exciting adventure anyone can go on.
>
> **Richard Branson**, founder, Virgin Group, *The Sunday Times*, 7 December 2014

Case insights with questions are woven throughout the book showing how organizations address real issues and apply the concepts explained in the chapter.

The numerous cases on social enterprises are denoted by this symbol.

(♀) Case insight   **Grameen Bank**

(⊞) Integrated social enterprise

Grameen Bank – meaning 'bank of the villages' in the Bangla language – was set up in Bangladesh in 1976 by Professor Muhammad Yunus, who originally set up a research project to study how to design a credit delivery system to provide banking services to the rural poor. In 1983 it became an independent bank. Grameen Bank provides tiny loans, called microcredit, without collateral to the poor. The aim is to leverage their skills to help them start and grow tiny businesses. It uses a local, group-based approach – called solidarity lending – to ensure that borrowers repay their loans and develop a good credit history. Each borrower belongs to a five-member group. The group is not required to give guarantees for loans to its members, and repayment is solely the responsibility of the individual borrower. However, the group and the centre ensure that everyone behaves responsibly and individuals do not get into arrears with their repayments. Of its borrowers, 96% are women.

Borrowers are encouraged to become savers, and the bank also accepts deposits. It also provides other services and runs several development-oriented businesses including fabric, telephone and energy companies. It seeks to establish a new sort of self-sustaining rural association that reduces dependency on external finance, increases development impact and spreads risk. Funding has come from different sources. Initially, donor agencies provided the bulk of capital at low interest rates but, by the 1990s, the bank was getting most of its funding from the central bank of Bangladesh. In 1976 Professor Yunus received the Nobel Peace Prize. The success of Grameen Bank has inspired similar projects in more than 40 countries around the world.

QUESTION:
1 How many stakeholders, each with different objectives, have to be brought together for this bank to operate effectively?

↻ Summary

> You need to recognize what are your personal drivers and constraints. These will influence whether entrepreneurship is for you and what you might want your business to become.

> You bring financial, human and social capital to your start-up. Financial capital for a start-up can be minimized through partnering with others and bootstrapping. Human capital is derived from your education, training and previous managerial or industry experience. Social capital is derived from your social skills and access to appropriate professional networks. The more capital you bring to the business – of any kind – the more likely you are to succeed.

> Most people have barriers to entrepreneurship (real and psychological). What they need is a strong 'push' or 'pull' to make them take the plunge.

> The entrepreneurial character has six traits: a high need for autonomy; a high need for achievement; an internal locus of control; drive and determination; creativity and innovation; and a willingness to take measured risks.

> These traits are influenced by your background and upbringing and are underpinned by the cultures of the different groups you associate with.

> Cognitive development theory emphasizes the situations that lead to entrepreneurial behaviour. Relevant concepts are self-efficacy, intrinsic motivation and intentionality.

These provide support for some of the entrepreneurial character traits from a different perspective.

> The concept of high internal locus of control is generalized self-efficacy. This motivates entrepreneurs and gives them the dogged determination and self-belief to persist in the face of adversity, when others just give in. Self-efficacy is affected by a person's previous experiences – success breeds success, failure breeds failure. This is the entrepreneur using their mental model or dominant logic as a basis for decision-making.

> Intrapreneurs have many of the qualities as entrepreneurs. They are results-orientated, ambitious, rational, competitive and questioning. They must have strong interpersonal and political skills and be adept at handling conflict and the politics of the larger organization in which they operate.

> Social entrepreneurs have many of the same qualities as entrepreneurs. They are driven by social purpose and are adept at recognizing social opportunity. They need a heightened sense of accountability to the wide range of stakeholders involved in the social enterprise.

> Civic entrepreneurs are similar to intrapreneurs and require similar levels of interpersonal and political skills. However, they probably need to be more patient because of the bureaucracy they are likely to face. A major issue for them is the lower level of risk that is acceptable within many of the services offered in the public sector and the related public accountability.

Summaries provide an overview of the main points covered in the chapter.

Activities encourage you to apply concepts or find out about the entrepreneurial environment.

✓ Activities

1 List the elements of financial, human and social capital you bring to a start-up business.
2 Take the GET test and discuss the results with your friends. Do they recognize these characteristics and the associated behaviours in you? What are the influences that might have contributed to your character? Reflect on the results. What are the implications for you? Write a report on whether you have an entrepreneurial character.
3 Repeat this activity by getting an entrepreneur to complete the test and having them reflect on the results.

💬 Group discussion topics

1 Is it better to start a business when you are young or to wait until you are older? Why is this?
2 What are the barriers to entrepreneurship you face? How might they be overcome?
3 What would 'push' or 'pull' you into entrepreneurship?
4 What sort of business might you like to start up?
5 What are the advantages and disadvantages of being an entrepreneur?
6 Are entrepreneurs born or made?
7 Can character traits really predict who might start up a business?
8 Which entrepreneurial character traits might have negative implications? What are they and how might they be countered?
9 What does self-efficacy mean? Is it a good or a bad thing for entrepreneurs?
10 Are entrepreneurs delusional?
11 Are entrepreneurs gamblers?

Group discussion topics allow you to think about the text material and develop your critical and reflective understanding of it and what it means in the real world.

☞ References

Acs, Z.J. and Audretsch, D.B. (2005) 'Entrepreneurship, Innovation and Technological Change', *Institute for Development Studies*, ISSN No. 5-5.

Alexander, J., Nank, R. and Strivers, C. (1999) 'Implications of Welfare Reform: Do Nonprofit Survival Strategies Threaten Civil Society?', *Non-profit and Voluntary Sector Quarterly*, 28(4).

Anderson, J. (1995) *Local Heroes*, Glasgow: Scottish Enterprise.

Asian Development Bank (2013) *Asia SME Finance Monitor*, Philippines: ADB.

Autio, E. (2007) *Global Entrepreneurship Monitor 2007 Global Report on High-Growth Entrepreneurship*, London, UK: London Business School; and Babson Park, MA: Babson College.

Full journal and book references are given at the end of each chapter, allowing you to explore the relevant research further. The author index at the back of the book allows you to find out about the contributions of particular academics.

🌐 www.palgrave.com/Burns-Entrepreneurship-And-Small-Business-4e

Go online to access additional teaching and learning resources for this chapter on the companion website. Click here in the ebook to complete a multiple choice revision quiz for this chapter.

Additional digital resources, include multiple choice questions embedded directly in the ebook at the end of every chapter, and more teaching and learning resources available on the companion website.

Meet the Entrepreneur videos offer you an insight into the real-life ups and downs of actual entrepreneurs.

MEET THE ENTREPRENEURS

Part 1: Entrepreneurship

In this first instalment of our video case studies, the entrepreneurs introduce themselves and their businesses. Click on the play buttons below to learn about their reasons for starting their own business, how they came up with the original idea, and what they think makes a good entrepreneur.

AJ Asver

 Cassandra Stavrou

 John Loughton

 Ross Beerman

 Sandra Wanduragala

 Scott Cupit

 Stefan Botha

Questions

> Who are the target customers for these businesses and why should customers buy their products or services?
> What entrepreneurial character traits can you spot in each of the interviewees?
> What were the push and pull factors that led each entrepreneur to start their own business?
> How important has national culture and/or location been to these entrepreneurs?
> Did these entrepreneurs spot opportunities or create them?

The full videos of each entrepreneur's story are available on the companion website.

Meet the Entrepreneurs

Accompanying this book are seven in-depth video case studies with successful entrepreneurs, covering a range of businesses and geographical locations. These videos interrogate the entrepreneurs on the experiences and challenges they have faced starting and managing their own businesses, and offer students an invaluable insight into life as an entrepreneur.

Following the lifecycle of each business, the videos have been divided into four sections that mirror the structure of the book, and can be found at the end of each Part, on pages 142, 292, 410 and 527. The videos draw out issues that have been discussed across different chapters, and allow a useful exploration of both common themes shared by all businesses as well as industry-specific issues. The accompanying questions invite you to critically analyse and compare what you have learned.

The full videos for each entrepreneur are also available on the companion website, if you would like to hear their story from start to end uninterrupted.

AJ Asver, co-founder, Scoopler/JustSpotted, USA

AJ is co-founder of the real-time search engine Scoopler and the celebrity-spotting website JustSpotted. Having grown up in the UK, AJ travelled to San Francisco in 2008 to turn his business dreams into reality. Spotting a clear business opportunity, AJ's original business idea shifted and so Scoopler became JustSpotted. Within three years of operation, JustSpotted was successful enough to be noticed and eventually bought by none other than search giant Google. In 2014, AJ left Google, after working there for three years, with plans to embark on a new start-up in the music space. And he's only just turned 30.

Cassandra Stavrou, co-founder, Propercorn, UK

www.propercorn.com/

Propercorn started in Cassandra's kitchen when she was just 25. After realizing that all '3pm slump' snacks either left her feeling guilty or dissatisfied, Cassandra set out to make a gluten-free popcorn range without the compromise. It would be "popcorn done properly".

Starting out with cold calls and endless nights packing boxes at her business partner, Ryan's, flat, Propercorn now has a team of 30 based in London and exports to six countries in Europe. Since first launching in the Google London headquarters in October 2011, Propercorn has emerged as one of the fastest growing brands in the UK, with Cassandra working tirelessly to create a dynamic business, grounded in passion and excitement for popcorn.

John Loughton, founder, Dare2Lead, UK

www.dare2lead.co.uk

John is a social entrepreneur, campaigner and motivational speaker. John founded award-winning leadership development company Dare2Lead in 2011, at the age of 23. John ran his first campaign aged 11 and has engaged world leaders such as Queen Elizabeth, the UN Secretary General and the President of the European Parliament, working in over 35 countries. In 2013 he was named Outstanding Youth of the World.

A business with strong social objectives, Dare2Lead is passionate about unlocking the success potential of organizations through corporate and management training while also making a positive difference in society by empowering young people through emerging leadership and development programmes. Their range of leadership development programmes combines real-life experiences of leadership and success alongside proven leadership and management tools. Their client base includes governments, NGOs, large corporates, small businesses and a range of public bodies.

Ross Beerman, co-founder and CEO, AllLife, South Africa

http://alllife.co.za

Ross has worked both in South Africa and internationally in the financial services sector. He worked in Corporate Finance and M&A in the USA, and returned to South Africa in 1998 to work in private equity. In 2001, Ross founded Theta Specialised Finance, a principal acquirer of distressed credit instruments, which was sold to a strategic buyer at the end of 2003. In 2004 Ross co-founded AllLife with the intent to provide life insurance to people living with HIV, based on the premise that properly designed systems and processes, combined with great people, could cost-effectively intervene to help clients manage their health and change their mortality. AllLife has delivered life insurance to tens of thousands of HIV+ people and has recently begun leveraging its IP, systems and processes to also deliver easily accessible life insurance to diabetics in South Africa and abroad.

Sandra Wanduragala, founder, and Selyna Peiris, business development director, Selyn Handlooms, Sri Lanka

http://www.selyn.lk/

In 1991, Sandra Wanduragala gave up her career as an attorney-at-law to start Selyn, in rural Sri Lanka. From the start, Selyn has been a family business. Sandra built the company alongside her brother, Hilary. Her daughter, Selyna (who the company is named after), is also now involved in the business.

Selyn is Sri Lanka's only fair trade–guaranteed handloom company, and one of the country's biggest social enterprises. Selyn has revived the traditional Sri Lankan craft of handloom weaving to create its wide product range, including fabrics, garments, jewellery, home accessories and children's toys. These products are sold locally in Sri Lanka and globally in key export markets in the European Union, the USA and parts of Asia. Selyn began with 15 women in a

small rural village but has now grown to around 1,000 members, 95% of whom are women. In addition to infrastructure, technical support and a guaranteed flow of work, members are offered services such as health camps, childcare facilities, and life skills, leadership and entrepreneurship development programmes. The Selyn Foundation extends beyond the business; it is a grassroots effort to relieve poverty and empower Sri Lankan youth and women by means of education, vocational training, credit-provisions and other developmental tools.

Scott Cupit, founder and managing director, Swing Patrol, UK and Australia

www.swingpatrol.co.uk

Swing-dance performer, teacher, choreographer and general enthusiast Scott founded Swing Patrol London, the dance school and events business, in 2009, based on his experience co-founding and running Swing Patrol Melbourne in his home country of Australia.

Scott has been recruited as Assistant Charleston Choreographer to Jenny Thomas on the hit UK television show *Strictly Come Dancing*, was crowned 2015 Dance Teacher of the Year, and has danced at both Buckingham Palace and 10 Downing Street. From a handful of students in a single venue, in just six years Swing Patrol London has grown to a team of over 54 teachers operating from over 40 venues across London, holding hundreds of social events each year and has developed corporate events and content-marketing functions. In 2014, Scott appeared on the popular UK television show *Dragons' Den*, and successfully secured investment from Deborah Meaden.

Stefan Botha, founder and director, Rainmaker Marketing, South Africa

www.rainmakermarketing.co.za

With several years of experience in the area of property development marketing, Stefan decided to start his own business in 2012, and so Rainmaker Marketing was born.

With a focus on building and transforming brands, Rainmaker Marketing provides a turn-key sales and marketing solution that specializes in property development marketing and hospitality branding. With a niche approach, and a comprehensive in-house team, the business has worked on large-scale property developments throughout South Africa, Mauritius and Mozambique.

DIGITAL RESOURCES

Interactive ebook

Included free with each print copy of this book is access to an interactive ebook.

The perfect companion to the print book, the ebook replicates the pages of the book and offers all the versatility you would expect, such as bookmarking and easy searching, but also offers added embedded multimedia content right at your fingertips, including:

> **Video summaries and interviews** offering you different insights into the field and practice of entrepreneurship:
>   > Part introductions with Paul Burns
>   > 'Meet the Entrepreneur' video case study instalments at the end of every Part
> **Multiple choice questions** integrated at the end of every chapter – a useful way to help you consolidate your learning and revise what you have just read.

Your unique code gives you access to the ebook for a whole year, and after the initial download, it can be read offline, giving you freedom and flexibility to use it on campus, at home, even on the bus! Visit **www.palgrave.com/Burns-Entrepreneurship-And-Small-Business-4e** for details on downloading your ebook. You'll never find yourself falling behind on the reading your lecturer assigns, with the book accessible anytime and anywhere from your mobile device or laptop.

Companion website

The companion website (**www.palgrave.com/Burns-Entrepreneurship-And-Small-Business-4e**) hosts a number of additional resources to aid teaching and learning.

Teaching resources

Instructors who adopt this book on their course gain access to a selection of password protected resources to help plan and deliver their teaching:

> Chapter-by-chapter PowerPoint slides, including relevant diagrams and figures, to use in lectures
> A chapter-by-chapter Instructor's Manual that includes:
>   > case notes
>   > links to useful websites
>   > video links to support teaching
> Teaching notes on the 'Meet the Entrepreneur' video case studies

Learning resources

For students, a number of tools are provided to help extend your discovery of entrepreneurship beyond the book.

> Full 'Meet the Entrepreneur' video case studies
> Flashcards of useful key terms in the book
> Bonus international case studies
> Guides to sources of further information & laws & regulations for businesses in the UK
> Links to other online sources of help & advice, including online tests
> Downloadable versions of the New Venture Creation framework & business plan

PART 1 ENTREPRENEURSHIP

Click on the play button in your ebook to watch a video interview of Paul Burns on the subject of entrepreneurship.

PART 2 START-UP

PART 3 GROWTH

PART 4 MATURITY

1 | ENTREPRENEURSHIP: THE SOCIAL AND BUSINESS REVOLUTION

Contents

Getty

Learning outcomes

When you have read this chapter and undertaken the related activities you will be able to:

> Critically analyse the changing commercial environment and how it impacts on entrepreneurship;
> Explain how the approach entrepreneurs take to management in a risky, uncertain environment differs from 'traditional' management;
> Define an entrepreneur and understand the different forms entrepreneurship might take;
> Define small firms and understand their characteristics;
> Explain why entrepreneurs and small firms are so important to the economies of modern countries;
> Understand the role of social and civic entrepreneurs and the issues they face;
> Understand the meaning of sustainable entrepreneurship.

 Case insights

Instagram	Kiran Mazumdar-Shaw and Biocon
Material Pleasures	
AirAsia	Grameen Bank
LED Hut	The Entertainer
Amanti Cupcakes	SBA Hydro
Monkey Music	Goodone

The new age of uncertainty

The old world order has changed and continues to change. Economic power is moving east from the USA and Europe to China and India. If the most startling evidence of this was the financial crisis of 2008 that plunged the mature Western economies into recession, the seeds of change were sown much earlier. So far the 21st century has seen enormous turbulence and disruption. There have been the unpredictable shocks caused by terrorist attacks around the world, followed by the wars in Afghanistan and Iraq. The upheavals caused by the so-called Arab Spring of 2011 continue to affect the Middle East, not least Syria. There have been natural disasters like the Icelandic volcano in 2010, the earthquake and tsunami in Japan in 2011 and the outbreak of Ebola in West Africa in 2014. There have been enormous shocks to the international monetary system precipitated by the banking crisis of 2008, which have particularly affected the Eurozone. There have also been some spectacular corporate failures, from Lehman Brothers in the USA to Royal Bank of Scotland (RBS) in the UK. Corporate integrity has come to be questioned. The unexpected failure of Enron in the USA in 2001, one of the most admired firms of the 1990s, became a benchmark for management greed and lack of integrity. But such scandals were not confined to the USA. Parmalat in Italy became the largest bankruptcy in Europe in 2003. The Olympus scandal of 2012 in Japan led to prosecutions. In addition, banks across the world have been rocked by a series of scandals that have led to fines and government intervention. Alongside this the 21st century has seen unprecedented volatility in just about every market, from commodities to exchange rates, from stock markets to bond markets. And behind this volatility is the uncertainty surrounding climate change and whether we have reached a 'tipping point' in global warming.

Underpinning the volatility is the development of global connectivity – an increasingly complex world full of interconnections formed by a truly global marketplace linked by new technologies that allow instant communication from almost anywhere. Small changes tend to be amplified in highly connected systems. Actions in one part of a market can have unexpected and rapid consequences in another part of it. And nobody, not even sovereign states, seem able to control this. And the pace of change has accelerated. Change itself has changed to become a continuous process of often-discontinuous steps – abrupt and all-persuasive. The ancient Chinese saw change as endless and an essential feature of our universe – a pattern of cyclical coming and going, growth and decay, winter and summer, the yin of night and yang of day. Somehow the West had forgotten this, believing instead that we could create stability and certainty, that change was a series of discrete events that moved us from one stable state to another. Economists based theories on it. And economists, politicians and managers focused on the ways that change could be controlled in a systematic way.

With the new age of uncertainty came austerity. Recession and stagnation became the order of the day after the banking crisis of 2008, leading to a persistent rise in unemployment and deepening income inequality. The shift from boom to recession simply made us realize our vulnerability in this new era. Commercial opportunities remain but competition is now as much about survival as growth. And, as global competition continues to increase, sources of competitive advantage are proving increasingly difficult to sustain over any period of time. So much so that it is the ability to create new sources of competitive advantage quickly, again and again, that is proving to be the only sustainable source of real competitive advantage. At the same time as seeking new sources of competitive advantage, businesses must continue to manage existing businesses. They must find ways of managing to achieve cost efficiencies while at the same time differentiating themselves from the competition. They must find ways to innovate at the same time as managing products at the mature stage of their life cycle. They must find ways of understanding and reconciling customer needs in both India and the USA, of reconciling global integration with local differentiation. And they must respond to changes in these needs quickly, just as they must react quickly to the actions of competitors.

The new age has also seen companies face new social pressures. Corporate scandals have led to cries for improved corporate governance and boardroom accountability. Excessive executive

> Sometimes people imagine that going into business is a smooth trajectory from struggling start-up to fully-fledged global brand. But that's never really the case. Growing a company is all about overcoming endless challenges, big and small. This is also what makes starting a business the most exciting adventure anyone can go on.
>
> **Richard Branson**, founder, Virgin Group, *The Sunday Times*, 7 December 2014

> We stand on the threshold of a new age – the age of revolution. In our minds, we know the new age has already arrived: in our bellies, we're not sure we like it. For we know it is going to be an age of upheaval, of tumult, of fortunes made and unmade at head-snapping speed. For change has changed. No longer is it additive. No longer does it move in a straight line. In the twenty first century, change is discontinuous, abrupt, seditious.
>
> **Gary Hamel**, 2000, *Leading the Revolution*, Boston: Harvard Business School Press

salaries and bonuses that bore no relationship to the performance of the organization, exemplified in the banks, have redoubled these cries. At the same time, companies have been pressurized to take a more socially responsible role. This pressure comes from many sources. Environmentalists want companies to reduce their 'carbon footprint' and espouse 'green' issues and become more sustainable. Social reformers want them to change some of their behaviours, for example exploitation of child labour in developing economies. Social activists want them to espouse 'corporate citizenship' programmes and undertake charity work in the community. Finally, ethical activists see many companies behaving in unacceptable ways and want business ethics to be re-established in the boardroom. All these issues have become bundled together under the umbrella of Corporate Social Responsibility (CSR). CSR is seen as increasingly important.

An age of change and opportunity

But for entrepreneurs change presents opportunities – and these changes have meant small entrepreneurial firms have flourished. For entrepreneurs CSR is an opportunity to be both ethical *and* to improve competiveness by differentiating themselves from competitors. Other factors have accelerated this trend towards smaller, more entrepreneurial firms. There has been the shift in most economies away from manufacturing towards the service sectors where small firms often flourish because of their ability to deliver a personalized, flexible, tailor-made service at a local level.

Technology has played its part. It has influenced the trend in three ways. Firstly, the new technologies that swept the late-20th-century business world have been pioneered by new, rapidly growing firms. Small firms have pioneered innovation in computers, the internet and mobile technologies, creating new markets for these innovations. Small firms have been at the forefront of developing mobile applications, or apps, because the costs of doing so are low but the gains from selling to a global market can be enormous. Secondly, these technologies have actually facilitated the growth of self-employment and small business by easing communication, encouraging working from home and allowing smaller and smaller market segments to be serviced. Indeed, information has become a product in its own right and one that can be generated anywhere around the world and transported at the touch of a button. Finally, many new technologies, for example digital printing, have reduced fixed costs so that production can be profitable in smaller, more flexible units. They have also simplified the routes to market so that small firms can sell to larger firms or direct to customers around the world, without the expense of putting in place a distribution network. And as large firms increasingly outsource non-core activities, the beneficiaries are often small firms.

As we have moved from an industrial economy to a knowledge economy, driven by new digital technologies, new commercial opportunities have continued to emerge both from technological and market innovation, sometimes breaking down established industry barriers and creating new and unexpected sources of competition. For example, the internet has caused many high-street retailers to radically reappraise their customer offering and will probably lead to the high street looking very different in the future. It has caused the music, video and print industries to reappraise how their products are distributed. It has caused disruption, generating as many opportunities as threats. Entrepreneurs have been quick to capitalize on these opportunities to establish new businesses with less capital than before.

This move to a knowledge economy has also meant that economies of scale (with costs declining as volumes increase) have become less important as a form of competitive advantage. For example, a high proportion of innovations in the pharmaceutical industry now come from small firms set up specifically to undertake research and

Fancy

development. Value is increasingly being created, not from physical assets, but from knowledge and the virtual assets it creates – a shift from assets that must be purchased and then restrict flexibility to ones that can be built up over time and used in many different ways. A high proportion of high-growth firms (called 'gazelles' by academics) hold intellectual property and intangible assets such as trademarks and patents (Department of Business, Enterprise and Regulatory Reform, 2008), and investment in so-called intangible assets such as computer codes, copyrights and patents is now 50% higher than investment in tangible assets such as plant and machinery, and is increasing.

These developments in technology have affected markets. Customers increasingly expect firms to address their particular needs. Market niches are becoming slimmer and markets more competitive – better served by smaller firms that can get close to their customers. The new technologies mean that these niche markets can be attacked globally, making them economic. Start-ups are also able to focus on them straight away without having to set up a costly international sales and distribution network. You can sell on the internet and subcontract delivery. The international start-up is now an everyday occurrence. This disruption has affected the way customers buy from the high street and in the supermarket. The high street has become a place to spend leisure time rather than shopping time – presenting opportunities for small service businesses. The advent of 'click and collect' has affected the whole retail trade, accelerating the trend towards smaller, local stores and away from supermarkets.

Social trends have also accelerated the growth of small firms. People want to control their own destiny more. After periods of high unemployment, they see self-employment as more attractive and more secure than employment. Redundancy has pushed many people into self-employment at the same time as the new 'enterprise culture' gave it political and social respectability. And, in an age of uncertainty people seek to control as many aspects of their economic security as possible. The growth of the 'new-age' culture and 'alternative' lifestyles, encouraged by worries about climate change, have also led to the development of a whole range of new self-employment and sustainable opportunities, albeit often at the periphery of the economy. And finally the role of entrepreneur has become respectable and admired.

Managing change and uncertainty

While large firms have increasingly found difficulty in dealing with this new order, start-ups and smaller ventures seem to find opportunities that these larger, more established firms find threatening. Even in this age of uncertainty and austerity they thrive, despite facing increasingly fierce competition. McMillan (2004) characterized what she called the 'traditional, classical, mechanistic' view of change as abnormal, potentially calamitous, an incremental linear event that is disruptive that can be controlled. She contrasted this to what she called the 'new, modern dynamic' view that change is normal, continuous, turbulent, both revolutionary and incremental, uncontrollable and non-linear but full of opportunities. The two views are contrasted in Table 1.1.

Table 1.1 Traditional vs modern views of change

Traditional, classical, mechanistic view of change		New, modern, dynamic view of change
Abnormal	vs	Normal
Incremental	vs	Both revolutionary and incremental
Linear	vs	Non-linear
Disruptive	vs	Turbulent
Potentially calamitous	vs	Full of opportunity
Cause and effect	vs	About learning and creativity
An event	vs	Continuous
Controllable	vs	Uncontrollable

The approach of managers in big companies to managing change was to employ the rational techniques of long-term planning and tight control systems. But they were finding it difficult to cope with the changing environment by the end of the 20th century. They cut budgets, closed plants, downsized or 'rightsized', deconstructed – and went out of business. The 'deconstruction' of larger firms into smaller, more responsive units concentrating on their core activities, often 'outsourcing' or subcontracting many of their other activities to smaller firms, has also contributed to the trend towards smaller firms. Large firms and even the public sector became leaner and fitter in the 1980s in a bid to reduce fixed costs and reduce risks. Small firms have benefited, although many may be seen as dependent on large ones.

But the core of the problem is that traditional management practices focus on efficiency and effectiveness rather than creativity and innovation – control rather than empowerment. They look for cost savings through scale efficiencies rather than differentiation through economies of small scale. They look for uniformity rather than diversity and stress discipline rather than motivation. And they often discourage what they see as the risk-taking associated with a market opportunity without the information to evaluate it, by which time the opportunity will have been seized by a small firm. Add all this to the danger that bureaucracy will swamp the organizations that practise this traditional form of management, that they will ossify, and you have the makings of disaster. No wonder big was no longer beautiful.

The entrepreneurial revolution

This new age of uncertainty has powerful implications for all organizations. Planning becomes problematic if you cannot predict the future, and strategic management faces completely new challenges as the linear models based on knowledge and information and used for decades seem increasingly unrealistic. And yet entrepreneurs not only cope but thrive.

Over the last 30 years, entrepreneurs establishing new ventures have done more to create wealth than firms at any time before them – ever! Of the current wealth of the USA, 95% has been created since 1980. And as we look around for role models, we realize that so many of our most successful corporations have been founded in our lifetime. Of the 100 largest public companies in the USA, 31 were founded by an entrepreneur during the post-war era, creating over four million jobs, and 29% of US firms on the Global FT 500 list were founded after 1950 (Sanandaji and Sanandaji, 2014). For example, Bill Gates started Microsoft in 1975, the late Steve Jobs started Apple in 1976, Michael Dell set up the Dell Corporation in 1984, Pierre Omidyar launched eBay in 1995 and Larry Page and Sergey Brin launched Google in 1996. And, although not to the same extent, this was not just happening in the USA. In the UK, Alan Sugar launched Amstrad in 1968, Richard Branson started his Virgin empire in 1972, James Dyson started selling his Dyson vacuum cleaners in 1976, the late Anita Roddick opened the first Body Shop in 1976 and Julian Metcalfe and Sinclair Beecham opened their first Pret A Manger in 1986. In India, Sunil Mittal started the first business that was to become Bharti Enterprises in 1976 and Kiran Mazumdar-Shaw started Biocon in 1978. These are now gigantic corporations that made their founders household names and millionaires.

Finally, people have begun to appreciate the contribution all small firms make to the economies of their countries. It was David Birch (1979) who, arguably, started this process with his seminal research which showed that 82% of new jobs in the USA, between 1969 and 1976, were created by small firms (under 500 employees). In fact, Haltiwanger et al. (2013) have shown that it is young, newly created firms rather than established small firms generally that create most jobs. Small, growing firms create jobs from which the rest of society benefits. They have outstripped large firms in terms of job generation, year on year. At times when larger firms have retrenched, smaller firms continue to offer job opportunities. It has been estimated that in the USA small firms now generate half of GDP and over half of exports now come from firms employing fewer than 20 people. What is more, they make up a large part of the voting population. Over 95% of enterprises are 'small', no matter how that is defined. No wonder our governments and media are so fascinated by them.

Entrepreneurship has become something that society, governments and organizations of all sizes and forms wish to encourage and promote. Whether it be creating a new venture or breathing life into an old one, whether it is creating new products or finding new ways to market old ones, whether it is doing new things or finding new ways of doing old things, entrepreneurial management – whatever that is – has become a highly valued skill to be nurtured, developed and encouraged. Fostering entrepreneurship in all aspects of their teaching is probably one of the major challenges facing business schools in the 21st century. Entrepreneurs themselves have finally been recognized as a vital part of economic wealth generation. They have become the heroes of the business world, embodying qualities that many people envy – freedom of spirit, creativity, vision and zeal. They have the courage, self-belief and commitment to turn dreams into realities. They are the catalysts for economic and sometimes social change. They see an opportunity, commercialize it, and in doing so become millionaires themselves.

> The mind-set that in a huge global economy the multinationals dominate world business couldn't have been more wrong. The bigger and more open the world economy becomes, the more small and middle-sized companies will dominate.
>
> **John Naisbitt**, 1994, *Global Paradox: The Bigger the World Economy, the More Powerful Its Smaller Players*, London: BCA

Entrepreneurial management

So, how do these successful entrepreneurs manage their businesses? The key is their different approach to dealing with risk and uncertainty. And at the core of this is a very personal approach to management generally – one that emphasizes that a new business is a social entity built around personal relationships and around one person, the founder, or as a colleague put it, 'two arms, two legs and a giant ego'. The key to understanding how any small firm is managed is to understand the owner-manager. Their personality and their behavioural characteristics will strongly influence this. It affects how customers and staff are handled and how decisions are made.

Getty

Successful entrepreneurs are good at developing relationships with customers, staff, suppliers and all the stakeholders in the business. They are able to form loyal relationships with customers. They tend to manage their staff by developing strong personal relationships rather than relying on formal structures and hierarchies. Formality reduces flexibility, so they manage informally, setting an example by their behaviour. This ability to form strong personal relationships helps them develop the partnerships and networks that are part of the social capital they create. It enables them to leverage the strategic skills of the partnership. However, there is always the danger of overdependence on the founder and too little delegation of authority as it grows.

These relationships are at the core of how entrepreneurs deal with the risk. While they are prepared to take measured risks, they always want to keep them to a minimum. Their network of personal relationships can give them early warning of a risk materializing. It can also alert them to new opportunities. It is a major source of knowledge and information. However, small firms typically approach decision-making differently than larger firms. They tend to adopt an incremental approach that is often seen as short-term. But, as we shall see, limiting commitment is an approach that helps mitigate risk in uncertain environments. Entrepreneurs tend to keep capital investment and fixed costs as low as possible, often by subcontracting activities. They tend to commit costs only after the opportunity has proved to be real and then only commit limited resources – the resources they can afford to lose. This may be prudent and reflect their resource limits, but it can mean losing first-mover advantage for a new product or service, which is why they frequently experiment and learn from a 'limited launch' into the market. Finally, entrepreneurs are adept at compartmentalizing risk, for example by separating out business ventures into separate legal entities, so that the failure of one does not endanger the survival of the others. We shall look at how risk can be managed in Chapters 9 and 10.

> It is not possible to draw a picture of the universe, but we know it and how fast it is moving and developing. It is like describing the shape of a large cloud in the sky, blown off by a strong wind. Yet we know its shape and where it is because we sense it. Although it is not entirely possible to describe it in a static way, a world-class entrepreneur can describe it and even capture a large chunk of it, converting it into raindrops or profit.
>
> **Kenichi Ohmae**, 2005, *The Next Global Stage: Challenges and Opportunities in our Borderless World*, New Jersey: Pearson Education

Entrepreneurs also develop strategy differently. They are often accused of not developing any strategy at all and are often seen as being intuitive, almost whimsical, in their decision-making. Economists find it difficult to understand and to model. It certainly does not fit well into 'logical' economic models such as discounted cash flow. The reason lies at the heart of any entrepreneurial venture – the greater degree of risk and uncertainty it faces. The result is a different approach that is just as logical but little understood. Although it may not be there at the launch of a business, successful entrepreneurs quickly develop a strong vision of what they want their businesses to become. Although they do not always know how they will achieve the vision because of the uncertain environment they face, they have strong 'strategic intent'. This is accompanied by a loose or flexible strategy underpinned by continuous strategizing – assessing the options about how to make the most of opportunities or avoid risks as they arise. By creating more strategic options they improve their chances of successfully pursuing at least one opportunity and avoiding most risks – albeit possibly at the expense of short-term profits. They keep as many options open as long as possible. The greater the number of strategic options, the safer they are in an age of uncertainty. We shall look at how entrepreneurs develop strategy in Chapters 6 and 12. Make no mistake; entrepreneurs to a large extent create their own luck.

Successful entrepreneurs find ways of reconciling these issues – ways of developing strategy without overcommitting to one course of action and ways of minimizing their investment in resources. They are adept at using networks of relationships to the full and mitigating the risks they face. They can stay flexible, able to grasp commercial opportunities quickly. And as their businesses have grown, these successful entrepreneurs have created organizational structures that are fleet of foot and flexible, structures that are able to adapt and cope with rapid change. McMillan (op. cit.) cast the net wide in searching for ideas about how to deal with change by saying that we need to look at quantum physics and complexity theory – which we shall indeed return to in Chapters 18 and 19 when we look at how entrepreneurial firms organize themselves.

 ## Case insight   Instagram

Entrepreneurial start-and-sell

Kevin Systrom and Mike Krieger became millionaires before the age of 30 by selling their start-up to Facebook for $1 billion in 2012, giving the pair $300 million in cash. The company was called Instagram and it had only 13 employees. Instagram is an online mobile photo-sharing, video-sharing and social networking service. Users can take pictures and videos, and share them on a variety of social networking platforms, such as Facebook, Twitter, Tumblr and Flickr. It is distributed as an app through the Apple App Store, Google Play and the Windows Phone Store and is supported by most mobile devices. Only two years earlier, the pair had secured seed funding with venture capitalists to work on the project, going 'live' shortly after. In 2011 they secured further funding that valued the company at some $25 million. The following year a further round of fundraising valued it at $500 million.

What Systrom and Krieger did was to link developments in technology and connectivity to unmet – perhaps even unthought of – customer needs. Systrom was a business management and engineering graduate and Krieger had studied symbolic systems, which combined computer science,

psychology and artificial intelligence with philosophy. They both used apps a lot and what they developed was a social media site where photos and videos – not words – could be easily uploaded, edited and shared with friends. Images are easier to generate than written words, and Instagram was the first app you could use to take photos and then instantly share them online. Some 65 million photographs are posted on the site every day and it has more than 200 million monthly active users. Instagram is famously used by the Kardashian sisters and Justin Bieber. Interestingly, in 2013, Instagram grew by 23%, while Facebook, its parent company, only grew by 3%.

❏ Visit the website: https://instagram.com.

QUESTIONS:

1 What is involved in matching technology with unmet customer needs?

2 What are the pros and cons of an entrepreneur selling-on a successful business quickly rather than growing it to significant size – for the entrepreneur, the business and society?

Defining the entrepreneur

This book will look at many different types of entrepreneurs in different contexts. The Oxford English Dictionary defines an entrepreneur as 'a person who attempts to profit by risk and initiative'. But this definition, while emphasizing risk and initiative, could cover a wide range of professions, including that of a paid assassin. The difference is more than just one of legality. The question to ask is, how do they make profit? The notion of entrepreneur has been crafted over many centuies, starting with Cantillon (1755), and has seen many different emphases (see Table 1.2). Over 200 years ago Jean-Baptiste Say, the French economist, said: 'entrepreneurs shift economic resources from an area of lower productivity into an area of higher productivity and greater yield' (1803).

But where does the perception of the opportunity to shift these resources come from? There are two generally accepted explanations of where entrepreneurial opportunities come from – the Schumpeterian view and the Kirznerian view. In the Schumpeterian view, opportunities emerge out of the entrepreneurs' internal disposition to *initiate or create change*. They are the innovators who 'shock' and disturb the economic equilibrium during times of uncertainty, change and technological upheaval. With Schumpeter the emphasis is on independent firm formation by entrepreneurs leading to this 'creative destruction'. By way of contrast, the Kirznerian view emphasizes opportunity recognition and implies that entrepreneurial profits are secured on the basis of *knowledge and information gaps* that arise between people in the market – called **information asymmetry** (Chapter 14) – all based within the general equilibrium or neoclassical model of economics, originally derived from Marshall (1890). In this view, entrepreneurs are alert, discovering opportunities by acting as an arbitrageur or a price adjuster in the marketplace. Kirzner's work is based on that of Knight, who discussed entrepreneurship's role in wealth creation with an emphasis on the ability to cope with risk and uncertainty. In the real world, both

> " I am often asked what it is to be an entrepreneur and there is no simple answer. It is clear that successful entrepreneurs are vital for a healthy, vibrant and competitive economy. If you look around you, most of the largest companies have their foundations in one or two individuals who have the determination to turn a vision into reality.
>
> **Richard Branson**, from Anderson (1995), *Local Heroes*, Glasgow: Scottish Enterprise. "

Table 1.2 The antecedence of modern entrepreneurship

Date	Author	Concept of entrepreneur
1755	Cantillon	Introduced the concept of entrepreneur from '*entreprendre*' (ability to take charge).
1803, 1817	Say	Emphasized the ability of the entrepreneur to 'marshal' resources in order to respond to unfulfilled opportunities.
1871	Menger	Noted the ability of entrepreneurs to distinguish between 'economic goods' – those with a market or exchange value – and all others.
1893	Ely and Hess	Attributed to entrepreneurs the ability to take integrated action in the enterprise as a whole, combining roles in capital, labour, enterprise and entrepreneur.
1911, 1928, 1942	Schumpeter	Envisioned that entrepreneurs proactively 'created' opportunity using 'innovative combinations' which often included 'creative destruction' of passive or lethargic economic markets.
1921	Knight	Suggested that entrepreneurs were concerned with 'efficiency' in the use of economic factors by continually reducing waste, increasing savings and thereby creating value, emphasizing their ability to cope with risk and uncertainty effectively and implicitly understanding the opportunity-risk-reward relationship.
1948, 1952, 1967	Hayek	Continued the Austrian tradition of analytical entrepreneurs, attributing to them capabilities of discovery and action, recognizing the existence of information asymmetry which they could exploit.
1973, 1979, 1997, 1999, 2009	Kirzner	Attributed to entrepreneurs a sense of 'alertness' to identify opportunities and exploit them accordingly.
1974	Drucker	Attributed to entrepreneurs the capacity to 'foresee' market trends and make a timely response.
1975, 1984, 1985	Shapero	Attributed a 'judgement' ability to entrepreneurs to identify 'credible opportunities' depending on two critical antecedents – perceptions of 'desirability' and 'feasibility' from both personal and social viewpoints.

Source: Based on Etemad (2004), pp 12–15.

Schumpeterian and Kirznerian approaches seem to be used by entrepreneurs – they both create and spot opportunities – and a few studies tell us when, how and by whom these approaches might be used (e.g. Craig and Johnson, 2006; Samuelsson and Davidsson, 2009). Indeed, Kirzner (2009) himself concluded that both approaches are needed to understand the nature of dynamic market processes.

Reconciling these views, we can say that entrepreneurs create value by exploiting some form of change – either shifting resources or, more directly, improving productivity. They can create this change themselves or spot it happening. In Chapter 4 we use the terms 'create opportunity' or 'spot opportunity' in our approaches to finding a business idea. Entrepreneurs can exploit change in technology, materials, prices or demographics. They provide an essential source of new ideas and experimentation that would otherwise remain untapped in the economy (Acs and Audretsch, 2005). We call this process innovation and this is an essential tool for entrepreneurs and one that creates wealth for an economy. We shall examine it in greater detail in Chapter 3. Entrepreneurs create new demand or find new ways of exploiting existing markets. They identify a commercial opportunity and then exploit it. They are agents of change. In essence, an entrepreneur is best defined by their actions:

> *An entrepreneur creates and/or exploits change for profit by innovating, accepting risk and moving resources to areas of higher return.*

Notice that our definition says nothing about starting a new venture or owning the enterprise that exploits change. Entrepreneurs could undertake these activities for established, larger firms while remaining in salaried employment, content for the profits (and risks) of their work to go to their employers. We call them **intrapreneurs** and we shall look at them again in Chapters 3 and 19. Owner-managers own the business they manage. Sole traders are owner-managers. Managers of companies owning over 50% of the share capital, and thereby controlling the business, are owner-managers. The term is also used loosely when a small group of managers own and control the business. However, not all owner-managers are entrepreneurs.

Notice also that our definition does not say whether profit is maximized. Profit is not always the prime motivation for creating a new venture. For many people it is simply a badge of success and the attraction of being an entrepreneur lies in being your own boss, doing what you want to do rather than what you are told to do. Some people spot a business opportunity – a product or a service that they do not see offered in the market or a way of doing something better or cheaper. Some people might be frustrated by characteristics of current products or services being offered that does not meet their needs. Some people, just a few, have a genuine 'eureka' moment when they come up with a new invention or have an idea that can revolutionize an industry. Whatever the source of their business idea, they feel motivated to do something about it – perhaps wanting to make a lot of money on the way. What defines the entreprenur is their willingness to act upon the idea.

In fact most new ventures do not grow to become the industry titans we discussed previously. More than 95% of small firms in Europe employ less than 10 people. Two-thirds employ only one other person. Academics recognize three start-up typologies:

> **Salary-substitute firms** – firms that are set up that simply generate an income comparable to what they might earn as an employee (e.g. plumbers, store owners etc.).
> **Lifestyle firms** – firms that allow the founder to pursue a particular lifestyle while earning an acceptable living doing so (e.g. sports instructors, artists etc.). In many cases self-employment is the conventional and accepted way of pursuing these life options.
> **Entrepreneurial firms** – these are the ones that bring innovative ideas and ways of doing things to the market. They are set up to grow from the start. Research shows that small business founders from the first two typologies can be distinguished from entrepreneurial founders based upon their goals because they tend to focus upon providing family income and entrepreneurial founders focus upon growth and profit (Stewart et al., 1999). Within this

group, young firms with the highest growth have been called 'gazelles' by academics. They are few in number but have a disproportionate importance to national economies, particularly in terms of employment (Autio, 2007). We shall return to look at them in Chapter 3.

There are also the firms that fall in the middle, doing well but perhaps not growing rapidly or to any great size. They might fulfil a valuable economic need, but there is a limit to the size of the market they serve. Often the entrepreneurs launching these sorts of ventures go on to become **serial entrepreneurs** – selling-on the successful business and going on to grow another, capitalizing on their ability to start a new venture and creating personal wealth from their sale rather than from its operation. Many entrepreneurs in our Case insights start a number of businesses. As you can appreciate, entrepreneurs and the small firms they manage are not homogeneous. Some entrepreneurs are successful and some are not. Each small firm is different and every small firm is organic – it will change over time and in different circumstances.

 ## Case insight   Material Pleasures

Lifestyle firms

In her mid-forties, Julie Spurgeon graduated with a first class honours degree in ceramic design from London's Central Saint Martin's College of Art and Design in the summer of 2008. As part of her final project to design a range of tableware she had to seek critical appraisal from retailers and industry experts. One of the firms she contacted was upmarket retailer Fortnum & Mason, and they were sufficiently impressed to commission a range of bone china tableware, called Material Pleasures, that was launched in August 2009.

The trademark Material Pleasures, which goes on the reverse of each piece, is registered (cost £200), and Julie joined Anti Copying in Design (ACID), which allowed her to log her design trail as proof against copying. Julie has had to pay for tooling and manufacturing costs herself. The moulds cost £5000 and the factory in Stoke-on-Trent required a minimum order of 250 pieces. The contract with Fortnum's involved exclusivity for six months. All this was funded with a £5000 loan from the Creative Seed Fund and a part-time job.

'In the future I'd like to continue creating specialist tableware, as well as handmade pieces. Material Pleasures stands for individual design, not big-batch production.' (Sunday Telegraph, 12 July 2009)

❑ Visit the website: http://materialpleasures.net/

QUESTIONS:

1 Would you agree that this is a lifestyle business? Is it likely to grow to a significant size?

2 What are the pros and cons of society offering training programmes, grants or subsidized finance for this sort of business – for the entrepreneur, the business and society?

 ## Case insight   AirAsia 1

Entrepreneurial firms

Former Time Warner executive Tony Fernandes set up Asia's first low-cost airline, AirAsia, in 2001 by buying the heavily indebted state-owned company from the Malaysian government for only 25p. He set about remodelling it as a short-haul, low-cost operator flying around Asia. It was the first low-cost airline in the Asian market, copying the idea from airlines in the West such as easyJet (see Case insight on page 173). The company expanded rapidly from a fleet of only two planes in 2002 to a fleet of over 180 planes flying to over 100 destinations and 22 countries by 2015. It created a completely new Asian market in low-cost air travel that is now enjoyed by millions of people.

In 2007, UBS research showed it to be the lowest cost airline in the world, with a break-even load factor of just over 50%. It achieves this through a crew productivity level that is triple that of Malaysia Airlines and an average aircraft utilization rate of 13 hours a day, involving an aircraft turnaround time of just 25 minutes. Now with hubs in Kuala Lumpur and Singapore, it has also established associate airlines in India, Japan, Thailand, Philippines and Indonesia.

❑ Visit the website: www.airasia.com.

QUESTION:

1 How can governments encourage or facilitate this sort of entrepreneurial endeavour?

Case insight   LED Hut

Serial entrepreneurs

Some entrepreneurs make a living from starting up new businesses and selling them on when they get to a certain size. They do not like large organizations and know what they are good at doing. Jonathan Ruff set up LED Hut in 2011. It sells a range of light products, including LED bulbs, mainly to trade buyers. By 2013 it had some 60 staff and made a profit of £750,000 on a turnover of £17 million. In 2014 he sold the company for £18 million to US retailer Batteries Plus Bulbs, agreeing to remain as CEO for two years. This was in fact Jonathan's fourth business venture. He started at the age of 17, selling mobile phone accessories on eBay before starting other businesses that he sold-on.

'I like building things from scratch. When a company gets to near 100 employees or sales of £40 million, it isn't for me.' (*The Sunday Times*, 7 September 2014)

❑ Visit the website: www.ledhut.co.uk

QUESTION:

1 What do you think motivates somebody to become a serial entrepreneur?

Notice also that our definition of entrepreneur says nothing about the purpose of exploiting change or the uses to which profit might be put. Some entrepreneurs have social or civic objectives and are willing to invest their own time and even risk their own capital for little or no financial return, with any profits generated being ploughed back to meet these objectives. They operate in social and civic enterprises and we shall return to them later in this chapter.

Defining small firms

You might argue that people starting up lifestyle and salary-substitute firms are not 'true' entrepreneurs because they are not motivated primarily by profit. But these small firms are the backbone of societies. That then begs the question of what is a small firm? As with the other terms, there is no uniformly acceptable definition of a small firm. Back in 1971, the Bolton Report (Bolton, 1971), which is usually held to be a definitive report on the state of small business in Britain at the time, made heavy weather of providing a statistical definition. Recognizing that one definition would not cover industries as divergent as manufacturing and service, it used eight definitions for various industry groups. These ranged from under 200 employees for manufacturing firms to over £50,000 turnover (in 1971) for retailing, and up to five vehicles or less for road transport. So many definitions clearly cause practical problems. What is more, definitions based on financial criteria suffer from inherent problems related to inflation and currency translation.

The European Commission coined the now widely used term 'small and medium-sized enterprise' (SME) and in 1996 defined it as an organization employing fewer than 250 people – a criterion that continues to be used for most statistical purposes. It defines these further categories:

	Number of employees
Micro	0–9
Small	10–49
Medium	50–249
Large	250 or more

The EU goes further to define the SME as having a turnover of less than €50 million and an annual balance sheet total of €43 million when it comes to establishing which SMEs might benefit from EU programmes, policies and competitiveness rules.

In the United States, the Small Business Administration sets small business criteria based on industry, ownership structure, revenue and number of employees. This is typically 500, although it can be as high as 1,500 in some industries.

Small firms in the UK

During much of the 20th century, the UK saw a decrease in the importance of small firms, measured in terms of the firms' share of manufacturing employment and output. The proportion of the UK labour force classified as self-employed was at its lowest point in the 1960s. It was no wonder that the Bolton Committee (op. cit.) concluded that 'the small firm sector was in a state of long-term decline, both in size and its share of economic activity'. Since the 1970s the situation has been reversed. Small firms have increased in importance, measured in terms of their number and their share of employment and turnover, and the number of small firms continues to rise, as does the number of people classified as self-employed. In 1979 there were only 2.4 million SMEs in the UK (see preceding definition). By 2014 this had grown to some 5.2 million.

UK business statistics are produced annually and are available online (www.statistics.gov .uk). In 2014 they showed that the number of businesses in the UK continues to increase, currently standing at some 5.2 million; 1.5 million (29%) were companies, 460,000 (9%) were self-employed partnerships and 3.3 million (62%) were sole proprietorships (Department for Business Innovation and Skills, 2014). Table 1.3 shows that 99.9% of these businesses were SMEs (all but 7,000) and they generated 60.1% of employment and 46.7% of turnover. However, while SMEs are the dominant form of business, the detailed statistics also show that 75.6% of all businesses in the UK had no employees (3.9 million). These comprise sole proprietors, partnerships with only self-employed partners and companies with only an employee/director. These businesses generated 17.3% of UK employment for their proprietors (4.3 million) and 6.6% of UK turnover (£231 billion). They have been the fastest growing form of business in recent years. Overall, the number of businesses with no employees has increased 68% (1.6 million) since 2000 – perhaps reflecting a preference to subcontract rather than take on full-time staff. These statistics reinforce the view that most UK small firms really are small, offering no more than self-employment. Most of these are probably lifestyle businesses. Few firms grow to any significant size. There are significant differences in start-up rates and growth rates for business according to gender and ethnicity. These issues are dealt with in Chapter 3.

There are also taxation (Value Added Tax – VAT) statistics that inform us about SMEs. These are produced annually and are available online from the Office of National Statistics in a series called 'Business Demography' (www.statistics.gov.uk). Information about VAT registrations and deregistrations is widely used as the best guide to patterns of change in the small-firm sector. They are also used in regional and local economic planning. However, these statistics measure only those firms that register for VAT, and because there is a relatively high registration threshold many very small businesses never register. Therefore, while changes in net stock of businesses provide valuable information on trends, the stock figures themselves are underestimates of the size of the business population.

The net change in business stocks is a figure that is often reported in national newspapers. It tends to be highly related to the state of the economy. Small firms are particularly vulnerable to economic changes because of their frequently precarious financing situation. In times when the economy is in

Table 1.3 UK businesses, employment and turnover, by size of business

	Businesses ('000)	%	Employment ('000)	%	Turnover (£million)	%
Micro	5,010	95.6	8,276	32.8	655,442	18.6
Small	195	3.7	3,807	15.1	514,895	14.6
Medium	31	0.6	3,075	12.2	476,864	13.5
Large	7	0.1	10,070	39.9	1,874,053	53.3
Total	5,243	100.0	25,228	100.0	3,521,254	100.0

recession there tends to be a net decrease in the stock of businesses and vice versa. The 1980s saw a large increase in the net stock of registered businesses, followed by decreases between 1991 and 1994. From 1995 onwards, net registrations have generally increased, with the numbers of companies and public corporations rising and sole proprietors and partnerships declining. The year 2014 saw a net increase of 96,000 registrations (2.26 million registrations – 2.17 million deregistrations), down from 108,000 businesses in the previous year (Office for National Statistics, 2014).

These statistics are also broken down by sector and region and do change. The highest registration rates tend to be in the 'business administration and support services' and 'professional, scientific and technical' categories, followed by 'finance and insurance' and 'information and communications'. For many years London has tended to have both the highest registration and deregistration rates and Northern Ireland the lowest rates. One interesting point is that regions with high registrations also tend to have high deregistrations – an effect called 'churning'. This indicates that high economic growth may cause or be caused by more firms coming into existence (higher registrations) at the same time as the resulting increased competition causing more firms to cease trading (higher de-registrations).

These VAT statistics have also been used to show that the most dangerous time for a new business is its first three years of existence. Almost 50% of businesses will deregister within that period – a statistic that remains fairly constant. This does not, of course, mean that the closures represent failure in terms of leaving creditors and unpaid debts. Most businesses are simply wound down. Some will close because the business ceases to be lucrative, others because of changes in the circumstances of the proprietor: death, retirement or changes in personal motivations. Some will simply close to move on to other, more lucrative opportunities. Indeed, many will start again and become serial entrepreneurs (Bosma and Levie, 2010; Hessels et al., 2010). This 'churning effect' of small firms closing and opening is part of the dynamism of the sector as they respond to changing opportunities in the marketplace and is why the net change in the stock of businesses is more important than the individual number of failures.

Cressy (2008) produced an interesting framework linking firm size, survival and subsequent growth. This predicted that smaller firms have a higher failure rate than larger firms but those that survive will then grow faster than larger firms – a prediction with strong empirical support. We shall explore this linkage through the lens of innovation in the next chapter.

Other studies have given an insight into the UK small firms sector. Small firms tend to have lower productivity than large firms, even in the same industry – a conclusion supported across Europe (Eurostat, 2009). Firms with fewer than 200 employees had 55% of the productivity (measured in value added per employee) of firms with 1,000 or more employees. In the computer and office machinery sectors, SME productivity is only one-third that of larger firms. These differences are largely because of lower capital backing. Research also indicates that SMEs have a disproportionately high number of 'bad jobs' with low pay and poor working conditions (McGovern et al., 2004) and higher accident rates (Walters, 2001). The availability of flexible working practices to encourage family-friendly working also appears arbitrary in SMEs (Dex and Smith, 2002). However, it would be wrong to characterize all SMEs as poor employers because there is enormous diversity of practice (Barrett and Rainnie, 2002; Ram and Edwards, 2003).

 ## Case insight   Amanti Cupcakes

UK start-ups

Tina Katsighiras started Amanti Cupcakes in 2013 selling sweet treats like cupcakes, brownies and scones through the social networking site Facebook – a low-cost way of testing out a business idea (Chapter 8). Working from her home in Prudhoe in the north of England, she takes orders online and bakes them on the day they are ordered for, delivering them to local residents at night. She also supplies a number of shops and cafes after samples she gave them free quickly sold out. The mum-of-two decided to leave her clerical job and start up her own business after her father

Continued...

Continued from previous page...

suffered a stroke. One year later and the business is doing well, with up to 50 home deliveries every evening and six shops and cafes placing regular orders.

'I just got up one morning and realised that my life wasn't going to change unless I did something about it. I'm half Greek and come from a long line of successful chefs. I even trained in catering after leaving school.

I had always enjoyed baking and people had always come to me for birthday and Christmas cakes, so I decided to follow that route.' (www.hexhamcourant.co.uk 16 October 2013)

QUESTION:

1 How would you describe this sort of start-up?

Case insight   Monkey Music

UK start-ups

Courtesy of Monkey Music

Angie Coates

Angie Coates' mother was a teacher and her father owned a small engineering firm. At the age of 11 Angie won a scholarship to study the oboe at the Guildhall School of Music and Drama in London, graduating with a music degree in 1988. She went on to become Head of Music at Thomas's London Day Schools. So, when she had a baby daughter it was only natural that she would want her to share her love of music. However, she was not happy with the baby music classes she found locally, so in 1993, with her daughter only a few months old, Angie started her own business, Monkey Music, based in London. Monkey Music started out offering music classes to infants and pre-school toddlers from a church hall in Dulwich, southeast London.

'I was a young mum and ready to change my lifestyle completely. I wanted to stop having to get up at 6.00 am every day to then leave my baby with a childminder before travelling to work. I wanted to do something fresh and exciting, for my daughter and for me.'

By 1998 she was struggling with the huge demand for her classes and was teaching over 500 children a week, so, on the advice of her lawyer brother, she decided to franchise the music curriculum, taking a percentage of the fee charged by the franchisee (Chapter 9). The Monkey Music programme is divided into four stages, each tailored to specific age groups for babies and young children from 3 months: Rock'n'Roll, Heigh-ho, Jiggety-Jig and Ding-Dong. Each class will take up a maximum of between 10 and 15 children. Class fees average at around £7.50.

'We take children through a very specific and progressive curriculum which comprises of a vast repertoire of especially composed songs and musical activities. Our curriculum supports all aspects of child development and classes are led by highly trained Monkey Music teachers. We start children very young so we support their social and emotional development as well as physical and language development ... Creativity is the most exciting part of Monkey Music.'

Monkey Music is widely recognized by the British franchise industry as an award-winning business, was winner at the British Franchise Association Franchisor of the Year Awards in 2005 and was a finalist in the same awards in 2010 and 2013. National parenting awards include winner of the Best National Pre-Schooler Development Activity in 2010 and 2013 and Best Toddler Development Class in 2008, with Monkey Music teachers winning numerous other parenting awards on a local level. Angie has decided not to dilute the product offering and to keep the product range simple and focused, with the website and teachers selling merchandise which extends the class experience: the soft Monkey and Baby Mo toys, class CDs and T-shirts. She feels that it is far too early to think of new product offerings.

By 2014 the business had nine staff based in Harpenden, just north of London. The network was generating sales of over £3 million. There were around 50 franchises with over 100 teachers running classes in more than 300 venues across the UK. The most successful franchise reported a turnover of £180,000 and profit of £70,000, and a significant number of franchises have remained under the same ownership for more than 10 years.

... And Angie now has five daughters.

❑ Visit the website: www.monkeymusic.co.uk

QUESTIONS:

1 What were Angie's motivations in starting up Monkey Music?

2 How did she keep the costs of starting the business down?

3 How much of a risk did she face in starting and then growing the business?

Small firms around the world

SMEs are the backbone of the economies throughout the world. They are increasing in number in most countries, as is their share of employment. Almost 99.9% of enterprises in the EU are SMEs. They generated 67.1% of employment and 57.6% of GDP or manufacturing value added (Eurostat, 2008). They employed on average 4.3 people, varying between 12 people in Slovakia and upwards of 7 in Estonia, Ireland, Latvia and Germany, to less than 3 in the Czech Republic and Greece. SMEs are a vital part of all EU economies. They dominate many service sectors, particularly hotels, catering, retailing and wholesaling, and are important in construction. What is more, SMEs in the EU display many of the same characteristics as those in the UK. Most display modest growth rates and only about 50% survive beyond their fifth year.

In the USA, SMEs (less than 500 employees) accounted for 99.9% of businesses in 2011, 48.5% of employment, and in 2008 they contributed 46% of GDP. What is more, it is estimated that they generated 63% of new jobs between 1993 and 2013 (www.sbecouncil.org/about-us/facts-and-data).

An EU report (European Commission, 2008) comparing EU to US SMEs found that US SMEs were on average larger than EU firms, with proportionately fewer micro firms generating less employment. It observed that entry, exit and survival rates were roughly comparable and that the main differences with the USA were:

1   New firms expand more rapidly in the USA than in the EU;
2   New firms display a higher dispersion of productivity in the USA than in the EU;
3   The more productive firms in the USA have a stronger tendency to increase their market shares than those in the EU.

The report concluded that the US market was probably therefore more competitive than the EU and had fewer barriers to growth. It is interesting to view the conclusions of this report alongside those of another by Sanandaji and Sanandaji (op. cit.). They looked at the careers and backgrounds of some 1,000 entrepreneurs who founded new firms and earned at least $1 billion between 1996 and 2010 – called 'SuperEntrepreneurs'. They observed that the proportion of SuperEntrepreneurs varied significantly across countries; Hong Kong had the highest, with about three SuperEntrepreneurs per million inhabitants, followed by Israel, the USA, Switzerland and Singapore. The proportion in the USA was roughly four times higher than in Western Europe. They noted what we already know, that self-employment does not necessarily lead to a growth business – our gazelles – observing that the USA had lower rates of self-employment than many other countries, for example Greece, Turkey, Spain, Portugal and Italy, and that self-employment in Silicon Valley is half that of the average of California. The implication is that policies aimed at encouraging self-employment do not necessarily lead to growth businesses, a topic we shall return to in Chapter 3.

The picture is much the same in other countries. Between 2007 and 2012, SMEs in Asia (less than 250 employees) accounted for 98% of businesses, 66% of employment and contributed 38% of GDP. It is estimated that 30% of Asia's total export value was by SMEs, with 41.5% from China (Asian Development Bank, 2013). In all countries the importance of SMEs is growing.

The picture can be more complicated to assess in countries where there is a large 'informal' sector that is not recorded in official statistics, such as Africa. The International Finance Corporation (part of the World Bank) estimates that formal and informal SMEs in Middle East and North Africa (MENA) countries comprise some 80–90% of businesses in most MENA countries. Typically they account for 10–40% of employment, according to the official statistics. However, this is likely to be a significant underestimation because it is estimated that the typical non–Gulf Cooperation Council (GCC) MENA countries employ as much as two-thirds of labour informally. In GCC countries this is to be only 6% (http://www.ifc.org/wps/wcm/connect/1e6a19804fc58e529881fe0098cb14b9/IFC+Report_Final.pdf?MOD=AJPERES). These figures vary considerably from country to country. For example, in the UAE, SMEs account for 95% of businesses, 42% of employment and 40% of GDP (http://www.go-gulf.ae/blog/dubai-sme-statistics/).

Global Entrepreneurship Monitor (GEM)

GEM is a research programme which was started in 1999 in 10 countries. By 2013, it surveyed more than 197,000 individuals and approximately 3,800 national experts on entrepreneurship across 70 economies, representing an estimated 75% of the world's population and 90% of the world's total GDP. It is a harmonized assessment of the level of national entrepreneurial activity in each of the countries. This activity is the product of two things: entrepreneurial opportunity (demand) and entrepreneurial capacity (supply). The two are linked. Without opportunity the capacity is wasted, and vice versa. These are in turn influenced by a nation's culture, economic infrastructure, education and demography. The GEM survey categorizes entrepreneurs under three headings:

> About to start up a business or have just done so within the last three months (nascent entrepreneurs) – the stage at which individuals begin to commit resources, such as time or money, to start a business or have already just done so;
> Already own or manage a business that has been established and is under 3.5 years old, but where the business is generating income and paying salaries or drawings;
> Already own or manage a business that has been established and is over 3.5 years old.

In addition, GEM identifies potential entrepreneurs by asking individuals if they expect to start a business within the next three years.

From this information a figure for total early-stage entrepreneurial activity (TEA) is calculated for each country as the proportion of nascent entrepreneurs and new business owner-managers (Figure 1.1). This is the measure of entrepreneurial capacity at any point of time – the propensity of individuals in a country to be entrepreneurial, given the social, cultural and economic conditions. Survey questions seek to understand the profile of TEA and how it is influenced by these conditions.

The 2012 UK GEM survey (Levie and Hart, 2012) was based upon over 11,000 working-age adults. It found that, for the first time since GEM began, almost one-quarter were engaged in entrepreneurial activity or intended to start a business within the next three years. The measured levels of entrepreneurial activity in the UK were generally higher than France or Germany, but lower than the USA:

> The TEA was 9.8%, compared to a historical average of about 6.0% (2002–2010). This compared to 5.2% in France, 5.3% in Germany and 12.8% in the USA.
> The level of nascent entrepreneurs was 5.7%. This compared to 3.7% in France, 3.2% in Germany and 8.9% in the USA.
> The level of owner-managers (established under 3.5 years) was 4.3%. This compared to 1.5% in France, 2.1% in Germany and 4.1% in the USA.

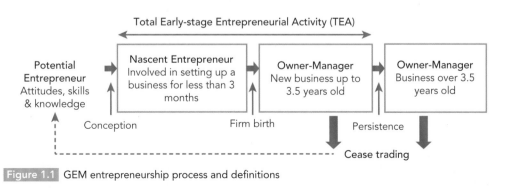

Figure 1.1 GEM entrepreneurship process and definitions

Source: Reprinted with permission from *Global Entrepreneurship Monitor 2014 Global Report* by Singer, Amoros and Moska.

> The level of owner-managers (established over 3.5 years) was 7.0%. This compared to 3.3% in France, 5.0% in Germany and 8.6% in the USA.
> The proportion ceasing to trade in the last 12 months was low, at 1.0%. This compared to 1.2% in France and Germany and 2.8% in the USA.

GEM came up with some interesting conclusions about gender and race to which we shall return in Chapter 3.

GEM is an enormous research endeavour generating quantitative data that can be used for both cross-sectional analysis and, probably most importantly, longitudinal analysis, allowing us to track individuals from entrepreneurial aspiration ('nascent entrepreneurship') to action. Obvious methodological problems exist. For example, GEM does not attempt to measure differences in culture. Also the use of a single questionnaire across all the countries is clearly problematic. Nevertheless, data from GEM is increasingly being pored over by econometricians eager to find statistical relationships of any kind. GEM reports can be downloaded free of charge from www.gemconsortium.org.

 ## Case insight   Kiran Mazumdar-Shaw and Biocon

Millionaire entrepreneur

Born in 1953 in Bangalore, India, Kiran Mazumdar-Shaw is one of the richest women in India. She is the founder of Biocon, a biotech company and India's largest producer of insulin. With a degree in zoology, she went on to take a postgraduate course and trained as a brewer in Australia, ahead of returning to India hoping to follow in her father's footsteps as a brewmaster. Despite working in the brewing industry in India for a couple of years, she never achieved her ambition, finding her career blocked by sexism. Instead, in 1978, she was persuaded to set up a joint venture making enzymes in India.

Kiran Mazumdar-Shaw started Biocon India with Irishman Les Auchincloss in 1978 in the garage of her rented house in Bangalore with seed capital of only INR 10,000. It was a joint venture with Biocon Biochemicals, Ireland. Eventually she found a banker prepared to loan the company $45,000 and, from a facility in Bangalore making enzymes for the brewing industry, started to diversify. It became the first Indian company to manufacture and export enzymes to the USA and Europe. This gave her a flow of cash that she used to fund research and to start producing pharmaceutical drugs. The early years were hard.

'I was young, I was twenty five years old ... banks were very nervous about lending to young entrepreneurs because they felt we didn't have the business experience ... and then I had ... this strange business called biotechnology which no one understood ... Banks were very fearful of lending to a woman because I was considered high risk.' (BBC News Business, 11 April 2011)

In 1989, Kiran met the chair of ICICI Bank, which had just launched a venture fund. The fund took a 20% stake in the company and helped finance its move into biopharmaceuticals. Shortly after this, Unilever took over Biocon Biochemicals and bought ICICI's stake in Biocon India, at the same time increasing it to 50%. In 1996 it entered the biopharmaceuticals and statins markets. One year later Unilever sold its share in Biocon Biochemicals, and Mazumdar-Shaw bought out Unilever and was able to start preparing Biocon India to float on the stock market, which it did in 2004, with a market value of $1.1 billion.

In 2003 Biocon became the first company to develop human insulin on a Pichia expression system. Since then it has obtained a listing on the stock exchange and entered into thousands of R&D licensing agreements with other pharmaceutical companies around the world. Today Biocon has a turnover in excess of INR 24,000 million. It has Asia's largest insulin and statin production facilities and its largest perfusion-based antibody production facility. It produces drugs for cancer, diabetes and autoimmune diseases and is developing the world's first oral insulin, currently undergoing Phase III clinical trials.

Kiran Mazumdar-Shaw has enjoyed many awards and honours. In 2010 TIME magazine included her in their 100 most powerful people in the world; in the same year the Financial Times had her in their list of the top 50 women in business. Passionate about providing affordable health care in India, she has funded the 1,400-bed Mazumdar-Shaw Cancer Centre, a free cancer hospital in Bangalore. Every year, she donates $2 million to support health insurance coverage for some 100,000 Indian villagers.

QUESTION:

1 How typical is this story? What are the chances of becoming a millionaire by starting your own business?

Social and civic entrepreneurs

It was Bill Drayton who first coined the phrase social entrepreneur in 1972 when he helped an Indian named Vinoba Bhave redistribute land so that more farmers could become landowners, contributing to their local communities – a process that eventually resulted in some seven million acres of land being given away. Today, he is the founder and CEO of Ashoka, an organization that was created to help support, connect and build up social entrepreneurs and their ideas. Social entrepreneurs usually operate as entrepreneurs within organizations whose primary purpose is social rather than economic – called social enterprises. Sometimes they create these organizations themselves but sometimes, like an intrapreneur, they will operate as entrepreneurs within an existing social enterprise. A social enterprise operates in a commercial way to achieve its social objectives, and any profits it generates are ploughed back to help achieve them. It is often also about creating social change at a community level, normally through voluntary or community groups. In the UK this has a long history, from Victorian hospitals to the modern-day hospice movement. The legal forms a social enterprise can take are outlined in Chapter 9. Social Enterprise UK, a national body representing social enterprises, says a social enterprise must satisfy six criteria. It must:

> Have a clear social or environmental mission set out in its governing documents;
> Generate the majority of its income through trade;
> Reinvest the majority of its profit;
> Be autonomous of the state;
> Be majority controlled in the interests of the social mission;
> Be accountable and transparent.

Social entrepreneurs have many of the qualities of commercial entrepreneurs; in particular they are innovative, often creating change by doing things differently. They operate at the intersection of the public and private sectors, pulling together resources from both but always with the purpose of serving their social mission. They might also pull in resources from the voluntary sector. The social enterprises they create are often locally based, but could be national or international.

Pearce (2003) tries to explain this myriad of interlinking concepts by talking about three systems of the economy – private, public and social – delineated in two dimensions – trading/non-trading and global/community-based, shown in Figure 1.2. The first system is the private sector, which concentrates on trading, with the objective of profit maximization. But even this has its legal and illegal sectors. It operates on anything from a local to a global basis. The second system is public services and government, which operates in a planned, non-trading way. It is characterized as bureaucratic and inefficient. It also operates on anything from a local to a global basis. The third system is the social economy, which includes social enterprise, voluntary and charity organizations and the family economy. This is usually far more community-based and can be both planned and based upon market trading. The use of the word 'system', rather than sector, in this context is deliberate because it is meant to imply that each system is not homogeneous.

It was estimated that in 2012 there were approximately 70,000 social enterprises in the UK contributing £18.5 billion to the UK economy and employing almost a million people (Department for Business, Innovation and Skills, 2013). The GEM 2009 Social Entrepreneurship Report (Terjesen et al., 2009) showed that in the UK the highest level of social entrepreneurial activity is among the youngest age group (18–24 years) at 4.4% – a result that has persisted for a number of years. However it is the people in the oldest age group (55–64 years) that are most likely to be running established social enterprises (1.7% involvement). The report shows no significant difference between women and men, and states that those most likely to be social entrepreneurs belong to the mixed ethnic origin group (6.3%) and combined black African and black Caribbean

" Social entrepreneurs are not content just to give a fish or teach how to fish. They will not rest until they have revolutionized the fishing industry.

Bill Drayton, founder, Ashoka, http://www.architectsofpeace. org/architects-of-peace/ bill-drayton "

Figure 1.2 The three systems of the economy

Source: Adapted from Pearce, J. (2003) *Social Enterprise in Anytown*, Calouste Gulbenkian Foundation. Reproduced with permission.

group (7.5%) – all higher than the percentage of the white population who play a part in social enterprise. The GEM results should, however, be treated with caution because the definition of social entrepreneur is so broad that it includes anybody trying to start or manage any form of social, community or voluntary activity.

Civic entrepreneurs operate within larger civic organizations in the public sector, such as government, local councils, schools, health authorities and police forces. They are therefore more like intrapreneurs and, just like intrapreneurs, their freedom of action may be limited by the rules and regulations of the organization they work for. However, like social entrepreneurs, their primary aim is social rather than economic. The terms social entrepreneur and civic entrepreneur have often been used in an almost interchangeable way, but they are different. The link is through the voluntary, community and not-for-profit sectors that straddle the public and private sectors, often working on the delivery of government initiatives.

Conflicts within social enterprise

There are inherent conflicts within a social enterprise. The first is the conflict between its social and commercial operations. The objectives of a social enterprise can be 'integrated' with its commercial operations or 'complementary' to them. An integrated model is one where surplus-generating activities simultaneously create social benefit, with one objective not getting in the way of the other. The art of integration, according to Fowler (2000), is to 'marry the development agendas with market opportunities and then manage them properly so that they are synergistic not draining'. Two examples of integration are the Grameen Bank (see Case insight on page 21) and the Big Issue (Case insight on page 80.). All too often, however, this is not the case and the one agenda 'contaminates' the other, perhaps leading to reduced efficiency and effectiveness on the commercial side or dilution of the social objectives on the other. When surpluses from the commercial activity are simply used as a source of cross-subsidy for the social objectives, rather than producing social benefits themselves, this can more accurately be called complementary social entrepreneurship.

Case insight   Grameen Bank

 Integrated social enterprise

Grameen Bank – meaning 'bank of the villages' in the Bangla language – was set up in Bangladesh in 1976 by Professor Muhammad Yunus, who originally set up a research project to study how to design a credit delivery system to provide banking services to the rural poor. In 1983 it became an independent bank. Grameen Bank provides tiny loans, called microcredit, without collateral to the poor. The aim is to leverage their skills to help them start and grow tiny businesses. It uses a local, group-based approach – called solidarity lending – to ensure that borrowers repay their loans and develop a good credit history. Each borrower belongs to a five-member group. The group is not required to give guarantees for loans to its members, and repayment is solely the responsibility of the individual borrower. However, the group and the centre ensure that everyone behaves responsibly and individuals do not get into arrears with their repayments. Of its borrowers, 96% are women.

Borrowers are encouraged to become savers, and the bank also accepts deposits. It also provides other services and runs several development-oriented businesses including fabric, telephone and energy companies. It seeks to establish a new sort of self-sustaining rural association that reduces dependency on external finance, increases development impact and spreads risk. Funding has come from different sources. Initially, donor agencies provided the bulk of capital at low interest rates but, by the 1990s, the bank was getting most of its funding from the central bank of Bangladesh. In 1976 Professor Yunus received the Nobel Peace Prize. The success of Grameen Bank has inspired similar projects in more than 40 countries around the world.

QUESTION:

1 How many stakeholders, each with different objectives, have to be brought together for this bank to operate effectively?

The second conflict arises around the issue of democratic accountability. It occurs particularly when the activities of the social enterprise are not integrated. A social enterprise operates at the boundary between public and private sectors, and there is an inherent conflict in the values and beliefs of the two sectors. The issues relating to social enterprise revolve around its commercial efficiency and effectiveness on the one hand and its democratic accountability on the other. There are difficulties with accounting for the two objectives and in particular making trade-offs between the two. It is the old issue of whether the (commercial) means always justify the (social) ends. It is therefore imperative for a social enterprise to decide on the core mission and realize what is peripheral – a means of achieving the ultimate mission. Unless this happens, social enterprises can avoid rigorous monitoring and democratic accountability. But this begs the question of who decides on the core mission, and how 'performance' in meeting the mission might be measured. The complex nature of the stakeholders' interests in most social enterprises means that these issues can be 'fudged' and are often the result of political influence. The danger particularly occurs when public funds are involved. Where these are channelled through another organization there is always the possibility of commercial gain, and without clear performance criteria and democratic accountability there is no way of knowing whether the public got value-for-money.

Fowler (op. cit.) was concerned about these conflicts, noting particularly that it is a risky framework for the development of recipients of international development aid – non-governmental organizations (NGOs). These organizations handle large amounts of public money. He doubted that they can handle the conflicts between social and commercial behaviour. He argued that retaining their moral underpinning and inspiration is vital and any involvement in income-generating activities will compromise this. He also feared that the social enterprise framework is not sustainable because they are so dependent on government aid. There is also the concern about what entrepreneurial activities the large amounts of public money they receive might be put to. Fowler is therefore more in favour of 'civic entrepreneurship', which he sees as providing 'civic, as opposed to public, legitimacy and economic viability from a broad base of citizen support'.

The third conflict concerns the nature of the objectives a social enterprise is set up to achieve. These may be clearly non-political, for example Jamie Oliver's Fifteen restaurant group and Cafédirect in the UK. However, they may also be seen as ways of encouraging some sort of 'social engineering', often originating from a government policy initiative. For example, the UK government has encouraged the formation of social enterprises for the delivery of services such as health and social care, fostering and adoption, transport and recycling – areas that traditionally have been seen as the responsibility of the public sector. This is partly because social enterprise is seen as innovative and efficient, but it is also partly as a way of getting extra, non-government funding into the service and, in extremis, can be seen as 'privatization'.

There are always lessons to be learned when the activities and approaches of one sector are compared to another, not least in a public sector that is often seen as overly bureaucratic. Eikenberry and Kluver (2004) acknowledged the need for the public sector to work with not-for-profit, community and voluntary organizations, observing that 'they are more than just tools for achieving the most efficient and effective mode of service delivery; they are also important vehicles for creating and maintaining a strong civil society'. Alexander et al. (1999) underlined the importance of their role as 'schools or laboratories of democratic citizenship' – training grounds for citizenship that involve people in socially beneficial activities that they would not otherwise engage in. However, sometimes politicians can use social enterprise as a way of forcing change on the public sector, and not always for the best reasons.

 ## Case insight   The Entertainer

A family business with values

Gary Grant bought a toy shop in the small town of Amersham in England in 1981. Today, The Entertainer is a UK-wide chain of stores with a turnover of £140 million and profits of over £7 million and plans to open franchise chains worldwide. It already has over 100 shops in the UK as well as two in Pakistan and one in Azerbaijan, selling a wide range of toys from Lego and all things *Frozen* to loom bands. Stores are sited in prime, high foot-fall, high-street locations and the average customer spend is only about £10. At a time when many UK retailers have seen sales stagnate, sales for The Entertainer continue to climb, and 20% of sales are now online.

The company is 100% family-owned, with headquarters close to Gary's home in Amersham. Gary is a committed Christian and gives 10% of profits to charity. He has been known to gather his staff together in prayer in troubled times, but more recently they have shared in generous bonuses – £1.5 million in 2014 – on top of awards for completing training hurdles or giving good customer service.

'In everything we do faith is central to our decisions. We have got the ability to put back into society. We pay UK taxes and don't dodge around it unlike some high-street names. There are no staff on zero hours contracts or profits siphoned into off-shore tax havens.' (*The Guardian*, 7 April 2015)

QUESTION:

1 How difficult is it to run your own business and maintain strong social and ethical values?

Sustainable entrepreneurship

The boundary between the public and private sectors is continually changing, and social enterprise is often at that boundary. However, private companies can also act to achieve social good. Indeed, as we shall see in Chapter 9, the legal formation of a social enterprise can be cumbersome and there are some pragmatic advantages to remaining a sole trader or private company, not least the avoidance of public accountability. There is a long history of entrepreneurs with social motivations – from the chocolate maker J. Cadbury & Sons with its Quaker values, to the jam maker Wilkin & Sons. More recently companies like Lush and Timberland have managed to combine business and social values successfully – and in the process enhance their brand image. But always the commercial objective came first, and always the entrepreneurs decided on the social mission and how it was to be met.

Another approach to this issue in recent years has been the emergence of what has become known as **sustainable entrepreneurship** – where issues of CSR, sustainability, ethics and good corporate governance are at the core of a 'for-profit' commercial enterprise. Entrepreneurship that emphasizes joint economic and ecological value creation only has been called **environmental entrepreneurship**, **eco-entrepreneurship** and **eco-preneurship**.

Sustainable entrepreneurship is about meeting the needs of today through profit without prejudicing the future. Porter and Kramer (2011) defined it as a 'unique' concept whereby sustainable business strategies focus on increasing both social and business value, broadening the scope of a business from more profit-driven goals to the creation of joint benefits and 'shared value'. These strategies are part of the overall strategy of the company – not just an 'add-on' – and come from its very reason for existence – its mission. Schaltegger and Wagner (2011) said that entrepreneurs who are sustainability-driven within their core business and contribute towards sustainable development can be called sustainable entrepreneurs. Kalam and Singh (2011) saw sustainability as having six dimensions:

> **Economic** – implying that the core business model is commercially sound and robust and the development tools are based upon the core competencies of the region;
> **Technological** – implying that technology will be the driving force behind the development tool;
> **Social** – reflecting the belief that the enterprise must partner with the local community and facilitate building capacity and improving living standards, rather than treating community members just as customers;
> **Environmental** – implying that the wide range of environmental issues such as reducing waste and pollution, protecting biodiversity, preserving natural resources etc. are all taken into account and the business should aim to have a beneficial or at least neutral effect;
> **Value** – implying that the development should be accompanied by the creation of a value-based society that reduces social conflict;
> **Learning** – implying that the development should create an infrastructure that facilitates learning and the transfer of knowledge, thereby encouraging innovation.

In sustainable entrepreneurship, innovation is aimed at finding 'efficient sustainable solutions for the most pressing problems of the world' (Weidinger et al., 2014). This might involve searching for new products, services or processes that alleviate poor social or environmental conditions, make more efficient use of energy and other natural resources, or harness otherwise underused resources that are in greater abundance, cheaper to produce or less harmful to society.

 ## Case insight   SBA Hydro

Sustainable entrepreneurship

SBA Hydro and Renewable Energy Private Limited develops and operates micro-hydro power plants, providing hydroelectric power to villages in the Himalayan Belt of northern India. These villages have, in the past, suffered long periods of blackouts and relied on polluting diesel generators for much of their power needs. SBA's customizable, flexible-use turbines harness the underused resources of fast-flowing Himalayan streams to produce clean energy. Working with the Indian government, the company adopts a cooperative-based approach to implement these projects, finding employment for many who would otherwise remain unemployed. It trains local staff to plan, construct, operate and maintain the stations, employing about 10 locals at each plant. SBA funds the building and development of the station and, after a period of 10 years, transfers the station fully to the local community. SBA also sells the electricity it produces to the national grid. After meeting their own energy needs, villages can feed the surplus energy to the state utility for use by towns and by bulk industrial and commercial consumers. This earns them much-needed revenue to ensure their own development.

QUESTIONS:

1 Is this an example of sustainable enterprise? Explain.

2 How does it differ from Grameen Bank?

Case insight   Goodone

Social or private enterprise?

Nin Castle and Phoebe Emerson met at Brighton University in 2001. Both Nin and Phoebe were doing fashion courses and they talked about setting up a fashion business but were uneasy about some of the ethical and environmental issues relating to the industry. Two million tonnes of clothes are sold annually in the UK, of which one million will end up in landfill sites when half of it is reusable. It was while at a nightclub in 2003 that they came up with the idea of Goodone. The idea was to design and produce innovative, quality, one-off clothing which was made from hand-picked, locally sourced, recycled fabrics. They called it 'up-cycling', 'innovatively combining new British and sustainable fabrics with reclaimed textiles'. They wanted to change perceptions of what recycled clothing can be by creating garments which did not look recycled.

Starting with only £1,000, in 2005 they made a deal with a local charity shop that allowed them to go through all the bags of textiles that were being sent to the rag factory at the cost of £1 a bag. They also acquired a disused car show-room in Brighton – a large open space into which they put two makeshift beds and a couple of second-hand sewing machines – and started their business:

'We had no funding, were living on housing benefit and doing part-time jobs to try and get the business up and running. In 2006 our first customers were local boutiques. We were full of enthusiasm and rather naive as we really thought that our tiny business could make an impact on the huge fashion industry.' (Nin Castle, *Daily Telegraph*, 5 February 2009)

Nin did the design work and Phoebe looked after the business side, both working on the manufacturing. Within a few months they decided to go on a three-day 'Creative Business' start-up course run by the National Council for Graduate Entrepreneurship (NCGE) and registered Goodone as a company. After a year in the car showroom, they relocated to Hackney in London so as to be in the 'fashion hub' of the UK. They also set up their own online shop.

In 2007 they won a £15,000 prize from NCGE, much of which was spent on repairing the sewing machines. However, the prize also generated a lot of free PR, and articles about the company appeared in the national press. These stimulated sales – Goodone fulfilled orders for clothes from the cult shop 'Side by Side' in Tokyo, Japan – and created more opportunities. They exhibited at the 'Fashion Made Fair' sale in Brick Lane, London, 'The Clothes Show Live' in Birmingham and the 'Margin' trade show in London, and started giving presentations to the London School of Fashion. They were awarded Manufacturing Advisory Service funding to develop the Goodone product line and brand and a London Development Agency SME Innovation Award, which gave them manufacturing consultancy from the London College of Fashion. Normally, lengths of cloth are sent to the manufacturer, but with recycled fabric every piece is different and that creates special problems. Goodone also began outsourcing some manufacturing to HEBA Women's Project, a London charity.

In January 2008 Phoebe amicably left the company to work in other areas of social enterprise and since then has become a lawyer working in the human rights field. Nin then went on to produce charity T-shirts by recycling old campaign T-shirts from Greenpeace, Shelter, Amnesty, Liberty and WWF. She spent August 2009 in South Africa working for the Tabeisa Project, designing and producing clothes in a township outside Cape Town for sale in the UK.

Goodone's mission statement sets out their aims:

'Goodone design and produce innovative, quality, one-off clothing which is made from hand-picked, locally-sourced, recycled fabrics. We aim to exceed people's expectations of what recycled clothing can be by creating

Courtesy of Goodone, Photographer Jessica Bonham

Continued...

Continued from previous page...

garments which don't look obviously recycled. Instead of "reworking" or "customising" existing pieces we design for production. Using our specialist knowledge in the deconstruction and reconstruction of garments, sustainable sourcing and production we are able to create a limitless amount of new clothing from old, which, dependent on the combination of coloured, patterned and textured fabrics chosen, will inherently always remain unique. This means we are able to mass-produce the one-off.

By using these recycled materials we are not only providing a creative and sustainable solution for waste reduction but also minimising energy use and the damage to environment caused by the production of new clothing. It is our goal to continue to build a reputable brand which is internationally recognised for pioneering the production of high-quality, innovative 'recreated' clothing, secondly, provide specialist consultancy, working with, instead of against, existing brands and retailers to solve their own waste issues, consequently impacting the industry on a bigger scale, and thirdly, to educate the next generation of fashion designers, entrepreneurs and consumers on the urgency and methods for designing, producing and consuming sustainably.'

Goodone's summer 2010 collection was shown at London Fashion Week and was offered at Topshop's website and flagship Oxford Street store. In the same year, Clare Farrell joined the Goodone team as co-designer. By 2014 Goodone was supplying outlets in London, Manchester, Brighton and Glasgow in the UK and internationally in Germany, USA, Switzerland, Canada and Spain. They were also selling from their website. The turnover is modest. Goodone employs part-time staff and makes use of interns. Both Nin and Claire also teach at fashion colleges and Goodone's income gets ploughed back into the business. Goodone is an example of a business with social objectives and one that has made the most of grants and support that are available to young enterprises.

❑ Visit the website: www.goodone.co.uk.

QUESTIONS:

1 Is this a social enterprise or just a socially ethical business?

2 Is Goodone successful? How do you measure this? What does money measure in this business?

3 Was it right that Nin and Phoebe should have been able to make so much use of grants and support?

⟳ Summary

› We are living in an age of uncertainty characterized by continuing, unpredictable and rapid change – change that is both incremental and discontinuous. It is an increasingly complex world full of interconnections formed by a global market place linked by technology allowing instant communication.

› While large firms find this environment challenging, small, entrepreneurial firms have thrived and, while their contribution to economic prosperity has become recognized, many entrepreneurs have become millionaires.

› The key to this success has been the ability of entrepreneurs to work with change to recognize and create opportunities.

› Entrepreneurial management is characterized as being a social activity that has a different approach to dealing with risk and uncertainty. Successful entrepreneurs generate strong relationships with stakeholders that allow them to mitigate risk and maintain flexibility of action. They develop strategy differently, creating strategic intent but maintaining a loose, flexible strategy and continuously strategizing and creating as many strategic options as possible.

› Entrepreneurs are defined primarily by their actions. They create and/or exploit change for profit by innovating, accepting risk and moving resources to areas of higher return.

› Small, entrepreneurial firms are a vital part of the economies of most Western countries; 95% of the wealth of the USA was created since 1980. SMEs generate 50% of GDP in the USA, and over 25% in the UK. In the EU they generate 67% of employment. But it is the fast-growing 'gazelles' that generate most of the employment growth.

› A small and medium-sized enterprise (SME) is one with fewer than 250 employees. A micro business has up to 9 employees, a small business up to 49 employees and a medium-sized business up to 249 employees.

› Until the 1960s the UK saw a decrease in the importance of small firms, although since the 1970s this has been reversed. SMEs are now an important part of the economies of all countries around the world. They generate significant employment and wealth. Nevertheless, most small firms in the UK are unlikely to grow to any size.

> A social enterprise operates in an entrepreneurial way to achieve social objectives, and any profit is ploughed back into the enterprise to help achieve them. They operate at the intersection of the public and private sectors – in the social economy.

> There can be conflicts within a social enterprise: between its social and commercial operations; around the issue of democratic accountability; and in the nature of the social objectives it is set up to achieve. Social enterprise can be seen as a way of diminishing the responsibilities of the state.

> Sustainable entrepreneurship is where issues of CSR, sustainability, ethics and good corporate governance are at the core of a 'for-profit' commercial enterprise.

✓ Activities

1 Write a report that critically analyses the changing commercial environment and how it impacts on entrepreneurship.

2 Research and write a report on the background and history of an entrepreneur who set up their own business and grew it successfully.

3 Update the statistics on small firms in Britain and in the EU. Alternatively, obtain similar statistics on the performance of small firms in your country. What does this tell you about recent developments? Summarize your findings in a report.

4 Access the latest GEM report for your country and summarize its findings in a report.

5 Research the history of a successful social enterprise and outline the reasons for its success in a report.

💬 Group discussion topics

1 Is now a good time to start your own business?

2 Do you dream of starting your own business? If so, why? If not, why not? What do you think will be the main challenges you would face?

3 List the pros and cons of running your own business.

4 What are the main challenges facing a start-up today?

5 Do you think the definition of an entrepreneur in this chapter is adequate?

6 How does an entrepreneur differ from an intrapreneur or a social entrepreneur?

7 Is an owner-manager of a small firm automatically an entrepreneur?

8 How does the management of a small firm differ from the management of a large one?

9 What are the characteristics of small firms that distinguish them from large firms and what are these implications? Do they mean that small firms really are sufficiently different to warrant special study?

10 Are small firms sufficiently homogeneous to justify special study? What further segmentation or classification might you suggest and what are the special and different characteristics of these segments?

11 Are all small firms worthy of special treatment? If so, which small firms and what sort of special treatment?

12 Why has the number of small firms been increasing in the UK since the late 1960s?

13 Is it good that so many businesses close in the first three years?

14 Should arts students who want to be self-employed be taught entrepreneurship?

15 Should all students at university be taught entrepreneurship?

16 What are the real defining characteristics of a small firm?

17 What are nascent entrepreneurs? What does their number tell us that start-up statistics do not?

18 Does social enterprise diminish the responsibilities of the state?

19 Are you content to see public money going to social enterprise? Explain.

20 Would you prefer to be a social entrepreneur, a commercial entrepreneur with social values or a sustainable entrepreneur? Explain.

☞ References

Acs, Z.J. and Audretsch, D.B. (2005) 'Entrepreneurship, Innovation and Technological Change', *Institute for Development Studies*, ISSN No. 5-5.

Alexander, J., Nank, R. and Strivers, C. (1999) 'Implications of Welfare Reform: Do Nonprofit Survival Strategies Threaten Civil Society?', *Non-profit and Voluntary Sector Quarterly*, 28(4).

Anderson, J. (1995) *Local Heroes*, Glasgow: Scottish Enterprise.

Asian Development Bank (2013) *Asia SME Finance Monitor*, Philippines: ADB.

Autio, E. (2007) *Global Entrepreneurship Monitor 2007 Global Report on High-Growth Entrepreneurship*, London, UK: London Business School; and Babson Park, MA: Babson College.

Barrett, R. and Rainnie, A. (2002) 'What's So Special About Small Firms? Developing an Integrated Approach to Analysing Small Firms Industrial Relations', *Work, Employment and Society*, 16(3).

Birch, D.L. (1979) 'The Job Creation Process', unpublished report, *MIT Program on Neighbourhood and Regional Change,* prepared for the Economic Development Administration, US Department of Commerce, Washington, DC.

Bolton, J.E. (1971) *Report of the Committee of Inquiry on Small Firms,* Cmnd. 4811, London: HMSO.

Bosma, N.S. and Levie, J. (2010) *Global Entrepreneurship Monitor, 2009: Executive Report,* Babson Park, MA, USA: Babson College; Santiago, Chile: Universidad del Desarrollo; Reykjavík, Iceland: Háskólinn Reykjavík University; and London, UK: Global Entrepreneurship Research Association.

Cantillon, R. (1755) *Essai sur la Nature du Commerce en General,* London and Paris: R. Gyles; translated (1931) by H. Higgs, London: Macmillan. See also Resources on Cantillon, available online at cepa.newschool.edu/het/profiles/cantillon.htm.

Craig, J.B.L. and Johnson, D. (2006) 'Establishing Individual Differences Related to Opportunity Alertness and Innovation Dependent on Academic-Career Training', *Journal of Management Development*, 25(1).

Cressy, R. (2008) *Determinants of Small Firm Survival and Growth,* in A. Basu, M. Casson, N. Wadeson and B. Yeung (eds), *The Oxford Handbook of Entrepreneurship,* Oxford: Oxford University Press.

Department of Business, Enterprise and Regulatory Reform (2008) *High growth firms in the UK: Lessons from an analysis of comparative UK performance,* BERR Economics Paper no. 3, London, UK: Department of Business, Enterprise and Regulatory Reform.

Department for Business, Innovation and Skills (2013) *Small Business Survey 2012: SME Employers,* London, UK: Department for Business, Innovation and Skills.

Department for Business Innovation and Skills (2014) *Statistical Release: Business Population Estimates for the UK and Regions 2014,* London, UK: Department for Business Innovation and Skills.

Dex, S. and Smith, C. (2002) *The Nature and Pattern of Family-Friendly Employment Policies in the UK,* Abingdon: Policy Press.

Drucker, P.F. (1974) *Management Tasks, Responsibilities, Practices,* New York: Harper & Row.

Eikenberry, A. and Kluver, J.D. (2004) 'The Marketisation of the Non-profit Sector: Civil Society at Risk?', *Public Administration Review,* 64(2), March/April.

Ely, R.T. and Hess, R.H. (1893) *Outline of Economics,* New York: Macmillan.

European Commission (2008) *European Competitiveness Report 2008*: available online at www.ec.europa.eu/enterprise.

Eurostat (2008) *Enterprises by Size Class – Overview of SMEs in the EU, Statistics in Focus, 31/2008,* available online at epp.eurostat.ec.europa.eu.

Eurostat (2009) *European Business Facts and Figures, 2009 Edition,* Luxembourg: Eurostat, available online at epp.eurostat.ec.europa.eu.

Fowler, A. (2000) 'NGDOs as a Moment in History: Beyond Aid to Social Entrepreneurship or Civic Innovation?', *Third World Quarterly,* 21(4).

Haltiwanger, J., Jarmin, R.S. and Miranda, J. (2013) 'Who Creates jobs? Small Versus Large Versus Young', *Review of Economics and Statistics,* 95.

Hamel, G. (2000) *Leading the Revolution,* Boston: Harvard Business School Press.

Hayek, F.A. (1948) 'The Use of Knowledge in Society', in Hayek, *Studies in Philosophy, Politics and Economics,* Chicago: University of Chicago Press.

Hayek, F.A. (1952) *The Sensory Order,* Chicago: University of Chicago Press.

Hayek, F.A. (1967a) 'Competition as a Discovery Procedure', in Hayek, *New Studies in Philosophy, Politics, Economics and History of Ideas,* Chicago: Chicago University Press.

Hayek, F.A. (1967b) 'The Results of Human Action, but not Human Design', in Hayek, *New Studies in Philosophy, Politics, Economics and History of Ideas,* Chicago: Chicago University Press.

Hessels, J., Grilo, I., Thurik, R. and Van der Zwan, P. (2010) 'Entrepreneurial Exit and Entrepreneurial Engagement', *Journal of Evolutionary Economics,* 21(3).

Hisrich, R.D. and Peters, M.P. (1992) *Entrepreneurship: Starting, Developing and Managing a New Enterprise,* Homewood, IL: Irwin.

Kalam, A.P.J.A. and Singh, S.P. (2011) *Target 3 Billion – PURA: Innovative Solutions towards Sustainable Development,* London: Penguin Books.

Kirzner, I.M. (1973) *Competition and Entrepreneurship,* Chicago: University of Chicago Press.

Kirzner, I.M. (1979) *Perception, Opportunity and Profit: Studies in the Theory of Entrepreneurship,* Chicago: University of Chicago Press.

Kirzner, I.M. (1997) 'Entrepreneurial Discovery and Competitive Market Processes: An Austrian Approach', *Journal of Economic Literature,* 35.

Kirzner, I.M. (1999) 'Creativity and/or Alertness: A Reconsideration of the Schumpeterian Entrepreneur', *Review of Austrian Economics,* 11.

Kirzner, I.M. (2009) 'The Alert and Creative Entrepreneur: A Clarification', *Small Business Economics,* 32.

Knight, F. (1921) *Risk, Uncertainty and Profit,* Chicago: University of Chicago Press.

Levie, J. Hart, M. (2012) *Global Entrepreneurship Monitor: United Kingdom 2012 Monitoring Report,* Aston Business School and the Hunter Centre for Entrepreneurship, University of Strathclyde.

Marshall, A. (1890) *Principles of Economics,* London and New York: Macmillan.

McGovern, P., Smeaton, D. and Hill, S. (2004) 'Bad Jobs in Britain: Non-standard Employment and Job Quality', *Work and Occupations,* 31.

McMillan, E. (2004) *Complexity, Organisations and Change,* London: Routledge.

Menger, C. (1871/1981) *Principles of Economics,* New York: New York University Press.

Naisbitt, J. (1994) *Global Paradox: The Bigger the World Economy, the more Powerful its Smaller Players,* London: BCA.

Office for National Statistics (2014) 'Statistical Bulletin: Business Demography, 2013', *Office for National Statistics,* November 2014.

Ohmae, K. (2005) *The Next Global Stage: Challenges and Opportunities in our Borderless World*, New Jersey: Pearson Education.

Pearce, J. (2003) *Social Enterprise in Anytown*, London, UK: Calouste Gulbenkian Foundation.

Porter, M.E. and Kramer, M.R. (2011) 'Creating Shared Value', *Harvard Business Review*, 3–17.

Ram, M. and Edwards, P. (2003) 'Praising Caesar Not Burying Him – What We Know About Employment in Small Firms', *Work, Employment and Society*, 17(4).

Samuelsson, M. and Davidsson, P. (2009) 'Does Venture Opportunity Variation Matter? Investigating Systematic Process Differences between Innovative and Imitative New Ventures', *Small Business Economics*, 33.

Sanandaji, T. and Sanandaji, N. (2014) *SuperEntrepreneurs: And How Your Country Can Get Them*, London, UK: Centre for Policy Studies.

Say, J.B. (1803) *Trait d'economie politique ou simple exposition de la maniére dont se forment, se distribuent, et se consomment les riches*; revised (1819); translated (1830) by R. Prinsep, *A Treatise on Political Economy: On Familiar Conversations on the Manner in Which Wealth is Produced, Distributed and Consumed by Society*, Philadelphia: John Grigg and Elliot.

Say, J.B. (1817) *Catechisme d'economie politique*; translated (1921) by J. Richter, *Catechism of Political Economy*, J.A.

Schaltegger, S. and Wagner, M. (2011) 'Sustainable Entrepreneurship and Sustainable Innovation: Categories and Interventions', *Business Strategy and the Environment*, 20 (4).

Schumpeter J.A. (1911) *Theorie der Wirtschaftlichen Entwicklung*, Munich and Leipzig: Dunker und Humblat; translated (1934) by R. Opie, *The Theory of Economic Development*, Cambridge, MA: Harvard University Press.

Schumpeter J.A. (1928) 'The Instability of Capitalism', *Economic Journal*, 38.

Schumpeter, J.A. (1942) *Capitalism, Socialism, and Democracy*, New York: Harper.

Shapero, A. (1975) 'The Displaced, Uncomfortable Entrepreneur', *Psychology Today*, 8.

Shapero, A. (1984) 'The Entrepreneurial Event', in C. Kent (ed.), *The Environment for Entrepreneurship*, Lexington, MA: DC Health.

Shapero, A. (1985) 'Why Entrepreneurship?', *Journal of Small Business Management*, 23(4).

Stewart, W.H., Watson, W.E., Carland, J.C. and Carland, J.W. (1999) 'A Proclivity for Entrepreneurship: Determinants of Company Success', *Journal of Business Venturing*, 14(2).

Terjesen, S., Lepoutre, J., Justo, R. and Bosma, N. (2009) *Global Entrepreneurship Monitor Report on Social Entrepreneurship Executive Summary*, Babson Park, MA, USA: Babson College; Santiago, Chile: Universidad del Desarrollo; Kuala Lumpur, Malaysia: Universiti Tun Abdul Razak; and London, UK: London Business School.

Timmons, J. (1999) *New Venture Creation: Entrepreneurship for the 21st Century*, Boston: Irwin/McGraw-Hill.

Walters, D. (2001) *Health and Safety in Small Enterprise*, Oxford: PIE Peter Lang.

Weidinger, C., Fischler, F and Schnidper, R. (eds) (2014) *Sustainable Entrepreneurship: Business Success through Sustainability (CSR, Sustainability, Ethics and Governance)*, Heidelberg: Springer.

www.palgrave.com/Burns-Entrepreneurship-And-Small-Business-4e

Go online to access additional teaching and learning resources for this chapter on the companion website. Click here in the ebook to complete a multiple choice revision quiz for this chapter.

The economics of entrepreneurship and public policy | 2

Getty Images/iStockphoto Thinkstock Images \ anyaberkut

Contents

Learning outcomes

When you have read this chapter and undertaken the related activities you will be able to:

> Explain the theories used to explain the growth in number and importance of SMEs;
> Explain the role of the entrepreneur in stimulating economic growth;
> Explain the links between creativity, invention, innovation and entrepreneurship;
> Explain the contribution of small firms to innovation;
> Explain the link between innovation and firm location;
> Explain how public policy can influence the volume of start-ups and their growth and how it can influence social enterprise;
> Critically evaluate the role of public policy towards SMEs and social enterprise.

Case insights

Web 2.0	Astex
Charles Babbage	Seven Stories National Centre for Children's Books
Chuck Hull	
James Dyson	Brompton Bicycle (1)
Gazelles	

The economics of entrepreneurship

You might ask whether there are any underlying theories to explain the growth in number and importance of small firms. Marxist theory predicts that capitalism will degenerate into economies dominated by a small number of large firms and society will polarize between those that own them and those that work in them. To a Marxist, the rise of small firms is just another, subtler way for this trend to manifest itself. Small firms are dependent upon larger firms for their custom and well-being; they absorb risk and push down pay and conditions for workers because they are rarely unionized. However, the successful growth of so many small firms since the 1980s, the increasing fragmentation of industries and markets, and the increasing popularity of self-employment by choice would seem to belie this theory.

People like Fritz Schumacher (1974) would have us believe that the growth of small firms is part of a social trend towards a more democratic and responsive society – 'small is beautiful'. To him the quality of life is more important than materialism. He was very much in favour of 'intermediate technology' – simpler, cheaper and easier to use – with production on a smaller scale and more locally based. However, the technologies that fuelled the growth of small firms at the end of the 20th century were far from simple and, for many, quality of life improved alongside material wealth.

This leads us to free-market economics. At one extreme, the growth of small firms can be seen as the triumph of the free market and the success of the 'enterprise culture' promulgated by politicians like Ronald Reagan and Margaret Thatcher. Increasing numbers of small firms were the natural result of increased competition and a drive to prevent private and public monopoly. But what exactly does economic theory have to say about the creation of small firms?

Traditional industrial economists would explain the growth of new firms in terms of industry profitability, growth, barriers to entry and concentration. However, they are more concerned with 'entry' to an industry, rather than whether this is by a new or an existing firm. They assume an endless supply of potential new entrants. They would say that entry to an industry is high when expected profits and growth are high. It is deterred by high barriers to entry and high concentration, when collusion between existing firms can take place. However, much of this work does not specifically consider the role of new or smaller firms. Indeed, Acs and Audretsch (1989) show that entry by small, primarily new, firms is not the same as entry by large firms and that the birth of small firms is lower in highly concentrated industries and ones where innovation plays an important part.

By way of contrast, labour market economists have been more interested in what influences individuals to become potential entrants to an industry by becoming self-employed. Psychologists have also contributed greatly to this work, which has focused on the character or personality of the individual, the antecedent influences on them, such as age, sex, education, employment status, experience and ethnicity, as well as other societal influences. As we shall see in the next chapter, this work has proved far more interesting and informative.

Entrepreneurship and economic growth

The link between entrepreneurship, or more specifically the creation of new firms, and economic growth has until recently been far from clear – as far as economists are concerned. Traditional theories tended to suggest that entrepreneurship impeded rather than encouraged growth. In Chapter 1 we looked at the different definitions of an entrepreneur developed through the centuries, particularly the views of Schumpeter, Knight and Kirzner. While Knight (1921) saw the entrepreneur as someone who was willing to bear risk for a reward, Kirzner (1973) emphasized their role as an intermediary and market-maker. Both Knight 's and Kirzner's works were based on the general equilibrium or neoclassical model of economics which focused on optimizing existing resources within a stable environment and treated any disruptions, such as the growth of entrepreneurial new firms that created whole new industries, as 'god sent' external forces.

By way of contrast, Schumpeter's work focused on the disruptive role of the entrepreneur as an innovator. And, while Kirzner added the important dimension of information, knowledge and opportunity recognition to the work of Schumpeter, it was Schumpeter who created the link between entrepreneurship, innovation and growth. He was the first person to challenge neoclassical economics. In his primary work he set out his overall theory of economic development – an endogenous process within capitalism of wrenching the economy out of its tendency towards one equilibrium position and towards a different one – a process of 'creative destruction' (Schumpeter, 1911). This fundamental phenomenon entails the development of new combinations of the means of production, which Schumpeter labels 'enterprise' but we could equally call 'innovation', while the individuals carrying them out are called 'entrepreneurs'. These new combinations 'as a rule … must draw the necessary means of production from some old combinations'.

Schumpeter was arguing against traditional economic theory which presumed that the economy always tended towards equilibrium and changes in that equilibrium could only occur through changes in the underlying conditions of the economy, such as population growth, changes in savings ratios, or external shocks, such as wars or natural disasters. The former were thought to change only slowly and the latter only occurred unpredictably. Schumpeter sought to explain the process of economic development as a process caused by enterprise – or innovation – and carried out by entrepreneurs.

For Schumpeter a normal healthy economy was one that was continually being 'disrupted' by technological innovation, producing the 50-year cycles of economic activity noticed earlier by the Russian economist Nikolai Kondratieff. Using data on prices, wages and interest rates in France, Britain and the USA, Kondratieff first noticed these 'long waves' of economic activity in 1925. Unfortunately he was executed by Stalin some 10 years later because he (accurately as it turned out) predicted that Russian farm collectivization would lead to a decline in farm production. It was therefore left to Schumpeter to study these waves in depth.

Schumpeter said that each of these cycles was unique, driven by different clusters of industries. The upswing in a cycle started when new innovations came into general use:

> Water power, textiles and iron in the late 18th century;
> Steam, rail and steel in the mid 19th century;
> Electricity, chemicals and the internal combustion engine in the early 20th century.

These booms eventually petered out as the technologies matured and the market opportunities were fully exploited, only to start again as a new set of innovations changed the way things were done. For the last 20 years of the cycle, the growth industries of the last technological wave might appear to have been doing exceptionally well. However, they were, in fact, just repaying capital that was no longer needed for investment. This situation never lasted longer than 20 years, and returns to investors then started to decline with the dwindling number of opportunities. Often this was precipitated by some form of crisis. After the 20 years of stagnation, new technologies emerge and the cycle starts again. By the time Schumpeter died in 1950 the next cycle of boom was starting, based upon oil, electronics, aviation and mass production. Another started in the 1980s based upon computers, software and mobile technologies including the internet.

The other factor is that innovation – particularly technological innovation – also seems to generate growth that cannot be accounted for by changes in labour and capital. Although the return on investment may decline as more capital is introduced to an economy, any deceleration in growth is more than offset by the leverage effects of innovation. Because of this, the rich Western countries have seen their return on investment increasing, while the poorer countries have not caught up.

But innovation does not happen as a random event. Central to the process are the entrepreneurs. It is they who introduce and then exploit the new innovations. For Schumpeter, 'the entrepreneur initiates change and generates new opportunities. Until imitators force prices and costs

It is clear that successful entrepreneurs are vital for a healthy, vibrant and competitive economy. If you look around you, most of the largest companies have their foundations in one or two individuals who have the determination to turn a vision into reality.

Richard Branson, founder, Virgin Group, from Anderson (1995)

into conformity, the innovator is able to reap profits and disturb equilibrium.' By way of contrast, early classical economists such as Adam Smith saw the entrepreneurs as having a rather minor role in overall economic activity. Smith thought that they provided real capital but did not play a leading or direct part in how the pattern of supply and demand was determined.

Aghion and Howitt (1992) produced a formal restatement of Schumpeter's theory of 'creative destruction' whereby new entrants replace existing inefficient firms. Other economists have emphasized the Schumpeterian assumption that innovation-based growth needs entrepreneurs and effective selection among entrepreneurs (Acemoglu et al., 2006; Michelacci, 2003). These theories of 'industrial evolution' have linked entrepreneurship and economic growth directly (Audretsch, 1995; Ericson and Pakes, 1995; Hopenhayn, 1992; Jovanovic, 1982; Klepper, 1996; Lambson, 1991). They focus on change as the central phenomenon and emphasize the role knowledge plays in charting a way through this. Innovation is seen as the key to market entry, growth and survival for an enterprise and the way entire industries change over time. What is more, in the UK it has been suggested that innovative businesses are the main drivers of employment (Cosh and Hughes, 2007).

Based on the work of Kirzner, Acs et al. (2004, 2005) and Audretsch (2007) expanded on the notion that the important feature of entrepreneurs is their role as 'knowledge filters', facilitating 'knowledge spill-overs' or 'knowledge transfers'. The information they need in order to innovate is crucial – being inherently uncertain, asymmetric (one party may have more than another) and associated with high transaction costs. However, Venkatarman (1997) observed that different people spot different opportunities because they possess different prior knowledge, and innovations introduced by entrepreneurs are related to their prior knowledge. As a result of these differences in knowledge, there are differences in the expected value of new ideas, and people therefore have a financial incentive to leave secure employment to start up a new enterprise in order to capitalize on a commercial idea that they believe in more than others. Once established, if economies of scale are important (Chapter 6), the enterprise must grow, simply to survive. In this way the economic performance of nations is linked to how well the potential from innovation is tapped – how well start-ups are encouraged and growth facilitated. And inherent in the process is churning – firms being displaced by newer, more innovative rivals.

These new evolutionary theories, supported by empirical evidence, therefore state that entrepreneurship encourages economic growth through innovation for three reasons:

1   It encourages competition by increasing the number of enterprises. While this increases growth in itself, it is a cumulative phenomenon because competition is more conducive to knowledge externalities – new ideas – than is local monopoly. And so entrepreneurship encourages entrepreneurship.
2   It is a mechanism for 'knowledge spill-overs' – transmission of knowledge from its point of origin to other individuals or organizations. Knowledge spill-over is an important mechanism underlying endogenous growth, and start-ups – entrepreneurs – are seen as being particularly adept at appropriating knowledge from other sources. In other words entrepreneurs spot opportunities and innovate.
3   It generates diversity and variety among enterprises in any location. Each enterprise is in some way different or unique and this influences economic growth.

Finally, it has been suggested that entrepreneurship has an important role in wealth distribution (Spencer et al., 2008). Here the distinction is made between the entrepreneurial innovation of small start-ups and the innovative activities of existing businesses, especially those that dominate the market, with new firms replacing existing firms on a regular basis. They emphasize the disruptive nature of the Schumpeterian view as leading to this redistribution of wealth and the continuing vitality of the capitalist system. Paradoxically, Schumpeter's vision was of an eventual decline in entrepreneurship and an increase in wealth concentration leading, eventually, to socialism. So far, this prediction has not proved to be true.

Case insight   Web 2.0

US high-growth web start-ups

Some of the fastest and highest-growth start-ups over the last decade have been based on the development of interactive websites, where users can generate their own content and interact with each other and form a virtual community – called Web 2.0. This is in contrast to websites that limit the user to viewing the content. Examples of Web 2.0 include social networking sites, wikis, blogs, video hosting sites, hosted services, mash-ups etc. Fast, high-growth start-ups face particular problems. Because of the uncertainties surrounding their market acceptance and their accelerated development, they need to plan for growth, particularly because they often need to raise considerable finance at inception. The lean start-up techniques outlined in Chapter 6 can help mitigate the risks they face. Nevertheless, there are many examples of highly successful Web 2.0 start-ups that have made their founders millionaires.

Facebook

This is arguably the best known Web 2.0 start-up. Founded by **Mark Zuckerberg with some friends** while at Harvard in 2004, it is an online social networking site based in Menlo Park, California. Its famously oversubscribed initial public offering in 2012 raised $16 billion, although share value subsequently slumped. It now has over 757 million active users every day, and revenues in 2014 were over $12.4 billion.

LinkedIn

This is another social networking site, but it is used for professional networking. Now headquartered in Mountain View, California and Dublin, Ireland, it was founded by **Reid Hoffman and a group of colleagues** in 2002 and launched in 2003. Its initial public offering in 2011 was also oversubscribed, but shares subsequently doubled in value.

It now claims to have approximately 300 million users, and revenues in 2013 were approximately $1.5 billion.

Twitter

This is a social networking and microblogging site that enables users to send and receive text message 'tweets'. Based in San Francisco, it was launched by **Jack Dorsey and others** in 2006. By 2013 it had over 500 million registered users (some 213 million active) who post some 340 million tweets a day, and it generated revenues of approximately $664 million, although after seven years the company has still not made a profit. So, for everybody using the site Twitter generates annual sales about one cent for each character in a Tweet. It has attracted considerable private and venture funding and was floated on the stock market in 2013, seeking to attract $1 billion – a company valuation of $12–20 billion.

Dropbox

This is a file hosting service founded by **Drew Houston and a friend** in 2007 and launched in 2008. It is based in San Francisco. It allows files to be stored 'in the cloud' – free up to a certain size and for a fee beyond that size. By 2014 it claimed to have over 300 million users, and revenues in 2013 were approximately $200 million.

YouTube

This is the well-known, widely used video-sharing website based in San Bruno, California. It was launched in 2005 by **Steve Chen, Chad Hurley** and **Jawed Karim**. The venture-funded start-up was purchased by Google only 22 months later, in 2006, for $1.65 billion.

QUESTION:

1 How easy is it to predict markets, sectors or industries that will enjoy this sort of growth?

Invention, innovation and creativity

At the macro level, entrepreneurship and innovation are seen to encourage economic growth. At the micro level, innovation is the prime tool entrepreneurs use to create or exploit opportunity. Firms that grow do so because they innovate in some way. In his book *The Competitive Advantage of Nations*, Porter (1990) said: 'Invention and entrepreneurship are at the heart of national advantage', adding that 'companies achieve competitive advantage through acts of innovation'. However, entrepreneurs – or more precisely start-ups – are not the only people who try to practise innovation. For all firms, of any size, innovation has become something of a Holy Grail to be sought after and encouraged. But what is the difference between innovation and invention? And how are they linked to creativity?

Fancy

> There are so few new ideas, so few new things that have not been done. But although the safe place to be is copying what others are doing, I think the people who succeed will be those with the boldness to do something in a totally different way. They take an idea and reinvent it.

Rachel Elnaugh, founder, Red Letter Days, *The Sunday Times*, 23 May 2004

Parkhurst (1999) defined creativity as 'the ability or quality displayed when solving hitherto unsolved problems, when developing original and novel solutions to problems others have solved differently, or when developing original and novel products'. Creativity can be directed towards many other ends, however, it underpins innovation. Amabile et al. (1996) called it the 'seed' of innovation that is important throughout the innovation process. McLean (2005) observed that without creative ideas, innovation is an engine without any fuel. And creativity is needed throughout the process of innovation.

We now move to innovation. Mintzberg (1983) defined innovation as 'the means to break away from established patterns', or in other words, doing things really differently. Kanter (1983) defined it as 'the generation, acceptance and implementation of new ideas, processes, products and services ... [which] involves creative use as well as original invention'. Mellor (2005) defined it simply as either 'creativity + application' or 'invention + application'. Invention is the extreme and riskiest form of innovation. It is usually associated with the development of a completely new or better product (e.g. the invention of the World Wide Web) or process (e.g. Henry Ford's assembly line for producing cars). But, arguably, it could also be associated with different forms of marketing and the development of completely new business models that help create new markets (e.g. the development of low-cost airline travel). However, examples abound of inventions that are not commercially successful, mainly because they did not satisfy a customer need. Thomas Edison, probably the most successful inventor of all time, was so incompetent at introducing his inventions to the marketplace that his backers had to remove him from every new business he founded. So the difference between invention and innovation is not just a question of scale, but also successful implementation.

Case insight   Charles Babbage

The inventor of the computer

Contrary to popular misconception, the computer was not 'invented' by IBM. The principles of the computer were defined by the English scientist Charles Babbage in 1830. He invented a mechanical analytical engine or universal calculator, which was programmed by punch cards, had a store of information (memory) and a calculating engine (processor). But Babbage was forever tinkering with his designs and he could not find anyone to pay him to make the machine. He did not seem to have sufficient motivation or faith in his designs to actually make an operational machine. What is more, he was generally irritable and disagreeable – it is said that he hated humanity. He therefore never found a backer who might have invested in its development. Instead Babbage went on to try to devise a foolproof system for betting on horses.

QUESTIONS:
1 Was Babbage an entrepreneur? Explain.
2 What personal qualities did he lack?

Case insight   Chuck Hull

The inventor of the 3D printer

By way of contrast, Chuck Hull, who was born in 1939, has gained fame and fortune out of his invention of the 3D printer, even though it has not yet come into everyday use. In the early 1980s he was working for a company that used UV light to layer plastic veneers onto table-tops and furniture. Like others within the industry, he was frustrated

Continued...

Continued from previous page...

by the length of time taken to produce even small plastic parts for prototypes of new product designs. He thought that if he could place thousands of thin layers of plastic on top of each other and then etch their shape using light, he might be able to produce three-dimensional objects quickly. Eventually he developed a system where light traced the shape of one layer of an object onto photopolymer – a material which changes from liquid to a plastic-like solid when light shines on it. Subsequent layers are then printed one on top of the other until the shape is complete. The whole process took a matter of minutes rather than the weeks involved in moulding and casting.

He patented his invention in 1986 and co-founded 3D Systems to commercialize the new method of production.

The first commercial product was produced in 1988. 3D Systems sells 3D printers, materials and software to companies that regularly produce prototypes, such as car manufacturers and aerospace and medical equipment design companies. It has been said that one day the technology could become the biggest advance in manufacturing since the industrial revolution. Chuck has over 100 patents to his name and is still chief technology officer of 3D Systems, the company he founded.

QUESTIONS:
1 Is Hull an entrepreneur? Explain.
2 What personal qualities does he possess that Babbage did not?

Innovation can therefore take three forms:

> **Product innovation** – improvements in the design and functional qualities of the product or service;

> **Process innovation** – improvements in how the product is produced, assembled or delivered, so that it is better or cheaper (e.g. the substitution of a cheaper material in an existing product);

> **Marketing innovation** – improvements in the marketing of the product or service (e.g. use of social media) or changes in the business model that might open up new markets (e.g. selling online as well as face-to-face). These are the sort of innovations entrepreneurs are particularly good at and, just occasionally, they can open up whole new markets that did not exist before.

Simply introducing a new product or service that has customers willing to buy it is not necessarily innovation. New cars are rarely truly innovative, despite what the marketing hype might say. However, the Model T Ford was truly innovative because it revolutionized the way cars were assembled. The Mini was truly innovative because it changed the way cars were designed and changed the way people perceived vehicle size. But how high a degree of innovation does there have to be for it to cross the line to become invention? When a sofa manufacturer produces a 'new' sofa, is that a new product? Economists would probably argue that it was not (because the cross elasticity of demand[1] is unlikely to be zero) – but the entrepreneur might disagree. What if the sofa manufacturer starts manufacturing chairs? At what point does the firm start producing genuinely new products? As Porter (1998a) observed, 'much innovation is mundane and incremental, depending more on an accumulation of small insights than on a single major technological breakthrough'. Innovation may be a hazy concept only because of the myriad forms it can take.

What constitutes innovation is therefore contentious. But even this fails to recognize that there is a second dimension to innovation, and that is how frequently it is practised. Arguably, a firm that practises frequent small-scale innovation is just as innovative as one that has the occasional large-scale innovation. And what is true is that the sum of many small, incremental innovations can have an enormous impact on competitive advantage (Bessant, 1999). Often these innovations are introduced during the later stages of the life cycle of a product or service so as to maintain or improve competitive advantage and extend its life. Indeed, there is evidence that the majority of commercially significant innovations are indeed incremental rather than radical (Audretsch, 1995). Many incremental changes can add up to a revolution. For example, Henry

> True innovation is rarely about creating something new. It's pretty hard to recreate the wheel or discover gravity; innovation is more often about seeing new opportunities for old designs.
>
> **Neil Kelly**, founder, PAV, *The Sunday Times*, 9 December 2001

---

[1] Cross elasticity of demand measures the responsiveness of demand for a product to the change in price of other related products. When there is zero elasticity of demand there is no relationship between the products. Thus if elasticity is not zero, customers require some price inducement to try the 'new' product.

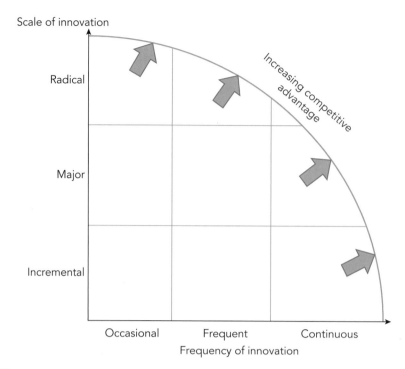

Figure 2.1 Innovative intensity

Ford's revolution in the car industry involved extensive incremental changes – to products and processes, component and factory design and in the way labour was organized in his factories.

This leads to the idea that the impact of innovation on competitive advantage might be measured on two dimensions – frequency of innovation and scale or degree of innovation. Together these measure the innovative intensity of the firm. This is shown in Figure 2.1. Frequent small-scale innovations may be just as financially lucrative as the occasional 'big-bang' breakthrough. What is more, these frequent small-scale innovations are less risky. Competitive advantage is therefore increased by pushing out the envelope in Figure 2.1, and truly innovative firms will tend to cluster along this envelope.

What is also true, however, is the vital role played by the entrepreneur in matching the innovation to a market need – existing or in the future. For example, the early success of the Apple Macintosh was based upon its use of the now ubiquitous mouse and its graphic user interface. However, this technology was invented by scientists at Xerox Palo Alto Research Centre (PARC) and had been tried out unsuccessfully in high-priced computers, such as Xerox Star and Apple Lisa. But it was the late Steve Jobs and Apple who successfully brought the redesigned mouse to the mass market. We shall return to the issues of innovation in business in Chapter 4, when we look at how to find a business idea.

 Case insight   James Dyson

Inventor and entrepreneur

James Dyson is the inventor of the revolutionary cyclone vacuum cleaner who challenged established large companies in the market to gain a market share in excess of 50%. He is a habitual inventor, also inventing the 'Ballbarrow', a

light plastic wheelbarrow with a ball rather than a wheel. The idea for the vacuum cleaner came to him in 1979 because he was finding that traditional cleaners could not clear all the dust he was creating as he converted an old house. Particles clogged the pores of the dust bags and reduced the suction. He had developed a small version of the large

Continued...

Continued from previous page...

industrial cyclone machines, which separate particles from air by using centrifugal force, in order to collect paint particles from his plastic-spraying operation for Ballbarrow. He believed the technology could be adapted for the home vacuum cleaner, generating greater suction and eliminating the need for bags.

Working from home, investing all his own money, borrowing on the security of his home and drawing just £10,000 a year to support himself, his wife and three children, he produced 5,000 different prototypes. However, established manufacturers rejected his ideas and venture capitalists declined to invest. In 1991 he took the product to Japan and won the 1991 International Design Fair prize. He licensed the manufacture of the product in Japan, where it became a status symbol selling at $2,000 a time. On the back of this, and 12 years after the idea first came to him, he was able to obtain finance from Lloyds Bank to manufacture the machine under his own name in the UK. Today Dyson products can be purchased worldwide, and James Dyson is one of the top 50 richest people in the UK, worth approximately £3 billion. He stepped down as chair of the Dyson Group in 2010.

QUESTION:

1 Is Dyson an entrepreneur? Explain.

The link between innovation and business growth

As already noted, young, high-growth firms – called 'gazelles' by academics – are few in number but have a disproportionate importance to national economies (Autio, 2007). Definitions vary depending on how growth is measured (e.g. sales, profit, employment), but in the USA it has been estimated that they compose less than 1% of all companies but generate about 10% of new jobs in any year. Indeed, the top performing 1% of all firms generate about 40% of all new jobs (Stangler, 2010). In the UK they were estimated to represent 2 to 4% of firms but were responsible for the majority of employment growth (Department of Business, Enterprise and Regulatory Reform, 2008).

Middle-sized firms generally have a disproportionate impact on national economies. In the UK, while they represented just 1% of firms they generated 30% of GDP and employed more than one-third of the workforce (GE Capital, 2012). And Europe lags behind the USA, where SMEs were on average larger and expanded more rapidly (European Commission, 2008). And while a higher percentage of UK firms achieve high growth than European firms, the UK still lags behind the USA (Department of Business, Enterprise and Regulatory Reform, op. cit.).

PHOTODISC

You might expect, therefore, for there to be a direct link between these gazelles and innovation. However, while there is some empirical support for a link between innovation and business growth, a number of studies have failed to find any direct *general* relationship (Coad and Rao, 2008; O'Regan et al., 2006). The problem is that finding a relationship is not straightforward because of *methodological* problems and problems surrounding the *measurement* of both innovation and growth. For example, any link with growth in profits is likely to be 'lagged', with innovation taking time – perhaps years – to feed back into growth in profits, although, as we have noted (Cosh and Hughes, op. cit.), innovation is positively associated with growth in employment. Then there is the issue of 'cycling' – the understandable tendency of firms to innovate in one period and then 'consolidate' in the next (Cefis, 2003) – a feature we shall return to in Chapter 12 in the context of setting strategy. Finally there is the question of causation. Even if there were an observable link, it does not necessarily prove causation: 'while small innovators may in aggregate grow faster than non-innovators this is not to suggest that innovation is a necessary, nor less a sufficient condition for growth or superior performance' (Freel, 2000).

So, finding evidence of a direct relationship between business growth and innovation is problematic. Indeed relationships between innovation and other factors would also seem to be complex. The rate of innovation (however measured) seems to vary between firms of different size, across industries and sectors depending on industry age and stability, and even location.

 ## Case insight   Gazelles

UK fastest, high-growth firms

Every few months *The Sunday Times* produces what they call the 'Fast Track 100' – a listing of Britain's fastest growing private companies by sales, measured by compound annual growth. Sales have to exceed £250,000 in the base year and £5 million in the final year, and there have to be more than 10 employees. It excludes technology firms. The listing changes with every new edition, but below are some examples of the companies that have been featured in 2014. What stands out is the diversity of sectors they range over. (Figures in brackets are the last reported turnover.)

Ambrey Risk (£123 million; security services)

Founded by John Thomson, Chris Charney and Mark Osborne in 2010, the company provides ex-military personnel to protect, and train others to protect, ships from pirates.

Anesco (£100 million; energy efficiency services)

Spun out of Scottish and Southern Energy in 2010 by Adrian Pike and Tim Payne, Anesco provides energy efficiency consultancy and installs and maintains domestic and solar panels.

Brompton Bicycle (£127 million; bicycle manufacturer)

Founded by Cambridge University graduate Andrew Ritchie (who also designed the bicycle) in 1988, the company now sells its distinctive range of folding bicycles around the world (Case insights, Chapters 2, 7 and 13).

Entier (£32 million; facilities management services)

Founded by Peter Bruce and four colleagues in 2008 to provide support services to oil and gas companies off the Scottish coast, it now offers a range of facilities management services, including catering and hotels, around the world.

JCB (£2,712 million; construction equipment manufacturer)

Founded by Joseph Cyril Bamford just after World War II, this remains a family owned and run business. It is a British manufacturing success story and is now the third largest construction manufacturer in the world (Case insight, Chapter 17).

Lily's Kitchen (£16 million; pet food manufacturer)

Founded by Henrietta Morrison in 2008, the company manufactures over 50 gourmet dog food lines which include ingredients like kelp, alfalfa and blueberries.

Loungers (£134 million; cafe bars and restaurants)

Founded in 2002 by three friends – Alex Reilley, Jake Bishop and Dave Reid – the company operates some 53 cafe bars and restaurants that are open all day.

Mind Candy (£47 million; online games developer)

Founded by Michael Acton Smith in 2004, this is a children's online games developer that is best known for its Moshi Monsters, who have become the most licensed property in the UK (Case insight, Chapter 10).

Thomsons Online Benefits (£33 million; software developer)

Founded by Michael Whitfield and Chris Bruce in 2000, the company develops software that is used by companies like Starbucks and Samsung to manage their employee benefit schemes.

TLC Group (19 million; care homes and hotels)

Founded in 2007, this is a care home and hotel group based around London and Cambridge. It is owned and run by the Popat family.

QUESTIONS:

1 Why is it more difficult to be included in this list as a business gets bigger?

2 What are the implications of this list changing every time it is published?

The link between innovation and firm size

Just as entrepreneurs are not defined simply as owner-managers, entrepreneurial firms are not defined, necessarily, in terms of size. Schumpeter said nothing about whether innovation could be best carried out by small or large firms. To him this was irrelevant. An entrepreneur could just as easily work in a large firm as in a small one. Indeed, later in his career Schumpeter (1950) seemed to credit larger, rather than smaller, businesses more with delivering economic growth. So, is there a link between innovation and firm size?

On the face of it, empirical evidence suggests that larger firms are more likely to be innovative than smaller ones. Indeed, EU data (European Union, 2007) showed that larger firms (250+ employees) were more likely to be innovative than smaller firms (10–49 employees). Data from the UK (Robson and Haigh, 2008) showed that larger firms (250+ employees) were more likely to conduct internal research and development (R&D) and contracted-out R&D. It also concluded that larger firms were also much more likely to introduce product, process or managerial innovations than smaller firms. Large firms seem to outperform small firms where resources are important – because of capital intensity or because of scale of spending on R&D, advertising etc. In particular they have better access to both internal and external finance than smaller companies. Indeed, for smaller companies there are just too many problems to sort out and larger firms have more resources, more money, more experience … more of everything to throw at a problem.

Overall, few small firms introduce really new products into their product range. Even fewer introduce really new products into the economy as a whole. This role is more likely to be undertaken by larger firms because of the resources they command. However, small firms can, and often do, introduce products or services that are clearly differentiated from those of the 'competition', to the point where one might question whether there is any direct competition. Indeed, this ability to differentiate clearly is a major element in their success. Small firms are most likely to provide something marginally different from the competition in terms of the product or service, and thus find a gap in the market. They are also far more likely to innovate in terms of marketing and customer service (often low-cost options). However, these small innovations might be highly valued by a small group of customers and therefore highly profitable. They frequently find new routes to market first, for example 'direct' selling, via the phone, with call centres located in low-cost areas, or via the internet, offering similar advantages through the 'virtual' organization. Small firms are often innovative in their approach to key account management and customer relationships. They find ways of networking with customers and suppliers so as to cut costs and lead times.

But studies of innovation and company size can appear contradictory. This can be because of the problem of measuring innovation. Some studies have used input measures such as R&D expenditure or number of R&D employees. However, such studies must be treated with caution because of the inability of small firms often to separate these inputs out. It has also been suggested that small firms conduct R&D more efficiently and introduce new products to the marketplace faster than big companies. For example, a US study found that small firms produce 2.4 times as many innovations per employee as large firms (Acs and Audretsch, 1990). Other studies have used output measures such as number of patents – an accurate but limited measure of innovative activity. They can also appear contradictory because they vary across different industry sectors. Whereas large firms have greater access to resources, smaller firms have behavioural advantages – a closeness to the market, a greater willingness to take risks, an ability to act quickly. And it is in sectors or industries where these characteristics are important that small firms are more important in terms of innovation.

The influence of industry structure

Just as some industries are more innovating than others, the importance of size of firm on innovation varies from industry to industry. Industry structure seems to influence the level of innovation (Santarelli and Piergiovanni, 1996). Studies have concluded that innovation is less likely in more mature industries that are highly concentrated and therefore dominated by larger firms (Acs and Audretsch, 1988; Dolfsma and van der Panne, 2008). In these industries larger firms were the dominant innovators. Indeed, in a review of the evidence, Symeonidis (1996) concluded that there was no evidence that either large firms or industries with high concentration were associated with high levels of innovation. He also observed that even if there was an association, this did not imply a causal relationship.

This raises the question of the nature of these innovations. You might speculate that in the concentrated industries they focus on incremental product innovations and cost-reduction process innovations. By way of contrast, in the less concentrated industries there was more likely to be **radical** or **disruptive innovation** – step changes in products, processes or the framing of markets. And in the less concentrated industries smaller firms tend to be the dominant innovators. Robson and Haigh (op. cit.) added support to this by showing that sales from new-to-market or new-to-the-business products represent a higher percentage of turnover in smaller compared to larger firms.

Established, larger firms have the advantage when it comes to incremental innovation. They have the product experience, established marketing channels and resource capabilities. That advantage can disappear with disruptive innovation – when the game changes in important and fundamental ways so that their product experience, marketing channels and resource capabilities become less important. It is no wonder then that so many small, entrepreneurial firms can thrive in this environment. Competitive advantage has to be built from scratch and that is where the entrepreneurial DNA becomes important. The main reason why existing, larger firms miss out on disruptive innovation is because they develop a **dominant logic** (or mental model) which dictates how the world is viewed. It filters the information received, subconsciously interpreting environmental data in a certain way. In fact, managers may only consider information that they believe relevant to the prevailing dominant logic in the organization or industry.

The influence of industry age and stability

In his study of a number of industries, Christensen (1997) characterized company mortality as happening in stable markets where companies were geared up to delivering more of what existing customers wanted. He observed that with each generation almost all of the previously successful large firms failed to make the transition effectively and were often squeezed out of the market or into bankruptcy, despite the fact they were often exemplars of good practice – ploughing a high percentage of earnings into R&D, having strong working links with their supply chain, working with lead customers to better understand their needs and develop product innovations, and delivering a continuous stream of product and process innovations that were in demand from their existing customers. The problem they had was their inability to identify and capitalize on the emergence of new markets with very different needs and expectations – one aspect of the problem of market disruption. Essentially these firms were too close to their existing customers, suppliers and technologies. The result was that they failed to see the long-term potential of newly emerging markets. What might have begun as a fringe business – often for something simpler and cheaper – moved into the mainstream and eventually changed the rules under which the mainstream businesses operated, so by the time the mainstream businesses realized this, they had lost their competitive advantage. Often, with the benefit of hindsight, the industry seemed to be driven by technological developments rather than market demand.

What seems clear is that innovative behaviour is not entirely related to firm size. It varies across industry sectors, depending on:

> **Innovation costs** – SMEs are less important where there are high resource costs. They are more active when resource costs are low, although they use these resources more efficiently than larger firms;

> **Size of markets** – SMEs thrive in industries where economies of scale are less important to customers than other factors such as marketing, service quality or variety, where low-cost innovation might be possible;

> Industry concentration, age and stability – SMEs are less important in stable, mature, high-concentration industries where the innovation focus has switched to efficiency and cost-reduction. They have a significant role to play by introducing disruptive innovation and creating new industries.

It has also been pointed out that the advantages of large firms are generally the disadvantages of small firms, and vice versa, and therefore collaboration or partnering between the two sizes of business can create powerful synergistic relationships (Vossen, 1998).

Storey and Greene (2010) concluded that 'once account is taken of sector, the life cycle of the technology and the innovation rate (e.g. innovations per employee), then the small business emerges in particular sectors as key "agents of change"'.

Innovation, location and network effects

There is evidence that innovation can be geographically concentrated in certain areas, particularly with respect to smaller firms, and this leads to 'clusters' of small firms that form mutually supportive networks. This is often referred to as 'innovative milieu' theory (Camagni, 1991; Keeble and Wilkinson, 1999). This theory is based on the assumption that knowledge is a crucial element in the process of innovation (Simmie, 2002) and, whereas large firms have their own R&D functions to help generate this, small firms have to rely on networking and a process of 'socialization' that allows them to collect information and accumulate knowledge (Capello, 1999). Geographical proximity facilitates this process of knowledge transfer, and hence these clusters of small firms can be observed (Keeble and Wilkinson, op. cit.; Porter, 1998b). Saxenian (1994) argued that it was the social networks embedded in the local community of Silicon Valley, based on strong ties of collaboration and informal communication and learning, that encouraged its economic growth.

Within these clusters, where there is the development and sharing of a common base of knowledge, 'collective learning' is taking place. This allows the firms to coordinate their actions so as to solve the technological and organizational problems they face (Lorenz, 1996, quoted in Keeble and Wilkinson, op. cit.). 'Collective learning' can be either conscious – as in research collaborations – or unconscious. Unconscious learning occurs where the skills and knowledge are vested in a workforce that is shared between the small firms. These clusters therefore attract similar small firms because it is a low-cost way of gaining knowledge. The newly emerging but fast-developing 'fintech' industry in the UK, which offers various forms of crowdfunding (see Chapter 14), is predominantly located around Canary Warf in the London.

More recently the interest in geographic location has focused on high-technology industries. The importance of these industries is underlined by the fact that investment in so-called intangible assets such as computer codes, copyrights and patents is now 50% higher than investment in tangible assets such as plant and machinery, and it is increasing. While the USA has its own Silicon Valley, Cambridge in the UK is home to a number of high-technology clusters and is an example of both types of learning. In computing, not only are there research collaborations between Cambridge University and the firms in the cluster, but there is also a skilled workforce graduating from the university and a group of academics willing to work part-time with them. Such is the strength of the cluster and importance of the university that Bill Gates endowed it with sufficient funds to finance new state-of-the-art computer laboratories. Universities generally are seen as an important source of knowledge and therefore important to the development of clusters, hence the various initiatives to encourage them to work more closely with industry. Universities generate 'public knowledge' and this 'spills over' into the commercial world through conferences and seminars, consultants, the personal networks of academics and industrial researchers (MacPherson, 1998), and commercial spin-offs (Mitra, 2000). This has been the reason for developing 'incubator units' and Science Parks for technology-based SMEs, often located adjacent to universities.

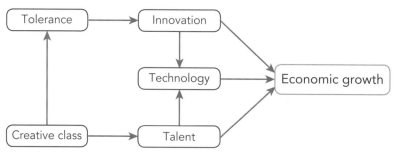

Figure 2.2   Technology, talent, tolerance and economic growth

Source: Figure 1 from Florida, R. and Tinagli, I. (2004), *Europe in the Creative Age*, Demos, p.12. Reproduced with permission.

Florida (2002; Florida and Tinagli, 2004) argued that some locations – particularly cities like London or Barcelona – attract talented, creative people he called 'the new creative class' and these people, in turn, attracted creative, innovative firms. He claimed that rather than people following jobs, the jobs will follow people with the appropriate talent, creating a virtuous circle of economic growth. He claimed that the ability to compete and prosper in the new global economy 'increasingly turns on the ability of nations to attract, retain and develop creative people', arguing that this new 'creative class' is drawn to a particular sort of place: 'open, diverse communities where differences are welcome and cultural creativity is easily accessed.' He argued that it is tolerance that attracts the creative class and they have the talent to develop new technologies. He observed that new knowledge-based economies thrive in locations and countries that combine these three elements – technology, talent and tolerance – to provide economic growth in the way shown in Figure 2.2.

These clusters may well generate a culture or subculture that encourages creativity, innovation and entrepreneurship, and underlying the culture is a process of networking and information exchange that encourages knowledge transfer and 'spill-overs'. As we shall see in Chapter 4, networking – in all its different ways – creates 'connectivity' and underpins creativity (Johnson, 2010). The idea is that innovation is not about a 'eureka' moment but more about the recombining of pre-existing ideas to create something new. Essentially this is a social process where strangers, different cultures and disciplines meet that exposes people to new ideas, information and knowledge from diverse networks of sources. A creative environment is one where these people – individuals and companies from different disciplines and with diverse ideas – come in contact with each other almost serendipitously. Stimulation is continuous. But you need the right environment for it to take place. Johnson uses the coral reef as the analogy for the perfect creative environment and how it encourages connectivity. The coral reef is a huge diverse ecosystem where, despite competition for resources, existence is dependent on cooperation and everything is recycled on a matrix

of calcium carbonate built up by the coral. Johnson makes the point that invention is time and environment dependent. It depends on the right circumstances that give it the possibilities. So the internet depends on computers, microwave ovens depend on electricity and people depend on their environment.

Networks can also be a way of meeting potential partners. Partnerships, strategic alliances and joint ventures are ways of mutually exploiting business opportunities where a firm may not have all the skills or resources necessary. Numerous academic studies have shown that there are real benefits from strategic alliances and partnerships for organizations of all sizes. For example, alliances can create economic advantage by leveraging market presence (Lewis, 1990; Lorange and Roos, 1992; Ohmae, 1989). And, as we have noted, high-growth firms rely heavily on building relationships with other firms, either through supply chains or formal strategic alliances (Department of Business, Enterprise and Regulatory Reform, 2008).

It will be interesting to see how far the internet, which facilitates 'global connectivity', affects the formation of geographic clusters in future years. Already the Cambridge cluster of technology enterprises and the people who work in them is said to have better 'connections' with similar clusters in other parts of the world than 'connections' with towns within a few miles in the UK.

 Case insight   Astex

The Cambridge cluster

Courtesy of Astex

Astex Therapeutics was set up in 1999. It was founded by Dr Harren Jhoti, who left GlaxoWellcome (now GlaxoSmithKline), and by two University of Cambridge Professors – Chris Abell and Sir Tom Blundell. Located in Cambridge, UK, the company focuses on the discovery and development of drugs, particularly in the area of oncology, using a technique called 'fragment-based drug discovery' – a technique pioneered by the founders and dubbed 'Pyramid'. It was partially seed-funded by the University of Cambridge and raised nearly £100 million of venture capital

funds, working in partnership with larger pharmaceutical companies to develop a number of new drugs.

In 2011 it merged with a NASDAQ quoted US company called Supergen, based in Dublin, California, whereupon the US company closed its US laboratory and concentrated its research in Cambridge where some 80 people were employed. Astex became a US quoted company with James Manuso of Supergen as chair and CEO until 2013. In 2013, Astex was bought by a Japanese pharmaceutical company called Otsuka for approximately $900 million. Its research and headquarters still operates from Cambridge with Harren Jhoti as President and CEO.

QUESTIONS:

1 How important is the link with Cambridge University for Astex? Explain.

2 In the age of the internet, how important is geographic proximity to sources of knowledge in encouraging innovation? Explain.

Social enterprise and social innovation

Just as SMEs are seen as vehicles for encouraging product or market innovation, social enterprises are often seen as ways of encouraging 'social innovation' – innovations that involve 'new ideas (products, services and models) that simultaneously meet social needs (more effectively than alternatives) and create more social relationships or collaborations … they are innovations that are not only good for society but also enhance society's capacity to act' (Bureau of European Policy Advisors, 2011). In other words, just like commercial SMEs, social enterprises need to create 'added value' by doing things differently or more effectively so that it can be applied additionally to the objectives of the social enterprise. And one of the characteristics of successful social enterprises is their ability to network and mobilize a wide range of supporting resources, often at a low cost. These are then brought together to enable the launch of the new social initiative.

There is a long history in the UK of voluntary and charitable involvement in community and social initiatives. The social entrepreneurship movement has called for these partnerships to take an even wider form, linking the public, social and business sectors to reconstruct welfare provision. This would involve not-for-profit organizations undertaking entrepreneurial ventures and the pooling of government welfare funding under the control of local communities. In an early call for a different approach, Leadbeater (1997) said what was needed was a 'new philosophy, practice and organization' of social welfare with social entrepreneurs in a pivotal role pushing through innovations. He concluded that the UK social welfare system was in need of radical reforms that empower disadvantaged people and encourage them to take greater responsibility for, and control over, their lives.

In the USA, the not-for-profit sector is much larger than in Europe, probably twice the size of that in the UK. Philanthropy, or charitable giving, is also far larger and better established, and the so-called Welfare State is an anathema. It is not surprising, therefore, that in the USA there is a subtle shift of emphasis towards the entrepreneurial management of not-for-profit organizations and how they compete for funds. Boschee (1998) talked about a 'tectonic shift' in the way that not-for-profit organizations saw themselves and were funded. Brinckerhoff (2000) actually said that social entrepreneurship was becoming one of the essential characteristics of successful not-for-profit organizations.

 Case insight   Seven Stories – National Centre for Children's Books

 Social enterprise

The Seven Stories – National Centre for Children's Books based in Newcastle upon Tyne is the first museum in the UK wholly dedicated to British children's books. It was founded by Elizabeth Hammill and Mary Briggs with the help of many authors, illustrators, publishers, teachers and librarians. Its aim is to collect, champion and celebrate children's literature and, in doing this, make a real difference to the children and families living nearby by improving childhood development and raising aspirations. They wanted to inspire local children to love books. In 2002 the charity purchased a seven-story Victorian warehouse in the Ouseburn Valley, about half mile from Newcastle city centre. The project cost £6.5 millon and was financed by grants from Newcastle City Council and Arts Council England, as well as donations from many other trusts and individuals.

The Centre is a not-for-profit charitable trust governed by a board of trustees. It is now run by 38 paid staff – paid for through grants, donations and self-generated income – and some 50 volunteers. It provides some 40 work placements annually. The Centre has exhibitions of books, drop-in family activities, storytelling, author and illustrator events – all intended to bring children's books alive – open to families and school parties. The museum charges for entry and has over 70,000 visitors annually.

It works with over 50% of the schools in the north east of England and 85% of schools in Newcastle. It has over 10,000 school visitors annually and reaches another 12,000 children, young people and grown-ups each year through its outreach work in schools and communities. It works with vulnerable children and families through partners such as Action for Children, St. Oswald's Hospice and local children's centres.

❏ Visit the website: www.sevenstories.org.uk

Damien Wooten © Seven Stories – National Centre for Children's Books

seven stories
National Centre for Children's Books

QUESTION:

1 Why is social innovation difficult and what might precipitate it?

Public policy towards SMEs

As we have observed, entrepreneurship and innovation are seen to encourage economic growth, despite the direct linkage being unclear, and successive governments around the world have been keen to craft public policies that encourage both. But can and should governments intervene, or should they just leave things to the invisible hand of the market? Casson et al. (2008) observe that entrepreneurship flourishes in liberal market economies that exhibit some or all of the following characteristics:

> Ownership rights for private property;
> Freedom of movement and association;
> Confidentiality specifically of business information;
> Protection of intellectual property rights;
> Access to impartial and competent courts to enforce these rights;
> A stable currency based on prudent control of the money supply;
> Democratic, stable government;
> Openness to immigration by entrepreneurs and skilled workers.

Given the existence of a liberal market economy, economists would generally say that 'market failure' is a necessary but not a sufficient condition for further government intervention and is therefore only justified when its benefits outweigh its costs. Examples of market failure might include the inability of individuals to accurately assess the private benefit to them of starting their own business, and the inability of financial institutions to offer finance to SMEs, for example because of their inability to accurately assess the risk of lending (see Chapter 14) or the over-dominance of large firms in some markets to the extent that competition is suboptimal.

Notwithstanding this, government economic policy in most countries tries to encourage the start-up, survival and growth of SMEs. They do this because of start-ups' ability to generate jobs (particularly when large firms might be shedding them) and the ability of entrepreneurs to increase innovation and improve productivity and growth (Van Praag and Versloot, 2007). It might also have something to do with owner-managers being a powerful political constituency. These policies generally fall into six categories:

> **The regulatory framework**
  These include all forms of taxation and social security, health and safety regulations, product and labour market regulation and bankruptcy regulation, as well as administrative burdens associated with market entry or growth (often referred to as 'red-tape').

> **Entrepreneurial capabilities**
  These include business education and skills training, entrepreneurial training, advice and mentoring and the general entrepreneurial infrastructure.

> **Enterprise culture**
  These include a wide range of influences on attitudes towards entrepreneurship and risk-taking. Policy initiatives might be targeted at the young or the general public.

> **Access to finance**
  These include grants, access to debt finance (through banks and crowdsourcing), including issues of collateral, credit unions and micro-finance and equity finance (crowdsourcing, business angels and venture capital), as well as stock markets.

> **R&D and technology**
  These include R&D investment incentives, university/industry interaction, technology diffusion, technology cooperation between firms, broadband access and patent systems.

> **Market conditions**
  These include competition policy and anti-trust laws including issues about access to domestic and foreign markets, as well as the degree of public sector involvement and government procurement policies.

In times when unemployment is high, encouraging start-ups is often seen as a way of reducing the jobless. This was the case in many countries as a result of the economic recession that started in 2008. Those starting these firms are 'pushed', sometime reluctantly, into self-employment as a way of earning a living. Using the framework above, governments may wish to influence this by improving entrepreneurial capabilities and access to finance. They may be offered grants, 'soft-loans' and training and advice as inducements. However, the 'salary-substitute' wage these businesses generate will often still be below the salary it substitutes, and self-employment is inherently risky because many firms do not survive long and few grow to any size. In times of growth, when unemployment is low, public policy might shift towards raising productivity and innovation. Using the framework above, the focus would shift to encouraging R&D and technology and improving market conditions through competition policy.

At this point it is interesting to return to the work of Florida (op. cit.) on how to encourage clusters of firms that are creative. The cities around which these are often based are at the heart of successful contemporary economies. The implication of Florida's work is that countries need to attract creative people in order to attract creative, innovative companies and encourage that virtuous circle of economic growth. He claims that this is achieved by fostering a culture of openness and tolerance and that he found a strong relationship between openness to gays, Bohemians and immigrants and the ability of cities and regions to innovate, generate high-technology industry and secure high value-added economic growth. It is not that these groups create the economic growth, rather that their existence is a proxy that indicates something about the culture of a community that encourages growth – one that is open to new people and new ideas. Florida's work is controversial not least because of the controversial implications across a wide range of public policies, including immigration. The work also has implications for city planners as they try to mirror the sort of environment these people like – with space for interaction like parks, cafes and small shops and with streets that are safe for these activities to take place.

Policy intervention

As you would expect, governments in different countries take different views about policy interventions, reflecting their view of the role of government generally. Dennis (2004) provides a useful framework for looking at this based on the degree of intervention – both assistance and impediments – that a government might be willing to make (Figure 2.3). This generates four policy options that he calls compensating, competing, nurturing and limiting. Highly interventionist governments like those in the EU are willing to put impediments in the way of SMEs by way of

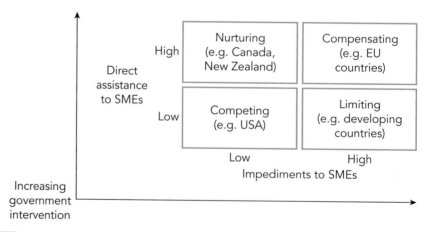

Figure 2.3 SME policy intervention framework

Source: Based on Dennis, 2004

rules and regulations, but at the same time will compensate them by offering direct assistance in many different forms – called 'compensating'. By way of contrast, non-interventionist (or free-market) governments like that in the USA may offer little direct assistance but at the same time have very low impediments (except with regard to minority rights and the promotion of technology businesses) – called 'competing'. Nurturing countries, like Canada and New Zealand, offer few impediments but many direct publicly funded incentives and assistance for SMEs. Limiting countries, like many African, East European and South American countries, create high impediments to SMEs but offer little assistance. One major impediment in developing countries is lack of property rights, which impedes ownership of both physical and intellectual assets and at the same time restricts borrowing potential.

Hölzl et al. (2006) provide a stylized typology (adapted and shown in Figure 2.4) for looking at the issue of whether governments should simply encourage more start-ups (Policy option 1) or increase the capabilities of existing SMEs (Policy option 2). The horizontal axis depicts the degree of success of the firm measured by their scale, and the vertical axis represents the number of firms achieving each stage. The strongly skewed shape of both curves reflects the decreasing number of firms that move from the idea stage to become growth businesses. There are many prospective entrepreneurs (latent or nascent), somewhat fewer actual start-ups, many of which fail, sometimes quickly. Even fewer firms will survive but not grow to any size and fewer still will go on to become growth businesses.

Policy option 1 (orange line) encourages more start-ups – converting more prospective entrepreneurs to actually 'take the plunge'. But this policy is likely to lead to many firms never actually trading and then more failing shortly after launch. In contrast, Policy option 2 (red dashed-line) diverts resources from encouraging start-ups to increasing the capabilities of surviving firms to exploit opportunities and grow. This is likely to lead to fewer start-ups but, more importantly, more firms that survive and grow. Which policy a government selects depends on their objectives and the shape of the two curves. There is also the issue of how you select surviving SMEs for Policy option 2, since most policy advisors would be sceptical about the ability of governments

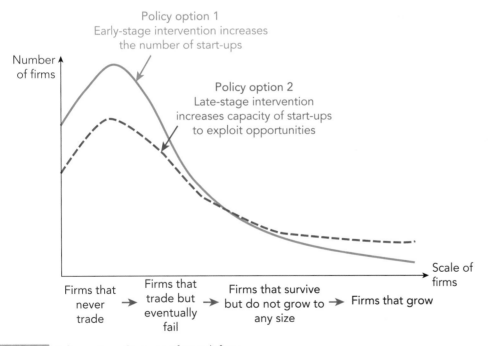

Figure 2.4 Policy options: Start-ups of growth firms

Source: Based on Figure 1 in Jovanovic, B. (2001) 'Fitness and Age: Review of Carroll and Hannan's "Demography of Corporations and Industries"', *Journal of Economic Literature*, 39, S, 105–119. With permission of Boyan Jovanovic and the American Economic Association.

to 'pick winners'. However, as with so many things in the real world, it is usually not a question of 'either/or', but rather what balance is the right balance between the two policies.

The effectiveness of policy intervention

This brings us to the issue of whether these sorts of policy interventions are effective or value-for-money to the taxpayer. Here we must distinguish between the micro-level interventions, like advice and assistance for SMEs, and the macro-level interventions, like taxation and regulation that affect the whole economy. We must also remember that policy effectiveness is determined, not only by the choice of policy, but also by how effectively that policy is delivered – a factor too often forgotten.

Most academics would seem unconvinced by the arguments for government micro-level intervention to encourage SMEs, observing that there is little evidence of success (Bill et al., 2009; Bridge et al., 2009; Davidsson, 2008; Storey and Greene, op. cit.). For them, governments cannot justify policy interventions related to provision of finance, training, advice and assistance etc. for particular groups or the general creation of an 'enterprise culture' – either in terms of effectiveness or value-for-money. The exception might be intervention to support technology businesses in terms of R&D and innovation because of information and knowledge imperfections. They might also agree with the case for a publicly funded loan guarantee scheme for SMEs for similar reasons. Both cases involve market imperfections caused by information asymmetry. However, we must remember that we live in a political economy and SMEs can be an effective political constituency in arguing for special treatment.

However, by way of contrast, most academics would agree that broader macro-economic policies that encourage a stable but growing economy, such as taxation, regulation and competition policy, can have a powerful effect on SMEs and particularly high-growth businesses, simply because they affect the economic environment in which they and all other businesses operate, and particularly because of the degree of uncertainty faced by SMEs (Storey and Greene, op. cit.).

Low tax rates (particularly capital gains tax) – These are often assumed to encourage SMEs, and would seem to be associated with a high proportion of 'super entrepreneurs' (millionaire entrepreneurs) within an economy (Sanandaji and Sanandaji, 2014).

Regulation – This is often seen as particularly onerous for SMEs, imposing burdens, costs and constraints on SMEs (e.g. Fletcher, 2001; Kitching, 2006, 2007). Some academics agree that there is a special case for deregulation for SMEs. Sanandaji and Sanandaji (op. cit.) see low regulation as also being associated with a high proportion of 'super entrepreneurs' within an economy. However, it has also been claimed that regulation does not necessarily constrain SME activity and performance and that it could create opportunities and enabling activities that might improve performance, depending upon the indirect reaction of other stakeholders – customers, suppliers, competitors, infrastructure providers and regulatory authorities (Kitching et al., 2013).

Competition policy – One example of regulation that might assist SMEs is in the area of competition policy. This is seen as a way of addressing 'market failure'. Market entry and exit barriers can lead to monopolies or oligopolies developing and other information or knowledge imperfections. Although the prime beneficiary of competition policy is consumers, SMEs can also benefit if they are affected by 'unfair' competition. This can be particularly the case in the provision of finance but also may apply to government procurement.

There is often a heated debate about immigration into particular countries. However, policies around this controversial area do affect entrepreneurial capabilities because, as we shall see in the next chapter, immigrants are often more entrepreneurial than the indigenous population. The problem is that, while high levels of immigration would seem to have a positive influence on entrepreneurship, they also have many other social and economic affects.

Social enterprise policy

Governments have many motivations for encouraging social enterprise. These include tackling social and environmental challenges, increasing levels of enterprise (particularly in developing economies), developing ethical markets and public sector reform. Among other things, the UK government sees social enterprise as part of its strategy for tackling long-term levels of deprivation and high rates of social exclusion. In 2001 it launched the Social Enterprise Unit within the Department of Trade and Industry. In 2006 this became the Office of the Third Sector under the wing of the Cabinet Office, with a Cabinet Minister responsible for the area. In 2010 this was renamed the Office for Civil Society, with responsibility for charities, social enterprises and voluntary organizations.

The priorities for the Office have changed with different governments, although its enduring policy has been to encourage a culture of social enterprise, providing advice and information and improving access to finance for social enterprises. Important new legal forms of social enterprise have been introduced (Chapter 9) as well as new sources of funding (Chapter 14). It also wishes to facilitate the way social enterprise works with government. Current priorities include:

> Increasing volunteering and social action (Community First);
> Increasing private charitable donations by making it easier to donate through payroll giving;
> Encouraging community action through recognition and awards (e.g. Queen's Award for Voluntary Service), and by funding the training of local community organizers;
> Encouraging the spin-out of government services through the formation of public service mutuals.

The issue with social enterprises is that the diverse nature of the motivations for encouraging them can sometimes appear altruistic, indeed naïve, while sometimes they appear highly political. For example, many people see the attitude towards social enterprise by the UK government in 2015 as a means of reducing the size of the public sector – a way of reducing public sector expenditure, rather than increasing public good. The spinning-out of government services has also been accompanied by reductions in government support. As a result, sometimes services have deteriorated and some of the organizations taking over these services have struggled to survive. Some charities have withdrawn from offering these spun-out services. Some organizations have even closed. For social enterprise to work there does need to be a mutuality of interest and motivation to increase public good. And where government is the major funder of the service this can create a very real tension.

At the root of this tension is the fact that social enterprises of any sort cannot be relied upon to deliver social objectives as a matter of policy because they rely too much on the philanthropic motives of individuals and/or governments. It has also been pointed out that, unlike its commercial counterpart, no economic case in terms of efficiency can be made to support a shift to social entrepreneurship and the market is not a legitimate benchmark to justify changes from a rights-based welfare system (Cook et al., 2003).

Eikenberry and Kluver (2004) were particularly concerned about the problems of what they call 'the methods and values of the market' being applied in both the public and the not-for-profit sector and the detrimental impact upon democracy and citizenship in the USA. They put their point strongly:

> For the public sector, an emphasis on entrepreneurialism is incompatible with democratic citizenship and its emphasis on accountability and collective action for the public interest (Box, 1999; Box et al., 2001; deLeon and Denhardt, 2000; Denhardt and Denhardt, 2000; King and Strivers, 1998). Furthermore, the market model places little or no value on democratic ideals such as fairness and justice (Terry, 1998). For the non-profit sector, marketization trends such as commercial revenue generation, contract competition, the influence of new and emerging donors, and social entrepreneurship compromise the non-profit sector's civil society roles as value guardians, service providers and advocates, and the builders of social capital.

The problem then is the mixing of social and economic objectives. There is no accepted framework to measure the two together and, in particular, the trade-off between them. What is efficient economically may be ineffective socially and vice versa, but where does the acceptable trade-off lie, and who decides? Social enterprises can therefore all too easily avoid rigorous monitoring both because of the lack of an accounting framework and because of the complexity of the interests of their diverse stakeholder base. In the commercial world it is simple. Owners generally look to get the maximum financial return on their investment and if a sole owner has different, perhaps lifestyle, objectives, they have no other owners who can object to their decision. Economists tell us that in a free and efficient market these entrepreneurial motivations maximize the financial returns for society. They generate economic growth – as economists measure it. However, there is no such theoretical framework for social enterprise that guarantees maximization of social returns – even if we could measure them.

 ## Case insight   Brompton Bicycle (1)

Growth through innovation

The quirky Brompton folding bicycle was invented by Cambridge University graduate Andrew Ritchie in 1976 and went into full production in 1988. He produced small volumes of the cycle himself from a small, cluttered factory under a railway arch in West London. It became a style icon, combining practical, lightweight design, durable engineering and careful assembly. It also became a profitable niche business, selling at a price premium despite the fact that by 2002 it still produced only about 6,000 cycles each year and employed 24 people. Not surprisingly, demand exceeded supply.

That all started to change in 2002 when Will Butler-Adams joined the firm as Managing Director aged only 28. He is still Managing Director today, and Andrew remains Technical Director. It was Will who introduced new ways of working, introducing budget plans and subcontracting parts of the manufacturing process such as the manufacture of wheels and frame to other UK manufacturers. This allowed more space to become available in the small factory in London, which is still where the bikes are assembled by hand.

'The idea was to outsource the non-core stuff, so that we could then lavish more attention on the core things, and do them better. And we could make more bikes.'

By 2014 Brompton had become the UK's largest cyclemaker, producing over 40,000 cycles a year and employing some 190 people. It offered seven basic models at prices ranging from almost £800 to over £2,000. Each one could be customized to suit personal requirements.

With a turnover of £28 million, it now exports some 80% of its bikes to 44 countries. Sales growth in 2013 was over 25%, with the largest increase in sales going to export. It sells Brompton bikes directly to the public through its website (where they can be customized). In the UK, USA, Canada and Ireland, it also sells through bicycle retailers. In other territories, it sells to distributors who operate their own dealer networks. It is now focusing its growth on exporting to the USA and in 2014 hosted retailers from nine US states. The company remains privately owned and all this growth has been achieved entirely organically and without outside finance. Will has no plan to relocate any production to the Far East to take advantage of cheaper labour costs:

'What we are doing by making the bikes in London is protecting our intellectual property. It's brilliant, and it really works. Of course we sell bikes in China, so someone could buy one and try to reverse engineer it. But it is not that simple – the complexity of our manufacturing process is such that it is not easy.' (BBC News Business, 15 July 2013)

Courtesy of Brompton Bicycle

Continued...

Continued from previous page...

The history of Brompton is an insight into amateur design that can find its way into the marketplace:

1975: A chance meeting with a backer of another folding bike business – the Bickerton – starts Andrew Ritchie thinking about the design of folding bikes.

1976: Brompton registered as a company after the building of a prototype. The prototype was quickly deemed too large.

1977: A more effective prototype was developed with larger wheels and a simpler, lighter folding mechanism.

1978–80: Andrew tries to find an established bicycle manufacturer to take up the novel design under licence. Despite initial interest, companies like Raleigh, then the largest bicycle manufacturer in the UK, turn him down because they were 'not convinced that a market existed, or could be created, for such an unusual machine'.

1980–81: The design was finalized and the first batch of 30 bikes was produced to order as Andrew worked doing design and engineering work for a local firm.

1981: Low-volume manufacturing of the Brompton started from a small premises in Kew, London.

1986: Funding secured to scale-up production.

1987: Brompton exhibited at the Cyclex event and won Best Product award.

1988: Full production started from a railway arch in Brentford. Having previously sold bikes directly to customers, Brompton appointed its first dealer.

1991: Production extends to a second arch in the same railway viaduct.

1993: The company moves to larger premises in Chiswick Park, London.

1995: Brompton awarded the Queen's Award for export. Since then the company has also been awarded the Queen's Award for Innovation as well as International Trade (**2010**).

1996: Brompton awarded 'Bike of the Year' by the German National Cycling Association (ADFC). Since then the company has received a number of awards including the Bike Biz Brand of the Year Award (**2010**).

1998: Brompton moves to its current factory near Kew Bridge, London.

2001: There is product innovation as Sturmey Archer gears are replaced by SRAM hubs.

2004: There is further product innovation as a long wheel base and improved hinge joints are introduced.

2005: A super-light upgrade is introduced, featuring an alloy headset and titanium forks, rear frame, pedal bolt and mudguard stays. New handlebars are offered for existing models.

2006: The first Brompton World Championship is held in Barcelona, Spain – an event that now takes place every year. The company now hosts cycling events around the globe.

2007: A new rear frame clip that allows the bike to be folded in two is introduced.

2009: Andrew receives the Prince Philip Award for Innovation.

2012: Brompton receives the British Inspiration Award for Innovation, Enterprise and Industry.

The company is also expanding into other areas of business. It opened its first UK store in Covent Garden, London in 2013, adding to sites in Kobe, Shanghai, Hamburg and Amsterdam. These stores allow it to get closer to its customers and experience what works best selling its bikes. It has also recently launched a bike rental scheme in 20 UK locations.

❑ **Visit the website where you can see the full product range, where the bike is manufactured and view many of the worldwide Brompton events: www.brompton.com**

QUESTIONS:

1 Was the Brompton bike an invention or an innovation?
2 What role has innovation played in the growth of the company?
3 How are the problems of linking innovation and company growth reflected in the history of the company?
4 Why has the company been successful and what are the lessons you learn from their success?

⊃ Summary

› Many politicians would claim that the growth of small firms is a manifestation of the success of free-market capitalism, although Marxist theory does seem to be able to accommodate it. But while industrial economists would have little to say to explain the phenomenon, labour economists and psychologists have been more successful by looking at the influences on self-employment.

> It was Schumpeter who first linked entrepreneurs with economic growth through innovation and 'creative destruction'. Historically there have been cycles of innovation that disrupted economies, causing rapid growth. These are usually technology-led and facilitated by entrepreneurial activity.

> Theories of 'industrial evolution' link entrepreneurship and economic growth through the tendency of entrepreneurial companies to increase competition, make the most of knowledge spill-overs and create increased diversity.

> Innovation can take three forms: product, process and/or market innovation. To be successful it must be linked to customer demand.

> Innovation is difficult to define. It is about doing things differently. Although scale of innovation is important, competitive advantage can equally be gained by frequent, incremental innovations – a strategy that is less risky and from which the majority of commercially significant innovations have come. It is scale and frequency of innovation that combine to produce competitive advantage.

> Invention is the extreme and riskiest form of innovation. But inventors are not necessarily entrepreneurial, and they may need the help of an entrepreneur or an entrepreneurial organization to link their invention to market demand. However, others may be an inventor, innovator and entrepreneur – all in one. While creativity is at the core of invention and innovation, so too is the ability to spot market opportunities – and this is a very important role for the entrepreneur.

> Social enterprises often use social innovation to achieve their objectives.

> Finding evidence of a relationship between innovation and business growth is problematic. Indeed, relationships between innovation and other factors would seem to be complex. The rate of innovation (however measured) seems to vary between firms of different size, across industries and sectors depending on industry age and stability, and even location.

> Small firms produce more than their fair share of innovations and seem to do it more efficiently than large firms. However, they tend to do this in sectors where resources, in particular capital, are less important. Innovation is not entirely related to firm size. It also relates to business activity, industry, nature of innovation and the type of company. Small and large firms have advantages in producing different types of innovation.

> Geographical proximity facilitates the process of knowledge transfer, and hence clusters of small firms can be observed, sharing 'collective learning' either through conscious or unconscious mechanisms. This underlines the importance of networks.

> Government economic policy in most countries tries to encourage the start-up, survival and growth of SMEs. However, most academics would conclude that there is little evidence of the effectiveness or value-for-money of micro-economic policy interventions. By way of contrast, most would agree that the broader macro-economic policies of taxation, regulation and competition policy can have a powerful effect.

> Governments have encouraged the development of social enterprises through legal and taxation changes and the provision of advice and finance, although the motivations for this can be diverse.

> A major issue with social enterprises is that they cannot be relied upon to deliver social objectives as a matter of policy because they rely too much on the philanthropic motives of individuals or governments. There is also the issue that, while commercial entrepreneurs operating in a free and efficient market might maximize the financial returns for society and generate economic growth, there is no such theoretical framework for social entrepreneurs that guarantees maximization of social returns.

✓ Activities

1 Research the government's current policies to encourage start-ups and the growth of SMEs. Distinguish between micro- and macro-economic policies.

2 Research the government's current policies to encourage the start-up and growth of social enterprises.

💬 Group discussion topics

1 Discuss the meaning of innovation.
2 Discuss the differences between creativity, invention and innovation, and the links with entrepreneurship.

3 Assess the case for frequent incremental innovation rather than infrequent radical innovation. Are the two mutually exclusive? How can these be measured on Figure 2.1?

4   Assess the advantages and disadvantages small firms have over large firms in innovation, and vice versa.

5   Discuss the effect the internet might have in changing the nature of the geographic 'clusters' of high-tech SMEs.

6   Discuss the ways entrepreneurship can help stimulate economic growth.

7   Assess the case for encouraging entrepreneurship. List the ways this might be achieved.

8   Discuss whether government policy should encourage start-ups and the growth of SMEs. If you believe it should, suggest specific policy interventions. Compare these to the policies uncovered as a result of Activity 1. If you do not, outline the role government intervention should take (if any).

9   Assess the case for all undergraduates undertaking enterprise courses at university.

10 Make the case for and against supporting female and/or minority entrepreneurship.

11 Discuss the arguments for and against business regulation.

12 Discuss the arguments for and against lower taxation for SMEs.

13 Discuss the reasons why social enterprise needs to be socially innovative. Provide examples of what this means and how it might be achieved.

14 Discuss whether government policy should encourage the start-up and the growth of social enterprises.

15 Discuss whether or not social enterprise should undertake activities that the state normally has responsibility to deliver.

☞ References

Acemoğlu, D., Aghion, P. and Zilibotti, F. (2006) 'Distance to the Frontier, Selection and Economic Growth', *Journal of the European Economic Association*, 4.

Acs, Z.J. and Audretsch, D.B. (1988) 'Innovation in Large and Small Firms: An Empirical Analysis', *American Economic Review*, 78(4).

Acs, Z.J. and Audretsch, D.B. (1989) 'Births and Firm Size', *Southern Economic Journal*, 55.

Acs, Z.J. and Audretsch, D.B. (1990) *Innovation and Small Firms*, Cambridge, MA: MIT Press.

Acs, Z., Audretsch, D., Braunerhjelm, P. and Carlsson, P. (2004) 'The Missing Link: The Knowledge Filter and Entrepreneurship in Endogenous Growth', *CEPR Discussion Paper 5409*, CEPR London.

Acs, Z., Audretsch, D., Braunerhjelm, P. and Carlsson, P. (2005) 'Growth and Entrepreneurship: An Empirical Assessment', *CEPR Discussion Paper 5409*, CEPR London.

Aghion, P. and Howitt, P. (1992) 'A Model for Growth through Creative Destruction', *Econometrica*, 60.

Amabile, T.M., Conti, R., Coon, H., Lazenby, J. and Herron, M. (1996) 'Assessing the Work Environment for Creativity', *Academy of Management Journal*, 39(5).

Anderson, J. (1995) *Local Heroes*, Glasgow: Scottish Enterprise.

Audretsch, D.B. (1995) 'Innovation, Growth and Survival', *International Journal of Industrial Organisation*, 13.

Audretsch, D.B. (2007) 'Entrepreneurship Capital and Economic Growth', *Oxford Review of Economic Policy*, 23(1).

Autio, E. (2007) *Global Entrepreneurship Monitor 2007 Global Report on High-Growth Entrepreneurship*, London, UK: London Business School; and Babson Park, MA: Babson College.

Bessant, J. (1999) 'Developing Continuous Improvement Capability', *International Journal of Innovation Management*, 2.

Bill, F., Johannisson, B. and Olaison, L. (2009) 'The Incubus Paradox: Attempts at Foundational Rethinking of the SME Support Genre', *European Planning Studies*, 17(8).

Boschee, J. (1998) *Merging Mission and Money: A Board Member's Guide to Social Entrepreneurship*, Washington, DC: BoardSource.

Box, R.C. (1999) 'Running Government like a Business: Implications for Public Administration Theory and Practice', *American Review of Public Administration*, 29(1).

Box, R.C., Marshall, G.S., Reed, B.J. and Reed, C.M. (2001) 'New Public Management and Substantive Democracy', *Public Administration Review*, 60(5), September/October.

Bridge, S., O'Neill, K. and Martin, F. (2009) *Understanding Enterprise, Entrepreneurship and Small Business*, Basingstoke: Palgrave Macmillan.

Brinckerhoff, P. (2000) *Social Entrepreneurship: The Art of Mission-Based Venture Development*, Hoboken, NJ: Wiley.

Bureau of European Policy Advisors (2011) *Empowering People, Driving Change: Social Innovation in the European Union*, European Commission, Brussels: EU.

Camagni, R. (ed.) (1991) *Innovative Networks: Spatial Perspectives*, London: Belhaven.

Capello, R. (1999) 'Spatial Transfer of Knowledge in High Technology Milieux: Learning versus Collective Learning Processes', *Regional Studies*, 33.

Casson, M., Yeung, B., Basu, A. and Wadeson, N. (2008) *Introduction*, in A. Basu, M. Casson, N. Wadeson and B. Yeung (eds), *The Oxford Handbook of Entrepreneurship*, Oxford: Oxford University Press.

Cefis, E. (2003) 'Is there Persistence in Innovative Activities?', *International Journal of Industrial Organization*, 21(4).

Christensen, C. (1997) *The Innovator's Dilemma*, Cambridge, MA: Harvard Business School Press.

Coad, A. and Rao, R. (2008) 'Innovation and Firm Growth in High-Tech Sectors: A Quantile Regression Approach', *Research Policy*, 37(4).

Cook, B., Dodds, C. and Mitchell, W. (2003) 'Social Entrepreneurship – False Premises and Dangerous Forebodings', *Australian Journal of Social Issues*, 38(1), February.

Cosh, A.D. and Hughes, A. (eds) (2007) *British Enterprise: Thriving or Surviving?*, Cambridge: Centre for Business Research, University of Cambridge.

Davidsson, P. (2008) 'Some Conclusions about Entrepreneurship and its Support', Paper presented at the World Entrepreneurship Forum, November, Evian, France.

deLeon, L. and Denhardt, R.B. (2000) 'The Political Theory of Reinvention', *Public Administration Review*, 60(2), March/April.

Denhardt, R.B. and Denhardt, J.V. (2000) 'The New Public Service: Serving rather than Steering', *Public Administration Review*, 60(6), November/December.

Dennis, W.J. (2004) 'Creating and Sustaining a Viable Small Business Sector', Paper presented at the School of Continuing Education, University of Oklahoma, 27 October.

Department of Business, Enterprise and Regulatory Reform, (2008) *High growth firms in the UK: Lessons from an analysis of comparative UK performance*, BERR Economics Paper no. 3, London, UK: Department of Business, Enterprise and Regulatory Reform.

Dolfsma, W. and van der Panne, G. (2008) 'Currents and Sub-currents in Innovation Flows: Explaining Innovativeness using New-product Announcements', *Research Policy*, 37(10).

Eikenberry, A. and Kluver, J.D. (2004) 'The Marketisation of the Non-profit Sector: Civil society at risk?', *Public Administration Review*, 64(2), March/April.

Ericson, R. and Pakes, A. (1995) 'Markov-Perfect Industry Dynamics: A Framework for Empirical Work', *Review of Economic Studies*, 62.

European Commission (2008) *European Competitiveness Report 2008*, available online at www.ec.europa.eu/enterprise.

European Union (2007) *Statistics in Focus: Community Innovation Statistics, Is Europe Growing More Innovative?*, 61/2007, Brussels: EU.

Fletcher, I. (2001) 'A Small Business Perception on Regulation in the UK', *Economic Affairs*, 21(2).

Florida, R. (2002) *The Rise of the Creative Classes: And How It's Transforming Work, Leisure, Community and Everyday Life*, New York: Basic Books.

Florida, R. and Tinagli, I. (2004), *Europe in the Creative Age*, London: Demos.

Freel, M.S. (2000) 'Do Small Innovating Firms Outperform Non-innovators?' *Small Business Economics*, 14(3).

GE Capital (2012) *Leading from the Middle: The Untold Story of British Business*, London; GE Capital.

Hölzl, W., Huber, P., Kaniovski, S. and Peneder, M. (2006) 'Neugründung und Entwicklung von Unternehmen, Teilstudie 20', in K. Aiginger, G. Tichy and E. Walterskirchen (eds), *WIFO-Weißbuch: Mehr Beschäftigung durch Wachstum auf Basis von Innovation und Qualifikation*, Vienna: WIFO.

Hopenhayn, H.A. (1992) 'Entry, Exit and Firm Dynamics in Long Run Equilibrium', *Econometrica*, 60.

Johnson, S. (2010) *Where Good Ideas Come From: The Natural History of Innovation*, London: Allen Lane.

Jovanovic, B. (1982) 'Favorable Selection with Asymmetrical Information', *Quarterly Journal of Economics*, 97(3).

Jovanovic, B. (2001) 'Fitness and Age: Review of Carroll and Hannan's "Demography of Corporations and Industries"', *Journal of Economic Literature*, 39, S, 105–119.

Kanter, R.M. (1983), *The Change Masters: Innovation and Productivity in American Corporations*, New York: Simon & Schuster.

Keeble, D. and Wilkinson, F. (1999) 'Collective Learning and Knowledge Development in the Evolution of Regional Clusters of High Technology SMEs in Europe', *Regional Studies*, 33.

King, C.S. and Strivers, C. (eds) (1998) *Government Is Us: Public Administration in an Anti-Government Era*, Thousand Oaks, CA: Sage.

Kirzner, I.M. (1973) *Competition and Entrepreneurship*, Chicago: University of Chicago Press.

Kitching, J. (2006) 'A burden on Business? Reviewing the Evidence Base on Regulation and Small Business Performance', *Government and Policy*, 24(6).

Kitching, J. (2007) 'Is Less More? Better Regulation and Small Business Enterprise' in Weatherill, S. (ed.), *Better Regulation*, Oxford: Hart.

Kitching, J., Hart, M. and Wilson, N. (2013) 'Burden or Benefit? Regulation as a Dynamic Influence on Small Business Performance', *International Small Business Journal*, 33(2).

Klepper, S. (1996) 'Entry, Exit, Growth and Innovation over the Product Life Cycle', *American Economic Review*, 86(3).

Knight, F. (1921) *Risk, Uncertainty and Profit*, Chicago: University of Chicago Press.

Lambson, V.E. (1991) 'Industry Evolution with Sunk Costs and Uncertain Market Conditions', *International Journal of Industrial Organisations*, 9.

Leadbeater, C. (1997) *The Rise of the Social Entrepreneur*, London: Demos.

Lewis, J.D. (1990) *Partnerships for Profit: Structuring and Managing Strategic Alliances*, New York: Free Press.

Lorange, P. and Roos, J. (1992) *Strategic Alliances: Formation, Implementation and Evolution*, Oxford: Blackwell.

MacPherson, A.D. (1998) 'Academic-industry Linkages and Small Firm Innovation: Evidence from the Scientific Instruments Sector', *Entrepreneurship and Regional Development*, 10(4).

McLean, L.D. (2005) 'Organizational Culture's Influence on Creativity and Innovation: A Review of the Literature and Implications for Human Resource Development', *Advances in Developing Human Resources*, 7(2).

Mellor, R.B. (2005) *Sources and Spread of Innovation in Small e-Commerce Companies*, Skodsborgvej: Forlaget Globe.

Michelacci, C. (2003), 'Low Returns in R&D due to Lack of Entrepreneurial Skills', *Economic Journal*, 113.

Mintzberg, H. (1983) *Structures in Fives: Designing Effective Organisations*, London: Prentice Hall.

Mitra, J. (2000) 'Nurturing and Sustaining Entrepreneurship: University, Science Park, Business and Government Partnership in Australia', *Industry and Higher Education*, June.

Ohmae, K. (1989) 'The Global Logic of Strategic Alliances', *Harvard Business Review*, March/April.

O'Regan, N., Ghobadian, A. and Gallear, D. (2006) 'In Search of the Drivers of High Growth in Manufacturing SMEs', *Technovation*, 26(1).

Parkhurst, H.B. (1999), 'Confusion, Lack of Consensus and the Definition of Creativity as a Construct', *Journal of Creative Behaviour*, 33.

Porter, M. E. (1990) *The Competitive Advantage of Nations*, New York: Free Press.

Porter, M. E. (1998a) *On Competition*, Boston, MA: Harvard Business School.

Porter, M. E. (1998b) 'Clusters and the New Economics of Competition', *Harvard Business Review*, Nov–Dec.

Robson, S. and Haigh, G. (2008) 'First Findings from the UK Innovation Survey 2007', *Economic and Labour Market Review*, 2(4).

Sanandaji, T. and Sanandaji, N. (2014) *SuperEntrepreneurs: And how your country can get them*, London, UK: Centre for Policy Studies.

Santarelli, E. and Piergiovanni, R. (1996) 'Analysing Literature-based Innovation Output Indicators', *Research Policy*, 25(5).

Saxenian, A. (1994) *Regional Advantage: Culture and Competition within Silicon Valley and Route 128*, Cambridge, MA: Harvard Business Press.

Schumacher, E.F. (1974) *Small Is Beautiful*, London: Abacus.

Schumpeter J.A. (1911) *Theorie der Wirtschaftlichen Entwicklung*, Munich and Leipzig: Dunker und Humblat; translated (1934) by R. Opie, *The Theory of Economic Development*, Cambridge, MA: Harvard University Press.

Schumpeter J.A. (1950) *Capitalism, Socialism and Democracy*, New York: Harper Row.

Simmie, J. (2002) 'Knowledge Spillovers and Reasons for the Concentration of Innovative SMEs', *Urban Studies*, 39, 5–6.

Spencer, A.S., Kirchhoff, B.A. and White, C. (2008) 'Entrepreneurship, Innovation and Wealth Distribution: The Essence of Creative Destruction', *International Small Business Journal*, 26(9).

Storey, D.J. and Greene F.J. (2010) *Small Business and Entrepreneurship*, Harlow: Prentice Hall.

Stangler, D. (2010) *High Growth Firms and the Future of the American Economy*, Kauffman Foundation Research Series: Firm Growth and Economic Growth, Kansas City, MO: Ewing Marion Kauffman Foundation.

Symeonidis, G. (1996) 'Innovation, Firm Size and Market Structure: Schumpeterian Hypotheses and Some New Themes', *OECD Economic Studies*, 27.

Terry, L.D. (1998) 'Administrative Leadership, Neo-managerialism, and the Public Management Movement', *Public Administration Review*, 58(3), May/June.

Van Praag, C.M. and Versloot, P.H. (2007) 'What Is the Value of Entrepreneurship? A Review of Recent Research', *Small Business Economics*, 29(4).

Venkatarman, S. (1997) 'The Distinctive Domain of Entrepreneurship Research: An Editor's Perspective', in J. Katz and R. Brockhaus (eds), *Advances in Entrepreneurship, Firm Emergence and Growth*, Greenwich, CT: JAI Press.

Vossen, R.W. (1998) 'Relative Strengths and Weaknesses of Small Firms in Innovation', *International Small Business Journal*, 16(3), 88–94.

www.palgrave.com/Burns-Entrepreneurship-And-Small-Business-4e

Go online to access additional teaching and learning resources for this chapter on the companion website. Click here in the ebook to complete a multiple choice revision quiz for this chapter.

3 | THE ENTREPRENEURIAL CHARACTER

Contents

Getty

Learning outcomes

When you have read this chapter and undertaken the related activities you will be able to:

> Understand your motivations for wanting to start your own business and the barriers you face;
> Critically assess the personal capital you would bring to your business;
> Understand and critically assess trait theory;
> Understand the entrepreneurial character traits and how they are developed;
> Critically assess whether you have an entrepreneurial character;
> Understand the qualities needed to be an intrapreneur and a social or civic entrepreneur.

Practice insight: Measuring your entrepreneurial tendency

Practice insight: Could you be an intrapreneur?

 Case insights

Souqalmal	Sadaf Gallery
Marc Demarquette	Golden Krust (1)
Hide My Ass!	Duncan Bannatyne
Adam Schwab and AussieCommerce Group (1)	John Bird and The Big Issue

What you need to be an entrepreneur

Never has it been easier to create a new venture. And never have the chances of success on a global basis been higher. But running it can be hard work. It is an all-consuming, 24-hour, seven-day-a-week activity – at least until you have a management team you can rely on. So it helps enormously if you enjoy what you are doing. You need commitment and dedication. You need stamina – '90% perspiration, 10% inspiration'. It can break up relationships and split families. It is risky, without guaranteed results. So, you need to be able to bounce back from setbacks, because there will be many. You need determination and persistence in situations where others might give up. You need to be emotionally tough – self-employment can generate a roller coaster of emotions. You need to be emotionally self-sufficient – it can be lonely. You need to be task-orientated – motivated to deliver the best product or service to your customers, all day, every day. You need to be attuned to the opportunities generated by your customers and the market you operate in. Most of all you need to be able to live with a degree of risk and uncertainty – you will always be the last one to get paid and then only if there is enough cash left over. If you crave certainty, routines and a regular pay cheque, entrepreneurship is not for you.

However, the rewards for being successful can be high, especially if you enjoy what you are doing. There is the freedom and independence you have on a day-to-day basis, the sense that you control your own destiny and that it is you who will benefit from your hard work. There is the sense of purpose that launching your own business brings and satisfaction that comes from your achievements. And for many of the most successful entrepreneurs it can bring wealth and even fame.

Motivation

All this means that it is important to understand yourself – your personal strengths and weaknesses, the make-up of your character. What are the emotions that go with entrepreneurship for you? What are your fears and aspirations? You start by understanding your motivation to start your own business. As we saw in the Chapter 1, people can start up many different kinds of organizations for many different reasons. You need to understand your own motivations for being an entrepreneur. Why are you considering it? What are your personal drivers? What do you want the business to become – a salary-substitute, lifestyle or entrepreneurial business? Or do you want it to achieve some social or civic objectives? In other words, what is your business purpose?

Of course, entrepreneurs often start out thinking they want to achieve one thing and then change it later as new opportunities emerge. Many people start out with what appears a business without growth prospects but go on to seize opportunities that present themselves. John Hargreaves is a docker's son who left school at 14 and started a market stall in Liverpool selling Marks & Spencer clothing seconds. He went on to found the Matalan clothing chain in the UK, a venture he sold for £1.5 billion in 2009. Alan Sugar, now well known in the UK for his appearances on *The Apprentice* TV show, founded the computer companies Amstrad and Viglen and is a millionaire. He started out boiling beetroot to sell from market stalls in London's East End.

Nevertheless, you need to match your personal motivations with the business you intend to set up now – not in 10 years' time. There is no point in setting up a business intended to grow rapidly unless you are willing and able to make the additional time and resource commitment. And you certainly will need to enjoy whatever your venture entails. You will spend enough time working in it.

You also need to consider any personal constraints or barriers that might affect your venture. Are you short of money, time or skills? What are your fears about self-employment? Many of these may originate from family or other commitments. It is important that your business fits in with what you want from your life and lifestyle. You need to have a balance between work and personal life that suits you. Without an acceptable balance, the stress and pressure may be too much.

> A good entrepreneur doesn't just run a business; they live and breathe it.
>
> **Martyn Dawes**, founder, Coffee Nation, Startups: *www.startups.co.uk*

> I wake up at 6 am, work for a couple of hours then take a break, maybe work 12 hours a day; weekends, four or five hours a day, even on holidays.
>
> **Adam Schwab**, co-founder, AussieCommerce, *Management Today*, July 2014

> You'll need passion, a belief in what you do and hard work to achieve it.
>
> **Emma Elston**, founder, UK Container Maintenance, *The Sunday Times*, 29 June 2014

> Fun is at the core of the way I like to do business and has informed everything I've done from the outset. More than any other element, fun is at the core of Virgin's success.
>
> **Richard Branson**, founder, Virgin Group, *Losing My Virginity* (1988), London: Virgin

> I wouldn't say it was at the cost of everything else, but when I am at work, I work hard and do long hours – and when I am not at work my mind still tends to be there anyway.
>
> **Mike Peters**, founder, Universal Laboratories, *The Sunday Times*, 11 July 2004

Start-up capital

Even if they are short of cash, every entrepreneur brings capital to their start-up. There are three kinds of capital: financial, human and social (Figure 3.1). The more capital you bring to the business – of any kind – the more likely you are to succeed (Unger et al., 2011). More specifically, human, social and financial capital are generally thought to be facilitators of innovation activity, particularly in high-technology firms (e.g. Koskinen and Vanharanta, 2002; Lee et al., 2010; Thornhill, 2006). But lack of one kind of capital can often be compensated for by an abundance of another.

Financial capital

Financial capital comprises cash and other assets or resources you bring to the business. The cash you have may be limited; however, it can probably go further than you think. The important thing to remember is that you do not necessarily have to buy and own a resource to be able to use it. Using resources that you may not own is called '**bootstrapping**' (Chapter 10). Entrepreneurs often commit only limited resources themselves – the resources they can afford to lose. They find ways of using resources that they do not own by partnering with others (Chapter 9). Actually, minimizing your ownership of resources reduces your risks and gives you more flexibility – it allows you to commit and de-commit quickly to new opportunities.

Human capital

Human capital comprises your skills, abilities, knowledge and experience. It is vital for any business. Knowledge and experience of a business or industry can be an invaluable source of business ideas. It can also give you an insight into the problems that you will face in business and it is always better to make mistakes at somebody else's expense rather than your own. If you do not have that experience, then education and training can alert you to the problems and give you the skills to overcome them. That is why so many people take training courses before they actually start up a business – it improves their chances of success. Human capital in the form of education and track record increases your credibility with financial backers. If you can demonstrate achievements, particularly in the industry that you want to start up in, it counts for a lot. It has also been shown that those entrepreneurs with more invested in their human capital are more likely to evolve and enjoy their business than those who invested less (Cassar, 2006).

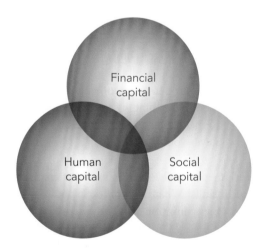

Figure 3.1   Forms of start-up capital

Social capital

This is derived from access to personal networks of friends and commercial contacts. It is about your ability to get on with people – your social skills. It is built on relationships, and this is at the core of the entrepreneurial approach to doing business – relationships with customers, employees, suppliers, the bank and landlord. It is social capital that enables you to build your credibility with all these stakeholders in your business. It is the personal touch that distinguishes entrepreneurs from the faceless, grey-suited managers of large firms. These relationships can build into an invaluable network of contacts and goodwill that can be used to generate knowledge and information on new opportunities or threats.

Networking has been found to be one of the most important factors underpinning long-term business performance (Cross et al., 2005; Hoppe 2010). It can affect profitability because it generates opportunities for social learning, spotting business opportunity and access to finance (Chan and Foster 2001; Cron et al., 2006; Shane, 2000). Networks can increase your flexibility and reduce, or give you early warning of, the risks you face. Networks also might yield up partners or ways of bootstrapping resources. They might provide you with your first customer, or provide you with low-cost or free office space. They might provide professional advice and opinion, often without charge. They might even provide you with the cash that the banker is so reluctant to provide.

 ## Case insight   Souqalmal

The importance of social and human capital

Born in Mauritius, Ambareen Musa holds an undergraduate business degree from RMIT University, in Melbourne, Australia, and a MBA from INSEAD, France. She started her first online business, an online property portal for international students in Australia, at the age of 21. She moved to London in 2004 to work for General Electric's financial arm, GE Money, where she worked in various roles including marketing, financial literacy, customer advocacy and e-commerce. She led the first online financial literacy initiative in the UK, Moneybasics.co.uk. Moving to the Middle East in 2008, she worked as a consultant for Bain & Company Middle East and focused on financial services projects such as growth strategies for banks in the region. She moved on to set up the consulting arm of MasterCard Middle East

and Africa, where she stayed for two years, before founding Souqalmal in 2012 in Dubai, United Arab Emirates.

Souqalmal is Arabic for 'money market'. The online site says that its aim is 'to create a transparent market place and empower consumers'. It allows consumers to compare some 3,000 products online including credit cards, car loans, insurances, SME loans, mobile phone plans, schools and nurseries in the UAE, Saudi Arabia and Kuwait. The site also has news and guides about the markets it covers. It has become the leading financial comparison website in the Middle East.

❏ Visit the website: www.souqalmal.com

QUESTIONS:

1 What human and social capital does Ambareen Musa possess?

2 How did her education and experience help her in starting up Souqalmal?

Triggers for entrepreneurship

Many people with a good business idea, capital and the necessary business skills never take the plunge into self-employment. They face barriers – some real and some psychological. Some people are just too risk averse. They fear the unknown and do not like uncertainty. If you have a family, you might fear the consequences of not having a regular income or losing what little financial capital you have.

What many people need is some sort of 'trigger' that either 'pushes' or 'pulls' them into it. Some people are 'pushed' into setting up their own business because they are made redundant, they find they just do not fit into the company they work for or, simply, that they have no alternative. Typically, these are situational factors that push you towards self-employment. Immigrants are often 'pushed' into being highly entrepreneurial. They have few alternatives. The USA, famed for its entrepreneurial culture, was built by immigrants and many millionaire entrepreneurs are first

```
┌─────────────────────────────────┐
│   Situational & psychological    │
│   barriers to entrepreneurship   │
│                                  │
│  > Need for regular income       │
│  > Fear of loss of capital       │
│  > No capital                    │
│  > Risk averse                   │
│  > Doubts about ability          │
└─────────────────────────────────┘
```

Business idea ──────────────────────────────────▶ Start-up

```
┌──────────────────────┐                    ┌──────────────────────┐
│     Push factors     │      Trigger       │     Pull factors     │
│                      │                    │                      │
│  > Unemployment      │                    │  > Independence       │
│  > Disagreements     │                    │  > Recognition        │
│  > Organizational    │                    │  > Personal           │
│    'misfit'          │                    │    development        │
│  > No other option   │                    │  > Wealth             │
└──────────────────────┘                    └──────────────────────┘
```

Figure 3.2 Barriers and triggers to entrepreneurship

> " We got the inspiration [for Lush] because we were broke. The previous business had gone bust. We had mortgages, three children and no money. So – make a living!
>
> **Mark Constantine**, founder, Lush, *RealBusiness*, 26 May 2009 "

or second generation immigrants. Sergey Brin, co-founder of Google, emigrated to the USA with his family from the Soviet Union at the age of six. Steve Jobs's father was Syrian. In the UK, six of the most successful wholesale medicine and drug supply companies were founded by Kenyan Asians – pharmacists – who came to Britain in the 1960/70s as forced immigrants and are now millionaires (Navin Engineer, Bharat Shah, Bharat and Ketan Mehta, Vijay and Bhikhu Patel, Ravi Kari and Naresh Shah).

Many people, however, are 'pulled' into starting up a business for more positive reasons. They yearn for independence and recognition of their achievements. This gives them drive and determination. They look for personal development. And the prospect of becoming rich might be attractive. Pull factors are typically psychological – they derive from your character traits and the influences on them. When 'push' and 'pull' factors combine it is little wonder that the result is a powerful trigger to create a new venture – as long as you have that all-important business idea. The combination of these triggers – the push and pull factors – and the barriers you face in setting up your own business are shown in Figure 3.2. It is no coincidence that the two peaks in the age of people becoming entrepreneurs are in their early 20s or their late 30s – coinciding with periods when barriers might be low because they have least to lose or face reducing family commitments as children leave home.

Case insight   Marc Demarquette

Triggers for entrepreneurship

Half French and half Chinese, Marc Demarquette was born and lives in London. He was a management consultant until a life-threatening incident necessitating facial reconstruction surgery caused him to reconsider his priorities.

'You don't get a chance to think in full-time employment. I came to the conclusion I hated what I was doing.'

His interest in catering led him to the prestigious Maison Lenôtre in Paris to learn the art of making chocolate and then to the Alps to work with a master chocolatier. In 2006, with the help of a £40,000 bank loan, he opened an up-market artisan chocolate shop, Demarquette, in Fulham, south west London, and a small production facility nearby. He sold his range of high-quality, award-winning chocolates through the store and its website as well as wholesale through other retailers like Fortnum & Mason.

Since launching the business, Marc has put approximately £170,000 of his own cash into it. In 2011 he closed the Fulham shop in the face of a threatened 100% rent increase, focusing instead on internet and wholesale business. He also

Continued...

Continued from previous page...

expanded his wholesale business overseas. By 2014, annual revenues exceeded £500,000 and he was employing five staff. He was still supplying Fortnum and Mason as well as Harvey Nichols and Selfridges – all high-end UK retailers, but more than half of his revenues now came from exporting to some 20 countries in Europe, Japan and the USA. In 2009 about one-third of his total revenues came through his website. By 2014, internet sales represented 40% of British revenues.

'I've always wondered whether I was the right person to steer the company or whether I am too close to the operation ... *You need to have nerves of steel but it has been a fantastic experience. I'm loving it. I just wish I had a couple of extra hours in the day to enjoy my own life.' (The Sunday Times,* 24 May 2009 and 28 September 2014)

❏ **Visit the website:** *www.demarquette.co.uk*

QUESTION:

1 What was Marc's trigger for entrepreneurship? Explain.

Myths about entrepreneurs

Many of the barriers to entrepreneurship are real, but the doubts about your ability can be unfounded. Entrepreneurs may be idolized in the press, but they are really just people, although they may have certain characteristics. Read et al. (2011) claim there are seven myths about entrepreneurs who 'see opportunities others don't, seize them faster, make better predictions and are brash risk-takers.' These lead to the usual objection to starting your own business – namely, 'I don't have an idea, money, entrepreneurial skills – and I'm afraid to fail.' These seven myths are:

> **Entrepreneurs have good ideas and you don't** – Ideas are easy to come by, but we never know how successful they will be, and that includes entrepreneurs.
> **Entrepreneurs are risk-takers** – They may be willing to accept risk, but they don't like it and limit and mitigate it in any way they can.
> **Entrepreneurs have money and you don't** – Just not true. Money does not guarantee success, and many money-starved start-ups have blossomed.
> **Entrepreneurs are extraordinary forecasters** – They are not. They are just willing to live with uncertainty but then organize themselves to cope with it, indeed, influence it.
> **Entrepreneurs are not like the rest of us** – They are, and entrepreneurial principles and skills can be taught.
> **Entrepreneurs are visionary** – Visions evolve as opportunities emerge. You define your own vision and measures of success. These will change over time and may expand beyond your current imagination. An unrealistic vision can be just an illusion.
> **You don't know how to take the plunge** – Hopefully books like this will show you how to do just that.

These myths create psychological barriers – a belief that you are not one of these 'special people'. It takes a degree of courage and self-belief to start your own business. However, some barriers can also be very real, arising from your situation. Perhaps you really do not have any capital or you have a family who rely on you for a regular income. Fear of the unknown is a strong de-motivator, but increasingly paid employment is not seen as a guarantee of regular income. As larger firms delayer, restructure and even just close, employees are increasingly realizing that there is no such thing as a 'job for life'. At least with self-employment you control some elements of your destiny. And, as this book will demonstrate, there are many good business ideas still out there, entrepreneurial skill can be learned and your risks are limited. Entrepreneurs really are not that 'special'.

Character traits of entrepreneurs

Your personal drivers and fears about entrepreneurship derive from your personal character. This influences the importance you place on 'pull' factors and how you react to 'push' factors. It is a source of many of the barriers you place in the way of being an entrepreneur. We do not completely understand how character traits develop and whether some might be 'hardwired' into your personality. However, they are at least in part the product of the many influences that have shaped and developed you over your life: from your parents to your nationality, from your education to your career. They are influenced by the different groups of society you operate in, their culture and norms of behaviour. And, while it might be possible to classify your character at a point in time, it can change over time and in different circumstances. Many researchers believe that entrepreneurs have certain identifiable character traits or personality dimensions that incline them towards setting up their own business and help them navigate through the uncertainties of entrepreneurship. What is more, some believe personality traits can be acquired or developed by individuals.

Research into the character traits of entrepreneurs is substantial and goes back some 40 years. While facing many methodological issues, which we shall return to later in this chapter, it has thrown up a number of overlapping personality dimensions. Figure 3.3 summarizes the six main entrepreneurial character traits, harvested from the numerous research studies indicated. Each is a necessary but not a sufficient trait. What is needed is the combination of all of them to be present.

Need for independence

Entrepreneurs have a high need for autonomy and independence. This is most often seen as the need to 'be your own boss'. It has been said that, once you run your own firm, you cannot work for anybody else. This is the most often cited entrepreneurial trait and supported by researchers and advisors alike. However, independence means different things to different people: doing things differently, being in a situation where you can fulfil your potential or controlling your own destiny.

An entrepreneur is unfailingly enthusiastic, never pessimistic, usually brave, and certainly stubborn. Vision and timing is crucial. You have to be something of a workaholic, too. You have to be convinced that what you are doing is right.

Chris Ingram, founder, Tempus, *The Sunday Times*, 17 March 2002

Entrepreneurs don't like working for other people … I was once made redundant by *Manchester Evening News*. I had a wife who had given up a promising career for me, and a baby. I stood in Deansgate with £5 in my pocket and I swore I would never work for anyone else again.

Eddy Shah, founder, Messenger Group, *The Times*, 16 March 2002

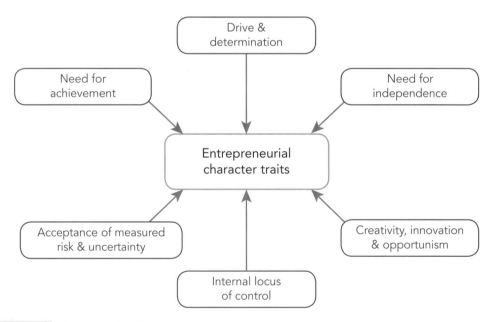

Figure 3.3 Character traits of entrepreneurs

Sources: Aldrich and Martinez, 2003; Andersson et al., 2004; Baty, 1990; Bell et al., 1992; Blanchflower and Meyer, 1991; Brockhaus and Horwitz, 1986; Brush, 1992; Buttner and More, 1997; Caird, 1990; Chell et al., 1991; Cuba et al., 1983; de Bono, 1985; Frank et al., 2007; Hansemark, 2003; Hirsch and Brush, 1987; Kanter, 1983; Kirzner, 1973, 1979, 1997, 1999; Korunka et al., 2003; McClelland, 1961; Pinchot, 1985; Rosa et al., 1994; Schein et al., 1996; Schumpeter, 1996; Schwartz, 1997; Shapero, 1985; Shaver and Scott, 1992; Storey and Sykes, 1996.

Need for achievement

Entrepreneurs have a high need for achievement. However, people measure their achievement in different ways, depending on the type of person they are: for example, the satisfaction of producing a beautiful work of art, employing their hundredth person or making the magic one million dollars. For many entrepreneurs, money is just a badge of success, validating their achievement. It is not an end in itself. What they are satisfying is their underlying need for achievement – recognition of their success. And while they may have a 'need' for achievement, that does not necessarily mean that they are actually high achievers, only that this 'need' creates a drive within them. If they have a high need but achieve little, then they can be profoundly unhappy.

Internal locus of control

Entrepreneurs have a high internal locus of control – a belief that they control their own destiny. They may believe in luck, but not fate. They believe that they can create their own destiny. This is underpinned by a high level of 'self-efficacy' – self-confidence (possibly unfounded) in their ability to complete a task successfully. In extremis, a high internal locus of control can also manifest itself in a desire to control everything and everyone around you. This can lead to a preoccupation with detail, overwork and stress, particularly if you feel you cannot trust those around you to complete the tasks delegated to them. This in turn can lead to a mistrust of subordinates, an unwillingness to delegate and an 'infantilization' of subordinates – they are expected to behave as incompetent idiots so that is the way they behave, not making decisions and not circulating information (Kets de Vries, 1985). The better ones do not stay long.

Drive and determination

Entrepreneurs have enormous drive and determination motivated by their need for achievement and underpinned by internal locus of control which gives them self-confidence in their ability to complete the task successfully. These three personality dimensions appear prominently in the academic literature. Because of their drive, entrepreneurs are proactive rather than reactive and appear more decisive. They act quickly. However, this trait can have its downside. Often entrepreneurs can also be easily diverted, for example by the most recent market opportunity. They also seem to do things at twice the pace of others, unwilling or unable to wait for others to complete tasks. They are often seen as restless and easily bored. Patience is certainly not a virtue many entrepreneurs possess. They seem to work 24 hours a day and their work becomes their life, with little separating the two. It is little wonder that this places family and personal relationships under strain. As a result, they can be difficult to work for and can be intolerant of those who do not share their enthusiasm.

A good example of an entrepreneur with these three character traits was the late Steve Jobs, co-founder of Apple. He was certainly driven and controlling. He was notoriously difficult to work for, wanting 'impossible' things done within 'impossible' time frames. He was labelled a 'control freak'. He was accused by many of being rude and abusive and even bullying in order to get his own way. He always believed he knew best and wanted things done his way – quickly.

As a child I never felt that I was noticed. I never felt that I achieved anything or that there was any expectation of me achieving anything. So proving myself is something that is important to me and so is establishing respect for what I have achieved.

Chey Garland, founder, Garlands Call Centres, *The Sunday Times*, 27 June 2004

I am motivated by my success, not money. But success is partly measured by money.

Wing Yip, founder, W. Wing Yip & Brothers, *The Sunday Times*, 2 January 2000

I actually don't believe in luck … I don't know anyone who got anywhere without hard work.

Lyn Lee, founder, Awfully Chocolate, *BBC News Business*, 8 November 2010

Being an entrepreneur is like being a juvenile delinquent … The more you tell us we can't do it; the more we want to prove you wrong … If we were to listen to people who keep telling us not to do it, then 77th Street would never have happened. Because in the early days everyone was telling us we would fail … Today we have proved everybody wrong.

Elim Chew, founder, 77th Street, *BBC News*, 20 December 2010

I'm often asked what sets successful entrepreneurs apart … a couple of key attributes are determination and common sense … anyone can make £100 million if they have the commitment and staying power. The beauty of being an entrepreneur is that, if the first idea doesn't work, you can come up with a second, and a third until you hit on a workable concept.

Duncan Bannatyne, serial entrepreneur, *Daily Telegraph*, 5 March 2009

When the going gets tough – pitch in and keep working. Nothing comes easy so you should expect it to get tough and to have to work hard.

Elizabeth Gooch, founder, eg solutions, *Launch Lab* (www.launchlab.co.uk), 13 January 2009

Purestock/ Punchstock/ Getty Images

Creativity, innovation and opportunism

The ability to be creative and innovative is an important attribute of entrepreneurs, particularly in growth businesses. But creativity can mean different things in different contexts. For entrepreneurs, creativity is focused on commercial opportunities. They spot an opportunity and then use creativity and innovation to exploit it. They tend to do things differently. But the degree of creativity that an entrepreneur has tends to reflect itself in the growth a business achieves. Generally, the more creative and innovative the entrepreneur is, the greater the growth potential of their business – a factor that distinguishes the entrepreneurial firms or 'gazelles' described in Chapter 1. One important aspect of this is timing – the ability to be in the right place at the right time. Timing is everything. Innovation that is before its time can lead to business failure. Innovation that is late results in copy-cat products or services that are unlikely to be outstanding successes. A question constantly asked about successful entrepreneurs is whether their success was due to good luck or good judgement. The honest answer in most cases is probably a bit of both. But, as we shall see, real entrepreneurs can help to make their own luck. We shall explore how to develop personal creativity in Chapter 4.

Acceptance of risk and uncertainty

Entrepreneurs are willing to take risks and live with uncertainty – things that can be very stressful for most people. They are willing to risk their money, reputation and personal standing if the business fails. And the entrepreneurial firms or 'gazelles' often seem willing to take the greatest risks to achieve their growth. However, that does not mean entrepreneurs are gamblers. They do not like risk and they will try to avoid or minimize the risks they face and insure against them. They have a distinctive approach to risk mitigation which involves gaining knowledge and information from networks and partnerships and the compartmentalization of risks. They have 'inside information' – real or imagined – that reduces the risk and uncertainty in their minds. They never really believe the business will fail and that they will be able to affect the outcome – their high self-efficacy and internal locus of control. They really do believe that they can succeed where others might have failed. The challenge is to ensure the information on which this belief is based is real, verifiable and can then be shared with others. The problem of different levels of knowledge is called information asymmetry and is important when it comes to raising finance (Chapter 14).

> You have to have nerves of steel and be prepared to take risks. You have to be able to put it all on the line knowing you could lose everything.
>
> **Anne Notley**, co-founder, The Iron Bed Company, *The Sunday Times*, 28 January 2001

> You have to be prepared to lose everything and remember that the biggest risk is not taking any risk at all.
>
> **Jonathan Elvidge**, founder, Gadget Shop, *The Sunday Times*, 17 March 2002

> We take risks – but they're always calculated.
>
> **Emma Elston**, founder, UK Container Maintenance, *The Sunday Times*, 29 June 2014

As observed, these personal character traits, particularly creativity and risk-taking, might be strongest in founders of growth firms. These character traits are likely to show themselves in the behaviours summarized in Table 3.1. How many of these do you exhibit?

There is one further quality that these entrepreneurs of growth businesses seem to have, although not necessarily at the launch of the business. They have or quickly develop a **vision** for the business. This is part of the fabric of their self-motivation. They are able to see what the business might become despite the odds. As we shall see in Chapters 7 and 18, it also helps them to bring others with them – employees and customers. It is an essential leadership quality.

Table 3.1 Behaviours associated with entrepreneurial character traits

Need for independence	Need for achievement	Internal locus of control
You are likely to be a person who:	You are likely to be a person who is:	You are likely to be a person who:
> Dislikes taking orders > Prefers to work alone & 'do their own thing' > Likes to make up their own mind & not bow to pressure > Can be seen as stubborn & determined > Prefers to do 'unconventional' things	> Restless & energetic > Task & results orientated > Persistent & determined > Forward looking & self-sufficient > Optimistic rather than pessimistic	> Believes they control their own destiny & discounts fate > Believes they create their own luck by hard work and effort > Is self-confident & shows considerable determination > Is willing to take advantages of opportunities that present themselves
Drive & determination	**Creative & innovative**	**Moderate risk-taking**
You are likely to be a person who:	You are likely to be a person who:	You are likely to be a person who:
> Is proactive rather than reactive > Acts decisively & quickly > Sets achievable goals & then works hard to achieve them > Is persistent & determined > Continues in a task despite setbacks > Is 'on the go' all the time > Is restless & easily bored	> Is curious & questioning > Is intuitive & imaginative > Is innovative with an abundance of ideas > Is sometimes a bit of a daydreamer > Enjoys change & the challenges it poses	> Makes decisions quickly > Can act on incomplete information evaluating likely costs against benefits > Accurately assesses their capabilities & then sets challenging but attainable goals > Is neither over nor under ambitious

Case insight   Hide My Ass!

Entrepreneurial character

Hide My Ass! (HMA!) began as a free proxy service created by Jack Cator. He originally created it as a way around school rules about using the internet. He wanted to unblock popular sites at the time like MySpace and other online games sites. The original HMA! masked the users' IP address by using proxy sites. By replacing their online identity, it allowed users to access sites that might be restricted from their home IP address, although it only worked on a site-by-site basis. It soon developed into a way people could get around censorship and access otherwise forbidden internet sites by appearing to be based in another country.

Jack enjoyed working with computers from an early age. He left school in 2005, aged 16, to enrol in a two-year technology course at college, where he developed HMA!. He worked from his bedroom at home and used income from advertisers to set up the service, using freelancers in eight countries. HMA! went online in the same year and, because it was a free service, rapidly gained users. In 2008, still running the business from his parents' house, Jack added a low-cost subscription-based virtual private network (VPN) to the otherwise free service. This protects the user's entire internet connection – including browser, online games and Skype – rather than simply their activity on individual sites. Because the free proxy service was so popular, the business

did not have to convert many of these visitors into paying customers to start generating substantial profits. What is more, regular, professional users became more frequent. Because it offers users anonymity, the service is now used by professional security firms tracking down hackers and virus writers. In 2011, he opened the company offices in London.

By 2014, Jack had built HMA! into an expert VPN service with the widest international server network of any other VPN company in the world. The parent company, Privax – of which Jack is CEO – now provides a VPN service to over 10 million users and 250,000 paying subscribers worldwide. It employs over 80 people based in London, and uses over 700 servers in some 130 countries. It also launched an app, Hide My Phone!, which allows users to rent mobile phone numbers temporarily, masking their country of origin. By 2014, Privax generated profits of £2.3 million on turnover of £11.5 million. In 2015, Jack sold HMA! for £40 million ($60 million) to AVG Technologies, a New York–listed Dutch company specializing in online privacy and internet security. One-third of the price was performance-dependent. Not bad for a 26-year-old, one-time rebellious school boy!

QUESTION:

1 What lessons do you learn from Jack Cator and HMA!?

Cognitive development theory

Cognitive theory provides an insight into how these character traits might have developed. Jean Piaget (1896–1980) is usually credited with the origins of the theory. He saw children's cognitive development as influenced both by biology and environmental experience. Children construct mental models (shortcuts or 'rules of thumb') of how the world around them operates and these models change as they experience discrepancies between the real world and their mental models. Cognitive theory therefore shifts the emphasis from the individual towards the situations that lead to entrepreneurial behaviour. In particular, it seeks to understand how people think and react in different situations. It seeks to understand the mental models or '**dominant logic**' that influences entrepreneurial behaviour and how they can be affected (it is also called cognitive heuristics). It is an important part of human capital but, as we shall see in the next chapter, can also act to constrain thinking. Some strands of cognitive theory reinforce ideas about how traits may influence behaviour.

Chen et al. (1998) argue that it is self-efficacy (a belief in their own capabilities) that motivates entrepreneurs and gives them the dogged determination to persist in the face of adversity, when others just give in. With this characteristic, entrepreneurs become more objective and analytical but tend to attribute any failure to outside factors such as insufficient effort or poor knowledge. Chen et al. argue that self-efficacy is affected by a person's previous experiences – success breeds success, failure breeds failure. This is the entrepreneur using their mental model or dominant logic as a basis for decision-making, even if the mental model is based upon relatively few experiences. Entrepreneurs appear to make extensive use of cognitive heuristics – simplifying strategies – in decision-making (Delmar, 2000). Because of this, successful entrepreneurs can often be seen as 'over-confident' (Forbes, 2005), particularly with regard to predicting a future outcome, to the point of escalating their commitment to it (Baron, 1998). Many studies observe that people who report overconfidence and high levels of self-efficacy therefore are more likely to become entrepreneurs (e.g. Chen et al., op. cit,; Koellinger et al., 2007; Krueger and Dickson, 1994). Generalized self-efficacy is effectively the same as the internal locus of control trait observed in entrepreneurs.

Delmar (op. cit.) outlines two other cognitive concepts that are relevant to your motivation to start a business. *Intrinsic motivation* suggests people who undertake tasks for their own sake perform better than those motivated by external factors ('pull' factors compared to 'push' factors). This strong inner drive – called type 'A' behaviour – amounts to almost compulsive behaviour. 'A' types tend to be goal-focused and exhibit high levels of drive, wanting to get the job done quickly. They also tend to try to proactively affect events (internal locus of control), focusing on the future when they are often not in control of the present. The second concept, *intentionality*, suggests people who intend to do things are more likely to do them than people who do not. This is the result of entrepreneurs' internal locus of control and is what underpins their drive and determination.

I thrive on adversity. I like it when the chips are down. When nobody believes that something can be done, I think, 'We are going to do this!'

Dale Vince, founder, Ecotricity, *The Daily Telegraph*, 27 May 2011

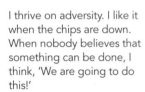 **Case insight   Adam Schwab and AusssieCommerce Group (1)**

Influences on entrepreneurship

AussieCommerce started life as a small website with one employee offering daily deals in Melbourne. Based on the Groupon model, the website, originally called Zoupon, sold everything from massages to restaurant offers. Launched by Adam Schwab and Jeremy Same in July 2010, by 2015 the business had grown to become the AussieCommerce Group, one of the largest umbrella e-commerce businesses in Australia and New Zealand comprising more than 15 websites.

Adam Schwab is the son of a builder and an accounting teacher. His first experience with the business world came

Continued...

Continued from previous page...

as an 11-year-old, when he realized there was a captive market selling lollipops to other kids on his school bus. Attending Caulfield Grammar School, he was friends with Jeremy Same. The pair would start a number of successful small ventures together, including DigiCat, which sold CDs containing copies of high-scoring assignments to students across Australia: 'this wasn't a huge business but relatively speaking, it was a nice little earner for a couple of 18-year-olds.'

After leaving school Adam studied Commerce/Law at Monash University where he also had a number of part-time jobs, including popcorn maker at a cinema (also with friend Jeremy), working in a supermarket and working as a nightclub host. During university he set up a business called DigiLaw, replicating the DigiCat model but this time selling law notes to law students. He even managed to convince the law bookstore to sell the product, leading students to believe that it was somewhat more official than it actually was. Despite being successful, the business was forced to close when the Dean of the law school banned students from buying and using it.

Courtesy of AussieCommerce Group

Adam Schwab and Jeremy Same

After leaving university, Schwab started work as a corporate lawyer specializing in mergers and acquisitions with Freehills. However, in late 2004, he and his friend Jeremy spotted a commercial opportunity in the property market in Melbourne – renting and furnishing inner-city apartments, which they would then offered to 'high-end' backpackers and travellers. With very little capital and an old trailer owned by his father, Adam scrounged cheap furniture to fit-out their first apartment. The pair soon realized that they would be able to make a reasonable margin by offering the apartments to small groups for shorter periods. The model would later morph into offering apartments to corporate clients under the Living Corporate brand: 'we could put four travellers in the apartment or one corporate client.' As the Melbourne property market was booming, Adam and Jeremy acquired six properties which would within a couple of years be sold for a profit of more than AUD 1 million. This cash would allow them to create a business that was scalable on an international basis.

Searching for ideas from around the world, Adam noticed the TopTable restaurant booking business in the UK (now a part of global travel giant, Priceline). In late 2009, Adam and Jeremy started working on MyTable, a similar discount-based restaurant booking site. However, halfway through development of the site, Jeremy, on a trip through the USA, noticed the success of Groupon and convinced Adam to change focus and launch Zoupon. This later became DEALS .com, and so the AussieCommerce Group was born. A year later, Adam and Jeremy developed MyTable into a takeaway food ordering website and then sold it to the Catch Group, to merge with EatNow, which in turn would merge with MenuLog and be sold in 2015 to UK-based Just Eat for AUD 855 million.

QUESTIONS:

1 Going from his history, what social and human capital does Adam Schwab possess?

2 What lessons do you learn about the entrepreneurial character from Adam Schwab?

Cognitive development theory emphasizes the influence of our background on our character. The influences are many and varied. They are 'learned' through our experiences of life and our experiences are framed by the cultures and subcultures of the different groups that we operate within – such as nationality, family, religion, work background etc. (Figure 3.4). Culture is about the prevalent norms, basic values, beliefs and assumptions about behaviour that underpin that group. And as we saw in the previous chapter, geographical proximity facilitates the transfer of knowledge and learning through the networks that develop. However, it is not only cultures but also the situations and stages of our life that seem to influence our propensity to be entrepreneurial.

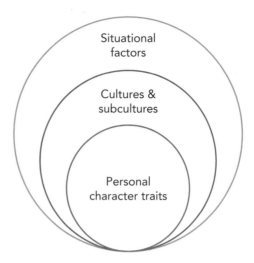

Figure 3.4 Influences on character traits

Evaluating the trait approach

Studies about entrepreneurial character traits have been widely criticized. A point that often draws dispute is that entrepreneurship is not consistently defined. Some studies have focused on nascent entrepreneurs – people who intend to go into self-employment (e.g. Korunka et al., op. cit.); some have focused on those who actually enter self-employment (e.g. Frank et al., op. cit.); and some on those entrepreneurs who run successful businesses (e.g. Baum and Locke, 2004). The studies also use a variety of inconsistent methods to measure personality traits (Delmar, op. cit.). What is more, some studies attempt to link only a single trait to entrepreneurship, while others attempt to link a number (multivariate studies). These multivariate studies have failed to identify a strong causal link between a single trait and entrepreneurship (Shook et al., 2003). Deakins (1996) highlighted a range of methodological problems:

> Traits are not stable and can change over time;
> Measuring personality traits requires subjective judgements;
> Measurement tends to ignore cultural, environmental and contextual influences;
> The role of education, learning, and training is often overlooked;
> Issues such as age, sex, race, social class and education can be ignored.

These issues led Delmar (op. cit.) to conclude that personality traits do not adequately explain the differences between individuals who engage in entrepreneurial activity and those who do not, implying all entrepreneurs do not possess all these traits and some people who are not entrepreneurs may have them.

Notwithstanding these criticisms, numerous meta-analyses of psychological studies using the widely accepted 'Five-Factor Model' of personality have consistently found robust linkages between personality traits and entrepreneurship – both the intention to start up a business and often its performance (e.g. Brandstätter, 2011; Collins et al., 2004; Rauch and Frese, 2007; Stewart and Roth, 2001, 2007; Zhao and Seibert, 2006; Zhao et al., 2010). The five factors in the model are openness, conscientiousness, extraversion, agreeableness and neuroticism. This model of personality seems able to account for different traits in personality without overlapping. All but one trait (agreeableness) can be found in Table 3.1, while the need for independence is not included in the 'Five-Factor Model'. High scores in these five traits indicate:

> **Openness** – An openness to experience and outside influences indicating a more curious, creative and inventive personality, compared to a more cautious, reserved approach (linked to the trait of creativity and innovation in Table 3.1);

> **Conscientiousness** – An organized, self-disciplined and driven approach to undertaking tasks with a strong aim for achievement compared to a more easy-going approach (linked to drive, determination and a need for achievement in Table 3.1);

> **Extraversion** – An energetic, assertive, outgoing personality with a 'can-do' view of life compared to a more solitary and introverted approach (linked to drive, determination and internal locus of control in Table 3.1);

> **Agreeableness** – A friendly, cooperative and compassionate personality compared to a more detached and analytic approach;

> **Neuroticism** – A sensitive, nervous and anxious personality compared to a more self-assured and confident approach (linked to internal locus of control in Table 3.1).

For example, Zhao et al.'s study (op. cit.) concluded that four of these traits were associated with both the inclination to start up a business and performance – a high degree of openness, conscientiousness, extraversion and a low degree of neuroticism. The study added that risk propensity, included as a separate dimension of personality, was positively associated with entrepreneurial intentions but was not related to entrepreneurial performance. Brandstätter's (op. cit.) meta-analysis of five prior meta-analyses endorsed this relationship and also reported differences between the traits of entrepreneurs and managers, who had a low degree of agreeableness. In the light of this research evidence, we can reasonably conclude that personality is an important influence on entrepreneurial behaviour.

 Practice insight Measuring your entrepreneurial tendency

The General Enterprise Tendency (GET) test provides you with the opportunity to reflect on whether you have an entrepreneurial character. It is a 54-question instrument that measures your personal character traits in five dimensions of entrepreneurial character – need for independence, need for achievement, internal locus of control, acceptance of measured risk and uncertainty, and creativity and innovation. It can be taken free online in about five minutes on www.GET2test.net.

The results are automatically analysed and a personal report on your character traits can then be printed out. It provides an indicative, although not a definitive, measure of your entrepreneurial tendency. The test was developed by Caird and Johnson at Durham University Business School over a number of years. Caird (1991a, 1991b) established the construct validity and reliability of the test by testing it on entrepreneurs and comparing it to occupational groups including teachers, nurses, civil servants, clerical workers and lecturers and trainers. Overall, entrepreneurs were found to be significantly more enterprising than the other groups, however they were not the only group to score highly on *individual* measures. Stormer et al. (1999) applied the test to 128 owners of new (75) and successful (53) small firms. They concluded that the test was acceptable for research purposes, particularly for identifying owner-managers, but it was poor at predicting business success. Either the test scales need to be refined for this purpose or the test did not include sufficient indicators of success such as antecedent influences on the individual or other factors related to the business rather than the individual setting it up. So, the GET scores need to be looked at overall rather than individually, and the test does not predict business success.

The influence of national culture

National cultures vary widely reflecting underlying core values, but measuring them in any meaningful way is extremely difficult. The most widely used dimensions of national culture are those developed by Hofstede (1981), who undertook an extensive cross-cultural study using questionnaire data from some 80,000 IBM employees in 66 countries across seven occupations. Although conducted about 40 years ago, it remains one of the most authoritative studies on national culture. From his research he established the four dimensions shown in Figure 3.5. It shows that there are dominant, measurable cultures in particular countries, although this will probably have changed over the intervening period.

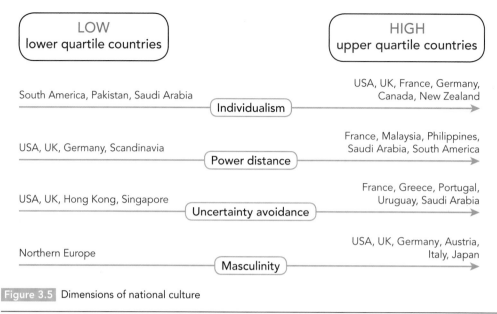

Figure 3.5   Dimensions of national culture

Source: Inspired by Hofstede, G. (1981) *Cultures and Organizations: Software of the Mind*, London: HarperCollins.

Individualism versus collectivism

This is the degree to which people prefer to act as individuals rather than groups. Individualistic cultures are loosely knit social frameworks in which people primarily operate as individuals. In these cultures the task prevails over personal relationships and the atmosphere is competitive. Collectivist cultures are composed of tight networks in which people operate as members of 'in-groups' expecting to look after, and be looked after by, other members of their 'in-group' and 'out-groups'. The atmosphere is cooperative within the 'in-group' although it may be uncharacteristically competitive with 'out-groups'.

Power distance

This is the degree of inequality among people that the community is willing to accept. Low power distance cultures endorse egalitarianism, relations are open and informal, information flows are functional and unrestricted and organizations tend to have flat structures. High power distance cultures endorse hierarchies, relations are more formal, information flows are formalized and restricted and organizations tend to be rigid and hierarchical.

Uncertainty avoidance

This is the degree to which people would like to avoid ambiguity and resolve uncertainty, and prefer structured rather than unstructured situations. Low uncertainty avoidance cultures tolerate greater ambiguity; prefer flexibility; stress personal choice and decision-making; reward initiative, experimentation, risk-taking and team-play; and stress the development of analytical skills. High uncertainty avoidance cultures prefer rules and procedures, stress compliance, punish error and reward compliance, loyalty and attention to detail.

Masculinity versus femininity

This defines quality-of-life-issues. Hofstede defined 'masculine' virtues as those of achievement, assertiveness, competition and success. These cultures reward financial and material achievement with social prestige and status. 'Feminine' virtues include modesty, compromise and cooperation. These cultures value relationships. Issues such as quality of life, warmth in personal relationships, service and so on are important. In some societies having a high standard of living is thought to be a matter of birth, luck or destiny, rather than personal achievement (they have an external locus of control), thus devaluing the 'masculine' virtues.

At a later date Hofstede and Bond (1991) added a fifth dimension – short/long-term orientation. A short-term orientation focuses on past and present and therefore values respect for the status quo. This includes an unqualified respect for tradition and for social and status obligations. A long-term orientation focuses on the future and therefore the values associated with this are more dynamic. They include the adaptation of traditions to contemporary conditions and having only qualified respect for social and status obligations. Clearly an entrepreneurial culture might be though of as one with a long-term orientation.

Hofstede's work is particularly interesting because it allows us to describe national cultures, albeit for IBM employees. In particular it allows us to describe what many people would see as the most entrepreneurial culture of all – that of the USA. The USA emerges as a highly individualistic, 'masculine' culture, with low power distance and uncertainty avoidance – one that is said to be conducive to entrepreneurship (Licht and Siegel, 2008). And indeed we recognize this. It is a culture that tolerates risk and ambiguity, has a preference for flexibility and is an empowered culture that rewards personal initiative. It is a highly individualistic and egalitarian, a culture that is fiercely competitive and the home of the 'free-market economy'. Assertiveness and competition are central to the 'American dream'. If there is a key virtue in the USA it is achievement, and achievement receives its monetary reward. It is an informal culture. According to the Declaration of Independence, all men are created equal, but they also have the freedom to accumulate sufficient wealth to become very unequal. The USA is the original 'frontier culture'. It actually seems to like change and uncertainty and certainly rewards initiative and risk-taking.

This, then, is the anatomy of an enterprise culture, one that encourages enterprise and entrepreneurship: highly individualistic, 'masculine', with low power distance and uncertainty avoidance. We might assume that countries with similar cultures encourage entrepreneurship and those at opposite extremes of these dimensions therefore probably inhibit entrepreneurship. The UK sits alongside the USA, although at the time of the study this was probably only the start of the structural changes, brought about by the government of Margaret Thatcher, that revived its stagnant economy and encouraged the growth of an 'enterprise culture' (Carr, 2000; Morris, 1991).

Interestingly, Saudi Arabia is at the opposite extreme to the USA on three of these dimensions. It has a collectivist culture, with high power distance (a respect for authority) and high uncertainty avoidance – a description that, by and large, still rings true. The Muslim religion and local tribal ties are important influences on the culture of most Gulf States.

Many academics and politicians believe that the impact of national culture upon aggregate levels of individual entrepreneurial activity could have significance for public policy. In a review covering 33 countries using Hofstede's dimensions, Shane (1992, 1993) concluded that national rates of innovation were positively correlated with individualism and power distance and negatively with uncertainty avoidance. Rinee et al. (2012) came to similar conclusions for individualism and power distance using the Global Innovation Index across

Getty Images/iStockphoto / Thinkstock \ Catherine Yeulet

66 countries. However, these studies have been questioned on a number of grounds (e.g. Hofstede's dimensions can change over time; Shane, op. cit.). What is more, the dimensions were correlated against innovation, not entrepreneurial propensity or start-up rates. However, in a review of the literature, Hayton and Cacciotti (2014) concluded that national cultural values did indeed 'influence, or at least correlate with individual motives, motive dispositions, traits and cognitions that are associated with being an entrepreneur.' What they could not find was any evidence of a causal

link, and this leads them to conclude that 'evidence for the mediating process linking culture and behavior remains sparse and inconsistent, often dogged by methodological challenges.'

Not only is culture an important influence on individuals, it is also an important influence on an organization. We shall return to the topic and see how it affects the organization and how it might be crafted through effective leadership in Chapters 18 and 19.

Case insight   Sadaf Gallery

The challenges facing entrepreneurs

Today, Sahar Al Kaabi is probably the best-known female entrepreneur in Oman. She is Chair of Sadaf Gallery, a company providing luxury home accessories, gifts for special occasions and flower arrangement services. She was the first woman to be elected to the Oman Chamber of Commerce and Industry and, in 2015, was appointed a member of the advisory board for the National CEO Program established with an aim to develop the next generation of Omani leaders and entrepreneurs. However, the road to entrepreneurship was not straightforward and Sadaf Gallery only succeeded the second time around.

Sahar graduated in Arabic literature in 1993 and initially worked for Oman Air as an assistant manager in the purchasing department. After two years she decided to leave her job because the working hours conflicted with her family and other obligations. She had just divorced and had three children to take care of. She also found that the job routine did not fulfil her ambitions and she needed to acquire new skills. These circumstances created a number of social, financial and psychological difficulties for her, and her family arranged for her to go on a holiday to the UAE. While visiting the city she saw a shop selling accessories, flowers, clays and toys, with a gift-wrapping service. This reminded her of her childhood because she was different from other kids due to her interest in different types of accessories and antiques rather than toys. This inspired Sahar to start a similar business in Oman as soon as she came back. She worked on a feasibility study due to her lack of business experience. She found that there was no direct competition and she could source the required capital through a family loan. She also selected Sadaf as a name for her business, meaning an amalgamation of light and darkness and representing the period between dawn and night that was consistent with her psychological state at that time.

In 1996 Sahar opened Sadaf Gallery in Muscat. However, Sahar was inexperienced and the business concept was new, and she was unable to promote it well to the right customers. Her customer base was limited and her financial obligations increased. As a result, she experienced financial problems resulting in a cash flow crisis. She closed the gallery in 1998.

Sahar travelled to Egypt for higher studies and returned to Oman in 2000, but her attraction to entrepreneurship had not diminished. At a jewellery exhibition arranged by her aunt she met a Bahraini businessman, who offered her the opportunity to market his product: a 'Holy Quran', written in 1.5 cm stone inlaid with precious stones. Sahar started to prepare a list of the companies, banks and governmental institutions which might find the product attractive. She started her promotion plan with the Diwan of the Royal Court – looking after His Majesty's Palace – where it might have been presented as a gift for guests. She did not succeed in selling the product, but she came to know the kind of gifts these organizations were looking for. She came to realize that banks needed special promotion items at reasonable prices, whereas the Diwan needed luxury Arabic perfumes, jewellery and watches and was willing to pay much more.

Sahar started looking for local dealers to provide souvenirs, luxury perfumes and jewelleries for both the Diwan and the banks. She arranged catalogues and provided prospective customers with samples in innovative packaging with customized designs, all subcontracted to a local designer who gave her products the unique designs that provided a distinct competitive advantage. The first contract from a bank was worth Omani Riyals 1,900 (about £3,200), the total cost was OR 1,200, giving her a profit of OR 700. A few months later she secured her first contract worth OR 7,000 from the Diwan of the Royal Court to supply them with perfumes, with a profit estimated of OR 3000. As she started to focus on the Diwan's needs, she found it prudent to investigate global brands that were not available in the local market. She travelled to Switzerland to attend a watch exhibition and to France to attend a perfumes exhibition in 2003. There she was able to build strong business relationships with watch and perfume producers for the purpose of marketing their products especially to the Diwan. She brought catalogues and perfume samples when she came back to Oman. She hired a Kuwaiti with experience in gift wrapping and flower arrangements and within five months was joined in the business by her sisters. She was able to reopen the gallery and this time sold a number of high-value gift items to a range

Continued...

Continued from previous page...

of consumers from all walks of life. Sahar also came up with an innovative idea of opening a ladies' coffee shop as a part of the gallery. According to Omani culture, women do not accompany men in their social gatherings and on weekends they do not have the opportunity to socialize.

In 2004, Sadaf Gallery was awarded OR 5,000 as the best youth project in the 'Intilaaqah' competition – a programme sponsored by Shell Oman to finance small projects. In 2008, Sahar was selected as deputy president to lead a Business Women's Association in Oman. Since then she has opened three more galleries in Oman, and another in Qatar with a Qatari partner. Currently she is upgrading the company website to enhance its competitiveness and to develop an online customer base.

'When you want to start something, you should study and have a good plan.' (*Times of Oman*: omaninfo.com)

QUESTIONS:

1 What factors made Sahar take up entrepreneurship?

2 What lessons did she learn that contributed to her success?

3 What is the importance of Sahar as a role model in Oman?

Social and demographic influences

In many ways the academic research on the other influences on entrepreneurship is even more confusing, and sometimes contradictory, than with personal character traits. There is a myriad of claimed influences that are difficult to prove or, indeed, disprove. There are simply too many variables to control and causal links remain questionable. The only really safe conclusion is that, except for a handful of influences, the research is inconclusive.

Education

One influence that comes through on many studies for both start-up and growth is educational attainment. Many studies show a positive association between the probability of starting up in business and increases in educational attainment (e.g. Levie, 2007). This may be because education increases your social capital. It might also be because it makes you more likely to question the status quo and more aware of opportunities around you. A review of high-growth firms in the UK and USA found that the education, experience and management skills of the founder were particularly high – typically they had degree-level qualifications and often an MBA (Department of Business, Enterprise and Regulatory Reform, 2008). The report also observed that half of the US entrepreneurs had previously founded a business, while two-thirds of the UK entrepreneurs had previously held a position as a company director. You might indeed question these findings given that Bill Gates, Steve Jobs and Michael Dell all dropped out of university to start their businesses and Richard Branson left school at the age of 16, but similar research in many countries tends to support this result. In the USA only 16% of 'the most successful entrepreneurs' in a study were found to lack a college degree, compared to 53% of the self-employed, and they were five times more likely to hold a PhD than the general population (Sanandaji and Sanandaji, 2014). In China, the 2012 Global Entrepreneurship Monitor report showed that 31% of prospective entrepreneurs had degrees or were graduates, 27% were from community colleges and 80% had prior work experience (Xavier et al., 2013). However, it must be said that not all studies support the view that education increases the probability of starting up in business, particularly in the international context (e.g. Le, 1999; van der Sluis et al., 2005).

"
Get as much professional training as you can before starting a business. Doing a MBA first really helped me.

Andrew Valentine, founder, Streetcar, *The Sunday Times*, 15 November 2009

"

Age

Although entrepreneurial activity is spread over all age groups, it peaks in the young (early 20s) and the middle-aged (late 30s). Research shows that these groups of entrepreneurs are most likely to be associated with growth companies. What is more, the proportion of young entrepreneurs is increasing. Youth brings creativity. However, age brings experience, knowledge and an invaluable network of relationships and contacts. Between the two, many people decide to bring up a family, with all the constraints that brings. The previously cited study (Department of Business, Enterprise and Regulatory Reform, op. cit.) concluded that high-growth firms tended to be founded by male entrepreneurs who start up the business in their 30s, following a period of management experience. The previously cited Chinese study showed that entrepreneurs tended to be younger with an average age of 31 (Xavier et al., op. cit.).

Family background

Studies have shown that a family business background, such as having a parent who was an entrepreneur or having worked in a family business, increases the probability of starting up in business (e.g. Athayde, 2009; Le, op. cit.; Levie, 2010).

Partnering

High-growth companies are also more likely to be set up by groups rather than by individuals, and these groups share in the management and ownership and therefore the success (or failure) of the business. Partnering with others to set up a business can bring the same advantages as age, i.e. knowledge, experience and networks. The previously cited report also observed that the highest growth firms relied heavily on building relationships with other firms, either through supply chains or formal strategic alliances (Department of Business, Enterprise and Regulatory Reform, op. cit.).

Digital Vision

Emigration and ethnicity

Ethnic minorities tend to have high self-employment rates in most Western industrialized countries. What is more, observation tells us that immigration to a foreign country is positively associated with entrepreneurship (a strong push factor). In China, overseas returnee entrepreneurs are seen as particularly important because they are usually highly educated and return to start up technology ventures (Wright et al., 2008). However, the data for different ethnic groups is not homogeneous and generalizations are therefore dangerous. The 2012 GEM Report (Levie and Hart, 2012) tells us that both first and second generation immigrants in the UK have significantly higher rates of early-stage entrepreneurial activity than others. This pattern is similar to France, but in the US, only first generation immigrants have higher rates. However, while minority ethnic–led businesses in the UK compose 7% of businesses (Department for Business, Innovation and Skills, 2013), rates for different ethnic groups are not uniform. Those for Asians (Indian, Pakistani, Bangladeshi etc.) and Chinese are higher than those for white males, while those for black Africans and black Caribbean people are lower, typically more comparable to white women. With some 200,000 Asian-owned businesses in the UK, Asians are recognized as the most likely ethnic minority group in the UK to become entrepreneurs and are represented across all sectors of business.

One reason for the high self-employment rate for Asians compared to black Africans and black Caribbean people appears to be family background and expectations. Traditionally, Asian families have valued the independence of self-employment. This seems to be changing, with second generation Asians in the UK being encouraged to enter more traditional professions. However, one of the problems with looking for a pattern is that these ethnic groups are no longer homogenous and there is a complex set of family, community and societal influences at play.

> We all had one thing in common – we came to a country where we had to make it and our families supported us. My wife didn't mind me working 14 hours a day on the business and not being home to read the children bedtime stories. But we had, and still have, a good relationship. We have no regrets.
>
> **Bharat Shah**, founder, Sigma Pharmaceuticals, *Kenyan Jewels* (www.alusainc.wordpress.com), 12 August 2008

Case insight   Golden Krust (1)

Immigrant entrepreneurs

Lowell Hawthorne used to work with his family in his father's bakery in St. Andrew, Jamaica. In 1981 he and many of his family immigrated to the USA where he joined the New York Police Department. Seven years later Lowell decided he wanted to start his own business, so he brought the family together and nine of them decided to start up what they knew most about – a bakery. However, the first problem was that they were unable to obtain any loan finance from the banks. Undaunted, the family pooled their resources (which involved family members having to remortgage their houses) to find $107,000. Golden Krust was launched in 1989.

Today, Golden Krust is known for its Jamaican patties – flaky, yellow rectangles of dough filled with spicy meat or fish – and the sauces to go with them. But for the first three years of its existence, while the company produced a range of Jamaican bakery products, it bought-in the patties from a West Indian restaurant chain. It was only when the supplier cut off supplies that Lowell was forced to find out about making patties himself – going to the UK to find out how to do it. Less than a year after this crisis, equipped with a baking method from Scotland, a chef named Mel and a new machine, sales exceeded $2 million for the first time. By 1996, as well as a bakery, the company had seven restaurants.

'As an immigrant, not understanding the system here made it more difficult ... Had I lived there and understood how it worked I think we would have gone through it easier.'

Today, Golden Krust remains a family business and has become the largest West Indian food chain in the USA. It still has its manufacturing base in New York, but it also operates as a franchisor and has a chain of more than 120 restaurants selling its patties in nine US states. Turnover exceeds $100 million. It now makes most of its money as a franchisor. This generates an up-front fee and a restaurant royalty of 5% on the turnover. The company also sells its patties wholesale to big distributors like Walmart and supplies New York's schools and prisons in an effort to expand the customer base beyond the West Indian communities.

'We have a 2020 vision: We want to make Caribbean cuisine mainstream by 2020.' (BBC News Business, 20 June 2012)

❑ Visit the website: www.goldenkrustbakery.com

QUESTION:

1 What were the motivations to launch Golden Krust and how does being a family business help or hinder it?

Gender

In a review of studies across many countries, Storey and Greene (2010) concluded that women are less likely to start businesses than men. GEM supported this conclusion for high-income countries, showing that the TEA (total early-stage entrepreneurship activity) rate for women in the UK was only about half that of men – lower than the USA (Levie and Hart, 2012). In 2012, women-led businesses in the UK made up only 19% of SMEs, although this was up from 14% in 2010 (Department for Business, Innovation and Skills, op. cit.).

Although the situation is changing quickly, research findings also consistently show women-owned businesses are likely to perform less well than men-owned businesses, however measured – turnover, profit or job creation (Department of Business, Enterprise and Regulatory Reform, op. cit.; Fairlie and Robb, 2009). Studies indicate one reason for this is because they have lower amounts of capital – human, social and financial (Brush, 2006; Fairlie and Robb, op. cit.; Parker, 2009). Women also devote less hours to the business, often working part-time (Carree and Verheul, 2009; Fairlie and Robb, op. cit.; Verheul et al., 2009). The reasons for these characteristics may be many and various, and some may be self-determined, related to family roles. There are also differences in business and industry choice. For example, women-owned businesses are concentrated in the retail and service sectors (Department for Business, Innovation and Skills, op. cit.; Carter and Shaw, 2006). Brush (2008) says this is because they tend to start up businesses that 'fit the feminine image'. She also observes that they frequently choose areas of business that tend to have higher failure rates and higher financial barriers.

> Not all women want to get to the top of the board. They want to reach a certain level with a fantastic job, but with time for family and life outside the business. Being at the top is not always the best position.
>
> **Mary Perkins**, co-founder, Specsavers, *The Guardian*, 28 October 2011

> I want to be a mother but also successful, so there has to be some kind of balance. There are times that I have realized I have not spent enough time with my husband or children all weekend because I have been doing business related things … There are more opportunities to start a business from home; something that suits women who are juggling careers and parenthood. … I think women have the ability to be multi-skilled – ironing and being on the phone at the same time – which gives them an advantage in balancing work and life.
>
> **Ruth Coe**, founder, Bespoke Beauty, *Startups*: www.startups.co.uk

> Men tend to be less emotionally attached and are therefore happy to move on and look for the next project. Hence, they are more likely to be serial entrepreneurs.
>
> **Duncan Bannatyne**, serial entrepreneur, *The Daily Telegraph*, 17 June 2009

Not surprisingly, therefore, only 7% of UK 'high-growth' firms (growing at over 20% per annum) were founded by women or teams which include women – 6% in the USA (Department of Business, Enterprise and Regulatory Reform, op. cit.). Notwithstanding this, women-owned businesses are among the fastest growing entrepreneurial populations in the world and make significant contributions to innovation, employment and wealth creation in all economies. They can be a force to be reckoned with. The Center for Women's Business Research (2008) showed that there were over 1 million women-owned businesses in the USA, employing 13 million people and generating almost $2 trillion in sales annually.

 ## Case insight   Duncan Bannatyne, serial entrepreneur

The entrepreneurial character

Duncan Bannatyne is probably best known in the UK because of his appearances on the BBC TV series *Dragons' Den* rather than his achievements as a serial entrepreneur. His life has, however, been a colourful one. He was born in 1949 into a relatively poor family in the town of Clydebank, Scotland. The second of seven children, his father was a foundry-man at the local ship yard. When told that the family could not afford to buy him a bicycle, Duncan tried to get a job delivering newspapers for the local newsagents, only to be set the challenge of finding 100 people who wanted a newspaper to be delivered. By knocking on doors he collected the names, got his newspaper round and eventually was able to buy his bicycle.

Duncan left school at 15 to serve in the Royal Navy. He served for five years before receiving a dishonourable discharge – after nine months detention – for threatening to throw an officer off a jetty. He spent his 20s moving from job to job around the UK, including taxi driving and selling ice creams, ending up in Stockton-on-Tees. It was there, in his early 30s, that Duncan's entrepreneurial career started when, using his personal savings, he bought an ice cream van for

£450. He built this business into a fleet of vans selling 'Duncan's Super Ices'. Even here he showed entrepreneurial flair. He was innovative – he started using a scoop that speeded up serving and made a shape like a smile in the ice cream, which the children loved. He was good at spotting opportunities – he bought one pitch in a local park for £2,000 which gave him profits of £18,000 in one summer. He eventually sold the business for £28,000, but not before he had spotted another opportunity. In the 1980s the government started helping unemployed people by paying their rent. Duncan used his profits from the ice cream business to buy and convert houses into bedsits for rent. He rented to the unemployed, so the rents were guaranteed by the government.

Duncan used the proceeds from the sale of the ice cream business – and almost everything else he owned – to move into the residential care homes industry with a business partner. He took out a bank loan, remortgaged his own home and started building up credit card debt. The building costs of the care home were to be financed by a 70% mortgage, but this would only be released when building work was complete and the home was available for occupation.

When building costs for the first home spiralled out of control and no more funds were available, he, his partner,

Continued…

Continued from previous page...

friends and family decided to finish the work themselves. The total costs for the care home came to £360,000 and nearly bankrupted Duncan. But the bank then valued the finished home at £600,000, giving a mortgage of £420,000. This meant that Duncan could recover his costs, pay off his debts and still have equity to put into the next care home. Using a mix of retained profits and borrowings, and by offering shares in the company, he expanded the number of homes.

'When I opened my first nursing home, I had considered newsagents and bed and breakfast establishments but then Margaret Thatcher started to revolutionise care for the elderly … I spotted an opportunity. I came to the conclusion that landlords who owned nursing homes could make a lot of money from the scheme. I took advantage and bought a plot of land with a bank loan and set up my first nursing home in Darlington as soon as I could. When that was full, I paid off all my debts, bought another plot and repeated the process until the portfolio included 45 homes.'

The company was called Quality Care Homes and it was eventually floated on the Stock Exchange. Duncan also went into children's nurseries with the Just Learning chain. In 1996 he sold Quality Care Homes for £26 million and Just Learning for £22 million. By now, however, he had expanded into health clubs with the popular Bannatyne's chain.

'I remember while I was working in the nursing home industry, I injured my knee and used to travel 30 minutes to a local gym in the North East for exercise and physiotherapy. While working on my knee, I also tried to work out the gym's business plan. I knew the membership fees and the number of members and I calculated approximately how much the building cost because I sat and counted the number of tiles on the ceiling and equated them to square footage in my nursing homes. I did the necessary sums and worked out that, if I opened my own health club, I would make a 35%-40% return on capital. It was a no-brainer.' (Daily Telegraph, 30 July 2009)

By buying plots of land next to the health club sites, Duncan expanded into the hotel business. He worked out that by sharing staffing, reception and other facilities he could save costs and offer hotel residents use of the health club facilities during their stay. So Bannatyne Hotels was born. Duncan has since acquired health clubs from Hilton Hotels, making his the largest independent chain of health clubs in the UK. Duncan's wealth is estimated to be approximately £175 million, making him the wealthiest of the Dragons in the Den.

QUESTIONS:

1 Why did Duncan become an entrepreneur?

2 What are the major influences on him and how have they affected his character?

3 What entrepreneurial character traits can you observe in him?

Intrapreneurs

Intrapreneurs share many of the characteristics of entrepreneurs (Hornsby et al., 1993). They need to be able to perceive an opportunity, have a vision for what it might become and then be motivated to run with it. However, they work within larger organizations and will probably come from within them. They are therefore likely to be hybrids, having to work hard to create entrepreneurial structures and cultures around them, but always having to communicate with more bureaucratic individuals in the organization that employs them. And they will probably only emerge if the organization 'permits' it.

Kanter (2004) found that intrapreneurs were comfortable with change, had clarity of direction, thoroughness, a participative management style and an understanding that they needed to work with others to achieve their goals. Ross and Unwalla (1986) said the best intrapreneurs are result-orientated, ambitious, rational, competitive and questioning. They dislike bureaucracy and are challenged by innovation but have an understanding of their organization and a belief in their colleagues. They are adept at politics and good at resolving conflict – and need to be because they will face a lot of it as they smooth the connections with 'conventional' management.

Pinchot (1985) also characterized intrapreneurs as goal-orientated and self-motivated, but he said, unlike entrepreneurs, they are also motivated by corporate reward and recognition. He observed that they need to be self-confident and optimistic, but may well be cynical about the bureaucratic systems within which they operate, although they do believe they can circumvent or manipulate them. In that sense they are good at working out problems within the 'system' –

> I consider myself to be a corporate entrepreneur. I have not created the company I am in charge of, but I have changed the way it is run and have made a real difference. I think times have changed and entrepreneurs don't have to be totally out on a limb. There are plenty of opportunities for entrepreneurialism in large companies too.
>
> **Diane Thompson**, Chief Executive, Camelot, *The Sunday Times*, 17 March 2002

or even bypassing the system – rather than leaving the organization. Like entrepreneurs they are strongly intuitive, but unlike entrepreneurs their corporate background means they are less willing to rely on intuition and more willing to undertake market research into a new project. Pinchot says they are also risk-takers and believe that, if they lose their jobs, they will quickly find new ones. However, he believes they are less willing to take personal risks than entrepreneurs. They are also sensitive to the need to disguise risks within the organization so as to minimize the political cost of failure. In terms of skills, Pinchot believed they are often good at sales and marketing and can bring those skills to bear both internally and externally. They are also able to delegate but are not afraid to roll their sleeves up and do what needs to be done themselves.

Intrapreneurs are adept communicators with strong interpersonal skills that make them good at persuading others to do what they want. In this respect they are similar to entrepreneurs in that they build and rely on relationships. This process of influencing without authority, based upon reciprocity, is at the heart of the skill of intrapreneurs (Cohen and Bradford, 1991). Intrapreneurs must be able to identify potential allies and understand their world and their motivations. They need to be able to use the language and motivations of potential allies to their own advantage. Once they understand this language, the intrapreneur can communicate more effectively on a personal level. For example, sport can often act as a bridge in these circumstances. They then start establishing a working relationship, in which exchanges of value might take place – a process of give and take. This takes time and they therefore need to be somewhat more patient than entrepreneurs. On a more Machiavellian level, once they understand the motivations of the potential ally, they can start to influence them.

 Practice insight Could you be an intrapreneur?

Gifford Pinchot (1985) proposed the eleven-question test below to see whether people might have what it takes to be an intrapreneur. He says that if you answer 'yes' to six or more it is likely that you are already behaving like an intrapreneur. See if you are one.

1   Does striving to make things work better occupy as much of your time as working on existing systems and duties?
2   Do you get excited about work?
3   Do you think about new business ideas in your spare time?
4   Can you see what needs to be done to actually make new ideas happen?
5   Do you get into trouble sometimes for doing things that exceed your authority?
6   Can you keep your ideas secret until they are tested and more developed?
7   Have you overcome the despondency you feel when a project you are working on looks as if it might fail and pushed on to complete it?
8   Do you have a network of work colleagues you can count on for support?
9   Do you get annoyed and frustrated when others cannot successfully execute your ideas?
10 Can you overcome the desire to do all the work on a project yourself and share responsibility with others?
11 Would you be willing to give up some salary to try out a business idea, provided the final rewards were adequate?

Social and civic entrepreneurs

In essence, social entrepreneurs are entrepreneurs in a social or not-for-profit context. The difference is that their prime motivation, aims and mission are social rather than commercial. They still pursue opportunities and continually innovate, but for the purpose of serving their social mission. As you might therefore expect, social entrepreneurs seem to enjoy most of the character traits and behavioural characteristics of their business counterparts. However, social enterprises are complex organizations that often have multiple stakeholders – clients, sponsors, donors, employees, government – and multiple service objectives. In a commercial business the objective is usually far more simple – to maximize the return to the owner. Not-for-profit organizations also face a rapidly changing environment in which they compete intensely with each other and even with other commercial organizations for monetary donations. They therefore must pursue dual strategies that involve commercial success by developing sustainable competitive advantage in order to fulfil their social mission. Thompson et al. (2000) described social entrepreneurs as having the following characteristics:

> They are *ambitious and driven*. They have been able to *clarify* and *communicate* an inspirational mission; around this they have *recruited* and *inspired* paid staff, users and partners, as well as an army of volunteers. They have known where they could acquire resources, some of which they have 'begged, stolen or borrowed.' But their vision has been for something which will *add value* for the underprivileged sections of the community. The development of relationships and *networks* of contacts has brought *trust*, visibility, credibility and cooperation which has been used as an intellectual base from which the physical and financial capital required to generate social capital could be found. *Creativity* invariably featured. By understanding and managing the inherent risks – the projects are often financially fragile with limited resourcing; and the targeted beneficiaries may be prone to stray – the social entrepreneurs have been able to overcome the inevitable setbacks and crises. (Emphasis in original)

The important extra dimension is one of social virtue and personal credibility – a demonstrable commitment to some social objective that gains the trust of the diverse range of stakeholders. Not-for-profit organizations are uniquely complex organizations. Mort et al. (2003) use this complexity to argue for the multidimensional nature of social entrepreneurship. They conceptualize a social entrepreneurship construct based upon the overlap of four elements: 'virtue' – a social mission; sound judgement; an ability to spot 'social opportunities'; and a pro-activeness and willingness to take risks. Firstly, the social entrepreneur is driven by a mission of 'creating better social value than their competitors which results in them exhibiting entrepreneurially virtuous behavior.' Secondly, they exhibit balanced judgement and an ability to see through the complexity of the situation they face. Thirdly, in a similar way to business entrepreneurs, they are able to recognize opportunities to create better social value that others cannot. Finally, just like business entrepreneurs, they display innovativeness, pro-activeness and risk-taking in their decision-making. Only when these four elements combine is social entrepreneurship created. Virtue is a key element in the construct. It underpins the social entrepreneur's balanced judgement. The authors defined it as 'positively good values such as love, integrity, honesty and empathy, which must be acted upon to become genuine virtues.' The social entrepreneur's attitudes and behaviours must have a virtuous dimension. This influences everything they do and gives them a 'coherent unity of purpose and action in the face of moral complexity.'

Civic entrepreneurs have to work within what are likely to be large organizations in the public sector and are therefore more like intrapreneurs. However, because public sector objectives are so diverse and unquantifiable, their interpersonal, political and even Machiavellian skills need to be even greater. Because the public sector is likely to be more bureaucratic than the private sector, they need to be even more determined to push through their changes but patient in terms of achieving their goals. Indeed, the changes and innovations they are tasked with pushing through may well not have originated (solely) with them.

Leadbeater and Goss (1998) observed that civic entrepreneurs know that they cannot succeed alone and are keen to involve other individuals or organizations with complementary skills. They are keen to work across traditional boundaries, within and outside their organization. They also need to be extremely adept at dealing with complex political situations and communicating with a wide range of stakeholders with differing objectives. To work effectively, a civic entrepreneur either needs to be highly placed or, like an intrapreneur, to have a high-level sponsor to protect them when times are difficult or vested interests are upset, and to help them to unblock the blockages to change as they occur. Sponsors will help secure resources, provide advice and contacts. They will need to nurture and encourage the civic entrepreneur, particularly early on in the life of the project or when things go wrong. They will need to endorse and create visibility for the project at the appropriate time and be good at managing the political and public dimensions of their work, building legitimacy as the project becomes successful. As Leadbeater and Goss (op. cit.) noted in their study of civic entrepreneurship:

> *In most cases the process of revitalization began with a joint effort by political leaders, managers, staff and users to rethink the organization's goals and purpose. This strategic sense of purpose was not confined to senior managers. They understood that this sense of purpose needed to be shared, ideally from the outset, by politicians, staff and users.*

A major difference with civic entrepreneurship is the degree of risk that is acceptable within the services offered in the public sector. Many of these – like education, health and social care – intimately affect people's lives. While innovation is obviously needed, otherwise organizations will stultify, what scale of innovation, given the related risks, should a civic entrepreneur be allowed to push through? Entrepreneurship involves the risk of failure, but if failure means that a person dies – as it might do in the context of healthcare – is that risk acceptable? The civic entrepreneur therefore has to be willing to live with this lower risk threshold and, at the same time, to be subject to the degree of public accountability that goes with it.

 ## Case insight   John Bird and The Big Issue

 ### Social Entrepreneur

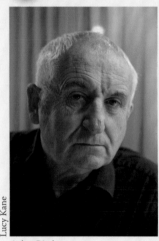

Lucy Kane

John Bird

Courtesy of Big Issue

The Big Issue is a magazine that is sold by homeless people on the streets of many UK towns and cities. It is probably the most prominent example of social entrepreneurship in the UK. It was created as a 'business solution to a social problem' by John Bird in 1991, and backed by Gordon and Anita Roddick, founders of The Body Shop. It is a limited company that donates its profits to the Big Issue Foundation, a registered charity that addresses the problems of the homeless. The Big Issue Foundation's mission is 'to connect vendors with the vital support and personal solutions that enable them to rebuild their lives; to determine their own pathways to a better future'. Since its launch, the enterprise has grown and become self-sustaining. By 2014, The Big Issue was helping some 2,000 individuals, selling over 100,000 copies per week. It claims to be read by 250,000 people. In 2013 it handed over more than £5 million to its vendors. The Big Issue has inspired other street papers in more than 120 countries, leading a global self-help revolution. A recent review of its activities has led it to also move into social trading.

The scheme started in London, based on a similar idea in New York. Its aim is to allow these people to work to earn a living, rather than begging – enabling them to address their personal poverty and retake control of their lives. The Foundation also aims to campaign on social exclusion issues. The magazine has many regular features including book, film, TV and play reviews. It prides itself on its ability to get exclusive personal interviews from celebrities and other well-known people and is sold to consumers on its quality rather than as a means of securing a charitable donation. It also secures income from advertisers in the magazine and its website.

However, the fact remains that The Big Issue is sold exclusively by the homeless on the streets, rather than in magazine stores or by volunteers. This makes the nature of the transaction somewhat unusual. When they are asked to buy, consumers come face-to-face with beneficiaries and can see that they are trying to help themselves out of their situation. Vendors are given training and there is a 'Street Support Team' to help them. They are first given a small number of magazines and thereafter have to buy copies to sell on at 50% of the cover price. One key aspect of the transaction is that the consumer is asked for a limited and relatively small financial contribution (the cover price was £2.50 in 2014). This legitimizes small donations. In this way, giving small amounts to a morally justified and legitimate cause is made easy. These factors have led researchers to conclude that 'the Big Issue is rarely bought for its own sake, simply as a quality product, but that its intrinsic value to the consumer does play a role in whether or not the initiative is supported. In other words, consumers buy it

Continued...

Continued from previous page...

because they believe that they are helping the homeless (to help themselves)' (Hibbert et al., 2002).

John Bird is the social entrepreneur behind The Big Issue. And it is his background that provides the clues to his commitment to social issues. Born in a two-bedroom house shared with a number of other families in a slum-ridden part of Notting Hill, London, just after World War II, he was the third of six boys in a poor Irish family. When his parents failed to pay the rent they were evicted and the family had to share a single room in his grandmother's house. He was made homeless at the age of five and lived in an orphanage run by the Sisters of Charity between the age of seven and ten.

'It tore the heart out of me. We were there three years. My brothers fitted in very well but I was a bit sensitive. I didn't see my father all through that time and I saw my mother perhaps once a month. When I went in there, I could tell the time. When I came out, I couldn't. It just threw me completely. I was always in trouble, always being beaten by the nuns. I really, really took it very hard. I hated my family. I hated everything.' (The Guardian, May 1994)

Many of his early activities, legal or otherwise, demonstrated entrepreneurial tendencies. At just three or four, he would go to Portobello Market with his brothers, picking up discarded orange boxes, breaking them up and selling them as kindling wood. He left the orphanage as a 10-year-old troublemaker and spent the next 15 years running away, sleeping rough in the streets of London and stealing whatever he could lay his hands on. Later, phoney charity collections and newspaper ads selling books that people would never receive were just some of his scams. He was also a shoplifter and burglar. Eventually he ended up in jail. However, at some point in his late 20s he started writing poems and mixing with student 'revolutionaries' who got him interested in political activism. He joined the Socialist Labour League and the Workers Revolutionary Party (WRP), working to overthrow 'the establishment'.

Although he knew nothing about the job, he started work as a printer when he left the WRP in the late 1970s. Not surprisingly, he got sacked from job after job, but learned a little in each, until eventually he had sufficient knowledge to set up his own small printing works. He liked being his own boss, working around 100 hours a week in his garage to make a go of the venture.

'I didn't realize I was an entrepreneur until about five years ago. I just thought I was mad … I was always coming up with new ideas, always inventing things, always doing this and doing that. And then people started talking about entrepreneurialism, maybe in 2000, and it was a bit like finding out you actually belong in a club.'

He turned his hand to writing and publishing, telling friends he was a businessman. However, almost everything he published went back to his roots, and the poverty and unfairness he had grown up with on the streets of London. The poor and homeless were a particular focus for his attention. Luck plays a part in the story. He and Gordon Roddick were old friends and, having seen a street paper being sold by homeless people in New York, Roddick thought Bird, with his experience of homelessness, running a business and printing magazines, might be interested in launching a similar venture in London. At that time the principle was that the magazine would operate as a business with both the sellers and the company making a profit. However, six months later The Big Issue was losing £25,000 a month. Bird did not give in, instead addressing the problem without sentiment in a very business-like way.

'I looked upon it as a challenge. I got rid of about ten people, I put the wages up of a few others and made them work harder.' (http://startups.co.uk, published 9 September 2008, updated 3 October 2013)

He also made the magazine a fortnightly rather than monthly publication, and keeping the cost of the publication at £0.50, doubled the price to the vendors. It worked and by the first anniversary in 1992, The Big Issue had turned a £1,000 profit. But breaking even wasn't the only challenge in the early days. Sellers physically attacked Bird and his staff when they learned they would have to pay for the magazine. Bird overcame this in his typically robust way, hiring a couple of the homeless men to act as bodyguards.

❏ Visit the website: www.bigissue.com

QUESTIONS:

1 What character traits do you observe in John Bird?
2 What are the major influences on him and how have they affected his character?
3 Is The Big Issue self-sustainable? If so, why is this important?
4 What do you think about the move into social trading?

⟲ Summary

> You need to recognize what are your personal drivers and constraints. These will influence whether entrepreneurship is for you and what you might want your business to become.

> You bring financial, human and social capital to your start-up. Financial capital for a start-up can be minimized through partnering with others and bootstrapping. Human capital is derived from your education, training and previous managerial or industry experience. Social capital is derived from your social skills and access to appropriate professional networks. The more capital you bring to the business – of any kind – the more likely you are to succeed.

> Most people have barriers to entrepreneurship (real and psychological). What they need is a strong 'push' or 'pull' to make them take the plunge.

> The entrepreneurial character has six traits: a high need for autonomy; a high need for achievement; an internal locus of control; drive and determination; creativity and innovation; and a willingness to take measured risks.

> These traits are influenced by your background and upbringing and are underpinned by the cultures of the different groups you associate with.

> Cognitive development theory emphasizes the situations that lead to entrepreneurial behaviour. Relevant concepts are self-efficacy, intrinsic motivation and intentionality.

These provide support for some of the entrepreneurial character traits from a different perspective.

> The concept of high internal locus of control is generalized self-efficacy. This motivates entrepreneurs and gives them the dogged determination and self-belief to persist in the face of adversity, when others just give in. Self-efficacy is affected by a person's previous experiences – success breeds success, failure breeds failure. This is the entrepreneur using their mental model or dominant logic as a basis for decision-making.

> Intrapreneurs have many of the qualities as entrepreneurs. They are results-orientated, ambitious, rational, competitive and questioning. They must have strong interpersonal and political skills and be adept at handling conflict and the politics of the larger organization in which they operate.

> Social entrepreneurs have many of the same qualities as entrepreneurs. They are driven by social purpose and are adept at recognizing social opportunity. They need a heightened sense of accountability to the wide range of stakeholders involved in the social enterprise.

> Civic entrepreneurs are similar to intrapreneurs and require similar levels of interpersonal and political skills. However, they probably need to be more patient because of the bureaucracy they are likely to face. A major issue for them is the lower level of risk that is acceptable within many of the services offered in the public sector and the related public accountability.

✓ Activities

1. List the elements of financial, human and social capital you bring to a start-up business.
2. Take the GET test and discuss the results with your friends. Do they recognize these characteristics and the associated behaviours in you? What are the influences that might have contributed to your character? Reflect on the results. What are the implications for you? Write a report on whether you have an entrepreneurial character.
3. Repeat this activity by getting an entrepreneur to complete the test and having them reflect on the results.

💬 Group discussion topics

1. Is it better to start a business when you are young or to wait until you are older? Why is this?
2. What are the barriers to entrepreneurship you face? How might they be overcome?
3. What would 'push' or 'pull' you into entrepreneurship?
4. What sort of business might you like to start up?
5. What are the advantages and disadvantages of being an entrepreneur?
6. Are entrepreneurs born or made?
7. Can character traits really predict who might start up a business?
8. Which entrepreneurial character traits might have negative implications? What are they and how might they be countered?
9. What does self-efficacy mean? Is it a good or a bad thing for entrepreneurs?
10. Are entrepreneurs delusional?
11. Are entrepreneurs gamblers?

12 In the context of entrepreneurship, what does creativity mean?

13 Are entrepreneurs control freaks?

14 Why are immigrants often entrepreneurial?

15 Why are women less entrepreneurial than men?

16 Can education and training make you more entrepreneurial?

17 What are the additional characteristics of growth businesses? Why are they important?

18 Does your country have an entrepreneurial culture?

19 How can an entrepreneurial culture be encouraged?

20 How are social and civic entrepreneurs different to commercial entrepreneurs?

☛ References

Aldrich, H.E. and Martinez, M. (2003) 'Entrepreneurship as a Social Construction: A Multi-Level Evolutionary Approach', in Z.J. Acs and D.B. Audretsch (eds), *Handbook of Entrepreneurship Research: A Multidisciplinary Survey and Introduction*, Boston, MA: Kluwer Academic Publishers.

Andersson, S., Gabrielsson, J. and Wictor, I. (2004) 'International Activities in Small Firms – Examining Factors Influencing the Internationalisation and Export Growth of Small Firms', *Canadian Journal of Administrative Science*, 21(1).

Athayde, R. (2009) 'Measuring Entrepreneurial Potential in Young People', *Entrepreneurship Theory and Practice*, 33(2).

Baron, R.A. (1998) 'Cognitive Mechanisms in Entrepreneurship, Why and When Entrepreneurs Think Differently Than Other People', *Journal of Business Venturing*, 13(4).

Baty, G. (1990) *Entrepreneurship in the Nineties*, Englewood Cliffs, NJ: Prentice Hall.

Baum, J.R. and Locke, E.A. (2004) 'The Relationship of Entrepreneurial Traits, Skills and Motivations to Subsequent Venture Growth', *Journal of Applied Psychology*, 89.

Bell, J., Murray, M. and Madden, K. (1992) 'Developing Expertise: An Irish Perspective', *International Small Business Journal*, 10(2).

Blanchflower, D.G. and Meyer, B.D. (1991) *Longitudinal Analysis of Young Entrepreneurs in Australia and the United States*, Working Paper no. 3746, Cambridge, MA: National Bureau of Economic Research.

Brandstätter, H. (2011) 'Personality Aspects of Entrepreneurship: A Look at Five Meta-analyses', *Personality and Individual Differences*, 51(3).

Brockhaus, R. and Horwitz, P. (1986) 'The Psychology of the Entrepreneur', in D. Sexton and R. Smilor (eds), *The Art and Science of Entrepreneurship*, Cambridge, MA: Ballinger Publishing Co.

Brush, C.G. (1992) 'Research on Women Business Owners: Past Trends, A New Perspective and Future Directions', *Entrepreneurship: Theory and Practice*, 16(4).

Brush, C.G. (2008) 'Woman Entrepreneurs: A Research Overview', in M. Casson, B. Yeung, A. Basu and N. Wadeson (eds), *The Oxford Handbook of Entrepreneurship*, Oxford: Oxford University Press.

Buttner, E. and More, D. (1997) 'Women's Organisational Exodus to Entrepreneurship: Self-Reported Motivations and Correlates with Success', *Journal of Small Business Management*, 35(1).

Caird, S. (1990) 'What Does it Mean to Be Enterprising?', *British Journal of Management*, 1(3).

Caird, S. (1991a) 'Self Assessments on Enterprise Training Courses', *British Journal of Education and Work*, 4(3).

Caird, S. (1991b) 'Testing Enterprising Tendency in Occupational Groups', *British Journal of Management*, 2(4).

Carr, P. (2000) *The Age of Enterprise: The Emergence and Evolution of Entrepreneurial Management*, Dublin: Blackwell.

Carree, M. and Verheul, I. (2009) 'Time Allocation by the Self-employed: The Determinants of the Number of Working Hours in Start-ups', *Applied Economics Letters*, 16.

Carter, S. and Shaw, E. (2006) *Women's Business Ownership: Recent Research and Policy Developments*, Report to the Small Business Service, London: DTI.

Cassar, G. (2006) 'Entrepreneur Opportunity Cost and Intended Venture Growth', *Journal of Business Venturing*, 21.

Center for Women's Business Research (2008), *Key Facts*, Washington, DC: Center for Women's Business Research, available online at www.nfwbo.org/facts/index.php.

Chan, S.Y. and Foster M.J. (2001) 'Strategy Formulation in Small Business: The Hong Kong Experience,' *International Small Business Journal*, 19(3).

Chell, E., Haworth, J. and Brearley, S. (1991) *The Entrepreneurial Personality*, London: Routledge.

Chen, P.C., Greene, P.G. and Crick, A. (1998) 'Does Entrepreneurial Efficacy Distinguish Entrepreneurs from Managers?', *Journal of Business Venturing*, 13.

Cohen, A.R. and Bradford, D. (1991) *Influence without Authority*, New York: Wiley.

Collins, C.J., Hanges, P.J. and Locke, E.E. (2004) 'The Relationship of Achievement Motivation to Entrepreneurial Behavior: A Meta-analysis', *Human Performance*, 17.

Cron, L.W., Bruton, D.G. and Slocum J.W. (2006) 'Professional Service Ventures, Performance, and the Gender Effect,' *Journal of Leadership and Organizational Studies*, 12(3).

Cross, R., Liedtka, J. and Weiss, L. (2005) 'A Practical Guide to Social Networks,' *Harvard Business Review*, 83(3).

Cuba, R., Decenzo, D. and Anish, A. (1983) 'Management Practises of Successful Female Business Owners', *American Journal of Small Business*, 8(2).

Deakins, D. (1996) *Entrepreneurs and Small Firms*, London: McGraw-Hill.

de Bono, E. (1985) *Six Thinking Hats*, Boston: Little, Brown and Company.

Delmar, F. (2000) 'The Psychology of the Entrepreneur' in S. Carter and D. Jones-Evans (eds), *Enterprise and Small Business: Principles, Practice and Policy*, 1st edn, London: Prentice Hall.

Department for Business, Innovation and Skills (2013) *Small Business Survey 2012: SME Employers: A Report by BMG Research*, London, UK: Department for Business, Innovation and Skills.

Department of Business, Enterprise and Regulatory Reform, (2008) *High Growth Firms in the UK: Lessons from an Analysis of Comparative UK Performance*, BERR Economics Paper no. 3, London, UK: Department of Business, Enterprise and Regulatory Reform.

Fairlie, R., and Robb, A. (2009) 'Gender Differences in Business Performance: Evidence from the Characteristics of Business Owners Survey', *Small Business Economics*, 33(4).

Forbes, D. (2005) 'Are Some Entrepreneurs More Overconfident than Others?', *Journal of Business Venturing*, 20.

Frank, H., Lueger, M. and Korunka, C. (2007) 'The Significance of Personality in Business Start-up Intentions, Start-up Realization and Business Success', *Entrepreneurship in Regional Development*, 19(3).

Hansemark, O.C. (2003) 'Need for Achievement, Locus of Control and the Prediction of Business Start-ups: A Longitudinal Study', *Journal of Business Economic Psychology*, 24.

Hayton, J.C. and Cacciotti, G. (2014) 'Is There an Entrepreneurial Culture? A Review of Empirical Research', *ESRC*, ESRC Research Paper 16, February.

Hibbert, S.A., Hogg, G. and Quinn, T (2002) 'Consumer Response to Social Entrepreneurship: The Case of The Big Issue in Scotland', *International Journal of Nonprofit and Voluntary Sector Marketing*, 7(3).

Hirsch, R.D. and Brush, C.G. (1987) *Women Entrepreneurs: A Longitudinal Study*, Frontiers in Entrepreneurship Research, Wellesley, MA: Babson College.

Hofstede, G. (1981) *Cultures and Organizations: Software of the Mind*, London: HarperCollins.

Hofstede, G. and Bond, M.H. (1991) 'The Confucian Connection: From Cultural Roots to Economic Performance', *Organizational Dynamics*, Spring.

Hoppe, M (2010) 'The Influence of Social Networks on Company Success for SMEs: An Empirical Investigation of the Online B2B-Network Xing', *Euram 2010*, 19–22 May, Rome.

Hornsby, J.S., Naffziger, D.W., Kuratko, D.F. and Montagno, R.V. (1993) 'An Interactive Model of the Corporate Entrepreneurship Process', *Entrepreneurship, Theory and Practice*, 17(2).

Kanter, R.M. (1983) *The Change Masters*, New York: Simon & Schuster.

Kanter, R.M. (2004) 'The Middle Manager as Innovator', *Harvard Business Review*, 82(7/8).

Kets de Vries, M.F.R. (1985) 'The Dark Side of Entrepreneurship', *Harvard Business Review*, November–December.

Kirzner, I.M. (1973) *Competition and Entrepreneurship*, Chicago: University of Chicago.

Kirzner, I.M. (1979) *Perception, Opportunity and Profit: Studies in the Theory of Entrepreneurship*, Chicago: University of Chicago.

Kirzner, I.M. (1997) 'Entrepreneurial Discovery and Competitive Market Processes: An Austrian Approach', *Journal of Economic Literature*, 35.

Kirzner, I.M. (1999) 'Creativity and/or Alertness: A Reconsideration of Schumpeterian Entrepreneur', *Review of Austrian Economics*, 11.

Koellinger, P., Minniti, M. and Schade, C. (2007) '"I Think I Can, I Think I Can": Overconfidence and Entrepreneurial Behaviour', *Journal of Economic Psychology*, 28.

Korunka, C., Franf, H., Lueger, M. and Mugler, J. (2003) 'The Entrepreneurial Personality in the Context of Resources, Environment, and the Start-up Process – A Configuration Approach', *Entrepreneurship Theory and Practice*, 28(1).

Koskinen, K.U. and Vanharanta, H. (2002) 'The Role of Tacit Knowledge in Innovation Processes of Small Technology Companies', *International Journal of Production Economics*, 80.

Krueger, N.F.J. and Dickson, P.R. (1994) 'How Believing in Ourselves Increases Risk Taking: Perceived Self-Efficacy and Opportunity Recognition', *Decision Sciences*, 25(3).

Le, A.T. (1999) 'Empirical Studies of Self-Employment', *Journal of Economic Surveys*, 13.

Leadbeater, C. and Goss, S. (1998) *Civic Entrepreneurship*, London: Demos.

Lee, S., Park, G., Yoon, B. and Park, J. (2010) 'Open Innovation in SMEs – An Intermediate Network Model', *Research Policy*, 39(2).

Levie, J. (2007) 'Immigration, In-migration, Ethnicity and Entrepreneurship in the United Kingdom', *Small Business Economics*, 28(2).

Levie, J. (2010) *Global Entrepreneurship Monitor Scotland 2009*, Glasgow: Hunter Centre for Entrepreneurship, University of Strathclyde.

Levie, J. and Hart, M. (2012) *Global Entrepreneurship Monitor: United Kingdom 2012 Monitoring Report*, Aston Business School and the Hunter Centre for Entrepreneurship, University of Strathclyde.

Licht, A.N. and Siegel J.I. (2008) 'The Social Dimensions of Entrepreneurship', in M. Casson, B. Yeung, A. Basu and N. Wadeson (eds), *The Oxford Handbook of Entrepreneurship*, Oxford: Oxford University Press.

McClelland, D. C. (1961) *The Achieving Society*, Princeton, NJ: Van Nostrand.

Morris, P. (1991) 'Freeing the Spirit of Enterprise: The Genesis and Development of the Concept of Enterprise Culture', in R. Keat and N. Abercrombie (eds), *Enterprise Culture*, London: Routledge.

Mort, G.S., Weerawardena, J. and Carnegie, K. (2003) 'Social Entrepreneurship: Towards Conceptualisation', *International Journal of Nonprofit and Voluntary Sector Marketing*, 8(1).

Parker, S.C. (2009) *The Economics of Entrepreneurship*, Cambridge: Cambridge University Press.

Pinchot, G. (1985) *Intrapreneuring*, New York: Harper & Row.

Rauch, A. and Frese, M. (2007) 'Let's Put the Person Back into Entrepreneurship Research: A Meta-analysis on the Relationship between Business Owners' Personality Traits, Business Creation, and Success', *European Journal of Work and Organizational Psychology*, 16.

Rosa, P., Hamilton, S., Carter, S. and Burns, H. (1994) 'The Impact of Gender on Small Business Management: Preliminary Findings of a British Study', *International Small Business Journal*, 12(3).

Read, S., Sarasvathy, S., Dew, N., Wiltbank, R. and Ohlsson, A.V. (2011) *Effectual Entrepreneurship*, London: Routledge.

Rinee, T., Steel, G.D. and Fairweather, J. (2012) 'Hofstede and Shane Revisited: The Role of Power Distance and Individualism in National-Level Innovation Success', *Cross-Cultural Research*, 46(2).

Ross, J.E. and Unwalla, D. (1986) 'Who is an Intrapreneur?', *Personnel*, 63(12).

Sanandaji, T. and Sanandaji, N. (2014) *SuperEntrepreneurs: And How Your Country Can Get Them*, London, UK: Centre for Policy Studies.

Schein, V., Mueller, R., Lituchy, T. and Liu, J. (1996) 'Thinking Manager – Think Male: A Global Phenomenon?', *Journal of Organisational Behaviour*, 17.

Schumpeter, J.A. (1983/1996) *The Theory of Economic Development*, New Brunswick, NJ: Transaction Publishers.

Schwartz, E.B. (1997) 'Entrepreneurship: A New Female Frontier', *Journal of Contemporary Business*, Winter.

Shane, S. (1992) 'Why do Some Societies Invent More than Others?', *Journal of Business Venturing*, 7.

Shane, S. (1993) 'Cultural Influences on National Rates of Innovation' *Journal of Business Venturing*, 8.

Shane, S. (2000) 'Prior Knowledge and the Discovery of Entrepreneurial Opportunities', *Organization Science*, 11.

Shapero, A. (1985) *Managing Professional People – Understanding Creative Performance*, New York: Free Press.

Shaver, K. and Scott, L. (1992) 'Person, Processes and Choice: The Psychology of New Venture Creation', *Entrepreneurship Theory and Practice*, 16(2).

Shook, C.L., Priem, R.L. and McGee, J.E. (2003) 'Venture Creation and the Enterprising Individual: A Review and Synthesis', *Journal of Management*, 29(3).

Stewart, W.H., Jr., and Roth, P.L. (2001) 'Risk Propensity Differences between Entrepreneurs and Managers: A Meta-analytic Review', *Journal of Applied Psychology*, 86.

Stewart, W.H., Jr. and Roth, P.L. (2007) 'A Meta-Analysis of Achievement Motivation Differences between Entrepreneurs and Managers', *Journal of Small Business Management*, 45(4).

Storey, D. and Sykes, N. (1996) 'Uncertainty, Innovation and Management', in P. Burns and J. Dewhurst (eds), *Small Business and Entrepreneurship*, London: Macmillan.

Storey, D.J. and Greene, F.J. (2008) *Small Business and Entrepreneurship*, Harlow: Pearson Education.

Stormer, R., Kline, T. and Goldberg, S. (1999) 'Measuring Entrepreneurship with the General Enterprise Tendency (GET) Test: Criterion-related Validity and Reliability', *Human Systems Management*, 18(1).

Thompson, J., Alvey, G. and Lees, A. (2000) 'Social Entrepreneurship – A New Look at the People and the Potential', *Management Decision*, 38(5).

Thornhill, S. (2006) 'Knowledge, Innovation and Firm Performance in High-Technology Regimes', *Journal of Business Venturing*, 41.

Unger, J.M., Rauch, A. and Frese, M. (2011) 'Human Capital and Entrepreneurial Success: A Meta-analytical Review', *Journal of Business Venturing*, 26.

van der Sluis, J., van Prag, M. and Vijverberg, W. (2005) 'Entrepreneurship Selection and Performance: A Meta-analysis of the impact of Education in Developing Economies', *World Bank Economic Review*, 19(2).

Verheul, I., Carree, M. and Thurik, R. (2009) 'Allocation and Productivity of Time in New Ventures of Female and Male Entrepreneurs', *Small Business Economics*, 33(3).

Wright, M., Liu, X., Buck, T. and Filatotchev, I. (2008) 'Returnee Entrepreneurs, science Parks, Location Choice and Performance: An Analysis of High-Technology SMEs in China', *Entrepreneurship Theory and Practice*, 32(1).

Xavier, S.R., Kelley, D., Herrington, M. and Vorderwulbecke, A. (2013) *Global Entrepreneurship Monitor, 2012 Global Report*, London; Global Entrepreneurship Research Association.

Zhao, H. and Seibert, S.E. (2006) 'The Big Five Personality Dimensions and Entrepreneurial Status: A Meta-analytical Review', *Journal of Applied Psychology*, 91.

Zhao, H., Seibert, S.E. and Lumpkin, G.T. (2010) 'The Relationship of Personality to Entrepreneurial Intentions and Performance: A Meta-analytic Review', *Journal of Management*, 36.

www.palgrave.com/Burns-Entrepreneurship-And-Small-Business-4e

Go online to access additional teaching and learning resources for this chapter on the companion website. Click here in the ebook to complete a multiple choice revision quiz for this chapter.

4 | DISCOVERING A BUSINESS IDEA

Contents

Image Source \ Image Source/Milk and Honey

Learning outcomes

When you have read this chapter and undertaken the related activities you will be able to:

> Explain what makes an individual creative and understand how creativity can be improved;
> Assess your own creativity;
> Understand the importance of developing knowledge and awareness and how to develop your discovery skills;
> Use a range of techniques to scan the environment for business opportunities;
> Use a range of techniques to come up with a business idea by either creating or spotting opportunity.

 *Practice insight*: Measuring your creativity

 *Practice insight*: How to run a brainstorming session

Practice insight: 15 characteristics of a good business idea

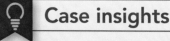 ## Case insights

Swarfega	TutorVista
OnMobile	The Million Dollar Homepage
Google (1)	DUPLAYS
Great Ormond Street Hospital	Nikwax
MamanPaz	Maggie's Centres
Summly App	Nuffnang
Swatch	Streetcar (now Zipcar)
Bloom & Wild	

Creativity

We explained in previous chapters that innovation is the prime tool entrepreneurs use to create opportunity. It is underpinned by creativity. But, if creativity underpins innovation, entrepreneurship and opportunity perception is the context in which it will flourish:

> 'Creativity is the starting point whether it is associated with invention or opportunity spotting. This creativity is turned to practical reality (a product, for example) through innovation. Entrepreneurship then sets that innovation in the context of an enterprise (the actual business), which is something of recognised value' (Bolton and Thompson, 2000).

For the entrepreneur, creativity is an essential tool that is used to seek out a business opportunity, finding unmet needs in the marketplace or finding innovative ways of meeting these needs. This chapter will explain how creativity can be encouraged and used to find a business idea.

Figure 4.1 depicts one way of looking at this. Only in quadrant 4 is there a winning combination of creativity and entrepreneurship. All other quadrants fail to achieve their full economic or commercial potential. In quadrant 3 there is a firm struggling with too many wasted ideas. It lacks an entrepreneurial orientation with the ability both to see the commercial application of the idea and to exploit it. In quadrant 2 there is a firm that lacks creativity but can at least copy and perhaps improve on the creative inventions coming from other firms if they have a commercial application. Firms in quadrant 1, lacking both creativity and entrepreneurship, are certain never to grow and indeed their very survival may be questioned. So, for the start-up it is about finding an innovative business idea, not a copy-cat idea, while being entrepreneurial in the approach to the market.

When you don't have a lot of money you've got to be creative about how you go about things … There's going to be a whole range of 'clever companies' that set up because creativity is now king, not cash.

Will King, founder, King of Shaves, *Real Business*, 1 July 2009

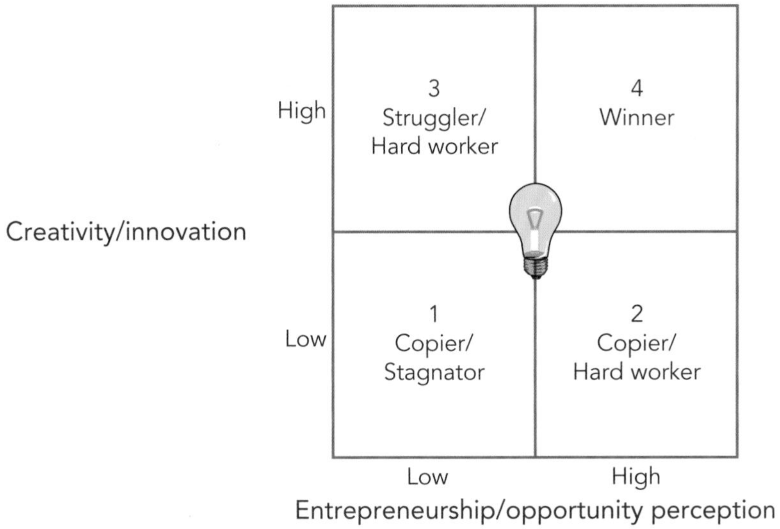

Figure 4.1   Creativity and entrepreneurship

Understanding creativity

We now better understand how the creative process works and how it can be encouraged. The brain has different parts which work in different ways and facilitate different human functions. One part – often referred to as the left brain – performs rational, logical functions. It tends to be verbal and analytic, operating in a linked, linear sequence (called logical or vertical thinking). Another part – often referred to as the right brain – is more intuitive and emotional. This is the part that is creative. It is non-verbal, linking images together to get a holistic perspective (called creative or lateral thinking). You use both sides of your brain, shifting naturally from one to the other in different situations.

Dominant left-brain thinkers tend to be rational, logical, analytical and sequential in their approach to problem-solving. Right-brain thinkers are more intuitive, value-based and non-linear in their approach. The cognitive styles are also reflected in the preferred work styles with left-brain thinkers preferring to work alone, learning about things rather than experiencing them and having the ability or preference to make quick decisions. By way of contrast, dominant right-brain thinkers prefer working in groups, experiencing things (for example, learning by doing) and generating lots of options in preference to focusing on making a speedy decision. People have a preference for one or other approach, but can and do switch between them for different tasks and in different contexts.

Normally the two halves of the brain complement each other, but many factors, not least our education, tend to encourage development of left-brain activity – logic. Kirby (2003) speculates that this may well explain why so many successful entrepreneurs appear not to have succeeded in the formal education system (e.g. Steve Jobs and Richard Branson). He argues that entrepreneurs are right-brain dominant. But he goes even further by speculating that there may be a link between this and dyslexia, observing that many entrepreneurs are dyslexic (e.g. Richard Branson) and language skills are left-brain activities. This is an interesting but unproved hypothesis.

However, the point is that most people need to encourage and develop right-brain activity if they wish to be creative. And this is possible, with training. To overcome the habit of logic you need to deliberately set aside this ingrained way of thinking. Creative or lateral thinking is different in a number of dimensions to logical or vertical thinking. It is imaginative, emotional, and often results in more than one solution because it explores different views of the problem. It can take discontinuous leaps and often restructures problems. By way of contrast, logical thinking is always seeking answers and often converges on a solution, usually without questioning the premise upon which the problem is based. It uses existing structures, concentration on approaches that it sees as 'relevant'. Edward de Bono (1971) set out some of the dimensions of difference. Figure 4.2 is based on his work.

People are inherently creative, but most of us stifle it because we find questioning leads to change and change is threatening. We all create rituals and routines that we feel comfortable with and these normally mitigate against questioning the status quo. These routines help us through the day. Being creative often takes people outside of their 'comfort zone'. They are uneasy with it. Sometimes blocks and barriers need to be attacked. These blocks can take many forms, but here are some:

> The belief that there is only one solution;
> The tendency to be practical and logical in looking for that solution;
> The tendency to think too narrowly and with too much focus – not thinking 'outside the box';
> The tendency not to question the premise on which a problem is based and therefore not to reframe it (not thinking 'outside the box' again);
> The tendency to accept the 'rules of the game' and the status quo unquestioningly;
> The reluctance to accept uncertainty and ambiguity;
> The unwillingness to appear foolish by suggesting unconventional approaches or ideas;
> The unwillingness to take risks in looking at different approaches or ideas;
> The lack of belief that you can be creative.

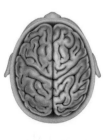

Logical	Creative
Seeks answers	Seeks questions
Converges	Diverges
Asserts best or right view	Explores different views, seeks insights
Uses existing structure	Restructures
Says when an idea will not work	Seeks ways an idea might help
Uses logical steps	Welcomes discontinuous leaps
Concentrates on what is relevant	Welcomes chance intrusions
Closed	Open-ended

Figure 4.2 Dimensions of creativity (logical vs. creative)

It is never easy to change an inherent tendency, but it can be done, and recognizing the blocks to creativity and then dismantling them is the first step.

 Practice insight Measuring your creativity

Find out how creative you are by taking the AULIVE creativity test. This is a 40-question instrument that measures your creativity in eight dimensions. It is available free online at www.testmycreativity.com. The analysis assesses your answers against answers from others with similar backgrounds and provides you with the opportunity to reflect on the results.

The dimensions are:

Abstraction – the ability to apply abstract concepts/ideas.

Connection – the ability to make connections between things that do not appear connected.

Perspective – the ability to shift one's perspective on a situation in terms of space, time and other people.

Curiosity – the desire to change or improve things that others see as normal.

Boldness – the confidence to push boundaries beyond accepted conventions; also the ability to eliminate the fear of what others might think of you.

Paradox – the ability to simultaneously accept and work with statements that are contradictory.

Complexity – the ability to carry large quantities of information and be able to manipulate and manage the relationships between such information.

Persistence – the ability to force oneself to keep trying to generate more and stronger solutions even when good ones have already been generated.

Generating knowledge and awareness

A prerequisite to all creative processes is the generation of knowledge and the awareness of different ideas. We are constrained in our thinking by our prior knowledge (Venkatarman, 1997), so we need to expand it. We need to seek it out. However, all too often we are unaware of the knowledge and information that is being generated around us. We then need time to mull over that knowledge and information. This subconscious 'incubation period' happens when you are engaged in other activities and you can let your mind work on the problem. The best activities are those that are instinctive and do not require left-brain dominance. Interestingly, sleep happens when the left brain gets tired or bored and during this time the right brain has dominance. Incubation therefore often needs sleep. The old adage, 'sleep on the problem', has its origins in an understanding of how the brain works. It is little wonder that so many people have creative ideas when they are asleep – the problem is trying to remember them. Creativity, therefore, can take time and needs 'sleeping on'.

In a thought-provoking book, Johnson (2010) did a good job of dispelling the romantic myth that good ideas are a result of serendipity – a 'eureka moment' for a lone genius:

> [Good ideas] come from crowds, from networks. … You know we have this clichéd idea of the lone genius having the eureka moment. … But in fact when you go back and you look at the history of innovation it turns out that so often there is this quiet collaborative process that goes on, either in people building on other people's ideas, but also in borrowing ideas, or tools or approaches to problems. … The ultimate idea comes from this remixing of various different components. There still are smart people and there still are people that have moments where they see the world differently in a flash. But for the most part it's a slower and more networked process than we give them credit for.

His central thesis was that new ideas rarely happen by chance. They take time to germinate and mature. Often the big idea comes from the 'collision' of smaller ideas or hunches and the chance of these 'accidental collisions' is increased with the exposure you have to more people and different ideas. So, while creativity underpins the generation of ideas, a prerequisite of this is connectivity – a connection with and an awareness of what is going on in the world in general. It generates new ideas, knowledge and information.

Case insight   Swarfega

Connectivity – re-using ideas

Not all ideas find a commercial application in the way they were originally envisaged and observation and connectivity can change the direction of an invention. Swarfega is a green gel which is a dermatologically safe cleaner for the skin. It is now widely used to remove grease and oil from hands in factories and households. But the original product, developed in 1941 by Audley Williamson, was not intended for degreasing hands at all. It was intended as a mild detergent to wash silk stockings, making them easier to put on. Unfortunately, the invention of nylon and its application to nylon stockings and tights rendered the product as obsolete as silk stockings.

Watching workmen trying to clean their hands with a mixture of petrol, paraffin and sand which left them cracked and sore led Williamson to realize that there was a completely different commercial opportunity for his product. He **observed** a need to help clean grease from workmen's skin and **connected** the characteristics of Swarfega with the ability to meet that need.

QUESTION:

1 How difficult is it to be as creative as Williamson?

Ideas, knowledge and information can come from many sources. Reading newspapers, magazines, journals and books and surfing the web are passive forms of connectivity. But essentially connectivity is a social process involving talking with people with different views of the world. Active connectivity involves meeting a diverse range of people – networking. Networks are important structures that can provide you with information about markets, professional advice and opinion, often without charge. This might involve attending meetings, clubs, seminars and conferences. It is likely to involve travel. Formal networks such as Chambers of Commerce, the Small Business Development Centers in the USA, and trade associations can be invaluable for this. Networks can also provide opportunities to form partnerships, either formally or informally, so as to better exploit an opportunity. The more exposed you are to these influences the more likely you are to be creative and innovative and spot opportunities. Indeed, as Johnson says, the driver of innovation over time has been the increasing connectivity between different minds and 'chance favours the connected mind'.

ALLEKO - iStockphoto.com

> That's how *we* learned: by travelling, meeting people, setting up appointments; it's a continuous process.
>
> **Manish Agarwal**, CEO, Reliance Games, *The Guardian*, 22 April 2015

> Contacts are important but you have to get out there and meet people. It can be difficult when you are absorbed in running a business. But there is always something to learn from meeting someone new and a lot to learn from meeting someone old. The right contacts can become an invaluable source of learning as well as an inspiration and support.
>
> **Jonathan Elvidge**, founder, Gadget Shop, *The Times*, 6 July 2002

Connectivity, therefore, extends beyond any industry or market context. It is not just about being aware of different approaches or perspectives on a problem, but also about getting the brain to accept that there are different ways of doing things – developing an open and enquiring mind. Many people almost have to give themselves permission to be creative – to think the unthinkable. Steve Jobs's interest in calligraphy is claimed to be the source for Apple's early development of a wide range of fonts on its computers. Some of the best business ideas have social origins, linking social need to commercial opportunity. For example, Cadbury, the chocolate maker, was founded in 1924 based on Quaker values with the aim of persuading people to drink chocolate rather than alcohol. Similarly, solutions to commercial problems or opportunities can come from unrelated disciplines. The ubiquitous Velcro fastening was conceived in 1941 by Swiss engineer George de Mestral. He got his inspiration from nature. After a walk, he observed that there were burrs of the burdock plant sticking to his clothes and his dog's fur. He looked at them under a microscope and observed they had hundreds of tiny 'hooks' that caught onto 'loops' on clothing or fur. From this he conceived the possibility of two materials being bound together.

The point is that ideas that are commonplace for one group can spark insight for another. It is all about being open to ideas from every source and not being inward looking. Large technology companies like Samsung and LG have active programmes to encourage staff to be exposed to ideas from a wide, and sometimes unusual, range of sources. This is one reason why partnering with other people can be so useful in stimulating innovation. One person exposes the other to different ways of doing things, different ideas, and from this there is the spark of creativity.

> I believe opportunity is part instinct and part immersion – in an industry, a subject, or an area of expertise … You don't have to be a genius, or a visionary, or even a college graduate to think unconventionally. You just need a framework … Seeing and seizing opportunities are skills that can be applied universally, if you have the curiosity and commitment.
>
> **Michael Dell**, founder, Dell Corporation, *Direct from Dell: Strategies that Revolutionized an Industry*, 1999, New York: Harper Business

Case insight   OnMobile

Right time, right place

Arvind Rao was working in the financial services sector in New York when he tried to launch a business developing value-added services – ringtones, wallpapers and apps – for mobile phones. Called OnMobile, it was originally incorporated in the USA in 2000 but failed to find a market. Not to be defeated, Arvind approached telephone operators in India with his ideas and found that his timing was perfect. India's mobile phone market was expanding rapidly. He quickly found one customer, then another.

OnMobile became the first Indian telecom value-added service company to go public when it was listed on the Bombay Stock Exchange and the National Stock Exchange of India in 2008 and is now India's largest value-added services provider. Based in Bangalore, India, it now has offices around the world.

❏ Visit the website: http://www.onmobile.com/

QUESTION:

1 What lessons do you learn from OnMobile?

Developing discovery skills

But entrepreneurship is not just about knowledge, awareness and connectivity. There are another set of skills you need to practice to discover entrepreneurial opportunities. In a six-year study of more than 3,000 US CEOs, contrasting 25 well-known entrepreneurs (such as Steve Jobs of Apple, Jeff Bezos of Amazon, Pierre Omidyar of eBay, Peter Thiel of PayPal, Niklas Zennström of Skype and Michael Dell of Dell Corporation) with other CEOs who had no track record for innovation, Dyer et al. (2009) found five 'discovery skills' that made these entrepreneurs particularly adept at linking market opportunity and innovation. They echo Johnson's approach. The five skills are:

1. Associating

Innovative entrepreneurs connect seemingly unrelated questions, problems or ideas from many different fields. They are able to recognise relationships among objects, processes, cause and effect, people and so on that others do not see, searching for different, unorthodox relationships that can be replicated in a different context. These relationships can lead to new ideas, products or services. So, the inconvenience of mixing different drinks to form a cocktail led to the (obvious?) idea of selling them ready-mixed. James Dyson (Case insight on page 36) was able to see that a cyclone system for separating paint particles could be used (less obviously?) to develop a better vacuum cleaner; doctors at Great Ormond Street Hospital were able to see that the efficiency of

Formula 1 pit stops could help them to improve patient care (see Case insight below). This often comes from mixing with people from diverse backgrounds and disciplines.

The minds of the entrepreneur CEOs in the study were able to make *connections* between seemingly unrelated things, transferring questions, problems or ideas from one discipline to another. They capitalized on apparently divergent associations. What is more, this ability to associate seemed to be something that could be encouraged through stimulation: 'The more frequent people in our study attempted to understand, categorize, and store new knowledge, the more easily their brains could naturally and consistently make, store and recombine associations' (Dyer et al., op. cit.). Associating links the attributes of connection, abstraction and perspective measured in the AULIVE test.

2. Questioning

Innovative entrepreneurs have the curiosity to challenge conventional wisdom, asking 'why?', 'why not?' and 'what if?'. The iconic Apple iPod was developed at a time when MP3 players were well established. Staff developing Apple's iTunes software for use with MP3 players formed such a low opinion of the ease of use of MP3s that they decided that they could do better. Most of the entrepreneur CEOs were able to remember the specific question they asked that inspired them to set up their business. They were also able to imagine opposites – apparent paradoxes – including some different future state and to embrace real-world constraints so that they became opportunities if they could be overcome. Questioning links the attributes of curiosity, paradox and boldness measured in the AULIVE test.

3. Observing

Innovative entrepreneurs observe common phenomena and people's behaviour, particularly that of potential customers. They scrutinize these phenomena, noticing fine detail and gaining insight into new ways of doing things. Ratan Tata observed a family of four perched on a moped and asked, why could they not afford a car? In 2009, after years of product development which involved new modular production methods, Tata Group launched the lowest-priced car in the world – the Nano. Effective observing requires the ability to handle complexity and shift one's perspective – abilities also measured in the AULIVE test. Observing is a prerequisite to associating. It is part of how associations are made. You need to observe detail to be able to associate it across boundaries.

4. Experimenting

Innovative entrepreneurs actively try out new ideas, creating prototypes and launching pilots. Where these do not work, they learn from any mistakes and try to use the learning in different projects. The Apple iPod started life as prototypes made out of foam-core boards, using fishing weights to give it the right feel. All the entrepreneur CEOs engaged in some form of active experimenting ranging from 'intellectual exploration' to 'physical tinkering'. One of their most powerful experiments was visiting, living and/or working overseas. This was all part of being exposed to new ideas and mixing with people from diverse backgrounds. Experimenting is one aspect of curiosity.

 ## Case insight   Google (1)

Experimentation

'Google's "just-try-it" philosophy is applied to even the company's most daunting projects, like digitizing the world's libraries. Like every new initiative, Google Book Search began with a makeshift experiment aimed at answering a critical question; in this case: how long does it take to digitize a book? To find out, Larry Page [co-founder of Google] and Melisa Mayer [a former senior Google executive] rigged up a piece of plywood with a couple of

Continued...

Continued from previous page...

clamps and proceeded to photograph each page of a 300 page book, using a metronome to keep pace. With Mayer flipping pages, and one half of Google's founding team taking digital snap shots, it took 40 minutes to turn the ink into pixels. An optical character recognition programme soon turned the digital photos into text, and within five days the pair had ginned up a piece of software that could search the book. That kind of step-wise, learn-as-you-go approach has repeatedly helped Google to test critical assumptions and avoid making bet-the-farm mistakes.' (Hamel, 2007)

QUESTIONS:

1 What are the barriers to experimentation?

2 How do you apply the principle to a start-up?

 ## Case insight   **Great Ormond Street Hospital**

Discovery skills

Ideas for innovations can come from unusual sources. The Great Ormond Street Hospital for children took its inspiration from watching the McLaren and Ferrari Formula 1 racing teams take only six seconds to turn a car around at a pit stop. Doctors at the hospital were concerned by the time they took to move patients from the operating theatre to the intensive care unit where they recovered. Delays in emergency handover could cost lives, so they contacted Ferrari to see how the process might be improved. Ferrari explained that their pit-stop procedure was kept simple, with minimal movements all planned in advance. In fact, it was so simple that it could be drawn on a single diagram. From that plan, every member of the Ferrari team knew exactly what they had to do and when to do it in a coordinated fashion. Ferrari videoed the hospital's handovers. When the doctors watched it they were shocked at the lack of structure. Ferrari concluded that, with an ever-changing team and unpredictable demand, the hospital's handover teams needed a simple formula they could understand and work to – just like a pit stop. And Ferrari helped the hospital to design it.

Courtesy of the Great Ormond Street Hospital

The hospital team **observed** the speed of the Formula 1 pit stop. They **associated** this activity with the process that they undertook to move patients into intensive care. They **questioned** whether they could use similar processes. And finally they **experimented** to see if it would work.

QUESTION:

1 What are the barriers to developing discovery skills?

---

5. Networking

These innovative entrepreneurs spent time finding and testing ideas with a network of diverse individuals in different countries. They do not just network with like-minded people. Networking is therefore about connectivity. It is a prerequisite for observing and associating.

As shown in Figure 4.3, these discovery skills link with Johnson's idea of connectivity to show how creativity can be encouraged and facilitated. These skills need to be practised so that you break away from the temptation to stick with your established mental models or dominant logic. They can be combined with a set of techniques that will actually help you spot a good business idea. They then take time to come to fruition – the incubation period. But first we need to look at the different ways you might come up with a business idea.

> Network. Meet people. Show a genuine interest in others. Don't talk too much. Listen more.
>
> **Raoul Shah**, founder, Exposure, *The Observer*, 29 September 2013

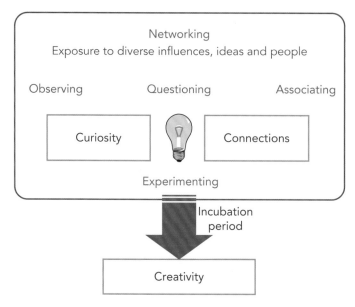

Figure 4.3 Connectivity and discovery skills

 ## Case insight   MamanPaz

Ideas from other countries

If you have been to Mumbai you may have come across the 'dabbawallah system' that delivers hot, home-cooked lunches to workers in their offices around the city. For reasons of taste and hygiene, most office workers prefer to eat home-cooked food in their workplace rather than eat outside at a food stand or at a local restaurant. The meals might come from central kitchens, work-from-home women or from home itself. It is estimated that the 'dabbawallah system' delivers 250,000 lunches each day using bicycles and the railways.

MamanPaz is an Iranian online equivalent of the 'dabbawallah system'. It offers Iranian meals cooked by actual mums to customers who prefer home-cooked meals to canteen food or takeaways. It was founded in 2014 by Tabassom Latifi, who was working for a corporate bank before she started the business. Originally she did everything herself, but within a year she employed four office staff and five motorbike delivery people. She uses a small work-from-home network of women to supply the meals and uses snap inspections of their kitchens and texted customer feedback to maintain quality. She currently supplies about 200 meals a day.

QUESTION:

1 Why is it important to adapt ideas from other countries to suit local circumstances?

Finding a business idea

The 'eureka moment', when a business idea is born, rarely happens by chance. Successful entrepreneurs are able to match opportunities in the marketplace with innovative ways of meeting those opportunities. They link opportunity with creativity and innovation. Successful entrepreneurial firms like Google or Samsung continually seek out ways of developing innovations that match commercial opportunities in a systematic way. Their success is not just down to good luck.

Generating good ideas is a numbers game: the more ideas you generate, the more are likely to see the light of day. Even at the development stage, it has been estimated that for every 11 ideas starting out on the process only one new product will be launched successfully, and perfecting that idea can take time. The idea is unlikely to be exactly right straight away, so you need to be willing to modify it before and after launch. This applies as much to the business model as to the product/service itself. This means that options need to be generated and considered at each stage of development and even after launch.

Often the only sure way of knowing whether the idea will make a lucrative business is to try it out – launch the business but minimize your risks in doing so (see '*lean start-up*' in Chapter 6). The more the business idea is original and different and without established competitors, the less likely is market research to yield an insight into demand because customers do not understand how it might be used. Steve Jobs was famously disdainful of market research, in particular, focus groups, preferring to rely on his own insight about what the market wanted – just as Henry Ford famously once said that if he had asked people what they wanted, they'd have said 'faster horses' rather than 'new-fangled' things called cars.

New venture typologies

So how do you go about searching for these business opportunities? This depends on the 'type' of new venture you want to start up. There are six generalized types of new venture, shown in Figure 4.4. Each has implications for how you go about finding a business idea and each requires a very different business model which influences the complexity of your business plan.

1. Copy-cat
You can introduce an already existing product or service into an existing market. Of course there is always room for competition in free markets but, unless you are significantly better than the competition in some way, you will probably be left to compete on price. This can be problematic if your competitors are large, well established and able to capitalize on economies of scale – since low price implies low costs. And you may therefore struggle. Most copy-cat start-ups do compete primarily on price and therefore have low profitability and rarely grow. They are often salary-substitute firms and compose the majority of small, owner-managed firms. However, each new venture must be considered on its own merits. For example, a new convenience/grocery store is entering a highly competitive environment where large supermarkets have enormous economies of scale and will be able to compete more effectively on price. However, if this were the only store on a new estate, with the nearest supermarket 10 miles away, then there is a good chance of making a healthy profit … that is until another copy-cat store starts up because there are no barriers to entry in this market.

2. Incremental product/service innovation
If you want your new venture to avoid competing primarily on price, the thing to do is to try to **spot** gaps in the market, perhaps by altering the elements of the product/service in some

> Innovation has more to do with the pragmatic search for opportunity than the romantic ideas about serendipity or lonely pioneers pursuing their vision against all the odds.
>
> **Nicholas Valery**, 'Innovation in Industry', *The Economist*, (1999)

	Existing market	Incrementally new market	Radically new market
Radical product/service innovation	4 Disruptive innovation		6 New-to-the-world industries
Incremental product/service innovation	2 Incremental product/service innovation		
Existing product/service	1 Copy-cat	3 Market expansion	5 Market paradigm shift

Figure 4.4 New venture typologies

> "
> True innovation is rarely about creating something new. It's pretty hard to recreate the wheel or discover gravity; innovation is more often about seeing new opportunities for old designs.
>
> **Neil Kelly**, founder, PAV, *The Sunday Times*, 9 December 2001
> "

significant way that adds value to customers. This avoids competing head-on with established businesses and should allow you to charge a higher price, at least until competitors appear. If you are able to safeguard your intellectual property on this innovation (Chapter 9), then you might sustain this strategy for longer. If you are able to create a market niche for your product/service, this could give you a sustainable competitive advantage and be very profitable – an entrepreneurial firm. Alternatively, it might allow you to establish a lifestyle business that allows you to do the things you enjoy while generating an adequate income. The danger here is that you are, by definition, competing against established suppliers, with recognized brands and distribution channels. Competition will be fierce and they may be able to copy your incremental innovation.

3. Market development

Another option is to **spot** incrementally new customers or markets not currently served by existing suppliers, for example in different geographical markets (both national and international). This offers considerable opportunities for new ventures as new products or services that originate in more developed markets eventually find their way into developing markets at a later date. Timing and local knowledge can be crucial when new products or services are introduced into any market. However, the danger here is always that the established supplier in the original market eventually moves into this new market and has sufficient resources and market presence to out-compete you. The challenge is therefore to move with sufficient speed that you dominate this new market before they try to enter it.

4. Disruptive innovation or invention

Introducing radically new products/services into existing markets will certainly confound the competition, particularly if your innovation can be safeguarded, but it is not something that all of us are able to do. It is often linked to technological developments. While most companies are continually making improvements and incremental innovations to their products and services, invention can be risky and takes both time and money. As we saw in Chapter 2, unlike James Dyson and his now ubiquitous cyclone vacuum cleaner, many inventors fail to make their invention commercially viable. However, entrepreneurs are often able to **create** market opportunity. Steve Jobs never invented anything himself but he revolutionized three industries – personal computers, music and film animations – because he was able to create commercial applications for innovations.

5. Market paradigm shift

This is when you **create** radically new markets by challenging the paradigms or conventions upon which an industry bases its whole marketing strategy. So, for example, the development of the low-cost airline industry involved no inventions or innovations, only different ways of doing things that involved minimizing the costs and therefore the price of air travel. In doing this companies like Southwest Airlines in the USA and easyJet and Ryanair in the UK created whole new markets for air travel that never existed before. Tony Fernandes later copied this business model very successfully in different markets with AirAsia.

6. New-to-the-world industries

And just sometimes radical new inventions **create** radically new markets. Tim Berners-Lee invented the World Wide Web in 1990, which in turn created new internet-based markets for information and changed the way we shop for many products and services. Like many inventors before him, Tim Berners-Lee did not make a fortune from this. Others, like the founders of numerous internet firms, such as Larry Page and Sergey Brin of Google or Jeff Bezos of Amazon, created businesses and made their fortunes based on his invention. Again it was the entrepreneur who saw the commercial application for their invention. As we saw in Chapter 2, new-to-the world industries have been created for centuries – water power, textiles and iron in the 18th century; steam, steel and rail in the 19th century; and electricity, chemicals and the internal combustion engine in the early 20th century. New-to-the world industries are disruptive and difficult to predict, but cause enormous economic booms that eventually peter out as the technologies mature and the market opportunities are fully exploited.

> "
> Reinventing the wheel is risky and usually money and time-consuming – both of which would-be entrepreneurs normally lack. However, improving something that is already on the market means there is a demand for the product and you can just do it better with some lateral, creative thinking. That's not to say entrepreneurs should be discouraged from trying something revolutionary. But if you look through history, almost every super successful entrepreneur took an existing idea or business and made it better.
>
> **Adam Schwab**, founder, Aussie Commerce Group, *www.BRW.com.au*, 29 July 2014
> "

The further you move away from being a copy-cat start-up (in either a vertical or horizontal direction), the higher the investment you are likely to need but also the higher the profit you are likely to make. However, while copy-cat start-ups can be very risky because of the strong competition, the greater the product/service or market innovation, the greater the risks you are also likely to face. 'Dot-com' boom was rapidly followed by a 'dot-com' bust at the end of the 20th century as many of the innovations were found not to have a viable market. Ideas that involve disruptive innovation or market paradigm shift are difficult to find and risky to launch as a business.

If you review these six new venture typologies you will see you have two options in finding a business idea:

> If you are looking for radical product/service innovation or to create radically new markets, you must **create** your opportunity, because it is unlikely that there is evidence of market need.
> If you are looking for incremental product/service innovation or to enter incrementally different markets, then you probably can **spot** an opportunity that meets an unfilled current or future market need. Spotting opportunity is easier than creating opportunity and can be just as profitable and less risky.

The reality is that the most successful business ideas are really just improvements rather than groundbreaking inventions. There is nothing wrong with this approach, because it is based on existing products or markets and therefore involves lower risk. Apple's success is based upon good design and improving product ease of use rather than invention. Apple 1 was a big improvement on other computers, with its graphic user interface and 'mouse', the iPod was a big improvement on MP3 players which had been available for years and the iPhone improved on mobile phone from Nokia and BlackBerry. Google entered a crowded search engine market then dominated by AltaVista and simply created a better product by using an improved search algorithm. It became commercially successful after it introduced its AdWords bidding system – invented by Idealab. Facebook entered the market well after social networking sites like Friendster and MySpace.

 ## Case insight   Summly

Creating opportunity – new ideas

Born in London to well-off parents but brought up in Australia for his first seven years, Nick D'Aloisio became adept at using the computer at an early age. It was his hobby. He used it to make animations and films and even apps. At age 15, he created an algorithm that formed the basis for an app called Trimit that summarized long articles down to tweet-lengths:

'I was using Twitter a lot on my phone, and was realizing there was a massive gap between the link on the tweet and the full story. If you could come up with a summary layer to show in Twitter, that would be awesome.'

Trimit enjoyed mixed commercial success but attracted good reviews, wide publicity and thousands of downloads. It was this that attracted the attention of Horizons Ventures, a venture company lead by Li Ka-shing, a Hong Kong billionaire and Asia's richest man. Horizons Ventures decided to invest $300,000 in the venture and this allowed D'Aloisio to recruit a small team in London to develop a completely redesigned version of the app which was launched as Summly beta in December 2011.

Summly summarizes news articles for mobile phone users. If they were interested enough, they can then read the full article on the original website. The idea was that the app created traffic for these websites from users of mobile phones interested in the stories and would create a market for this content with a wider, younger demographic:

'There is a generation of skimmers. It's not that they don't want to read in-depth content, but they want to evaluate what the content is before they commit time. Especially on a mobile phone – you don't have the phone, or cellular data, or screen size to be reading full-length content.' (The Guardian, 29 March 2013)

Less than a year later, funding of £1 million was secured to further develop the app. Working with partners such as Stanford Research Institute, D'Aloisio also managed to obtain the help and support of a network of technology experts and celebrities such as Ashton Kutcher, Wendi Deng, Mark Pincus, Brian Chesky, Stephen Fry and Yoko

Continued...

Continued from previous page...

Ono. The full Summly app was launched in November 2012 and reached number nine in the free iPhone app chart in the same month, and within one year it attracted more than one million downloads and more than 250 publishers, including News Corp.

In 2013, still aged only 17, D'Aloisio sold Summly to Yahoo, reportedly for $30 million (£19 million). Yahoo wanted to integrate the app into a wider range of their services, and Nick and his team joined Yahoo to help with this development. The first product using Summly was launched by Yahoo in January 2014.

QUESTION:

1   What are the barriers to creating opportunity?

Creating opportunity

Creating a business opportunity that has not existed before involves radical product or market innovation and can lead to the development of new-to-the-world industries – boxes 4, 5 and 6 in Figure 4.4. It is more difficult and riskier than spotting opportunity because there is no guarantee that the market need will finally materialize. It requires vision and self-belief aplenty, and is likely to take time and resources. It requires a high degree of creativity and innovation. However, the returns for success are likely to be high.

Disruptive innovation/invention is a step change in products, processes or the framing of markets. Generated by major inventions, they can have large-scale disruptive effects on markets, industries and even economies. For example, although Henry Ford did not invent the car, he did revolutionize the way cars were produced and sold, moving from craft-based to being assembled on a production line and from wealthy customers to an affordable car for every man. He created a new commercial market. This involved extensive incremental changes – to products and processes, component and factory design and in the way labour was organized in his factories. This disruptive innovation created the mass market for cars that we know today. But where did he get his vision of the future from? How was he able to break away from the established thinking of how a car should be made and who it should be sold to? When disruptive innovation creates radically new markets, fortunes can be made (and lost) quickly. That short window of opportunity might frame some of your start-up strategies. This form of innovation can therefore be highly profitable but very risky. It requires a leap in creative imagination from mere possibility to commercial reality that can be difficult for many people. And to stand any chance of seeing the light of day most inventors need to partner with an entrepreneur.

Market paradigm shift happens when entrepreneurs challenge the conventional ways of marketing a product/service. In most sectors there are factors that managers believe are critical to the success of their business. These paradigms become part of the dominant logic of an industry. But circumstances and the environment can change while the managers running the industry do not adapt their way of thinking. For example, Microsoft arguably missed the internet revolution. It, rather than Google, could have dominated the search engine market, but new developments that threatened to cannibalize their main source of revenue – the Windows Operating System and the Microsoft Office suite – were not allowed to surface. Instead, all resources were targeted at defending Microsoft's existing dominance of the software market.

To see an opportunity for market paradigm shift you need to be constantly questioning the status quo. You need to ask the question '*why* are things done this way?' followed by the question '*why not* do them a different way?'. This willingness to continually question the status quo is one of the five fundamental 'discovery skills' exhibited by successful entrepreneurs that we discuss earlier in this chapter. Sometimes doing things differently can add value for the customer without involving extra costs – indeed sometimes doing things differently can reduce costs – while still giving you the opportunity to charge a high price. You can approach the task of challenging market paradigms by systematically looking at sectoral, customer and performance conventions and continually asking the questions 'why?' and 'why not?'.

> We learned the importance of ignoring conventional wisdom … It's fun to do things that people don't think are possible or likely. It's also exciting to achieve the unexpected.
>
> **Michael Dell**, founder, Dell Corporation, *Direct from Dell: Strategies that Revolutionized an Industry*, 1999, New York: Harper Business

Market paradigm shift is probably easier to create than invention and can be just as profitable. Based on a sample of 108 companies, Kim and Mauborgne (2005) estimated that, whereas only 14% of innovations created new markets, these innovations delivered 38% of new revenues and 61% of increased profits. So how might you go about creating completely new markets? Ian Chaston (2000) argued that you have to systematically challenge established market conventions and develop new solutions. Kim and Mauborgne called this 'blue-ocean strategy' – market needs that are currently unrecognized and unmet. Companies creating blue-ocean strategies never benchmark against competitors, instead they make this irrelevant by 'creating a leap in value for both the buyers and the company itself'. They **create** uncontested market space, **creating** new demand and making competition irrelevant. Kim and Mauborgne contrasted this to 'red-ocean strategy' which involves gaining competitive advantage in existing, often mature markets. They acknowledge that 'red oceans' cannot be ignored, but they criticize conventional marketing strategy as being too focused on building advantage over competition in this way.

None of this was new. Based upon a study of firms that had challenged established big companies in a range of industries, Hamel and Prahalad (1994) claimed that these firms had succeeded in creating entirely new forms of competitive advantage by asking three key questions:

> What new types of customer benefits should you seek to provide in 5, 10 or 15 years?
> What new competencies will you need to build or acquire in order to offer these benefits?
> How will you need to reconfigure your customer interface over the next few years?

Chasing 'blue oceans' involves questioning the dominant logic in an industry – challenging market paradigms. Chaston's approach to this is simple: understand how conventional competitors operate and then challenge their approach by asking whether a different one would add customer value or create new customers – our 'why?' and 'why not?' questions. There are many conventions that can be challenged. Chaston suggested three categories:

1   **Sectoral conventions**
    These are the strategic rules that guide the marketing operations of the majority of firms in a sector, such as efficiency of plants, economies of scale, methods of distribution and so on. Kim and Mauborgne (2005) talked about reorientating analysis from *competitors* to *alternatives*. So, for example, insurance used to be sold through high-street insurance brokers until Direct Line came along in the UK, challenged the conventional wisdom and began to sell direct over the telephone, then on the internet. Now this is the norm.

2   **Performance conventions**
    These are set by other firms in the sector such as profit, cost of production, quality and so on. Kim and Mauborgne argued that both value enhancement and cost reduction could be achieved by redefining industry problems and looking outside industry boundaries, rather than simply trying to offer better solutions than rivals to existing problems as defined by the industry. In the 1960s, Japanese firms ignored Western performance conventions en masse and managed to enter and succeed in these markets.

3   **Customer conventions**
    These conventions make certain assumptions about what customers want from their purchases, for example price, size, design and so on. Kim and Mauborgne talked about reorientating analysis from *customers* to *noncustomers*. Body Shop redefined the cosmetic industry's 'feel-good factor' to include environmental factors. Companies like Southwest Airlines, Ryanair and easyJet pioneered low-price air travel and redefined the airline industry.

To find disruptive innovation or ways of changing market paradigms you need to be able to think creatively 'outside the box'. You need to be able to generate new ideas and knowledge, a vision of the future that links market opportunities to your key capabilities. You need to be able to challenge conventions and be open to new ideas. You need to be able to deal with rapidly changing and disparate information in a wide range of new technologies and in diverse, fragmented and often geographically widespread markets. You need to be able to chart a way through often uncertain political and unstable regulatory environments. And in these circumstances, knowledge and information are powerful sources of opportunity and innovation. But remember, creating opportunity can be risky because there is no guarantee that the market will agree with your vision of the future.

 ## Case insight   Swatch

Creating opportunity – market paradigm shift

Swatch created a whole new market for cheap watches by daring to be different. In the 1980s, cheaper watches like Citizen and Seiko competed by using quartz technology to improve accuracy and digital displays to make reading the time easier. The industry competed primarily on price and functional performance. People usually owned just one watch. Swatch set out to change the market and make affordable fashion accessories that were also accurate timepieces.

SMH, the Swiss parent company, set up a design studio in Italy whose mission was to combine powerful technology with artwork, brilliant colours and flamboyant designs. To start, Swatch had to be affordable, so costs had to be kept low. Consequently, it was designed with fewer components than most watches. Screws were replaced by plastic mouldings. It was made in large volumes in a highly automated factory, enabling labour costs to be driven down to less

than 10%. Swatch changed the reason for buying a watch from the need to tell time to the desire to be fashionable. They differentiated themselves not on the function of the timepiece but on its design and also its emotional appeal – a lifestyle image that made a statement about the wearer. In doing this they encouraged repeat purchases because each watch was a different fashion accessory making a different statement about the wearer. Because it was offered at an affordable price, people were encouraged to buy more than one watch. The company used innovative guerrilla marketing techniques (see Chapter 8) to bring the watch to the market under several different designs. Swatch has built up a core of loyal customers who repeat-purchase their watches. New Swatch designs come out every year.

❏ Visit the website: http://www.swatch.com/

QUESTION:

1 How difficult is it to change the way you think about a product or market?

> It's always an opportunity when you see a big market that hasn't changed much.
>
> **Ning Lee**, founder, Made.com, *BBC News Business*, 3 November 2011

Spotting opportunity

While creating opportunity is hard, spotting opportunity in a systematic way is easier, and there are tools and techniques that you can help you. This may involve incremental product/service innovation and market expansion. The main source of opportunity is change. So, if you are looking for opportunity, look for change – changes in technology, law and regulation, market and industry structures, demographics, culture, moods and fashions all create market opportunities that entrepreneurs can exploit. As we have already observed, the internet was an enormous source of business opportunity. Reviewing the environment for change is therefore a prime source of business ideas, and a technique called a PESTEL analysis can help you with this (see next section). Of course, opportunity can also exist where markets are failing to meet changing customer needs – through dominant logic, laziness, ignorance or just because it takes time for the market information to be acted on. Entrepreneurs are often closer to customers and listen to what they say, and they recognize and act on market opportunity quicker than established firms.

Drucker (1985) believed that innovation could be practised systematically through a creative analysis of change in the environment and the opportunities it generates. He listed seven 'basic symptoms' of change that can be used to search systematically for entrepreneurial opportunities alongside the PESTEL analysis:

1 **The unexpected**
   This can be unexpected success or failure or an unexpected event. Nobody can predict the future, but an ability to react quickly to changes is a real commercial advantage, particularly in a rapidly changing environment. Information and knowledge are invaluable.

2   **Incongruity**
    This is the difference between what actually happens and what was supposed to happen.
    Plans go wrong, and unexpected outcomes produce opportunities for firms that are able to
    spot them.

3   **Inadequacy in underlying processes**
    Processes are taken for granted despite the fact they can be improved or changed. This is
    essentially improving process engineering – especially important if the product is competing
    primarily on price.

4   **Changes in industry or market structure**
    Unexpected change, perhaps arising from technology, legislation or other outside events, cre-
    ates an opportunity to strategize about how the firm might cope and, as usual, first-mover
    advantage is usually worth striving for.

5   **Demographic changes**
    These could be population changes caused by changes in birth rates, wars, medical improve-
    ments and so on.

6   **Changes in perception, mood and meaning**
    These changes can be brought about by the ups and downs of the economy, culture, fashion
    etc. In-depth interviews or focus groups can also often give an insight into these changes.

7   **New knowledge**
    This can be both scientific and non-scientific. This amounts to the disruptive innovation and
    challenges to market paradigms that we discussed previously.

One way you can discover inadequacies in underlying processes (Drucker's symptom 3) or
question market paradigms is by analysing the value chain in an industry (Figure 4.5). Behind this
is the idea that real advantages in cost or differentiation can be found in the chain of activities that
a firm performs to deliver value to its customers. The value chain comprises five primary activities:

1   Inbound logistics (receiving storing and disseminating inputs)
2   Operations (transforming inputs into a final product)
3   Outbound logistics (collecting, storing and distributing products to customers)
4   Marketing and sales
5   After-sales service

and four secondary or supporting activities:

1   Procurement (purchasing consumable and capital items)
2   Human resource management
3   Technology development (R&D etc.)
4   Firm infrastructure (general management, accounting etc.).

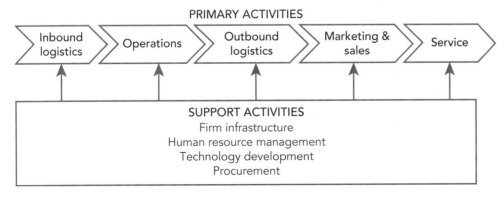

Figure 4.5 Value chain

Each generic category can be broken down into discrete activities unique to a particular firm or industry. By looking at the costs associated with each activity and trying to compare them to the value obtained by customers from the particular activity, you can seek to identify any mismatches. Entrepreneurial opportunities exist when customers might derive greater value by changing the value chain, even if this involves increasing costs, or if costs can be reduced without affecting the value to the customer. For example, low-cost supply may be linked to proximity to a key supplier of raw materials or labour (see TutorVista Case insight on page 103). Another example might be where a high-quality product might be let down by low-quality after-sales service – the value to the customer not being matched by sufficient investment. Entrepreneurial firms can add value to the customer in a number of ways, not least by developing the close relationships they offer to both customers and suppliers. A particularly effective entrepreneurial strategy is to identify a sector in which the relationships are weak and to create value by tightening them up.

Another major source of new ideas is new business ideas introduced in other parts of the world. Good ideas take time to spread, and the window of opportunity to exploit an idea is not the same around the world. As we saw with the OnMobile Case insight earlier, you need to be in the right place at the right time to be successful. What might be a good idea today in one market might only be viable in another some years later. And the spread of the internet makes exploitation of overseas markets a real possibility for some start-ups. On the other hand, in some countries start-ups have benefited from local restrictions on foreign competition. The Google equivalent in China is Baidu and in Russia it is Yandex. Both copied the Google model. Instead of Amazon, in China you would go to Alibaba and in Iran you would go to Digikala. Instead of Facebook, in China you would go to Qzone, RenRen, PengYou or Kaixin. Opportunities exist everywhere.

 ## Case insight   Bloom & Wild

Reimagining the value chain

All photos courtesy of Bloom & Wild company

Aron Gelbard

Starting the company in 2013, Ben Stanway and Aron Gelbard took the inspiration for their online florist business, Bloom & Wild, from the inefficiencies they found when they researched the supply chain for cut flowers. Flowers typically wilt after 14 to 16 days of being cut. And yet the supply chain from field to customer can involve four middlemen – exporter, auctioneer, wholesaler and retailer. Each middleman can take a couple of days to move the flowers on, which means that their life in the home is reduced to only a week or so. Not only do these middlemen add costs to the flowers, but they also reduce their value to customers.

Bloom & Wild's business model involves customers ordering flowers online a few days in advance, so that growers can then cut them to order. They are then placed in small vials of water to keep them fresh and inside a net to keep the size down, and then finally inside a specially designed box that can fit through a standard letter box. Sending the flowers by post in this way means that customers do not have to be at home to receive them and they should last twice as long as flowers bought in shops. There is one final advantage – the costs of the middlemen are cut out, making flowers from Bloom & Wild generally cheaper. So, at a stroke, the new model solves issues of price, longevity and convenience. Videos on the company's website even give ideas about flower arrangement. The only downside is that the model cannot deal with last-minute buys for that 'nearly forgotten' event.

❏ Visit the website: https://www.bloomandwild.com/

QUESTION:

1 What do you need if you are to reimagine a value chain?

Case insight   TutorVista

Spotting opportunity – developing the supply chain

Based in India, Krishnan Ganesh launched TutorVista in 2006. It offers a very 21st century service. The company uses the internet to connect students in high-wage cost countries like the USA and Britain with private tutors from low-wage cost countries like India. It is completely dependent on the internet and the widespread availability of home computers. TutorVista is an intermediary. The part-time tutors are mainly employed full-time as teachers in schools and work from home for TutorVista – a remote business model that allows the company to keep capital and running costs to a minimum and minimize risks. Teachers are vetted and quality is monitored. The company markets the service directly using Google search advertisements. When somebody searches for tutor support in any subject an advertisement for TutorVista comes up. When they click on the website they can talk to staff about the service.

And yet Krishnan had no experience of the education sector. He got the idea when he was travelling around the USA and was shocked to hear a media debate about 'the crisis in the US school education system'. He investigated (asking the question 'why?') and realized that personal tutors in the USA were charging $40–$60 an hour and were regarded by most people as unaffordable. That got him to ask the question: 'Why not link teachers from India, where wage rates are lower, to the market demand in the USA?'

In 2011, the publisher Pearson increased what was a smaller stake in TutorVista to a 76% majority stake, paying $127 million. It acquired the remaining shares in 2013.

❏ Visit the website: http://www.tutorvista.com/

QUESTION:

1 What are the barriers to spotting this sort of opportunity?

Exploring change to find a business idea

There are many techniques designed to help explore change and generate new commercial ideas. As we have already said, generating ideas is a numbers game – the more ideas you come up with, the more likely you are to find one that is viable. So it is worth distinguishing between those techniques designed to generate volume and those designed to improve quality. Some techniques are more applicable to spotting opportunity, others to generating opportunity.

Brainstorming

This is one of the most widely used, basic techniques, designed to generate volume and used for either **spotting** or **creating** opportunity. It is practised in a group. In the session you do not question or criticize ideas. You suspend disbelief. The aim is to encourage the free flow of ideas – divergent thinking – and as many ideas as possible. Everyone has thousands of good ideas within them just waiting to come out. But people inherently fear making mistakes or looking foolish in front of others. Here making 'mistakes' and putting forward ideas which don't work is not only acceptable, it is also encouraged. You might start with a problem to be solved or an opportunity to be exploited. You encourage and write ideas down as they come – there are no 'bad' ideas. All ideas are, at the very least, springboards for other ideas.

 Practice insight How to run a brainstorming session

1 Describe the outcome you are trying to achieve – the problem or opportunity – BUT NOT THE SOLUTION. This could be a broad area of investigation – new ideas and new markets can be discovered if you don't follow conventional paths.

2 Decide how you will run the session and who will take part. You need an impartial facilitator who will introduce things, keep to the rules and watch the time. They will restate the creative process if it slows down. The group can number anywhere from 4 to 30. The larger the

Continued...

Continued from previous page...

number, the more diverse the inputs but the slower (and more frustrating) the process – so around 12 members is probably ideal.

3   Set out the room in a participative (i.e. circular) and informal style. Comfortable chairs are important. Refreshments should be available continuously. Make certain there are flip charts, coloured pens etc., or, if you want to be high tech, you can use some of the specialist software that is available (e.g. Brainstorming Toolbox). Each person should also have a notepad so they can write down ideas.

4   Relax participants as much as possible. The style is informal. The rules of engagement should be posted clearly for all to see and run through so that everybody understands:

> Quantity counts, not quality – postpone judgement on all ideas;
> Encourage wild, exaggerated ideas – all ideas are of equal value;
> Build on ideas rather than demolish them.

5   When the ideas have dried up – it might take a little time for them finally to do so – close the session, thanking participants and keeping the door open for them should they have any ideas later.

6   Open the session by asking for as many ideas as possible. Get people to shout out. Write every one down on the flip chart and post the sheets on the wall. Encourage and engage with people. Close down criticism. Try to create group engagement.

7   Analyse the ideas posted. Brainstorming helps generate ideas, not analyse them. What happens from here is up to you. Sometimes the people who generated the ideas can also help sort them, but remember to separate out the sessions clearly. Perhaps excellent ideas can be implemented immediately, but do not forget to investigate the interesting one – no matter how 'off the wall'.

For more information on the technique visit: www.brain storming.co.uk.

 ## Case insight   **The Million Dollar Homepage**

Brainstorming

The Million Dollar Homepage is a single webpage that is divided into 10,000 boxes, each 100 pixels in size. Space was sold to advertisers at $1 for each pixel, providing a montage of company logos. Advertisers were promised that the page would remain online for at least five years. The idea for the page came to Alex Tew, a Nottingham Trent University student in the UK, in 2005. He had brainstorming sessions before he went to bed each night, writing the ideas down on a notepad. The site took just two days to set up and cost £50. Alex sold the first blocks of pixels to his brothers and friends and used the money to advertise the site. The site address began to appear in internet blogs and chat rooms and, following a press release, a BBC technology programme ran a short feature on the page in September 2005. By January 2006, Alex was a millionaire.

❏ Visit the website: http://www.milliondollarhomepage.com/

QUESTION:

1   Was this just good luck?

PESTEL analysis

A PESTEL analysis is a widely used tool to help thinking about future developments in the wider environment. This in turn can be used to **spot** commercial opportunities that these developments generate. The analysis looks at the changes that are likely to occur in the areas spelled out by the acronym PESTEL:

Political changes like local or central government elections, political initiatives (for example on price competitiveness), new or changed taxes, merger and takeover policy and so on.

Economic changes such as recession, growth, changes in interest rates, inflation, employment, currency fluctuations and so on.

Social changes such as an ageing population, increasing inequality, increasing work participation from home, 24-hour shopping, increasing crime, increasing participation in higher education, changing employment patterns, increasing number of one-parent families and so on.

Technological developments such as increasing internet bandwidth, the coming together of internet technologies, increasing use of computers and chip technology, increasing use of mobile phones, increasing use of surveillance cameras and so on.

Environmental developments such as climate change, waste and pollution reduction, species reduction and so on.

Legal changes such as health and safety rules, changes in employment laws, food hygiene regulations, patent laws and so on.

The technique is often shortened to 'PEST' or 'SLEPT' by dropping the 'legal' and 'environmental' elements of the acronym.

The trick is to brainstorm about how these developments might create business opportunities not currently being met. Take for example the development of the internet and mobile networks. The ability to download films and music has questioned the viability of shops selling DVDs and CDs, but created opportunities for new devices (netbooks, tablets, smartphones etc.) and services (particularly niche services) linked to the internet and mobile networks. The development of internet shopping generally might cause developers to rethink the purpose and structure of our town centres. It might cause individual shops to re-engineer the way they meet customer needs – most shops have websites and many offer internet shopping alongside conventional shopping.

Futures thinking

This is another technique often used to think about the future. For example, based on the changes identified by a PESTEL analysis, it can help develop further insight into the implications of that change, ahead of defining the commercial opportunity. It tries to take a holistic perspective developing a vision about the future state after the change has taken place. From this, the commercial opportunities can be identified, again using brainstorming. Current constraints to action are ignored, and in this way the barriers to change are identified. Some barriers may indeed prove to be permanent or insurmountable, but many might not be. Objections are therefore outlawed and disbelief suspended at the initial ideas stage. Only later on might options get discarded once the barriers are considered. The key to thinking about the future is not to assume it will necessarily be like the past. Change is now endemic and often discontinuous.

So, for example, you might start thinking about the future of a particular form of retailing in five years' time, given the impact of the internet and smartphone. Will bricks-and-mortar retailing continue to exist? If so, how will it combine with these technological developments? What will it look like, where will it be located and what services will it need to offer? How will it attract customers? These and many more questions might help to 'flesh out' a picture of what it might look like and what you need to do to survive and prosper in the future.

Mind maps

This is simply a map of related ideas from one original idea. It helps develop and refine a business opportunity, whether it is **spotted** or **created**. It can be used by an individual or by a group. As with brainstorming, you have to suspend disbelief and simply generate related ideas that might not have been encapsulated in the original. It can help you 'think outside the square' and generate relationships that might not initially have been apparent. Creativity is about making connections between apparently unconnected things, and mind maps can be particularly helpful in doing this. A simple example related to the opening of a shop is shown in Figure 4.6. This shows how mind maps can also be used to look at the complex activities that need to be undertaken in order to launch a new business.

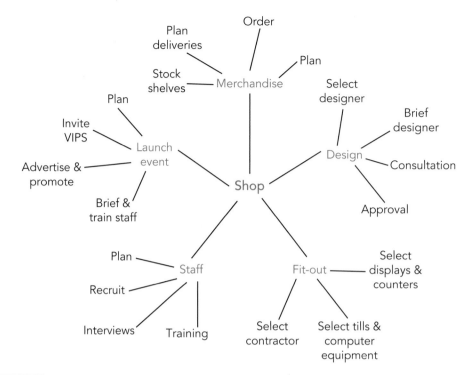

Figure 4.6 Mind map

Figure 4.7 shows a four-step, systematic process for **spotting** a commercial opportunity and generating a business idea based upon a PESTEL analysis, futures thinking and using brainstorming and mind mapping techniques.

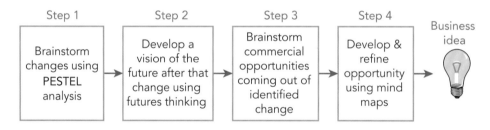

Figure 4.7 Exploring change to find a business idea

Case insight   DUPLAYS

Spotting opportunity – unmet demand

In many countries in the Middle East, locals prize jobs in the public sector rather than in private business. It is not surprising therefore that many start-ups originate from the large expatriate populations. And where better to find a business idea than from the unmet needs of the people

you come from? While working as expatriates in Dubai in the United Arab Emirates, Canadian-born Davinder Rao and Indian-born Ravi Bhusari wanted to make friends and play sport but found that most social activities revolved around going to bars or visiting shopping malls. They had already organized some 20 expat friends to play Frisbee on a regular basis and reasoned that if they wanted to do this, other expats might be interested as well and, what is more, there might be a business opportunity. So, in 2007 they started

Continued...

Continued from previous page...

DUPLAYS. From this small beginning, the company has grown and now organizes sports such as football (soccer), beach volleyball, basketball, touch rugby, netball, cricket, Frisbee and golf, often with related social events. They offer nightly league matches and weekend tournaments organizing facilities, equipment, staffing and scheduling.

> *'Most of the institutionalised activity seemed to revolve around shopping malls or going for drinks or brunches. We figured plenty of people like to play sport and so the secret was to meet that need and build a website and a business that helped people discover what was out there.'*

The notorious red tape in many countries of the Middle East can make it hard to start a new business. DUPLAYS's founders discovered that the bureaucracy can be especially difficult for expats to negotiate without local connections. However, while many countries require expats starting a business to have a local partner, Dubai has a free-zone system without this requirement, meaning founders can own 100% of the business. Nevertheless, DUPLAYS's founders still found that raising finance was difficult.

> *'Attracting money can be harder as an expat. You can understand it from the investor's perspective. If an expat has a business and it goes belly-up, then they can walk away, go back home or to another country. They have less reputational risk, so for investors, that can be scary.'*

Since 2007, DUPLAYS has grown to over 70,000 members playing over 29 recreational sports. It now has branches in cities in the UAE (Dubai, Abu Dhabi and Al Ain), Saudi Arabia (Riyadh and Jeddah), Qatar (Doha) and India (Delhi and Guraon), and claims to rank as one of the largest adult sport and social clubs in the world. In fact, much of its income now comes from organizing corporate events for international organizations such as Castrol, Gillette, Samsung, Volkswagen and also local companies. Being based in an international business hub has proved crucial to DUPLAYS's success in this market, while Dubai's tax-free status has not hurt either. The company has also expanded into what it calls 'corporate wellness', organizing events, leagues and complete wellness programmes for organizations to get employees healthy and active, using sport and activity to help with team-building. Clients include Al Hilal Bank, Dubai Airport, Emirates Aluminium and First Gulf Bank.

> *'We're proud that although we're expats, we're building a company that is good enough to export. That's a great feeling.'* (BBC Business News, 14 April 2013)

❏ Visit the website: http://duplays.com

QUESTION:

1 What are the barriers to spotting this sort of opportunity?

Exploring existing products to find a business idea

Thinking inside the box

Boyd and Goldenberg (2013) believe that innovation in existing products or services can also be pursued systematically using five simple 'templates' for looking at their characteristics. They call it 'thinking inside the box':

> **Subtraction** – You can innovate by taking out features of a product that do not add value for some segments of the market. This is the approach taken by low-cost airlines.

> **Division** – Dividing the functions of a product can be innovative. For example, the dividing out of the control features on many electronic products and placing them into a remote control provided more convenience and allowed the products to become smaller/slimmer.

> **Multiplication** – Taking some characteristic or feature of a product and duplicating it can be innovative. For example, 'picture-within-picture' TVs allow people to watch more than one programme at a time.

> **Task unification** – Bringing together multiple tasks into one product or service can add value for customers. For example, sunscreen products added facial moisturizers (and vice versa) to unify a task.

> **Attribute dependency** – Two or more apparently unrelated attributes can be correlated with each other. For example, smartphones now provide information that depends on your geographic location and, for example, the speed of your windscreen wiper or volume of your radio can vary with the speed of your car.

Analogy

This is a product-centred technique that attempts to join together apparently unconnected or unrelated combinations of features of a product or service and benefits to the customer to come up with innovative solutions to problems. It is therefore designed to provide more focused ideas that create opportunity out of unsolved problems for customers. Analogies are proposed once the initial problem is stated. The analogies are then related to opportunities in the marketplace. It is operated in a similar way to brainstorming. George de Mestral's connection between the properties of burdock seed and the need to stick and unstick things is an example of analogy that led to the development of Velcro.

To build an analogy, ask some basic questions:

> What does the situation or problem remind you of?
> What other areas of life or work experience similar situations?
> Who does these similar things and can the principles be adapted?

Often the analogy contains the words '... *is like* ...', so you might ask why something 'is like' another? For example, why is advertising like cooking? The answer is because there is so much preamble to eating. Anticipation from presentation and smell, even the ambiance of the restaurant you eat it in, are just as important as the taste and nutritional value of the food itself. They 'advertise' the food to be eaten.

Attribute analysis

Sometimes a product can be inadequate and simply not work properly, presenting a fairly obvious opportunity for a new, better product. However, sometimes the deficiencies can be more subtle. Attribute analysis is another more focused product-centred technique designed to evolve product improvements and line extensions – used as the product reaches the mature phase of its life cycle. It therefore can be useful in spotting opportunities arising from inadequate existing products or services. It uses the basic marketing technique of looking at the features of a product or service which in turn perform a series of functions but, most importantly, deliver benefits to the customers. An existing product or service is stripped down to its component parts and then you explore how these features might be altered, using brainstorming. You need to focus on whether those changes might bring valuable benefits to the customer. Nothing must be taken for granted. You can then develop and refine these changes using mind mapping.

Image Source \ www.imagesource.co

So, for example, you might focus on a domestic lock. This secures a door from opening by an unwelcome intruder. The benefit is security and reduction/elimination of theft from the house. But you can lose keys or forget to lock doors, and some locks are difficult or inconvenient to open from the inside. A potential solution is to have doors that sense people approaching from the outside and lock themselves. You could have a reverse sensor on the inside – they unlock the door when someone approaches (which could be activated or deactivated centrally). The exterior sensor could recognize 'friendly' people approaching the door because of sensors they carry in the form of 'credit cards' or they could be overridden by a combination lock. The lock could be linked to a door that opens automatically.

Figure 4.8 shows a three-step, systematic process for spotting a commercial opportunity and generating a business idea based upon analysing the attributes of an existing product or service and using brainstorming and mind mapping techniques.

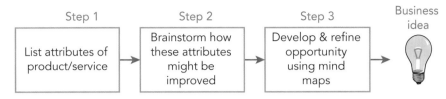

Step 1	Step 2	Step 3	Business idea
List attributes of product/service	Brainstorm how these attributes might be improved	Develop & refine opportunity using mind maps	

Figure 4.8   Exploring inadequate products to find a business idea

Gap analysis

This is a market-based approach that attempts to produce a 'map' of product/market attributes based on dimensions that are perceived as important to customers, analysing where competing products might lie and then spotting gaps where there is little or no competition. Depending on scale, this can be used to spot or create opportunity, particularly in the form of redefining market paradigms. Because of the complexity involved, the attributes are normally shown in only two dimensions. There are a number of approaches to this task:

> **Perceptual mapping** – This maps the attributes of a product within specific categories. So for example, the dessert market might be characterized as hot vs cold and sophisti-cated vs unsophisticated. Various desserts available on the market would then be mapped onto these two dimensions. This could be shown graphically (see Figure 4.9). The issue is whether the 'gap' identified is one that customers would value being filled – and means understanding whether they value the dimensions being measured. That is a question for market research to attempt to answer.

> **Non-metric mapping** – This maps products in generic groups that customers find similar and then tries to explain why these groupings exist. A classic example would be in the soft drinks market where products might be clustered and then described simply in terms of the widely used generic groups 'still' vs 'carbonated' and 'flavoured' vs 'non-flavoured'. The key here is also finding the appropriate dimensions that create opportunities for differentiating the product. The mapping of soft drinks on the two dimensions above is unlikely to reveal any gaps in the market.

> **Repertory grid** – This is a more systematic extension of this technique using market research. Customers are asked to group similar and dissimilar products within a market, normally again in pairs. They are then asked to explain the similarities and dissimilarities. The sequence is repeated for all groups of similar and dissimilar products. The explanations are then used to derive 'constructs' which describe the way in which people relate and evaluate the products. These constructs form a grid that can be used to map the products, using the words used by the customers themselves.

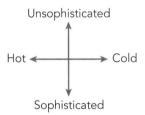

Figure 4.9   Perceptual mapping

Figure 4.10 shows a four-step, systematic process for spotting or creating a commercial oppor-tunity and generating a business idea based mapping the attributes of an existing product or service using brainstorming and identifying gaps in the market.

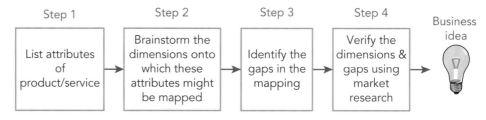

Figure 4.10 Finding a business idea using gap analysis

 ## Case insight   Nikwax

Spotting opportunity – inadequate products

Born in 1954, Nick Brown was a keen hiker who walked regularly in the Peak District and Scotland. But he was unhappy with the waterproofing products available in shops, because they just did not keep the water out of his boots. He was also a bit of a chemist, doing A-level chemistry at school. Consequently, as a teenager he used to mix together various ingredients from his shed and the local hardware store in a saucepan to form a boot wax. He would then use it to coat them before going hiking. And it worked. He had dry feet and the boots did not soften up and lose their essential supportive feature.

However, it was a prolonged period of unemployment after leaving university with a third class degree in anthropology at the age of 22 that forced him to turn his invention into a business. In order to earn some money he boiled up the boot wax he had invented in his north London flat and sold it to a local shop at twice what it cost to produce. He produced the wax in a discarded tea urn, using a primus stove, a jug and materials bought from a local store. The wax was then poured into tins which he silk screened by hand.

'It was a low point for me. I stepped back and asked myself what I had done. I had done nothing well ... I had already supplied a local store with a few pots of it. When they sold out quickly I realised this was something I could do.' (*Sunday Times*, 25 May 2014)

He used a £200 overdraft to buy a van and travelled around selling the wax directly to stores during the day, returning to make the wax at night. He focused on exports early on, travelling to Europe on an Interrail card to sell directly to shops and going to trade shows to push his product. Turnover grew quickly and he started employing staff, but the banks refused to provide finance, believing he was overtrading (see Chapter 11). He therefore financed the growth of the business internally through retained profits. Nikwax was so effective that it set the standard for a range of aftercare products under the Nikwax brand. Nikwax was the first company in the world to produce a range of water-based products for restoring waterproofing in the home. The range grew to include products for many other uses where waterproofing was required, from ropes to tents.

Today Nikwax, founded in 1977, employs 114 staff and has a turnover of £10 million. Nick still owns 92%, with the rest owned by employees. Of its sales, 70% come from abroad, and it has offices in the UK, USA, Australia and Poland.

❏ Visit the website: www.nikwax.com

QUESTION:

1 How easy is it to explore the adequacy or inadequacy of an existing product?

Finding an idea for a social enterprise

The same principals and process outlined in this chapter to find a commercial business idea can be applied to finding an idea for a social enterprise. The only difference is that you are looking for a social rather than market need. You can spot unmet social needs simply by observation – noticing the needs around you – but they might also arise out of change. You can create opportunity by reconfiguring the way existing services are delivered, in such a way as to create added-value that can then be applied to your social objectives.

Just as with self-employment, the spur to set up social ventures can be a 'pull-factor', such as an emotional personal experience like bereavement. This can be an extremely effective and motivating driving force. The spur can equally be a 'push-factor', like the current UK government's push to spin out many government welfare services through the formation of public service mutuals. Neither motivation diminishes the basic requirement for social need to exist. And in meeting this need, you need to be as socially innovative as possible. Otherwise, why do it? So, you need to think through how these social needs can be delivered more effectively so as to improve the social welfare of those targeted.

One final thought at this point is that you do not have to be a social enterprise to achieve, at least some, social goals. As we shall see in Chapter 7, commercial business can also achieve social objective through social responsibility measures and philanthropy. Being a social enterprise creates some legal restrictions and responsibilities that commercial enterprises do not have (Chapter 9), against which any advantages have to be weighed.

Case insight   Maggie's Centres

 Social enterprise

Every year, over 300,000 people are diagnosed with cancer in the UK alone. Maggie's Centre, or to give it its formal name, the Maggie Keswick Jencks Cancer Caring Centres Trust, offers free practical, emotional and social support to people with cancer and their families and friends. It was set up by Maggie Keswick Jencks, a landscape designer with an international reputation, just before her death from breast cancer in 1996. Maggie lived with advanced cancer for two years before her death. During that time she used her knowledge and experience to create a blueprint for a new type of care. Maggie's Centres are built around her belief that people should not 'lose the joy of living in the fear of dying'.

The first centre was built in Edinburgh in 1996. Since then it has grown rapidly and by 2014 had fifteen centres around the UK and a further four planned. The centres are based upon ideas about cancer care originally laid out by Maggie around the principle that design affects how we feel. All of the centres are designed by leading architects. Each is unique, being built around a kitchen on an open-plan basis – no closed doors – and designed to be friendly,

welcoming and full of light – calming spaces. Each centre is staffed by health professionals, including a cancer nurse and a psychologist, and a fundraiser. Each centre is located next to a NHS cancer hospital. In 2013, Maggie's supported over 25,000 people newly affected by cancer and received some 125,000 related visits.

Maggie's now also provides online support for cancer patients. This offers the same kind of support offered by the centres, with blogs and online advice managed by professional psychologists.

Maggie's programme of support has been shown to strengthen the physical and emotional well-being of people with cancer. Since 2000, the work of the Centres has been commended by the NHS Cancer Plan, NICE and the Cancer Reform Strategy. In 2013 it was highlighted as 'best practice' by the UK National Cancer Survival Initiative Report by the Department of Health.

❑ Visit the website: www.maggiescentres.org.uk

QUESTIONS:
1 Can the approaches outlined in this chapter develop an idea for a social enterprise?
2 How would you apply them to Maggie's Centre?

The idea generation process

So, all good business ideas are based upon commercial opportunities, underpinned by market need. You can *create* opportunities through radical product or market innovation, but when you do so there is probably little or no evidence of market need. Your innovation creates a need that did not exist before. However, you can *spot* opportunities by spotting change which leaves unmet customer needs or systematically analysing product or service characteristics to see how they can add value to the customer. If you can introduce product or market innovations to meet these needs, you may have a viable business opportunity. As shown in Figure 4.11, to be successful both approaches must be linked to customer needs. So, for example, the invention of a butter stick that could be squeezed out of a plastic stick, much like glue, tried to create a business opportunity but failed to find a market need. By way of contrast, the undisputed market for instantaneous transportation has so far failed to result in the invention of a Star Trek–like teleport device.

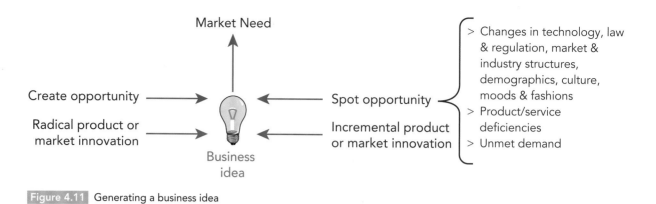

Figure 4.11   Generating a business idea

Case insight   Nuffnang

Spotting opportunity – matching with your skills

Timothy Tiah Ewe Tiam

When he graduated from the London School of Economics, Cheo Ming Shen wanted to use his newly acquired skills to set up a new venture in in his home country of Singapore, taking advantage of Asia's underdeveloped online and social media market:

'I look for business opportunities that I think can work in the internet space and then I go develop it, and then market it and sell it as a business.'

He applied his business and internet skills in his home country where he had more local knowledge. His first venture was based upon his observation that there were a lot of blank spaces on blogs:

'In Asia there are hundreds of thousands of blogs ... it's a fad that has taken off in such a way that ... the West hasn't seen ... This was a big chunk of internet space that wasn't being monetized. It represented a huge audience collectively but nobody could ... effectively put them together ... The blogs are a very interactive medium so it's a very personal medium as well ... When someone sees advertising ... they're more likely to click.' (BBC News Business, 16 November 2010)

Cheo Ming Shen

Founded with his partner Timothy Tiah Ewe Tiam, Nuffnang acts as an intermediary between advertisers and bloggers. Bloggers are paid for each unique visitor or sponsored post and Nuffnang takes a percentage. The simple idea required little capital to establish as a business and became profitable within its first year. It has proved so successful that it has expanded to Malaysia, the Philippines, Australia, Thailand, China and the UK. The founders now have six internet-based businesses based in Singapore.

QUESTION:

1 How important is local knowledge in spotting opportunity?

You can develop the skills to spot market opportunities, and there are techniques to help with this. Essentially, the process of generating ideas involves three stages:

1 You need to ensure that you are exposed to as many diverse and different ideas, influences and people as possible and that you are aware and alert to these influences. A general sense of awareness and openness is also important. Even when exposed to diverse influences, most people walk through life blinkered to what is happening around them.

2 You need to recognize market opportunities by observing how consumers go about their daily lives and questioning whether their needs can be met 'better' (or at all) in a different way. You need to practise the skills and techniques outlined in this chapter that encourage you to question ('why?' and 'why not?') and experiment. You need to think about things that

are happening around you and how they might affect the future. You need to question the status quo and ask why things cannot be done differently.

3   Finally, you need to formulate and reformulate your business idea so that there is a commercially viable business model – something we shall return to in the next chapter. Not all products work to start with, and not all ideas are commercially viable to start with. Howard Head, the inventor of the steel ski, made some 40 different metal skis before he found one that worked consistently. Recognizing market opportunities by observing how consumers go about their daily lives and questioning whether their needs can be met 'better' in a different way is an important first step, but experimenting with the connection so as to perfect the product/service and the business model is vital.

All of this takes time. You need time to think and ponder, time to incubate ideas. Incubation time happens when you are engaged in other activities, including sleep, and you can let your subconscious mind work on the problem. Time is also needed to make the connections or associations between opportunities and your capabilities. There is an element of serendipity here. But the longer the time and the more the potential connections, the more likely the ideas are to germinate. This process of reformulation of the business idea is one that repeats itself well into the concept phase of product development, even into the point where you develop your business model and the use of discovery skills facilitates this process.

 Case insight   Streetcar (now Zipcar)

Market paradigm shift

Andrew Valentine studied modern languages and anthropology at Durham University. While there, he and a friend set up a student radio station, Purple FM. After graduating, he joined the shipping company P&O and worked for them for six years, while doing a part-time MBA. But in 2002 Andrew got itchy feet and, together with a friend, Brett Akker, decided he wanted to set up his own business rather than work for other people. The problem was he did not have a business idea. So he and his partner set about searching systematically for the right business. They spent 18 months researching many ideas for a business, from organic food to training courses, meeting twice a week, before coming up with the final idea:

> 'We looked at hundreds of ideas. We were basically trying to identify gaps, so we were looking at how society was changing and what was missing. Our business had to have potential, be capable of being scaled up and play to our strengths. We kept looking until we found something that matched our criteria.'

The final idea came from something Andrew read about in the USA – a car-sharing club, but one with a commercial orientation. It piggybacks on environmental concerns about pollution and problems city dwellers face in driving and parking in their cities. The idea is that members of the car-sharing club can rent a car for as little as half an hour, replacing the need to buy. There is a one-off membership fee with an annual renewal charge, and members then rent the cars by the hour. Cars are parked in un-manned, convenient locations just off residential streets and are ready to drive away using a smartcard to open the door and start up – eliminating the need to go to an office to collect and return keys. Members can make car reservations online or by phone at any time they need one, and cars are available 24 hours a day. The cars are kept clean, serviced and fuelled – ready to go.

> 'I read about a similar business overseas and immediately thought, what an amazing idea. There were a couple of other companies already running this kind of service in Britain but they weren't doing it the way we imagined we would be able to do it. We thought we could be more effective.'

Once they had the idea, they spent four months holding market research focus groups to test out the business model and developing financial projections to estimate the resources they would need:

> 'We were satisfying ourselves that not only would it work but that there was enough demand for it … Brett and I share a healthy level of permanent dissatisfaction with the service. This means that we are constantly working at making it better and improving everything. I really enjoy the creativity of growing a business.' (The Sunday Times, 15 November 2009)

Initially called Mystreetcar and based in Clapham, South London, the business was finally launched in 2004 on the back of their savings, £60,000 of outside finance

Continued...

Continued from previous page...

and £130,000 of lease finance to purchase the first eight cars. They did not see their competitors as car rental companies, but rather car ownership. It turns car ownership (a product) into a service and is seen by many as a 'greener' alternative because it encourages less road use. The business model challenges the basic paradigm of having to own a car to be able to use it at short notice, even for the shortest journey.

Initially they did everything themselves, working almost a 24-hour day. They handed out leaflets at train and tube stations in the early mornings, eventually getting family and friends to help. They answered the phone and signed up members, meeting them to show how to use the cars. They even washed and maintained the cars themselves. They offered a 24-hour service to members so, to start with, one of them had to be near to a phone all day, every day. After three months they had 100 members, each having paid a membership deposit and an annual joining fee, so they went out and leased 20 more cars at a lease cost of £300,000.

The company changed its name simply to Streetcar and, in 2007, Andrew and Brett gave up 43% of the business to Smedvig, a venture capital company, who invested £6.4 million. By 2009, Streetcar had a turnover of £20 million with some 1,300 cars based in six UK cities. In 2010, the

US company Zipcar (a company launched in 2000) bought Streetcar for $50 million (£32 million), giving the founders $17 million (£11 million). Zipcar subsequently purchased similar businesses – Carsharing in Austria and Avancar in Spain. And, in 2013, Avis, the third largest car-hire firm in the world, bought Zipcar for $500 million (£307 million) – a 50% premium on its share value. At this point Zipcar had 767,000 members in the USA and Europe.

'By combining Zipcar's expertise in on-demand mobility with Avis Budget Group's expertise in global fleet operations and vast global network, we will be able to accelerate the revolution we began in personal mobility.' Scott Griffiths, chair and chief executive, Zipcar, *The Guardian,* 2 January 2013.

❏ Visit the website: www.zipcar.co.uk

QUESTIONS:

1 What benefits does Streetcar offer to its customers? How are these different to car ownership and traditional car hire?

2 How does Streetcar shift the paradigm of car ownership and car hire?

3 Why did Zipcar buy Streetcar? Why did Avis buy Zipcar?

 Practice insight 15 characteristics of a good business idea

The best business ideas generate high profits and involve low risk. Unfortunately, very few such opportunities exist. However, here is a checklist of 15 characteristics of a commercially viable idea:

1 **Identified market need or gap** – the idea must meet a clearly identified market need to be commercially viable. This chapter should help you find this.

2 **No or few existing competitors** – the more innovative your product/service and markets, the fewer competitors, and the higher the price you are normally able to charge. However, remember it is always possible that there are no competitors because there is no viable market for the product/service. We shall look at this in Chapter 5.

3 **Growing market** – it is always easier to launch a business into a new or growing, rather than declining, market. Of course, it may be that you are launching a business that will create a completely new market. We shall look at this in Chapter 5.

4 **Clearly identified customers and a viable business model** – if you don't know who you are selling to, you won't know how to sell to them, which means you

probably will not succeed. You need to go about building your business model systematically. And remember you may be selling to more than one market segment. We shall look at this in Chapter 6.

5 **Low funding requirements** – the lower the funding requirement, the easier it is to start up and the less you have to lose if the idea does not work. We shall look at this in Chapter 6.

6 **Sustainable** – the business must be built on solid foundations so that it has longevity. We shall look at this in Chapter 7.

7 **High profit margins** – the more innovative your product/service and your market, the higher your margin is likely to be. We shall look at this in Chapter 7.

8 **Effective communications strategy** – once you know who you are selling to, and why they should buy from you, you need to be able to communicate a persuasive message to them and build a loyal customer base. We shall look at this in Chapter 8.

9 **Not easily copied** – if it can be, protect your intellectual property. However, often getting to the market quickly and developing a brand reputation is the best

Continued...

Continued from previous page...

safeguard. We will go into ways to safeguard your ideas in Chapter 9.

10 **Identifiable risks that can be monitored and mitigated** – the future of a start-up is by definition uncertain. Identifying risks is the first step to understanding how they can be monitored and then mitigated. The more options you have identified, the greater your chance of success. We shall look at this in Chapter 10.

11 **Low fixed costs** – low fixed costs mean lower risk, should volume reduce. It gives you flexibility. A combination of high profit margin and low fixed costs (high profit, low risk) is always very attractive. We cover this in greater detail in Chapters 10 and 11.

12 **Controllable** – putting in robust operating and financial controls increases your chances of survival and success, and ultimately will add value to the firm. The major imperative in the early years is to monitor and manage cash flow. We cover this in greater detail in Chapters 10 and 11.

13 **Management skills that can be leveraged** – you need to have the appropriate management skills, and if you do not, you need to acquire them or recruit or partner with others with the appropriate skills. We shall look at this in Chapters 8, 12 and 18.

14 **Scalable** – small projects can usually get off the ground easily, but bigger projects can be problematic because they are just 'too big'. In which case, you need to see whether the project can be broken down into smaller projects that can be implemented when the original idea is proved – scalability. The idea is to avoid as much risk as possible for as long as possible – but to make sure you do not miss the window of opportunity completely. This is all a question of judgement and changing market conditions, so you need to remain flexible and think through how you might scale up the project when it proves successful. We shall look at this in Chapters 12 and 13.

15 **Financeable** – if you do not have sufficient resources yourself, the project needs to be able to attract finance. We shall look at this in Chapter 14.

Many of these characteristics will only become apparent as you develop your business model. In doing this you need to be flexible and develop strategic options as you go through the process. If the preferred option turns out to be unattractive or impossible, you can then return to consider the other options you have come up with. Chapter 15 will show you how this can be turned into a business plan that will put forward your best business model.

You will be reminded of these characteristics as you work through this book.

⊃ Summary

> Creativity is a 'right-brain' activity that involves lateral as opposed to vertical thinking. It is intuitive, imaginative and rule-breaking.

> Developing business ideas involves creativity. You can improve this by developing your discovery skills: associating, questioning, observing, experimenting and networking.

> Connectivity is a prerequisite to creativity. It generates new knowledge and information. Networking is an important element in developing this.

> There are six new venture paradigms: a copy-cat strategy, incremental product/service innovation, market expansion, disruptive innovation, market paradigm shift and new-to-the-world industries.

> A copy-cat strategy implies competing primarily on price, and this means that the business is likely to have low profitability and limited growth potential. Any other paradigm involves product/market innovation – changing the product/service or its market to a greater or lesser degree.

> You can find good business ideas by either creating opportunity or spotting it. In both cases the idea must be linked to a market need, whether or not it is yet exhibited.

> Creating opportunity involves radical product or market innovation. Radical innovation involves creating new business opportunities that have not existed before: developing disruptive innovation, market paradigm shift and/or new-to-the-world industries. This is difficult and risky. You can challenge industry paradigms by questioning sectoral, performance and customer conventions.

> Spotting opportunity involves analysing change. Change creates opportunities. These opportunities may involve incremental product or market innovation.

> Symptoms of change are: the unexpected, the incongruity, inadequacy in underlying process, changes in industry or market structure, demographic changes and changes in perception, mood and meaning.

> Opportunities also exist in questioning the value chain in an industry to see where additional value can be created (for customers and/or the firm) in some meaningful way.

> There are techniques that can help you can spot opportunities arising from change. These include brainstorming, PESTEL analysis, mind mapping and futures thinking. Figure 4.7 shows how these techniques can be used systematically to generate business ideas.

> There are techniques that can help you can spot opportunities arising from inadequate products. These include 'thinking inside the box' as well as techniques of analogy, attribute analysis and gap analysis. Figures 4.8 and 4.10 show how these can be used systematically to generate business ideas.

> The same principals and process outlined in this chapter to find a commercial business idea can be applied to finding an idea for a social enterprise. The only difference is that you are looking for a social rather than market need.

✓ Activities

1 Take the AULIVE creativity test and discuss your results with group colleagues.
2 Select any day-to-day object (e.g. a paper clip). Undertake a group brainstorming session to see how many uses you can find for it. Repeat the activity with another object.
3 In a group, use the PESTEL acronym to explore major changes that your society will face in the next five years. From these, select one and explore the business opportunities that might arise out of it. Repeat the process for a number of these major changes.
4 If you do not have a business idea, go through the processes in Figures 4.7 (Exploring change to find a business idea), Figure 4.8 (Exploring inadequate products to find a business idea) and/or Figure 4.10 (Finding a business idea using gap analysis) to find one. This is best done in a small group.
5 Write down as clearly as possible a description of your product or service idea. Also write down:

> Its features;
> The customer demands will it meets;
> Where it falls in the new venture typologies (Figure 4.4);
> Further development work still needed on you product;
> A description of the types of customers that you think will purchase your product or service and why you think they will buy it;
> The names of competitors and why their product or service is not as good as yours.

💬 Group discussion topics

1 Compare the barriers *you* face to being creative with the barriers faced by the rest of the group. Compile a list of the major barriers and how they might be overcome.
2 Using your AULIVE creativity test results as a base, discuss whether these dimensions adequately measure creativity compared to other measures covered in the text. Is there any overlap with the GET2 test dimensions (Chapter 3)?
3 Discuss whether people can be trained to be more creative. If so, explain how.
4 Discuss how you might improve your 'connectivity' and discovery skills. Are there exercises that might help?
5 Discuss how creativity and innovation is shown in entrepreneurship.
6 Discuss whether creative skills are good in all organizations. Explain why they might be important or not in different occupations.
7 Discuss how easy or difficult it is to find business ideas based on the different sorts of new venture typologies in Figure 4.4.
8 Discuss why it is so important to be different to competitors.
9 Discuss the importance of motivations in finding a business idea that you will enjoy.
10 Discuss the difficulties you face in finding a social enterprise idea.

☞ References

Bolton, B. and Thompson, J. (2000) *Entrepreneurs: Talent, Temperament, Technique*, Oxford: Butterworth-Heinemann.

Boyd, D. and Goldenberg, J. (2013) *Inside the Box: A Proven System of Creativity for Breakthrough Results*, London: Profile Books.

Chaston, I. (2000) *Entrepreneurial Marketing: Competing by Challenging Convention*, Basingstoke: Palgrave.

de Bono, E. (1971) *Lateral Thinking for Management*, Harmondsworth: Penguin.

Dell, M. (1999) *Direct from Dell: Strategies that Revolutionized an Industry*, New York: Harper Business.

Dyer, J.H., Gregersen, H.D. and Christensen, C.M. (2009) 'The Innovator's DNA', *Harvard Business Review*, December.

Drucker, P. (1985) *Innovation and Entrepreneurship*, London: Heinemann.

Hamel, G. (2007) *The Future of Management*, Boston, MA: Harvard Business School Press.

Hamel, G. and Prahalad, C.K. (1994) *Competing For the Future: Breakthrough Strategies for Seizing Control of your Industry and Creating the Markets of Tomorrow*, Boston, MA: Harvard Business School Press.

Johnson, S. (2010), *Where Good Ideas Come From: The Natural History of Innovation*, London: Allen Lane.

Kim, W.C. and Mauborgne, R. (2005) 'Blue Ocean Strategy: From Theory to Practice', *California Management Review*, Spring, 47(3).

Kirby, D. (2003) *Entrepreneurship*, London: McGraw Hill.

Valery, N. (1999) 'Innovation in Industry', *The Economist*, 5 (28).

Venkatarman, S. (1997) 'The Distinctive Domain of Entrepreneurship Research: An Editor's Perspective' in J. Katz and R. Brockhaus (eds), *Advances in Entrepreneurship, Firm Emergence and Growth*, Greenwich, CT: JAI Press.

🌐 www.palgrave.com/Burns-Entrepreneurship-And-Small-Business-4e

Go online to access additional teaching and learning resources for this chapter on the companion website. Click here in the ebook to complete a multiple choice revision quiz for this chapter.

5 | RESEARCHING AND EVALUATING THE BUSINESS IDEA

Contents

Getty Images/iStockphoto Thinkstock Images \ christingasner

Learning outcomes

When you have read this chapter and undertaken the related activities you will be able to:

> Define and describe your market or industry;
> Assess the degree of competition in your market/industry and the effect on profitability;
> Identify and evaluate the strengths and weaknesses of your competitors;
> Review future trends in your industry and assess how they might affect you, and from this develop critical success factors for your business.

 *Practice insight*: Undertaking desk and field research

 *Practice insight reminder*: Characteristics of a good business idea

Case insights

Indian video gaming industry	Novo Nordisk
Online dating industry	Bill Gates and Microsoft
Temple & Webster	Amazon, Apple, Facebook, Google and Microsoft
Alibaba, Tencent and Baidu	
Digikala, Aparat and Takhfifan	

The importance of research

Market research is essential before you launch a business. Just imagine being a football manager and not knowing anything about your team (your customers), who you are about to play against and how many players they are allowed to have (your competitors) or even the size of the pitch and duration of the game you are about to play (the nature of the market and industry). And then there is the little matter of the rules of the game (the laws affecting the industry). In such circumstances your chances of success would be slim. The President of Harvard Business School once said that if you thought knowledge was expensive, you should try ignorance.

As we have seen, you can either create opportunity or you can spot opportunity, but in both cases your creative skills must be linked to a market need. So, you need to find out about market need – who your customers might be and why they should buy from you. You also need to find out about your competitors – who they are and what their strengths and weaknesses might be. This all helps minimize risk and uncertainty and provides some basis on which to make the decisions about marketing strategy. For a start-up, any information is probably of value, but the key question that needs to be answered is: why should anyone buy from you rather than from your competitors?

Your backers will expect you to have a thorough understanding of your market/industry and the trends within it. Based on this they will expect you to have identified your customers and competitors and estimated the size of your market. If you are launching a new product, not only will they expect it to actually work as you say, but they will also probably expect some market testing (field research) to gauge customer reaction to it, compared to competitors' products.

There are a number of ways you can undertake market research and we shall cover them later in this chapter; however, before you get down to this level of detail you need to look carefully at the industry or market in which you propose to operate. Unless you start out to create a completely new-to-the-world industry, it is likely that there will be an existing market or industry that sells similar goods or services to the ones you propose. Understanding this industry will help you start to fine-tune and evaluate your idea. It will give you an insight into your potential customers and how to reach them. It will help you identify and assess that competition and start to develop your business model and competitive strategy. Indeed, understanding the shortcomings of companies in an industry can sometimes yield new business opportunities which may lead you to come up with a better or completely different business idea.

Defining your market or industry

The first challenge is to identify and define your market or industry. Most markets or industries have some underlying structural conditions that help define them and that influence the degree of competition within them. The first step in industry analysis therefore is to describe the key elements of the industry's structure. However, defining the industry you are in can be more difficult than you think. An industry is any group of firms that supplies a market, but markets are rarely homogeneous. After all, they are made up of customers with a wide range of needs. An industry is likely to comprise a number of markets or, more accurately, market segments. The competition within these segments can be very different, and as a result the profitability of individual companies within an industry can vary widely.

For example, the car industry comprises many market segments – hatchbacks, family cars, luxury cars, sports cars, SUVs etc. Do cars in each of these sectors compete against each other? Is Jaguar, a UK producer of luxury sedans and sports cars, a competitor of Honda, a Japanese producer of hatchbacks and family cars? There are clear market boundaries between segments and there is the question as to what extent a car and a car producer in one segment competes against another. Similarly, a local convenience or grocery store located, say, 10 miles from the nearest other shop might not be competing directly against supermarkets, despite being in the food retail industry, because of its location. So, geographic boundaries to a market might also apply. The criterion here again is substitutability – are customers willing to travel to the supermarket? However, to some extent, markets and industries can overlap. For example, does the ready availability of video conferencing mean that it is somehow substituting for business travel – and the computing industry therefore competing with the travel industry?

So, an industry is likely to comprise a number of markets. Drawing the boundaries of your industry and the market segments within it is therefore a question of judgement. It is an important judgement that will define who you think you compete with and, probably, the marketing strategies you therefore put in place. The judgement rests on an accurate identification of your customers, which we cover in the next chapter, and their willingness to buy similar products or services.

Market/industry typologies – life cycle

In order to describe your industry or market you need to understand some terminology. However, this is more than just terminology. The three market and/or industry typologies outlined in this chapter have implications for the firms within them and the opportunities they generate for newcomers. This first set of typologies refer to the stage the market or industry is at in its life cycle (Figure 5.1).

Completely new (market paradigm shift)

This is the new market resulting from a market paradigm shift or radical innovation. The market is not proven and demand is very difficult to estimate. Processes and procedures are yet to be developed. There are no competitors.

Implications:

> High risk, but also potential for high returns;
> Customers difficult to identify;
> No competitors;
> Gaining first-mover advantage very important;
> Opportunity to dominate the market;
> Likely to be high marketing costs (customers may not understand product/service benefits).

Emerging

This is a market where there is proven demand but the size of the market is still uncertain. The market is growing. Processes and procedures have still not become fully established. There are still no dominant brands or market leaders.

Implications:

> Few competitors;
> Customers starting to be identified;
> First-mover advantage still significant;

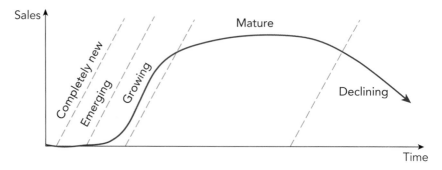

Figure 5.1 Market life cycles

> Opportunity to redefine processes and procedures that are not operating effectively;
> Still opportunity to dominate the market;
> Marketing costs still likely to be high;
> Barriers to entry probably in the process of being established.

Growing

This is a market where there is proven and growing demand – market research would show it to be attractive. Processes and procedures are still developing as new competitors enter the market. Competition is fierce, as companies battle to penetrate the market and gain market dominance. Dominant brands and market leaders are beginning to emerge at the same time as some companies are going out of business.

Implications:

> Growing number of competitors;
> Product/service extensions likely to be emerging;
> Buying patterns becoming established;
> Aggressive marketing strategies in a fiercely competitive market;
> Dominant brands beginning to emerge;
> Competitive pricing;
> Market looks good on paper, but entrants may be too late unless their product/service is based upon significant innovation.

Mature

This is an established market with well-documented characteristics. It is large but growth is slow or non-existent. There are established processes and procedures, buying and repeat-purchasing patterns. Few new customers are entering the market. Competitors are established. There is limited innovation. Industry might be fragmented or consolidated (see below).

Implications:

> Well-established competitors (market might be fragmented or consolidated);
> Defensive pricing possible (meeting or beating new entrants);
> Difficult to break into market, competition strong;
> Opportunity to innovate based on existing product/service;
> Opportunity to innovate based upon process or after-sales service;
> Opportunity to innovate based upon established marketing processes.

Declining

This is a well-documented, declining market with established processes, procedures and buying patterns. There is a declining number of customers and competitors. Product range is narrowing as weak lines are dropped. There is no innovation. Industry might be fragmented or consolidated (see below).

Implications:

> Market has a limited life expectancy;
> Declining range of products;
> Opportunity to consolidate market by becoming dominant player (probably by buying out competitors);
> May be opportunity to establish niche if reducing competitors means demand is still high;
> May be opportunity to cut costs by re-engineering production process to reflect reducing market demand;
> May be opportunity to buy stock at 'distress prices' from companies going out of business and sell on at a profit;
> Opportunity for radical product/service innovation.

It is usually easier to sell in an emerging or growing rather than a declining market, but it can be hard going if your market is completely new. Backers may tend to prefer emerging rather than completely new markets simply because it proves that demand does exist.

Market/industry typologies – concentration

There are a second set of typologies that overlap with life cycles and these refer to the concentration of competitors.

Fragmented

This is a market where there are a large number of competitors of about the same size, usually in a mature or declining industry.
    Implications:

> Well-established competitors;
> Competitive pricing, limited profitability;
> Opportunity to consolidate industry and become market leader (probably by buying out competitors).

Consolidated

This is a market where there are a few, large competitors, usually in a mature or declining industry.
    Implications:

> Well-established competitors;
> Defensive pricing possible (meeting or beating new entrants);
> Barriers to entry are likely to be high;
> Few entrepreneurial opportunities other than radical product or market innovation.

It is far easier to start up in a fragmented rather than a consolidated market. However, consolidation often happens as industries mature and decline, when some opportunities for mergers or acquisitions start to emerge.

Market/industry typologies – geographic extent

The final set of overlapping typologies refer to the geographic extent of the market/industry.

Local, regional or national

This is often a new or emerging market; it may become global in time.
    Implications:

> Gradual geographic roll-out allows marketing mix to be fine-tuned, but at the expense of first-mover advantage;
> Market dominance easier in smaller geographic markets;
> Some markets (e.g. technology-based) can develop geographically over time from developed to developing countries.

Global

This is a market that is international from the start. We look at this in greater detail in the next chapter.
    Implications:

> Competitors quickly become established in foreign markets;

> Opportunities exist for foreign start-ups where others have followed a local, regional or national strategy;
> Internet-based new ventures have the opportunity to 'go global' at start-up;
> 'Going global' at start-up can be very expensive;
> Opportunity to expand on a country-by-country basis, varying product/service offering as appropriate.

It is traditionally easier to start up in a local market and gradually spread your market, but global start-ups are becoming easier to establish because of the internet, allowing products or services targeted at very specific, small customer segments to be sold globally. Sometimes thinking locally can also mean losing the window of opportunity for a good business idea by allowing competitors to gain a national or global foothold.

 Case insight   Indian video gaming industry

Market research

India may now be a technology giant with its own billion-dollar companies like Tata Consultancy Services (TCL), Wipro and HCL, and it is also home to big development centres for multinational companies like Microsoft, Nvidia, Ubisoft, Zynga, Electronic Arts, Disney, Playdom, Sony and Digital Chocolate, but until recently it has not developed much of a home-grown video gaming industry. However, things are changing rapidly. It was in the late 1990s when companies like **Dhruva Interactive** and **Indiagames** started developing video games, mainly for the large multinationals who would subcontract specific graphics tasks, such as modelling racing cars, to local studios in India. These worked like factory production lines, exploiting India's cheap but skilled labour force. There were probably only a couple of dozen firms then, but by 2015 India had over 250 video gaming companies, mostly recent start-ups with about half employing under five people – an industry worth about $890 million and growing rapidly. Inspired by the success of hit games like Doodle Jump, Angry Birds and Cut the Rope, Indian companies are now both developing and marketing entire games themselves for local and the international markets. The focus is now on developing intellectual property rather than subcontracting.

'In the last two years it has changed, mostly because of the emerging start-up community. We have Flipkart, which is India's Amazon, we have OlaCabs, which is India's Uber – these companies have shown that technology-driven concepts can flourish here. That has trickled down to the game development community, so we're seeing a lot of small studios springing up and taking risks. India has traditionally been a risk-averse society; we were told: 'if you don't take a job in a big company, you probably won't get married.' But the tech sector has opened up really quickly. Studios are now saying: if other tech start-ups are doing well, why can't

gaming?' (Abhinav Sarangi, co-founder All In A Day's Play, *The Guardian*, 22 April 2015)

This change is not only to do with the culture within India, it is also to do with the democratization of game publishing and smartphone penetration. Today you can publish a game simply by becoming a developer registered with Apple or Google. And with an Android smartphone costing about £50, the increase in smartphones has been meteoric:

'We took eight years to reach an installed base of 80 smartphones, and then this year we're adding 100 million more … We have the cheapest 3G in the world, and it's going to get cheaper because 4G is coming. We have very cheap Android smartphones coming in … Last year, India had about 1.2 billion downloads on Android. It's the fourth-largest market for Android.' (Rajesh Rao, http://venturebeat.com/2014/, March 2014)

Founded in 1997, **Dhruva Interactive** is one of the early companies in this rapidly coming-of-age gaming industry. The company still undertakes subcontract work on many well-known games that are published mainly by Western companies. However, it has also created its own games like Bazzle and Conga Bugs, and its founder, Rajesh Rao, has started his own separate incubator, the Game Tantra Incubator, to invest in new game start-ups. Dhruva has two studios in Bangalore and employs over 300 people. Founded in 2007, **Yellow Monkey Studios** has developed many games including the tile-sorting puzzler *Socioball*, which features a map editor that allows players to create their own levels and then share them via Twitter. Founded in 2008, **Gamiana Digital Entertainment** publishes Vinashi, a multiplayer online strategy game based on Indian history. Launched in 2011, **Reliance Games** is already an international developer and publisher of games, specializing in movie licences such as *Hunger Games: Catching Fire* and *Pacific Rim*. **99Games**, based in Udupi, has developed 15

Continued…

Continued from previous page...

games for both the domestic and global market, including *Star Chef*, a fast-moving cooking action game with 40,000 daily users. **On The Couch**, a small firm based in Mumbai, produced *Rooftop Mischief*. Other prominent gaming start-ups include **HashCube Technologies**, **MadRat Games**, **Moonfrog Labs**, **Hashstash Studios**, **Rolocule Games**, **Octro**, **Growl Studios** and **All In A Day's Play**.

Foreign giants are also starting to make games in India. The French company **Ubisoft** has been in Pune since 2008 with a large studio of over 300 employees. Once just a subcontract studio, it is now making its own games such as the Indian smartphone music game *Just Dance Now*, tying up endorsements deals with Bollywood stars.

Easy-to-play arcade and casual games like Angry Birds, Candy Crush and Temple Run dominate the Indian mobile market at around 85%. The market is driven by the growth in the mobile network. Games are targeted at this market because of the low entry cost for the value-conscious Indian customer. This gives smaller firms an edge because they can monitor user ratings and then alter the games quickly to reflect their interests. There are currently three constraints to the growth of the industry:

1   **Payment methods** – Barely 8% of Indians have credit cards and over 90% of mobile users are on prepaid contracts, meaning that the Western model of relying on customers to make seamless in-app purchases through online app stores does not work. Credit card remains the sole payment mechanism for iOS and Android systems. Also, the networks would struggle with the data load, because much of India's mobile infrastructure is still operating at 2G speeds; however, there are third-party wallet companies like Paytm and MobiKwik that could be used to overcome the problem. Direct-operator billing is another answer to the problem, and Google has been trying to set up deals with Indian telecom companies, but so far without success. Yet another possibility would be to integrate the direct-operator billing into in-app purchases, but all of this begs the second challenge.

2   **Pricing** – The average disposable income in India is low and the minimum Google in-app purchase threshold of £0.55 is just too high for the market – perhaps by a factor of 10! As a result, the ad-funded business model dominates the Indian gaming market (see the Practice insight into internet business models in Chapter 6), at least until a game becomes a 'hit' with customers. If a game is successful, income can also come from distribution deals, selling the intellectual property of a game to a publisher and from brand licensing.

3   **Funding** – Like the movie industry, gaming is hit-driven, which means unknown start-ups have problems raising finance, with venture capitalists often expecting them to be profitable with a single game. They still often depend on subcontract work to finance the development of their own games. Founder of Hashstash, Sunil Kinshuk, started the company in 2011 with £1,000 of his own money and only by 2015 was in talks with venture capitalists to raise a further £50,000. However, in contrast, Gamiana raised just under $1 million in 2011 from the Indian Angel Network on the back of its successful Jamia and Vanashi games.

The video gaming industry is high risk, high reward, and India has a substantial knowledge infrastructure and a skilled, low-cost workforce to exploit it. If these three constraints can be removed, it may well explode.

QUESTIONS:

1   Using the typologies outlined above, how would you describe the Indian video gaming industry?
2   What are the strengths and weaknesses, threats and opportunities facing the industry?
3   Under what circumstances might this be an attractive market for a start-up?

 ## Case insight   Online dating industry

Assessing competition

Mintel estimate that the online dating industry in Britain alone has grown by 73.5% since 2009 and in 2015 could be worth £165 million, growing to more than £300 million in four years' time (*The Sunday Times*, 8 February 2015). The market in the USA is far larger, estimated to be £1.3 billion ($2 billion), and the potential internationally is huge, with market growth in Eastern Europe, Russia, Asia and South America highlighted as particularly attractive as the market reaches the mature phase of its life cycle in other countries. Little wonder then that there are hundreds of new websites and apps trying to cash in on this emerging market, raising large amounts of venture funding. It is estimated that in 2015 there were already more than 1,400 dating websites and apps. The trouble is that with so many entrants, competition is fierce and the fall-out in terms of business failures is large.

Continued...

Continued from previous page...

Matthew Pitt, operations director at Global Personals, which is involved with more than 7,500 dating sites globally, warned,

'If you are thinking of joining the industry now, you are very unlikely to be successful – unless you have very deep pockets and a differentiated dating offering. Nowadays it's a mature industry with a few large players dominating the mainstream markets and smaller independents doing OK because they've got a strong brand. The latter will find it increasingly tough going forward because they cannot match the investment in technology and resources that the larger sites can to keep their sites at the forefront.' (*The Huffington Post (UK)*, 26 October 2012)

Typically, sites ask you to upload details of yourself, with photos and perhaps videos. They also ask you to submit a profile of the person you are looking for. They then match couples using computer algorithms that may allow for factors like location, age, social demographics, religion, sexual orientation etc. Some sites use psychometric personality tests to help match, for example Match.com uses the Myers-Briggs test. In recent years, niche sites have been set up to cater for particular groups of people. The range of niche characteristics is wide, for example disabilities, professions, sexual orientation, lifestyle activities, even dietary requirements. However, the sites are driven by volume of traffic, and the more specialist the niche, the smaller the community being served.

The industry uses three basic business models to generate income (see the Practice insight into internet business models in Chapter 6). The most common is a subscription model. Others use the 'freemium' model, offering free sign-up but a subscription or fee (perhaps using prepaid virtual credits) to contact other people. Many sites also generate income from advertising. They may also offer additional services such as sending real or virtual gifts or background checks.

Established companies in the industry include Tinder, Match.com, eHarmony, Plenty of Fish and Zoosk, and niche sites like Mature Dating and Christian Mingle.com. Despite established competitors, there are still new entrants to the industry. The challenge they face is to find how they can be different and unique compared to their competitors. One such entrant is **Happn**, which was launched in France in 2014 by Didier Rappaport. It raised $8 million venture funding from DN Capital to allow it to open sites in the UK, Spain, Italy, USA and Mexico within a year of its launch. Their USP (unique selling proposition) is that it locates nearby potential partners and allows members to track them in real time – for example somebody passing close by, using the same roads on their daily commute to work or regularly visiting a particular cafe or bar – and ask them for a meeting. It uses a 'freemium' business model (free to women) with a charge for getting in touch. Another 2015 US entrant to the industry is **Whim**, which raised $200,000 from family, friends and the seed fund 500 Startups. Founded by Katey Nilan and Eve Peters, this app aims to speed up the process of dating and eliminate the need for messaging, waiting and planning. Users indicate who they like and when they are free, and the app then arranges times and places for the various meetings. A third US entrant in 2015 is **Bumble**, whose USP is that only female users can start conversations with prospective partners.

Only time will tell whether any of these online dating sites and apps will succeed. That will depend on a number of factors. For example, how significant is their USP to customers? How easily is it copied and how will the major competitors react if they are successful? How important is market scale and brand? But with the industry already fragmenting and consolidating, the competition is fierce. Although the potential rewards are high, so are the risks.

QUESTIONS:

1 How important is geographic location?
2 Under what circumstances might this be an attractive market for a start-up?
3 What do you think are the important things these start-ups need to do in their first year of existence?
4 If the three companies highlighted are successful, what might be the competitive reaction they face? How might they combat or react to this?
5 Would you like to have been the founder of these businesses? Give the reasons for your answer.

Market research

You need to find as much relevant information as you can about your markets, your industry and your customers and competitors. There are two ways you can do this – desk research and field research. All of the market and industry information discussed so far you should be able to obtain through desk research, although you may have to use your judgement to analyse it in the way you want.

Desk research

Desk research is what it says – research that you can do from a desk, at home or in a library, using the computer and internet or journals etc. Desk research is cheap, quick to do and is usually good for getting background information. However, it will not be specific to your business, can be incomplete or inaccurate and may well be out of date. Information on markets, sectors and industries is published in newspapers, trade magazines, industry surveys and reports, trade journals or directories, many of which will be available on the internet. There are websites that provide all sorts of information but ultimately the prime source of information in the UK is the British Library, where most national and regional economic and business data and information is housed. Desk research can provide information on product developments, customer needs or characteristics, competitors and market trends. However, for many start-ups local information is of far more importance than regional or national information and that might come from Chambers of Commerce and other local sources of help and advice.

Clarifying who will be your customers should enable you to better focus your promotion and marketing efforts. It might also help you to identify both new customers and, eventually, new products or services. Desk-based market research should help you estimate the size and growth of your market. You might intend to sell your product/service to private or business customers. It should help you understand the profile of both these types of customers. A private customer profile might include personal characteristics (demographics) such as age, gender, socioeconomic group, occupation, geographic location and other characteristics of the home, stage in family life cycle, and so on. Similarly, an industrial profile might include type of business, size, sector/industry, location, nature of technology, creditworthiness and so on. It might involve understanding why, where and when customers buy, the structure of established distribution channels and the nature of economic and other environmental trends that might affect the industry. Remember, you need to understand what the conventions in a market or industry are – even if you intend to try to change them. Clearly, while you might be able to find this information for an established market/industry, it is far more problematic for new or emerging markets.

Knowing who your competitors are is just as important. Desk research should provide not only names but also information on competitors' product/service offerings, size, profitability, even their operating methods (e.g. whether restaurants are takeaway, self-service etc.). However, judgement is always needed. For example, a pizza restaurant may face competition from a whole range of other local restaurants, not just those offering pizza. Understanding why customers buy from competitors gives a further insight into the needs of customers and ideas about how you might combat competition.

Field research

Field research involves going out and collecting new information – usually about customers – that is not publicly available. It can involve conducting face-to-face individual or group interviews, telephone surveys or administering text, email or postal questionnaires. This can provide a lot of valuable and unique information. Simple observation and discussion will go a long way without costing much other than time. However, its informality means that the samples of people you approach may not be representative of your customer base and your questioning may be less than precise. To be more reliable, you have to ensure that your respondents represent your potential customers. You also need to structure your questions so that the subject areas are covered comprehensively and consistently, so that there is no ambiguity and you can compare answers from one respondent to another. Your questions should not 'lead' respondents by implying an answer to the question. And the design of your questionnaire should facilitate interpretation and possible data processing. A very simple piece of advice is to always test out a questionnaire before using it 'for real'.

But informal field research can be invaluable, particularly for start-ups dealing directly with the public. Visiting competitors at their place of business, perhaps buying their product or service and talking to other customers, will give an insight into how they operate. For retailers, location is obviously very important. Once prospective premises have been identified, check out the local trade. Find out how many and what type of customers pass by the location. Are shops in the immediate vicinity an advantage or disadvantage? The world's biggest retailer, Walmart, was founded by Sam Walton who famously went to rival K-Mart stores with a notepad and pencil to note down exactly what they did and how they did it and then improve on it. Location can be important for other businesses, for example proximity to customers or a workforce. Many start-ups locate where the owner-manager happens to live. Some locate where the owner-manager wants to live. Neither is a positive decision, unless there are sufficient customers.

However, sometimes, as we observed in the last chapter, the only sure way of knowing whether the idea will make a lucrative business is to try it out – launch the business but minimize your risks in doing so. The more original the business idea, the less likely market research is to yield an insight into demand, simply because customers do not understand how the product or service might be used. For some start-ups the easiest and cheapest way to undertake market research is to test-market and launch the business in a low-cost way, constantly reviewing what is happening and how customers react, and refining the product or service offered to them. We outline this approach (called lean start-up) in the next chapter. However, this can still be an expensive way of doing market research if things go wrong, and some basic market research is probably essential for just about any start-up.

> I would have spent more time researching my idea. Although I couldn't afford it at the time, it would have saved me a lot of effort if I had recognized that customers wanted top quality gourmet coffee through machines rather than the instant product that was part of my original business plan.
>
> **Martyn Downes**, founder, Coffee Nation, *Startups*: www.startups.co.uk

---

 Practice insight Undertaking desk and field research

Desk and field research have different roles in market research. Desk research provides valuable general background information, while field research provides specific information. Their main characteristics are summarized below.

	Desk research	**Field research**
Uses	Background information on: > Industries and markets > Environmental and market trends > Competitors > Customers > Distribution chains > Supply chains > Product development > National and regional economic data	Specific information on: > Customer/consumer needs, satisfactions and dissatisfactions > Consumer reaction to products in development > Direct trial of competitors' product/service performance > Customer reactions to competitors' product service performance > Premises investigation
Sources/techniques	> Newspapers and magazines > Trade magazines, journals and directories > Industry surveys and reports > Government reports > National statistics	> Observation and discussion > Face-to-face interviews > Focus groups > Telephone interviews > Text, email or postal questionnaires
Advantages	> Cheap > Quick > Good for background information, particularly on industries and markets	> Reflects your needs > You control quality > Up to date
Disadvantages	> Not specific to your business > Can be out of date > Can be incomplete or inaccurate	> Can be expensive and/or time consuming > Competitors may find out what you are up to > Can be complicated (e.g. sampling, question structure)

Continued...

Continued from previous page...

Field research

The different techniques used in field research also have different characteristics. These are summarized below.

	Personal interview & focus group	Telephone interview	Questionnaire
Quality of information	Very good	Good	Good
Quantity of information	Good	Fair	Good
Speed of collection	Good	Very good	Poor
Likely response rate	Good	Good	Poor
Cost (money and/or time)	High	Fair	Fair

The construction of questionnaires in field research involves using different types of questions for different purposes. There are four basic types of questions:

> **Closed question** – This requires a specific yes/no answer (often by ticking a box) and is best used where factual information is required. It can be used to build quantitative data on responses. For example, 95% of respondents said 'yes'. It takes little time for respondents.

> **Multiple choice question** – This is where the respondent has a number of options from which to choose. It is also best used for factual information. For example, 'Select the frequency of your monthly visits to this shopping centre' (respondents would then normally be presented with options and asked to tick the appropriate box).

> **Scaled question** – This is where respondents are asked to evaluate or rate some characteristic on a quantitative scale. For example, 'Rate the quality of service on a scale of 1 (very poor) to 5 (very good)' (often by ticking a box). It takes relatively little time for respondents, but predefines the dimensions of measurement.

> **Open question** – This requires the respondent to amplify an answer, often expressing an opinion. It is often used in conjunction with a closed question to provide some insight or depth to quantitative data. It is often used when seeking a better understanding of buyer behaviour. It takes time for respondents to answer.

Questions should be in a logical sequence, moving from general to specific, from factual to opinion- or behaviour-based, from least sensitive to most sensitive. They should try to influence respondents as little as possible.

A guide to sources of information and advice is provided on the website accompanying this book.

Case insight   Temple & Webster

Spotting gaps in the market

Photographed by Denise Braki

Brian Shanahan

Brian Shanahan's father first planted the entrepreneurial seed in his mind by saying that the only way he would make money or be happy would be by running his own business. However, when Brian left school he went to work for accountants KPMG and then for JP Morgan in corporate finance, where he stayed for about seven years. He had always been interested in computers and enjoyed writing programmes.

He had also witnessed the growth of online retailing firsthand at JP Morgan, so when the opportunity to become Chief Financial Officer of eBay Australia came up in 2005, he leapt at it. There he learned all about online marketing, customer experience, PR and all aspects of e-commerce. He joined Gumtree International in 2008, responsible for building the brand in the classified ads market across seven countries, including Australia.

However his father's advice was always at the back of his mind, so when Brian met Conrad Yiu at a digital dinner one night, the two got talking about what they wanted to do with their careers and found they shared the same ambition. Unlike many people, they decided to do something about it and started doing research into online

Continued...

Continued from previous page...

retailing opportunities, joining up with two other like-minded friends, Adam McWhinney and Mark Coulter. According to Telsyte, a specialist e-commerce research house, online retail sales were expected to exceed AUD 30 billion by 2016 – twice the level in 2011. At the time, existing online retailers like eBay and Amazon tended to be 'horizontal providers' – offering everything but not specializing in any particular category. Brian had done a lot of research into these shopping categories during his time at eBay and Gumtree, and he discovered that there was a lot of demand in the homewares category but very few providers. Only some 3% of retailers had migrated to online sales. The four decided that this was the market they would target. And so, homeware and furniture retailer Temple & Webster was born in 2011.

They decided that the company would be the 'expert' in this category and set about creating a brand that represented this, one that is a little old fashioned and about attention to detail, showing customers the care they wanted to provide. They wanted a brand name that was Australian and spoke to Australian heritage and came across the names of William Temple and John Webster, two furniture designers who were commissioned in the 1820s to design two ceremonial chairs for the governor of New South Wales, Lachlan Macquarie. They developed that brand image using 'beautiful' print advertising, television and online video that attempted to create an emotional link with members and potential customers.

They decided that the website would offer high discounts on premium exclusive products but that they would use a subscription model – a members-only site – because they wanted to establish an element of exclusivity and capture people who are interested in their homeware category, not just a particular product. Traditional retailers have to drive traffic to their sites, paying for customers to come back again. A members site means that members can be contacted directly and regularly with special offerings without paying fees to intermediaries.

The four co-founders provided the seed capital to launch the business and did not take a salary for the first six months. However, by Christmas 2011, it was evident that the idea was going to work. Today Temple & Webster has over 850,000 members. It generated AUD 10 million in its first full year of trading, doubling that to AUD 28 million in the second year and then AUD 50 million in 2015.

Brian says that one of the biggest challenges initially was finding potential suppliers:

'Online was still a new channel for them and they didn't quite understand the flash-sale business model, and in

Styled by Adam Powell Photographed by Denise Braki

particular, the need to reserve products for sales. We invested a lot of time in educating them about the process … Mind-sets have definitely changed. These day's suppliers come to us instead of the other way around. The size of our database and the volume of sales that we do in a week is more than what a lot of wholesalers would do in a year with their retail partners.'

He attributes the company's strong growth to three factors:

'People, people and people – This means focusing absolutely on our customers and what they want, building and nurturing the right relationships with our trading partners and hiring and retaining staff that are the right cultural fit, and have a passion for the business.' (http://www.sparke .com.au, 16 October 2014)

❏ **Visit the website: http://blog.templeandwebster.com.au/**

QUESTIONS:

1 What do you think was the reaction of established brick-and-mortar furniture retailers to the success of Temple & Webster? What strengths and weaknesses does Temple & Webster have compared to them?

2 How might the company combat this competitive reaction?

Styled by Jono Flemming Photographed by Denise Braki

Estimating your market size

Estimating the size of a new market created by disruptive innovation or market paradigm shift can be almost impossible. However, as we have just observed, even estimating the size of a segment of an existing market can be difficult. Market research can provide only so much data. If you wish to introduce a new smartphone app, the fact that there are over 1 billion smartphones worldwide is not entirely relevant. Your app might be in English, which limits the market size, and it might be developed for only one operating system. Then there is the question of the channels through which the app will be sold. All of these factors limit the market that you are attacking – even before the question of whether you are likely to achieve your target market penetration.

You can measure a market size in either value or volumes (units), but you need to distinguish between the different types of market shown in Figure 5.2.

1   **Potential market** is the size of a general market that might be interested in buying a product (e.g. one billion smartphones);
2   **Total Available Market (TAM)** is the size of your prospective market – those in the potential market who might be interested in buying your particular product. This reflects the total sales of competing products (e.g. English apps for a particular operating system);
3   **Served Available Market (SAM)** is the size of the target market segment you wish to serve within the TAM (e.g. particular app function);
4   **Penetrated market** is the size of the SAM you capture.

SAM is the market segment(s) you are targeting, given any restrictions such as demographics, geography, language, technology etc. Your market share is therefore your penetrated market divided by SAM. If you are seeking funding, your backers will expect you to try to describe both your TAM and SAM and estimate their size and the trends within them. They will expect you to be able to explain and justify how you will achieve your penetrated market.

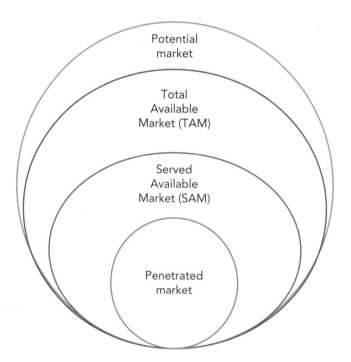

Figure 5.2   Market size definitions

Identifying your competitors

Of equal importance is the identification of your competitors. You should be able to name them. There are three types of competitors:

> **Direct competitors** – those offering similar or identical products or services. These are the most important because they compete directly and you need to understand just how you are different and better than them and how you will convince their customers to switch to you.

> **Indirect competitors** – those offering close substitutes. Where you have an innovative product or service you may have no direct competitors but still need to persuade customers using the 'inferior' competitor offering to switch.

> **Future competitors** – those who could enter your market in the future. If your new venture is successful it will attract competitors. You need to think who they might be and how they might be countered.

Desk research might enable you to evaluate existing competitors in terms of their product/service offering, size, profitability, operating methods and distribution channels. You need to form an assessment of the strengths and weaknesses of competitors' products/services compared to your own. Ultimately you will have to make some judgements about whether they are attacking the same customer segments as you and the quality of their value proposition. How are you different? How sustainable is your competitive advantage? These are issues we shall return to in the next chapter.

You should also assess the influence competitors have over the market – the level of industry competitiveness. With disruptive innovation or market paradigm shift it may just be that there is no real, direct competition – at least until new entrants to the market appear. Which brings us to looking at the barriers to entry in the market and, in particular, the legal protection your product/service might enjoy (Chapter 9). Again, if you are seeking funding, your backers will expect you to have a thorough understanding of your competitors (real or otherwise) and their strengths and weaknesses, compared to you. After all, you will be battling against them in the market.

> The ability to play your own game rather than playing the game of a competitor is exactly where you want to be as a company.
>
> **Jeff Weiner**, CEO, LinkedIn, *The Sunday Times*, 14 July 2013

Assessing industry competitiveness

Porter (1985) developed a useful structural analysis for looking at an industry, assessing the degree of competition within it and therefore its profit potential. He described five forces at play:

1 **Competitive rivalry in the industry**

   The competitive rivalry of an industry is central to the analysis. Rivalry will depend on the number and size of firms within it and their concentration (fragmented vs consolidated), its newness and growth (point in life cycle) and therefore its attractiveness in terms of profit and value added together with intermittent overcapacity. Crucially important is the extent of product differentiation, brand identity and 'switch costs' – the costs of switching to another product. The greater the competitive rivalry, the less the ability of a firm to charge a high price.

2 **Threat of substitutes**

   How likely are customers to stop buying your product/service? This revolves around relative price performance of substitutes, the switch costs and the propensity of the customer to switch, for example because of changes in tastes or fashion. The greater the threat of substitutes, the less the ability of the firm to charge a high price. So, for example, a small firm selling a poorly differentiated product in a price-sensitive, fashion market would find it difficult to charge a high price.

Pixtal

3 **Threat of new entrants**
Barriers to entry keep out new entrants to an industry. These can arise because of legal protection (patents and so on), economies of scale, proprietary product differences, brand identity, access to distribution, government policy, switch costs, capital costs and so forth. Switch costs are the costs of switching to another product. A firm whose product is protected by patent or copyright may feel that it is relatively safe from competition. The greater the possible threat of a new entry to a market, the lower the bargaining power and control over price of the firm within it.

4 **Power of buyers**
This is determined by the relative size of buyers or customers and their concentration. The fewer there are, the higher their buying power. It is influenced by the volumes they purchase, the information they have about competitors or substitutes, switch costs and their ability to backward integrate or develop their own source of supply. The extent to which the product they are buying is differentiated in some way also affects relative buying power. The greater the power of the buyers, the weaker the bargaining position of the firm selling to them. So, for example, if buyers are large firms, in concentrated industries, buying large volumes with good price information about a relatively undifferentiated product with low switch costs, they will be in a strong position to keep prices low. Thus, if you are selling to the big supermarket chains they will squeeze your margins.

5 **Power of suppliers**
This is also determined by the relative size of firms and the other factors mentioned above – the fewer there are, the higher their power. So, for example, if suppliers are large firms in concentrated industries, with well-differentiated products that are relatively important to the small firms buying them, then those small firms are in a weak position to keep prices, and therefore their costs, low.

Two important points stand out from Porter's analysis. Firstly, the higher the degree of differentiation and inbuilt switch costs for your product/service, the more likely your business is to succeed. Secondly, there is the question of the number of competitors you face (concentration). Typically, the fewer competitors you face, the more likely you are to succeed – although this might mean there is a very limited market for your product/service. However, this generalization depends on the market power of these competitors. If you are entering a market where there are few competitors, they might combine to deter your entry. You need to think very carefully before entering a market dominated by a few big companies because they will have well-established market positions and the resources to fight off new entrants.

Case insight Alibaba, Tencent and Baidu

The internet market in China

Despite its recent slowdown, the Chinese economy has still grown at just under 10% a year for over 30 years, overtaking Japan in 2010 to become the world's second-largest economy and expected to overtake the USA shortly. New ventures and the SME sector have fuelled a significant part of that growth, and nowhere has this been more evident than in trade conducted on the internet. The internet has exploded in China, and with it the opportunity to do business in new ways with customers who have been badly served in the past. It is estimated that by 2015 the e-commerce market

Continued...

Continued from previous page...

in China will be approximately £300 billion, rivalling the size of that in the USA and many times larger than Britain and Japan, even combined. But the relatively underdeveloped nature of China's existing markets has meant that, rather than being the disruptive innovation that it has been in the West, in China these internet companies have often filled a void, with relatively little competition. Western companies have often been hindered in filling this void because of legal and cultural constraints.

As many Western firms have found (see B&Q Case insight on page 336), doing business in China is not easy. They have faced many bureaucratic institutional barriers in a country where there is heavy state intervention. China was ranked 91 out of 181 by the World Bank in terms of difficulty of doing business (World Bank, 2012). The report states that it takes Chinese entrepreneurs on average 13 procedures and around 33 days to start a business, compared to an OECD average of 5 procedures and 12 days. Although Chinese entrepreneurs are able to navigate China's institutional environment more easily than Westerners, they can be hindered by the weak property rights and still need good 'connections' at the right level in government. Chinese firms began by copying Western models, but soon started to adapt to local needs and develop their own characteristics. And, as we observed in Chapter 3, highly educated, overseas returnee entrepreneurs, often scientists and engineers trained in the West, have been at the forefront of starting-up technology ventures.

The industry in China is now dominated by three internet conglomerates: Alibaba, Baidu and Tencent. China has a high degree of state intervention and control, and these companies work closely with state agencies. They regulate the content of much of the internet in China and are able to spread the costs of regulation over a broad revenue base. This means the nature of their dominance of the market is different to the internet market in the West. They seem to be able to easily resist foreign competition within China. What is more, they seem to prefer to build their own versions of popular new internet services (often copied from the West), rather than buying out competitors, as tends to happen in the West. It is feared that this will discourage Chinese start-ups, not least because finance might be hard to come by. These factors might combine to increase the dominance of these companies, but the fear is that this will be at the cost of innovation.

Alibaba Group is China's equivalent of eBay or Amazon, whose combined turnover, at over £250 billion, it now exceeds. It was founded by Jack Ma in 1999 and remains a privately-owned, Hangzhou-based group of internet businesses. In 2014 it offered shares to the public in the USA (see Case insight on page 378). The Alibaba Group includes online retail sites, shopping search engines, payment systems, e-commerce businesses, business-to-business portals and cloud computing services. The original **Alibaba** continues as a global business-to-business site – now the largest in the world – that is often used by overseas businesses to tap into China's manufacturers. Founded in 2003, alongside Alibaba is **Taobao**, now China's largest consumer-to-consumer and business-to-consumer online shopping platform. It claims to have some 370 million registered shoppers, three out of four online sales in China and one out of two packages posted. It also offers services that allow others to trade – instant messaging, payment systems and logistics. Profits mainly come from advertising. Originally it competed with eBay China by not charging transaction fees, but it really took off and started generating revenues by overcoming the biggest barrier to online shopping in China – trust – by creating an escrow payment service called **Alipay** in 2004, with payment withheld until goods were delivered. There are many part-time traders on Taobao, and students in particular seem to have taken to trading on the website. Introduced in 2008, its sister site, **Taobao Mall** (or **Tmall**), is a huge online 'shopping mall' where only professional sellers are allowed. For example, United Cosmetics is one of the thousands of 'shops' on the 'mall'. Its large offices are on the outskirts of Hangzhou and house hundreds of 'beauty consultants' who handle customers' online queries. Other high-end brands offered are Burberry and Estée Lauder. In 2009, Alibaba launched **Alibaba Cloud Computing**, offering cloud computing services. In 2011, it launched **Juhuasuan**, another shopping website but one specializing in 'flash sales'. It also launched **eTao**, a comparison shopping site. In 2006, eBay withdrew from China. In 2005, Alibaba acquired China Yahoo! through an exchange of shares, enabling it to offer a portal with news, email and search facilities. Yahoo remains a major shareholder.

Tencent is the fourth-largest internet company in the world, after Google, Amazon and eBay. It was founded in 1998 by Ma Huateng and Zhang Zhidong and is now a public company based in Nanshan District, Shenzhen. It started as a copy of the ICQ chatroom, targeting young people. It still offers a chat service but also offers many other services and is becoming something of an internet conglomerate. Its many interests include social networks, web portals, e-commerce and multiplayer online games. It also sells virtual goods, like dresses for avatars or weapons for online games that are bought with virtual money (Q coins) that accountholders buy for real money. It is rapidly expanding into smartphone services with offerings like **WeChat**. Because it has almost 700 million user accounts and is so diversified, it now derives income from a wide range of sources including advertising, products (real and virtual) and virtual and mobile services.

Continued...

Continued from previous page...

Baidu offers a range of web services such as Chinese-language search engines for websites, audio files, images and videos, similar to Google, as well as an encyclopedia similar to Wikipedia. It now claims to be the number one search engine in China. It was launched in 2000 by Robin Li and Eric Xu (both returning Chinese nationals) and is now a public company based in Haidian District of Beijing. Baidu offers a government information and laws search service as well as offering the facility to search through news websites. It also has a licence to become a full news website itself. Baidu Youa is a shopping and e-commerce site and Baidu Movies allows TV programmes, videos and movies to be downloaded. It also has a social networking service called Baidu Space. It offers cloud storage services. Baidu Encyclopedia claims to be the biggest in the world by users. Only registered users can edit articles, and this and its other search engine editorial activities have opened it to claims of heavy censorship. Baidu derives its income mainly from advertising models such as pay-for-placement and pay-per-click.

There are, of course, many other Chinese internet companies, many which copy Western businesses. For example, Sina Weibo is a copy of Twitter but it allows users to attach comments, pictures and videos to their messages. It also recruited thousands of celebrities to use its service. It worked closely with regulators when it was set up and, as a result, it can quickly stop certain users from logging on and blocking posts containing certain terms. Youku is a copy of YouTube, but mixed with Hulu and Netflix. While individuals can post videos, much of its content is made professionally by television companies or the company itself. Youku needed several licences to start up and has had to develop its own 'monitoring system', with editors viewing all clips before posting. However, it is interesting but perhaps not surprising, given the level of state intervention and control, that the dominant Western internet companies like Google, Amazon, eBay and Twitter have not been able to secure the Chinese market. The question is whether there is space for more local start-ups.

QUESTIONS:

1 How and why is the Chinese internet market different than the market in the West?

2 Because of its high growth rate, China is an attractive market for start-ups generally, but is that the case for internet start-ups?

3 Explain when and why global, national, regional and/or local market structures and conditions might be important to a start-up.

4 What level of industry or market analysis should you undertake for your start-up?

 ## Case insight   Digikala, Aparat and Takhfifan

The internet market in Iran

In 2013 *The Economist* said that the most promising overseas markets for e-commerce would be 'low-trust, under-banked emerging economies' (*The Economist*, 23 March 2013). Because of religious restrictions and international sanctions, doing business in Iran can be difficult, and finding start-up funding can be particularly difficult (see Hamijoo Case insight on page 375). But it has not stopped a spate of e-commerce start-ups. Internet and smartphone usage is very high in Iran, with over half of its 80 million population having access to the internet and smartphones and some 70% of its population under 35 years old. Indeed, *Internet World* estimates that there are 46 million internet users in Iran – representing almost half the total number in the entire Middle East. Internet speeds can be a problem because of restricted bandwidths, and there is still online censorship blocking sites like Facebook, Twitter and YouTube. However, Iranians can get around blocked addresses by using virtual private networks (VPNs) like Hide My Ass! (see Case insight on page 65). E-commerce can also face the problem that Iran is isolated from the outside world financially and Iranians do not have access to international credit cards; however, they do have Iranian bank debit cards, which work online within Iran.

Digikala is an online Iranian e-commerce site similar to Amazon. Founded by two brothers, Hamid and Saeed Mohammadi, in 2007, it has become the biggest e-commerce platform in the Middle East with some 750,000 visitors each day and over 2.3 million subscribers. Almost 90% of Iran's e-commerce takes place on the site. It was launched from a small rented office in Tehran with a group of seven people, offering only two products – mobile phones and digital cameras. Today, it has 760 employees and is operating in more than 20 Iranian cities, shipping more than 4,000 orders a day. One of its major

Continued...

Continued from previous page...

local competitors is Bamilo, a joint venture between South Africa's MTN telecom company and Germany's Rocket Internet, which also started a site similar to eBay called Mozando. If sanctions were to be lifted, Hamid Mohammadi does not see Amazon as a threat, as Digikala is too well established:

> 'I don't think Amazon is a threat to us. Even if they do see Iran as so big a market, they would have to establish a Persian-language Amazon. I think lifting sanctions would be more of an opportunity for people like us than a threat ... The situation in Iran is quite exceptional, there is a huge market for start-ups, something you can't easily find in other countries, and maybe that's why so many of the Iranian diaspora are returning to Iran.'

Aparat is an Iranian version of YouTube. Five million videos a day are watched on the site and it gets about 150 million hits a month. It recently introduced a new free-of-charge service called Filimo, a version of Netflix. Founded by Mohammad-Javad Shakouri Moghaddam in 2005, it is part of Sabaldea, a company that is also behind a number of other successful internet projects, including Cloob.com, a Persian-language social-networking site with over 3 million users, and Mihanblog.com, a free blog-hosting service. Sabaldea was launched with a staff of 3 and now has some 65. If sanctions were to be lifted, Shakouri Moghaddam hopes that many of its users will stay loyal:

> 'Of course the absence of YouTube here has helped us to grow, but even if the filtering were lifted our emphasis on original content means we will be less affected.'

Takhfifan is an Iranian version of the deal-of-the-day website Groupon, offering discounts on a range of products and services, from restaurants and coffee shops to theatres and concert tickets. It claims to have over a million email subscribers and offers 20 to 25 deals a day. Founded in 2011 by Nazanin Daneshvar, who left her job in a German investment bank to return to Iran, together with her sister, it now has some 60 employees:

> 'Four years ago, people in Iran didn't know what start-ups were or they associated them with fraud, but now they are taken seriously and people show trust.' (*The Observer*, 31 May 2015)

QUESTIONS:

1 How and why is the Iranian internet market different to the market in the West? How is it different to China?

2 What might be the effect on these businesses if sanctions are lifted and at the same time Western competitors have access to the Iranian market?

3 Is Iran an attractive market for an internet start-up? Explain.

4 What are the challenges facing an internet start-up in Iran?

Industry futures

Once you have looked at the market and industry you will be entering you can start to assess the strengths and weaknesses of your product or service against those of competitors. You can extend this to look at the strengths and weaknesses of your business compared to your competitors. Ultimately, however, your interest in market and industry analysis is about trying to predict the future – the threats and opportunities you might face. This is the classic SWOT analysis (strengths, weaknesses, opportunities and threats), which we shall look at in greater detail in Chapter 12. This seeks to identify the overlap between the business environment and a firm's resources. In other words, a match between your firm's strategic or core competencies, capabilities and resources and market opportunities.

The weakness with the SWOT analysis is that it can focus too much on the current market and industry situation. It does not provide you with any tools to help you look at the future, which is where your real interest lies. Unless there are structural reasons, current levels of profitability in an industry are unlikely to be a good predictor of the future because competitors are likely to enter an attractive industry. So, you need to understand the current industry and market structures and then look at how they might change in the future.

Some of the techniques we used in the last chapter to find a business idea can equally be applied to how your industry might look in, say, five years' time, after you have entered the market:

1   The PESTEL analysis can used to identify the future influences on the industry (you might have already done this).
2   You can then apply these influences to the broad trends you have identified through research into the industry. Is the industry expanding or contracting? Is it consolidating or fragmenting? Is competition intensifying or are products becoming more differentiated?
3   The futures-thinking technique can then be used to build up a scenario of how direct and indirect competitors might react to your entry into the market and where future competitors might come from. How will all this affect the industry? How will this affect you?
4   You can then brainstorm to explore how you might react to these trends and competitors. What strategies might you adopt? Will you need to modify or change your product/service idea? Will you need to identify and enter new markets?

 ## Case insight   Novo Nordisk

Scenario planning

In 2006 the Danish multinational Novo Nordisk, the leading provider of diabetes treatments in the world, commissioned the Institute for Alternative Futures to produce four scenarios for what was seen as a looming twin epidemic of diabetes and obesity in the Western world.* Currently, 20.8 million Americans have diabetes. The study estimated that this will more than double to 50 million by 2025 unless action is taken. The scenarios were designed to show the impact of various courses of action, to show how serious this twin epidemic could become if the West stayed on its current path, to illustrate the range of options available for averting the crisis, and to demonstrate how learning to meet the challenge of diabetes and obesity could play

a major role in the evolution of the healthcare system. Starting with a scenario that assumed a continuation of the status quo (which would result in 50 million diabetics in the USA by 2025), each of the subsequent scenarios progressively incorporated more diabetes control factors and laid out the consequences of these actions, with the fourth scenario showing the most comprehensive approach to control.

* Diabetes & Obesity 2025: Four Future Scenarios For the Twin Health Epidemics, Institute for Alternative Futures, June 1 2006.

QUESTION:

1   What are the best- and worst-case scenarios that might affect your business idea?

Scenario planning is another technique that tries to assess how possible future situations might impact on a firm. Although its origins lie in the military, its use in business dates from the late 1960s and is widely attributed to Herman Kahn and Anthony Wiener of the RAND Corporation. Trends and drivers of change are identified from the PESTEL analysis and built into scenarios. These situations must be logically consistent possible futures, usually an optimistic, a pessimistic and a 'most likely' future, based around key factors influencing your firm. Optional courses of action or strategies can then be matched to these scenarios. In effect, the scenarios are being used to test the sensitivity of your start-up strategies. They also allow assumptions about the status quo of the environment to be challenged. After the financial crisis of 2008, Lego started using scenario planning as part of its annual budgeting process, allowing it to build contingency plans for each 'crisis' scenario that it identified.

This review of the future should generate a series of threats and opportunities that you may face in five years' time. You need to think through how you might cope with them. These in turn generate **strategic options** that you might undertake if the risks or opportunities actually materialize. The more strategic options that you can identify, the more flexibility you have. They are sources of real value to you and potential investors. Companies that present many options and/or opportunities are more attractive than those with fewer. In the same way, resources that can be used in a number of different ways are more attractive to own, as opposed to rent or buy in, than those with limited use.

Case insight   Bill Gates and Microsoft

Looking to the future

In 1995, five years before he stepped down as CEO of Microsoft, Bill Gates wrote an internal memo that has become increasingly pertinent:

> 'Developments on the internet over the next several years will set the course of our industry for a long time to come ... I have gone through several stages of increasing my views of its importance. Now I assign the internet the highest level of importance. In this memo I want to make it clear that our focus on the internet is crucial to every part of our business. The internet is the most important single development to come along since the IBM PC was introduced in 1981.'

By 2014, Microsoft had only just started to focus on the importance of the internet and was falling behind competitors. With sales of Windows and Microsoft Office falling sharply, it had been forced to announce a 'far-reaching realignment of the company' to enable it to respond more quickly to change, 'focusing the whole company on a single strategy'. This involved disbanding product groups, making redundancies and reorganizing itself into functional lines such as engineering, marketing, advanced strategy and research. Will this work or will it be too little, too late? Only time will tell.

QUESTION:

1   How difficult is it to 'predict' the future?

Your review of current and future competition should also start to generate a series of **critical success factors** – things you need to get right to ensure your survival and success. They might come out of your scenario planning and will certainly be amplified and developed as you develop your business model. The sort of questions you are seeking to answer are:

> What drives competition?
> What are the sectorial, performance and customer conventions that competitors adhere to and how important are they to customers?
> What are the main dimensions of competition?
> How intense is competition?
> How can you be different and obtain competitive advantage?

 ## Case insight   Amazon, Apple, Facebook, Google and Microsoft

Defining a new market

The boundary between markets and industries can become very blurred in the fast-moving technology-driven world of the internet, making the identification of competitors sometimes difficult. This is particularly the case when the real fight is for an emerging market that, as yet, is not formally defined. This is the case with the battle currently under way between the five US giants of the digital age: Amazon, Apple, Facebook, Google and Microsoft. In the past these companies have provided hardware, software and various products and services, each content to 'stick to the knitting' and focus on its core market. However, new hardware such as tablet computers and smartphones linked by Wi-Fi and 3G/4G networks, and new software in the form of apps, are breaking down these barriers.

The battle now is to become the sole provider of all our digital requirements, offering a vast range of services tailored to our 'needs', all day, every day, anywhere, from the best online platform – a kind of digital utility. The reward is not just the profit from the goods or services that may be purchased but also the digital footprint of users (identified by their IP address) – their internet surfing and buying habits, likes and dislikes, times of day on the internet and even their location. All of this is collected automatically in real time. It is very valuable to advertisers and salespeople alike, allowing them to offer targeted advertising at particular times of day in particular geographic areas. This has been popularized as:

> Amazon knows what you read.
> Apple knows what you buy.
> Facebook knows what you like.
> Google knows what you want.
> Microsoft knows where you live.

These firms aim to provide the best online platform for the delivery of 'universal internet services'. The more services

Continued...

Continued from previous page...

these companies offer, the more customers they are likely to attract, and the more advertising revue they are likely to earn. However, each of the Big Five is coming to this new market from different existing markets with new products and services and very different strengths and core competences.

Amazon started life selling books online and now sells almost everything (see Case insight on page 353). However, with the introduction of the Kindle, which allows the purchase and reading of books online, it entered the hardware market (it subcontracts production). The introduction of the colour touchscreen Kindle Fire, usefully preloaded with your Amazon account details, not only makes this easier, it comes with social networking that connects you to others who purchase the same books and films. Amazon also offers a new app shop, online payment system, TV and film streaming and cloud computing facility. Amazon is a fierce acquirer of smaller companies to help it grow and achieve market dominance.

Apple started life designing and manufacturing computers (see Case insight on page 484). It has become an iconic designer brand offering premium-priced electronic gadgets ranging from its computers to the iPod, iPhone and iPad. It recently integrated Twitter into all its devices. Apple redefined how music was sold through iTunes. It sells books through iBooks. It also offers a wide range of apps for its devices. It has launched a web-enabled Apple TV, selling films and TV programmes through iTunes. It has also launched its own cloud computing facility called iCloud. Apple is also sitting on $100 billion of cash, more than any of the other four companies. However, unlike other companies, Apple has a track record of working on its own to grow.

Facebook, the ubiquitous social network site, is the newcomer to this group. It is constantly improving itself and now offers many of the features of Google+. It has launched its own email system – described as 'broader, more social' than Gmail. It even has Facebook credits, a virtual currency used to play computer games. It is also about to launch its own Facebook phone, from which photos and status updates can be uploaded to your Facebook page at a click. In a strategic alliance with Netflix (the films and TV website), Spotify (the music streamer) and Zynga (the computer gamer), it intends to launch Facebook TV, Facebook movies, Facebook music and Facebook games. It is exploring whether to offer its own internal search service based on the data provided by Facebook subscribers rather than computer algorithms. Facebook's stock market launch in 2012 was estimated to have raised over $5 billion – small change compared to Apple, but still a substantial nest egg.

Google has become not only the name of a search engine and company but also the name for what we do when we search the internet for information (see Case insights on pages 92, 304 and 519). As well as information searches, it also offers maps, images and many other services, including its own internet portal. Google also has Gmail, which is well established in the market, and Gmail+ is designed to make this more social, in direct competition with Facebook. It has its Chrome internet browser, and, in 2012, its Android operating system had more users than Apple's iPhones and accounted for over half of worldwide smartphone sales. It now sells smartphones and tablet computers under its own brand, although manufacturing is subcontracted to partners. It has Google Music offering music downloads and owns YouTube, where you can watch and rent TV programmes and films, and has plans to launch Google TV. It has its own online payment system called Google Wallet. Google has a history of partnering with others and using acquisition to help it grow.

Microsoft predates the other four companies, starting as the supplier of the ubiquitous Windows Operating System and then the Microsoft Office suite of software. It also has the internet browser Internet Explorer and email system Outlook Express. Many computers come with its software already installed, including the internet browser – which has been the subject of some anti-trust actions. It offers server applications and cloud computing services like Azure. It has entertainment systems including the Xbox video gaming system, the handheld Zune media player, and the television-based internet appliance MSN TV. Microsoft also markets personal computer hardware including mice, keyboards and various game controllers such as joysticks and gamepads. Arguably, it missed the internet revolution, and since then it has been playing catch-up by expanding, often by acquisition, into search engines such as Bing. It purchased the video communications company Skype, and has entered into a strategic alliance with Nokia to produce smartphones with its own Microsoft operating system – the Windows Phone. It is also imitating Apple and starting to open its own retail outlets.

So, Amazon started life as an internet retailer, Apple as a hardware supplier, Facebook as a social network, Google as an internet search engine and Microsoft as a software developer. But the question is: where will this convergence of competition lead? Will there be one winner? And what will we call this new industry?

QUESTIONS:

1 Why are these industries/markets converging?

2 How might you describe this new industry/market, using the typologies outlined in this chapter?

3 These companies are in the same industry as the Chinese firms Alibaba, Tencent and Baidu (see previous case); however, are they in the same market? How do the markets differ?

4 Do you see these companies facing competition from Alibaba, Tencent and Baidu in the future? What form might this take?

The go/no-go decision

This is the point to take stock whether you actually do want to launch a new venture. You start by asking yourself whether this is what you really want to do and whether you are well suited to being an entrepreneur. We looked at the typical character traits of entrepreneurs in Chapter 3. Do you have these traits? Does being an entrepreneur fit with your aspirations for your life at this time? Do you have the skills and capabilities needed? Are you confident that you can assemble the resources you need (human, social and financial)? Sometimes the business idea might be good, but you might not be the right person to take it to the market. If this is the case, you might need to find a partner or you might be able to sell the idea on. Most people base their business upon skills, experience or qualifications that they have already gained from a previous job or through a hobby. Often they think that their employer is not making the most of some opportunity. Sometimes they have an idea but cannot persuade their employer to take it up, so they decide to try it themselves. Often they have contacts in the industry they believe they can exploit to their own advantage. These are positive factors that 'pull' people into entrepreneurship. Equally people can be 'pushed' into entrepreneurship because they have few alternatives, for example because they are made redundant. Whatever your motivations, you need to undertake an honest evaluation of your personal viability as an entrepreneur.

PhotoDisc/Getty Images

The next step is to look at the practicality of the idea. You may have a business idea but the product or service concept probably needs to be developed; it needs to be specified in detail and then tested. Is it technically feasible to produce the product or service at a cost that allows adequate profits to be made? You may have to prepare a product prototype, although in the case of a service this is likely to be the same as a detailed product specification. Developing a prototype is a process of experimentation, where numerous iterations of an idea are created and tested to see whether they provide the desired result. Prototypes used to be complicated and expensive to produce but now can be developed relatively inexpensively in early stages using computer simulations (Google even provides a tool called Sketchup). All the time, practicality must be weighed against what you believe the market needs and what competitors are currently offering. And at some point you will have to make the decision about whether this product or service is really what customers want – a market-testing process best made based upon market research and/or limited-launch feedback.

> You need to figure out how you can be better or different. What are you doing that hasn't been done before?
>
> **Troy Collins**, founder, Endource, *The Sunday Times*, 5 March 2015

Underpinning the process is the constant need to check the commercial viability of the business idea. You need to assure yourself that there is a viable market for your product or service. Who are your customers and why will they buy from you? You might be able to assess viability through various forms of market testing, for example trying out a retail idea as a 'pop-up' stall. And then there are your competitors. How will you compete against them? How are you different? Will you be able to capitalize on this idea as quickly as existing firms? A good business idea has a window of commercial opportunity. Too early or too late and it is unlikely to be successful, and it will only have a finite life cycle. Even if you intend to launch a social enterprise, you need to know the costs and revenues and assure yourself that these are 'satisfactory'. Will your business be profitable? Commercial viability usually hinges on the profits the firm makes compared to the risks it faces. This will determine whether it can be funded.

Figure 5.3 shows this screening process – from the idea phase to concept phase and finally to launch phase. It is iterative. The practicalities of producing the product or service must be weighed against the needs of customers and the commercial viability of the concept. Commercial viability is never certain, particularly at this stage, but studying the market and industry should give you some clues and the Practice insight in the previous chapter highlights the characteristics of the best business ideas. Commercial viability hinges on the effectiveness of your business model and the strategies you develop to launch and grow your business. However, even at this stage a 'go' decision is not certain because you need to produce detailed plans about how the product or

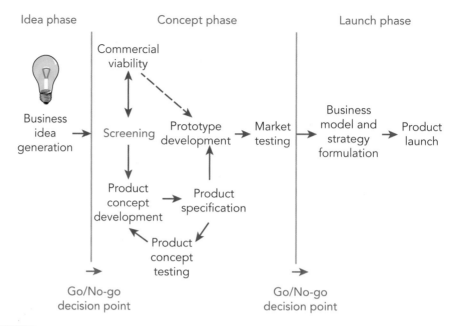

Figure 5.3 The screening process ahead of the go/no-go decision

service will be produced, operated, marketed and financed – in other words a business plan. And the detail in this might lead you to alter some elements of the business idea and, in extremis, even abandon it. Nevertheless, the business plan is something you need to develop before you launch.

 Practice insight reminder Characteristics of a good business idea – 2 & 3

2 **No or few existing competitors** – the more innovative your product/service and markets, the fewer competitors, and the higher the price you are normally able to charge. However, remember it is always possible that there are no competitors because there is no viable market for the product/service.

2 **Growing market** – it is always easier to launch a business into a new or growing, rather than declining, market. Of course it may be that you are launching a business that will create a completely new market.

⊃ Summary

> You need to identify and be able to identify and describe the characteristics of the market or industry within which you will operate. Commonly used typologies include life-cycle, concentration and geographic extent. However, drawing the boundaries of your industry can be difficult and is a question of judgement. Porter's Five Forces will help you assess the degree of competition within it.

> Desk research is cheap and quick. It should help you estimate the size of your market and identify your competitors.

> Your Total Available Market (TAM) is the size of your potential market – those who might be interested in buying your particular product. This reflects the total sales of competing products. Your Served Available Market (SAM) is the size of the target market segment you wish to serve within the TAM. Your penetrated market is the size of the SAM you actually capture. Your market share is your penetrated market divided by SAM.

> The profitability of individual companies within an industry can vary widely implying that your choice and, just as important, execution of strategy is probably more important than your choice of industry.

> Your interest in industry analysis is about trying to predict the future – the threats and opportunities you might face. You can use techniques such as PESTEL

analysis, brainstorming, futures thinking and scenario planning to help you do this.

> This analysis should generate a series of threats and opportunities and strategic options that you might undertake if they actually materialize. The more strategic options that you can identify, the more flexibility you have. It should also generate a series of critical success factors – things you need to get right to ensure survival

and success. These will be amplified and developed as you develop your business model.

> Deciding whether a business idea is viable involves checking against your own aspirations and capabilities, considering the practicality of the idea, and evaluating its commercial viability. The screening process is shown in Figure 5.3. Although there are characteristics of a good business idea, ultimately commercial viability can only be assessed by drawing up a comprehensive business plan.

✓ Activities

1 Undertake research into your industry and/or market. Using the typologies outlined in this chapter, describe its characteristics. Assess the degree of competition within it.

2 Assess the future of your industry and/or market in five years' time using the techniques outlined in the chapter (you might try 'best-case' and 'worst-case' scenarios). List the risks you might face over this period and how they might be mitigated. List your critical success factors – the things you need to get right to ensure your survival and success.

3 Bearing in mind some of the techniques outlined in the previous chapter, review activities 1 and 2 to assess whether any new business opportunities emerge from your analysis.

4 Estimate the size of your market (SAM and TAM).

5 Using the 15 characteristics of a good business idea listed in the Practice insight in Chapter 4, evaluate the attractiveness of your business idea on a scale of 1 (not attractive) to 5 (very attractive). Total your scores and reflect and evaluate the result.

💬 Group discussion topics

1 Why is market research important? What information can it generate for a start-up?

2 How do you define an industry and a market?

3 What information can you get from desk/field research? How would you use the different sorts of information? What are the advantages and disadvantages of each?

4 Market research tells you nothing of importance about a radical innovation or completely new markets. Discuss.

5 How important is market research as the business grows? What information might you be looking for?

6 The better your idea, the more likely there is to be competition. Discuss.

7 Is it easier to start up in a fragmented or a consolidated market?

8 Competition is always fiercest in the most attractive markets/industries – those where there is greatest customer demand, and therefore profit potential. Discuss.

9 Why are there business opportunities in mature and/or declining markets?

10 At what stage(s) are industries likely to develop a 'dominant logic' and become complacent?

11 Should a start-up always be attracted to an industry where there is little competition?

12 Is it better to have big company or small company competitors?

13 Why might an entrepreneur perceive themselves as having no competition?

14 If the future is so important, what is the point of looking back and doing market research?

15 What would it take to get you to start up your own business?

👉 References

Porter, M.E. (1985) *Competitive Advantage, Creating and Sustaining Superior Performance*, New York: Free Press.

World Bank (2012) *Doing Business 2013: Smarter Regulations for Small and Medium-Size Enterprises*, Washington, DC: World Bank Publications.

 www.palgrave.com/Burns-Entrepreneurship-And-Small-Business-4e

Go online to access additional teaching and learning resources for this chapter on the companion website. Click here in the ebook to complete a multiple choice revision quiz for this chapter.

Meet the Entrepreneurs

Part 1: Entrepreneurship

In this first instalment of our video case studies, the entrepreneurs introduce themselves and their businesses. Click on the play buttons below to learn about their reasons for starting their own business, how they came up with the original idea, and what they think makes a good entrepreneur.

AJ Asver

Cassandra Stavrou

John Loughton

Ross Beerman

Sandra Wanduragala

Scott Cupit

Stefan Botha

Questions

> Who are the target customers for these businesses and why should customers buy their products or services?
> What entrepreneurial character traits can you spot in each of the interviewees?
> What were the push and pull factors that led each entrepreneur to start their own business?
> How important has national culture and/or location been to these entrepreneurs?
> Did these entrepreneurs spot opportunities or create them?

The full videos of each entrepreneur's story are available on the companion website.

PART 1 ENTREPRENEURSHIP

PART 2 START-UP

Click on the play button in the ebook to watch Paul Burns discussing the challenges of starting up.

PART 3 GROWTH

PART 4 MATURITY

6 | START-UP: DEVELOPING THE BUSINESS MODEL

Contents

Practice insight: Internet business models

Practice insight: Lean start-ups for merchants

Practice insight reminder: Characteristics of a good business idea

PhotoDisc/Getty Images

Learning outcomes

When you have read this chapter and undertaken the related activities you will be able to:

> Understand the meaning of the terms 'effectuation' and 'lean start-up';
> Understand the importance of developing a planning framework for your new venture and how a business model is developed and used for this purpose;
> Understand the difference between features and benefits, and how features might be engineered to provide valued benefits for customers;
> Identify and describe your customer segments;
> Understand the importance of channels of distribution to the marketing mix;
> Define your value proposition for each customer segment;
> Describe how these value propositions fit into an overall marketing strategy.

Case insights

MOMA	Dell Corporation
Pinterest	easyJet (1)
TruffleShuffle	Quad Electroacoustics
Figleaves	Morgan Motor Company
The Pub (1)	Escape to the Cape

Bringing your idea to life

So you have a business idea that looks viable. And by now you should have knowledge of how your industry and market operates. The challenge is to bring this idea to life – how to make it happen. And here we can learn some lessons from other successful entrepreneurs. Sarasvathy (2001) undertook a study of how 27 successful US entrepreneurs approached business decisions. The subjects all had at least 15 years of entrepreneurial experience, including successes and failures, and had taken at least one company public. They were presented with a case study about a hypothetical start-up with the founder facing 10 decisions. The rationale for these decisions was then explored in more detail. Some years later the same research was conducted on a group of successful professional managers in large organizations, allowing contrasts and comparisons to be made between entrepreneurs and managers.

The conclusion was that these entrepreneurs came to decisions based upon something that was christened 'effectual reasoning' or 'effectuation' (making something happen) – quite in contrast to the causal or deductive reasoning used by the professional executives. Effectuation has gained popularity by contrasting itself with what might be called traditional principles of management. Sarasvathy came to five main conclusions about how successful entrepreneurs approach decision-making in their uncertain, rapidly changing environment.

1   While the executives set goals and sought to achieve them sequentially and logically, the entrepreneurs' goals were broad and evolved over time based on whatever personal strengths and resources they had, creatively reacting to contingencies as they occurred – reflecting the approach to strategy development outlined in Chapter 1. They start with the resources they have and go to market quickly. They do not wait for perfect knowledge or the perfect opportunity. They learn by doing.

2   While executives wanted to research opportunities and assess potential return before committing resources, entrepreneurs were far more inclined to go to market as quickly and cheaply as possible and assess market demand from that – an approach labelled 'affordable loss', representing the maximum amount they could afford to lose in the event of failure. They set an 'affordable loss', evaluating opportunities based upon whether that loss was acceptable, rather than trying to evaluate the attractiveness of the predicable upside. We explain this in more detail in Chapter 10.

3   The entrepreneurs did not like extensive, formal research and planning, particularly traditional market research. This was explained in terms of them not believing that the future was predictable (and the upside therefore could be evaluated), preferring instead to believe in their own ability to obtain the information needed to react quickly to changing circumstances. They believed that while they could not predict the future, they could control it (a high internal locus of control), or more precisely, 'recognize, respond to, and reshape opportunities as they develop'. They use uncertainty to their advantage by developing contingencies and remaining flexible rather than slavishly sticking to existing goals. However, it was significant that they did adopt more formal structures as their businesses grew and, as the study put it, they became both 'causal as well as effectual thinkers'.

4   Also prominent was the entrepreneurs' propensity to partner with stakeholders – customers, suppliers and advisors – to help them shape the business – reflecting the importance of building relationships. New ventures rarely have the resources to undertake all the tasks required to make the business work, so partnering gives them an important extra resource (Sorenson et al., 2008). They use networks of partnerships to generate knowledge, leverage resources and make the future become the reality. By way of contrast, the executives tended to know exactly where they wanted to go and then follow that set path without seeking partnerships.

5   It was noticeable also that the entrepreneurs were less concerned about competitors than the executives. This might be explained in terms of their inherent self-confidence, but the study explained it in terms of them seeing themselves as on the fringe of a market or creating an entirely new market through some sort of disruptive innovation. They believed they were different or better than competitors in a way that gave them a differential advantage.

As overwhelming as it might seem, if you have vision and you believe you have a unique product, then go for it. You need to take risks and accept that you will not succeed every time but that's part of the process. When it comes right, it's an amazing journey.

Wayne Edy, founder, Inov-8, *The Sunday Times*, 15 March 2015

When looking for a chess partner, find a grandmaster.

Zhang Ruimin, CEO, Haier Group *Strategy, + Business*, Issue 77, Winter 2014

There are lessons to be learned from this research. In particular, the approach to developing strategy and decision-making is subtly different to traditional frameworks. Although the entrepreneurs in the study did not like extensive, formal research, we have already seen that there are many quick, cheap and less 'formal' ways of finding out about your industry and market. The ultimate test, however, is the marketplace itself. And the challenge is to launch your business and test your idea within your 'affordable loss'.

Case insight   MOMA

Bringing an idea to life

Tom Mercer

Tom Mercer is a Cambridge University graduate whose first job was as a management consultant with Bain & Company in London. Before going to work, he would blend a liquid mixture of yogurt, oats and fruit for his breakfast in his flat in London. But it took time and he was often late for work. Then it suddenly struck him that his problem was actually a good business idea – pre-prepare the blend so that people could eat it at home or as they travelled to work. So he decided to try out the idea, with the help of friends, by giving it to commuters arriving at Waterloo station, London, to try to get their feedback. He stayed up most of the night before, cutting up fruit, blending it with oats and yogurt and then pouring it into water bottles he had picked up from Tesco. The feedback was positive and Tom left Bain & Company to start MOMA in 2006.

The original idea was to sell the yogurt, oat and fruit mix – now called 'Oatie Shakes' – to early-morning commuters from colourful carts at high footfall points, like stations around London. The first MOMA cart opened at Waterloo East station, and by 2008 there were nine carts, employing mainly students wanting to earn extra money. MOMA also sold into a number of London offices and shops, including Selfridges. The breakfast mixes were prepared in Deptford, South East London, then driven to central London to be sold from MOMA's carts in the early morning.

After the 2008 recession, MOMA started to refocus its marketing away from selling directly to customers from its carts and onto selling via retailers. It is now sold through supermarkets like Waitrose and Tesco as well as being available in trains, planes and coffee shops across the UK. The product range was also broadened to include bircher muesli and porridge. By 2015 the MOMA brand had gone through two redesigns and three London-wide marketing campaigns. Not bad for something that started as a pop-up stall on a train station.

❏ Visit the website: http://www.momafoods.co.uk

QUESTION:

1 What do you learn about bringing an idea to life from the case of MOMA?

Courtesy of MOMA

New Venture Creation Framework

Entrepreneurs may not like formal planning – in the big-company sense – but a simple framework for developing a start-up is extremely useful. It needs to be minimalist and easy to use, illuminating the issues and helping you to develop broad, flexible strategies. It needs to provide a link between experience and strategy, facilitating learning by doing. For the less practised, such a framework helps organize and develop what would otherwise be an unstructured and disjointed experience.

To help with this, Burns (2014) developed the 'New Venture Creation Framework', shown in Figure 6.1 – a simple eight-stage pictorial presentation showing the flows around a business and designed to facilitate start-up planning. Once the business idea is generated in stage one, the remaining seven stages of this Framework focus on the development of a **business model**. A business model is the plan for how a business competes, uses its resources, structures its relationships, communicates with customers, creates value and generates profits (George and Bock, 2011). The New Venture Creation Framework mirrors an approach developed for large companies by Osterwalder and Pigneur (2010), which they call a 'Business Model Canvas'. Central to both approaches is the development of an innovative business model – which should form the core of your business idea. The business model within the New Venture Creation Framework comprises the following elements:

> You jump off a cliff and you assemble an airplane on the way down.
>
> **Reid Hoffman**, co-founder, LinkedIn, *BBC News Business*, 11 January 2011

Market segments and the value proposition

At the core of a business model is the identification of different groupings of customers with similar characteristics – called **market segments** – and the motivations each segment has for buying your product or service – called the **benefits** they are seeking. Pulling these benefits together for each segment is called your **value proposition**. Before you develop this, you need to understand the structure of the market and industry you are entering and the value propositions they are currently offering customers. We shall cover this later in this chapter.

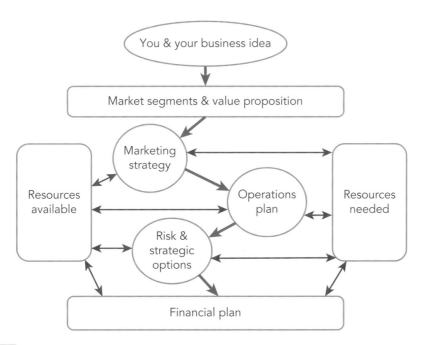

Figure 6.1 The New Venture Creation Framework

Source: Burns (2014)

Marketing strategy

Your marketing strategy describes how you will deliver your value proposition to each of the customer segments you have identified. The tool for delivering this is called the **marketing mix** – price, promotion/communication, service, distribution channels, branding etc. A good marketing strategy helps you develop **competitive advantage** against other companies in your market. This section needs to cover your core strategy as well as your strategy for the launch and the subsequent growth of the business. We shall cover this in Chapter 7 and 8.

Operations plan

The operations plan highlights the practical things you need to do to launch a new venture. These range from legal to operating issues, including **partnership** opportunities. It should identify those key activities you need to undertake to ensure success. We shall cover this in Chapter 10.

Risk and strategic options

Launching a new venture involves taking risks – and the business model should tease out the major risks you face and how they might be mitigated or avoided entirely. It should identify the **critical success factors** that underpin the operations of the business and the different ways of doing things should circumstances change or be different to those anticipated – called **strategic options**. These are valuable because circumstances can, and do, change. We shall cover this in Chapter 10.

Resources available and resources needed

This defines the resources you bring to the business – **human, social, intellectual and financial** – and the resources you need. A major component of this is your ability to pull together and lead a management team. We shall cover these aspects in Chapters 14 and 18.

Financial plan

This shows the **profit** the business should generate and how it will be used. It shows the **cash flow** of the business and the external finance that is required. It is a set of **financial forecasts** – revenues, related costs and resulting financial structures of the business. We shall cover this in Chapter 11.

Even if your core business idea has merit, unless you find and persuade customers to buy it and can then deliver it to them, you do not have a viable business. Even then, you have to persuade them that your product/service is so good that they want to buy it again and again. To do this you need marketing, operations and financial plans, based on the resources you need and have access to. You also need to identify and minimize the risks you face.

Viewed holistically, the Framework can help you identify patterns and understand the processes needed to deliver them. It allows you to alter elements and ask those all-important 'what if?' questions. For example, you will need to operationalize your marketing strategy and to do that you will need the appropriate resources. Some may already be available to you whilst others may need to be sourced externally. However, if you cannot obtain the resources you need, you may have to adapt your original marketing strategy. Similarly, the results of your market segmentation will probably influence the development of your value proposition(s), and this could well cause you to adapt and improve your original business idea.

The great advantage of developing a business model in this way is that it is (relatively) quick to develop and easy to change. It allows you to explore in a structured way innovative alternatives and options – always trying to understand the linkages and implications of different/product market offerings, whilst allowing you to test new models against established ones. You can experiment with different versions to see which critical assumptions are most realistic (revenue model, pricing, sales, costs etc.). Only when you are satisfied with this model would you ever think of perhaps going on to write a formal business plan. The real challenge, of course, is to develop an innonative business model and then implement it effectively.

There are three well-known generic business models that will be covered in greater detail later in this chapter: low price/low cost, high differentiation and customer focus. These combine to produce the niche business model of highly differentiated products/services offered in small volumes at a relatively high price. This will also be covered in detail later in this chapter. However, other business models can be just as successful. For example:

> Bringing together different market segments that derive value from the presence of each other. This is called the network effect or 'multisided platforms';
> Offering free product/services – where non-paying customers are financed by other parts of the business model or other customer segments;
> Open business models – where value is created through collaboration between partners.

 Practice insight Internet business models

The business model is crucial to success for all firms. The way internet firms make money largely defines their business model. Typically there are six ways of doing this:

> Direct sales model – where products or services are sold directly online (e.g. Amazon);
> Advertising model – where the internet firms are paid for ads being placed on their website (e.g. YouTube);
> Pay-per-click model – where they are paid for clicks onto an advertiser's link (e.g. Google);

> Subscription model – where customers subscribe for the online product or service (e.g. *The Times* newspaper);
> Freemium model – where there is a basic service that is free but extras or premium services are charged for (e.g. SurveyMonkey);
> Affiliate model – where the website hosting ads is paid commission on sales by online retailers or other people trying to sell things (e.g. eBay).

 Case insight   Pinterest

Linking a business idea to a business model

Founded in 2010 by Ben Silbermann, Paul Sciarra and Evan Sharp, Pinterest has attracted investments that value the company at $11 billion, despite the fact it has only just begun to generate revenue. Pinterest is a visual bookmarking tool that helps people discover and save creative ideas. Users collate (or 'pin') and share images on themed digital pinboards – for example, fashion, photography, cooking, home or garden improvements etc. The site is highly visual, unlike many other text-heavy social networks. 'Pinners' are encouraged to browse pinboards that interest them for images from others who share their interest. According to comScore, there are 70 million monthly active users on Pinterest.

The inspiration for the idea came when Silbermann and Sciarra were working on a failed idea for a shopping app called Tote. They noticed that instead of buying through

the app, users emailed pictures of products to each other. People liked pictures and they wanted to get ideas and inspiration from them. The challenge was to turn this into something that made money.

'There has been so much remarkable work on search – on making it so that you can find what you're looking for and you can retrieve it really quickly. But there has been little work done on helping people discover things when they may not know exactly what they are looking for … From very early on with our investors, we were clear that the goal of the service was to help people discover things that were meaningful to them. That motivation falls closely in line with the goals of lots of businesses and advertisers.' (The Sunday Times, 6 July 2014)

Because Pinners have an obvious hobby interest, advertising can be highly relevant and targeted, thus commanding a premium price. Because Pinners browse

Continued...

Continued from previous page...

Ben Silbermann, Evan Sharp

Pinterest for attractive images and ideas, it has a very different feel to conventional search engines, such as Google, that are designed to deliver specific information. Sites like Google build profiles of their users by mining the data they generate. But that means that their targeted advertising can often feel intrusive and therefore counterproductive for advertisers. People come to Pinterest to plan the things that they'd like to do in the future -- whether it's something they'd like to buy, a recipe they'd like to make, or a place they'd like to go. They just click on the pins they wish to investigate further. Therefore, it's a huge opportunity for marketers to be a part of the process in helping Pinners take action on the Pins that they find online. And, whilst Pinterest also has pins promoted by companies, a Promoted Pin looks just like any other Pin in the system with the exception of a note that says 'promoted', making a Promoted Pin less obtrusive than other ads. Companies have been pinning for years, setting up their own pinboards on Pinterest to showcase their own products. And in 2014 the company launched a self-serve platform that enables companies to create their own Promoted Pins that can be posted to other boards.

With an estimated 55 million regular users, Pinterest has caught not only the attention of investors but also the big advertisers. However, now that they have devised a revenue-generating business model, the question is: how will the search engines that they hope to take revenue from react? In the past they have often bought up the best new ideas.

Courtesy of Pinterest

❏ Visit the website: www.pinterest.com

QUESTIONS:

1 Which of the six internet business models would you apply to Pinterest?

2 The inspiration for Pinterest came from a failed idea for an app called Tote. What are the potential effects on an entrepreneur of a failure like this?

Lean start-up

One approach to the challenge of launching a business with limited resources (within your 'affordable loss') that has been popularized by Ries (2011) is called 'lean start-up'. He coined the phrase for new ventures that minimize the lead time as well as their investment in a new product/ service launch. The idea is that the product/service is not launched in a 'perfect state' but rather in its 'minimum viable' state, then is refined using customer feedback in an iterative fashion to further tailor the product/service to the specific needs of customers – a process he called 'validated learning'. In this way, valuable time and money are not invested in designing features or services that customers do not value. This approach should give the start-up first-mover advantage and minimizes costs while, importantly, reducing market risks when the product/service finally reaches a wider market. The key to the approach is close customer relationships and developing mechanisms to receive their feedback.

Ries gave the example of the start-up strategy of Nick Swinmurn, who founded the US online shoe retailer Zappos. Instead of building a website and a large database of footwear, he tested his business idea by taking pictures of shoes from local stores, posting them online and selling them directly to customers. If they purchased the shoes through his website he would then buy the shoes from the stores at full price. Although he did not make a profit, this quickly validated his business idea, with minimum cost and risk.

The lean start-up idea was originally developed for high-tech businesses, based upon the way companies like Google develop new products, but has gained popularity generally. It reflects the 'parallel' new product development model – where product development and concept/market testing go side-by-side – and embraces elements of the 'lean manufacturing' philosophy. The approach mirrors entrepreneurs' incremental approach to decision-making – gaining knowledge as they proceed – and the way they limit their financial exposure as much as possible.

The idea of small-scale market entry and trial in order to gain market information prior to full product launch for a start-up is not new (Chaston, 2000). What is more, the advent of the internet means that the opportunities to do this are increasing. The idea that risk is related to the time taken to launch a new product/service is not new either (Burns, 2005) – too early and you risk being ill-prepared and turning customers against it, too late and you lose first-mover advantage. Inaction can cost dearly, so launch timing is critical. Ries said this depended on having a 'minimum viable product' – one that allows a start-up to collect the maximum amount of validated learning about customers with the least effort. But this is a matter of judgement. If the product/service is so underdeveloped that customers reject it, even a limited launch can spell disaster later and ruin the brand name.

The idea works well for some products – for example software – where new features can be trialled on the back of the core product. This is an approach often taken by Google. However, if the core product does not function, you risk customer rejection. For high-investment innovations (often disruptive innovations), the product must be substantially right the first time. Ask Apple if they would have been happy to launch a 'minimum viable' iPhone.

We fully believe that the cost of inaction is greater than the cost of a mistake. So we move quickly and learn through trial and error. Trial, test, analyze. Then repeat.

Brian Shanahan, founder, Temple & Webster, *http://www. sparke.com.au,*16 October 2014

 Practice insight Lean start-ups for merchants

There are many low-cost ways of testing market demand for a product. In the UK we have 'car-boot sales', in the USA, 'garage sales', in Canada, 'trunk sales', and in many countries, products are just sold by the side of the road. Indeed you can make a living selling things in this way. In the UK you can find out where your local car-boot sale is taking place by simply looking on the internet – www.carbootjunction.com. More recently, as the high streets have more and more vacant shop sites, we have started to see 'pop-up', temporary shops (and even restaurants) testing out new marketing concepts. However, the internet has meant that you can now reach a far wider group of customers than these physical markets and at a relatively low cost. Sites like Amazon, eBay and Alibaba can be used to sell goods and offer a low-cost way of testing market demand. They also offer to host 'storefronts' for small merchants where 'buy-it-now' goods can be offered. This allows you to achieve visibility and brand loyalty which was previously only gained through traditional advertising or local shoppers.

However, while these sites can offer an international reach, the fees they charge are increasing and the growth of social media means that new lower-cost outlets are now emerging. For example, there are thousands of Facebook pages dedicated to buying and selling products. The FaceBay community page (known as Fbay) was launched in 2010 and now has tens of thousands of members. To join you simply 'like' the page and then you can trade with members. These sites can be geographically based, thus facilitating the exchange of goods and services for cash.

Indeed, there are likely to be a number of locally-based internet trading sites around where you live: simply Google 'for sale' and your postcode or zip code to find them. For example, in Bristol in the UK there is a site where some 500 mothers buy, sell and give away things like clothes, toys or furniture, mainly for children. This, like many groups, is open only to members, so you need to join before you can participate. Twitter is also an increasingly popular and free way of trading: simply enter '#forsale', then another '#' followed by the place you live. You can find anything from properties to computer games offered for sale in this way. Many classified ads websites now also have their own official Twitter accounts. The important thing with all these low-cost ways of buying and selling is that there is no official system of vetting and it really is a case of 'buyer beware' – hence the importance of location.

You can find other sites where you can buy and sell goods in the UK by visiting www.alternatives-to-ebay. co.uk. These include www.preloved.co.uk, where you can advertise second-hand goods free with no selling fees and www.gumtree.com, where you can advertise certain types of goods free. There are also apps that enable users to sell goods such as 'Shpock', a UK app launched in 2014. 'Zapper' is a free-to-download app from iTunes that sells DVDs, CDs, games, mobiles or electronic devices by scanning in the bar code. The app then immediately gives you a price and, if you accept this, you can send the goods to Zapper free of charge and they will forward payment.

Case insight   **TruffleShuffle**

Lean start-up

Pat Wood

In 2004, Pat Wood's retro Dukes of Hazard T-shirt, bought from a US website, aroused so much interest at his local pub that he wondered whether it might form the basis of a business. He bought another for £10, listed it on eBay and sold it within 24 hours for £20. And that was how the business was born. He bought the domain name truffleshuffle .co.uk and started selling retro T-shirts online from his one-bedroom flat.

'Every time I sold a T-shirt I'd buy two more. I thought if I could make a couple of hundred pounds a month I would be happy.'

The website attracted a lot of interest and within months he was receiving 30 orders a day. However, Wood kept his full-time job in IT, packing T-shirts in the evening with his girlfriend Claire, who was studying law at university.

'I'd get all my mates to come over on a Friday night to put T-shirts in envelopes and I'd pay them in pizza, while Claire and I coped with demand by just not sleeping.'

Wood finally decided to leave his job in 2005 when turnover reached £100,000 a month.

'I didn't want to put all my eggs in one basket, so I stuck it out as long as possible, but in the back of my mind I knew I had a business that was able to provide me and Claire with a salary, so I took the leap.' (*The Sunday Times*, 27 July 2014)

Wood generally bought T-shirts from the USA and resold them in the UK. If a T-shirt did not exist for a TV show, he would obtain a licence to use particular images. And gradually the proportion of own-made T-shirts grew. He also started selling to retailers such as Topshop and Next. He developed a second website for band T-shirts and now sells a range of clothing as well as novelty and gift items. In addition to selling on his own website, he also sells worldwide through Amazon and eBay. Although the business was cut back for a couple of years following the 2008 recession, today it takes approximately 24,000 orders a month and has a turnover of £3.5 million. Based in Avonmouth, UK, it employs 14 staff.

❏ Visit the website: www.truffleshuffle.co.uk

QUESTION:

1 What are the advantages of lean start-up? What is the link with the discovery skill of experimentation (Chapter 4)?

International start-ups

Most SMEs are short of capital, and many practice 'lean start-up' without realizing it. Indeed, most SMEs serve predominantly local markets – not surprising given the high proportions that are service businesses. However, increasing numbers of businesses are now selling internationally from day one (Anderson et al., 2004). They enter different countries at once, often for both exporting and sourcing. The internet has made this easier, particularly for internet business like the Summly app (see Case insight on page 97) or e-commerce merchants like TruffleShuffle. Selling to a very small target or niche market in one country can raise issues of viability. Selling to the same niche market globally can dramatically change the equation and offer the opportunity of high profits, because of economies of scale. However it was not always like this, and for businesses that need to establish a physical presence in other countries, for example to deliver a service or product to customers, many of the barriers still exist.

Most physical start-ups that are born global do so because they either see unmet demand and a market opportunity or can derive some significant form of competitive advantage from being international. Entrepreneurs can capitalize on international market imperfections by linking resources from around the world. Oviatt and McDougall (1994) identified three groups:

> **New international market makers** – who simply moved goods from one country to another where there was higher demand. This can now sometimes be done using the internet as a sales platform rather than establishing a physical presence in another country (e.g. Nikwax Case insight on page 110);
> **Geographically focused start-ups** – who focus on using foreign resources like raw materials, people or financing to service the needs of other countries more cheaply. The TutorVista Case insight on page 103 showed how this could be done by a lone entrepreneur, and the Alibaba business-to-business network (see Case insight on page 137) is an example of how manufacturing partners can be found in China;
> **Global start-ups** – who just perceive themselves as global businesses from inception and derive some form of significant competitive advantage from doing so (e.g. Hide My Ass! Case insight on page 65).

Aggarwal (1999) observed that many of the start-ups in this final category conduct business in high-technology niche markets. This might be expected, given that the ever accelerating pace of technological advancement means that product life cycles are shortening and first-mover advantage in all markets becomes vital. Anderson et al. (2004) found strong support for the idea that 'the degree of environmental dynamism' in an industry is related to internationalization. In addition, the size of start-up investment often creates a need to achieve economies of scale across as wide a market as possible, despite producing a niche product. However, in a review of the literature and a study of 12 high-technology international start-ups, Johnson (2004) found many factors influenced the decision to internationalize, and concluded that, while this was a factor, the main reasons were:

> The international vision of the founders;
> The desire of the founders to be international market leaders;
> The identification of specific international market opportunities that needed to be exploited quickly;
> The possession of specific international contacts, networks and sales leads.

To be successful, international start-ups must have both local and international knowledge and make extensive use of international business networks or contacts (Johnson, op. cit.; Oviatt and McDougall, op. cit.). For a start-up these often rest with the founder(s). They are therefore personal, usually with a relationship that is built up over time and based on trust. And virtual relationships based on the internet are no substitute for this. These networks can be vital in providing insights into effective market entry and competitive strategies (Coviello and Munro, 1995). Used properly, they can leverage up the capabilities of the start-up (Laanti et al., 2007). Zhou et al. (2007) argued that home-based social networks play a mediating role in the relationship between inward and outward internationalization, allowing firms to go international more rapidly and profitably. They do this by providing opportunities for:

> Knowledge of and information about foreign market opportunities;
> Obtaining advice and experiential learning;
> Gaining referral trust and solidarity – also often leading to a partnership, alliance or joint ventures to reduce the risk in exploiting an opportunity. We explore the legal form these might take in Chapter 9.

Many academics agree that there is a positive relationship between internationalization and firm performance (e.g. Chelliah et. al, 2010; Kuhlmeier and Knight, 2010; Lu and Beamish, 2001). Kuhlmeier and Knight (op. cit.) linked four dimensions of internationalization to performance – relationship quality, cooperation, trust, and commitment – claiming these help to improve the international performance of SMEs especially in export markets. Zahra et al. (2009) suggested that having a wider international market scope exposes SMEs to a 'rich network of information that encourages and enhances future product innovation'. In other words, internationalization has many benefits beyond simply financial.

Of course some start-ups often start locally and grow by expanding their geographic and market base more gradually, moving from exporting to having sales agents, offering a licence or franchise, to organizing a joint venture before eventually opening a subsidiary. We explore this progression – sometimes called the **stage model of internationalization** – in Chapter 13. To operate successfully in overseas markets involves knowledge of both customers and competitors and may involve changing elements of the value proposition to better suit local conditions. In many ways each new country is a start-up in its own right.

 Case insight   Figleaves

Using the internet to penetrate overseas markets

Michael Ross, Chief Executive of Figleaves, a UK online retailer of women's lingerie, has managed to penetrate one of the most difficult markets in the world – the USA. Launched in 1999 as Easyshop, selling women's clothing, the company changed its name the following year after it decided to focus on lingerie. But the secret for Figleaves was that, when it launched in the USA, it was already its second largest market because it sold on the internet and American women were not concerned that the lingerie they ordered came from Britain.

Figleaves has negotiated a number of online marketing deals and web links to maximize the exposure its site enjoys. US deals are negotiated by a salesperson who flies out once a month from the UK. The company even has a concession within Amazon. Its 'Shock Absorber' bra was launched in the USA together with Amazon, by holding a tennis match between Amazon's founder, Jeff Bezos, and the tennis star Anna Kournikova. One feature of the Figleaves website is the facility to purchase in a number of different currencies. Figleaves now claims to be the global leader of 'multi-brand intimate apparel e-tailers'. The website features 250 brands and more than 30,000 items of lingerie, swimwear, sleepwear, activewear, menswear and hosiery.

❏ Visit the website: www.figleaves.com

QUESTION:

1 How important is local knowledge in penetrating an overseas market?

Identifying your market segments

Returning to the development of the all-important business model, the first step is to identify your customers, what they want and why they will buy from you. A business will only succeed if it offers customers a value proposition that meets their real needs or solves real problems for them. The initial target market should also be the group of customers that most need your solution to their problem because other solutions are less satisfactory. While customers are all individuals, it is usually possible to group them in some way that is useful in terms of targeting, for example by identifying their different group needs or problems. These are called market segments. Normally, it is only possible to communicate with customers economically through these groups. The key for a start-up is to identify and focus limited resources on just three or four clearly defined, important and sizeable market segments. The marketing mix, marketing and communications strategy, can then be tailored to the needs of customers in these different segments. Of course you will not turn away customers who do not fall into these segments; it is just about focusing your limited resources where they are likely to have the greatest return.

There are many ways of segmenting markets and there are no prescriptive approaches. Market segments match groups of customers with their product/service wants or needs – the benefits they are looking for. The segment can be any one, or a combination of, descriptive factors. The descriptive factors for private customers might include personal demographics (e.g. age, gender, socioeconomic group, occupation, stage in family life etc.), geographic location (particularly important for retail start-ups), channels of distribution used to get to the customers etc. For business markets, they might include type of business, size, location, nature of technology and so on. You are looking for groups of customers with similar needs that can be identified and described in some meaningful and useful way. You a looking for a gap in the market, where the needs of a particular segment are not being met as well as they could be.

To be viable a market segment must be:

1   Distinctive with significantly different needs from other segments. Without this the segment boundaries are likely to be too blurred.
2   Sufficiently large, or willing to pay a high enough price, to make the segment commercially attractive. It may be that a gap in the market exists because it is not commercially viable.
3   Accessible. The gap in the market might not exist in reality because the segment cannot be reached – through communication or distribution channels.
4   Defendable from competitors. If the segment is not defendable, for example because you are selling a copy-cat product, prices and profits will quickly reduce as competition increases.

Market segments vary in size. The slimmer the market segment that the product or service is tailored to suit, the higher customer satisfaction is likely to be, but so too, is cost – and therefore price. We all like personal service and the ultimate market segment comprises just one customer. However, this might not be a commercially viable segment. The trend is towards slimmer and slimmer market segments, particularly since the internet has made it easier to link customers with similar needs in different geographic areas. The danger facing firms selling to slim market segments is their overreliance on a small customer base. If tastes change, the segment might disappear.

Vary your markets. Think about how your product could fit into different markets. Clippykit works for retail, the promotions industry and education.

Calypso Rose, founder, Clippykit, *The Daily Telegraph*, 6 February 2009

Defining your value proposition

Your value proposition is why customers buy from you rather than from another company. Customers buy a product or service because it provides a benefit or solves a problem for them. The features or characteristics of the product or service must combine to deliver that benefit to the customer, or they will not buy it. And different market segments might be looking for different benefits. The features of a car combine to provide the benefit of transport, but different customers are looking for more than just transport – which is why there are numerous types of cars and many producers.

Vargo and Lusch (2004) argued that customers essentially purchase services rather than goods, and goods should therefore be viewed as a medium for delivering or 'transmitting' services. They defined service as 'the application of specialized competences (knowledge and skills) through deeds, processes, and performances for the benefit of another entity or the entity itself'. In this way, companies manufacturing cars are not in the business of selling cars but in the business of providing 'mobility services' through the cars that they manufacture – a concept adopted by Andrew Valentine with Streetcar (see Case insight on page 113).

If all industries are service industries, it becomes vital for them to understand the service that consumers are seeking. This requires a shift in focus from the product to the consumer and an understanding of their needs, but more particularly how these translate into a service they value. You need to understand the core benefits a customer is looking for when they purchase a good or service and then engineer the features to deliver those benefits. And these features can take many forms, both physical and psychological. Focusing on the benefit-needs of your market segments and delivering distinctive, differentiated value propositions to each of them is at the very core of developing your marketing strategy. Unfortunately, many owner-managers like to define their products in physical terms and therefore think they are selling one thing, only to find customers are buying something else.

Features can be translated into benefits by exploring their meaning. For example:

Feature		Benefit
Our shop takes credit cards	*Which means*	You can budget to suit your pocket
Our shop stays open later than others	*Which means*	You get more choice when to shop
Our shop is an approved dealer	*Which means*	You can be guaranteed that we know and understand all technical aspects of the product
Our shop is a family business	*Which means*	You get individual, personal attention from somebody who cares

Listing the features of a product or service can be the start of the process of understanding the benefits that the customer is seeking from them. However, it is more convincing to start with the benefits that customers are looking for and then construct features that provide those benefits. Which actually comes first is a little like the chicken or the egg question.

Tailoring your marketing mix

The next stage in developing your value proposition is to understand what your product/service features are and how they might deliver the benefits a customer or consumer wants. One widely used technique or language for describing the features of a product or service is the marketing mix or the 'Five Ps', a convenient shorthand for: product/service (functional specification, design etc.), price, promotion (or communication), place of sale (including distribution channels) and people (or related service). Features included in this classification are shown in Table 6.1. Customers buy benefits, not features, but all of the features can provide benefits to the customer and therefore enhance the value proposition. The customer buys the marketing mix as a package, and the mix must be consistent to reinforce the overall benefit that the customer is looking for. The marketing mix is only as strong as its weakest link. So, for example, a low price for a quality product might jeopardize sales because it sends a confused message and questions credibility. A high price can be charged for a quality product, but the other elements of the marketing mix still need to be consistent with this.

For a start-up, which is likely to be short of money, the founding entrepreneur is central to the whole marketing mix. Of necessity, their approach to marketing will probably be very much hands-on and face-to-face. They might use their network of contacts to find customers and suppliers. They might develop strong personal relationships with customers to secure repeat sales. This can be a distinct competitive advantage over larger firms that adds value to the customer.

Table 6.1 Marketing mix

Product/service	Price	Promotion	Place	People
> Quality	> List price	> Communication	> Location	> Relationships
> Performance	> Discounts (volume, loyalty etc.)	> Advertising	> Layout	> Service
> Design	> Auction	> PR	> Distribution channels	> Advice
> Newness or novelty	> Negotiated	> Word-of-mouth	> Retail/wholesale	> Support
> Colours	> Payment terms	> Fairs & exhibitions	> Internet	> Partnerships
> Sizes	> Sales and special offers	> Sponsorship	> Telephone	
> Specification	> Differential or segment pricing	> Competitions	> Face-to-face selling	
> Customization		> Point of sale displays		
> Packaging		> Brand		
> Convenience				

Indeed, one particularly effective entrepreneurial strategy is to identify a sector in which customer relationships are weak and to create value by tightening them up. In the longer term, this relationship can evolve into a distinctive brand. Customer relationships are an important part of the marketing mix and marketing strategy.

While any individual element of the marketing mix may not be unique and can often be easily copied, elements of the mix can be combined to produce something unique and distinctive. It is the combination that is unique, not the individual elements, and this can provide a differential advantage over competitors. If the combination is sufficiently unique, it may challenge existing market paradigms. Establishing a brand that captures the elements of uniqueness can itself add value to the value proposition. And building switch costs for customers into the value proposition – costs of changing supplier – can also enhance your competitive position by discouraging them from buying from competitors. Rather than building in costs into your proposition you could offer additional benefits for customer loyalty.

> Be very sure you have something unique that can't be replicated easily.
>
> **Angie Coates**, founder, Monkey Music, *The Sunday Times*, 30 November 2014

Linking features and benefits with marketing mix

The final step then is to be able to engineer the features of a product or service to deliver distinctive benefits that customers value, and craft these into some sort of strategy. But features can be many and varied, covering all the elements of the marketing mix, and combined in almost endless variations. Let us take as an example pens. One type of pen is the cheap, disposable ballpoint, bought simply as a writing implement. Clearly, its core value proposition to end-use customers is based upon low price/cost, and the pen manufacturer needs to drive down costs and drive up volumes. Pens of this sort sell for a few pennies in volumes of 100+, but for much more (although still very cheaply) when sold individually. These pens typically have a low-cost, functional plastic shell, usually with a cap. Two end-use market segments might be private customers and organizations with employees needing pens. The characteristics of these segments and the routes to market are shown in Figure 6.2. Our pen manufacturer needs to understand the benefits these two segments are seeking. They are looking for a pen that writes satisfactorily and can be conveniently purchased, but is also cheap and therefore disposable. If new technologies produce cheaper, more convenient ways of writing or passing messages, these customers may stop purchasing pens altogether – which is happening because of smartphones and computers.

However, our pen manufacturer also needs to understand the routes to market, shown in the lower part of Figure 6.2. Channels of distribution are important for this product and each channel will be looking for different benefits – typically profit and product availability. If they do not get the benefits they are looking for, the end-use customers may never be offered the product, no matter how good it is.

Consider the route to market for the single-purchase private customer (segment 1A). Convenience of purchase is their primary consideration. No advertising or promotion is expected and service is non-existent, as pens are probably sold on a self-service basis. Other elements of the marketing mix are relatively unimportant, so there is strong price competition from manufacturers of similar pens. These customers purchase the pen through retailers like newsagents or stationers. Retailers buy in bulk through wholesalers. The benefit that retailers, like wholesalers, are looking for is profit – which means the higher the margin to them, the more attractive the product and the more prominent they are likely to display the pen. Indeed they may be persuaded to stock only this pen rather than those of competitors (called '**supply-push**'). The margin must however be sufficient to satisfy both wholesaler and retailer. The retailers might be encouraged to purchase the pens because of 'free' point of sale displays. At the same time, just-in-time deliveries, with increased delivery reliability and improved distribution times, may allow wholesalers to both decrease their inventory costs and at the same time reduce stock-outs – real benefits that help differentiate this manufacturer from others.

Private customers buying in large volumes (segment 1B) and organizations buying for their employees (segment 2) may buy these pens in bulk from wholesalers. They expect lower prices

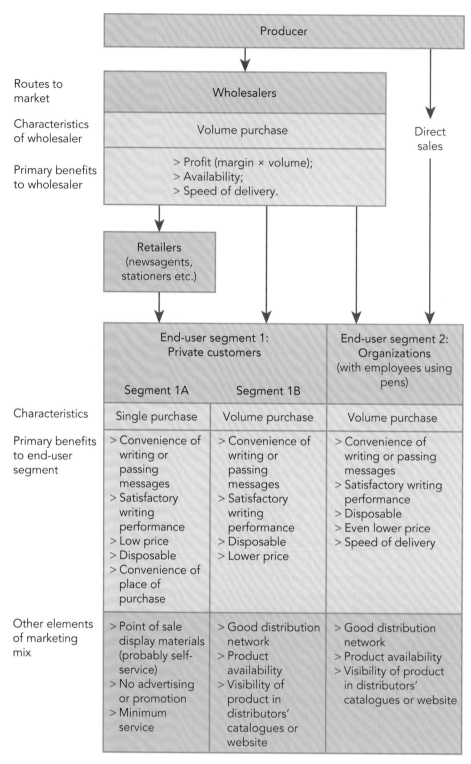

Figure 6.2 Features, benefits and marketing mix

than those offered by the retailer, as well as speedy, reliable delivery. Pens selling through this distribution channel will not need point of sale display materials but may need different packaging. Discounts may be offered based upon volumes purchased. The wholesaler may need to invest in a catalogue, website, advertising and a direct sales force. The pen must be prominently displayed, or at least easily found, in the catalogue or website. The pen manufacturer might also decide to sell direct to these end-users, but they would have to invest in a catalogue, website, advertising and a direct sales force – things that may not be their core activities.

One way of stimulating end-user demand is to advertise directly to the end-user and persuade them to seek out the product from the distributor (called '**demand-pull**'). This only works if the product they are seeking is highly differentiated (e.g. through branding), so it is unlikely to work for this sort of pen. The less differentiated the product, the more likely this strategy is to work. However, an innovative start-up may decide to bypass the established distribution channels and sell directly to the end customer. But this is likely to involve extra costs (advertising, distribution, delivery etc.), which may not be commercially viable.

Channels of distribution

This disposable pen example underlines the fact that customers buy benefits, not features, and you need to understand the benefits offered to both end-use customers and distributors. You must tailor your marketing mix to suit the needs of customers and consumers at each stage in the chain. This is what your marketing strategy should articulate in a coherent, consistent way. Each element of the marketing mix needs to be consistent with the others. And your marketing strategy will have implications for other elements of your business model, from the operations plan to the resources you will need. It will determine costs and revenues and have implications for the risks you will face.

Your channels of distribution need careful consideration. Using retailers, wholesalers or agents may extend your market reach, but each link in the chain is important and is looking for benefits, of which profit is probably the most important element. You do not control your distribution channels directly, you influence them – and they eat into your profits. On the other hand, if you decide to sell directly to customers, your revenues may be higher but so too are your costs. Direct sales costs might include: your own direct sales-force, costs of developing your website, online and/or telephone sales team, advertising and mail/delivery costs. The typical channels of distribution for consumer goods and for business-to-business sales are shown in Figure 6.3.

There is no one 'best' way to distribute a product or service and, as we have seen in the previous chapter, deciding to do it differently than the competition can prove profitable if the customers value the difference, and you can keep competitors from copying you for a sufficient length of time. Low-cost airlines such as easyJet changed the way passengers bought their tickets by insisting they could only book their flights online or by telephone, thus cutting out any intermediaries and the margin they might expect. Of course, other airlines have now copied this direct route to market.

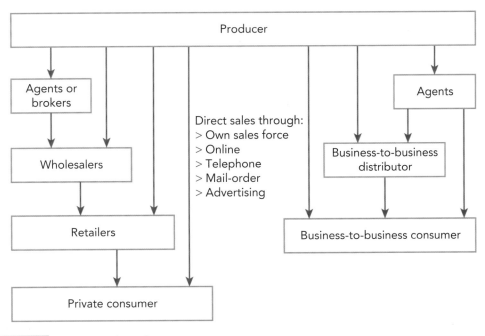

Figure 6.3 Distribution channels

Understanding customer and consumer benefits

Not all pens are the same and not all customers are consumers of the product/service. Some pens are bought by a customer as a gift for the ultimate consumer. And, again, we need to offer benefits to both the customer and the consumer. While a gift pen must perform the basic function of writing, it is likely to look very different and to have a very different marketing strategy, with a value proposition based upon high differentiation rather than low price. Two market segments and the benefits they are looking for are shown below, in Figure 6.4. The routes to market are

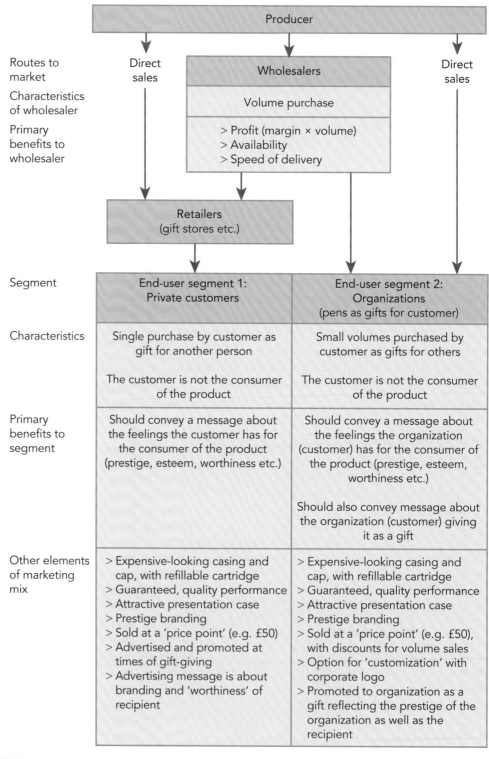

Figure 6.4 The difference between customer and consumer benefits

likely to be the same as the disposable pen, although in this case retailers are likely to be gift shops or department stores. Smaller gift shops might go through a wholesaler, while department stores might purchase direct from the manufacturer. As in the previous example, retailers and wholesalers are looking for profit, but in this case from smaller volumes at a higher price.

For both the customer and consumer, the pens must be functional and well-made, high quality and elegantly designed. The other elements of the marketing mix are also important. The pen will have prestige branding with guaranteed quality performance. It will come housed in an attractive gift presentation case and is advertised and promoted at times of gift-giving as prestigious and something that values the 'worthiness' of the recipient. If sold in a shop, it will probably be kept in a glass display stand that can be accessed only with the help of a shop assistant. If the pen is sold to an organization, the organization will probably want the opportunity to be associated with the brand by having their name put on the pen, although they will probably still expect a discount if ordering in bulk.

Getty

The point here is that the customer wants to spend, say, £50 on a prestigious gift for the consumer – one that conveys a message to them about the feelings of 'worthiness' the customer has for them. The brand and what it conveys are probably more important than the functionality of the pen itself. This is the benefit they are looking for. A low price is not consistent with the message and the benefit sought. And a box of 500 cheap, disposable ball pens is not a substitute gift, even though they are likely to last longer than the expensive pen. They just do not provide the right benefits. Competition comes from other gifts costing £50 that convey a similar message.

Putting together a bundle of benefits through a consistent marketing mix for each target market segment is the key to an effective marketing strategy. It is not easy. There is no blueprint to work from since most products/services and their markets are different. And, while studying your industry can tell you how competitors currently do things, this is no guarantee for the future. Indeed, daring to do things differently can be very profitable.

 Case insight   The Pub* (1)

Value propositions and market segments

You might think that a pub (a bar selling food and alcoholic and non-alcoholic drinks) is a very English institution. However, it faces all of the challenges facing any retail outlet. In particular, it faces high fixed costs related to its physical location and its serving staff. These costs need to be paid even if there are no customers. To compensate for this, gross margins can be high – 60 to 70% – so the operational imperative is to attract customers throughout the day.

To meet this challenge, an English high-street pub chain developed a two-level marketing strategy – one at the corporate level and one at the pub level to help local pub managers. Each pub was located in a prime, high-street, town-centre location, close to shopping centres and offices. Each pub was large, with areas with different seating, lighting etc. in different areas, allowing it to change the ambiance and target a number of different market segments. The pub chain needed to maximize the number of customers it attracted throughout the day. The local pub strategy outlined in Table 6.2 was designed to target different market segments at different times of the day. It highlighted the value proposition for each segment and the main elements of the marketing mix needed to attract that segment.

Continued...

Continued from previous page...

Table 6.2 An outline local-level marketing strategy for a pub

Segments	Shoppers	Office workers	Pensioners & unemployed	Office workers	Students	Regulars	Young, pre-clubbers
- Time	11.00 – 17.00	12.00 – 14.00	14.00 – 17.00	17.00 – 19.00	Any time	19.00 – 22.00	21.00 – 24.00
- Male/female	10/90%	40/60%	90/10%	60/40%	50/50%	60/40%	60/40%
Value proposition	A comfortable, safe, value-for-money place to eat & drink	A quick, value-for-money place to eat lunch	A comfortable, value-for money place to spend time	A lively atmosphere to meet friends after work	A relaxed, value-for-money place to meet friends	A welcoming place to meet friends for value-for-money food and drink	A fashionable, lively place to meet friends
Marketing mix							
- Main products	Coffee, tea, soft drinks & food	Food, range of drinks	Alcoholic drinks	Wide range of alcoholic drinks	Alcoholic drinks	Food, range of drinks	Wide range of alcoholic drinks
- Service	Friendly	Fast	Low priority	Friendly	Low priority	Friendly	Fast
- Price	Value-for-money	Competitive	Low-price beers	Attractive 'happy hour'	Value-for-money	Value-for-money	Low priority
- Ambiance	Safe, clean & comfortable	Clean & comfortable	Warm, TV, newspapers	Up-beat, lively	Relaxed, safe	Friendly, home away from home	Lively, up-beat with music & promotions
- Importance of location	High	High	Low	High	Moderate	Moderate	High
Critical success factors	Safe, clean & comfortable environment	Rapid service. Value-for-money food	Low price beers	Up-beat, lively ambiance with 'happy hour'	Relaxed, safe environment with other students	Friendly service and ambiance. Value-for-money food. Recognition as 'regulars'	Lively, up-beat ambiance with music & promotions

*The Pub is a real company, but the name is fictitious.

QUESTIONS:

1 Does the marketing plan convey the imperatives of the marketing mix effectively? What is it designed to deliver? Outline some of the details that might have been omitted.

2 Why is the location and size of the pub important for this marketing strategy to work?

Generic business models

As introduced at the beginning of this chapter, there are three well-known generic business models – low price/low cost, high differentiation, customer focus – and these combine to produce the niche business model of highly differentiated products/services offered in small volume at a relatively high price. These are models consistent with fundamental ways of creating sustainable competitive advantage. They greatly affect your business model. Porter (1985) called them 'generic marketing strategies'. Treacy and Wiersema (1995) called them 'value disciplines'. They are shown in Figure 6.5.

Low price/low cost

This is where customers value low price more than anything in the marketing mix. In this case, low price can only be achieved through low costs and if there are economies of scale to be achieved, a firm must achieve them quickly to survive (see easyJet and Dell Case insights on page 165). Operational excellence is needed to achieve this. These sorts of products are virtually commodities. What is more, new flexible manufacturing technologies with just-in-time scheduling and the internet which allows customers to 'design' products' to their own specification have meant that efficiency can be combined with variety. Fierce competition for market share is likely to lead to a market with a few dominant big players that are efficiency- and cost-focused. You enter an established market like this at your peril because a new venture is unlikely to have either the experience or the economies of scale that established competitors have.

High differentiation

This is where customers value the other elements of the marketing mix more than price and are therefore willing to pay a premium. Often the key elements of differentiation are the ability to offer the best quality or most innovative products (e.g. Apple or Rolls Royce), but the more product/service benefits you offer, the more ways you will be different to competitors. Start-ups need to differentiate themselves from competitors in ways that are important to customers (Gebauer et al., 2011). Those with strong differentiation should move quickly to establish themselves, often with premium branding, and can thrive with this offering (see Quad Electroacoustics Case insight on page 167).

Customer focus or intimacy

This is where the fifth 'P' (people or service) is important and the customers are provided with a product/service more closely tailored to their specific requirements. The key to having a customer focus is the ability to have a close relationship with them – understanding their needs – and it goes hand-in-hand with effective market segmentation. It is often based on good customer service (e.g. Coutts Bank). Customer loyalty is high and there is the opportunity to develop a strong brand. Economies of scope can be significant, allowing a business with a strong brand to spread its costs over different products – for example by giving a range of products a prestige brand image. Despite the opportunity for economies of scope, small companies can thrive with this offering (see Morgan Motor Company Case insight on page 168).

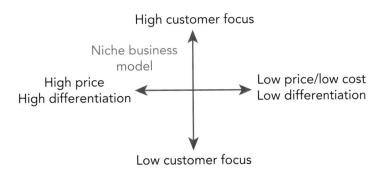

Figure 6.5 Value disciplines or generic business models

Table 6.3 Value disciplines and business imperatives

Low price/low cost	High differentiation	Customer focus
> Maintaining cost leadership through economies of scale > Continually driving down costs > Achieving high sales volumes > Improving efficiency > Standardization	> Understanding the basis for the differential advantage > Building on the differential advantage > Building barriers to entry > Building the brand > Continuous innovation > Encouraging creativity and innovation	> Maintaining close relationships with customers > Keeping in touch with and understanding changes in customer needs > Maintaining customer loyalty > Maximizing sales to existing loyal customers (economies of scope) > Building the brand

Each of the value disciplines has different **business imperatives** – shown in Table 6.3. Business imperatives are the things that you need to keep on top of, or risk failing to deliver your value proposition. Business imperatives can become the **critical success factors** for your business – things you must get right to survive. These imperatives can be conflicting, particularly between low cost/low price and the other two propositions, and need the application of judgement. For example, a low-cost/low-price airline would never want to compromise on safety, despite it being an easy way to cut costs. However, usually the conflict is not so dramatic and there are ways of resolving the conflict. For example, some large companies with product ranges based on different value propositions have unbundled their activities and set up separate organizations focused on those products with similar core value propositions. In this way, managers of these organizations have clear imperatives.

Treacy and Wiersema (op. cit.) say that once you have identified your core discipline or model, there are four questions that you need to answer:

1 For each dimension, what proportion of customers focus on it as their primary or dominant decision criterion? In other words, how important is each value discipline or business model to each market segment?

2 Which competitors provide the best value in each of these value or model dimensions? In other words, who is your major competitor in each discipline or model?

3 How do you compare to the competition on each dimension?

4 If you fall short of the value leaders in each dimension, how can this be remedied? Of course, if you do fall short, the real question is whether you can compete at all, or whether you have constructed a sufficiently different value proposition to create a new market not currently catered for.

Different business models can exist successfully side by side in the same industry if it is sufficiently large and heterogeneous. For example, the business model for low-cost airlines like Southwest Airlines, easyJet and AirAsia is very different to that of flagship carriers like Delta, British Airways and Emirates. Yet both business models survive, appealing to different target market segments. Dell and Apple co-exist in the personal computing market but with completely business models serving different market segments with different value offerings. There is certainly no golden formula for success.

Competitors will, however, usually try to copy successful business models and today's novel business idea can often prove to be tomorrow's norm. So the question is: for how long can the elements of differentiation be sustained? Performance against competitors needs to be continually reviewed. Value propositions need to be continually reinforced but also improved. They might also need, eventually, to be changed, and doing this goes to the core of the skills, capabilities and competencies a company has and the strategies it should employ.

The **core competencies** of a business are the resources or capabilities it has that can lead to competitive advantage over its rivals. For a start-up these will revolve around the skills and capabilities of the founder, the opportunity they have identified and the uniqueness of the way they intend to service the market they have identified. The more unique these competences are, the more difficult they are to copy and the more successful the start-up is likely to be (Rassmussen et al., 2011). They can be combined with **strategic assets** of a business – valuable assets such as equipment, trademarks, patents, brand (see Chapter 7) etc. – to create **sustainable competitive advantage**. The more unique and difficult they are to copy, the greater the competitive advantage and the greater the chances of success. They greater the competitive advantage of the business, the more highly it is likely to be valued by investors (Teece, 2010).

 ## Case insight   Dell Corporation

Changing your value proposition

Dell has adopted both a low-price/low-cost and a customer focus value proposition (selling direct and allowing customers to configure their own computers). Dell was a market leader in the provision of value-for-money computers in the 1990s because it integrated its supply chain with its online retail operations. Its fully integrated value chain – a business-to-consumer-to-business (B2C2B) business model – meant that customers could configure their own computers and order online while suppliers had real time access to orders and deliveries, so that Dell could receive stock information on a just-in-time basis, keeping the assembly line moving while minimizing its costs. Dell patented many of the innovations in this integrated value chain but ultimately competitors were able to copy many of these technological developments and integrate their supply chains so as to achieve similar cost savings.

This element of Dell's differential advantage has become less effective, and the question is whether Dell's direct relationship with customers is now of higher value than its low-price/low-cost proposition. If it is, then Dell might also want to sell other digital consumer electronics and office automation equipment direct to customers. And why should it not subcontract more of its assembly, focusing rather on the core strength that the customer values – the direct relationship? Again, this is something it has started doing. This raises many questions about the scope of Dell's activities and the nature of its business domain. But, as we saw in the Case insight about Amazon, Apple, Facebook, Google and Microsoft in Chapter 5, companies continually question this.

QUESTION:

1   What are the barriers within a large organization to changing a previously successful business model?

 ## Case insight   easyJet (1)

Low-cost/low-price business model

One firm that has successfully followed the low-cost/low-price business model is easyJet. It was founded by Stelios Haji-Ioannou, a MBA from London Business School, in 1995 with £5 million borrowed from his father, a Greek shipping tycoon. easyJet copied the business model of the US carrier Southwest Airlines, changing the marketing paradigm for the industry, and in doing so created a whole new market for low-cost airline travel in Europe. The company has transformed the European air travel market and has beaten off many rival imitators. Today it is a leading European airline. easyJet was floated on the stock market in 2000, making Stelios £280 million in profit. Only seven years after

founding the company and still owning 29%, Stelios realized that he was not suited to managing a public company and was better suited to being a serial entrepreneur, so in 2002 he resigned as chair, aged only 35. He was to be replaced by Sir Colin Chandler, aged 62, part of London's financial establishment as chair of Vickers Defense Systems, deputy chair of Smiths Group and director of Thales.

A central strategy of being low-price is being low-cost, and that has a number of implications for the way easyJet and its rivals are run. Aircraft are leased rather than owned. Low costs come from two driving principles – firstly, 'sweating' or making maximum use of the assets, and secondly, high operating efficiency. easyJet flies 'point-to-point' (average trip length about 1,000 km), without the connecting

Continued...

Continued from previous page...

flights and networks that the heritage carriers, like British Airways (BA), have to worry about. easyJet flies its planes for 11 hours a day – 4 hours longer than BA. Their pilots fly 900 hours a year, 50% more than BA pilots. In terms of operating efficiency, it means:

> Aircraft fly out of low-cost airports. These are often not the major airport serving any destination and can be some distance from the destination;
> Aircraft are tightly scheduled. Rapid turnaround is vital. Low-cost airlines aim to allow only 25 minutes to offload one set of passengers and load another, less than half the time of heritage rivals;
> Aircraft must leave and arrive on time (they will not wait for passengers), and if there are delays they can have horrendous knock-on consequences for the timetable. Nevertheless, punctuality is varied, with the low-cost carriers just as good as full-fare airlines on some routes;
> There is no 'slack' in the system. easyJet admits to having 'one and a half planes' worth' of spare capacity compared with the dozen planes BA has on standby at Gatwick and Heathrow. If something goes wrong with a plane, it can lead to cancellations and long delays;
> There are fewer cabin crew than full-fare rivals, and staff rostering is a major logistical problem;
> All operations and processes must be slimmed down and made as simple as possible.

In terms of customer service, it means:

> Ticketless flights;
> A single class, therefore with more seats on each plane, with no 'frills' such as complimentary drinks, meals or assigned seats – all additional services must be paid for;
> Baggage allowances are lower than heritage carriers and there is no compensation for delays or lost baggage;
> Transfers not guaranteed, because the planes could be late;
> Aerobridges for boarding and disembarking are generally not used, because these add cost;
> Concentration on point-to-point flights, whereas the full-fare, heritage airlines tend to concentrate on hub-and-spoke traffic.

One of the fears about low-cost airlines has been that they will be tempted to compromise on safety for the sake of cutting costs. The British Airline Pilots Association has claimed that pilots of low-cost airlines have been tempted to cut corners to achieve flight timetables. The industry is all too aware that the low-cost US airline ValuJet went bankrupt after one of its planes crashed in 1996, killing all 110 people on board. However, by partnering with some of the best-known maintenance providers in the industry, easyJet makes safety its first priority. In common with other low-cost operators, it operates a single type of aircraft. This offers economies of purchasing, maintenance, pilot training and aircraft utilization.

easyJet has started moving away from being the lowest-cost carrier to adding customer value, for example by flying to airports nearer to major cities. AirAsia is now generally regarded as the lowest-cost airline in the world, with Ryanair, a competitor of easyJet, not far behind. Interestingly, Ryanair has so little faith in its timetable that it advises passengers not to book connecting flights.

easyJet is generally regarded as having an excellent branding strategy – originally based on PR around its founder – and having one of the best websites in the sector. It is aggressive in promoting its brand and running advertising promotions that maximize seat occupancy. It realizes that planes must have a high seat occupancy to be economic. To this end, it is particularly inventive with pricing, encouraging real bargain hunters onto the less popular flights during the day and promoting early bookings with cheaper fares. easyJet has been at the forefront of using the internet for virtual ticketing, and now sells all of its tickets online. This means it does not have to pay commission to travel agents, and check-in can be quicker and more efficient. Its website has been held up as a model for the industry and many have copied it. easyJet also tries to get more sales from every passenger visiting its website and sell other services such as airport car parking, car hire and hotel bookings.

The industry in Europe has seen some fierce price wars as competitors battled for market share in a fast-growing market where there were economies of scale to be had. easyJet has been aggressive in buying out competitors (e.g. Go in 2002) and purchasing new routes and landing rights – which can be difficult to secure – giving it a comprehensive European network and securing the economies of scale that it needed. These days the low-cost airline industry is well established and far more difficult to enter. AirAsia entered the market in 2002, copying the successful low-cost model but in a new market without competitors.

❏ Visit the website: www.easyjet.com

QUESTIONS:

1 Who are easyJet's target market segments and what is the core value proposition it offers?
2 Which market segments might it not appeal to?

Continued...

Continued from previous page...

3 What are the operational imperatives for easyJet – the things it needs to get right to enable it to deliver the value proposition? How are these are achieved?

4 How important is low cost compared to other elements of the value proposition?

5 How do you go about compromising the core value proposition?

6 If you start to compromise your core value proposition, how far do you have to go before it is no longer core?

Niche business models

Companies that offer both high differentiation and high customer focus are said to have a niche business model. Market focus involves understanding in depth the needs of relatively few customers, and therefore there is more scope for differentiation. It often involves targeting smaller markets, and therefore there are more opportunities for smaller businesses. This is the strategy that research tells us is most likely to succeed for a start-up because it can charge higher prices and is more likely to sustain its differential advantage because the smaller market segment does not attract competitors, at least initially. What is more, as discussed earlier, the internet has meant that market niches can be global and that means that while there may be a clear identification of the needs of a few customers, the global size of this market segment could be quite large. And once the start-up dominates one market niche it can move on to another.

There is usually a trade-off between price and the other elements of the marketing mix. The stronger or more distinctive and different these other elements, the higher the price you are normally able to command. Too many small firms compete primarily on price because they do not understand how the other elements might add value to the customer and they believe the other elements of their marketing mix are insufficiently different from their competitors.

One small firm producing motor components found itself competing unsuccessfully against a large multinational that consistently undercut it on price. It decided that it could not survive with a value proposition relying on operational excellence/low cost and decided it needed a rethink. It researched its customers and the market and found there were many opportunities for products manufactured to a high technical specification in which quality and supplier reputation were more important than the price charged – a product leadership/differentiation value proposition – so it decided to switch its strategy. Low volumes and high price for specialist products proved to be a more sustainable strategy and, over time, it was able to develop close relationships with a few of its regular customers and became an established niche player in what otherwise might be seen as a highly competitive industry.

Following a niche business model involves maximizing your value proposition to a closely defined target customer group. It involves understanding the needs of this group – the benefits they are really looking for – and translating that into a marketing mix. The smaller the group, the more homogeneous their needs are likely to be. So you may want to look again at your original target market to see whether it can profitably be broken down into smaller market niches. Meeting the needs of each new niche may involve either adding costs, by adding more valued product features, or subtract costs, by eliminating less valued features. For each niche there is the question of the price they are willing to pay for this improved and differentiated product – a topic we shall cover in the next chapter. This iterative process is likely to have implications for the resources you need and some of the needs of the different market niches you identify may not be profitable to target. It is all a question of judgement.

> If you set up a company selling widgets like the bloke down the road and the only difference is that's yours are cheaper, you'll make a living but that's all you'll achieve. If you can be truly differentiated and unique, then you've really got something.
>
> **Martyn Dawes**, founder, Coffee Nation, *Startups*: wwwstartups.co.uk

Case insight   Quad Electroacoustics

Niche business model

One Huntingdon-based family company that has been very successful in differentiating its products and selling to a small but lucrative market segment is Quad Electroacoustics. Originally founded in 1936 by Peter Walker as an 'acoustical manufacturing company' to produce 'public address' systems, today its silvery-grey, bizarrely sculptured audio equipment looks like no other. It sounds superb as well. While Japanese 'competitors' bring out new models every year, Quad's stay the same and last forever. Its original

electrostatic loudspeaker was in production for 28 years. Quads is a byword for quality, reliability and design originality – but the equipment is not cheap. Current models sell for over £3,000, and still 70% of Quad's sales are exported, especially to Europe, USA and Japan.

❏ Visit the website: www.quad-hifi .co.uk

QUESTIONS:

1 Why is this a niche business?

2 What are the pros and cons of this business model for Quad?

Case insight   Morgan Motor Company

Niche business model

One company that arguably could make even higher margins by charging a higher price for its products is the Morgan Motor Company. Founded in 1909, it is the world's oldest privately owned car manufacturer, making a quintessentially British sports car. Every Morgan is hand-built and looks like it came from the 1930s. Each car is different, with a choice of 35,000 body colours and leather upholstery to match. It takes seven weeks to build a car, and customers are invited

to the factory to see the process. Morgan sells only about 500 cars a year, half overseas, and demand exceeds supply, cushioning the company from the vagaries of demand. Morgan is a unique car manufacturer in a niche market.

❏ Visit the website: www.morgan-motor.co.uk

QUESTIONS:

1 Why is this a niche business?

2 What are the pros and cons of this business model for Morgan?

Case insight   Escape to the Cape

Niche business model

Escape to the Cape is a venture set up by Shaheed Ebrahim in 2010 in South Africa. The tourism industry is a fiercely competitive business in South Africa, but the company offers guided tours around Cape Town with a difference. Shaheed spent about $4,000 to register his company and get a website and then took out a mortgage of $32,000 to buy his 7-seater bus which he equipped with the latest internet technology. As well as having an expert guide, the bus is equipped with Wi-Fi and clients can borrow a complimentary tablet computer that then allows them to go online to email, Facebook or Tweet their family and friends with emails, photos or videos of their tour. They can even talk to them using Skype. Every

seat has a facility to charge any mobile device. The bus has its own fridge offering a range of drinks including complimentary chilled water. Shaheed won the Emerging Tourism Entrepreneur of the Year award in South Africa for 2011/12.

'There are hundreds of tour operators out in Cape Town but the difference is that we've taken technology that's available and put it onto our tours, thereby enhancing the tours'. (BBC News Business, 31 January 2013)

QUESTIONS:

1 Why is this a niche business?

2 What are the pros and cons of this business model for Escape to the Cape?

 Practice insight reminder Characteristics of a good business idea – 4 & 5

4 **Clearly identified customers and a viable business model** – if you don't know who you are selling to you won't know how to sell to them, which means you probably will not succeed. You need to go about building your business model systematically. And

remember, you may be selling to more than one market segment.

5 **Low funding requirements** – the lower the funding requirement, the easier it is to start up and the less you have to lose if the idea does not work.

↻ Summary

> Effectuation is a term that refers to how entrepreneurs think: they have broad goals based on resource availability and react opportunistically to situations; they set 'affordable loss' and react quickly rather than evaluating thoroughly; they do not like traditional, formal planning; they build networks and partner with others; and they are less concerned with completion, believing they can overcome it.

> The New Venture Creation Framework outlined in Figure 6.1 provides a framework to help you find, explore, develop and refine your business idea. At the core of the framework is a holistic business model. The more innovative your business model, the more successful you are likely to be.

> Lean start-up involves minimizing the investment and lead time in launching a new product, ensuring only that it is in a 'minimum viable state' and then using feedback to better tailor the product to customer needs.

> You need to define your value proposition to your identified market segment(s). This summarizes the benefits offered by the product/service and is supported by the features and underpinned by the marketing mix.

> There are three well-understood business models: low-price/low-cost, high differentiation, customer focus. These combine to produce the niche business model of highly differentiated products/services offered in small volume at a relatively high price to a focused target market. These are models consistent with fundamental ways of creating sustainable competitive advantage.

> Different business models with different value propositions can exist happily side by side in the same industry, appealing to different target markets.

> The core competencies of a business are the resources or capabilities it has. They can be combined with strategic assets of a business to create sustainable competitive advantage. The more unique these competences are, the more difficult they are to copy and the more successful the start-up is likely to be.

> Marketing strategy is made up of elements of the marketing mix as they relate to the customer segments they are targeted at. Strategy is just a series of related tasks that, taken together, have coherence and give direction. The marketing strategy delivers the value proposition to these target market segments.

> You can sell directly to customers or through distribution channels. If you sell through channels, you might gain wider distribution but you lose profit and may lose control over communication to customers.

> 'Supply-push' is when you create incentives to intermediaries in your distribution channels to sell your product. 'Demand-pull' is when you create incentives directly with end-use customers who then 'pull' the product through the distribution channels.

✓ Activities

1 List and describe the customers you will be selling to, noting any common groupings or segments.
2 List the features of the product(s) and translate these into benefits for your customer segments.
3 Evaluate the importance of each of these benefits to each of your customer segments.
4 Describe the value proposition to each of your target market segments.
5 Explain how a business model based upon this value proposition can be delivered. List the most important drivers of your value proposition – the critical success factors on which your business will depend.

💬 Group discussion topics

1 Is effectual reasoning logical?
2 If entrepreneurs do not like traditional, formal planning, why should you develop a framework to explore the launch of your business?
3 What are the advantages and disadvantages of using a flexible framework like the New Venture Creation Framework to explore the launch of your business?
4 The cheapest way to undertake market research is to start up and monitor your progress. Discuss.
5 Lean start-up only works for high-technology businesses. Discuss.
6 What are the advantages and disadvantages of internationalization early in the life of a business?
7 What are the barriers to reaching an international market?
8 Why are high-technology firms more likely to internationalize early in their life?
9 What are the barriers to trading on the internet?
10 Every product or service is different. Discuss.
11 We spent most of the 20th century creating mass markets and will spend most of the 21st breaking them down. Discuss.
12 Is market segmentation an art or science?

13 How can you group together customers in a useful way?
14 Customers buy services not products. Discuss.
15 Customers always want the cheapest product. Discuss.
16 Different customers are happy to pay different prices for the same product. Discuss.
17 Which strategy is best – 'supply-push' or 'demand-pull'?
18 What is the difference between the marketing mix, the value proposition and the business model?
19 What are the advantages and disadvantages of a business model relying on customer focus?
20 What are the advantages and disadvantages of a business model relying on low cost/low price?
21 What are the advantages and disadvantages of a business model relying on differentiation?
22 What are the advantages and disadvantages of the niche business model?

☛ References

Aggarwal, R. (1999) 'Technology and Globalisation as Mutual Reinforcers in Business Reorienting Strategic Thinking for the New Millennium', *Management International Review*, 2(1).

Anderson, S., Gabrielsson, J. and Wictor, I. (2004) 'International Activities in Small Firms: Examining Factors Influencing the Internationalization and Export Growth of Small Firms', *Canadian Journal of Administrative Sciences*, 21(1).

Burns, P. (2005) *Corporate Entrepreneurship: Building an Entrepreneurial Organization*, Basingstoke: Palgrave Macmillan.

Burns, P. (2014) *New Venture Creation: A Framework for Entrepreneurial Start-ups*, Basingstoke: Palgrave Macmillan.

Chelliah, S., Sulaiman, M. and Yusoff, Y.M. (2010) 'Internationalization and Performance: Small and Medium Enterprises (SMEs) in Malaysia International', *Journal of Business and Management*, 5(6).

Chaston, I. (2000) *Entrepreneurial Marketing: Competing by Challenging Convention*, Basingstoke: Palgrave Macmillan.

Coviello, N.E. and Munro, H.J. (1995) 'Growing the Entrepreneurial Firm: Networking for International Market Development', *European Journal of Marketing*, 29(7).

Gebauer, H., Gustafsson, A. and Witell, L. (2011) 'Competitive Advantage through Service Differentiation by Manufacturing Companies', *Journal of Business Research*, 64(12).

George, G. and Bock, A.J. (2011) 'The Business Model in Practice and its Implications for Entrepreneurship Research', *Entrepreneurship Theory and Practice*, 35(1).

Johnson, J.E. (2004) 'Factors Influencing the Early Internationalisation of High Technology Start-ups: US and UK Evidence', *Journal of International Entrepreneurship*, 2.

Kuhlmeier, D.B. and Knight, G. (2010) 'The Critical Role of Relationship Quality in Small- and Medium-Sized Enterprise Internationalization', *Journal of Global Marketing*, 23(1).

Laanti, R., Gabrielsson, M. and Gabrielsson, P. (2007) 'The Globalization Strategies of Business-to-Business Technology Industry', *Industrial Marketing Management*, 36.

Lu, J.W. and Beamish, P.W. (2001) 'The Internationalization and Performance of SMEs', *Strategic Management Journal*, 22(6).

Osterwalder, A. and Pigneur, Y. (2010) *Business Model Generation: A Handbook for Visionaries, Game Changers and Challengers*, New Jersey: John Wiley & Sons.

Oviatt, B.M. and McDougall, P.P. (1994) 'Towards a Theory of International New Ventures', *Journal of International Business Studies*, 25 (First Quarter).

Porter, M. (1985) *Competitive Advantage: Creating and Sustaining Superior Performance*. New York: The Free Press.

Rasmussen, E., Mosey, S. and Wright, M. (2011) 'The Evolution of Entrepreneurial Competencies: A Longitudinal Study of University Spin-Off Venture Emergence', *Journal of Management Studies*, September, 48(6).

Ries, E. (2011), *The Lean Startup: How Today's Entrepreneurs Use Continuous Innovation to Create Radically Successful Businesses*, New York: Crown Publishing.

Sarasvathy, S.D. (2001) 'Causation and Effectuation: Toward a Theoretical Shift from Economic Inevitability to Entrepreneurial Contingency', *The Academy of Management Review*, 26(2).

Sorenson, R.I., Folker, C.A. and Brigham, K.H. (2008) 'The Collaborative Network Orientation: Achieving Business Success Through Collaborative Relationships', *Entrepreneurship Theory and Practice*, 32(4).

Teece, D.J. (2010) 'Business Models, Business Strategy and Innovation', *Long Range Planning*, 43 (2/3).

Treacy, M. and Wiersema, F. (1995) *The Discipline of Market Leaders*, Reading, MA: Addison-Wesley.

Vargo, S.L. and Lusch, R.F. (2004) 'Evolving to a New Dominant Logic for Marketing'. *Journal of Marketing*, 68(1).

Zahra, S.A., Ucbasaran, D. and Newey, L.R. (2009) 'Social Knowledge and SMEs' Innovative Gains from Internationalization', *European Management Review*, 6(2).

Zhou, L., Wu, W. and Luo, X. (2007) 'Internationalization and the Performance of Born-Global SMEs: The Mediating Role of Social Networks', *Journal of International Business Studies*, 38(4).

⊕ www.palgrave.com/Burns-Entrepreneurship-And-Small-Business-4e

Go online to access additional teaching and learning resources for this chapter on the companion website. Click here in the ebook to complete a multiple choice revision quiz for this chapter.

ADDING VALUES TO THE BUSINESS MODEL | 7

Image Source \ Image Source/Milk and Honey

Contents

- Your values
- Your vision
- Your mission
- Creating value through values
- Branding your values
- Corporate social responsibility (CSR)
- CSR and financial performance
- Building the brand
- Setting your prices
- Price and volumes
- Summary

Learning outcomes

When you have read this chapter and undertaken the related activities you will be able to:

> Identify the values on which your start-up is based;
> Develop a vision for your start-up and write its mission statement;
> Understand the basis for values-based marketing;
> Understand how ethics and CSR can make good commercial sense and underpin the brand values of the product/service;
> Understand how brand values can be communicated through your communications strategy;
> Set your selling prices.

 *Practice insight*:
7 rules for communicating a vision

 *Practice insight*:
How to write a mission statement

 *Practice insight*:
10 rules to integrate values and marketing

 *Practice insight reminder*:
Characteristics of a good business idea

💡 Case insights

easyJet (2)	Brompton Bicycle (2)
Golden Krust (2)	Ecotricity
Adrenaline Alley (1)	Abel & Cole
Starbucks	Richard Branson and Virgin (1)
South Beauty	Xtreme SnoBoards (1)
Zound Industries	Lush

Your values

Just as it is important that you understand why you want to start a business and what you want from it, it is also important that your business reflects your vision and values. After all, you will be spending much of your time developing it and, in many ways, it is an extension of you and your personality. Most people find it very difficult to live their lives within organizations that do not share their values and beliefs. Indeed, this is often a reason for starting up your own business. This chapter will start to formalize the reasons you want to set up a business, which we first considered in Chapter 3. It will develop the vision you have for the business and the values upon which it is based. It will also show you how strong, ethical and social values can also enhance your business model, creating a clear brand identity. In doing this you may be able to charge a higher price for your product and create commercial as well as social value.

Values are core beliefs. The values you set for your business set expectations regarding how you operate and treat people. They may well have an ethical dimension. Historically many of the most successful Victorian businesses, such as Cadbury, Barclays Bank or John Lewis, were based upon Quaker values and many Victorian entrepreneurs went on to become great philanthropists (see Titus Salt Case insight on page 435). Values form part of the cognitive processes that will help shape and develop the culture of your business. Shared values form a bond that binds the organization together – aligning and motivating people. Organizations with strong values tend to recruit staff who are able to identify with those values and thus they become reinforced. They also help create a bond with customers and suppliers alike that can underpin a strong brand identity.

You articulate values not only with words but also by practising what you preach – 'walking the talk'. It therefore follows that it is very difficult to pretend to have values that are not real. You will be caught out when you fail to practice them. Values are not negotiable and need to be reinforced through recognition and reward of staff. They need to be embedded in the systems and structures of your business, so that everybody can see clearly that you mean what you say. Every organization develops a distinctive culture that reflects certain underlying values, even if they are never made explicit. If you do not make your values explicit there is always the risk that they might be misunderstood and you end up with an organizational culture that you are unhappy with. This is why many successful companies actually write down their values. Your values also need to be reflected in the strategies you adopt when you launch the business – your ethical underpinning and social policies. In other words, your values need to be reflected in your value proposition.

Your vision

It is important to create a vision for what the business might become – important for your motivation and that of all the stakeholders in your business. Your vision for the business should be based around and grounded in your business purpose. A vision is a shared mental image of a desired future state – an idea of what your enterprise can become – a new and better world. It must be attractive and aspirational and one that engages and energizes people, including yourself. However, it must be sufficiently realistic and credible that it is believable – stretching but achievable. It is usually qualitative rather than quantitative (that is the role of the objectives). Vision is seen as inspiring and motivating, transcending logic and contractual relationships. It is more emotional than analytical, something that touches the heart. It gives existence within an organization to that most fundamental of human cravings – a sense of meaning and purpose. It can be intrinsic, directing the organization to do things better in some way, such as improving customer satisfaction or increasing product innovation. It can be extrinsic, for example beating the competition.

Hamel and Prahalad (1994) studied firms that had successfully challenged established big companies in a range of industries. They said that to reconcile this lack of fit between aspirations and resources the successful firms used 'strategic intent'. This necessitates developing a common vision about the future, aligning staff behaviour with a common purpose and delegating and decentralizing decision-making. They argued that 'the challengers had succeeded in creating entirely new forms of competitive advantage and dramatically rewriting the rules of engagement.' They were daring to be different. Managers in these firms imagined new products, services and even entire industries that did not exist and then went on to create them. They were not just benchmarking and analysing competition, they were creating new marketplaces that they could dominate because it was a marketplace of their own making.

Ohmae (2005) used the Japanese word *kosoryoku* to describe what is needed to develop entrepreneurial strategy in an uncertain environment. He explained that it meant something that combined 'vision' with the notion of 'concept' and 'imagination', but unlike imagination, it has no sense of daydreaming but is rather an ability to see what is invisible and shape the future so that the vision succeeds: 'It is the product of imagination based on realistic understanding of what the shape of the oncoming world is and, pragmatically, the areas of business that you can capture successfully because you have the means of realizing the vision.'

> Reach for the stars and you will get there (or at least close). Aim low and you'll get there too.
>
> **Elizabeth Gooch**, founder, **eg** solutions, *Launch Lab* (www.launchlab.co.uk) 13 January 2009

 Practice insight 7 rules for communicating a vision

Kotter (1996) gave seven principles for successfully communicating a vision:

1 **Keep it simple:** Focused and jargon-free.
2 **Use metaphors, analogies and examples:** Engage the imagination.
3 **Use many different forums:** The same message should come from as many different directions as possible.

4 **Repeat the message:** The same message should be repeated again, and again, and again.
5 **Lead by example:** Walk the talk.
6 **Address small inconsistencies:** Small changes can have big effects if their symbolism is important to staff.
7 **Listen and be listened to:** Work hard to listen, it pays dividends.

Your mission

The formal statement of business purpose is called a mission statement. The mission statement says what the business aims to achieve and how it will achieve it. It therefore usually defines the scope of the business by including reference to the product/service, value proposition, customer groups and the benefits they derive. This stops you straying into markets where you have no competitive advantage, clarifies strategic options and offers guidance for setting objectives. Often it encompasses the values upheld by the organization. Like a vision statement, a mission statement should be short and snappy.

Vision and mission statements for a social enterprise are no different than those for a commercial enterprise, except of course for the social purpose. So for example, we saw in Chapter 3 that the mission statement for The Big Issue Foundation was: 'to connect vendors with the vital support and personal solutions that enable them to rebuild their lives; to determine their own pathways to a better future'.

Case insight   easyJet (2)

The mission statement

We looked at easyJet in the last chapter. Its mission statement is:

To provide our customers with safe, good value, point-to-point air services. To effect and to offer a consistent and reliable product, and fares appealing to leisure and business markets on a range of European routes. To achieve this we will develop our people and establish lasting relationships with our suppliers.

QUESTION:

1 Is this a good mission statement?

Enduring   Changing

VALUES ⟶ MISSION ⟶ VISION ⟶ STRATEGY ⟶ TACTICS

Long term   Short term

Figure 7.1 Values, mission, vision, strategies and tactics

The mission and vision of your business must be consistent with your values. All three go hand in hand, one reinforcing the other. You can then start to build the strategies that enable you to achieve your vision. This includes your business model and your marketing strategies. Finally, the tactics are the activities you conduct day-to-day, like promotion or sales campaigns. As shown in Figure 7.1, while strategies and tactics might change rapidly in an entrepreneurial firm, mission, vision and values are more enduring. Together, they form the 'road map' that tells everyone where you are going and how you might get there, even when one route is blocked in the short term.

 Practice insight How to write a mission statement

Mission statements can take many forms, but Wickham (2001) suggested the following generic format:

(*The company*) aims to use its (*competitive advantage*) to achieve/maintain (*aspirations*) in providing (*product/business scope*) which offers (*value proposition*) to satisfy the (*needs*) of (*customer segments*). In doing this the company will at all times strive to uphold (*values*).

 Case insight   Golden Krust (2)

Blending vision, mission and values in a commercial enterprise

We looked at Golden Krust in Chapter 3. Here are its vision, mission and values.

Vision: Golden Krust exists to provide the taste of the Caribbean to the world.

Mission:

- To provide consumers with authentic, tasty Jamaican patties and relevant Caribbean cuisine in convenient settings and sizes;
- To provide customers with outstanding customer service and reliable predictability at every touch-point;
- To provide employees with an environment that is rewarding, fun and aspirational;
- To provide communities in which we operate with a corporate citizen of which they can be proud;
- To provide stakeholders with a superior return on their investment.

Values:

- Our customers are at the core to our success;
- Integrity, value and fun are hallmarks to our approach to business;
- All stakeholders should benefit from their association with Golden Krust.

QUESTION:

1 Are the vision, mission and values of Golden Krust consistent?

Case insight   Adrenaline Alley (1)

 Blending vision, mission and values in a social enterprise

Based in Corby in Northamptonshire, Adrenaline Alley is Europe's biggest urban sports park. Although it is run as a commercial business, it is a charitable social enterprise and a Company Limited by Guarantee (explained in Chapter 9). We will look at Adrenaline Alley again as a Case Insight in Chapter 12. Here we focus on its vision, mission and values.

Vision: To expand our thriving centre for urban sports and community use bringing change that makes a real difference to people's lives, and provide opportunities for other communities to develop social enterprises in the same way.

Mission: To provide safe, secure and manageable facilities addressing the needs of local communities and to be recognized as a leading provider of urban sports using a range of partnerships to become a sustainable social enterprise.

Values:
Delivering our mission as a team, we strive to be:

- Approachable and honest – always willing to listen and learn;
- People focused – operating for the benefit of our community and participants;
- Accessible – willing to go the extra mile to ensure everyone can participate;
- Affordable – always striving to reduce costs;
- Versatile! – adapting the business to the needs of our customers.

❑ Visit the Adrenaline Alley website on: http://www.adrenalinealley.co.uk/

QUESTION:

1 Are the vision, mission and values of Adrenaline Alley consistent?

Case insight   Starbucks

Changing your mission statement

When the founder, Howard Schultz, returned to retake control of struggling Starbucks in 2008 he was keen to signal change and to innovate. The first thing he did was change the mission statement. As a start-up, Starbucks' mission statement had been:

To establish Starbucks as the premier purveyor of the finest coffee in the world while maintaining our uncompromising principles while we grow.

Howard Schultz changed it to reflect that they had outgrown the original and now needed something else to aim for:

To inspire and nurture the human spirit – one person, one cup and one neighborhood at a time.

QUESTION:

1 Why was the change in mission statement needed?

Creating value through values

Your values and vision are tools that create identity for your business. And if this identity is attractive to customers it can create value as part of your value proposition. At the very least, a clear identity for the business means that customers know what they are buying and, if they like it, facilitates a repeat purchase. But identity can do more than this. As we have seen, customers buy a product/service because the marketing mix provides them with a range of benefits that they value. These benefits can be psychological as well as physical. For example, a successful sole trader might offer a *reliable, friendly* service that differentiates them effectively from the competition. The personal relationship they establish with their customers epitomizes the reliability and friendliness of the service they deliver. And this relationship underpins the customer loyalty that is generated. The challenge is to extend it beyond the single-person business.

This reflects a move away from seeing the customer as someone with whom to have an arm's-length transaction – just somebody to sell to. It is part of the development called 'values-based marketing' that seeks to actively use customers to help sell existing product/services and develop new ones. This is based upon establishing a good relationship with customers – one that is underpinned by mutual self-interest, where there is something in it for both the customer and the company with each helping the other in certain ways. Relationships are built on good communication – a topic we shall return to in the next chapter – and technology has made this easier on a mass basis. Indeed, the development of the internet and social media has made this possible and affordable on a global basis.

Piercy (2001; 1999) was one of the first academics to observe that, as customers become increasingly sophisticated, marketing should move away from just relationship to values-based strategies that reflect customer priorities and needs: 'Achieving customer loyalty with sophisticated customers is the new challenge and we are only just beginning to realize what this means. It will mean transparency. It will mean integrity and trustworthiness. It will mean innovative ways of doing business. It will mean a focus on value in customers' terms, not ours. It will require new types of organization and technology to deliver value.'

Piercy characterized marketing strategy and the search for customer loyalty as progress from transactional and brand approaches to relationship and values-based strategies. These are illustrated in Figure 7.2.

Values-based marketing (also called **Marketing 3.0**) has been characterized as a holistic approach to marketing based upon combinations of segmentation approaches. It places a *participative* customer at its centre – a customer that is not only king, but also market research head, R&D chief and product development manager – for example through open source innovation like Starbucks' Ideas website: http://mystarbucksidea.force.com/. Customers are actively involved as advocates of the product/service – for example through social network sites. In this way the customers' involvement is leveraged far beyond the simple purchase of the product/service. This only happens if the organization is continually engaged in dialogue with customers through as many media as possible.

Piercy suggested that the sources for this values-based strategy are:

> **Management vision:** Clarity in direction and purpose, effectively communicated through a wide range of communication media.
> **Market sensing and organizational learning:** Understanding and responding to the external world using all the networks and channels of communication possible.
> **Differentiating capabilities:** Using core competencies to build differential advantage.

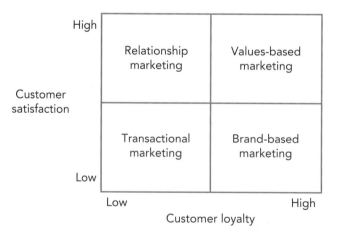

Figure 7.2 Values-based marketing

Source: From N.F. Piercy (2000) *Tales from the Marketplace: Stories of Revolution, Reinvention and Renewal.* With permission from Taylor & Francis.

> **Relationship strategy:** Managing the network of relationships and channels of communication used for market sensing to achieve superior performance.
> **Reinventing the organization:** Changing the organization form and processes to sustain and renew this strategy.

Kotler et al. (2010) were also keen advocates of values-based marketing. Rather than seeing values as an 'add-on', they envisaged marketing and values as being integrated, without separation. They asserted that companies need to focus on creating products/services and entire organizational cultures, which are customer values-based at a more multidimensional, fundamental level, starting with their values, mission and vision. They claim that, in a world where similar products/services can increasingly be relied upon to satisfy consumer needs, the only way to differentiate yourself and add value for the customer is to also address their spiritual needs. They argued that, to deliver this and thrive in this interlinked world, companies must collaborate with each other, with their shareholders, channel partners, employees and customers.

So, you need to appeal to customers' heads, hearts and spirits. The key to this is customer participation and involvement, using all the channels of communication created by the internet, mobile and social media, and then partnering where necessary to deliver real value to customers.

> *Compartmentalizing social responsibility is not the way to go. I think the model for starting employee engagement activities has to be embedded in everything we do.*
>
> **Richard Branson**, founder, Virgin Group, *www.hrmagazine. co.uk*, 13 July 2010

 Practice insight 10 rules to integrate values and marketing

Kotler et al. (op. cit.) gave 10 principles that they claim integrate marketing and values:

1 Love your customers and respect your competitors.
2 Be sensitive to change and ready to change yourself.
3 Guard your name, and have a clear identity.
4 Customers are diverse; first find those who benefit most from your product/service.
5 Always offer a good product/service at a fair price.
6 Always make yourself available and spread the news about your product/service.
7 Find your customers, keep and grow them.
8 Whatever your business, remember it is a service business.
9 Continually refine your business processes – quality, cost and delivery.
10 Continually gather information, but be wise in making your final decisions.

Branding your values

Your values need to be linked to your value proposition. But doing this is only part of the challenge. The other part is communicating this 'values-enhanced' value proposition to customers and consumers. This can be complicated. One way of shortcutting the process is to develop a brand that encapsulates the value proposition and everything it, and the company, stands for. In this way the customer's script is written for them and articulation is easier. This is the way to create sustainable competitive advantage by clearly differentiating yourself from competitors in the eyes of customers and consumers. It is what companies like Apple have achieved with their brand identity. Apple is a lifestyle brand that stands for design excellence, simplicity and ease of use. It identifies the owner of its products as part of the exclusive Apple 'tribe' and therefore builds a relationship of loyalty with them. Values-based marketing involves having both a strong brand identity and good customer relationships. It uses these things to the mutual advantage of both customer and company. The advantages of branding to both customers/consumers and product/ service providers are shown in Table 7.1.

> *Customers relate to brands and the values it stands for more than the tangible aspects of a product.*
>
> **Richard Branson**, founder Virgin Group, *The Guardian, Media Planet*, May 2015

Table 7.1 Advantages of branding

For customers and consumers	For product/service provider
> Easier product/service identification > Clearer communication of value proposition > Aids with product/service evaluation > Reduction in risk when purchasing (homogeneity of offering) > Can create additional interest or character for the product/service	> Conveys emotional aspects of the value proposition > Promotes product/service loyalty > Helps target marketing > Defends against competitors (creates differential advantage) > Allows higher price to be charged > Increases power in distribution channels

Getty

> When you've got single-digit market share – and you're competing with the big boys – you either differentiate or die … The idea of building a business solely based on cost or price was not a sustainable advantage.

Michael Dell, founder, Dell Corporation, *Direct from Dell: Strategies that Revolutionized an Industry*, 1999, New York: Harper Business

You and your rival have access to virtually all the same resources. Only by constantly thinking of new ways to reorganize these factors can you differentiate yourself. It's like poker. Everyone has the same number of cards. It's how you play your hand that matters..

Zhang Ruimin, CEO, Haier Group, *Strategy + Business*, Issue 77, Winter 2014

Differentiation means setting out to be unique in the industry along some dimensions that are widely valued by customers. These can be based upon the product or service and can be tangible (observable product/service characteristics such as function, quality, design, performance or technology etc.) and/or intangible (customer needs such as status, exclusivity etc.). Often differentiation is more sustainable when based not just on tangible factors, which are replicable, but also on intangible factors, which are not. So, for example, Mercedes-Benz cars and Dom Pérignon champagne differentiate themselves through product quality and status in the respective sectors. The UK retailer Lush differentiates itself through its bright, fun shopping environment, novel products and ethical values (see Case insight on page 192). Even companies competing primarily on price attempt to differentiate themselves not just through brand recognition. Dell may not have differentiated products but also attempts to differentiate itself on speed of delivery, uniqueness of personal systems configuration and other elements of service, while still maintaining a competitive price (Case insight on page 165). McDonald's has a very recognizable brand associated with value-for-money meals but also tries to differentiate itself, in part, through consistency and quality of service (speed, cleanliness and so on). You can differentiate yourself therefore by 'bundling' these things in different ways – so long as the customer values the 'bundle' and cannot create the 'bundle' easily themselves.

Branding is not something that just large organizations can afford. The name of a local tradesman is often their 'brand' and that name may stand for many things like quality of service. They will place great store on their local reputation. What is more, a good tradesman will take time to develop a personal relationship with their customers – something big companies have difficulty doing – and that relationship will be based on trust and respect. When customers have a good relationship with a reputable tradesman they will often recommend them personally to friends. And all of this costs infinately less than the expenditure large companies make in developing their brand.

Nevertheless, differentiation adds costs – even if it is just taking time to talk to customers – and it is essential that the benefits to the customers are seen by them as outweighing the costs. It is also essential that the product or service is clearly identified as being different. Design is an important element in this. As with Apple, good design can help improve the functional performance of a product. It can also make the product distinctive. Good design is aesthetically pleasing and conveys emotions that functionality cannot. The Apple brand achieves all these things. SMEs may not have the money to spend on design that Apple has, but, nevertheless, design is not something that can be ignored, particularly if it is part of your value proposition.

Clear branding can do the same. Consumers tend to form relationships with brands in much the same way as they form relationships with people (Aaker et al., 2004). A brand should be the

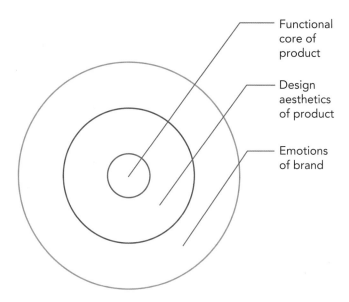

Functional
core of
product

Design
aesthetics
of product

Emotions
of brand

Figure 7.3 Layers of differentiation

embodiment of the product or service value proposition to customers. It tells you what you are buying but also what you want from the purchase. So, for example, the Mercedes-Benz, Jaguar and BMW brands tell you that you are buying a car but, more importantly, all convey quality and status. Virgin is the embodiment of Richard Branson: brash, entrepreneurial, different, anti-establishment. Effective brands, therefore, are emotional, appealing to the heart as much as the head. However, many so-called brands fall far short of this instant recognition of values and virtues, being little more than expensive logos. What do the Barclays, Shell or the BT brands convey, other than the knowledge of what the firm sells? Brands should be more than just logos that identify the products sold. They should represent the very identity – the persona – of the product sold. And, just as you are more than a head, body, two arms and legs, so too any product/service should be more than the sum of its parts. The challenge is to create that brand identity.

Design and branding add extra layers to a differentiated product – shown in Figure 7.3. The functional qualities of the product/service can be enhanced through the aesthetics of design and reinforced by the emotional values associated with the brand. The more points of differentiation from competitors you have the more sustainable your competitive advantage. Hi-fi manufacturer Bang & Olufsen uses aesthetics of design as well as status. Apple combines a high quality, easy-to-use product with elegant design, a fashionable, desirable brand – and a high price. Again, good design may cost money but it is not just for large companies. South Beauty (see Case insight below) understands that the design of its restaurants – its décor, layout and ambiance – is just as important as the quality of its food and service if it is to be able to charge higher prices than other restaurants. The important thing is that all the elements that contribute to the brand image are consistent.

> More than ever, consumers expect brands to be environmentally aware. They want to invest financially and emotionally in a product and, at start-up, you can't ignore that.
>
> **Chris Holmes**, founder, Woodbuds, *The Sunday Times*, 28 June 2015

 Case insight   South Beauty

Creating an identity

Zhang Lan opened her first restaurant specializing in Sichuan cuisine in in the 1990s in Beijing with $20,000 of savings. Today, South Beauty is a chain of some 40 restaurants employing thousands of people. It offers high-quality, high-price dining in luxurious surroundings. From the first restaurant Zhang Lan realized that a restaurant was about more than just food. The presentation of the food was important – it had to look good as well as taste good.

Continued...

Continued from previous page...

Service had to be first class. The design of the interior had to match the prices being charged and create the right ambiance. Today the flagship restaurant is the opulent Lan Club in Beijing, with an interior designed by the French designer Philippe Starck. Location was also important, and the first restaurant was located near to government buildings, and government officials frequently visited with important guests. However, creating a clear identity and branding it were the key factors that would help her grow the chain. She has tried to create a brand that appeals to her target market – 'business, white-collar people'. She chose an opera mask as the logo for South Beauty, echoing the consistent theme of quality and luxury that she hopes is embodied in the brand.

QUESTION:

1 How important are service, ambiance and brand to a restaurant?

 ## Case insight   Zound Industries

Differentiation by design

 zoundustries Zound Industries was founded in 2008 by eight individuals with different backgrounds in design, product development, finance, marketing, sales and business. Despite its youth it is already making a mark in the technology industry by bringing distinctive design to bear on headphones, merging the function of a sound-source with fashion accessories targeted at different markets. It is one of the fastest growing companies in Sweden, with offices in New York and Shenzhen, where most of the equipment it sells is manufactured. Co-founder and President Konrad Bergström explained:

'Eight years ago, when you were choosing your sneakers and the right shirt and then you just put on your ugly headphones. You didn't think about it, because the headphones showed that you liked music. And then when someone started to work with it and then make nice headphones that were more in line with design... then all of a sudden everybody started to say "oh, I can't wear these headphones because they don't look cool" ... It's not only about technology, it's a combination of technology and brand and design.' (*The Guardian*, 25 September 2014)

'The big dinosaurs of headphones or electronics still look at headphones as a technical product. If you search on the web, they are seen as a technical product. What we try to do is be the best in other aspects. Be best in design, be best in functionality but also be best when it comes to sound. What we are working really hard on is building these soft values, that if you use our products it says something more than just functionality. You are connecting in some way.' (www.highsnobiety.com, 3 May 2013)

Zound's mission is 'making electronics fashionable and fashion electronic'. Not that long ago it was the brand of trainers you wore that defined your lifestyle and 'tribe'. Today it is your headphones, and Zound has helped create this. Zound produces four brands of headphones and mini-speakers, each range targeted at a different market, although you can only really appreciate these different products by viewing them on the website:

Urbanears: Launched in 2009, this is the biggest brand. It is fashion-orientated, quirky and fun at a mid-point price range. It was voted one of the 'CoolBrands' of 2014/15 in the *Sunday Times* annual survey. These headphones feature many useful functional design details as well as using a range of materials and textile wrap cords that give them a feeling closer to a garment than a technological product. There are also distinctively designed mini-speakers;

Coloud: Targeted at the young and active, this range offers a colourful, cheaper alternative to Urbanears. It is a headphone equivalent of a Swatch watch. Zound has partnered with Nokia to make these headphones from a smaller number of components and keep costs low. Triangularity is a distinctive theme that runs throughout

Continued...

Continued from previous page...

the Coloud range, from the logo to the packaging to the angles in the headphone design;

Marshall: Launched in 2010, this is a brand licensed from the much-respected amplifier company. It is a quality range of headphones and speakers that sells to the high end of the market. It mirrors the distinctive look of Marshall amps and, by working with Marshall Amplification, also mirrors the distinctive sound quality;

Molami: Launched in 2011, this is an ultra-high-end, female-focused fashion range, distinctively angular and incorporating materials like leather and silk. Zound boasts that the range can be worn as a stylish fashion accessory that complements any outfit, whether or not it is being used as a headphone. It was launched in cities around the world in the same way a fashion house might show off the latest season's designs. It is regularly featured in fashion magazines.

Courtesy of Zound Industries

To support and promote its products Zound hosts high-profile Swegie events showcasing Swedish design, culture and creativity that coincide with fashion weeks in cities around the world, making certain they all have a 'celebrity' feel.

Zound set its sights on going global from its very beginning. Its vision is 'to be the world-leading lifestyle headphone manufacturer'. The company's strategy has been thought through systematically. Its distinctive design-led products are targeted at specific markets: 'From the time a product is developed to the day it is sitting on a store shelf, it has been strategically thought through how to create, market, and distribute it and which brand the product will be sold under. This way, multiple demographics are reached.' It has developed new products and new markets with relentless effectiveness.

Zound's success has also been based on its ability to partner with others. Starting at the very beginning the founders had a range of skills and experience. They describe themselves as a 'collective'. It has sought additional capital systematically at different stages of its growth, starting in 2009. It has partnered with different distributors in different countries and even produced joint-branded products with the retailer H&M. In 2014 Zound announced a partnership with Swedish telecom operator TeliaSonera, who acquired a stake in Zound. The aim is to bundle fashion headphones, audio speakers and device accessories together with TeliaSonera's mobile telecommunications.

By 2014 the company had sold over 8 million pairs of headphones in over 20,000 stores including Apple Stores in the USA and Canada, and Selfridges, Colette, FNAC and Media Market in Europe. Thousands of articles have featured the company's products, in publications such as *Vogue* (US), *Elle* (US) and *Time*.

The company believes software and hardware can be integrated into headphone design, delivering the same functionality as smartphones but as a fashion accessory. It plans to extend its Urbanears and Coloud headphone brands into the smartphone market in 2015. The move from audio products to smartphones is driven by the observation that smartphones have now become commodities, in the same way that headphones did 20 years earlier, and the market is ready for something different and distinctive that is both functional and fashionable. Further into the future, the company is also considering expanding into wearables.

❏ Go to the website on: www.zoundindustries.com

QUESTIONS:

1 Describe who you think is the target market for each of the four brands.

2 What is the value proposition for each target market?

3 How are the company's products differentiated from those of competitors?

4 If this is a fashion brand, is it sustainable? If so, how?

Corporate social responsibility (CSR)

Values in the corporate world translate not only into the culture of an organization and its brand but also into strategies and actions that have an ethical and social, rather than just a profit, dimension. The areas of business ethics, social responsibility and environmental sustainability have now been subsumed within what is called corporate social responsibility (CSR). This can include philanthropy, but we shall look at the nature of entrepreneurial philanthropy in greater detail in Chapter 17. It is now widely accepted that many business practices can have negative social and environmental side effects. There is a hierarchy of virtue for companies practising CSR, shown in Figure 7.4. At its base is CSR that delivers profit to the company. Next is CSR that comes through compliance with the law. Finally, there is CSR that is discretionary, based upon ethical norms and a desire to do the best thing for the community and society as a whole. Fortunately, elements of the hierarchy are not mutually exclusive and there can be commercial benefit in many forms of CSR.

Figure 7.4 CSR hierarchy of virtue

Case insight   Brompton Bicycle (2)

Environmental policies

Like a number of companies, Brompton Bicycle (reread Case insight on page 50) is concerned about its impact on the environment. Their website states that they are committed to:

> Striving to continually improve their environmental performance and integrating environmental management best practice and managing business operations to prevent pollution. For example, end-of-life recycling of bicycles is being investigated and the company plans to introduce a scheme shortly.

> Reducing their consumption of resources and improving their efficient use while managing waste generated from operations according to the principles of reduction, re-use and recycling. For example, waste from the manu-

facturing process – mainly metal – is collected and, where possible, recycled. All paper, cardboard, aluminium and plastics are recycled.

> Measuring and taking action to reduce the carbon footprint of the business. Cranfield University conducted an audit of Brompton's operations, allowing anyone to see how separate parts of the supply chain contribute to the 'carbon footprint' of the bike they buy, and how far they would have to ride their Brompton to offset the carbon that went into its manufacture and distribution. This assessment was carried out in compliance with PAS 2050, the official standard for calculating a product's carbon output.

> Giving due consideration to environmental issues and energy performance in the acquisition, design, refurbishment, location and use of buildings. For example,

Continued...

Continued from previous page...

all lights and heating boilers have been replaced by energy-efficient ones. Solar power is used to heat water and heating is controlled by an energy-efficient system.

> Ensuring environmental, including climate change, criteria are taken into account in the procurement of goods and services. For example, the company switched its renewable energy electricity supplier to Ecotricity (see Case insight on page 184).

> Promoting the principle of sustainable transportation and the integration of cycling in local and government planning strategies. As an example of good practice,

the company provides bikes for employees at heavily subsidized costs.

> Complying with all relevant environmental legislation.

Go to the website where you can read Brompton's policies and what they are doing to achieve them: www.brompton.com

QUESTION:

1 Why are these policies in the interest of Brompton as well as society in general?

2 At what levels of the CSR hierarchy in Figure 7.4 does the company operate?

Kotler and Lee (2005) suggested that the more a firm can benefit from CSR the more it will be inclined to integrate it on a strategic decision-making level, thus increasing its effectiveness in promoting its social causes. Looked at strategically, CSR can be used to both bring social and economic goals into alignment and to leverage capabilities and relationships in support of charitable causes (Porter and Kramer, 2002). This can create additional value for both the company and the causes it supports. Porter and Kramer later argued that, without such a strategic integration, the result will be 'a hodgepodge of uncoordinated CSR and philanthropic activities disconnected from the company's strategy that neither make any meaningful social impact nor strengthen the firm's long-term competitiveness' (Porter and Kramer, 2006). CSR and any philanthropic activities therefore need to be integrated into the overall strategy and strategy development of the firm. They should also be integrated into the formulation of the firm's corporate identity (Van de Ven, 2008). As well as helping to achieve altruistic aims, strong CSR policy can have three sound commercial benefits:

1. Increased sales, brand identity and customer loyalty

While any product must first satisfy the customer's key buying criteria – quality, price etc. – a strong CSR brand can increase sales and customer loyalty by helping to differentiate it (see Abel & Cole Case insight on page 185). Customers are increasingly drawn to brands with a strong CSR profile and CSR has become an element in the continuous process of trying to differentiate one company from another. A strong CSR brand can even create its own market niche for an organization. On the other hand, a bad CSR image can severely damage sales, as BP found after the Gulf of Mexico oil spillage in 2010, and research certainly suggests that consumers will punish firms that are perceived to be insincere in their social involvement (Becker-Olsen et al., 2006). It is because consumers tend to form relationships with brands that explains why the motivation behind CSR initiatives matters so much to them (Van de Ven, op. cit.). It mirrors personal relationships and is based heavily on trust and respect.

2. Reduced operating costs and productivity gains

Sustainability is about measuring and controlling inputs and many environmental initiatives therefore reduce costs (e.g. reducing waste and recycling, having better control of building temperatures or reducing use of agrochemicals). Yahoo! saved 60% of its electricity costs in the USA simply by opening windows where servers are located so as to let the hot air out. General Electric started a programme of becoming more sustainable ('greener') in 2004. By 2008 this initiative had yielded $100 million in cost savings. Waste-reducing cost savings can come from looking at raw materials usage, the manufacturing process, packaging requirements, transport needs, maintenance and the use of disposal methods. Actions to improve working conditions,

We're really noticing people's perceptions changing. More than ever they want products that are sustainable but without sacrificing style or quality.

Heather Wittle, founder, Beyond Skin, *The Sunday Times,* 28 June 2015

Planet Mark is a mark that assures customers that the organization it is purchasing from is active in improving its environmental and social performance. Established in 2013 by the Eden Project and the sustainability consultancy Planet First, businesses achieving the mark are then helped to monitor their environmental impact and lessen it, as well as encouraging their employees, customers and stakeholders to take action.

Visit the website: http://www.planetfirst.co.uk/planet-mark/

The **Institute of Corporate Responsibility and Sustainability (ICRS)** is a not-for-profit professional membership body established in 2014 by a number of leading companies to help promote CSR and sustainability through seminars and other events.

Visit the website: https://icrs.info/

lessen environmental impact or increase employee involvement in decision-making can improve productivity. For example, actions to improve work conditions in the supply chain have been seen to lead to decreases in defect rates in merchandise. Many social initiatives can increase employee motivation and cut absenteeism and staff turnover. An increasing number of graduates take CSR issues into consideration when making employment decisions. And caring for employees pays dividends. According to one newspaper, Southwest Airlines, the only airline in the USA never to lay off employees is now the largest domestic airline in the USA, with a market capitalization equivalent to all of its domestic competitors combined (Pfeffer, 2010).

3. Improved new product development

A focus on CSR issues can lead to new product opportunities. For example, car manufacturers are striving to find alternatives to fossil fuels, while developing conventional engines that are more and more economical. Innovation linked to sustainability often has major systems level implications, demanding a holistic and integrated approach to innovation management. As well as reducing costs, General Electric's sustainability programme yielded 80 new products and services that generated $17 million in revenues between 2004 and 2008.

 ## Case insight   Ecotricity

Environmental opportunities

Dale Vince

Born in 1961, Dale Vince was once a New Age hippie. He dropped out of school aged 15 and at the age of 19 toured Britain and Europe for a decade in a peace convoy. These days he is better known as a millionaire entrepreneur who owns Britain's largest green energy company, Ecotricity. Founded in 1995, Ecotricity generates electricity from its wind turbines around the UK, as far apart as Dundee and Somerset, and sells the 'green' energy to domestic and corporate customers, including Sainsbury's, Tesco and Ford.

Vince used to mend vehicles and improvise mobile shelters from scrap in his hippie days. He also built wind turbines to take to music festivals to power sound systems. The idea for large-scale turbines came to him on a hill near Stroud in Gloucestershire where his home – a former army lorry – was powered by a small wind turbine. He thought, why not build a full-sized, permanent wind turbine in the field?

'All us hippies used to say "Why don't they build big wind turbines?" One day I thought, who are "they"? So I dropped back in to build windmills.'

Originally he planned only to build turbines for other people, but, having failed to get backing from his local electricity company, he decided to build a turbine on adjacent land and connect it to the national grid. However, the electricity company wanted to charge him £500,000 to connect it. He persisted and negotiated the price down to £27,000.

'It took a long time to get that down. And I still had to borrow some money. The big banks here in Stroud looked at me like I was crazy.'

He finally borrowed the money from a 'green' bank, Triodos. But this was at least partly because he had started generating a regular income by welding masts for other electricity companies.

'I thought about going to people with a good cause and asking for funding as a charity. But having a business model was better.' (Daily Telegraph, 27 May 2011)

Ecotricity is still based in Stroud and employs almost 200 'co-workers'. It is a private company 100% owned by Vince and very much a family business. His two sons work in the office, his brother helps design the turbines and his sister deals with customers' inquiries. Even his father and brother-in-law and sister-in-law work for the firm. The company operates a 'not-for-dividend' model, reinvesting income directly into new sources of renewable energy. It claims to reinvest almost £400 per customer, per year. In 2010 it raised funds directly from the public by offering four-year 'EcoBonds' with a preferential rate of interest for customers. With some 1,800 applicants offering a minimum £500 investment, half of them customers, the offering was a great success. In the same year, Vince handed over day-to-day management to a team of directors, some recruited from major energy companies.

Continued...

Continued from previous page...

In 2013 Ecotricity got the go-ahead to build the UK's fourth largest wind farm. It has also diversified into other sustainable energy areas such as electricity from a solar farm and gas from food waste using an anaerobic digester. In 2012, Ecotricity announced that it has invested in a pump-to-shore wave energy machine called Searaser.
Visit the website: www.ecotricity.co.uk.

QUESTION:

1 Is Ecotricity anything other than a commercial business? If so, how does it differ?

CSR and financial performance

The quest to link corporate CSR directly to financial performance and/or share price performance spans some 40 years and has often been contradictory and confusing. Nevertheless, in a review and assessment of 127 empirical studies Margolis and Walsh (2003) concluded that there was a positive relationship between CSR and financial performance, a result supported in a meta survey by Orlitzy et al. (2003). Looking at investment portfolios, Ven de Velde et al. (2005) concluded that high sustainability-rated portfolios (ones that integrated environmental, social and ethical issues) performed better than low-rated portfolios. What is more, an Economic Intelligence Unit Survey in 2008 showed that the vast majority of US business leaders and their boards of directors now accept a clear relationship between CSR and financial performance (Business Green, 2008).

More recently, in a review of the literature Carroll and Shabana (2010) conclude that on the whole a positive relationship exists between CSR and financial performance, 'but inconsistencies linger'. This is because financial performance is effected by many other internal and external variables, not all controlled by the firm. What is more, 'the benefits of CSR are not homogeneous, and effective CSR initiatives are not generic'. They concluded that CSR activities need to be part of a coherent and consistent strategy that is directed at improving both stakeholder relationships and social welfare. They talk about 'a convergence between economic and social goals' – where social good is crafted into creating economic value. Kurucz et al. (2008) summarized the four ways CSR can add value:

1 Reducing costs and risk (waste, hazards etc.);
2 Strengthening legitimacy and reputation, particularly through branding;
3 Building competitive advantage through reputation and branding;
4 'Creating win-win situations through synergistic value creation' – linking economic and social goals.

 Case insight   Abel & Cole

Using CSR to create differential advantage

Abel & Cole may be the UK's largest organic food delivery, but that was not how it started. In 1985 Keith Abel was studying history and economics at Leeds University and selling potatoes door-to-door to make some money. He was a good salesman and that meant he could charge more for the potatoes than the supermarkets. Keith went on to City University, London, to study law. Unfortunately, he failed his bar exams and decided he might as well team up with a

Continued...

Continued from previous page...

friend, Paul Cole, and start doing the same thing to make some money – no notion of organic food, just making money. A Devon-based farmer, Bernard Gauvier, approached them to sell his organic potatoes. They cost more, but after a week of selling them Keith realized that nobody asked the price. He decided to investigate the differences between organic and non-organic products, and went to see what his regular supplier was spraying on his potatoes. Keith was 'pretty appalled' at what he saw. The organic idea slowly started to creep into his consciousness and he started to 'push' the organic side of the business – after all, he was good at selling, and he was delivering the produce to the door of the customers. The customers responded by buying more and asking for other things. Bernard persuaded Keith and Paul to start putting together organic vegetable boxes and by 1991 Abel & Cole converted to selling only organic vegetables, buying them directly from farmers.

Sales took off in the 1990s and they started to employ people. Unfortunately, while sales increased, the result was mounting losses. Things came to a head when unpaid debts caused the Inland Revenue to threaten them with bankruptcy. Paul decided to leave and set up his own wholesale company, while Keith decided to retake his bar exams – and passed. Then Keith realized that he could not practise law if he was declared bankrupt. Threatened with losing the family house, Keith's father-in-law, Peter Chipparelli, then chair of Mobil Oil in South America, decided to bail him out. This may have focused Keith's mind because he started taking advice, first from his father-in-law then from social entrepreneur Alan Heeks, who introduced him to his 22-year-old daughter, Ella, who stayed to do work experience and went on to become Managing Director only three years later.

The success of the company is due to the consistency of its marketing mix. Its ethical, eco-conscious profile is assiduously nurtured. Vegetables are organic, local (never air-freighted), seasonal and ethically farmed. They are delivered in a recycled cardboard box by a yellow bio-fuel van, together with a newsletter which includes lively vegetable biographies and hints on how to deal with some of the more obscure vegetables in the box. The company prides itself on employing the formerly long-term unemployed and offers them bonuses for cutting waste. It gives to charity. Customers can deposit keys with the company so that vegetable boxes are left safe and sound indoors. Prices are high, but not outrageously so because the 'middle-man' has been cut out of the distribution chain. Customers are middle-class, and shopping from Abel & Cole is definitely fashionable.

In 2007 the private equity firm Phoenix Equity Partners bought a stake in the company, valuing it at over £40 million. However, the recession of 2008 took its toll and, as consumers tightened their belts, sales slumped dramatically. In 2008 Abel & Cole made a loss of £13.8 million. This led to the main holder of company debt, Lloyds Bank, taking control in a debt-for-equity swap. Keith Abel remained in managerial control and bought back into the company shortly afterwards. By 2011 it was again making profits – £2.5 million on sales of £9.3 million – and in 2012 the company was bought by the William Jackson Food Group, a 180-year-old family business that makes Aunt Bessie's Yorkshire puddings. Keith remained in managerial control.

❑ Visit the website: www.abelandcole.co.uk

QUESTIONS:

1 Describe Abel & Cole's target market and their value proposition.
2 How does the marketing mix contribute to the value proposition?
3 Why can Abel & Cole charge relatively high prices?
4 What dangers does a company like this face?

Building the brand

As we have seen, in a world where products and services are often all too homogeneous, a good brand is a powerful marketing tool that must be the cornerstone of any strategy of differentiation that also helps cement customer loyalty. Over 50% of consumers say that a known and trusted brand is a reason to buy a product (Blasberg et al., 2008; Hess et al., 2011). And it is therefore no surprise that distinctive branding can increase the value of a company. The brand must reflect the promise of your value proposition and the personality of organization that offers it. Support for social and ethical causes can reinforce this, and it often makes good commercial sense. Building a brand takes time. It is built up through effective use of communication media and is recognized through the brand or company name and logo.

At this stage you may not have a recognizable brand like the ones cited, but you do have yourself and that can start to shape the identity of your start-up. In many ways shaping the identity of a start-up is easier the fewer people you have working with you. You have your personal values and beliefs to build on, underpinned by what the big companies call CSR. The trick is to understand what these values and beliefs are and make them explicit and clear, to ensure that they are reflected not only in what you do, but how you do things. They need to be clear to customers, employees, distributors and suppliers alike. And they need to be sincerely felt values and beliefs, otherwise you will be quickly found out and any trust you may have built up will disappear quickly.

The identity of your business should reflect the culture within it – its personality. You create the culture of your business through your leadership and you need to ensure that you create the culture and identity you want. This involves being consistent in words and actions. It requires an emotional intelligence that does not always come naturally but can be nurtured. It will take time to develop, but you need to start immediately. We discuss these leadership skills and how they can affect the culture of your business in Chapters 18 and 19. Your brand should reflect this identity and one of the best ways to do that is to use yourself to promote the brand. In Britain, probably the best known proponent of this is Richard Branson. His companies, under the Virgin name, are closely associated with him and what he personally stands for.

Brand and company names need to be distinctive and easy to remember, say and even spell across different cultures and nationalities. This implies short names are best. It is important that they do not have negative associations and that names do not mean bad things in other languages. Names should be supportive of your value proposition. This is not always easy or straightforward. 'Freeserve' was a good brand name for one of the first UK internet service providers – it was free. However, in 2004 it was changed to 'Wanadoo' because the name was easier to market across Europe. In 2006 it was again changed to 'Orange' as the company's product offering was expanded to include internet and telecommunications. Because it adds value to the company, your brand name and logo can and should be trademark protected if possible (Chapter 9).

There are no hard and fast rules about using the company name as a product name. Sometimes this works, particularly when it is a one-product company, but there are examples of successfully using different company and product names alongside each other. 'Burger King' is a successful company brand that describes at least the major part of the company's product range. It is associative – suggesting some characteristic or benefit of the product, albeit sometimes in an indirect way. In this way 'iPhone' is another associative product brand name, but this time is used alongside the company name 'Apple', which has a different set of brand associations. This is a freestanding name that has built brand value over a number of years. Some company names have been less successful in transferring across product ranges. For example the Dyson brand name is based upon the inventor/entrepreneur James Dyson, but is still very much associated with vacuum cleaners, although the company now offers a range of electrical products.

> The key thing is never to do anything which discredits the brand, like ripping off the public or doing something which you'd feel uncomfortable reading about.

Richard Branson, founder, Virgin Group, *The Observer*, 14 September 2014

Branding is valueless if consumers get home and are disappointed with the product.

Simon Smith, Head of Brand, The Saucy Fish Co., *The Observer*, 29 September 2013

Case insight   Richard Branson and Virgin (1)

Building the brand

Richard Branson is probably the best known entrepreneur in Britain today and his name is closely associated with the many businesses that carry the Virgin brand name. He is outward-going and an excellent self-publicist. He has been called an 'adventurer', taking risks that few others would contemplate. This shows itself in his personal life, with his transatlantic power boating and round-the-world ballooning exploits, as well as in his business life where he has challenged established firms like British Airways and Coca-Cola.

He is a multimillionaire with what has been described as a charismatic leadership style.

His company, Virgin, is also probably one of the best known brands in Britain, with 96% recognition, and is well-known worldwide. The Virgin name has found its way onto aircraft, trains, cola, vodka, mobile phones, cinemas, a radio station, financial services, fitness studios and the internet. It is strongly associated with its founder, Sir Richard Branson – 95% can name him as the founder. Virgin believes their brand stands for value for money, quality, innovation, fun and a sense of competitive challenge. They believe they

Continued...

Continued from previous page...

deliver a quality service by empowering employees and, while continuously monitoring customer feedback, striving to improve the customer's experience through innovation. According to Will Whitehorn, then director of corporate affairs at Virgin Management:

> *'At Virgin, we know what the brand name means, and when we put our brand name on something, we're making a promise. It's a promise we've always kept and always will. It's harder work keeping promises than making them, but there is no secret formula. Virgin sticks to its principles and keeps its promises.'* (*The Guardian*, 30 April 2002)

The brand has been largely built through the personal PR efforts of its founder. Branson realized the importance of self-publicity very early in his career when the BBC featured him in a documentary called 'The People of Tomorrow' because of his first venture, *Student* magazine. Since then he has become known for his, often outrageous, publicity stunts, such as dressing up as a bride for the launch of Virgin Bride. According to Branson:

> *'Brands must be built around reputation, quality and price ... People should not be asking "is this one product too far"' but rather, "what are the qualities of my company's name? How can I develop them?"'* (*Losing my Virginity*, 1998, London: Virgin)

As to what these qualities are for Virgin, Branson gives us a candid insight into at least one of them:

> *'Fun is at the core of the way I like to do business and has informed everything I've done from the outset. More than any other element fun is the secret of Virgin's*

success.' (J. Andersen, *Local Heroes*, 1995, Glasgow: Scottish Enterprise)

Virgin has a devolved structure and an informal but complex culture based upon the Virgin brand. It is the brand that unifies the different companies in the group. Branson believes that finding the right people to work with is the key to success and the Virgin brand is so strong that it helps attract like-minded staff. He believes that it is not qualifications that matter in people, but rather their attitude. He calls them 'Virgin-type' people – staff who will enjoy their work and are customer-focused. And their enthusiasm for the brand rubs off on the customers. As Branson says:

> *'Our brand values are very important, and we tend to select people to work for us who share these values ... For as much as you need a strong personality to build a business from scratch, you must also understand the art of delegation ... I started Virgin with a philosophy that if staff are happy, customers will follow. It can't just be me that sets the culture when we recruit people. I have a really great set of CEOs across our businesses who live and breathe the Virgin brand and who are entrepreneurs themselves.'* (www.hrmagazine.co.uk, 13 July 2010)

QUESTIONS:

1 What is the essence of the Virgin brand? Why is it important to the company?

2 How is it developed and maintained?

3 How important is Richard Branson to the brand? What might happen when he retires?

Setting your prices

The more valued the brand to customers and consumers, the higher the price you will be able to charge. Setting price is a crucial element of the marketing strategy, but it is an art rather than a science. You may have one list price for your product or different prices for different market segments. Alternatively, you may operate an auction or negotiate the price of your product. You may offer discounts for types of purchases such as volume or loyalty and even prompt payment. There may be special offers at sales times.

The underlying principal is that the price charged for a product or service ought to reflect the **value-to-customer** of the package of benefits. The value can be different to different customers and in different circumstances. Take, for example, the price charged for emergency, compared to routine, plumbing work. A premium price reflects the benefit to the customer of preventing the house being flooded. However, the features of that emergency service, as reflected in the marketing mix, must reflect the benefits the customer is looking for; for example, ease of telephone call-out, 24-hour fast and efficient service, clear-up, facilitation of insurance claims and so on. Similarly, a low-cost airline like easyJet is able to charge a range of different prices for what is essentially the same service, transportation from one place to another, for example by offering early booking or off-peak fares. However, there is usually a **going rate** charged by competing firms for a similar product or service.

One factor in the pricing decision is the costs you face. Many people use what is called **cost+** or **full-cost** pricing. This takes the total cost of producing a product or delivering a service and divides it by the predicted number of units to be sold, to arrive at the average cost, to which a target mark-up is then added. Some costs, often called overheads, are **fixed**, and do not change with volume (e.g. depreciation of equipment, rent and some salaries). So what happens if predicted sales volumes are not achieved? The same fixed costs have to be spread over smaller volumes; implying that you need to charge a higher price to recover the overheads – a strategy that itself is likely to lead to falling sales. The reverse is true if volumes are greater than predicted.

Another benchmark is the **variable cost** of the product or service – the cost of producing one additional unit (e.g. the costs of materials or components and piece-work labour). You cannot charge just your variable cost because you are not recovering those fixed overhead costs. Unless price is above variable cost, there is no incentive to produce, because each additional unit sold would incur an additional loss. However, if you want to charge a range of prices to different market segments, these can be as low as your variable cost, so long as the average price you charge is above your full-cost. The lower your variable cost, the greater discretion you have in pricing. This is why off-peak tickets on low-cost airlines can be so much lower than peak fares. The extra variable cost of taking a passenger off-peak, when the plane is not full, is very low.

Pricing is therefore a question of judgement. Figure 7.5 shows the pricing range. Minimum short-term price is set by the variable cost, but long-term viability is set by the full-cost price. However, these ignore the customer. To make a profit, the average value-to-customer price needs to be above this. However, this can be made up of a range of prices to different segments, some of which might be below full cost (segments A, B and C).

Since it is always easier to lower prices than to raise them, it is important not to under-price your product/service. The price you charge should reflect the value-to-customer (Figure 7.5). Indeed most consumers, including business consumers, associate high price with high quality (Anderson, 2010). So, charging too low a price can mean that your customers associate too low a quality with your product or service. However, if customers show resistance to this higher price you can always offer a one-off, introductory discount – but this needs to be consistent with your launch strategy (see next chapter). In this way you have established the market price and can remove the discount in due course. If you can do this on a customer-by-customer basis, it should help you establish the actual value-to-customer. When you then try to remove the discount, you can reappraise the effect on demand. However, for most product/services, the lower your price, the higher your sales are likely to be. The question is whether that will lead to higher profit – and that is not always the case.

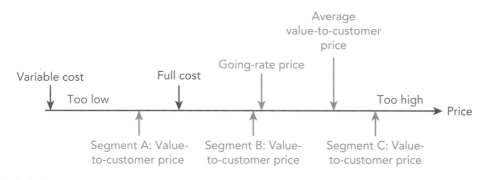

Figure 7.5 The pricing range

Case insight   Xtreme SnoBoards (1)

Costs and pricing

Xtreme SnoBoards* is a Case insight we shall return to in later chapters as we build up the company's financial forecasts. The company was set up by two young snowboarding enthusiasts to manufacture a specialist snowboard that they have perfected after two years of development. The founders undertook a detailed costing exercise that showed that the average material costs for each board was £32 and the average variable factory overhead was £5 per board (consumables, electricity etc.). Total variable costs are therefore £37 per board. The founders intend to pay themselves £36,000 in the first year and to employ three factory workers at an annual cost of £70,000, giving a total wage bill of £106,000. The factory is leased at an annual cost of £14,000 and depreciation of equipment, spread over eight years, is calculated at £8,700.

The average costs of producing a board is shown below based on target production of 3,780 units:

Variable costs:		
Direct materials		£32.00
Direct factory costs		£ 5.00
		£37.00
Fixed costs:		
Direct labour	£106,000	
Factory overhead	– depreciation	£ 8,700
	– factory lease	£ 14,400
	£129,100 ÷ 3,780 =	£34.15
Total average cost of producing each board		£71.15

The boards have been tested and used by professionals in competition and proved to be particularly responsive – so much so that a number of retailers have contacted the company to enquire about placing orders. There are three variations of board, designed for different conditions. The pair have researched their market and lined up two national retail chains and one overseas distributor who have placed advanced orders for the board at the price of £135 per board, net of delivery costs. These retail chains

intend to sell the boards at about £400. The founders therefore estimate that each board should make a contribution of £98 towards the fixed costs of direct labour and factory overheads (a contribution margin of 72.6%: £98 divided by £135) and a profit of £63.85 (a profit margin of 47.3%: £63.85 divided by £135), before other running costs for the business.

QUESTIONS:

1 How relevant are the costs of producing the board to the pricing decision?

2 Give some examples of what 'other running costs' are likely to be. Are they fixed or variable costs?

3 Based on these figures alone, what do you think of this business?

4 How can a shop justify setting a retail selling price of £400 for boards that cost them £135?

* Xtreme SnoBoards is a fictitious company.

Price and volumes

How demand reacts to changes in price is determined by the 'cross elasticity of demand'. The more differentiated the product or service, the more price-inelastic is demand – the volume sold does not vary greatly with changes in price. The more the product or service is a commodity, the more price will be elastic – sales volumes will be affected by price changes. Price elasticity may sound a highly theoretical concept, but the practical applications of it are important.

Table 7.2 shows the increase in sales volume required to maintain the same level of profitability as a result of a price reduction. This depends on the **contribution margin** (sales price minus variable cost, expressed as a percentage of the sales price - see Xtreme SnoBoards Case Insight opposite) before the price cut. If the contribution margin is only 20% and you were tempted to cut prices by 15%, you would have to increase sales volume by a massive 300% – a quadrupling of sales – just to generate the same profit as before. The higher the margin the less the effect, but even at 40% margin, you would still have to increase sales by 60%.

Table 7.2 The effect of price reduction on profit

		Contribution margin		
		20%	**30%**	**40%**
	−5%	+33%	+20%	+14%
Price reduction	**−10%**	+100%	+50%	+33%
	−15%	+300%	+100%	+60%

In contrast, Table 7.3 shows the decrease in sales volume that could sustain the same level of profitability in the face of a price increase. The same 20% margin could see a reduction in sales volume of 43% if prices were to be increased by 15% and would still generate the same level of profit. Of course the effect is less the higher the margin, but even at 40% margin, you could afford to loose 27% of your sales volume. However, if you cut overhead costs at the same time (why maintain the same level of staff with less work?) you should see profits actually increase. Alternatively, you might decide to improve the level of service offered by redirecting these overheads so as to justify the higher price. Either way, lower volumes might mean that stock holdings and other capital costs will reduce, an important consideration if capital is scarce.

Table 7.3 The effect of price increases on profit

		Contribution margin		
		20%	**30%**	**40%**
	+5%	−20%	−14%	−11%
Price increase	**+10%**	−33%	−25%	−20%
	+15%	−43%	−33%	−27%

As you can see from these tables, if you are working on slim margins, lowering prices may well lead to increased sales volumes, but it may also lead to lower profits. On the other hand, increasing prices may lead to increased profits, despite lower sales volumes. They show that the lower your contribution margin, the less able you are to reduce your price and the more vulnerable you are to price competition. In contrast, the higher your contribution margin, the lower the increase in volume needed to justified a price reduction and therefore the greater your discretion in terms of offering discounted prices. This can make differential pricing particularly attractive (segments A, B and C in Figure 7.5).

The contribution margin a product or service typically commands varies enormously from market to market, product to product, sector to sector. This is not just because of market demand, but also because of the high fixed overhead costs that some businesses need to cover in order to make a profit. Margins in the bricks-and-mortar retail or leisure sector are likely to be high because of the high fixed overhead costs they face in staffing and running their buildings. Just think of the costs you face to lease and run a prime-site, high-street store before you make a single sale. Many retailers try to operate with contribution margins of over 60%, allowing them considerable price flexibility for regular store 'sales'.

High fixed-cost businesses face the risk that these costs might not be met by the income generated from sales. Consequently, there is an increasing trend to try to 'share out' these fixed overhead costs as far as possible by partnering with other businesses such as suppliers, for example having just-in-time supplies which cut down stock-holding costs. While you might not be able to share costs with a customer, you might be able to get them to guarantee a certain volume of sales in return for a lower price (and lower contribution margin for you). This is why suppliers are happy to offer lower prices to the larger supermarkets and retailers in exchange for volume guarantees and why subscription-based business models might be attractive.

These calculations underline the importance of understanding the costs related to your business. Your financial structure influences the business model, the funding you need and the risks you face. We shall return to this in Chapter 11.

 ## Case insight   Lush

High differentiation strategy

If you walk down any high street in the UK – and many in a wide range of overseas countries – you might suddenly have your attention taken by a very distinctive, honeyed smell that causes you to look around and notice the bright, inviting shop front from which it emanates – a shop called Lush. Despite its ubiquity, Lush was only started in 1994. Yet today it has over 900 stores in over 50 countries, and its founder, Mark Constantine, has become a multimillionaire. It remains a privately owned family business and all seven shareholders work for Lush.

The story of Lush is intimately bound up with another very similar retailer called The Body Shop. In fact, you might, in passing, think that the shop front (if not the smell) bears more than a passing resemblance to The Body Shop, originally founded by Anita Roddick in 1976 and sold by her to the multinational L'Oréal (part of the Nestlé group) in 2006 for £652 million. And you would be right; not only the look but also the culture and ethics of the business are similar to The Body Shop, at least in its early years.

The link is the founder of Lush – Mark Constantine – and his is a very entrepreneurial rollercoaster of a story. Born in 1953, Mark was thrown out of his home by his mother and stepfather at the age of 17 and initially lived rough in the woods in Dorset, UK, before moving to London. He got a job as a hairdresser but started developing natural hair and skin products in his small bedroom. His ambition was to turn this into a business making and selling natural cosmetics, but it was not until he was 23 years old that he stumbled on his first success. He had read about The Body Shop in the press and sent Anita Roddick

some samples, including a henna cream shampoo 'which looked a bit like you'd just done a poo'. She had just opened her second shop. They met, got on well together and she placed her first order for £1,200 worth of products. At the age of 24 this was the real start of his first company, Constantine and Weir, set up with his wife, Mo, and Elizabeth Weir, then a beauty therapist and now retail director and shareholder of Lush. The company became The Body Shop's biggest supplier of cosmetics and Mark is credited for many of the elements of the company's ethical brand image, in particular its opposition to animal testing, that The Body Shop and Anita Roddick built up over those early years.

However, The Body Shop became uncomfortable with the formulations of many of its products being owned by another company and, in 1988, it bought Constantine and Weir for £6 million. Mark put the money into a new company, Cosmetics to Go, a mail-order company he had already started. The company never made a profit in any of its years of trading and went into bankruptcy in 1994. Faced with no money and a family to maintain, Mark started selling the bankrupt stock from a shop in Poole. This was the start of Lush.

As the business grew, new finance was injected by Peter Blacker, of British Ensign Estates, and Lush's finance director, Andrew Gerrie, who now sits on the board. They put in 'modest sums' but, cleverly, Mark set the exit value of these investments at the time, so that they could be bought out. Mark never forgot these ups and downs, and part of the firm's mission statement (prominent on the wall of its shops) states that 'we believe in the right to make mistakes, lose everything and start again'.

Continued...

Continued from previous page...

Lush does more than just make and sell cosmetics through its own shops. The distinctive elements of the marketing mix might be small individually but add up to give it a uniqueness that differentiates it from competitors. And, while cosmetics have always delivered a 'feel-good' feeling, Lush has added an environmental and social responsibility dimension to this value proposition.

> Its range of hand-made soaps, shampoos, shower gels, lotions, bubble bath and fragrances are 100% vegetarian, 83% vegan and 60% preservative free. They are made in small batches based upon shop orders from fresh, organic fruit and vegetables, essential oils and safe synthetic ingredients in factories around the world. Stores do not sell products older than four months. In addition to not using animal fats in its products, Lush is also against animal testing and tests its products solely with human volunteers. Moreover, Lush does not buy from companies that carry out, fund or commission any animal testing.
> The distinctive smell of a Lush shop is caused by the lack of packaging – which is environmentally sound – and Lush offers a free face mask for returning five or more of their product containers. The aim is to have 100% of their packaging recyclable, compostable or biodegradable.
> Lush shops are fun places, often with promotions and campaigns going on inside and outside. It supports many campaigns around animal welfare, environmental conservation, human rights and climate change.
> Some products, like 'bath bombs', are stacked like fruit and others such as soap are sold like cheese, wedges stacked on shelves and sold by weight wrapped in greaseproof paper. These attractive, bright displays give Lush shops the feel of old-fashioned market stalls or sweet shops.
> The shops are staffed by enthusiastic young people who are trained not to 'sell' but to help people select products by providing comprehensive product information, which includes who at Lush made the product.
> Lush donates around 2% of its profits to charity, supporting many direct action groups such as Plane Stupid, a group against the expansion of UK airports, and Sea Shepherd, a group that takes action against Japanese whaling ships. Often it launches products specifically to support these groups. Profits from the sale of 'Guantanamo Garden', an orange foaming bath ball, were donated to the human rights charity Reprieve, which helped Binyam Mohamed, a British resident who was held at Guantanamo Bay. It launched a Charity Pot moisturizer, giving the entire proceeds to charities

such as the Dorset Wildlife Trust and the Sumatran Orangutan Society.

The founders of Lush have some strong ethical beliefs that are reflected in their lifestyle and the values of the company. These values are stated on their website:

> We believe in buying ingredients only from companies that do not commission tests on animals and in testing our products on humans.
> We invent our own products and fragrances, we make them fresh by hand using little or no preservative or packaging, using only vegetarian ingredients and tell you when they were made.
> We believe in happy people making happy soap, putting our faces on our products and making our mums proud.
> We believe in long candlelit baths, sharing showers, massage, filling the world with perfume and in the right to make mistakes, lose everything and start again.
> We believe our products are good value, that we should make a profit and that the customer is always right.
> We also believe words like 'Fresh' and 'Organic' have an honest meaning beyond marketing.

Lush never advertises. Its growth has been organic. It owns its businesses overseas in various joint ventures, including the USA, Japan and Australia. In 2001 Lush tried to buy The Body Shop, but the Roddicks turned down the offer. It is listed regularly in *The Sunday Times* 100 Best Companies to work for. The business is still based in Poole, Dorset, and run from a small office above the first shop. Mo still designs cosmetics. One son, Simon, is head perfumer, and another, Jack, does the online marketing. Daughter Claire works for the charity Reprieve, to which Lush donates. The Constantines have lived in the same house now for 25 years. Mark does not hold a driving licence and has never owned a car. He often cycles to work. His hobby is bird songs and he has published a book on the subject. Mark is proud of Lush:

'Lush has been the most lucrative and successful thing I have ever done. There have been some innovative products that have helped propel the business, including bath bombs and the dream cream. The fact that the products don't have packaging helps boost profits. It is both an environmental and economic decision. The model is that if you don't package, you have enough money to put into your product and can give better value to the customer.' (The Sunday Times, 20 April 2014)

❑ Visit the website: www.lush.co.uk

Continued...

Continued from previous page...

QUESTIONS:

1 Who are Lush's target market segments and what is the value proposition it offers?

2 Which market segments might it not appeal to?

3 What are the operational imperatives for Lush – the things it needs to get right to enable it to deliver the value proposition? How these are achieved?

4 What does the Lush brand represent and how does is reflect the value proposition?

5 How does the company seek to differentiate itself from competitors? How real and sustainable are these elements of competitive advantage?

6 What is the role of ethics in the value proposition for Lush? How important are they to Lush? How might they be safeguarded?

 Practice insight reminder Characteristics of a good business idea – 6 & 7

6 **Sustainable** – the business must be built on solid foundations so that it has longevity.

7 **High profit margins** – the more innovative your product/service and your market, the higher your margin is likely to be.

⊃ Summary

> Your values and beliefs should underpin the business. They set expectations for how to operate and treat people – customers, employees, partners and suppliers. They should be reflected in your value proposition to customers.

> A mission statement is a statement of purpose for your business. This should be underpinned by your values.

> Developing a vision for the future of your business is important. This is a shared mental image of a desired future state. It must be attractive but credible – acknowledging the tension created by a realistic appraisal of the current situation. It is communicated as a vision statement.

> Values-based marketing seeks to develop customer relationships and is usually underpinned by a strong brand identity. It encourages customers to become loyal advocates of a product/service by involving them in aspects of marketing and product development.

> You can differentiate your product/service through its functional capabilities, its design and its brand.

> Branding identifies the product/service offering to the customer and is the start of developing a relationship

based upon trust that mutually benefits the customer and company.

> Your brand identity should reflect the value proposition you present to customers and be underpinned by the values that you hold. Effective branding adds value to the customer and the organization.

> As well as being worthwhile in its own right, CSR can be used to underpin your brand identity by providing evidence of your values and beliefs. It can also make sound commercial sense in other ways.

> Your brand should reflect the personality of your organization – its culture – and this will take time to establish. You create the culture of your organization through your leadership, and the culture of the organization is likely to reflect your personality.

> The price you set for your product/service should reflect the value to the customer, but will be influenced by your costs and the 'going rate'. It may be possible to charge different prices to different markets segments, reflecting the value to them of the product/service. In setting these prices you need to understand your cost structures and be able to estimate the price elasticity of demand.

✓ Activities

1 Compare and contrast the mission statements for easyJet, Golden Krust and Starbucks.

2 List your values; beliefs; and ethical, social and environmental concerns. How can these be reflected in your value proposition? How can this be communicated to your target market(s)?

3 Write down your vision for the business.

4 Using Wickham's pro-forma, write a mission statement for the business. Are your values, vision and mission consistent?

5 Based on your mission statement and underpinned by your values, write down words that convey the message you want your brand to convey. Craft this into a simple, coherent message for customers and write down how this might be effectively communicated.

6 Brainstorm a name for your business. Ideally it should reflect the message from the previous exercise.

7 Estimate your fixed and variable costs. Compare these to the prices you intend to charge for your product or service in different market segments. Estimate the volume of sales you need to achieve to make an acceptable profit.

🗩 Group discussion topics

1 Why are values in business important? Are they ever dangerous?

2 Why are ethics in business important?

3 Can you make more money being ethical or unethical in business?

4 The law defines the extent of our ethical and social responsibility. Discuss.

5 The law says that avoiding tax is legal but evading it is illegal. Large multinationals like Starbucks, Google or Dell are therefore perfectly within their rights to move profits around the world to countries with low tax rates. Discuss.

6 SMEs cannot move profits around the world to countries with low tax rates. Companies that do this have an unfair competitive advantage. Discuss.

7 Is it ethical to make profit from ethical and social values?

8 Marketing is just about selling. Discuss.

9 Why is branding so important?

10 What makes a good brand?

11 Is creating a brand more or less difficult for SMEs than for a big company?

12 How can SMEs develop a brand without the resources big companies have to publicize it?

13 How can you 'communicate' a brand image?

14 Why are people willing to pay quite high prices for bottled water when it is free from the tap?

15 Costs determine price. Discuss.

16 Is there really a limit to the price you can pay for a product or service?

17 Can you really sell less and make more profit?

18 How can you charge different prices for the same product or service?

☛ References

Aaker, J., Fournier, S. and Brasel, S. (2004) 'When Good Brands Do Bad', *Journal of Consumer Research*, 31(1).

Anderson, J.C. (2010) 'Purchasing Higher-Value, Higher-Price Offerings in Business Markets', *Journal of Business-to-Business Marketing*, 17(1).

Becker-Olsen, K.L., Cudmore, B.A. and Hill, R.P. (2006) 'The Impact of Perceived Corporate Social Responsibility on Consumer Behavior', *Journal of Business Research*, 59(1).

Blasberg, J., Vishwanath, V. and Allen, J. (2008) 'Tools for Converting Consumers into Advocates', *Strategy and Leadership*, 36(2).

Business Green (2008), 'US Execs: CSR Initiatives do Boost the Bottom Line', available online at http://BusinessGreen.com.

Carroll, A.B. and Shabana, K.M. (2010), 'The Business Case for Corporate Social Responsibility: A Review of Concepts, Research and Practise', *International Journal of Management Reviews*, available online at http://academia.edu.

Hamel, G. and Prahalad, C.K. (1994) *Competing For the Future: Breakthrough Strategies for Seizing Control of Your Industry and Creating the Markets of Tomorrow,* Boston, MA: Harvard Business School Press.

Hess, J., Story, J. and Danes, J. (2011) 'A Three-Stage Model of Consumer Relationship Investment', *Journal of Product and Brand Management*, 20(1).

Kotler, P. and Lee, N. (2005) *Corporate Social Responsibility: Doing the Most Good for Your Company and Your Cause*, Hoboken, NJ: Wiley.

Kotler, P., Kartajaya, H. and Setiawan, I. (2010) *Marketing 3.0: From Products to Customers to the Human Spirit*, Hoboken, NJ: John Wiley & Sons.

Kotter, P. (1996) *Leading Change*, Boston, MA: Harvard Business School Press.

Kurucz, E., Colbert, B. and Wheeler, D. (2008), 'The Business Case for Corporate Social Responsibility', in A. Crane, A. McWilliams, D. Matten, J. Moon and D. Seigel (eds) *The Oxford Handbook of Corporate Social Responsibility*, Oxford: Oxford University Press.

Margolis, J.D. and Walsh, J.P. (2003), 'Misery Loves Companies: Social Initiatives by Business', *Administrative Science Quarterly*, 48.

Ohmae, K. (2005) *The Next Global Stage: Challenges and Opportunities in our Borderless World*, Upper Saddle River, NJ: Prentice Hall.

Orlitzy, M., Schmidt, F.L. and Rynes, S.L. (2003), 'Corporate Social Performance: A Meta-Analysis', *Organization Studies*, 24.

Pfeffer, J. (2010) 'Layoffs are Bad for Business: The Downside of Downsizing', *Newsweek*, 15 February.

Piercy, N.F. (1999) *Tales from the Marketplace: Stories of Revolution, Reinvention and Renewal*, Oxford: Butterworth-Heinemann.

Piercy, N.F. (2001) 'The Future of Marketing Is Strategizing' in S. Dibb, L. Simkin, W.M. Pride and O.C. Ferrell, *Marketing: Concepts and Strategies*, Boston, MA: Houghton Mifflin.

Porter, M.E. and Kramer, M.R. (2002) 'The Competitive Advantage of Corporate Philanthropy', *Harvard Business Review*, December.

Porter, M.E. and Kramer, M.R. (2006) 'Strategy and Society: The Link between Competitive Advantage and Corporate Social Responsibility', *Harvard Business Review*, 12.

Van de Ven, B. (2008) 'An Ethical Framework for the Marketing of Corporate Social Responsibility', *Journal of Business*, 82.

Ven de Velde, E., Vermeir, W. and Corten, F. (2005), 'Corporate Social Responsibility and Financial Performance', *Corporate Governance*, 5(3).

Wickham, P.A. (2001) *Strategic Entrepreneurship: A Decision-Making Approach to New Venture Creation and Management*, Harlow: Pearson Education.

🌐 www.palgrave.com/Burns-Entrepreneurship-And-Small-Business-4e

Go online to access additional teaching and learning resources for this chapter on the companion website. Click here in the ebook to complete a multiple choice revision quiz for this chapter.

LAUNCHING YOUR BUSINESS

Contents

Stockbyte/ PunchStock/ Getty Images

Learning outcomes

When you have read this chapter and undertaken the related activities you will be able to:

> Assess the skills needed for a start-up and how they might be met;
> Understand the different ways of employing people and how to go about recruiting them;
> Draw up a job description and a person specification;
> Understand the benefits of using professional advisors;
> Understand the factors that influence the selection of an effective team and identify your own preferred Belbin Team Role;
> Understand the customer buying process and how the marketing mix can be used to encourage customers to become an advocate of your product/service;
> Understand how to find prospective customers throughout your distribution chain;
> Enhance your face-to-face sales skills;
> Write a press release;
> Draw up a communications campaign that helps launch your business;
> Develop a marketing strategy that launches the business.

Case insights

Huddle	Good Hair Day
BicycleSPACE	Clippy
The Fabulous Bakin' Boys (now The Fabulous Bakers)	Jack Wills: University Outfitters

Practice insight: 6 tips for dealing with objections

Practice insight: 6 tips for closing a sale

Practice insight reminder: Characteristics of a good business idea

People, people, people

Every business is primarily about people – as customers and as employees. This chapter is about both finding and attracting people to work with as partners or staff and customers. Many start-ups do not employ anybody to start with, but the only way you will grow is by recruiting appropriate staff, including managers, to deliver your product/service to more and more customers. Selecting, developing and managing staff will become a key activity – something many entrepreneurs have a problem with. When there is more than one founder, the issue of working with the other partners so as to become an effective management team can be just as challenging. And as a business grows it will face challenges and problems that mean the founder needs to adapt and change the way they manage the business. There are a number of 'stage models of growth' that seek to describe the challenges that they face as the business grows. These are covered in Chapter 12. The more rapid the growth, the more difficult this will be. And all of these changes need to be properly managed alongside the day-to-day delivery of customer service. It is little wonder that so few firms grow to any size. Some entrepreneurs even decide not to grow their business because they realize they cannot manage these changes or because they prefer to move on to another start-up.

Recruiting the right people to work with is crucial to the success of your business – the bigger the start-up, the more important the team. Team members can bring a range of skills, capabilities, knowledge and networks that complement and leverage the founder's experience. Industry experience can be vital in a new venture, particularly if the experience comes from a competitor – which is why Yahoo! recruited Marissa Mayer as its president and CEO in 2012. Mayer was one of Google's earliest employees and vice president of search products. It might take time to attract everyone you need and you might even have to launch the business with some key posts unfilled, but it is important that you recruit the best people and plug any skill gaps in some way.

You start by developing a skills profile for the business and identifying where the gaps exist. You might do this pre-launch and, say, for three years' time. These are operational skills and therefore depend on the nature of your business (Chapter 10). However, you will also need to have coverage of the core functional disciplines of business – sales, marketing, accounting etc. You may also be looking for specific market or industry skills. Depending on the size of your start-up, you may have to be flexible and live with a degree of overlap and indeed cope with some gaps, at least in the short term. It is therefore useful to classify the skills in your profile as 'key', 'important' or 'desirable'. Recruiting appropriate people with key skills, particularly pre-launch, may be a critical success factor (Chapter 10).

You can recruit people to work on a number of different bases:

> **Full/part-time** – Not all people want to work full-time and, for a start-up, each full-time employee can represent a large increase in fixed costs. So, employing part-time staff can be attractive, particularly if they are willing to work shifts and in-fill to meet customer demand, in which case you can specify the number of hours they work.

> **Regular hours/shift work** – Office workers might expect to work regular 'nine-to-five' hours, but in many industries, such as hospitality, shift-working is the norm and part-time work is common. The determinant factor here is what is required to provide the necessary customer service.

Getty Images/Ron Chapple Studios RF Thinkstock Images \ Ron Chapple Stock

> **Fixed-wage or salary/commission/piecework** – Employing full-time, fixed-wage or salary employees increases the fixed costs of your venture. While this may be necessary to attract the 'right' sort of person – particularly your management team – many types of jobs or even industries have different ways of working. Salespeople expect part of their remuneration to come from commission or bonuses based upon meeting their sales targets – the more they sell, the more they earn. Some workers expect to be paid on a piecework basis – they are paid for the volume they produce.

At some point you might be expected to draw up a job description for an employee listing the things they have to do and what they will be held accountable for in this role. This can problematic in a small, growing business where the nature of the tasks to be undertaken can change day-to-day and over time. Job descriptions can be made flexible. However, in some countries employees expect quite detailed and specific job descriptions. For example, the Swedish home furnishing store IKEA does not give employees job titles or precise job descriptions and this caused it a major problem when it first launched in the USA, where employees are used to clear roles and responsibilities. The resulting high staff turnover rates caused IKEA to change its recruitment processes so as to highlight the company's culture and values. Prospective employees who were not comfortable with this could therefore withdraw during the process.

Based upon the list of duties in the job description, you can then produce a person specification that lists the criteria on which to base selection of the person. This is an important document against which you can assess the suitability of a candidate for a post. Table 8.1 gives you a checklist of characteristics that might be included in this document. You can split these into 'essential' and 'desirable'. In most countries employees are expected to be given a contract of employment which outlines their terms and conditions of employment. In the UK this must be done within two months. What goes into this contract is prescribed by law. There are also a plethora of regulations and laws that regulate how you recruit, employ and dismiss employees.

Table 8.1 Person specification checklist

Person specification checklist

> Educational attainment	> Personal attributes (e.g. flexibility etc.)
> Experience (e.g. retail sales etc.)	> Personal characteristics (e.g. friendly etc.)
> Knowledge (e.g. marketing etc.)	> Personal circumstances (e.g. able to work
> Skills/abilities (e.g. team-working etc.)	evenings)

Finding a team

Finding and attracting a new venture team is rarely straightforward. Why should they join a risky start-up, particularly if they have a secure job in an established company? The answer lies in part with your persuasive power but also with the remuneration package you offer them. You may be short of cash to start with, but if you are successful there should be plenty of money to go around later on. So the answer may be to offer incentives such as target-linked bonuses, shares or share options. Most of the really successful start-ups, like Apple, have distributed shares to key managers early in their development.

Sometimes the new venture team will share the ownership of the business between them from the start. The share each has might reflect the cash, intellectual property or simply the time and effort they have put in to get the business off the ground – called '**sweat equity**'. The terms of a shareholders' agreement should specify how this is done, as well as anticipating future issues

The ability to find and hire the right people can make or break your business. It is as plain as that ... The right people in the right jobs are instrumental to a company's success.

Michael Dell, founder, Dell Corporation, *Direct from Dell: Strategies that Revolutionized an Industry*, 1999, New York: Harper Business

Table 8.2   Typical topics included in a Shareholders' Agreement

Topics in a Shareholders' Agreement

> Nature of the business
> Identity, role and title of founders
> Legal form of business
> Distribution of shares between founders
> Consideration paid for shares or ownership share of each founder (for cash or other consideration)
> Intellectual property signed over to company by founders
> Rights to appoint and remove directors
> Dividend policy
> Terms to protect minority shareholders
> Terms regulating the raising of capital (to avoid diluting existing shareholding)
> Conditions affecting founders regarding the valuation and disposal of shares, including buy-back clauses
> Other limitations on directors' and/or shareholders' freedom of action
> Resolution of disputes between shareholders

> You start out with a mission or dream and then you have to work out how you are going to get there. Any time that you choose to partner with anybody you make that choice to accelerate your growth, with the impact that has in some degree on your independence.
>
> **Kristian Segerstråle**, co-founder, Playfish, *The Sunday Times*, 22 November 2009

facing the founders. A shareholders' agreement only applies to those signing it, while the articles of association govern all future shareholders. Typical topics included in such an agreement are shown in Table 8.2.

Whatever the package you put together, you will need to seek out your potential team. Your network of contacts is always a good starting point – family, friends and professional contacts. You may need to advertise. However, rather than using the traditional media such as newspapers, an increasingly important mechanism is social media. You can use your Facebook or LinkedIn account to broadcast to friends or contacts that you are setting up a team and what skills, capabilities and knowledge you are looking for. Some companies use Twitter for recruiting. The range of communications media available are covered later in this chapter. Once you have people interested in joining your team, you need to shortlist those that meet your person specification and then interview those shortlisted to assess their suitability.

There has been considerable research into what makes a successful new venture team where ownership is shared. This has repeatedly shown the importance of cohesion and '**shared cognitions**' – shared goals and effective communications and transfer of knowledge between partners. 'Shared cognition' improves collective understanding within a group, and helps individuals with different functional backgrounds to reach consensus. This can improve decision-making quality and the general performance of the business (Smith et al., 2005; West III, 2007). It can also cut down on conflict within the partnership group (Burgers et al., 2009) and increase partners' 'reciprocal credibility and coordination' (Zheng, 2012), both positively effecting performance. Conflict generally takes two forms – relationship conflict and task conflict (Jehn and Bendersky, 2003). While conflicts over tasks can sometimes be productive and beneficial, relationship conflicts are rarely beneficial and may erode cohesion within the team negatively effecting performance (Gelfand et al., 2008). These studies underline the importance of being very careful in selecting partners and basing decisions not just on task competences but also on shared goals and good interpersonal relationships that can make for a cohesive partnership team.

However, sometimes, no matter how hard you try, you may be unable to find the 'right person' for the role you have identified. In these cases it may be possible to 'buy in' these roles through professional advisors, at least temporarily.

Using professional advisors

There are likely to be gaps in the professional knowledge and skills of any start-up. Professional advisors can be an invaluable source of this knowledge, skills and advice as well as providing an additional network of contacts for the founders. They might be persuaded to join a start-up for many reasons. They may be simply friends or family, willing to help because of the relationship with the founders. They might relish the challenge of helping a start-up. Professional advisors can also be hired or, in some cases, paid for by other bodies such as government. The types of professional advisors you might employ include:

Accountants – Accountants can help produce your financial plan (Chapter 15). They can then help produce your regular financial statements and then help analyse and interpret them (Chapter 11). Often they have access to industry financial norms that you can use to benchmark your performance. Indeed, the whole financial administration of your business can be subcontracted, including the issuing of sales invoices and collection of cash, the payment of purchase invoices and payroll administration. Accountants also offer tax advice and will handle the filing of information with appropriate bodies. They usually have a network of contacts who can help with finance and funding, from loan to equity capital. Every business needs to succeed financially to remain viable and having reliable accounting information is vital. The more ambitious your aims for your venture, the more likely you are to need good financial advice early on.

Lawyers/attorneys – Lawyers can help with anything involving the law. They can advise on the legal requirements of establishing the form of business organization you select or the various business licences or permits you might require. They can advise on safeguarding your business idea. They can help you draw up legal contracts – with staff, partners, suppliers or customers. They can be invaluable in drawing up a shareholders' agreement for the founding team. Often, like accountants, they have a network of contacts who can help with finance, from loan to equity capital, and sometimes they offer tax services. However, also like accountants, good lawyers can prove to be expensive, so it is always best to understand how they charge their fees before they start any work.

Business consultants – General business consultants can offer advice on marketing or strategic planning. They can help you draw up your business plan. Often they can provide access to other sources of help and advice, particularly at a local level, including specialist advice on specific industries or topics such as exporting. Local consultants can also provide invaluable access to local networks of other owner-managers and providers of capital. Some consultants might be 'free', paid for by government to help small firms. Most Western countries have services offering help and support to SMEs. In England this is provided through the Business Link network, in Scotland by Business Gateway, in Wales by Flexible Support for Business and in Northern Ireland by Invest Northern Ireland. In the USA it is provided by the Small Business Administration through its Small Business Development Centres.

Using advisors on a 'pay-as-you-go' basis can offer an attractive way of accessing a range of knowledge, skills and networks that a new venture might not be able to afford to employ on a full-time basis. The relationship with these advisors might be informal or formal – relying on a contract for service. However, skills gaps can also be addressed through:

> Your board of directors (Chapter 9);
> Different forms of partnership (Chapter 9);
> Equity investors, such as Business Angels (Chapter 14).

However advisors are used, new ventures can benefit by surrounding themselves with high-quality advisors to tackle the challenges they face. They add to the credibility of the management team and can persuade providers of finance to invest. The more ambitious your start-up, the more important this is.

This range of ways of meeting your need for people and the knowledge, skills and networks that they bring is summarized in Figure 8.1.

Have great advisers and listen to them. You don't have to take their advice but it's valuable to have other voices.

Sara Murray, founder, Confused.com, *The Sunday Times*, 1 February 2009

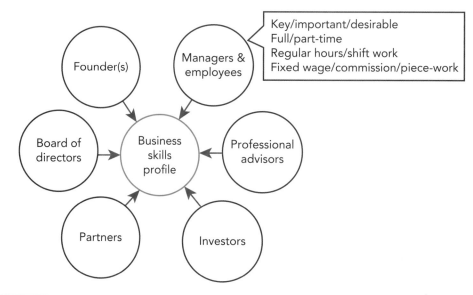

Figure 8.1   Meeting your skills needs

Selecting and developing the team

The ability to work effectively as a team is important. Team members bring with them information and experiences, as well as technical and management knowledge. Selecting an effective team will therefore depend upon the skills profiles and individual job descriptions and person specifications you develop. However, research suggests that demographic diversity such as age, gender and functional background is not as important for entrepreneurial team effectiveness as team process variables – how the team functions and their commitment to achieving overall goals (Chowdhury, 2005). The personal chemistry between members of the team is important. For a team to be effective, individuals need to have the right mix of a certain set of personal characteristics. Meredith Belbin (1981) identified three 'personal orientations', each of which translate into three 'team roles'. Each team role has positive qualities and allowable weaknesses. Individuals are naturally suited to two or three of these roles, yet all nine elements need to be present in a team for it to work effectively.

Thinking orientation

1   **Plant** – This is the team's vital spark and chief source of new ideas – creative, imaginative and often unorthodox. However, they can be distant and uncommunicative and sometimes their ideas can seem a little impractical.
2   **Monitor-Evaluator** – This is the team's rock – introvert, sober, strategic and discerning. They explore all options and are capable of deep analysis of huge amounts of data. They are rarely wrong. However, they can lack drive and are unlikely to inspire or excite others.
3   **Specialist** – This is the team's chief source of technical knowledge or skill – single minded, self-starting and dedicated. However, they tend to contribute on a narrow front.

People orientation

4   **Coordinator** – This is the team's natural chair – mature, confident and trusting. They clarify goals and promote decision-making. They are calm with strong interpersonal skills. However, they can be perceived as a little manipulative.

5   Team-Worker – This is the team's counsellor or conciliator – mild mannered and social, perceptive and aware of problems or undercurrents, accommodating and good listeners. They promote harmony and are particularly valuable at times of crisis. However, they can be indecisive.

6   Resource Investigator – This is 'the fixer' – extrovert, amiable, six phones on the go, with a wealth of contacts. They pick other people's brains and explore opportunities. However, they can be a bit undisciplined and can lose interest quickly once initial enthusiasm has passed.

Action orientation

7   Shaper – This is usually the self-elected task leader with lots of nervous energy – extrovert, dynamic, outgoing, highly strung, argumentative, pressurizes seeking ways around obstacles. They do have a tendency to bully and are not always liked. However, they generate action and thrive under pressure.

8   Implementer – This is the team's workhorse – disciplined, reliable and conservative. They turn ideas into practical actions and get on with the job logically and loyally. However, they can be inflexible and slow to change.

9   Completer-Finisher – This is the team's worry-guts, making sure things get finished – sticklers for detail, deadlines and schedules. They have relentless follow-through, picking up any errors or omissions as they go. However, they sometimes just cannot let go and are reluctant to delegate.

Chell (2001) suggested that the 'prototypical entrepreneur' might be a mix of three Belbin roles: plant (creative, ideas person), shaper (dynamism, full of drive and energy) and resource investigator (enthusiastically explores opportunities). She then suggested that the first team member to recruit should primarily be an implementer (reliable, efficient and able to turn ideas into practical action). The implementer will need a completer-finisher (conscientious, delivers on time), a team-worker (cooperative and unchallenging) and possibly a specialist (with particular knowledge or skills) working under them.

The challenge is to select the team and then to build cohesion and motivation. A cohesive team works together effectively because of its collective commitment to an agreed goal. Cohesive teams have been linked to greater coordination during team-working as well as improved satisfaction and productivity (Mach et al., 2010). The need for a cohesive team is particularly true for the partners team in a new venture as it has been shown to lead to superior business performance – providing a more stable and solid foundation of interpersonal relationships that produces synergistic behaviour and improves coordination (Ensley et al., 2002; Lechler, 2001; Thye et al., 2002). In most cases building a cohesive team involves building consensus towards the goals of the firm – perhaps easier between partners – while balancing multiple viewpoints and demands. However, too great a reliance on achieving consensus can lead to slow decision-making, so a balance is needed that will strain the interpersonal skills of the leader. In the best entrepreneurial firms, leadership seems to work almost by infection. The management team seems to be infected by the philosophies and attitudes of the founder and readily buy into the goals set for the firm, something that is helped if they share in its success.

Successful entrepreneurs build strong relationships with their team. Personal relationships are based upon trust, and trust is the cornerstone of a good team and an effective organizational culture. It is imperative that the management team trust you. This involves having transparent vision and values, being firm but fair, flexible but consistent. It involves being straightforward – doing what you say and meaning what you say – 'walking the talk'. It involves being open and spontaneous, honest and direct – being an authentic leader. While always placing the interests of the firm first, it also involves being supportive of individuals and having their interests at heart. Trust takes time to build and needs to be demonstrated with real outcomes, but it can be lost very quickly by careless actions and then takes even longer to rebuild. We shall return to issues around organizing and managing a team in Chapter 12 and to issues about leading them in Chapter 18.

Download the Belbin Team Roles questionnaire from: *www.belbin.com*

It takes real team spirit to take on challenges and win, and it also builds true camaraderie. It is this togetherness, above and beyond any other factor, that set great businesses apart from the also-rans.

Richard Branson, founder, Virgin Group, *Sunday Times*, 7 December 2014

The best teams stand-out because they are teams, because the individual members have been so truly integrated that the team functions with a single spirit. There is a constant flow of mutual support among the players, enabling them to feed off strengths and compensate for weaknesses. They depend on one another, trust one another. A manager should engender that sense of unity. He should create a bond among his players and between him and them that raises performance to heights that were unimaginable when they started out as disparate individuals.

Alex Ferguson, manager, Manchester United FC, 1999

In order to sell a product or service, a company must establish a relationship with the customer. It must build trust and support the customer's needs, and it must deliver a product that delivers the promised benefits.

Jay Conrad Levinson, *Guerrilla Marketing*, London: Piatkus Books, 1984

The customer journey

Just as with staff, you will need to seek out and attract customers. A good business idea and a persuasive value proposition does not guarantee success on their own. Customers will not queue up at the door of a start-up if they are unaware of its existence. Indeed, even if they are aware, they still might take some persuading to try a new, unproved product or service. As a newcomer to the market, you have little or no credibility or reputation. Even if you have a brand, customers will not initially recognize it. And then you still need to persuade them to purchase it again, and again. At least your brand should help them do this. But building that relationship that underpins an effective brand will take time. You need to attract the customer segments you are targeting and persuade them to start the journey to become the valuable loyal customers we discussed in the previous chapter. It is not easy or straightforward, even if you have the best product/service in the world. To do this you have to use all the tools in your marketing armoury – price, promotion, place and people – and in different ways, at different times and in different circumstances. How you go about this all depends on who your customers are.

The journey a customer takes in becoming a regular customer can be broken down into the four-stage process shown in Figure 8.2.

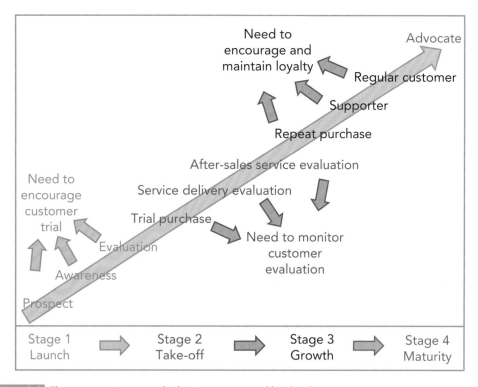

Figure 8.2 The customer journey – the buying process and loyalty chain

Stage 1: Launch

Once your prospective customer becomes aware of your product they will evaluate the value proposition it offers. They need to be made aware and encouraged to make that all-important first trial purchase. Often characterized as a buyer-behaviour model, this was broken down into a three-stage process called the AIDA model by Strong (1925): firstly, the cognitive stage, where the customer needs to be made aware of your product; secondly, the affective stage, where they need to have their interest stimulated and a desire to purchase generated; and, finally, the behaviour stage, where action to buy needs to be triggered.

Stage 2: Take-off

Once they have purchased your product/service, customers will evaluate whether you have delivered the value proposition that you promised. Remember, it will be the whole marketing mix that they then evaluate, including service delivery and after-sales service. And while they will be evaluating your offering, you should be checking to see if they are happy with it.

Stage 3: Growth

If the value proposition that is delivered meets their expectations then they may be persuaded to repeat purchase and become regular customers. Again, they will need some encouragement.

Stage 4: Maturity

The objective is to move the customer up the loyalty chain from regular customer to a supporter who thinks positively about the product/service, and ultimately to become an advocate. This is a customer who is so loyal that they are willing to recommend the product/service to others, and even bring in new customers or help with product development. Even at this stage their loyalty cannot be taken for granted. It must be encouraged and maintained.

As explained in the previous chapter, to take the customer through this journey you should be aiming to build a relationship with them – a relationship based on shared values. To achieve this you need to enter into a dialogue with them wherever they are on the loyalty ladder. The nature of that dialogue will be different, depending where they are on the ladder. Your communications strategy can help move customers up the loyalty ladder – creating awareness, stimulating need, creating brand awareness and loyalty and facilitating dialogue.

Ideally, relationships are based upon one-to-one and face-to-face interaction, but they can be influenced by various media. Indeed, in today's interconnected, knowledge-based society you can use a range of mass communications media to initiate, develop and maintain these relationships. And mass media becomes vitally important in communicating with mass markets, where the logistics of communicating face-to-face are problematic. Nevertheless, whether you are selling face-to-face or to mass markets, the objective is to build a long-lasting relationship with customers, rather than just selling them something on a one-off basis.

Finding your first customers

Finding the first customer is crucial, and if your network of contacts includes prospective customers or family or friends who might introduce you to them and use your network, it can short-circuit the problem you have with a lack of credibility. It all depends on who are your prospective customers and how you get to them.

Much of business-to-business selling is face-to-face, particularly when you are looking for that first order. Selling into distribution networks also often involves face-to-face selling. You start by identifying who specifically in the company you need to sell to. You need to find out the name of the buyer of your type of product/service and make an appointment to see them. Even this requires a degree of 'selling', just to get an appointment, because these are busy people with established suppliers. They need a reason to see you. And then you need to master some basic selling skills to turn these prospects into customers.

Face-to-face selling can be necessary for mass consumer markets but, because there are so many people, finding prospective customers that meet your marketing segmentation profile can be extremely time consuming. Of course you can sometimes buy in lists of prospects that meet your marketing segmentation profile and contact them directly – by phone, email or text. You may need to 'qualify' these leads – assess their real potential – before you commit too much time trying to sell to them. You might be able to obtain referrals. This can be particularly valuable once you are established and satisfied customers are willing to help. However, you need to persuade these prospective customers to show some interest in your product/service so they can be sold to. And this is particularly the case if you are counting on prospects contacting you rather than the other way round. There are many communications techniques you can use and there is a wide range of communications media. What media to use depends on the target market you wish to reach and the product/service you are offering. For example, if your target market is young males, digital new media, using the internet and smartphones, can be very effective and good value. However, if your target market does not use the internet or consume online content, this media will not work. Sometimes old-fashioned media such as flyers and posters can be more effective. Once you have identified the media, you need to decide on the message. Why should the prospect contact you, even if they see your message?

Case insight   Huddle

Getting noticed, getting used and getting customers

Courtesy of Huddle

Alastair Mitchell

Huddle is a cloud-computing system that allows documents, music and other data to be securely stored and accessed via the web. Its collaborative software allows users to share documents online and across multiple devices securely (on desktops via Microsoft Office applications, on the move with Android, iPhone and iPad apps), making it suitable for use by any organization where security is a concern. In fact, since its inception in 2006 it has become the global leader in cloud collaboration and content management, being used by over 100,000 organizations – ranging from NASA to Beats by Dre – in over 180 countries. Huddle now employs over 170 staff in London, San Francisco, New York and Washington, DC, has raised nearly $90 million in funding and has seen sales double year-on-year.

Huddle's co-founder is serial entrepreneur Alastair Mitchell. Born in 1977 and a graduate of Southampton University, his first start-up was an online media business and his second was an online commodities exchange. Both were

reasonably successful. He started Huddle with Andy McLoughlin, a Sheffield University graduate and friend whom he played badminton with. It was financed from £25,000 of savings and venture capital.

The company grew rapidly through users inviting colleagues either in the same workplace or from other organizations to work with them collaboratively using Huddle. Any individual could join for free but companies were charged a fee. This worked so well that most of the departments in the British civil service found themselves using the system extensively to share data and work collaboratively, resulting in a large British government contract. Since then it has repeated the success in the USA and is now also working with the Department of Homeland Security and the National Geospatial-Intelligence Agency to further develop its software.

❏ Visit the website: www.huddle.com

QUESTIONS:

1 What are the advantages and disadvantages of Huddle's early approach to generating customer awareness and purchase?

2 Would you continue to use the same model once you had gained established users?

3 Can this model be applied to other types of products? If so, give some examples.

Developing your sales skills

Most entrepreneurs will have to sell face-to-face at some stage – either to other businesses or to consumers. To sell face-to-face you need to identify the prospective customer by name and then be able to meet with them. This is easy to say but usually more difficult to arrange. Corporate buyers have busy schedules and established suppliers. Personal buyers often try to avoid salespeople. They need a reason to meet you – a hook that offers them something that they need.

It sounds obvious, but the first thing is to make certain you have identified the benefits this specific customer is looking for and thoroughly understand your value proposition. You must do some basic research on the prospect and, if relevant, the company they represent. The larger the potential sale, the more important the research and the longer you should spend on it. You want to build a relationship quickly. Knowing a few personal details about the prospect can help break down barriers quickly. But a professional relationship is based on mutual self-interest – you both want something – and trust that you both can deliver what you promise (in your case the value proposition and in their case cash payment). If possible, send them information on your company and your product/service in advance. A brochure can be very useful. At the meeting you need to establish what they want – the 'problem' they have – and how your product/service can solve the problem for them. You need to be able to:

> Ask questions and listen to the answers;
> Be clear about how your product/service will solve their specific 'problem' and be able to demonstrate its features either directly or with the help of photographs or brochures;
> Back up the claims you make about your value proposition with proof, for example by providing references or testimonials from satisfied customers;
> Handle objections and concerns;
> Close the sale.

Buyers are unlikely to eagerly buy your product or service on just your say-so. They will have doubts. How will the product or service really perform? Why should they trust what you claim? Ultimately this will boil down to a question of trust. And the bigger the expenditure you are asking them to make, the greater this barrier will be. However, there are techniques that can help you deal with 'objections' and persuade customers to buy and try your product or service.

 Practice insight 6 tips for dealing with objections

Some objections are fundamental – the customer does not want your product/service. But some are just raising other problems that you might be able to solve. There are six other types of objection or concerns, some of which can be dealt with. They are:

1 **Feature objection** – Some of the features do not meet the customer's approval. This might be overcome by emphasizing the positive reasons for these features.

2 **Information-seeking objection** – The customer wants more information about the product/service, often about proving your claims for it. This gives you the opportunity to provide that information.

3 **Price objection** – This might be fundamental or a buying signal and the start of negotiations. If they are seeking a lower price, try stressing the product benefits compared to competitors and value-for-money. If this

does not work, try offering a discount only in exchange for something else like a larger order.

4 **Delay objection** – The customer wants to put off making a decision. This is difficult if the delay is genuine and you need to find out the reason. If necessary, arrange a return visit.

5 **Loyalty objection** – The customer may have an established relationship with a competitor. Stress the benefits of the product; do not 'knock' the competitor but try to find reasons why they should change supplier, for example because they are not receiving the service they ought to. Always keep in contact as it may just take time to convince them to try you.

6 **Hidden objection** – The buyer prevaricates for no obvious reason. It is important to get to the unstated objection and deal with it, so ask questions.

Even when you have overcome these 'objections', some people have problems recognizing 'buying signals' from customers and can continue relentlessly through a sales meeting long after the customer actually wanted to buy the product or service. They just need an invitation to do so. Buying signals can be many and various: the customer becoming interested and animated, positive body language such as leaning forward or wanting to pick up or try the product. If interest is confirmed by asking a few questions, the whole process can be short-circuited and you can go to the most important stage of all – closing the sale. Again, there are techniques that help you do this without appearing too 'pushy' or impolite.

Selling to well-informed customers can be particularly difficult. They may have sought out online reviews or gathered expert advice from independent sources rather than relying on what you might tell them. They come to a sales meeting with a decision already half made and, after clarifying a few points that confirm they want to buy your product, often try to go straight to a price negotiation. The approach to take here is called 'insight selling' and involves trying to disrupt these pre-meeting decisions. Firstly, it involves trying to establish relationships with prospective customers well ahead of the meeting in their 'learning' phase so that you are seen as an expert consultant with valuable knowledge. Secondly, it involves using this position to disrupt and 'reset' customer thinking by challenging their assumptions, perhaps by identifying undisclosed problems they might face. In this way, the buying decision is a joint one, with the salesperson adding value by action as an expert consultant in the process.

 Practice insight 6 tips for closing a sale

There are six well-known techniques used for closing the sale:

1   **Trial close** – You can try this one immediately when you see a buying signal. This close uses the opportunity of an expression of interest to ask a further question which implicitly assumes a sale. For example, 'It is the quality of the product that has convinced you, hasn't it?' The trial close ends with a question, and if the answer is positive then you can proceed straight to close the sale.

2   **Alternative close** – This forces the customer to a decision between options. For example, 'Do you want an initial order of 1,000 or 2,000?' or 'Can we deliver next month or would you prefer next week?'

3   **Summary close** – This is useful if the buyer is uncertain about the next step. It summarizes what has been said and sets out the next steps. For example, 'So those are the advantages our service offers over the one you are using at the moment, and I think you would agree we are better in every respect. Do you agree?'

4   **Concession close** – Concessions are usually on price. They may secure orders but should not be given away too early, only at the end of the meeting when you judge it necessary to tip the balance in your favour. Always try to get something in exchange for a price concession. For example, 'And if you place an order this month, there is a special 5% discount.'

5   **Quotation close** – Often you have to provide a formal quote at the end of the sales interview. If this is the case, then it should be followed up with another visit to the customer to clarify the main points, answer any queries and secure the sale.

6   **Direct close** – Sometimes it is actually necessary to ask for the order directly – and then remain silent and listen to the answer. If the answer is 'no', a follow-up question should illicit some objections that you might be able to overcome.

Communications media

This brings us back to the importance of building relationships with prospective customers – not an easy task for a brand new start-up. And you can use a range of mass communications media to initiate, develop and maintain these relationships. Indeed, there has never been a greater choice of communications tools, and it grows every year. Some of these are listed in Table 8.3.

Table 8.3 Communication tools

Word-of-mouth	Newspaper advertising	Posters
Relationships and networks	Radio advertising	Flyers
Social networks and media	TV advertising	Hoardings/billboards
Blogging	Internet advertising	Direct mail
Guerrilla marketing	Sponsorship	Email
Publicity and public relations	Telephone	Texting

Word-of-mouth recommendation

This is spread through your relationships and networks and can be a very effective way of promoting a local start-up. It is a low-cost option that involves personal time and effort. It is extremely effective because, essentially, you are using advocates to promote your business. Family and friends might be able to help you initially but, once you are established, unpaid customer recommendation is very powerful. And, where word-of-mouth works well within a limited geographic location, social networks can take over to spread the word to a wider audience.

Social networks and media

This is a term that covers any communication hosted on the internet or on smartphones, such as texting, tweeting or blogging. It includes social networking sites such as Facebook, Twitter and YouTube. Social media can spread word-of-mouth recommendations very cheaply. It is extremely fast and can reach enormous audiences. The word 'viral' has been used to describe how messages can get passed around, causing revolutions in some countries. For consumer goods, word-of-mouth promotion using web-based social media networks – viral marketing – has been found to be more effective in developing brand identity through what is sometimes referred to as 'shared values', 'tribal identity' or 'emotional dialogue' rather than traditional mass-market advertising that focuses on product characteristics (Watts and Perreti, 2007). It is therefore a powerful tool.

Social media sites can be used in a number of ways, for example by establishing a presence and creating a community around your product/service. Usually linked to your own website, it can be used to establish a dialogue with customers, solicit feedback from them, build brand awareness and even generate sales leads. If used effectively, it can help harness the 'advocate effect' by building a 'community' of interest around your product/service. You can generate interest by constantly providing new topics for discussion or by organizing events or contests. Blogging is one way of familiarizing people with your product/service and building an emotional bond with them. You can set up a blog free through Wordpress.com. For it to work, a blog must be constantly refreshed with new content. It must be interesting, informative and fun. It must deal with more than just your company's product/service and reach out to address other lifestyle or industry issues of more general interest. It is unlikely to work if used as a medium for straightforward advertising. Chat rooms and discussion forums can also be cheap ways of developing relationships with customers. You might even email friends and family and ask them to promote your business. Many larger organizations now expend considerable resources on developing an internet presence through blogging and other social networking sites, generating artificial excitement and web traffic around their message.

Some social media sites also take advertising, which can be a useful way of reaching your target market. For example, Facebook allows start-ups to deliver targeted advertisements based upon key words in personal profiles and geographic location. But remember, if you are using the internet to promote your business, you need to have an attractive website and one that customers can navigate easily around (see Chapter 10).

Another approach to using social media to promote your product/service is to offer a free phone app that is useful or entertaining. If an app is something your target market uses it can be extremely effective because it will be shared and talked about. For example, in 2010 Volkswagen launched the new Golf GTI in the USA using exclusively a mobile platform, targeting young males. It offered a free app for a game featuring the new car. Within five days the app had been downloaded 800,000 times and had become the number one free app download on Apple's iTunes App Store in 36 countries.

Guerrilla marketing

This is a term that refers to any low-cost approach to creating awareness of a product/service using any of the media in Table 8.3. It relies on time, ingenuity and novelty, rather than cash, to get the message taken up and passed on. It might adopt unconventional ways to do this, such as publicity

Personal recommendation still counts for a lot. As my first boss told me: 'Make one person happy and they'll tell four others. Make one person unhappy and they'll tell seven others.' Never underestimate the power of word of mouth.

Raoul Shah, founder, Exposure, *The Observer*, 29 September 2013

I believe that one of the most important things is to spread the word in your personal network. Get your personal network working for you. A personal recommendation is so much more valuable than any kind of advertisement you can make.

Dieter Burmester, founder, Burmester, *BBC News*, 23 February 2012

stunts, graffiti, flash mobs etc. For example, notoriously, BMW attached a styrofoam copy of a Mini Cooper to the side of a skyscraper in central Houston, Texas, as part of a guerrilla marketing campaign. The idea is to create a 'buzz' around the product/service so that potential customers want to find out more and are eager to search out where it can be seen and/or purchased. One approach is to encourage the spreading of rumours related to a product/service. The campaign might use social networks and mobile technologies to encourage the buzz or the rumours to spread and 'go viral'. The whole idea is to involve prospective customers in promoting the product/service by doing something unusual and memorable, at the same time building a relationship with them.

Publicity and public relations (PR)

This involves getting media to recognize what you are doing and write news articles or record radio or TV features about it. It is therefore likely to reach a wider audience than your network of relationships. The key is to find something that is newsworthy or interesting. You must prepare press releases and be prepared to give interviews. A major advantage is that PR is free, and because you do not pay for it, these articles or programmes will have greater credibility than advertising which is often seen as self-serving and simply trying to increase sales (Smith, 2009). However, the problem is that you do not control the content of the article or feature, and prospective customers may be left interested in the product/service but not knowing how to purchase it or contact you. Worse still, there is a danger that the published article or feature might be negative or critical. And sometimes your story will not be run because other, more newsworthy events have happened on that day. If you have the cash, one option is to hire a professional PR company to manage your message.

You can get PR from the human interest story associated with your start-up, promoting yourself as a successful local entrepreneur. The combination of an interesting personality and a 'David and Goliath' story of taking on larger competitors can be irresistible. Richard Branson has been particularly good at this, ever since he launched his first magazine – *Student* – at the age of 18. He has used PR to establish the Virgin brand. As we saw in the previous chapter, Branson's exuberant personality and newsworthy publicity stunts mean that he often grabs the headlines. He launched Virgin Atlantic, identifying himself with the brand and positioning himself as the entrepreneur competing against the established competitor British Airways – a 'national carrier' that had government backing and a near monopoly on transatlantic air travel.

You might be able to get PR because of the novelty of your new product/service. Another approach is to have a celebrity launch the product or open new premises. You might also get specialist media to review your product by sending them a free sample. Apple used PR by getting respected computer and technology experts to review their new products prior to launch.

Advertising

Advertising a new product/service launch can be through a range of media such as newspapers, magazines, radio, TV, internet, flyers, posters, hoardings, direct mail, emails etc. Advertising can be expensive and there can be large-scale economies, but it can guarantee a wide audience – which is important for consumer goods and services. Most start-ups are unlikely to enjoy a large advertising budget, so extensive media advertising of the sort often seen for a new car model launch is unlikely to be an option. However, low-cost advertising such as posters and flyers – delivered to homes or placed under car windscreen wipers – can be extremely effective for a locally based business. They can create product/service awareness and tell customers where you are located and, if combined with a message that encourages a trial purchase, can quickly stimulate sales.

Highly focused advertising can be very cost-effective, for example through trade press or the focused pay-by-click advertising offered by Google and Bing. Pay-by-click allows you to advertise on the screen only when certain search words are used. It also allows you to place adverts on other peoples' websites – where they offer related products or services. With pay-by-click you only pay when your advertisement is clicked on.

Case insight   BicycleSPACE

Building customer relationships as a retailer

Erik Kugler and Philip Koopman opened their BicycleSPACE cycle store in Washington, DC in 2010. But with so much competition, this set out to be a cycle store with attitude, indeed passion, aiming to build 'a cycling community' around the shop using social networks. The retailer organizes regular group maintenance workshops and bike rides, such as the monthly 'full-moon' rides and a recent Halloween 'night of the cycling undead' attended by hundreds of cyclists. These are organized as social outings and are accompanied by music and food and refreshments.

'People can find all the products we sell online, and are often so well-read and knowledgeable. They've looked up every detail and come in knowing so much. To sell to those people you have to appeal to something greater – we're selling a lifestyle and an experience. People want to be part of something and come to a place where they'll be taken care of. We're really a social gathering spot and an essential place to learn about bikes, use them and have a good time.' (BBC News Business, 3 March 2013)

❏ Visit the website: www.bicyclespacedc.com

Courtesy of BicycleSPACE

QUESTIONS:

1 What role does the internet play in building customer relationships for BicycleSPACE?

2 Does it replace face-to-face relationship-building for BicycleSPACE?

Case insight   The Fabulous Bakin' Boys (now The Fabulous Bakers)

Building customer relationships as a manufacturer

Gary Frank lost his job as a Wall Street trader and was made redundant because of the stock market crash of 1987. Two years later he decided to move to Britain and, with his brother Jon, set up a company called the Delicious Doughnut Company, using funds from friends, family and a bank. However, doughnuts proved to be less popular in Britain than he expected, and company performance was lacklustre. Consequently, in 1997 they decided to drop doughnuts and move into muffins, flapjacks and cupcakes, creating a new image and re-branding the company with the name The Fabulous Bakin' Boys. They also changed the packaging and invested heavily in marketing and promotion to help persuade the supermarket chains to 'push' the company's products.

Being a small company meant that it had to rely mainly on in-store promotions, but the internet enabled it to open direct links with the consumers. The Fabulous Bakin' Boys website contained a database of jokes, cheeky postcard advertisements and online games such as Muffin Munchin and Cake Invaders that could be downloaded or 'mailed to a mate' as part of a viral marketing campaign. However, you could only do all this after you had registered. Once registered you received regular mail-outs. Online ordering was also possible. In 2007, the company started baking its own products, having bought out the assets of its major supplier, who had gone into administration.

The company was hugely successful in a market that was generally seen as stagnant. By 2012, The Fabulous Bakin' Boys had become one of Europe's leading muffin makers. With a turnover of about £20 million, it was supplying most of Britain's leading supermarkets. Aiming to double the size

Continued...

Continued from previous page...

of the business by 2015, the company announced ambitious plans to extend its product range and decided to invest £3 million in new packaging plant. However, rapid expansion can lead to problems if it is not managed properly. Not only was the plant 18 months late, but the company also overspent by 100% on it. New product development was put on hold and money was diverted from marketing to fund the equipment overspend. In 2014, The Fabulous Bakin' Boys went into administration but was immediately bought by the Dutch food company Daelmans Group and renamed *The Fabulous Bakers*. They retained the workforce, plant and customer base and even kept the website relatively unchanged. Only Gary and Jon lost their jobs.

❏ Visit the website: http://thefabulousbakers.com/

QUESTIONS:

1 What lessons are to be learned from the failure in 2014 of the original Fabulous Bakin' Boys?

2 What role does the internet play in building customer relationships for the company?

3 Does this replace face-to-face relationship-building?

Developing a communications campaign

You need to develop a communications campaign as part of your launch strategy. This can be aimed at your end-use customers as well as your distribution channels. Your campaign needs to be slightly different at each stage in Figure 8.1. However, underpinning it is the need to develop sustainable customer relationships and create a clear brand identity. Your strategy must both deliver and receive communications with customers, but ultimately it should be designed to open up a dialogue. Customer listening is important at all stages. The major aims at each stage are:

Stage 1

This is the launch stage of the business, where creating awareness of the product/service and persuading your first customers to purchase it are important. You need to get customers to understand what the product/service does for them and create a desire to at least try it. It is about:

- Creating brand awareness – getting customers to recognize that your brand, among others, meets their needs and should be considered;
- Stimulating brand purchase – persuading customers to buy your brand.

Stage 2

This is the take-off stage of the business when you are still trying to persuade more customers to try your product/service at the same time as persuading those who have tried it to repeat purchase. It is about:

- Creating brand attitude – getting customers to recognize how your brand is different to others;
- Facilitating brand purchase – having decided to buy your brand, the customer needs to know where the product can be purchased and at what price.

Stage 3

This is the growth stage of the business. This stage is about continuing to facilitate brand purchase and restating brand attitude and identity, reinforcing your value proposition so that regular customers are convinced that they are making the right purchase decision.

Stage 4

This is the final stage of creating brand advocacy. It is about cementing the relationship with the customer, involving them in prospecting, encouraging new customers and product/service development.

People no longer want to be sold to; they want companies to help them find an informed way to buy the right product or service at the right price. They will watch ads, but often online rather than on TV, and they're much more likely to view ads that friends have recommended. When something goes wrong with a product, they want to be able to reach the company instantly and get a quick solution. How companies adapt to this energetic and sometimes chaotic world will define their future success. The website, Facebook page, blog and Twitter feed are no longer add-ons to a business's communication budget. They should be central to its marketing strategy, and used in coordination with other marketing efforts.

Richard Branson, founder, Virgin Group, *http://www.entrepreneur.com/article/218098*, 8 February 2011

You need to develop a communications campaign that integrates with your overall launch strategy and moves customers through these four stages. Remember that, while there may be short-term objectives at each stage, the longer-term aim is to develop close customer relationships based on shared values. Developing such a campaign involves six steps:

1   Identifying the target market you wish to communicate with.
2   Identifying the media that reaches this target market.
3   Defining your communications objectives.
4   Developing and refining your communications message – words and images.
5   Setting the budget (money and other resources). Deciding whether the media that reaches your target market is appropriate for your message and is within your budget.
6   Preparing your communications plan – media, dates, times etc.

If your communications campaign is expensive, you would be well advised to test it out through focus groups before you launch it. And once the campaign is over you should evaluate it against the objectives you set in step 3.

Creating awareness

While all start-ups need to create awareness, how you approach this will depend on the type of business you are launching. Refer back to the start-up typologies in Figure 4.4 (on page 95). The more radical the product/service innovation, the more likely the start-up is to create genuine public interest. You are also likely to be able to use PR when you are introducing a product/service that exists elsewhere into a new market. Such developments are newsworthy in their own right and mean that you can use PR to your advantage. But even here, few companies would trust the public to beat a path to their door on the back of a news story. There is no guarantee that it will be accurate, nor is there any guarantee that they will explain where potential customers can buy the product/service. So it is important that you provide the media with information on what the product/service is and why it is newsworthy. This involves producing and distributing a press release and possibly organizing a press conference or launch event. This can be supported by a range of other activities that utilize as many of the communication media as time and money permit.

Few product launches enjoy the level of anticipation and pre-ordering of Apple products – and certainly Apple plans these launches meticulously. Even before the launch of a new product Apple ensures that there is promotion of the product, normally through a mix of free PR (pre-launch feature leaks, pre-launch product reviews etc.) and a theatrical launch event supported by media advertising. But then Apple has a brand recognized for design and innovation that has an established band of loyal customers and advocates – something that takes time to create and is not an option for a start-up. So you need to be creative in organizing such events and motivate customers and press to attend. And the lesson is clear – you need to create awareness of your product or service before the customer will even consider purchasing it – and you do not leave it to chance. You need to consider all the communications media discussed in the previous section.

With any product/service launch it is important to get the right message to prospective customers. The message you want to convey to your target market segment is that you have a value proposition that meets some, as yet unmet, need they have or meets it better than other products or services. They need to be told about your product/service, what it can do for them – the benefits – and where they can buy it. However, if your product or service is entirely novel you may have to limit the awareness message to what the product does, explaining the benefits offered. In both cases you want to create sufficient curiosity that prospective customers will consider purchasing it when they see the product or service on sale.

For those start-ups where the product innovation is incremental, the job of creating awareness is more difficult because the launch is less newsworthy. That means PR is less likely to bear results and you might focus more on the other communications media. However, you still have options that might get results. Some businesses are lucky enough to be able to have a celebrity launch their product/service – sometimes free and often found through their network of contacts. Celebrity launches can be extremely effective, particularly for shops because they attract potential shoppers. A celebrity might also be persuaded to endorse the product/service, but do remember that they are putting their reputation on the line. Alternatively, never underestimate the newsworthiness of your personal entrepreneurial story. Many newspapers run regular small business pages and are looking for inspiring stories to fill their pages.

As we have already discussed, social media can be a very cheap way of generating interest in a new business, but you need to have a 'hook' to get people interested even with this medium, and you need to find a way of finding the addresses to send your message to. Posters and flyers can do the same thing for local businesses. One way to short-circuit the early stages in the process outlined in Figure 8.1 is to get customers to jump straight to the evaluation or trial 'purchase' stage by offering them free or discounted samples or trials. This is only appropriate for low-price products/services that generate repeat sales. And it is most appropriate for products/services that are only incrementally different to those offered by existing competitors. In many cases it needs to be linked to incentives offered to the distributors offering the product/service.

 Case insight   Good Hair Day

Start-up marketing strategy

Good Hair Day (GHD), part of Jemella Group, was started by Martin Penny in 2001. Based in West Yorkshire, the company has revolutionized the hair industry with an iron that straightens hair between two heated ceramic plates. But when Martin first took the idea to his bank, asking for a £50,000 loan, the bank manager was sceptical, seeing the product as 'just another set of hair tongs'. The only way Martin got the money was on the strength of his track record running an environmental consultancy. But Martin decided on two important strategies that were to underpin the subsequent success of his business:

1   Not to manufacture the product himself, but to have it manufactured in Korea where costs were lower. This way, he could focus on sales and keep his fixed costs to a minimum.
2   Not to sell through the high street but to target firstly up-market London West End hair salons and then salons across the UK. The 'hair styling irons' were sold both for salon use and to customers by the salons themselves. Customer prices were high but so too were the margins for the salons. Despite product costs being relatively low, using this route to market differentiated GHD tongs from 'just another set of hair tongs'. It was seen as professional, special and up-market.

Since they used hair stylists, many celebrities such as Madonna, Victoria Beckham, Jennifer Aniston and Gwyneth Paltrow used GHD tongs, and the company benefited from celebrity endorsements. These helped to give it a certain exclusive cachet that then helped sell GHD products to the general public. The company claims that the iron is now used in more than 10,000 UK salons – 85% of the market. Based on this success GHD is now diversifying into other haircare products such as shampoo, conditioner and styling gel, and has launched a new brand called 'Nu:U', aimed at the mid-price, mass salon market.

❏ Visit their website: www.ghdhair.com

QUESTION:

1   What were the important elements of the start-up marketing strategy for GHD?
2   How important is it that other elements of GHD's strategy are consistent with these? Give some examples of consistent strategies.

Getting customers to buy

Figure 6.3 (on page 159) outlined the different ways of getting your product/service in front of customers – your channels of distribution. Selling through a distribution chain such as shops, agents or distributors eats into your profit margins but allows you to expand your reach, benefiting from your partners' strengths. Getting end-use customers to buy your product means incentivizing each stage of your distribution chain. While you might be able to contact distributors directly to create awareness of your product, they will need an incentive to stock it. They will be interested in the uniqueness of your product and will also react to whether customers are already seeking it out because of your customer awareness campaign ('demand-pull'). 'Demand-pull' communication strategies focus on your end-use customer. They create demand for the product and pull it through the distribution chain. However, they can be prohibitively expensive for many start-ups and therefore restrict the available market.

© Royalty-Free/Corbis

Ultimately, these channels are interested in profit, so they might be persuaded to stock your product, particularly if initially it is offered on a sale-or-return basis. Indeed, they might help promote your product if you offer them an extra initial discount or bonus ('supply-push'). With 'supply-push' your launch strategy will need to influence each link in the distribution chain. However, unless accompanied by other promotional activity, such as point of sale displays etc., this can leave decisions about promotion activity entirely with the distributor. This can lead to unintended consequences, such as distributors entering into local price promotions that are not consistent with other elements of your marketing mix. This underlines the important point that your launch strategy must be consistent with your overall strategy and should seek to coordinate 'push' and 'pull' incentives. The advantages and disadvantages of using distribution channels and a supply-push strategy are summarized in Table 8.4.

'Demand-pull' can be stimulated using all the communication media covered earlier. The message is different from an awareness campaign (although the two can be linked) because you now want to get people to try out and evaluate your product/service. The first customers to buy a new product/service have been characterized as 'innovators' – people who think for themselves, like novelty and try things. Innovators constitute only 2 or 3% of the market.

As we noted in the previous chapter, you can also encourage people to try out your product/service through pricing. For example, if the product or service it relatively low price and customers are likely to repeat purchase, free samples/trials or special introductory price offers may persuade customers to try it and then, if they like it, buy it again. Offering introductory discounts, rather than offering your product/service at a low price, allows you to re-establish your market price more easily after introduction. Customers will accept the removal of a discount far more easily than an increase in price. This strategy is usually necessary when differences to existing product/services are not great and customers need an incentive to switch.

By way of contrast, if your product/service is sufficiently unique or novel, it may be possible to premium price at launch, particularly if customers are unlikely to repeat the purchase

Table 8.4 The advantages and disadvantages of using distribution channels and a supply-push strategy

Advantages	Disadvantages

> Fewer buyers to communicate with:
  - time with buyer important;
  - relationships with buyer important.
> Less capital needed to invest in direct consumer communication, distribution etc.
> Potential to leverage market in line with distribution channels, gaining wider market coverage quicker than otherwise.
	> High-value, infrequent purchases by buyers are high-risk:
	  - need for detailed information about buyer;
	  - need for accurate identification of buyer incentives (product characteristics, point-of-sales displays, frequency of delivery, financial incentives etc.).
	> Lack of direct influence and control over end-consumer.
	> Buyer may have dominant negotiating position regarding price.
	> May de-emphasize brand and not cement product loyalty with consumer.

quickly. This creates a certain status associated with ownership of the product or service. You can then effectively lower the price later by including more features but keeping the price the same. This is the strategy used by Apple, with new versions of its products carrying new and better features. With this sort of product you can also afford to be selective about distribution, going into new channels as the product ages. So, for example, a film is shown first in cinemas, then on pay-to-view channels, and finally it becomes available on video or through download, usually with the price reducing progressively over time.

Once a customer makes a purchase they will evaluate your product/service against the promises you held out to them. Are the value propositions you advertised real? Does the product/service meet their expectations? Is the service delivery at each stage of the distribution chain appropriate? Remember the customer may not repeat buy if just one of your channels of distribution does not meet their expectations in some way. So, as well as making your first sales, you need to start evaluating your customers' reaction to your product/service and correcting any weaknesses in your value proposition. Indeed, doing this effectively could be your first step in establishing a relationship with customers. You can use face-to-face trials, evaluation questionnaires or feedback sheets. If you can get a contact address, tell them when any weaknesses are corrected. If there are no weaknesses, then these are prospective repeat-buy customers.

 ## Case insight   Clippy

Minimizing start-up costs

Calypso Rose graduated from a technical theatre course at a drama school and got a job in television production. It was while she was working in this job that she made the first see-through bag with pockets to display her collection of Polaroid photographs. She never intended to start up a business; however, the frequency of inquiries from people on where they could buy something similar prompted her to start thinking about it as a serious possibility. When her parents offered to lend her £2,000 to make the first 250 bags she decided to take the plunge, aged just 22, and Clippy was born.

Calypso decided to work from home to keep her overheads and breakeven low. Her mother, Clare, also helped with the business, meaning Calypso did not have to hire any employees. She found a UK manufacturer through Kelly's online directory, deciding that this was better than going to China to find a supplier. The UK manufacturer could turn around orders more quickly and, once she established a track record, would offer normal trade terms for payment, thereby helping her cash flow and reducing her risk.

Initial sales were mainly to family and friends – many of the people who had asked where they could buy the first bag. The official launch of Clippykit (now called Clippy) was at Olympia's Spirit of Christmas Fair in 2004. She established a website, customized a large bag with a sign saying 'stop me and buy one' and took a small stall on Portobello Road in London, a popular fashion and antiques market, to see if her business idea would work. She had done everything she could to minimize her risks and now wanted to see

if the bag would really sell. She sold all 250 bags in the first month. Working from home and only using the initial £2,000, she managed to build a turnover of £180,000 in the first year. In 2004, at the age of 22, she was voted London Young Business person of the year.

Calypso was worried from the start that the idea could be easily copied – after all, it was just a plastic bag with pockets for photographs – and that a bigger company with more resources could roll out an imitation product more effectively than her. So the idea was to push sales as quickly as possible but also to establish a fashion brand. A major breakthrough came when the fashionable Notting Hill boutique Coco Ribbon decided to sell her bags. Things got even better when celebrities such as Helena Bonham Carter, Jools Holland and Jamie Oliver started carrying Clippy bags. The bags have even been used as a 'goody bag' at the Brit Awards and the Orange Prize.

It also became clear early on that the concept behind the bags was flexible and could be applied to other products like makeup bags, lamp shades, wallets and umbrellas. Another development was that the products themselves could be personalized, and Calypso started offering kits to help people do that.

Calypso has been very adept at promoting the product herself. For example, in 2009, working with an enterprise organization called Make Your Mark, 650 girls in London took part in a competition to personalize a Clippy bag with an issue that was relevant to them.

The range of Clippy products had grown. With the company turnover being over £500,000, Calypso employs

Continued...

Continued from previous page...

two full-time and one part-time staff. The bags are sold through conventional wholesale and retail markets – through about 250 independent boutiques. They are sold as fashion items and promotional products, often customized for the promotion event. However, about a quarter of sales come from the website, which shows how the products can be used, hosts competitions and has a Calypso blog. You can also sign up for a regular newsletter.

❏ Visit the website: www.clippykitlondon.co.uk

QUESTIONS:

1 Who is the target market and what is the value proposition for Clippy? What are the key elements of competitive advantage in this value proposition?

2 Is this a 'lean start-up'? What did Calypso do to keep her start-up costs to a minimum?

3 What did she do to promote her product while keeping her costs to a minimum?

4 What are her growth options? Would you change the business model?

Penetrating your market

Your business will grow through a combination of repeat sales (for appropriate products) and new customers. Repeat sales will be built on the relationship you develop with customers, particularly as competitors emerge. New customers will come from a combination of promotional activity (including face-to-face selling), finding new distribution channels and using existing customers willing to act as your advocates in some way. Reputation spreads, but can take time.

While your first customers have been characterized as innovators, these will be followed by second-wave customers characterized as 'early adopters' – people with status in their market segment and opinion leaders. These constitute about 14%. They choose new products carefully. They adopt successful products, making them acceptable and respectable. As your product/service attracts more customers, it will attract more attention from competitors. They may adapt their marketing strategy and even change their product/service characteristics so as to compete more directly with you. So, your marketing strategy may need to adapt and change to suit this.

The appropriate strategy to adopt at this stage depends, in part, on the competitive position you find yourself in. Referring back to the new venture typologies in Figure 4.4 (on page 95), the more radical the product/service innovation or market you are creating, the more likely you are to be in a dominant market position at start-up. This should reflect itself in a low level of competition you face.

Strong competitive position

If you are in a strong competitive position you need to expand as rapidly as possible, investing in whatever is the basis for value offering and developing your brand identity. There is a window of opportunity for you to capitalize on your first-mover advantage before competitors copy you. In terms of the value disciplines outlined in Chapter 6:

> If your core value proposition involves high differentiation then you should further differentiate yourself from the competition, creating and building your brand. You will probably have been able to charge a premium price at launch and you should have been investing those profits in this from the start. Despite your high differentiation, as competitors emerge, your price may need to come down, either directly or, more likely, by improving the product's value in some way. Second-generation electronic products are typically better in some way (e.g. storage capacity for computers) but at the same price.

> If your core value proposition involves cost leadership (low price) then you must obtain the necessary economies of scale as quickly as possible to gain that dominant position. This involves investing in ways of keeping your costs low and, at the same time, expanding your sales through aggressive marketing, including price promotions.

So, the key to success is gaining rapid market dominance, at the same time as building those close customer relationships. To attract more innovators and early adopters you need to make an intensive push on distribution. This might involve organizing frequent sales promotions, continually finding new channels of distribution, expanding into new geographic areas etc. Customers and distributors love to sell products or services that have proved successful elsewhere. It reduces their risk. As we saw in Chapter 6, some, particularly high-technology, start-ups are international from the start. However, most move into overseas markets more gradually, starting by exporting products through independent channels like sales agents. We shall return to the issue of international expansion in a Chapter 13.

Weak competitive position

If you are not in a strong competitive position then your expansion needs to be more cautious. You need to plan to combat competition from the launch, with a view to profitability. One attractive option is to find a market niche within a competitive industry. Often in these circumstances a start-up is better advised to ignore the mass market, trying instead to carve out a smaller but distinctive market niche for itself – at least in the short term. This often avoids the high fixed costs usually associated with mass markets. It also often means that a higher price can be charged for the product/service, albeit on a smaller volume which, as we saw in the previous chapter, can result in higher profits. And often that niche is bigger than the founder ever imagined. Serial entrepreneurs go on to found one business with 'limited' potential after another, often selling them on.

While competition will certainly show itself at this stage, the real battleground will come later over the **early and late majority** of customers. They each make up about a third of customers and are more conservative, with slightly higher status and are more deliberate, thinking purchasers. They only adopt the product after it has become acceptable and will shop around and compare different product/service offerings. By this stage some competitors will have become established, while others will have fallen by the wayside. Those remaining will compete aggressively. This is the stage where your dominant market position and a well-recognized brand will really start to pay dividends. We shall address some of the challenges of marketing at this stage in Chapter 13.

 # Case insight   Jack Wills: University Outfitters

Low-cost marketing

Launched only in 1999 by Peter Williams and Rob Shaw, the Jack Wills brand has an old-world university association. It was originally known for selling hoodies (emblazoned with the names of universities), tracksuit bottoms, rugby shirts, hoodies, pyjamas and party dresses – primarily to well-off youngsters:

'I had just left university and I thought the years between 18 and 21 were amazing because you've got all the independence and freedom of being adult but you haven't quite entered the adult world. I looked back and realized I didn't appreciate how amazing those years were and I wanted to create a brand that epitomised that – for the person who has an aspirational response to that 18-21 British university thing.'

Using the trademark 'Jack Wills – University Outfitters', the brand has a 'public school' or 'preppy' image – and high prices reflect this, although they do offer a 25% discount to registered students. However, the business started life as a simple shop in the seaside town of Salcombe in Devon – a town without any university but plenty of well-off visitors (known humorously as Chelsea-on-Sea). The founders invested £40,000 in the venture, taken mainly from their credit cards, which left them little spare cash for anything else. So, they lived above the store.

Today, the founders are millionaires. And, with sales of over £120 million and over 60 stores in the UK and some 20 overseas in the USA, Ireland and Hong Kong, the Jack Wills brand is now better known for selling a modern 'take' on traditional 'British' clothes such as men's blazers and women's tweed jackets – 'playing off the tensions between old and new, formal and casual'. These often incorporate aspects of traditional British military and sporting design. The company uses navy blue and pink colour schemes in its packaging and for some of its products. They still sell sports-orientated clothing (for sports such as polo, rugby and

Continued...

Continued from previous page...

rowing) but the shops have evolved to also sell expensive designer clothes and hats – often developed in collaboration with well-known partners like Liberty or Fox Brothers – as well as toiletries, cushions, bed linen and towels.

With many stores located in university towns, the shops are often housed in historical buildings. The interiors feature dark wood tables and display cases, faded Persian rugs and yellowed posters, designed to mirror the image of all-things British. And products like bowler and pork-pie hats and silk headscarves help emphasize the eccentric and 'dandy-ish' Britishness of the brand. The company logo features a pheasant with a top hat and walking stick, known as Mr Wills.

Curiously, Jack Wills' approach to marketing today can look remarkably similar to its approach when the founders opened the first store – an approach that sets the brand apart from competitors. Back in 1999 the founders could not afford an expensive advertising campaign. Instead they gave away branded hoodies and rugby shirts to 'influencers' in the town – kids that others would admire – and would pay them to go around giving away branded T-shirts. Jack Wills clothes became 'cool'. Overt advertising would have detracted from the brand image. Today the company employs teams of 'seasonnaires' to roam beaches, ski resorts and university campuses and spread the brand – but never to sell. They rely on word-of-mouth and viral marketing. A year before the Jack Wills store opened in Nantucket, off Cape Cod in the USA, a team of seasonnaires spent the summer 'seeding' the market.

'They are the mouthpieces of the brand. They have often worked in stores and their job for the summer is to make friends, throw parties and be in the right places to seed the brand.'

The company also sponsors certain more exclusive university sports events (and related entertainment) such as polo matches between Cambridge and Oxford, Harvard and Yale, Eton and Harrow. It also hosts exclusive 'events' such as the annual seasonnaires' party. The company website lists its brand values as:

British – *'Britishness anchors all that we do; we're inspired by its history and tradition, blending old and new to create something that's distinctly ours. Wherever we go in the world, we'll always stay true to our British roots.'*

Entrepreneurial – *'The business began with two friends taking a risk. That pioneering approach and commercial instinct remains. And we will retain it, however large we become.'*

Innovative – *'Creativity, and the desire to be leading edge, drives us. It makes our day jobs more exciting, and ensures that we keep inspiring our customers too.'*

Responsible – *'Integrity and decency is at our core; it's inherent in us to act properly and treat everyone, whether our people, our suppliers or our customers, with respect.'*

Excellence – *'It's not just about our high quality product: we believe in excellence in everything we do, it's that simple.'*

Today, T-shirts are old-hat. Instead they give away neon yellow 'party pants' branded with different locations:

'The product is amazing but if you kind of boil it down to what's really special – and what people talk about – it's the party pants ... They sort of define us because it's not just a bunch of clothes, it's the best summer they've ever had, the best university experience or just the best winter trip because we're embedded in their lifestyle ... There's an inherent naughty rebelliousness in everything that we do.' (Peter Williams, *The Sunday Times*, 16 September 2012)

❏ Visit their website: www.jackwills.com

QUESTIONS:

1 Who are the target market segments for Jack Wills and what is the value proposition it offers?

2 Which market segments might it not appeal to?

3 What are the operational imperatives for Jack Wills – the things it needs to get right to enable it to deliver the value proposition? How are these achieved?

4 Is the marketing mix consistent? Why is this important? What are the brand values?

5 Why has the company's original approach to creating brand awareness translated so well into a longer-term advertising/promotions strategy?

6 What are the advantages and disadvantages of this approach?

 Practice insight reminder Characteristics of a good business idea – 8 & 13

8 **Effective communications strategy** – once you know who you are selling to, and why they should buy from you, you need to be able to communicate a persuasive message to them and build a loyal customer base.

13 **Management skills that can be leveraged** – you need to have the appropriate management skills, and if you do not, you need to acquire them or recruit or partner with others with the appropriate skills.

⊃ Summary

> Any business is primarily about people. You need to develop a skills profile for your business – the skills, knowledge and networks that are needed to launch and operate your business. You meet your skills needs through people – founder(s), employees, partners, investors, professional advisors and the board of directors.

> Using professional advisors can be an attractive way of accessing a range of knowledge, skills and networks. Surrounding yourself with high-quality advisors can help tackle the challenges of growth and add to the credibility of your management team.

> Using your skills profile, you can draw up job descriptions for key roles and, based on these, person specifications that profile the skills, knowledge and attributes of those who might be able to undertake these jobs.

> Picking an effective team is also about assembling a mix of different personalities that can work together as a team. Belbin identified three orientations and nine team roles that are needed:

> • Thinking orientation: plant, monitor-evaluator and specialist.

> • People orientation: coordinator, team-worker and resource investigator.

> • Action orientation: shaper, implementer and completer-finisher.

> You must make a prospective customer aware of your product/service and then persuade them to purchase it.

> Once they have purchased your product/service they will evaluate whether you have delivered your value proposition. They may then be persuaded to repeat purchase and become regular customers.

> Eventually they may become a supporter who thinks positively about the product/service, and ultimately they may become an advocate of it. You need to encourage this progression through building a relationship with your customers.

> You can build this relationship through face-to-face contact with customers and through your communications

strategy. Communications media include your personal networks, internet and social media, PR and advertising.

> The more radical your product innovation or the market you are creating, the more likely your start-up is to be of interest to the general media. However, they can also be interested in the human interest side of a business start-up. Media need to be made aware of the launch of your business. You can do this through a press release and a product launch event.

> You can sell directly to customers or through distribution channels. If you sell through channels, you might gain wider distribution but you lose profit and may lose control over communication to customers.

> To sell your product or service face-to-face with a customer you need to sell its benefits: be clear about how it will solve the customer's specific 'problem' and be able to demonstrate its features; be able to back up the claims you make about your value proposition with proof; be able to handle objections and concerns; and, finally, close the sale.

> 'Supply-push' is when you create incentives to intermediaries in your distribution channels to sell your product. 'Demand-pull' is when you create incentives directly with end-use customers who then 'pull' the product through the distribution channels.

> Price incentives can be effective in stimulating trial purchases of low-priced, repeat purchase products, particularly when the differences from existing products is small.

> If your product/service is sufficiently unique it may be possible to charge a premium price at launch.

> Your strategy for penetration may involve further sales promotions, expanding into new geographic areas, finding new channels of distribution etc.

> The more innovative your product or market, the more important it is to capitalize on your first-mover advantage and maintain your market dominance through rapid market penetration and growth. Building brand loyalty is the ultimate aim as the regular customer becomes an advocate for your product/service.

✓ Activities

1 Identify the skills needed for your business and how they might be met:
1.1 List the skills, knowledge and competences required for your business, pre-launch, and the job roles these translate into. Make sure all skills etc. are covered by these roles.

1.2 Classify roles as 'key', 'important' or 'desirable'.
1.3 Classify roles as 'full/part-time' and 'regular/shift work' and note any special remuneration arrangements.
1.4 Identify the roles the founder(s) will take and identify the resulting role gaps.

1.5 Identify which roles or skill gaps might come from professional advisors, partners, the board of directors and/or providers of finance.

1.6 For the remaining role gaps, prepare a brief job description and person specification.

1.7 List the areas where you will need professional help and advice.

2 Decide on terms of employment and job advertisements:

2.1 Decide on remuneration levels (including bonuses and incentives) for all posts, including those occupied by founders.

2.2 If your new business is a limited company, decide which members of the new venture team will become shareholders. Draft the main features of a shareholders' agreement. Remember that you will need to ask the advice of a lawyer about this before anything is signed.

2.3 List their goals, performance measures and targets.

2.4 Draft job advertisements for job gaps and decide how these will be advertised.

3 Download the Belbin Team Roles questionnaire from www.belbin.com and get your existing new venture team to complete the test. List the implications of this for you and the rest of the team.

4 List as many novel ideas for making prospective customers aware of your product or service as you can.

5 List the ways you will take prospects through the stages of the customer journey in Figure 8.1.

6 Detail your communications strategy: target media 'communication objectives' communications message, budget and communication plan.

7 List the main elements of your launch campaign and identify the critical success factors.

8 Write a press release announcing the launch of your business.

9 Team up with two other students: one to act as a buyer (end-use customer or distributor) and one as an observer. Conduct a role-playing sales meeting lasting 5 minutes. **Seller:** Provide the buyer in advance of the meeting with a one-page summary of your product/service and its value proposition. Plan your meeting using the outline in this chapter. Try to close the sale.
Buyer: Make certain you understand your role. Remember you have been identified as a prospect and therefore you are interested the product/service; however, prepare some objections that the seller will have to counter.
Observer: Observe the sales meeting and give feedback on what worked or did not work and how it might be improved.

Group discussion topics

1 What is the difference between marketing and selling?
2 If you have a great product or service all you need to do is make customers aware of it and they will flock to buy. Discuss.
3 Relationships are based on trust. How do you build trust with customers?
4 How do you get a customer to become an advocate of your product or service?
5 Is social media the most cost-effective way of promoting your product or service?
6 You can build trust by using social media. Discuss.
7 Advertising is the most expensive way of one person talking to another. Discuss.
8 Advertising is all about gimmicks – getting noticed. Discuss.
9 PR is free and influential. Discuss.
10 Would you pay a reporter or newspaper to give you PR?
11 What is the role of pricing in persuading customers to make a trial purchase?
12 Compare and contrast the communication strategy for a highly priced technology-based product with that for a low-priced consumable.
13 How can you have one communications strategy if you have a number of different products or different market segments that you are selling to?
14 How does the communications strategy fit in with the overall marketing strategy?
15 What methods of selling would you consider unethical?
16 If sales are important, salespeople should be remunerated based on the sales they generate. Discuss.
17 Business is all about sales, nothing else matters. Discuss.
18 A complaint is a complaint. Can how a business handles complaints ever be a positive influence on reputation?

References

Belbin, R.M. (1981) *Management Teams – Why They Succeed and Fail*, London: Heinemann Professional Publishing.

Burgers, J.H., Jansen, J.J.P., Van den Bosch, F.A.J. and Volberda, H.W. (2009) 'Structural Differentiation and Corporate Venturing: The Moderating Role of Formal and Informal Integration Mechanisms', *Journal of Business Venturing*, 24(3).

Chell, E. (2001) *Entrepreneurship: Globalization, Innovation and Development*, London: Thomson Learning.

Chowdhury, S. (2005) 'Demographic Diversity for Building an Effective Team: Is it Important?', *Journal of Business Venturing*, 20(6).

Dell, M. (1999) *Direct from Dell: Strategies that Revolutionized an Industry*, New York: Harper Business.

Ensley, M.D., Pearson, A.W. and Amason, A.C. (2002) 'Understanding the Dynamics of New Venture Top Management Teams: Cohesion, Conflict, and New Venture Performance', *Journal of Business Venturing*, 17.

Ferguson, A. (1999) *Managing My Life,* London: Hodder & Stoughton.

Gelfand, M.J., Leslie, L.M. and Keller, K.M. (2008) 'On the Etiology of Conflict Cultures', *Research in Organizational Behavior*, 28.

Jehn, K.A. and Bendersky, C. (2003) 'Intragroup Conflict in Organizations: A Contingency Perspective on the Conflict-outcome Relationship', *Research in Organizational Behavior*, 25.

Lechler, T. (2001) 'Social Interaction: A Determinant of Entrepreneurial Team Venture Success', *Small Business Economics*, 16.

Levinson, J.C. (1984) *Guerrilla Marketing*, London: Piatkus Books.

Mach, M., Dolan, S. and Tzafrir, S. (2010) 'The Differential Effect of Team Members' Trust on Team Performance: The Mediation Role of Team Cohesion', *Journal of Occupational and Organizational Psychology*, 83(3).

Smith, K.G., Collins, C.J. and Clark, K.D. (2005) 'Existing Knowledge, Knowledge Creation Capability, and the Rate of New Product Introduction in High-technology Firms', *Academy of Management Journal*, 48(2).

Smith, R.D. (2009) *Strategic Planning for Public Relations*, 3rd edn, New York: Routledge.

Strong, E. (1925) *The Psychology of Selling*, Maidenhead: McGraw-Hill.

Thye, S.R., Yoon, J. and Lawler, E.J. (2002) 'The Theory of Relational Cohesion: Review of a Research Program', *Advances in Group Processes: Group Cohesion, Trust and Solidarity*, 19.

Watts, D.J. and Perreti, J. (2007) 'Viral Marketing for the Real World', *Harvard Business Review*, May.

West III, G.P. (2007) 'Collective Cognition: When Entrepreneurial Teams, Not Individuals, Make Decisions', *Entrepreneurship: Theory and Practice*, 31(1).

Zheng, Y. (2012) 'Unlocking Founding Team Prior Shared Experience: A Transactive Memory System Perspective', *Journal of Business Venturing*, 27(5).

Legal foundations

PhotoDisc/ Getty Images

Learning outcomes

When you have read this chapter and undertaken the related activities you will be able to:

> Safeguard your business idea;
> Decide on the appropriate legal form for your business or social enterprise;
> Understand the responsibilities of the board of directors of a company;
> Understand the value of partnerships, joint ventures and strategic alliances;
> Understand the advantages and disadvantages of franchising and what is involved in establishing one as either a franchisee or a franchisor.

Case insights

Trunki	Ahmed Khan and McDonald's
Xmi	The Body Shop franchise
Tiger	The Good Care Group
Specsavers	

Practice insight: Advice on safeguarding IP

Practice insight: Advice on forms of business

Practice insight: Advice on social enterprise

Practice insight: Advice on taxation

Practice insight reminder: Characteristics of a good business idea

Safeguarding your business idea

One of the important things you need to think about is whether you can safeguard the 'intellectual property' (IP) of your business idea. There are a number of ways you can do this: patents, trademarks, copyrights, industrial design rights and, in some countries, trade secrets. The justification of these rights is that they encourage the creation of IP and pay for associated research and development. It is claimed that there are substantial benefits in terms of economic growth for countries that encourage IP protection, whether or not it is a form of monopoly. A report by Shapiro and Pham (2007) observes that, while economists trace 30 to 40% of all US gains in productivity and growth over the course of the 20th century to economic innovation in its various forms, today, some two-thirds of the value of America's large businesses can be traced to the intangible assets that embody ideas, especially the IP of patents and trademarks. They claim that 'IP-intensive industries produce 72% more value added per employee than non-IP-intensive industries and create jobs at a rate 140% higher than non-IP intensive industries, excluding computers/electronics'. The authors go on to say that 'promoting and protecting new IP should be a high priority for US policymakers'.

However, some critics characterize these rights as intellectual protectionism or monopoly and argue that public interest is harmed by protectionist legislation (Levine and Boldrin, 2008). Contrary to Shapiro and Pham's study, Dosi et al. (2006) observed that, despite the doubling of patent registrations and a tripling of related legal costs of enforcement in the USA in the 1990s, there was no observable step-change in the levels of innovation or profitability. From a managerial rather than a policy perspective, strong intellectual property rights (IPR) can also have some significant disadvantages. In particular, they can inhibit collaborative working on innovation because collaborators want to safeguard their own IPR, despite the possibility that collaboration might generate far greater value. Indeed, one study concluded that the use of IPR has a *negative* effect on a strategy of long-term value creation, the positive influences being lead time, secrecy and tacitness of knowledge (Hurmelinna-Laukkanen and Puumalainen, 2007). Tidd and Bessant (2013) conclude: 'Firms need to balance the desire to protect their knowledge with the need to share aspects of knowledge to promote innovation … Theoretical arguments and empirical research suggest that from both a policy and management perspective, *only a limited level of IPR is desirable to encourage risk taking and innovation*.'

So, the message for an existing business is that you should not rely too much on IPR, and certainly do not let it get in the way of networking or collaborative working where external knowledge is an important part of your systematic innovation. Secrecy may be just as strong a tool as IPR. Indeed, sometimes, if they can be maintained, trade secrets, such as the formula for Coca-Cola, are more effective than any form of legal safeguard since, by definition, if you register a 'secret', it is no longer secret. Only if your product can be 'reverse-engineered' in some way to expose its 'secret' is registration probably the best option.

However, for a start-up, the IP you have on your business idea may be one of the few real assets available to you, and in seeking finance for your idea you will have to expose it to many people, some of whom may be less scrupulous than others. In this case you would be well advised to seek the maximum IPR you can find. Nevertheless, being first to market is sometimes more effective in creating competitive advantage than IPR on an idea that has missed its window of commercial opportunity.

Modern use of the term IP goes back at least as far as 1888, with the founding in Berne of the Swiss Federal Office for Intellectual Property, but the origins of patents for invention go back even further. No one country can claim to have been the first in the field with a patent system, although Britain does have the longest continuous patent tradition in the world. Its origins date from the 15th century, when the Crown started making specific grants of privilege to manufacturers and traders. They were given open letters marked with the King's Great Seal called 'Letters Patent'. Henry VI granted the earliest known patent to Flemish-born John of Utynam in 1449, giving him a 20-year monopoly on a method of making stained glass.

Intellectual property law

IP law varies from country to country. It is complex and usually comprises a multiplicity of individual pieces of legislation generated over a number of years. Because of this, if you think IP is important to your business, take legal advice. With the exception of copyright, if you want to protect your IP in other countries you will generally need to apply for protection in that country. Generally, however, four fundamental methods of protection are offered in most countries: patents, trademarks, industrial design rights and copyright. A simplified guide to these is given below, but details may vary from country to country.

 Practice insight Advice on safeguarding IP

The World Intellectual Property Organisation, an agency of the United Nations, produces the *Guide to Intellectual Property Worldwide* (available at www.wipo.int). In the UK information on regulations and laws can be obtained from the Intellectual Property Office (IPO) (www.ipo.gov .uk). Detailed UK legislation can be viewed on this site, as well as practical help with searches and registering your IP.

Patent

A patent is intended to protect new inventions. It covers how they work, what they do, how they do it, what they are made of and how they are made. It gives the owner the right to prevent others from copying, making, using, importing or selling the invention without permission. The existence of a patent may be enough on its own to prevent others from trying to exploit the invention. However, should they persist in trying to do so, it gives you the right to take legal action to stop them exploiting your invention and to claim damages. And herein lies the problem for cash-strapped start-ups. Can you really afford the legal fees involved in pursuing such a claim? Nevertheless, the patent allows you to sell the invention and all the IP rights, license it to someone else but retain all the IP rights, or discuss the invention with others in order to set up a business based on the invention.

The IPO says that for the invention to be eligible for patenting it must be *new*, have an *inventive step* that is not obvious to someone with knowledge and experience in the subject and be capable of being *made* or *used* in some kind of industry. If a patent is granted, it lasts for 20 years but must, in the UK, be renewed every year after the fifth year. Patents are published by the IPO online after 18 months, which makes people aware of patents that they will eventually be able to use freely once the patent protection ceases. This also can be seen as a disadvantage, and you should remember that there is no legal requirement for you to file a patent; you can always decide to keep your invention secret. This is undoubtedly cheaper, but if the invention enters the public domain then you may lose your rights to it. However, in dealing with individuals you might approach regarding an unpatented invention, such as prospective partners, suppliers or financial backers, you may ask them to sign a confidentiality agreement (also known as a non-disclosure agreement) which legally binds them not to disclose company secrets. You can also require employees to sign such an agreement.

The IPO lists some things for which a patent cannot be granted such as:

> A scientific or mathematical discovery, theory or method;
> A literary, dramatic, musical or artistic work;
> A way of performing a mental act, playing a game or doing business;
> The presentation of information, or some computer programs;
> An animal or plant variety;
> A method of medical treatment or diagnosis;
> Anything that is against public policy or morality.

™ Trademark

A trademark is a sign – made up of words or a logo or both – which distinguishes goods and services from those of competitors. The IPO says that a trademark must be *distinctive for the goods and services provided*. In other words, it can be recognized as a sign that *differentiates* your goods or service from someone else's. Once registered, a trademark gives you the exclusive right to use your mark for the goods and/or services that it covers in the country in which you have registered it. You can put the ® or ™ symbol next to it to warn others against using it. In the USA you can use the ™ symbol without a registration process, but it limits the 'exclusivity' to your local market. To get national exclusivity for specific categories, formal registration ® is required and you must prove a formal transaction has taken place within six months of registration. In all cases, trademark registration must be renewed every 10 years and cannot be maintained if it is not being used on a continuous commercial basis.

As with a patent, a registered trademark may put people off using the trademark without permission and allows you to take legal action against anyone who uses it without your permission. However, in the UK a trademark also allows Trading Standards Officers or the police to bring criminal charges against counterfeiters illegally using it. As with a patent, you can sell a trademark, or let other people have a licence that allows them to use it. In the UK, even if you don't register your trademark, you may still be able to take action if someone uses your mark without your permission, using the lengthier and onerous common law action of 'passing off'.

It is worth mentioning that, just because a company has its name registered does not mean that that name is a registered trademark – company law is different from trademark law. Similarly, being the owner of a registered trademark does not automatically entitle you to use that mark as an internet domain name, and vice versa. This is because the same trademark can be registered for different goods or services and by different proprietors. Also, someone may have already registered the domain name, perhaps with its use being connected with unregistered goods or services. To search or register a domain name you should apply to an accredited registrar (available from the Internet Corporation for Assigned Names and Numbers, www.icann.org).

The IPO say that trademarks cannot be registered if they:

> Describe goods or services or any characteristics of them, for example, marks which show the quality, quantity, purpose, value or geographical origin of the goods or services (e.g. Cheap Car Rentals or Quality Builders);
> Have become customary in this line of trade;
> Are not distinctive;
> Are three dimensional shapes, if the shape is typical of the goods you are trading. This can be very subjective. For example, whilst Toblerone has been able to trademark the shape of its chocolate bars, Kit Kat recently had its claim to trademark the shape of its bars rejected by the UK IPO;
> Has a function or adds value to the goods;
> Are specially protected emblems;
> Are offensive;
> Are against the law (e.g. promoting illegal drugs);
> Are deceptive.

® Registered design

If you are creating products or articles, which are unique because they look different from anything else currently available, then you might want to protect the look by registering it as a design. A registered design is a legal right which protects the overall visual appearance of a product in the geographical area you register it. The registered design covers the things that give the product a unique appearance, such as the lines, contours, colours, shape, texture, materials and the ornamentation of the product (e.g. a pattern on a product or a stylized logo). It is a valuable asset that allows you to stop others from creating similar designs. It does not offer protection from what a product is made of or how it works.

Registering a design gives you exclusive rights for the look and appearance of your product. This may be enough on its own to stop anyone using your design, irrespective of whether they copied it or came up with the design independently. Once a design is registered you can sell or license it and sell or retain the IP rights. In the UK, **Design Right** and **Community Design Right** may also give you automatic protection for the 'look' of your product.

The IPO say that to be able to register a design it must:

> Be new – in the UK a design is considered new if no identical or similar design has been published or publicly disclosed in the UK or the European Economic Area;

> Have individual character – this means that the appearance of the design (its impression) is different from the appearance of other already known designs.

© Copyright

Copyright allows you to protect your original material and stops others from using your work without permission. It can be used to protect any media:

> Literary works such as computer programs, websites, song lyrics, novels, instruction manuals, newspaper articles and some types of database;

> Dramatic works including dance or mime;

> Musical works;

> Artistic works such as technical drawings, paintings, photographs, sculptures, architecture, diagrams, maps and logos;

> Layouts or typographical arrangements used to publish a work (e.g. for a book);

> Sound or visual recordings of a work;

> Broadcasts of a work.

Copyright does not protect ideas, only how you 'publish' your ideas, for example in writing, in which case the words cannot be copied. This happens automatically in most countries, which means that you do not have to apply for it so long as it falls within one of the categories of media protected, but it also means there is no official copyright register. Although not essential, you should mark the material with the © symbol, the name of the copyright owner and the year in which the work was created (e.g. © 2016 Paul Burns). Copyright owners may also choose to use technical measures such as copy protection devices to protect their material. In the UK, in addition to or instead of copyright protection, a database may be protected by the 'database right'. Trademarks can be both registered designs (for the artwork) and copyright. You can only copy a work protected by copyright with the owner's permission, even when you cross media boundaries (e.g. crossing from the internet to print).

As copyright owner you have the right to authorize or prohibit any of the following actions in relation to your work:

> Copying the work in any way (e.g. photocopying, reproducing a printed page by handwriting, typing or scanning into a computer, and taping live or recorded music);

> Renting or lending copies of the work to the public, although in the UK some lending of copyright works falls within the Public Lending Rights Scheme and this does not infringe copyright;

> Performing, showing or playing the work in public (e.g. performing plays and music, playing sound recordings and showing films or videos in public);

> Broadcasting the work or other communication to the public by electronic transmission, including transmission through the internet;

> Making an adaptation of the work (e.g. by translating a literary or dramatic work, or transcribing a musical work or converting a computer program into a different computer language).

If you have copyright of a work, you can sell or license it and sell or retain your ownership. You can also object if your work is distorted or mutilated. As with other forms of IP protection, the existence of copyright may be enough on its own to stop others from trying to copy your material.

If it does not, you have the right to take legal action to stop them exploiting your copyright and to claim damages – that is if you can afford to go to court. Copyright infringement only occurs when a whole work or substantial part of it is copied without consent. However, what constitutes a substantial part is not defined and may therefore have to be decided by court action. Copyright is essentially a private right and therefore the cost of enforcing it falls to the individual.

Case insight   Trunki

Combating counterfeiters

Courtesy of trunki.com

The Trunki is a fun suitcase that looks like an animal and is designed for children. It is estimated that 20% of three-to-six-year-olds in the UK own one. It was an idea that Rob Law came up with in 1998, but it has proved so successful that it has attracted many imitations. In 2013 his company, Magmatic, finally won a lawsuit in the UK against PMS International, a Hong Kong company that had been selling a Trunki-style product. The UK High Court ruled that PMS's Kiddee Case breached

Law's design rights in that the 'overall impression' created by the Kiddee Case, including the horn-like handles and clasps resembling the nose and tail of an animal, was similar to the designs underpinning the Trunki. As a result of this, Magmatic was able to take out an injunction preventing the sale of Kiddee Cases throughout Europe and forcing PMS to destroy remaining stocks. PMS may also be liable to damages to compensate Magmatic for lost sales.

❏ Visit the website: www.trunki.com

QUESTION:

1 Why has Magmatic been successful in using the law to combat counterfeiting?

Case insight   Xmi

Combating counterfeiters

Ryan Lee set up Xmi in Singapore to manufacture and sell small, portable speakers he had developed that were capable of filling a room with high-quality music. His first product, the X-mini, was launched in 2006:

The recently launched thumb-sized speaker, the X-mini™ WE.

'There was no other small speaker that was better than this at the time. That is why we demanded the (price) premium. Customers are willing to pay for quality.'

Lee minimized the costs he faced in his new venture. Even today he operates from what used to be a bar in Singapore's central business district. He also subcontracted manufacture to companies in China, having considered companies in Indonesia and Vietnam:

'Not everything can be done in these countries, and on top of that

The original X-mini™.

Courtesy of Xmi

they are not even as good at assembly. So you're going to pay more for an inferior product.'

Despite the high price, demand was strong and the product proved successful. However, within six months he started receiving calls from distributors in Europe asking for a discount because they had been offered what looked like identical X-mini speakers at a much lower price. Upon investigating, he found that, although these imitations had plastic casings that were identical to the X-mini, they had far poorer sound quality,

Continued...

Continued from previous page...

different packaging and did not carry the company's serial numbers. Once he had convinced his distributors that these were fake, inferior products the problem disappeared, but it did make Lee aware that there was a black market for fake X-minis. His reaction was to change suppliers to ones with a reputation for trustworthiness. He also started to manufacture some of the highly sensitive components himself as well as splitting up components among different suppliers. But ultimately he feels that the only way to combat these fakes is to keep one step ahead by constantly innovating and improving the product:

'I'd rather throw my money to the engineers, not to the lawyers. You innovate faster than your fakes. That's how you play the technology game.' (BBC News Business, 25 March 2013)

❑ Visit the website: http://www.x-mini.com

QUESTIONS:

1 In what circumstances is safeguarding your IP through legal means worthwhile?

2 How might you combat counterfeiting through commercial means?

Legal forms of business

Starting up in business is inherently risky and how you structure your business has implications for how much risk you face personally. The three most popular legal forms of business are: sole traders (almost 60% of businesses), partnerships and limited liability companies. Their advantages and disadvantages are summarized in Table 9.1. In many countries a business needs a licence to operate, which can normally be obtained from the local council. In the UK certain types of business, such as those selling food or alcohol, employment agencies, mini cabs and hairdressers, need a licence or permit.

 Practice insight **Advice on forms of business**

You can get more information on legal forms of business online. The UK site also provides an interactive guide on the permits and licenses you need (click on 'licenses').

UK: www.gov.uk/set-up-business-uk
And: www.companieshouse.gov.uk
USA: www.sba.gov

Table 9.1 Advantages and disadvantages of different forms of business

	Sole trader	Partnership	Limited liability company
Advantages	> Easy to form > Minimum of regulation	> Easy to form > Minimum of regulation	> Limited liability > Easier to borrow money > Can raise risk capital through additional shareholders > Can be sold on > Pays corporation tax (which can be lower than personal tax)
Disadvantages	> Unlimited personal liability > More difficult to borrow money > Pays personal tax	> Unlimited personal liability > More difficult to borrow money > Pays personal tax > Unlimited personal liability for debts of whole partnership > 'Cease trading' whenever partners change	> Must comply with Companies Acts > Greater regulation > Greater disclosure of information

Sole traders

This is the business owned by one individual. The individual is the business, and the business is the individual. The two are inseparable. A sole trader is the simplest form of business to start – all that is needed is the first customer. It faces fewer regulations than a limited company and there are no major requirements about accounts and audits, although the individual will pay personal taxes which are based upon the profits made by the business.

There are two important limitations, however. The first is that a sole trader will find it more difficult to borrow large amounts of money than a limited company. Lending institutions prefer the assets of the business to be placed within the legal framework of a company because of the restrictions then placed upon the business. It is, however, quite common for a business to start life as a sole trader and incorporate later in life as more capital is needed.

The second disadvantage is that the sole trader is personally liable for all the debts of the business, no matter how large. That means creditors may look both to the business assets and the proprietor's assets to satisfy their debts. However, this disadvantage may be overcome by placing family assets in the name of the spouse or another relative.

Partnerships

Some professions, such as doctors and accountants, are required by law to conduct business as partnerships. Partnerships are just groups of sole traders who come together, formally or informally, to do business. As such, it allows them to pool their resources: some to contribute capital, others their skills. Partnerships, therefore, face all the advantages of sole traders plus some additional disadvantages.

The first of these disadvantages is that each partner has unlimited liability for the debts of the partnership, whether they incurred them personally or not. Clearly, partnerships require a lot of trust. The second disadvantage is that the partnership is held to cease every time one partner leaves or a new one joins, which means dividing up the assets and liabilities in some way, even if other partners end up buying them and the business never actually ceases trading.

Generally, if you are considering a partnership you would be well advised to draw up a formal partnership agreement. It is very easy to get into an informal partnership with a friend, but if you cannot work together, or times get hard, you may regret it. If there is no formal agreement, then in the UK the terms of the Partnership Act 1890 are held to apply. Partnership agreements cover such issues as capital contributions, division of profit and interest on capital, power to draw money or take remuneration from the business, preparation of accounts and procedures when the partnership is held to 'cease'. Solicitors can provide a model agreement which can be adapted to suit particular circumstances.

Limited liability companies

A company is a separate legal entity distinct from its owners, shareholders, directors and managers. In the UK it must be registered with Companies House in accordance the provisions of the Companies Acts (www.companieshouse.gov.uk). Certain companies must be registered with the Financial Conduct Authority (www.fca.gov.uk). It can enter into contracts and sue or be sued in its own right. It is taxed separately through corporation tax (in the USA this is an election). There is a divorce between management and ownership, with a board of directors elected by the shareholders to control the day-to-day running of the business. There need be only two shareholders and one director, and shareholders can also be directors.

The advantage of this form of business is that the liability of the shareholders is limited by the amount of capital they put into the business. However, banks are likely to ask for personal

Getty

guarantees from the founder(s) to get around this problem. A company also has unlimited life and can be sold on to other shareholders. Indeed, there is no limit to the number of shareholders. Therefore, a limited company can attract additional risk capital from backers who may not wish to be involved in the day-to-day running of the business. Also, because of the regulation they face, bankers prefer to lend to companies rather than sole traders. However, in reality, the founder of a start-up business is unlikely to avoid having to give personal guarantees for the loans a company raises. Clearly this is the best form for a growth business that will require capital and will face risks as it grows.

Nevertheless, there are some disadvantages to this form of business. In the UK under the Companies Acts, a company must keep certain books of account and appoint an auditor. It must file an annual return with Companies House (where all company records are kept in the UK) which includes accounts and details of directors and shareholders (https://www.gov.uk/government/organisations/companies-house). This takes time and money and means that competitors might have access to information that they would not otherwise see. Companies whose shares are traded publicly on a stock market are called 'public' (as opposed to 'private') limited companies and face additional regulation.

The easiest and cheapest way to set up a company is to buy one 'off the shelf' from a Company Registration Agent. This avoids all the tedious form-filling that is otherwise required. It also saves time. Agents will also show you how to go about changing the company's name if you want to. To find out more simply conduct an internet search for 'Company Registration Agent'.

In the USA there are also 'corporations'. These are also separate legal entities but organized under the authority of the state as either 'C Corporations' (C Corp) or 'Subchapter S Corporations' (S Corp). These are broadly similar to limited liability companies. The major difference between a C Corp and an S Corp is their tax treatment. C Corps are subject to double taxation at both the corporate and shareholder level. S Corps do not pay tax; instead all profits or losses are passed through to individual shareholders. Therefore, losses in a C Corp reside with the company and cannot be deducted from shareholders' other sources of income – unlike an S Corp (a limited liability company can elect for different tax treatments). Because of this, private investors tend to prefer these two legal forms if there are losses at start up. However, most venture capital funds will not invest in S Corps because the number of investors is restricted to 100 – unlike C Corps or limited liability companies, where there is no restriction. So, your planned funding structure may affect the legal framework you adopt, although a company can change its legal form later in life.

Corporate governance

If you decide to establish your start-up as a limited company, corporate governance – that is, the responsibility for overseeing strategy and ensuring its efficacy – rests legally with the company's **board of directors**. Its legal duties and responsibilities arise out of common law and statute, varying from country to country, and may also be detailed in the bylaws of an organization.

Directors have a fiduciary duty – a legal duty of loyalty and care – to act honestly and in good faith, exercise skill and care and undertake their statutory duty. They must act in the best interests of the company and its shareholders. This may seem an academic distinction if there are only two shareholders (e.g. yourself and your spouse) and one of these is the sole director of the company (e.g. yourself). However, even if this is the case, you must realize that you have certain legal responsibilities and, if your start-up is larger or you have aspirations for it to grow, then your board of directors may comprise more than just yourself. It might include other key members of your executive management team, who might also be shareholders, and even non-executive directors – outside directors who are not employees and part of your executive management team. Often, if you have obtained equity funding for your start-up, one of the conditions will be the appointment of specified non-executive directors. For example, if you obtain funding from a 'business angel' (an individual investing equity in a firm on a professional basis), they will normally expect to be appointed a **non-executive director**. In fact, non-executive directors have a valuable role in bringing different skills, an independent and objective perspective and a new network of contacts that can contribute to organizational knowledge and learning. They can also

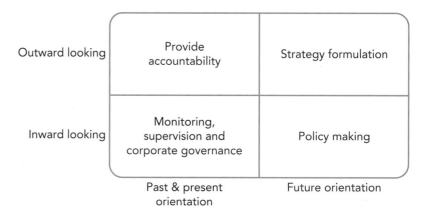

Figure 9.1   Role of the board of directors

act as an early warning system for potential future difficulties and can be particularly valuable in helping to resolve conflict in family firms.

The broad functions of the board are summarized in Figure 9.1, using the dimensions of inward/outward looking and past/future orientation:

Future orientation – Arguably the prime function of the board is to be outward looking and future orientated – to review and guide corporate strategy and policy. This might include over-all strategic planning, approval of strategies or investments in key areas, changes in the scope or nature of operations, major company decisions and so on. They are also responsible for how these translate into internal policies for the organization such as annual budgets, performance objectives, changes in organizational structure, compensation policy for key objectives, risk policy and so on.

Past and present orientation – The board then monitors performance against these strategies and policies and the ensuing risks it faces, as well as compliance with the law. These responsibili-ties include ensuring the integrity of the company's accounting and financial reporting systems, monitoring and supervising management performance, planning for management succession, providing proper accountability to other stakeholders in the firm, for example by appointing audi-tors and approving the annual financial statements, as well as ensuring that the company complies with all aspects of the law.

While establishing corporate strategy and policy may be the most important job for the board, it is unlikely that it will be given the appropriate weighting in terms of time allocation. Most boards, particularly in larger companies, spend too much time on the other functions, particu-larly monitoring management performance and legal compliance.

The board becomes more important where there is separation between day-to-day manage-ment and ownership of the firm and there are multiple stakeholders. Their role therefore becomes very important once a company grows to the point where it is floated onto a stock market. Once this happens the board needs to function in a more formal way. For example, in Europe separat-ing the role of chief executive or CEO from that of the board chair is considered good practice – to help avoid potential conflicts of interest between stakeholders and executive directors. For the same reason most of the *Financial Times* Stock Exchange (FTSE) companies comply with the recommendation that they have non-executive directors, although in small unquoted companies the proportion is much smaller. In the USA, the Sarbanes-Oxley Act introduced new standards of accountability on US public companies that made directors directly responsible for internal control, facing large fines and prison sentences in the case of accounting crimes.

To help boards develop and operate more effectively, the Chartered Management Institute (CMI) in the UK published a useful set of best practice checklists based upon a model of board-level competencies. Twenty-three board-level skills were identified and grouped together under the four key headings shown in Figure 9.2. These generic competencies need to be balanced and tailored to particular circumstances and specific functional board roles.

> Floatation gives a public face to your business and access to finance that is so often the key to development. But there needs to be a lot more atten-tion to strategy.
>
> **Elizabeth Gooch**, founder, **eg** solutions, *The Sunday Times*, 23 November 2008

Strategy **Guiding strategic direction** > Strategic thinking > Systems thinking > Awareness of external environment > Entrepreneurial thinking > Developing the vision > Initiating change > Championing causes	Operations **Exercising executive control** > Governance > Decision-making > Contributing specialist knowledge > Managing performance > Analysing situations > Awareness of organizational structure
Culture **Developing organizational culture** > Customer focus > Quality focus > Teamwork focus > People resource focus > Organizational learning focus	People **Practicing 'human' skills** > Communicating > Creating a personal impact > Giving leadership > Promoting development of others > Networking

Figure 9.2   Chartered Management Institute model of board-level competencies

Source: From Allday, D. (1997) *Check-a-Board: Helping Boards and Directors become More Effective.* Reproduced by permission of CMI. Copyright © CMI. All rights reserved.

Partnerships and joint ventures

Partnerships, strategic alliances and joint ventures are ways of exploiting a business opportunity where you may not have all the skills or resources to pursue it yourself. Partnerships can be broader than described earlier as a form of doing business (sole traders coming together to trade) and do not necessarily involve unlimited liability. In its simplest form, you might decide to sub-contract manufacturing or use a sales agent or distribution channels to sell your products. These are all forms of partnerships – where there is mutual advantage to be gained from some form of collaboration. The actual form these collaborations take can vary from informal to formal, underpinned by legal contract.

Partnering with others or organizations in setting up a new ventures simplifies the operating tasks you face and mitigates your risks. Since assets are owned or contributed by all the partners, the financial resources needed and the associated risk are spread and flexibility is increased. True partners can become part of a team pursuing a particular opportunity, even though not part of the same legal entity. They can help you in unexpected ways and you can often leverage their capability and resources – to your mutual advantage. So, just as you try to develop relationships with customers, you should try to develop them with other business entities. View your suppliers as partners, rather than just suppliers of a resource. But there are a wide range of partners and partnerships.

 Case insight   Tiger

Developing a partnership business model

TIGER The price-point retail model was invented in the USA. Typically it is a model operated by variety stores, selling a range of inexpensive household goods. Single price-point means that goods sell at one price, for example one dollar, pound or euro. And the name of the store then often reflects its value offering. The UK's Poundland claims to have introduced the concept to Europe in 1990 and is still the largest single-price discount retailer. Value and discount retailers have seen a boom in sales since the recession started in 2008/09.

Tiger is a Danish version of this retail concept. It sells toys, stationery and hobby and craft goods like knitting needles

Continued...

Continued from previous page...

All photos courtesy of Tiger company

and glitter glue. The products are own-branded, simple and colourful and most retail at less than £5. Tiger stresses its Scandinavian, functional-but-aesthetic design. The store itself is light, colourful and fun – laid out to be appealing to passers-by and to encourage impulse buys once inside. It has been likened to an Ikea marketplace. In the UK, Tiger has been called the 'posh-Poundland'; however, whereas you might go to Poundland for necessities, you would go to Tiger for 'affordable indulgences'. Lennart Lajboschitz opened the first store in Copenhagen in 1995. Since then it has grown to almost 500 stores in 24 countries.

Tiger expands by offering 50:50 'partnership' with local partners who are offered exclusive territories that might be large cities, regions or even small countries. For example, the UK is split into four territories: Southeast, Midlands, Wales and Scotland. These joint ventures are owned 50% by Zebra A/S (Owner of the Tiger chain) and 50% by the local partner. Zebra A/S is responsible for concept, goods and marketing, while the local partner is responsible for all operations and providing local know-how. Partners are expected to have comprehensive retail experience, local know-how and networks, an ability to run a minimum of 5–10 stores and access to at least €75,000.

❏ Visit the website: www.tiger-stores.com/tiger_partner.html or www.tigerstores.co.uk

QUESTION:

1 Why is this partnership model attractive to Tiger and to its partners?

Strategic alliances are a form of partnership whereby separate organizations come together to pursue an agreed set of objectives. They can be an effective way of sustaining competitive advantage and are particularly important in relation to innovation, where the partners have different competencies that they can apply in pursuing a commercial opportunity. There are often explicit strategic and operational motives for alliances such as gaining access to new markets. Jaguar partnered with the Williams racing team in 2011 to produce a new hybrid electric/petrol supercar. Nokia partnered with Microsoft to rejuvenate its smartphone offering in 2012 with the Lumia. Some start-ups have based their international expansion strategy almost entirely on foreign alliances.

A more formal strategic partnership is called a **joint venture**. This usually has a degree of direct market involvement and therefore needs to be underpinned by some form of legal agreement that determines the split of resource inputs and rewards. Often the joint venture takes the form of a separate legal entity to either of the parties involved. Richard Branson has been particularly adept at using joint ventures as a basis for rolling out new business ideas. He partnered with Deutsche Telecom to create Virgin Mobile and Delta Airlines owns 49% of Virgin Atlantic. Some developing countries do not allow foreign companies to set up in their country, only allowing joint ventures with local organizations, believing this to be a way of restricting foreign competition.

Numerous academic studies have shown that there are real benefits from strategic alliances and partnerships for organizations of all sizes. A government survey in the UK concluded that: 'in both the UK and the USA we observe that the highest growth firms rely *heavily* on building relationship with other firms either through supply chains or strategic alliances' (Department of Business, Enterprise and Regulatory Reform, 2008). Another US survey found that more than half of the fastest growing firms in the USA formed multiple partnerships to support their business models, resulting in 'more innovative products, more profit opportunities and significantly high growth rates' PricewaterhouseCoopers, 2002).

Alliances can create economic advantage by leveraging market presence (Lewis, 1990; Lorange and Roos, 1992; Ohmae, 1989). An example is **one**world, a strategic alliance of a dozen airlines including British Airways and American Airlines whose primary purpose is to encourage passengers to use partner airlines. Alliances can also provide vertical integration and scale economies at a greatly reduced cost (Anderson and Weitz, 1992). In its simplest form this is the arrangement a distributor has with a manufacturer when they have sole distribution rights.

The potential disadvantages of partnerships and alliances include loss of intellectual proprietary information, increased management complexities, increased financial and organizational risk, increased risk of becoming overdependent on the partner and partial loss of decision-making autonomy (Barringer and Harrison, 2000).

 Case insight   Specsavers

Developing a partnership business model

Specsavers was founded in 1984 by Doug and Mary Perkins, who met at Cardiff University. They started the business in their spare bedroom in Guernsey where they had moved to after selling their small chain of West Country opticians. In the early 1980s the UK government deregulated professional services, including opticians, allowing them to advertise for the first time. Doug and Mary seized the opportunity to try to launch a national chain of opticians. They opened their first stores in Guernsey and Bristol, followed rapidly in the same year by stores in Plymouth, Swansea and Bath. They wanted the company to establish its brand so that it would be seen as offering a wide range of stylish, fashionable glasses at affordable prices. They wanted Specsavers to be seen as trustworthy and locally based but with the huge buying power of a national company that meant savings could be passed on to the customer. Now with over 1,600 outlets worldwide and a turnover of £1.5 billion, Specsavers is the largest privately owned opticians in the world and the Perkins family are believed to be billionaires.

Specsavers has used an interesting joint venture approach to grow its business, a strategy which minimizes its capital requirements and the risks it faces. It enters into joint ventures with individual opticians, meaning that each joint venture is a separate legal entity. When the new company is formed, an equal number of 'A' shares and 'B' shares are issued. All the 'A' shares in the company are issued to the practice partners. All the 'B' shares are issued to Specsavers Optical Group. If there is more than one director in the business, for example an optometrist and a dispensing optician or retailer, then the 'A' shares are divided between the two parties. 'A' shareholders are delegated responsibility for the day-to-day running of the store. As a 'B' shareholder, Specsavers provides supporting services, expertise,

experience and information. As the number of practices has grown, so has the range of support services provided to practices, so that partners receive full support in all aspects of their business, tailored to their requirements. These can include property services, practice design, practice start-up, buying and distribution, retail training and professional recruitment as well as support in producing accounts, audits and tax returns. Individual opticians can sell on their 'A' shares, subject to certain conditions.

A typical joint venture start-up may cost in excess of £150,000, depending on location and practice size. In an equal partnership between two optician partners, each would be expected to provide the business with a loan of at least £20,000. Specsavers will match this loan. Specsavers Finance will provide a further five-year loan for the remainder of the capital. Personal collateral is not required by Specsavers Finance to secure this loan. Specsavers and the partners sign a specific finance agreement. Loans are repaid from practice profits, sometimes within three years.

Specsavers claim the following advantages for opticians from this joint venture approach:

> A lower level of financial commitment from the opticians compared to a franchise.
> If targets are met the initial loan can be repaid from operating surpluses.
> Unlike a brand partnership or franchise, a joint venture partnership gives the partner the possibility of selling their shares in the future.
> The partner can end the relationship when they want.

❏ Visit the website: www.specsavers.co.uk

QUESTION:

1 List the advantages and disadvantages of this form of joint venture to both Specsavers and its partners.

Franchising

Franchising is a form of legal partnership. A franchise is a business in which the owner of the name and method of doing business (the **franchisor**) allows a local operator (the **franchisee**) to set up a business under that name offering their products or services. The terms of the relationship between franchisor and franchisee are set out in the franchise agreement. For franchisors it is a way of rolling out a business format rapidly without the need for large amounts of capital. It is popular with franchisees who are less entrepreneurial but wish to run their own business.

Franchisors need a proven, robust business model with an infrastructure to support local franchisees. One key principle is that the franchisor shall have operated the business concept with success for a reasonable time, and in at least one pilot unit before starting the franchise network. In exchange for an initial fee (anything from a few thousand to hundreds of thousands of pounds) and a royalty on sales, the franchisor lays down a blueprint of how the business is to be run: content and nature of product or service, price and performance standards, type, size and layout of shop or business, training and other support or controls.

Franchisees expect a detailed operations manual and operating systems and hands-on help in their start-up. They pay all the costs of establishing the business locally. Since the franchise is usually a tried and tested idea, well known to potential customers through its brand, the franchisee should have a ready market and a better chance of a successful start-up. Indeed, only about 10% of franchises fail.

 ## Case insight   Ahmed Khan and McDonald's

Franchisees

In 2011 the average McDonald's in Britain turned over £1.5 million per annum. A McDonald's franchise costs between £125,000–325,000, depending upon size and location (the average cost of a franchise in Britain is about £50,000), plus an additional one-off fee of £30,000. Monthly charges include rent, based on sales and profitability, a service fee of 5% of sales plus a contribution to national marketing (4.5% of sales in 2011). Terms are for 20 years (most franchises are for 5), franchisees are not permitted to hold other franchises and there is a compulsory nine-month, unpaid training programme for new franchisees.

Ahmed Khan left school at 18 to work in McDonald's in his home town of Southend-on-Sea. He became a supervisor and progressed until, at the age of 33, he bought his first McDonald's franchise for £240,000, using £60,000 of his own money and borrowing the balance from the bank. By the age of 44 he had five outlets in Newcastle upon Tyne:

'Having worked for McDonald's, I knew what someone could achieve by owning a franchise. The most appealing thing is the near-guaranteed profits, and the potential to expand. My dream is to own 10 or 15 stores.' (The Sunday Times, 24 July 2011)

QUESTION:

1 List the advantages and disadvantages to Ahmed of buying a McDonald's franchise.

There are hundreds of franchises in the UK and tens of thousands of franchisees. Franchising can be an effective way of rolling out a business model quickly by leveraging the capabilities and capital of franchisees. Most established franchisors are members of the British Franchise Association, which has a code of conduct and accreditation rules, based on codes developed by the European Franchise Association. Table 9.2 summarizes the advantages and disadvantages of being a franchisee and a franchisor.

 ## Case insight   The Body Shop franchise

Developing a franchise business model

Although The Body Shop is now owned by L'Oréal, the first store was opened by Anita Roddick in a back street in Brighton in 1976. It sold only about a dozen inexpensive 'natural' cosmetics, all herbal creams and shampoos, in simple packaging. Anita thought it would only appeal to a small number of customers who shared her values. Her husband, Gordon, even went off to ride a horse across the Americas about a month after it opened. But Anita was wrong. It proved to be a huge success. However, while this idea was novel at the time, it was easy to copy. The firm's initial roll-out owed much to Anita and Gordon Roddick's

Continued...

Continued from previous page...

clear focus on where their competitive advantage lay. They realized that their idea could be easily copied and success would only come from developing the brand and a rapid expansion. Unfortunately, they had little cash to do either. It was Gordon who had the idea of making The Body Shop a franchise, which meant that franchisees purchased the rights to open a The Body Shop® store and managed the shop themselves. The Roddicks initially decided not to manufacture their products or even invest in a distribution system, but rather to concentrate on getting the franchise formula right, developing the brand and protecting it from imitators.

Today, The Body Shop remains an international franchise chain of shops. The Body Shop International Ltd is the franchisor. Traditionally, franchisees paid an initial fee plus an annual operating charge for a fixed term, for a renewable franchise. Franchisees would buy a 'turn-key' system with a tightly controlled retail format providing shop fitting and layout, staff training and a stock control system, even help with site identification. The Body Shop International, of course, would also make a margin on the products it

sold to the franchisees. Franchisees receive regular visits from company representatives who provide assistance with display, sales promotion and training. Information packs, newsletters, videos and free promotional material are made available, and franchisees return a monthly report on their sales. This enables the company to monitor both trading results and the local sales performance of individual products. The company closely monitors the use of the Body Shop trademark in all franchisees' literature, advertising and other uses.

❏ Visit the website: www.thebodyshop.com

QUESTIONS:

1 How is this sort of franchise different from the joint venture partnership offered by Specsavers? Are the differences important?

2 Review the Lush Case insight, Chapter 7 (on page 192). How does Lush differ from Body Shop? What are the advantages and disadvantages of the two forms of business?

Table 9.2 Advantages and disadvantages of being a franchisee or franchisor

	Franchisee	Franchisor
Advantages	> Business format proved; less risk of failure > Easier to obtain finance than own start-up > Established format; start-up should be quicker > Training and support available from franchisor > National branding should help sales > Economies of scale may apply	> Way of expanding business quickly > Financing costs shared with franchisees > Franchisees usually highly motivated since their livelihood depends on success
Disadvantages	> Not really your own idea and creation > Lack of real independence > Franchisor makes the rules > Buying into franchise can be expensive > Royalties can be high > Goodwill you build up dependent upon continuing franchise agreement; this may cause problems if you wish to sell > Franchisor can damage brand	> British Franchise Association rules take time and money to comply with > Loss of some control to franchisees > Franchisees can influence the business > Failure of franchisee can reflect on franchise > May be obligations to franchisee in the franchise agreement

Legal forms of social enterprise

You can still have ethical and social objectives in a commercial limited liability company (or indeed as a sole trader or partnership). Many companies, of all sizes, do. In small companies these may be explicit or simply implied. In larger companies this is often part of corporate social responsibility (CSR), with explicit policies, strategies and objectives. If the primary aim of your start-up is social good, there are six legal forms of social enterprise in the UK. Their advantages and disadvantages are summarized in Table 9.3. These come with some benefits but many restrictions, the primary one (except for unincorporated associations) being that *all* the profits of the venture must be ploughed back into these activities. This can make raising capital difficult, unless you obtain finance specifically offered to social enterprises.

 Practice insight Advice on social enterprise

You can get more information about social enterprise in the UK online:
  www.gov.uk/set-up-a-social-enterprise.

UnLtd provides advice, training and support as well as funding for social enterprise:
  https://unltd.org.uk/

Unincorporated associations

These are informal associations of individuals that can form (and re-form) quickly – similar to sole traders or informal partnerships. They enjoy great freedom because they are not regulated. They are not registered with anybody, but they can apply for charitable status, which means they have to comply with the regulations of the Charity Commission (www.charity-commission.gov.uk). They can trade but cannot own assets or borrow money because an association has no legal status. However, it may be possible to set up a trust to legally hold ownership of property and assets for the community they are intended to benefit. Because these associations are unincorporated, each individual in the association is personally liable for any debts or loans.

Trusts

These are run according to the social objectives set out in the trust deed. Many organizations involved in health and social care and education are structured as trusts. Trusts are unincorporated

Table 9.3 Advantages and disadvantages of different forms of social enterprise

	Unincorporated Association	Trust	Charitable Social Enterprise	BenCom	CIC	CIO
Advantages	> Easy to form > Minimum of regulation > Can apply for charitable status	> Can hold assets > Can apply for charitable status	> Benefit from charitable status	> Can apply for charitable status	> Has limited liability status > Can hold assets but must have an 'asset lock'	> Benefit from charitable status > Can hold assets but must have an 'asset lock'
Disadvantages	> Unlimited personal liability > Cannot own assets or borrow money	> Must have trust deed > Must register with Companies House > Greater regulation > Greater disclosure of information > Profits cannot be distributed	> Must register with Companies House or FCA > Surpluses must be reinvested > Trustees cannot be paid > Profits cannot be distributed	> Must be registered with Companies House or FCA > Can raise funds by issuing shares > Profits cannot be distributed	> Must be registered with Companies House or FCA > Must issue annual community interest report and accounts > Profit distribution regulated > Cannot be registered charity	> Must be registered with Charities Commission > Profits cannot be distributed

bodies. Trustees manage the trust on behalf of the community for which it was set up, which will be laid down, along with the trust's social objectives, in the trust deed. The trust can hold assets but it cannot distribute any profits. However, trustees are personally liable for any debts or loans. Trusts may need to register with Companies House and, because they have social objectives, they can apply for charitable status through the Charity Commission.

Charitable social enterprises

These are set up wholly for charitable purposes that benefit the public. They must be registered with Companies House or the Financial Conduct Authority (FCA). They are regulated by Charity Commission regulations (HM Revenue & Customs in Northern Ireland and the Office of the Scottish Charities Regulator in Scotland). Charities benefit from tax and rate relief, and any surplus must be reinvested. The founder of a charity shapes its creation but not its strategic direction or operation. The charity is run by directors or trustees, who cannot be paid for their work. They shape its strategic direction.

Community benefit societies (BenComs)

These are incorporated 'industrial and provident societies' (cooperatives) – legal entities set up with social objectives, which conduct business for the benefit of their community. They are run and managed by their members, but profits cannot be distributed among members and must be returned to the community. BenComs can raise funds by issuing shares to the public and can be registered as charities. They are regulated by the FCA in the UK and must submit annual accounts. BenComs are different from cooperatives in that cooperatives operate for the mutual benefit of their members – which is not necessarily the same as the community – and therefore cannot be registered as charities.

Community interest companies (CIC)

These are essentially limited liability companies, registered with Companies House or the FCA, but with extra requirements. They can be limited by shares or by guarantee. They must demonstrate their social and environmental impact each year by issuing an annual community interest company report alongside the annual accounts. They must operate transparently and not pay directors excessive salaries. Profit distribution is also regulated; companies limited by guarantee may not distribute profits, whereas those limited by shares can do so under certain circumstances. CICs must have an asset lock, which means that profits or assets cannot be transferred for less than their full market value. People who start a CIC can steer the business as they see fit because they will be directors. More information can be found at www.cicregulator .gov.uk.

A CIC cannot be a charity. However, it is common for it to run alongside one. So, for example, it is common for a social organization to have two forms: a CIC, which runs in a business-like way while giving the community a stake in how it is run, and a charitable social enterprise to which the CIC's profits are transferred and which decides how they are spent. This dual form can maximize tax advantages. It also means that the charity can apply for grant funding that will help to get projects up and running, while the income generated by the CIC means that the organization is not totally dependent on these grants or the goodwill of donors or government.

Charitable incorporated organizations (CIO)

These are a newer form of incorporated organization that is set up for charitable purposes and therefore reports to the Charity Commission rather than Companies House or the FCA. Like CICs they must benefit local communities and have an asset lock. They are not able to distribute profits or assets to their members. Unlike CICs which have directors, CIOs have charity trustees. CICs and charitable social enterprises can convert into CIOs.

Case insight   The Good Care Group

Social objectives in a commercial business

Fiona Lowry set up The Good Care Group in 2009 because she felt the elderly and vulnerable should have the opportunity to stay at home and be cared for rather than go into residential care homes. This belief was born out of the experience in searching for care for her own parents and the realization that there were very few home care providers delivering a truly high-quality service. Lowry's ambition is to establish an organization that is able to drive up standards, professionalize home care and lead the way in the care sector.

With headquarters in London, the limited liability company now has some 400 live-in carers on its books and a turnover of £5.6 million. Home care services are available throughout England and Scotland, and they are delivered on a local basis through regional care teams. Carers are employees – not agency staff. Only about 5% of applicants

are accepted as carers. They are properly trained and given ongoing professional development. All employees are given the opportunity to be shareholders and almost all have taken it up. Lowry is chief executive on a board of 4 directors and 12 managers. Lowry is the biggest shareholder, with 20%. The company has no bank debt.

Lowry has had a successful career in the BBC and the private sector but this is not the first time she has made money out of a business which also had social objectives. In 2005 she founded Oracle Care, which provided residential and educational support for young people aged 10–18. She grew the business before selling it to the management team in 2012.

❏ Visit the website: www.thegoodcaregroup.com/

QUESTION:

1 Do social and commercial objectives coexist easily within The Good Care Group?

Taxation

All commercial businesses are liable to tax and there are a number of different taxes all organizations may have to deal with. All new businesses need to inform the tax authorities of their existence but particularly those with employees, where arrangements to deduct tax from wages may have to be made.

Practice insight Advice on taxation

You can get more information on business taxation online.

UK: www.hmrc.gov.uk
USA: www.sba.gov

Value Added Tax (VAT)

This is a form of sales tax that is common throughout the European Union. If your turnover is above a certain level you must register for VAT (in 2015/16 the level was £82,000 in the UK). If your turnover is above this, VAT must be charged on all goods or services you supply, but at the same time VAT on the goods or services you receive can be deducted from the amount you pay to the government. Different countries have different rates and there can be different rates for different sorts of products or services (in 2015/16 the standard or main rate of VAT in the UK was 20%). Certain goods or services may also be 'exempt' from VAT, which means that VAT is not charged on the goods or services you supply, but you cannot claim back VAT on the goods or services you receive.

Corporation tax

Limited liability companies pay corporation tax on their profits (in the USA this is by election). This can be imposed at the country and/or state level. There are rules about how profit is calculated for tax purposes and these vary from country to country. Tax laws are usually complicated. Some expenses are not tax deductible for tax and normally there are set rates of depreciation for fixed assets. Companies (as well as sole traders and partnerships) are legally entitled to *avoid* paying taxes by maximizing allowances, exemptions etc., but it is illegal to *evade* paying the appropriate taxes. The rate of corporation tax also varies from country to country and can increase with taxable profit (in 2015/16 the main rate was 20% in the UK). Shareholders receiving dividends from the company (paid out of profits) are charged income tax. In the UK the way this is calculated ensures that this income does not face corporation as well as income tax. In the USA, C Corps are subject to double taxation.

Income tax for sole traders and partnerships

Sole traders and partnerships pay income tax on their business profits. Although the expenses that can be deducted to arrive at your income as a sole trader or partner are similar to those for corporation tax, the detailed regulations and rates of tax can differ from country to country. Because there are often different rates of personal income tax depending on levels of income, personal income tax rates are often higher than corporation tax rates. In 2015/16 UK income tax rates after all personal allowances were 20% (up to £31,786), 40% (£31,786–£150,000) and 45% (above £150,000).

Local taxes

Most countries have local taxes. In many countries this takes the same form as corporate or income tax. In the UK it takes the form of a lump-sum tax based on the size of your business premises and is called 'Business Rates'.

Income tax due from employees

In many countries businesses are responsible for collecting income tax from employees and remitting it to the government (in the UK this is called the Pay-As-You-Earn or PAYE system).

Charities

Registered charities are normally exempt from tax on their income and exempt from VAT, but they have to deduct income tax from employees (PAYE).

 Practice insight reminder Characteristics of a good business idea – 9

9 **Not easily copied** – if it can be, protect your intellectual property. However, often getting to the market quickly and developing a brand reputation is the best safeguard.

⟳ Summary

> You may be able to safeguard the IP on your business idea through patent, trademark, registered design and copyright. However, this can be expensive and time consuming. Sometimes being first to market is more effective in creating competitive advantage. You can get employees or third parties to sign a confidentiality or non-disclosure agreement which prevents them from disclosing your idea.

> There are three legal forms of business: sole trader, partnership and limited liability company. Their advantages and disadvantages are summarized in Table 9.1.

> Responsibility for corporate governance legally rests with the board of directors. Directors have a fiduciary duty to act honestly and in good faith, exercise skill and care and undertake their statutory duty. They must act in the best interests of the company and its shareholders.

> Partnerships, strategic alliances and joint ventures can be very important for new ventures, particularly in the context of innovation and market penetration. They can enhance your business model without requiring additional capital outlay by:

  • simplifying operations;

  • leveraging your knowledge and capabilities;

  • spreading your risk.

› As a franchisor, franchising can be an effective way of rolling out a business model quickly by leveraging the capabilities and capital of franchisees. As a franchisee it can be a low-risk way of obtaining a tried and tested business model. The advantages and disadvantages are summarized in Table 9.2.

› There are six forms of social enterprise: unincorporated associations, trusts, charitable social enterprises, community benefit societies, community interest companies and charitable incorporated organizations. Their advantages and disadvantages are summarized in Table 9.3.

› All commercial businesses are liable to tax and there are a number of different taxes all organizations may have to deal with.

✓ Activities

1 Evaluate whether the IP of your business idea can be safeguarded in any way.

2 List the areas of activity in your business where partnership is possible and the types of partnership that are practical (partnership, strategic alliance and joint venture). For each area and type of partnership write down the advantages and disadvantages.

🗩 Group discussion topics

1 Is spending time and money on legally safeguarding your IP worthwhile?

2 How might you go about protecting your IP without resorting to law?

3 A big company with plenty of resources can always 'steal' your idea, even with legal safeguards. Discuss.

4 Under what circumstances might a partnership business form be more attractive than a sole trader form?

5 What are the advantages and disadvantages of having external directors on your board?

6 What are the advantages and disadvantages of partnering with other individuals or organizations?

7 Why and for what sort of businesses is being a franchisor an attractive way of rolling out a business quickly?

8 You never get rich being a franchisee. Discuss.

9 Is it better to set up a new venture with social objectives as a commercial enterprise or social enterprise?

10 What are the advantages and disadvantages of each of the legal forms of social enterprise?

11 There are only two certainties in life – death and taxes. Discuss.

12 Avoiding or minimizing tax is legal but evading it is illegal. But is it really ethical to avoid tax, for example by diverting income to another country with lower tax rates?

☛ References

Anderson, E. and Weitz, B. (1992) 'The Use of Pledges to Build and Sustain Commitment in Distribution Channels', *Journal of Marketing Research*, 29 (February).

Barringer, B. and Harrison, J. (2000) 'Walking the Tightrope: Creating Value Through Interorganizational Relationships', *Journal of Management*, 26(3).

Department of Business, Enterprise and Regulatory Reform, (2008) *High Growth Firms in the UK: Lessons from an Analysis of Comparative UK Performance*, BERR Economic Paper, 3 (November).

Dosi, G., Maengo, L. and Pasquali, C. (2006) 'How Much Should Society Fuel the Greed of Innovators? On the Relations Between Appropriability, Opportunities and Rates of Innovation', *Research Policy*, 35.

Hurmelinna-Laukkanen, P. and Puumalainen, K. (2007) 'Nature and Dynamics of Appropriability: Strategies for Appropriating Returns on Innovation', *R&D Management*, 37.

Levine. D. and Boldrin. M. (2008) *Against Intellectual Monopoly*, Cambridge: Cambridge University Press.

Lewis, J.D. (1990) *Partnerships for Profit: Structuring and Managing Strategic Alliances*, New York: Free Press.

Lorange, P. and Roos, J. (1992) *Strategic Alliances: Formation, Implementation and Evolution*, Oxford: Blackwell.

Ohmae, K. (1989) 'The Global Logic of Strategic Alliances', *Harvard Business Review*, March/April.

PricewaterhouseCoopers (2002) 'Partnerships Have Big Payoffs for Fast Growth Companies', *Trendsetter Barometer*, 26 August.

Shapiro. R. and Pham. N. (2007) *Economic Effects of Intellectual Property-Intensive Manufacturing in the United States*, World Growth, available online at www.sonecon.com/ docs/ studies/0807_thevalueofip.pdf.

Tidd, J. and Bessant, J. (2013) *Managing Innovation: Integrating Technological, Market and Organizational Change* (5th edn), Chichester: John Wiley.

🌐 www.palgrave.com/Burns-Entrepreneurship-And-Small-Business-4e

Go online to access additional teaching and learning resources for this chapter on the companion website. Click here in the ebook to complete a multiple choice revision quiz for this chapter.

Operations and risk

Getty

Learning outcomes

When you have read this chapter and undertaken the related activities you will be able to:

> Identify the key activities needed to launch and operate different sorts of business;

> Prepare Gantt charts and undertake critical path analysis;

> Undertake a risk management process that identifies, assesses, mitigates and monitors the risks faced by business;

> Understand how risk might be reduced through networks and partnering, financial and legal structures and appropriate approaches to financing the venture;

> Understand the importance of keeping contribution margins high and fixed costs low;

> Identify the critical success factors and strategic options for your business.

 Case insights

Ice Cream Mama	Richard Branson and Virgin (2)
Cotton On Group	Gordon Ramsay
Made.com	Mind Candy and Moshi Monsters
Smak Parlour	Kirsty's

Contents

- Managing the business
- Business model imperatives
- Key operating activities
- Retail imperatives
- Internet business imperatives
- Manufacturing business imperatives
- Service business imperatives
- Identifying risks
- Assessing risks
- Mitigating risks
- Monitoring risks
- Generic risk management strategies
- Risk management, strategic options and critical success factors
- Operating plans and critical paths
- Summary

Practice insight: Search engine optimization

Practice insight: Business-to-business contacts

Practice insight: 10 guidelines to reduce product waste

Practice insight reminder: Characteristics of a good business idea

Managing the business

Managing a business is concerned with handling complexity in processes and the execution of work. It is linked to the authority required to manage, somehow given to managers, within a form of hierarchy. The founder of a business assumes this authority, whether or not they are capable of exercising it. In fact, as we have noted, the style of management they initially adopt is likely to be informal, relying on strong personal relationships with employees rather than formal structures which might impede flexibility. Often they manage by example.

Back in the 19th century Max Fayol defined the five functions of management as planning, organizing, commanding, coordinating and controlling. Today, these sound very much like the skills needed to lead a communist-style command economy. Fayol's work outlined how these functions required certain skills which could be taught and developed systematically in people. Management on a day-to-day basis is therefore about detail and logic. It is about efficiency and effectiveness. Management and leadership are different and distinct terms, although the skills and competencies associated with each are complementary. We look at how the entrepreneur needs to develop these leadership skills in Chapter 18.

The purpose of a business is to deliver products or services to customers and that means you have to understand how to do that, even as a manager. If you want to start a plumbing business, you need to understand how to plumb as well as managing other plumbers. And, while every business is different, as Fayol believed, there are some generic approaches to managing this product/service delivery. At the same time, by starting a business you are facing risks that could lead to business failure and loss of money. And as we noted in Chapter 3, while entrepreneurs accept risk-taking, they do not like it and will strive to avoid and minimize it. Once more there are some generic approaches to managing these risks.

The founding entrepreneur has to be both a manager and a leader, and one of the important qualities of both is the ability to plan. This involves being able to prioritize activities and decide which is more important than another. These priorities vary from business to business, and prioritization is a question of judgement. Nevertheless, it is vital that the founder is able to do this and, ultimately, compile a list of **critical success factors** – things that are essential to get right if the business is to survive and grow. Critical success factors are distilled from **key operating imperatives** – key things that you need to do, although not all are critical. Which *imperatives* are *critical* is a question of judgement. It is not just about urgent tasks – most are urgent for a start-up. It is not just about efficiency – although this is likely to be important and take up much of the working day. It is not just about identifying factors that might set you back – there will be many of these. It is about deciding which things might fundamentally affect the success of the venture.

These key operating activities will come from elements of the business model, including marketing and operational activities, and the risks that the business faces. Some you will need to have completed *prior* to your business launch. For example, you might need a working prototype or your business model might have implications for the assets you need to own (licences, patents etc.) or you might need to secure key contracts with partners or customers. Some will be part of your day-to-day activities. This chapter is about managing operations, managing risk and providing an insight into which key operating activities might also be critical success factors for a start-up.

Business model imperatives

Your business model and the operating imperatives associated with the three core value propositions are likely to form some of your critical success factors (Table 6.3 is reproduced on the next page as Table 10.1). For example, Amazon originally set out to be a low-cost online retailer of books, so it located in Seattle, a major distribution hub for several large publishers. Companies with a differentiated product, like Apple, continuously innovate while building their brand based upon what they see as their differential advantages, such as design simplicity. Companies with a

Table 10.1   Value disciplines and business imperatives

Low-price/low-cost	High differentiation	Customer focus
> Maintaining cost leadership through economies of scale > Continually driving down costs > Achieving high sales volumes > Improving efficiency > Standardization	> Understanding the basis for the differential advantage > Building on the differential advantage > Building barriers to entry > Building the brand > Continuous innovation > Encouraging creativity and innovation	> Maintaining close relationships with customers > Keeping in touch with and understanding changes in customer needs > Maintaining customer loyalty > Maximizing sales to existing loyal customers (economies of scope) > Building the brand

strong customer focus like Virgin continually seek out new opportunities for brand extension, and Virgin does this while reinforcing its brand through the image of its founder, Richard Branson. Dell has a low-cost focus, so one of its key activities includes supply chain management. Should this focus change, as it is doing, then the importance of the supply chain will be reduced and other imperatives will emerge.

You start by considering how the generic marketing imperatives in Table 10.1 translate into key operating activities for your business. The Case insights into easyJet in Chapter 6 (on page 165) and Lush in Chapter 7 (on page 192) give you examples of marketing imperatives. For example, easyJet, like other low-price airlines, must keep its cost low, and this has numerous operations implications – from ticket pricing to luggage allowance, turnaround time to staff rostering, website design to branding. The question is whether any of these are critical to the success of the business. Critical success factors change, and the answer to the question will probably be different today compared to easyJet's early years. One enduring critical success factor for any airline is safety.

Key operating activities

Key operating activities are the most important things that you need to get right to make your business model work. They have implications for all aspects of the business, including the resources you need. Every business has its own key activities upon which its competitive advantage probably hinges. Some of these will need to be completed prior to your business launch, for example selecting an appropriate location for a retail business or obtaining appropriate licences. Others are key operating activities for the life of the business, for example keeping an up-to-date and engaging website or maintaining service levels. These may change over time as the business develops. But they are the day-to-day operating issues that you need to get right to deliver your customer value proposition. Some will be critical success factors. However, key activities cascade down an organization and what might be important or critical for a department within a larger business might not be of the same importance for the business overall. Paying salaries and wages on the due date is critical to many employees but is unlikely to feature on the key activities or critical success factors list for your business. It is all a matter of judgement.

Key pre-launch operating activities

If you hope to sell an innovative product, you probably will need to at least have a working prototype before trying to get finance, and you certainly need to have refined that prototype and be able to deliver the product in the required volumes before you go to market. However, you do not necessarily need to manufacture or even assemble the final product, just as you do not necessarily need to retail it directly to customers yourself. Some key pre-launch activities have implications for future operations. For example, eBay's business model requires them to have an efficient and effective web platform. This was needed at start-up, but the platform continues to be developed so the company can maintain its competitive position. Google's original business model required a working word-search algorithm. Today they need to keep at the forefront of internet-based search and retrieval technology and developments. Dell set out to be a low-cost provider of computer equipment and developed an innovative B2C2B integrated supply chain to facilitate this. Now this is commonplace and they are struggling to differentiate themselves.

Key operating activities

These are specific to each business, but there are some generalizations that can be made for specific industries – retail, internet, manufacturing and service. The location of a bricks-and-mortar retail business is a vital decision, just as the effective operation of the website is a vital activity for a virtual retail business. Many service businesses such as consultancies are based around some key skills, knowledge or problem-solving abilities, and training might therefore feature as a key updating activity. Production activities that underpin quality or efficiency might dominate the key activities for a manufacturing firm.

Retail imperatives

Launching a retail business – a shop, restaurant, bar etc. – poses a particular set of challenges. For any retailer, the 'place' element of the marketing mix is very specific and very important. The location must provide access to your target market. If you want the casual shopper or diner, you might locate in the high street or at a transport hub (like MOMA in Chapter 6) – wherever there is high footfall. High footfall locations are called prime sites and can be expensive. However, just because there are lots of people passing a location, it does not mean that those people are potential customers for the product/service offered by your business. If you are selling something that customers will seek out and you can rely on it 'pulling' them into the shop or restaurant then you can afford to be located at a secondary site, with lower footfall. You often see stores relying on infrequent purchases (furniture, cars, do-it-yourself etc.) located in secondary locations. Secondary locations have much lower rent and rates than primary locations. However, there may be additional costs associated with 'pulling' customers into that location.

Sometimes small retailers group together in areas which have lower rent and rates and establish their own customer 'pull' because of the charm the area has or because of the variety offered.

Table 10.2 Factors affecting the location decision of a retailer

Factors affecting location decision for a retailer

> Size of population in local area;
> Demographic and nature of population;
> Footfall outside specific location;
> Visibility of site;
> Proximity of 'magnets' such as anchor stores or transport hubs;
> Strength of competition;
> Consistency with customer value proposition;
> Site costs;
> Availability of parking;
> Availability of public transport;
> Potential for expansion;
> Nature of legal agreement (e.g. lease term, rent reviews etc.).

Retailers offering similar products/services can also group together to establish specialist 'quarters' such as a jewellery quarter or restaurant quarter.

For any retail outlet the frontage is the equivalent of a huge advertising hoarding or billboard for the products/services sold. It therefore needs to reflect the value proposition to customers. The ambiance is also very important – design, hygiene, layout etc. – and must also reflect the value proposition. It must be consistent with the rest of your marketing mix. If you are selling on price – for example like the Poundland stores in the UK – you do not need expensive frontage or point of sale displays because it is not consistent with the low-price value proposition. On the other hand, you may still need to locate in prime sites.

The launch of a new retail outlet needs to attract potential customers into the building. They therefore often have opening events, perhaps with celebrities or even bands, trying to generate a party atmosphere with banners, balloons, special decorations etc. Shops often have opening sales. While shoppers might just browse, drinkers or dinners will want to try out the products on sale, so special opening price discounts might be offered. Rather than relying on price offers, exclusive bars or restaurants might have special opening events which only selected people are invited to, creating an atmosphere of exclusivity. And while prime-site shops might rely on attracting passing customers, other retailers will need to promote their opening event.

While increasingly transactions are electronic, any business handling cash needs to ensure that there are safeguards in place to prevent theft. Staff theft is particularly problematic in bars. Increasingly, cameras are being used to supplement electronic cash registers. Cameras are also used extensively to discourage shoplifting. Table 10.3 provides a checklist of possible key activities for a retailer, based upon the mind map in Figure 4.6 on page 106. It is split between pre-launch activities and day-to-day operations.

Fancy

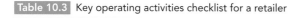

Table 10.3 Key operating activities checklist for a retailer

Retailing: Key operating activities checklist

Pre-launch	Operations
> Location	> Merchandising
> Licences and leases	> Stock control
> Store design and fit-out	> Promotions
> Merchandising and stocking	> Security (cash and shoplifting)
> Internet sales and website	> Service levels
> Sales staff recruitment and training	
> Credit/debit card merchant account	
> Launch event	

 ## Case insight   Ice Cream Mama

Retail location

After graduating from Sultan Qaboos University in Oman, Rami Al Lawati went to Australia to get a Bachelor's degree in Accounting and then to the UK to obtain an MBA. Returning to Oman he took a job with Omantel, the country's largest telecommunication provider. He met and married Huda, who had a degree in media studies and

digital technology. However, he was not happy in his job so he resigned after less than a year and decided to start a new venture with his wife using his business skills and the technological expertise of his wife. The company, called ProShots, provided high-quality photographic services, often using well-known photographers, for occasions such as weddings and birthdays, charging an equally high price for its services. However, the business was beset with

Continued...

Continued from previous page...

problems – for example, it used predominantly female photographers from East Asia and obtaining visas proved problematic – and therefore faced profitability and liquidity problems. Rami decided to change ProShots' focus, targeting instead corporate events. He also broadened its scope, renaming it Pro Group with a number of 'divisions'. Pro PR dealt with social media solutions, Pro Design designed communication material and Pro Events offered events management. The company also embarked on making documentaries for clients. However, while the company was quite successful in growing its turnover, it was not very profitable.

Never daunted, Rami continued to search for market opportunities and finally decided on ice creams. This was perhaps an obvious choice for such a hot country as Oman, but the market was dominated by international firms like Baskin-Robbins and a Pakistani creamery chain called Tropical. Rami decided that, in order to be different, he would capitalize on the popularity of homemade ice creams and focus on the traditional Omani way of making ice cream. Rami's mother used to make ice cream, so he started by copying her recipe and asked her permission to name the shop after her. She refused, so instead he named it Ice Cream Mama. The first shop opened in 2012 offering only two flavours: rosewater and laban. It sold out in the first day. By 2015, Ice Cream Mama had four stores in Muscat at popular locations.

'We believe that Oman is one of those countries that are very rich in culture in terms of food, fashion and so many things. But it hasn't been exposed to the world in a branded way and that's the gap I found in the market, it is the first traditional ice cream company from the GCC to be branded,' said Huda al Lawati.

One of the keys to its success has been selecting the right location. These must have high foot-falls with children and younger people. Ice Cream Mama stores are located near cinemas and malls. Rami and Huda have been careful to promote a distinctive Omani brand image. To make it feel more urban, street styles, including graffiti, are incorporated into the decor. The stores are also decorated with local scarves and motifs. Stores now offer a wide range of local and international flavours, but new local flavours like halwa, date and chai karak are launched regularly with much fanfare. As a result, Ice Cream Mama has become a popular brand in Oman, particularly among younger people, and has over 20,000 followers on Instagram.

Pro Group still exists but it is now funded by Ice Cream Mama. Rami and Huda want to take the venture abroad and are negotiating with clients in Dubai, Doha and Kuwait to open stores.

QUESTIONS:

1 What are the elements of Ice Cream Mama's marketing mix?
2 Why has it been successful?
3 Will the concept transfer to other countries?

Courtesy of Ice Cream Mama

Restaurants will need to develop attractive menus and make certain they have the chefs to deliver them. Waiting staff will need to be trained. Hygiene will be an important consideration and they will need to obtain a hygiene certificate from the local authority. Any retailer selling alcohol needs to obtain a licence from the local authority. Table 10.4 provides a checklist of possible key operating activities for a restaurant or bar.

Table 10.4 Key operating activities checklist for a restaurant or bar

Restaurant and bar: Key operating activities checklist

Pre-launch	Operations
> Location	> Hygiene
> Licences and leases	> Promotions
> Restaurant/bar design and fit-out	> Cash control
> Menu design	> Stock control (food and drink)
> Chef recruitment	> Staff rostering
> Staff recruitment and training	> Menu rotation
> Credit/debit card merchant account	> Service levels
> Website	> Customer security
> Launch event	

 ## Case insight   Cotton On Group

Critical success factors

Back in 1991 Nigel Austin was studying business at university and was short of cash, so he started selling acid-wash denim jackets from the boot of his car at the markets in Geelong, Australia. He bought the jackets from his father, a clothing wholesaler. The jackets sold well and, finding trading addictive, he decided to open a shop. Twenty-four years later he is still selling denim jackets – as well as T-shirts, jeans, checked shirts, dresses, sweaters, bras, undies and homewares. The difference is that his Cotton On Group (CoG) has grown to more than 1,300 stores – 760 in Australia alone – selling eight international brands in 19 countries, including the USA and South Africa. Sales in 2015 were approximately AUD 1.51 billion. CoG is what is often called a 'value fashion retailer' – selling fashionable, everyday, basic leisure clothing at value-for-money prices and quality. CoG is known for its intimate knowledge of its target customers, who are young and value-conscious, and its ability to keep abreast of new trends in the industry together with its ability to move quickly to meet them. However, the company remains a privately owned family business with relatives of Nigel and his wife holding many key positions in management. Its global headquarters still remain in Geelong.

Critical to the retail model is the timing of design, production and planning. The key to CoG's success lies in its supply chain and sourcing strategy, which allows it to offer quality products at the cheapest possible prices, and its ability to find and open stores that are relatively inexpensive, so that the capital investment is relatively low and there is a rapid pay-back period. CoG was one of the first Australian retailers to move to direct sourcing and adopt a fully vertically integrated business model. This allows for rapid replenishment of stocks and generates a higher margin. Products are manufactured by some 170 suppliers at 330 factories, mainly in China and Bangladesh, and are sent by sea freight to seven distribution centres in Melbourne, Brisbane, South Africa, China, Singapore, California and New Zealand.

Austin, who had worked in his father's Hong Kong office tracking down reliable suppliers, still uses some of them.

'We ended up having this perfect storm of comp sales growth through better replenishment systems and margin growth, so that was where the growth really kicked in. EBITDA (earnings before interest tax depreciation and amortisation) just took off, which funded more growth.'

However, direct sourcing also exposed the company to supply chain and reputational risk arising from the various scandals arising from the use of cheap labour and unsafe working conditions. Despite establishing an ethical sourcing programme some years earlier, CoG was criticized in Australia for being slow to sign an international fire and building safety agreement which compelled retailers to improve fire safety conditions and pay for factory workers in Bangladesh.

'The delay in signing the fire and safety accord was so we could do our own due diligence. We wanted to make sure if we were going to sign and commit to five years it was going to enhance our own program.' (www.brw.com.au, 2 April 2015)

Range reviews are conducted for each brand every quarter. Products are designed by a team of some 60 designers and trend forecasters, with a turnaround time between design and manufacture of two to eight weeks, depending on the category. New products are delivered to stores daily and new ranges arrive every week.

Cotton On Group contributes to the Cotton On Foundation (see Case insight on page 436).

❑ Visit the website: http://www.cottonongroup.com.au/

QUESTIONS:

1 What have been the critical success factors for Cotton On Group?

2 How might these factors change in the future as it continues to expand internationally?

Internet business imperatives

Many businesses trade on the internet, and that can get you access to international markets immediately. According to IMRG, the industry body for global e-retailing, in 2011 British consumers spent £68 billion on online goods and services, and this is growing rapidly. Selling on the web offers the opportunity to do business 24 hours a day, seven days a week – worldwide. It also offers you the chance to build relationships and develop an understanding of individual customers' buying patterns. The pure internet firm does not require the major fixed costs of a retail business like the high-street site and the shop-floor staff – but many traditional bricks-and-mortar businesses are now also trading on the internet, trying to offer customers the best of both worlds. At the moment, internet-based retail is most successful for branded products where the features are already understood, or for 'low-touch' products or services such as music downloads, books, airline or theatre tickets where, once again, customers understand precisely what they are buying. Almost half of all computers are now sold online, compared to less than 10% of clothing and footwear.

The key to successful trading here is a good website – one that gets people to visit and then revisit. Of course you can trade on other ready-built e-tail platforms such as Amazon and eBay. However, you may want to control content and presentation and to have your own web presence – and these platforms charge for their services. Indeed, your Microsoft software contains a basic website writing tool on Microsoft Office Live, where you will find links to free web design tools. If you do not want to build your own website from scratch you can buy skeleton sites that you can customize yourself or employ professional web designers. You can spend as much as you want to design and set up your own website. A basic one might cost as little as £500 but a good one could easily cost £20,000. If you search online you will find many website design services, but try asking friends and colleagues for recommendations.

Your website should enable customers to order quickly and easily. A site with a difficult sales process is likely to lose customers before they reach the checkout. It should also be easy to navigate, so customers do not get frustrated and leave without even attempting to make a purchase. Data and transaction security should also be a priority, and potential customers should be assured that their details will be kept safe. The content of the website needs to be updated regularly so as to maintain customer interest. It should also present a 'human face' and, better still, build a community of interest that encourages the visitor to communicate with you, ideally leaving their email address. You can then communicate with them directly. Just as in the real world, you should try to build a relationship with your customers, and we saw in Chapters 7 and 8 that the internet can be an important part of a communications campaign that helps build a loyal customer base around your brand.

You need to get customers to visit your site in the first place; just as with bricks-and-mortar businesses, you need to create awareness. Internet businesses often seem to forget this. You can create awareness of your site by using all the media outlined in Chapter 8, particularly advertising in print media or on other websites. As we have seen, services such as Google AdWords can be very cost-effective because they operate on a 'pay-per-click' basis. Social media such as blogs, chat rooms and discussion forums can also be cheap ways of getting customers to become aware of your website.

Optimize your website. Keep driving customers to your website using PR and marketing and make your site sticky. It's your portal to world markets.

Calypso Rose, founder, Clippykit, *The Daily Telegraph*, 6 February 2009

 Practice insight Search engine optimization

Search engine optimization (SEO) software is available to download.
Google offers a free tool for analysing your website traffic: www.google.com/analytics

This is a key-word research tool: www.compete.com
These sites offer guides and tips on SEO: http://searchengineland.com/guide/what-is-seo and www.seochat.com
This site offers free SEO tools: www.seolite.com

Table 10.5 Key operating activities checklist for an internet business

Internet business: Key operating activities checklist

Pre-launch	Operations
> Web design and navigation > Search engine optimization > Website advertising and promotion > Credit/debit card merchant account > Transaction security > Merchandising and stocking > Launch advertising and promotion	> Promotions > Social media promotions (e.g. blogs, chat rooms and discussion forums) > 'Community' building activities > Website update > Stock control

All internet businesses need to ensure that potential customers searching the web for sites such as theirs get links to their site as quickly as possible. Search engines thrive on content, and the more relevant content with keywords or phrases, the more likely your site is to be featured on a search. However, few people searching the web look beyond the first couple of pages of results. 'Search engine optimization' (SEO) ensures that you catch any potential customers searching for your type of product on search engines such as Yahoo or Google as quickly as possible. However, SEO can be expensive if you employ a company to do it. On the other hand, you can learn how to do it yourself with the help of a good book, an online course and some specialist software, which helps you monitor the traffic on your own website. Table 10.5 provides a checklist of possible key operating activities for an internet business.

 ## Case insight Made.com

Business models and risk

Made.com is an online furniture store. It was set up by Ning Li, a serial entrepreneur with experience of furniture selling in France, where he imported furniture from China. Made.com works directly with designers to custom-make exclusive products for customers. Putting the furniture retail market online has helped revolutionize what he calls a 'dusty industry' where retailers were reluctant to take risks with new designs and designers. The internet changed that, allowing experimentation with minimal risk and improving the speed of response to changing trends:

'If a new designer comes to see us with a new amazing table that looks risky, we say 'Why not?' because the only risk that we have is taking the photo. We put it online, if it doesn't sell, we pull it off. And if it sells, then everybody wins ... The internet allows us to launch products much faster than traditional business ... Speed is king ... The speed of designing new products and also renewing your catalogue is key... to keep people's interest... keep them coming back to the website.' (BBC News Business, 3 November 2011)

QUESTION:

1 How can the internet be used to help minimize risk for your business?

Manufacturing business imperatives

There are five types of operations processes involved in manufacturing or production:

Project

This is the production of one-off, large-scale products to meet the specific requirements of a client, for example buildings. Normally the project is built or manufactured on-site around the needs of the client, because it is not practical to move it once it is produced. Operational issues include effective resource delivery to and allocation around the site and the coordination of a large number of interrelated activities. The challenge is to deliver the project on time and on budget. Because it is one-off, specialist knowledge of this sort of project and accurate costing are vital.

Jobbing

This is one-off production to meet the specific requirements of a client, but the process can be undertaken in a factory and then shipped to the client, for example the production of a machine tool. This would normally make the organization of operations easier. The challenge remains to deliver the project on time and on budget, and specialist knowledge and accurate costing is vital.

Batch

This is where there is sufficient volume of production to justify organizing production in the most efficient and effective way. There is a degree of task repetition, but volumes rarely justify the investment of time in task analysis. An example is the manufacture of components that go on to be assembled into a bigger, more complicated product.

Line

This is where there is a further increase in volume, with a regularity of order that justifies the investment in task analysis and dedicated resources, for example the production of a limited range of clothing. Assembling subcomponents (which may come from subcontractors) to form the final product is usually an important part of the process. Organizing these processes in the most efficient and effective way is important.

Getty

Continuous

This is where volumes have increased to such an extent that an inflexible, dedicated process is in place to run all day, every day, with a minimum of shut downs, for example the production of consumer durables like washing machines. This is something that a small business would not normally be involved in.

Manufacturing and assembly can be complicated and often requires expensive machinery. So the first question to ask is whether you need to undertake the task yourself or whether you might have the process undertaken more cheaply, more quickly and to a higher standard by subcontracting the operation to a specialist? The answer lies in the particular knowledge, skills and capabilities upon which your business is based. If these are not based in manufacturing, then looking for a subcontractor might be a good idea.

 Practice insight Business-to-business contacts

Most manufacturing businesses require machinery and equipment of some sort. You can use trade magazines to search out suppliers. Quality control is likely to be an important operating issue and there are UK/international quality standards that may help (BS/ISO 9000 series). You will need to source raw materials. Business-to-business directories can help you source suppliers from around the world:

Applegate: www.applegate.co.uk
Alibaba: www.alibaba.com
Kompass: www.kompass.co.uk

Operating imperatives in manufacturing do vary considerably. Project and jobbing manufacture requires a high degree of specialist knowledge and skill and may require expensive specialist equipment. Project management skills are also important. There is the opportunity to differentiate and brand the business based upon this. Small businesses seem attracted to batch manufacturing, probably because the batches are not sufficiently large to warrant pursuing efficiencies and economies of scale. However, batch manufacturing can involve high volumes and a relatively wide range of products with different orders competing for the same processes and therefore control can be complex. Line manufacturing involves the ability to organize assembly and manage repetitive, routine operations efficiently and effectively. Cost control, plant utilization and economies of scale are likely to be important. Table 10.6 provides a checklist of possible key operating activities for a manufacturing business.

Table 10.6 Key operating activities checklist for a manufacturer or service business

Manufacturer and service business: Key operating activities checklist

Pre-launch	Operations
> Premises lease > Licences > Premises design and layout > Equipment purchase > Staff recruitment and training > Materials and stocks > Safety procedures	> Quality control > Stock control > Safety checks **Project and jobbing** > Project management > Knowledge and skills update **Batch** > Scheduling and processing of orders > Handling complexity **Line** > Staff control > Efficiency studies

 Practice insight 10 guidelines to reduce waste

Many academics and business people have observed that what is good for the environment can also be good for business. Sustainability means doing more with fewer resources, and that reduces costs. Scott (2010) gives the example of Walmart, which demanded that its 60,000 suppliers reduced packaging by at least 5% and as a result expected to reduce solid waste by 25% and shave $3.4 billion off operating costs. General Electric decided to become 'greener' in 2004. By 2008, 'green' practices had reduced costs by $100 million and yielded a portfolio of 80 new products and services that generated $17 billion in annual revenues. Here are Scott's 10 guidelines to reduce product waste:

1 Carefully design the product to minimize resources so it can be re-used in a closed-loop system.

2 Design products so they can be disassembled easily.
3 Reduce the use of hazardous inputs.
4 Switch to non-hazardous manufacturing methods.
5 Reduce the amount of energy required in manufacturing and use sustainable energy.
6 Use newer, cleaner technologies.
7 Use sustainable, re-manufactured, recycled or scrap materials in the manufacturing process.
8 Improve quality control and process monitoring.
9 Find ways to get the product returned for disassembly and harvesting of parts.
10 Reduce packaging or use recycled materials.

Service business imperatives

The most important imperative for a service business is the ability to deliver that service, and that depends upon the knowledge, skills and abilities of those delivering the service. All service businesses involve people, and their training is important. This training might reflect the specialist nature of the service – for example in consultancy and training. It might reflect the service process – for example where efficiency and effectiveness is important. Where direct contact with the client is involved, training should help develop the interpersonal skills of staff and their ability to manage client relationships as well as other staff.

Perhaps surprisingly, service delivery has some similarities with manufacturing. Larger consultancy assignments take the form of projects and require the same degree of coordination and control. A tailor-made training programme is similar to jobbing. A computer bureau that processes different clients' work is, in effect, a batch manufacturer. A fast-food restaurant has more than a passing similarity to line manufacturing. Table 10.6 therefore acts as a checklist of possible key operating activities for both a manufacturing and service business.

Identifying risks

It's easy to take a risk when it's just a couple of founders working from a garage; risk taking is part of a start-up's DNA. When your business grows, you still need to take risks, except there's a lot more at stake. Sometimes 'betting the company' is essential, but other times the reward needs to be weighed up against the risks for shareholders, customers and clients. We take lots of risks but only when the odds are in our favour.

Adam Schwab, founder, Aussie Commerce Group, *The Sydney Morning Herald*, 28 April 2014

You cannot start a business without taking risks. By launching your business you are inherently making a judgement – explicitly or implicitly – that you can overcome any risks that you might face. But have you really identified the risks that you face? How will you know if or when they materialize? And have you got contingency plans to deal with them should they materialize? Anybody reading your business plan will expect that you have. Risk often goes hand-in-hand with return. The higher the returns your business offers, the higher the risks that it is likely to face. So, just as financiers evaluate your financial projections (and the likelihood of achieving them), they also evaluate the risks that you face and your ability to deal with them.

Risk is inherent in business. While it cannot be avoided, it can be managed – or, more accurately, identified and even quantified so that it can be managed down to acceptable levels. This might involve putting in place appropriate controls or at least monitoring early warning of potential problems materializing. If risks can be avoided, then less time is spent 'fire-fighting' when they materialize.

You start by trying to identify the key risks that you face. Of course you cannot hope to predict all eventualities, but the more you try to anticipate them, the more you are able to generate both plans to deal with these risks and strategic options about the changes in direction that might result. Risk can take a number of forms. The risks associated with a particular course of action or achieving particular objectives might be identified. The corporate risks an organization faces might be identified. These risks may come from:

> External incidents (such as flood, fire and pandemic illness etc.) – These can be difficult to predict and the probability of occurrence might be low. However, the possible impact might be so great – for example loss of life – such that you need contingency plans to deal with them. Some of these risks will be generic risk to an industry. For example, the reaction of competitors.
> Internal incidents (such as the loss of sources of supply, malfunction of a major machine and product contamination etc.) – These can be many and varied, depending on the operations of your business. A good place to start look for possibilities is in your key operating activities.

You can try simply brainstorming the risks you face but another approach that can be useful is scenario planning (Chapter 5). Based on the threats an organization faces, scenarios can be explored about the results of these threats materializing. Table 10.7 gives you a checklist of possible risks that a start-up might face. It is not exclusive and in no particular order of priority. However, no matter how thorough your analysis, you can never expect to identify every possible risk. As has been said, the only two certain things in life are death and taxes, and one or two multinationals are working to reduce the latter.

Table 10.7 Risks checklist

Risks checklist

> Pre-launch delays – are any of the pre-launch key activities likely to cause delays?

> Competitors – what are they doing?

> Competitive advantage – is it being eroded?

> Market – how is it changing?

> Customer value proposition – is it being delivered?

> Product/service quality – is it adequate?

> Customer service – are they satisfied?

> Cash flow – is it adequate?

> Sales – are you meeting targets?

> Profits – are you meeting targets?

> Operations – are key activities under control?

> Productivity – is it meeting targets?

> Administration – are processes and procedures working well?

> Brand identity – is it being established?

> IP – is it secure?

> Technology – how are changes affecting you?

> Investment – do you need more?

> Stocks/inventory – are they adequate or too much?

> Merchandising – is it under control?

> Debtors/receivable – are they under control?

> Interest rates – how will changes affect you?

> Exchange rates – how will changes affect you?

> Management – are the team managing well?

Identifying the risk is only the start of the process, because not all risks are the same. Also important is the probability of the risk materializing. If the probability is very low, is there any point in preparing contingency plans? The answer may be 'yes' – if the impact on your business was large. And then there is the question of how the risks can be reduced or avoided and what you need to do to monitor these risks. Effective risk management is therefore a five-stage process:

1 Identifying the risks (internal or external);
2 Evaluating the probability of the risk materializing;
3 Evaluating the impact of that risk materializing;
4 Deciding how the risk might be mitigated (reduced or avoided);
5 Deciding what early warning signs might be monitored to identify that the risk is materializing.

Assessing risks

Risk management is about prioritization. Ideally the risks with the highest probability of occurrence and the greatest loss to the organization are handled first and those with the lowest probability of occurrence and the smallest loss are dealt with last (2 and 3, above). However, superimposed on this is the issue of whether the risks are controllable or not – whether they can be mitigated in some way. Figure 10.1 shows a useful way of classifying risks along these three dimensions. Any risks that have a major impact on the business are undesirable, but those which are very likely to happen pose the greatest danger (quadrant D). By way of contrast, risks with a low impact and a low likelihood of occurrence (quadrant A) pose the least risk. The third dimension is controllability. Some risks may be under your control or influence; others might be completely out of your control.

Generally, the less you control or influence the risk, the greater the danger it poses to your business. In this way the risk matrix becomes a Rubik's cube, with the greatest danger being in the cube with the highest impact, highest likelihood and least controllability (quadrant G). These risks cannot be mitigated but must be closely monitored. The risks that are very likely to happen

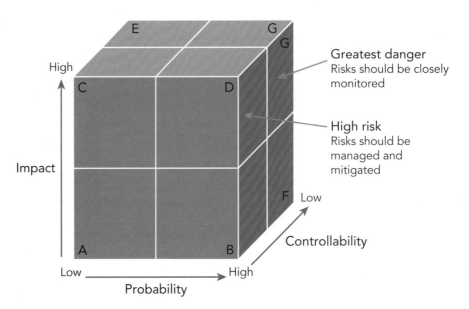

Figure 10.1 Risk classification

and have a major impact on the organization but can be controlled (quadrant D) will be the focus of managerial action to mitigate them.

Figure 10.1 classifies risk probability as either low or high and risk impact as either low or high. In reality it is often very difficult to quantify the probability of a risk materializing beyond a simple low (1), medium (2) or high (3). The monetary impact of the risk materializing might be just as difficult to establish beyond a similar low (1), medium (2) or high (3). The composite **risk factor** is defined as the probability of occurrence multiplied by the impact of the risk event. Using the simple classifications above, the highest composite risk factor is therefore 9 (3×3) and the lowest is 1 (1×1). This 1 to 9 scale can then be reclassified as low (1–3), medium (4–6) and high (7–9). This is called a **risk index**. The higher the index number, the greater the impact and the probability of the risk happening. These are the really dangerous risks. The question is how might you control or mitigate them?

Mitigating risks

Once you have your risk index, you can decide what to do about the risks you face. You have four options:

1 **Attempt to eliminate the risk**
   You might withdraw completely from the area of activity that generates the risk – an unlikely course of action initially for an entrepreneurial business. However, you need to at least continue to monitor these risks because at some point in the future you might change this decision.

2 **Attempt to reduce the risk**
   You might increase internal controls, training or supervision depending on the nature of the risk. Alternatively, you might select strategic alternatives that are less risky. Many of these strategies might involve transferring or sharing the risk with others, for example by partnering.

3 **Transfer the risk**
   There are many useful techniques that can be used to transfer both internal and external risks (e.g. insurance, foreign exchange or interest rate hedging). For example, companies constantly 'insure' against currency fluctuations – a risk they neither control nor influence – by buying forward in the currency market. As we saw in Chapter 9, partnering in all its forms

> If there are some obvious risks to your business model from the start, put in place some strategies to mitigate them.
>
> **Richard Branson**, founder, Virgin Group, *The Guardian, Media Planet*, May 2015

(e.g. subcontracting, outsourcing, franchising etc.) is an extremely effective way of transferring risk. For example, when developing a new product, you might find ways of spreading the risk by finding strategic partners or forming strategic alliances. This will also diminish the resources needed to exploit the opportunity but it will almost certainly reduce the return that you achieve.

4   **Accept the risk**

   You might simply accept all the risks in quadrant D. If you accept the risk completely, all you can attempt to do is plan to manage the risk and put in place early-warning indicators of it materializing, although this might be uneconomic if the impact on the organization is small. Many industries have inherent risks that need to be accepted if you decide to operate in that sector.

The most dangerous situation in business is where you have a high likelihood of occurrence, together with a high impact – a high risk index – in a situation where you have little control (quadrant G in Figure 10.1). In this situation you might consider any of options 1 to 3, but even if you end up accepting the risk it is vital that you monitor it and then take corrective action if it materializes. Quadrant G probably represents the situation you might face with competitors if your business proves successful – and you really need to have some plans and strategic options to deal with this (option 2).

Monitoring risks

All organizations have to accept some residual risk associated with their operations. However, you will need to monitor those risks with the highest risk index numbers, particularly those that are least controllable. As we saw in Chapter 3, entrepreneurs are good at gathering information by networking with customers, suppliers and other professionals. This can give you foreknowledge of risks materializing. You just need to be as aware of risks as opportunities and to ensure that you monitor them in a systematic way.

For those risks with the highest risk index numbers, you need to identify parameters or events that indicate an increased likelihood of the risk materializing – called **key risk indicators**. These need to be monitored on a regular basis so you can then take remedial action. To be effective, key risk indicators must be easy to monitor as part of your regular activity, highlighting when corrective action is needed and providing guidance on what action is needed. Cash flow is an obvious simple example of a key risk indicator. The risk is bankruptcy – you need cash to pay your bills – and cash flow measures your ability to do this. Most start-ups need to monitor their cash flow on a regular and frequent basis. We deal with this in the next chapter.

If the reaction of competitors is a major risk to your business, you need to develop a risk indicator that will measure this and put in place processes to ensure that it is monitored. For example, supermarkets regularly and routinely monitor the prices competitors charge for a typical basket of products. Without doing this they risk being uncompetitive and losing customers to rivals.

Generic risk management strategies

There are a number of generic strategies that can be used to manage and mitigate risk:

Partnering and other forms of networking

Partnerships, strategic alliances, joint ventures and franchising, like any form of networking, can provide knowledge and information about the risks you might face, how they might be mitigated and what you might select as your key risk indicators. They are all based on the strong personal relationships you are able to develop with stakeholders. These are ways of actively mitigating and sharing risk.

Strategic options

Creating strategic options is about contingency planning. It is about creating as many options for future courses of action as possible. It is about maintaining as much flexibility as possible for as long as possible so as to better deal with an uncertain and rapidly changing commercial environment. Many of these strategic options will come out of your review of risks and how to deal with them. The more strategic options you have, the lower the risks you are likely to face. We will look again at them in Chapter 12.

Affordable loss and lean start-up

Sarasvathy (2001) observed that entrepreneurs tended to go to market as quickly and cheaply as possible and assess market demand from that – an approach labelled 'affordable loss' (see page 145). They set an 'affordable loss', evaluating opportunities based upon whether that loss was acceptable, rather than trying to evaluate the attractiveness of the predictable upside. They decided what they were willing to lose rather than what they expected to make and therefore do not have to worry about the accuracy of predictions. Affordable loss can be calculated with certainty, depending on your situation. The idea is to decide what loss is acceptable to you, should the business fail. This defines the maximum extent of your loss from the very beginning and helps shape the start-up in terms of its risk/return profile. It is a two-step process. Firstly, set your acceptable level of risk (affordable loss), then push to maximize the return this will make, as shown in Figure 10.2.

The approach is linked to the concept of lean start-up (Ries, 2011 – see page 150). Using lean start-up you can gain the maximum information about viability by small-scale market entry. As you gain more information, you might set higher levels of affordable loss. Lean start-up allows you to assess the viability of the business model you developed. This is part of your '**commercialization risk**' – the unique risk associated with developing a new product and insuring customer acceptance. You can also help minimize your commercialization risk through the knowledge and information you gain by networking and partnering. The challenge then is to leverage up your affordable loss through knowledge and partnerships and only finally through external finance to find a start-up strategy that is achievable. Both these concepts were covered in Chapter 6.

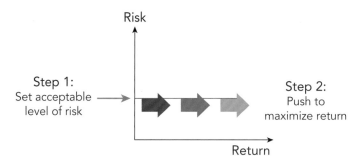

Figure 10.2 Setting risk and maximizing return

Borrowing and bootstrapping

One way of maximizing your return is by using other people's money as well as your own. As we shall show in Chapter 12, so long as the return you are able to make on this investment exceeds the rate of interest you are paying, then borrowing pays. However, when the reverse happens, you have to foot the bill and find the difference. And if the business should fail, it may be that you will have to repay the borrowing from your own personal funds. It all comes back to the relationship between risk and financial return. Normally, the higher the risk, the higher the financial return. So, if you really want to minimize your risk, you will have to minimize your borrowings and this may affect your financial return.

The reality is that the lower your external funding – including borrowing – requirement, the easier it is to start up and the less you might lose if the idea does not work. The funding you need is partly determined by the assets you need to start up and your 'affordable loss' – the amount you are willing to invest in the business. There has got to be a way of bridging any gap. However, if you can minimize your commitment of resources for as long as possible, you also minimize your funding requirement. This has implications for how you approach decision-making but you also need to realize that you do not need to own a resource to be able to use and control it. Sometimes changes to your business model can help minimize your borrowings. You may be able to borrow or rent the resource or partner with others who provide it. If you do not own a resource, you are in a better position to commit and de-commit quickly, giving you greater flexibility and reducing the risks you face. In the USA, minimizing the resources or assets that you own but still use and control is called 'bootstrapping'. To bootstrap you need to tap into as wide a network of contacts as possible.

 ## Case insight　Smak Parlour

Business models and risk

Abby Kessler and Katie Lubieski met at Drexel University studying design and merchandising. They moved to New York to work in the garment industry but soon returned to Philadelphia to design and sell edgy T-shirts to some 20 stores around the city. Some eight years ago they opened a fashion boutique in the Old City district of Philadelphia selling low-price clothing and jewellery targeted at younger women. It was successful and they thought about expansion, but the high costs and risks put them off until they heard about 'fashion trucks' in Los Angeles. These are simply box trucks that have been turned into mobile shops and follow a trend in mobile vending in the USA started by gourmet food trucks.

The cost of the truck is $20,000–$30,000, and it costs about $70,000 to make the truck into a shop (including air conditioning, fit-out, changing room, skylight and stocks), depending on what you want. But the overhead costs are then very low. You do not have to pay for leases or utilities, only the vehicle running costs (insurance, fuel etc.) and parking permits (anything from free to $1,000 per day, depending on location). And you can take the shop to the young customers that Smak Parlour targets, advertising its daily location to its loyal customer base on social media sites. You can also visit fairs, festivals and conventions.

❏ Visit the website: www.smakparlour.com

QUESTIONS:
1 What is the link between lean start-up and risk minimization?
2 List the ways you can minimize the risks facing your business.

High margins and low fixed costs

As we saw in Chapter 7, high contribution margins offer greater pricing discretion, which gives you the opportunity to price in different market segments differentially, thus maximizing sales volume. At the same time, low fixed costs mean lower risk of loss, should sales reduce. Both give you greater flexibility. So the two most important principles in any new venture, allowing you to keep your financial risks as low as possible are:

> **Keep your contribution margins as high as possible** – As we have observed, high contribution margins generally can only be achieved through strong differential advantage, and they allow you also to tailor prices for different market segments, thereby maximizing sales.
> **Keep your fixed costs as low as possible** – Fixed cost can come from operating costs, such as depreciation of fixed assets, or interest on borrowings. High fixed operating or overhead costs are called high operating gearing. High financing costs are called high **financial gearing** (or **leverage**). It follows that if you keep your investment in fixed assets low – and particularly your borrowings to finance them – then your fixed costs will be low. High interest payments could easily become a quadrant G risk in Figure 10.1. If turnover goes down, interest payments remain fixed and therefore reduce profit. Indeed, sometimes interest rates, and therefore interest payments, can go up when turnover, and therefore profit, are already reducing. This

is the classic situation that is created when interest rates are increased in order to decrease overall demand in the economy. The result is that small firms are squeezed by facing both higher interest costs and reducing sales.

There is a tension between a high contribution margin and low fixed costs. Firms with high margins are often associated with high fixed costs. For example, their high differential advantage may come from a high investment in technology or marketing. At the same time, firms competing primarily on price may be keeping their costs low through economies of scale, which are normally associated with investment in fixed assets such as plant and machinery. Because of this tension, the important thing is in not the absolute level of contribution margin and fixed costs but the relationship between them. This is measured by your **breakeven point** – a ratio that will be explained in the next chapter.

Compartmentalizing risk

A simple strategy followed by many entrepreneurs is to compartmentalize their business risks by setting each operation up as a separate legal entity. Should one fail, it will not endanger another. Serial entrepreneurs do this as a matter of course, partly because they intend to sell off each business at some point in the future. But other less obvious businesses, such as the Virgin Group, operate as holding companies that own (or partly own) numerous subsidiaries.

> The ideal business has no fixed overheads, commission only sales, large volume and low overheads
>
> **David Speakman**, founder, Travel Counsellors, *The Sunday Times*, 6 December 1998

Case insight   Richard Branson and Virgin (2)

Compartmentalizing risk

Richard Branson is probably the best known entrepreneur in Britain. Now in his sixties, his business life started as an 18-year-old schoolboy when he launched *Student* magazine, selling advertising space from a phone booth. His views on risk are interesting. In many ways he has been expert at minimizing his personal exposure to risk. He launched *Student* by writing to well-known personalities and celebrities – pop and film stars and politicians – and persuading them to contribute articles or agree to interviews. He persuaded a designer to work for no fee, negotiated a printing contract for 50,000 copies and got Peter Blake, the designer of The Beatles' Sgt Pepper's album cover, to draw the cover picture of a student. His first Virgin record shop was 'given' to him rent-free.

Today Branson's Virgin Group is made up of more than 20 separate umbrella companies, operating over 370 separate businesses. If any one were to fail it would not affect the others. Branson shares ownership with various partners. For example, Virgin Atlantic is 51% owned by Branson, with the remainder by the US carrier Delta Air Lines. Virgin contributes the brand and Richard Branson's PR profile, while the partner provides the capital input – in some ways like a franchise operation – and often the operational expertise. However, Branson is not afraid to commit his own (or borrowed) money when needed, for example when Virgin Atlantic was reprivatized.

As a result of this strategy, Branson and Virgin have seen some notable failures, but the brand has survived intact. The most widely publicized was Virgin Cola, launched in 1994 and closed down in 2012. Virgin Vodka suffered the same fate and was part of the entire Virgin Drinks subsidiary that was eventually closed. Virgin Vie was a cosmetics venture that was launched in 1997 and wound up in 2010. Virgin Clothing was probably the shortest-lived venture. Offering men's and women's clothing, it was launched in 1998 but was wound up in 2000. Virginware, a venture selling female lingerie, was similarly disastrous, closing down in 2005. Indeed, some of Branson's companies have themselves 'subcontracted' the brand to insulate themselves from commercial risk. For example, when Virgin Atlantic launched Little Red in 2013 – a small, UK-based domestic airline – it subcontracted all operations to the Irish company Aer Lingus on a 'wet lease' basis, meaning that they supplied the crew and aircraft, albeit in Virgin livery. Little Red closed down in 2014.

While he may tolerate risk and accept failure because it goes with being entrepreneurial, Branson continues to try to mitigate it throughout his business empire:

'One thing is certain in business; you and everyone around you will make mistakes. When you are pushing the boundaries this is inevitable – but it's important to recognise this. We need to look for new ways to shape up to the competition. So we trust people to learn from mistakes; blame and recriminations are pointless. A person who makes no mistakes, makes nothing.' (www.hrmagazine.co.uk, 13 July 2010)

QUESTION:

1 Why has the Virgin brand remained recognised and respected, despite these failures?

Case insight   Gordon Ramsay

Business models and risk

Gordon Ramsay is a famous TV chef with hit shows in the UK and USA such as *Hell's Kitchen*, *Kitchen Nightmares* and *Hotel Hell*. But that did not stop his business, Gordon Ramsay Holdings, from nearly failing in 2010/11 because he adopted the wrong business model and the wrong business partner. Most celebrity chefs license a partner such as a restaurant chain to use their name. They lend their name, create menus, hire key staff and undertake some promotion. In return, the chef receives a fee plus a percentage of turnover. However, the model Ramsay used was to set up and operate all the restaurants around the world himself and pay rent to the restaurant chain – potentially more lucrative but also more risky. This meant his capital costs and therefore borrowing was very high, and when the recession of 2008 hit, his fixed interest costs could not be met by his operating profits. What is more, often Ramsay committed to spend time at these restaurants – time that he did not have because of his TV appearances.

The result was a loss of £4.1 million in 2011, which meant that the company breached its loan agreements. Ramsay also fell out spectacularly with his father-in-law, Chris Hutchinson, who used to run the firm, accusing him publicly of siphoning off £1.4 million of company funds to support a secret family. After an acrimonious court battle,

Ramsay bought his 30% stake in the firm, costing the firm some £5 million. Ramsay had then to inject £2.5 million of his own money into the company to prevent it from going into bankruptcy.

Ramsay found a new partner, Stuart Gillies, who took 10% of the company that was renamed Gordon Ramsay Group. Many of the restaurants around the world were closed and debt was repaid. The business model was also changed to one that is more conventional and lower risk. The Group no longer put up capital. They take a fee for Ramsay's name and between 6 and 8% of turnover. Ramsay takes no salary from the group but his media earnings, which exceed £15 million a year, go through a separate company. Ramsay spends most of his time working on TV and books that create the brand that pulls customers into his restaurants. As a result of these changes, profits of the Gordon Ramsay Group started growing again: £1.4 million in 2012, £2 million in 2013 and £5 million in 2014. The company was able to expand again overseas, opening restaurants in Las Vegas, USA, the Middle East and returning to Asia.

Source: Adapted from *Sunday Times Magazine*, 14 July 2013

QUESTION:

1 What lessons do you learn from Gordon Ramsay's experience?

Risk management, strategic options and critical success factors

You can apply the risk management framework outlined in this chapter to your key operating activities. Your critical success factors should be the key activities needed to address the risks falling into quadrants D and G in Figure 10.1 – high risk and greatest danger. If they are controllable, you need to prepare action plans – decide what actions are required, who is responsible for undertaking them and establish timelines for their completion. However, you also need to prepare some strategic options – the actions you need to take if these critical factors do not go according to plan. This is particularly the case if you have highlighted any critical success factors over which you have little or no control, for example with competitive reaction. Preparing scenarios of 'worst-possible' cases in advance of them happening allows you to prepare contingency plans rather than trying to react after the event.

This risk management framework can be used to highlight the downside risks facing both your launch and your growth strategies (to be developed in Chapter 12). However, the framework can be turned on its head and used to look at business opportunities and strategic options, seeking to identify those with the highest impact (profit), highest probability (of success) and highest controllability (quadrant D, again). Once more, you need to prepare action plans – decide what actions are required, who is responsible for undertaking them and establish timelines for their completion. And what are the critical success factors? You can even use the Gantt chart technique we shall look at in the next section to help you plan this. You then need to generate some strategic options, should things not go according to plan. The whole process is a continuous one that involves a concept called 'strategizing' that we shall cover in the next chapter.

Your success will depend on your ability to mitigate and manage both the commercialization and more general business risks you face – both pre- and post-launch. The key risks you face need to be highlighted in the business plan. How you deal with them will lead to the development of your critical success factors, underpinned by detailed action plans, and strategic options. Both critical success factors and strategic options need to also be highlighted in your plan. This framework can equally be applied to your growth options. Successfully dealing with critical success factors are key milestones for a business. They are things to be celebrated when they are dealt with.

Case insight   Mind Candy and Moshi Monsters

New product development risk

Risk-taking is a recurrent theme in Michael Acton Smith's life. He was almost suspended from school for organizing a betting ring on school football games. His favourite book, *The Newtonian Casino*, is about college students who tried to beat the house by having microprocessors hidden in their shoes. His first job after university was with Goldman Sachs, with whom he hoped to become a market trader. And he always wanted to make money, as a child trying to breed chickens and koi carp, putting on BMX shows and producing a magazine.

> 'A lot of people approach life being very afraid of risk, always erring on the side of caution, and I think that's very sad. Only by putting yourself out there and getting out of your comfort zone do you grow as a person.'

Michael met Tom Boardman at university in the UK. Both started out in full-time employment but wanted to launch their own business based on ideas they had for gadgets and gifts. That did not happen until 1998 when they were both in their early twenties. They decided to raise money for their venture by taking part in medical trials for a new drug and borrowing £1,000 from Michael's mother. Working out of a rent-free attic, they started the online gadget and gift retailer Firebox.com. The business really took off when they offered a novelty chess set made of pieces that doubled as shot glasses. Firebox.com continues to sell a diverse range of obscure but 'cool' novelty products. But by 2004 Michel was bored and decided he wanted to develop something different. He secured £10 million in backing to set up another company called Mind Candy whose first project was an online-offline game called Perplex City – a global treasure hunt with £100,000 buried somewhere in the world with clues given in various media such as websites, text messages, magazines, live events etc. The game received critical acclaim, being nominated for a BAFTA in 2006, but it failed to catch on and ate through money. With only £1 million left, the second project was make or break.

In 2007 he launched Moshi Monsters, an online, interactive, cartoon-based world using tiny digital pet monsters that children could nurture. Players, typically aged between 6 and 12, pick one of six pet monsters and then travel around Monstro City completing puzzles to earn 'rox', the local currency that they use to improve the monster's home. While doing this, children can chat, upload stories and share drawings. It has been likened to a Facebook for kids. It proved to be a great success. By 2012 it had over 80 million players around the world and had expanded offline into a range of spin-offs such as toys, books, phone apps, a kids' magazine, a Nintendo DS video game, a music album, membership and trading cards and many other things children can purchase. Turnover in 2012 was £46.9 million. The business model involves membership subscriptions, but it is the associated merchandise that generates around half of Mind Candy's revenue. By 2013, Moshi Monster characters had become the most-licensed property in the UK. In December 2013, *Moshi Monsters: The Movie* was released and Mind Candy was estimated to be valued at £200 million.

Both the children's games market and the online gaming market are notoriously fickle and the question was whether Michael could continue to refresh Moshi Monsters with new ideas quickly enough. To help it do this he set up Candy Lab, an ideas incubator, described as a 'cross between Xerox Park and Willy Wonka's chocolate factory with new types of toys, new types of brands and new mobile games'. Michael's ultimate vision was to 'build the largest entertainment brand in the world for this new digital generation of kids'. He believed he had a blueprint for launching new games: start with the website and then branch out into merchandising, music and video:

> 'The bets you make are much smaller. The lead times are much shorter and the amount of capital you have to invest to find out if it's a hit or a loss are much lower.' (*The Sunday Times*, 8 July 2012)

However, company results were set to disappoint. In 2014 Mind Candy reported a loss of £2.2 million for the previous year, resulting from falling revenues from its Moshi Monsters licensing business – the movie had not

Continued...

Continued from previous page...

been as successful in the USA as it was hoped – and the firm's significant investment in mobile apps. Later that year Michael Acton Smith stepped down as Chief Executive of the company, saying he wanted to focus on a 'more creative role' within the company rather than its day-to-day running. Divinia Knowles, who had been at the company for eight years as Chief Operating Officer, took over as president, saying that her role was to raise the profile of other products such as World of Warriors, a role-playing game aimed at older children, and PopJam, a social photosharing app. Analysts said the company had been slow to adapt to the mobile games market, in particular the 'freemium' business model – the approach that gives away products for nothing, but encourages small payments within an app or other type of game. Later in 2014, venture capital firm Spark Ventures, which owned 2% of the company, wrote down the value of its investment by 60% saying:

'Mind Candy has continued to disappoint, missing budgeted revenues and reported sales [for 2014] substantially behind previous years.'

Mind Candy responded by saying that 2014 had been a year of transition:

'We have put the right building blocks in place for future growth, with a diversified product set that takes full advantage of opportunities in mobile, and a business that is the right shape to enable growth.' (Daily Telegraph, 12 December 2014)

❑ Visit the website: http://mindcandy.com/

See how Mind Candy develops new games: http://playtesting .mindcandy.com/

QUESTIONS:

1 What lessons do you learn from this case?
2 What are the risks now facing Moshi Monsters? How might they be mitigated?
3 What are the advantages and disadvantages of Michael's blueprint for launching new games? Are there prerequisites for it to work?
4 Could this blueprint apply to other products? If so, what kind?

Operating plans and critical paths

You need a broad, 'high-level' version of the operating plan to go into a business plan. This should identify major linkages and critical paths, including high-impact quadrant D risks and opportunities. Below the high-level plan you will have a number of detailed action plans about things that are still important, although not to those who will read your business plan. The operations plan should produce a series of milestones – operating objectives that are measurable and time deadlines for meeting them. Behind these will go a lot of detailed planning (and hard work) that do not show themselves in the business plan. We have split our operating plan into two parts: pre-launch – the things that need to be in place before you launch the business – and operations – the things you need to get right on a day-to-day basis, including the action plans coming out of your review of risks.

Each major activity in the lists you will develop can then be broken down into more detail, showing linkages and critical paths. The activities can then be ordered, with critical and high-risk ones scheduled as early as possible. **Gantt charts** are an excellent way of showing these linkages. Figure 10.3 shows a highly simplified Gantt chart based upon the pre-launch key activities checklist for a retailer based on the mind map in Figure 4.6 (page 106) and Table 10.3 (page 247), assuming the store location is already decided upon.

Photoalto

> Against each activity a block of time is drawn that represents the estimated length of time it will take to complete the task.
> The maroon arrows show the linkages between these activities.
> The orange arrows indicate the critical path along which each activity must be complete before the next begins.

The critical path is the longest path through the diagram and is the shortest possible time to complete the task – in this case opening the store. Unless the time taken for tasks can be shortened, this

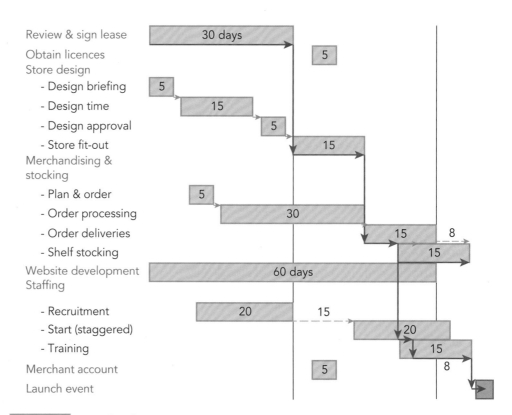

Figure 10.3 Gantt chart for opening a store

will take 68 days. If any task along the critical path line overruns, then the opening will be delayed. As you can see from the chart, the last two weeks of August and the beginning of September are congested periods of activity when staff are joining, stocking shelves and undertaking training prior to the store opening.

At the moment there is no slack built into these schedules. An added sophistication would be to build in fastest and slowest completion times and then check the effect on the critical path time. And it is very easy to fit dates into the format. You can go on to assign responsibilities and costs for the various tasks, going on to identify the risks that might delay completion of any activity. If this all seems a daunting task, there are computer programs that can help you with this sort of project planning.

You might produce a number of operating and action plans for different levels of your business. Your 'high-level' operating plan to go in the business plan would show key operating activities with their critical success factors. High-impact risks (and opportunities) would be clearly identified and strategic options developed. 'High-level' plans should be split into pre-launch and operational activities. A simplified Gantt chart for these key activities will illustrate clearly what needs to be done and when. If needed, you can write a brief line-by-line commentary. These key activities become your operational objectives – milestones in the development of your business. In our example one milestone might be to open the first store on 9 September.

 ## Case insight   Kirsty's

Simplifying operations and minimizing risk

When Kirsty Henshaw appeared on the UK TV show *Dragons' Den* in 2010 to get equity backing she knew exactly what she wanted. She asked for £65,000 in exchange for 15% of the business, but was happy to give away 30% because she wanted the involvement of two Dragons with experience and a network of contacts in this sort of business – Peter Jones and Duncan Bannatyne.

Continued...

Continued from previous page...

Kirsty was a 24-year-old, single mother from Preston, Lancashire, who left university without completing her Sports Therapy degree some two and a half years before her appearance on *Dragons' Den*. She started her business from her kitchen less than a year before appearing on television. Her son suffers from severe food allergies and intolerances and could not even eat an ice cream without becoming ill. Kirsty wanted a healthy, additive-free frozen dessert for her son but found that there was nothing really available from the supermarkets. Over a couple of years she developed two sorts of frozen desserts that not only tasted good but were low fat, low calorie and free from dairy, sugar, gluten, artificial additives, soya, cholesterol and nuts – one was eventually branded Coconuka and the other Coconice. She invested £20,000 of her own money while holding down two jobs. Producing food for sale in the UK is not straightforward, and she took advice from her local Business Link, the Trading Standards Institute and the Food Standards Association. She had her packaging and a website developed through a £3,000 government grant. And she only started producing her first products after she had secured distribution through a national wholesaler of health foods in December 2009. She also sold her products direct to customers through her website. But this was relatively small volumes which she batch produced in her own kitchen.

She knew that when she went on *Dragons' Den* looking for equity investment she would need not only a track record of sales, but also evidence of potential and plans for how to meet potential demand. She believed these products were unique and had national sales potential. But she also realized that she would face big problems with production and distribution at this scale. She therefore made two important operational decisions. Firstly, she decided that, to really make an impact she must sell into the national supermarket chains, and, secondly, that the only way she could meet this sort of demand would be to subcontract production. Kirsty had no expertise in this sort of large-batch/line production and this decision would allow her to focus on two important aspect of the business where she did have expertise – product development and sales. She also realized that, if (or when) the product was successful, competitors would soon copy her, therefore gaining market share with a branded product in the supermarkets as quickly as possible was vital.

Kirsty's sales in the months up to her *Dragons' Den* appearance had been some 2,500 units, giving her a profit of over £2,500. But the business plan she produced for the Den showed a profit projection of £300,000 for the year. The difference was a supermarket contract. Over a period of months, Kirsty had visited buyers at Tesco, the largest supermarket chain in the UK, who tasted the product and liked it, confirming that it was indeed unique to the UK market. At the same time, it emerged that some staff at Tesco liked the product so much that they had been purchasing it online. Tesco offered to give the product a trial in their stores ... so long as Kirsty could guarantee availability. Tesco would trial the product in 400 stores and each store would take 4 cases per week. Each case has 12 units and each unit has a margin of just over £1. The potential was obvious. So the next step was to find somebody to produce the product for her. Always thinking big, Kirsty approached the largest ice cream manufacturer in Europe to see if they could manufacture these sorts of volumes. Using the name of Tesco to the full, the company agreed to produce the product ... so long as she would guarantee the volumes.

So all the elements of the jigsaw puzzle were in place, but she decided that she now needed not only some venture capital but also some commercial expertise to help put these deals together and roll out the product – which is where the Dragons came in. Kirsty was looking not only for cash but also some commercial and industry experience, and Peter Jones provided the food manufacturing, distribution and retailing experience she needed while Duncan Bannatyne, through his fitness clubs, provided an opening to a health food market that she had not yet tackled.

The first thing Peter Jones did was to negotiate the subcontract deal with her manufacturer. They re-estimated first year sales at some 1.5 million units, giving a turnover of £5 million. Sales have taken off since then and Kirsty's products are now available in all five leading UK supermarkets. Indeed, in 2013 her product range was extended to include a range of healthy ready-meals. The company also changed its name from 'Worthenshaws' (the name it appeared under on *Dragons' Den*) to 'Kirsty's'.

❏ Visit the website: www.kirstys.co.uk

QUESTIONS:

1 Who is the target market for Kirsty's and what is the value proposition? What are the key elements of competitive advantage in this value proposition?

2 How did Kirsty go about simplifying the operational issues she faced?

3 How did she minimize the risks she faced?

4 Identify the risks the company now faces and its key operating imperatives. List the critical success factors.

5 What are Kirsty's growth options? Would you change the business model?

Practice insight reminder Characteristics of a good business idea – 10, 11 & 12

10 **Identifiable risks that can be monitored and mitigated** – the future of a start-up is by definition uncertain. Identifying risks is the first step to understanding how they can be monitored and then mitigated. The more options you have identified, the greater your chance of success.

11 **Low fixed costs** – low fixed costs mean lower risk, should volume reduce. It gives you flexibility. A combi-nation of high profit margin and low fixed costs (high profit, low risk) is always very attractive.

12 **Controllable** – putting in robust operating and financial controls increase your chances of survival and success, and ultimately will add value to the firm. The major imperative in the early years is to monitor and manage cash flow.

↻ Summary

> You need to identify the key activities to be undertaken to ensure the success of your venture. Some will need to be completed pre-launch, and some will be key operational activities that derive from your business model and its core value proposition.

> Your critical success factors are those key activities that you must get right to ensure the successful launch and day-to-day operation of your business.

> You need to identify the resource and operational implications of these key activities and develop detailed action plans as to how you will deal with them.

> Risk management involves five things:

  1. Identifying the risks (internal or external).

  2. Evaluating the probability of the risk materializing.

  3. Evaluating the impact of that risk materializing.

  4. Deciding how the risk might be mitigated (reduced or avoided).

  5. Deciding what early warning signs need to be monitored to identify if the risk materializes.

> You can evaluate risk by the probability of it occurring and the impact it will have and develop a risk index. You can then decide on the degree of control you have over it.

> Risks come from internal and external incidents. You need to identify the highest risks you face (those with the highest risk index number) and put in place the appropriate procedures to monitor the associated risk indicators.

> There are four ways of dealing with risk: attempt to eliminate it; attempt to reduce it; transfer or share it; accept it.

> There are a number of generic strategies to reduce risk. Your network of professional contacts can be used to bring you knowledge and information, including early warning of risk materializing. Partnering with others can be used to spread your risk.

> Your financial structure affects risk. You should keep your contribution margin as high as possible and your fixed costs as low as possible.

> You can decide on your 'affordable loss', and keep external funding to a minimum by bootstrapping. It may be possible to compartmentalize risk by setting up different parts of the business as separate legal entities.

> The risk management framework can be applied to analysing both downside risks and your growth options or opportunities.

> Critical success factors also emerge out of you analysis of risk and what needs to be done to manage it. Strategic options are the contingency plans you have in place should things go wrong.

> A 'high-level' operating plan provides details of key pre-launch and day-to-day operating activities and highlights the critical success factors. High-impact risks (and opportunities) would be clearly identified and strategic options developed.

> Key activities can be shown in a Gantt chart that shows linkages between activities and identifies the critical path. The critical path is the longest path through the chart and is the shortest possible time to complete the task.

✓ Activities

1 List the key operating activities you need to undertake to ensure the success of your venture pre-launch and ongoing, post-launch. List the resources and operational implications from these.

2 Select one key activity and draw up a Gantt chart, identifying the critical path.

3 Assign a risk index to each key operating activity identified in Activity 1 and identify which are the high-risk activities you face and whether these are controllable or not.

4 From Activities 1 and 3, identify your critical success factors and determine what the relevant milestones are.

5 Identify strategic options coming out of these activities.

🗩 Group discussion topics

1 In what sense can a sole trader also be a manager?

2 It has been said that the three most important decisions for a retail business are location, location, location. Discuss.

3 Ignoring the products for sale, what are the characteristics of a retail website that would encourage you to revisit it? What characteristics would cause you not to return? What is the relative importance of these?

4 Why are the imperatives for a service and manufacturing business so similar (Table 10.6)?

5 What types of business are the most complicated to launch: retail, internet, service or manufacturing? How might this complexity be simplified?

6 When does a 'key activity' become a 'critical success factor'?

7 If you focus too much on risk you will ignore opportunities. Discuss.

8 Can you really predict the risks a business might face?

9 If you cannot measure risk, you might as well ignore it. Discuss.

10 Setting an 'affordable loss' is a little too much like gambling – all or nothing. What is needed is a way of gauging how much and when to invest in a business. Discuss.

11 Who might a start-up partner with and what would be the advantages of this partnering?

12 How might you go about structuring a business with high margins and low fixed costs?

☛ References

Ries, E. (2011) *The Lean Startup: How Today's Entrepreneurs Use Continuous Innovation to Create Radically Successful Businesses*, New York: Crown Publishing.

Sarasvathy, S.D. (2001) 'Causation and effectuation: Toward a Theoretical Shift from Economic Inevitability to Entrepreneurial Contingency', *The Academy of Management Review*, 26(2).

Scott. J. (2010) 'The Sustainable Business', *Global Focus* vol 04, EFMD.

 www.palgrave.com/Burns-Entrepreneurship-And-Small-Business-4e

Go online to access additional teaching and learning resources for this chapter on the companion website. Click here in the ebook to complete a multiple choice revision quiz for this chapter.

11 | FINANCIAL MANAGEMENT

Contents

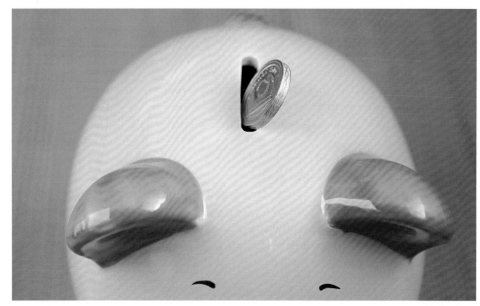

Image Source

Learning outcomes

When you have read this chapter and undertaken the related activities you will be able to:

> Understand the relevance and importance of different measures of financial performance;
> Understand how profit is arrived at and the difference between it and cash flow;
> Understand how the income statement and balance sheet are drawn up and the information contained in them;
> Develop the financial forecasts for a new venture – income statement, cash flow statement and balance sheet;
> Calculate break-even point and understand its relevance and importance;
> Use financial information to help with decision-making;
> Understand how financial information can be used to monitor and control performance.

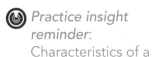 *Practice insight*:
3 tips for controlling debtors (receivables)

 *Practice insight reminder*:
Characteristics of a good business idea

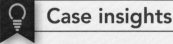 **Case insights**

| Xtreme SnoBoards (2) | The Pub (2) |

Financial objectives

For any venture to survive and grow it needs to be financially viable and it needs to have good financial control. This can mean a number of different things. For it to be attractive to an equity investor – and the founder – it needs to be profitable and efficient. For it to survive it needs to be sufficiently liquid to enable it to pay its bills. And all of these things mean that stakeholders are interested in the risk that a new venture faces. Therefore, SMEs need to be able to produce information that allows these things to be measured and controlled. This involves looking at a range of different concepts and measures.

> **Profitability** – Profit is the difference between your sales or turnover and your costs. A commercial business would normally want profits to be as high as possible. However, profit is not the same as cash. You may not have received payment for your sales nor indeed paid your costs. You can therefore be profitable, but illiquid – or vice versa. The two things are different. Profit measures how *all* the assets of the business have increased through your trading activities (sales – costs), not just cash. It is true that eventually the profit should turn into cash but meanwhile bills and wages have to be paid, and if you do not have the cash to pay them you may go out of business. Profitability is shown in the **income statement** of a business.

> **Efficiency** – Efficiency measures how profitably a business is using its assets. It is a measure of the *quality* of the profit you generate using these assets. Since those assets are paid for by the investors – including you – then it will be a significant influence on whether you can obtain finance. If the return you make (profit ÷ assets) is less than the going rate of interest, you are better off putting your money in the bank. Assets are shown in the **balance sheet** of a business. It is perhaps, therefore, obvious that to be efficient you need to be as profitable as possible by using the minimum of assets. There are a number of measures of efficiency using the technique called **ratio analysis**, explained in Chapter 12. Notice, however, that since cash is also an asset, there is a tension between being highly efficient and highly liquid.

> **Liquidity** – Liquidity measures a firm's ability to meet routine, short-term financial obligations. The most liquid of all assets is cash, and the **cash flow statement** shows how quickly it is estimated to come into and go out of the business. Cash flow is the life blood of a business; it pays the bills and the wages. Without adequate cash flow the firm might go out of business. The cash flow statement shows when cash from your sales comes in and when you make the expenditures associated with your costs and capital investments, such as buildings or plant and machinery. It also shows cash inputs from loan or share capital. There are other measures of liquidity that we shall deal with later.

> **Risk** – There are two sorts of risk measured in the financial statements. Operating gearing (or leverage) is the level of operating fixed costs (costs that cannot be altered easily, such as the cost of a lease on a premise), compared to your profitability. This is usually measured by your **break-even point**. Financial gearing (or leverage) is the level of your interest payments (which you cannot affect), compared to your profitability. It can also be measured by the amount of borrowing you have compared to your total assets. You have little discretion over these two sorts of fixed costs. The higher they are, the higher your risk of making a loss, should sales or turnover fall below a certain level.

The financial objectives of a commercial business will usually involve being highly profitable and efficient, while maintaining adequate liquidity and minimizing operating and financial risk. The challenge is quantifying these things and then achieving them. For a social enterprise with social objectives, profitability and efficiency may be constraints rather than elements to be maximized. However, whether it is a commercial or social enterprise the principles of financial management remain the same.

"The business side of any company starts and ends with hard-core analysis of its numbers. Whatever else you do, if you don't understand what's happening in your business factually and you're making decisions based on anecdotal or gut instinct, you'll eventually pay a big price.

Bill Gates, *Business @ the Speed of Thought*, New York: Time Warner, (1999)"

Understanding profit

Financial statements comprise three elements, each providing different, but consistent information:

> Income statement;
> Balance sheet;
> Cash flow statement.

How a business actually performs is measured by its historical financial statements, usually produced annually. These are used as a basis for taxing the business. Companies in the UK must submit them to Companies House, where they are publicly available. Financial statements are also used to control the business, and most well-managed firms will produce monthly income statements and monitor their cash flow on an even more regular basis.

The profit for any item sold is the difference between unit selling price and unit cost. You may have sold goods on credit. Total profit is the difference between total sales and total costs. It is important to realize that profit is not the same as cash. You may have sold goods on credit. Total profit tells you how **all** the assets of a business have grown (or shrunk) through trading – not just about changes in cash – and, as already pointed out, you can make a profit but have no cash, for example because the person who has bought the good or service has not yet paid for it.

Figure 11.1 shows how 'money' (often called 'funds') flows around a business. 'Money' comes in and goes out of the business as profits are made. This can take the form of cash but it can equally take the form of a 'promise-to-pay'. But at the same time 'money' might be spent on other things like assets or to pay taxes – but again this might be 'money' you owe rather than a cash payment. This 'money' is therefore not just cash, since you might owe 'money' or be owed it. It represents the growing assets – *all* assets – that the business owns, and this trading cycle is how it is created and accumulated or retained.

Start at 1 and work through the diagram in the sequence below:

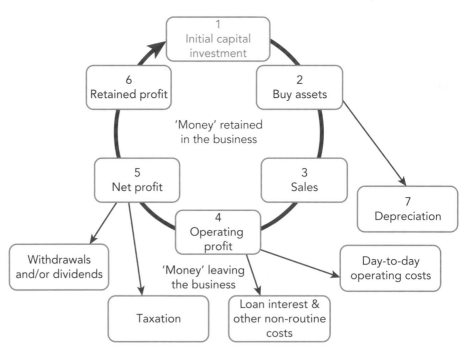

Figure 11.1 The 'money' generation cycle

1   A start-up needs to find capital in the form of cash. This could be a sole trader's own cash or, for a company, shareholders contributing share capital, both perhaps supplemented by bank borrowings.

2   This is now invested in assets to be used in the business. The assets will comprise long-term or fixed assets such as plant and machinery, office equipment, computers, vehicle and so on, and assets for use on a day-to-day basis. They will also include stocks (or inventories) of goods for resale, stocks of consumables to be used in the office, and, of course, cash to pay the bills. These are called current assets. The initial investment of cash has now turned into other assets, but all this 'money' is still retained in the business.

3   The assets are then used to generate sales. Goods are resold, services are rendered – sometimes for cash, sometimes on credit. This is the first stage on the way to making profits.

4   Of course, making sales is not enough to guarantee profits. Sales might be high, but if day-to-day business costs (paid for in cash or on credit) are higher, then a loss rather than a profit will emerge. So there is a need for management to control day-to-day costs and produce an operating profit. Other non-routine costs, such as loan interest, might also have to be deducted. All this 'money' leaves the business.

5   The result is net profit. This is still not, necessarily, cash because customers might owe you money or you might not have paid all your bills. However, it does represent an increase in the total assets of the business. If the business is established as a sole trader, cash may now be withdrawn. If the business is a limited company, corporation tax is paid and then dividends may be paid to shareholders. Sole traders pay income tax on the profits of the business and shareholders pay income tax on their dividends.

6   The balance of retained profits represents an increase in the capital of the business. However, this capital is still not, necessarily, cash. It can take the form of any assets. This is important as a business will need a constant flow of capital to replace existing assets which are used up and to expand and grow.

Boxes 3, 4, 5 and 6 are reported in the income statement (sometimes called the profit or profit and loss statement), but boxes 1 and 2 are reported in the balance sheet. The cash flow statement tells you only how one asset within the balance sheet – cash – has changed over the period. The income statement, therefore, does not tell you about new capital you might have introduced into the business nor the assets that the business might own in order to generate profit. It tells you about how the business goes about using its assets to increase their value. If those assets are being used in the business the profit statement needs to recognize that there is a cost associated with this as the asset wears out and reduces in value. Whereas the cash cost of the asset is recognized in the cash flow statement when the cash is spent, the cost of the asset needs to be allocated, somehow, over its life to the profit statement. Therefore, when you sell your product you recognize its cost when you make a sale. But how do you allocate the cost of a long-term, fixed asset over its life?

7   **Depreciation** is a way of showing this in the profit statement and is a major difference between profit and cash flow. The simplest method of calculating depreciation is called 'straight-line', which writes off the asset in equal amounts over its life. For example, if the asset cost $10,000 and has a working life of five years, at which time it can be sold off for $2,000, the annual depreciation would be:

$$\frac{\text{Initial cost} - \text{final residual value}}{\text{Life of fixed asset}} = \frac{\$10,000 - 2,000}{5} = \$1,600 \text{ per annum}$$

As shown in Figure 11.2, the value of the asset would go down by $1,600 each year. At the end of year one it would have a value of $8,400, year two $6,800 and so on, until year five when it would be $2,000. Each year the depreciation expense of $1,600 would be reported in the income statement. Although this is 'money' leaving the business, it does not represent any cash expenditure – that takes place when the asset is purchased.

| $1,600 | Written-off the value of the asset in year 1 as depreciation expense, asset value now $8,400 |

| $1,600 | Written-off the value of the asset in year 2 as depreciation expense, asset value now $6,800 |

| $1,600 | Written-off the value of the asset in year 3 as depreciation expense, asset value now $5,200 |

| $1,600 | Written-off the value of the asset in year 4 as depreciation expense, asset value now $3,600 |

| $1,600 | Written-off the value of the asset in year 5 as depreciation expense, asset value now $2,000 |

| $2,000 | Residual value of asset |

Figure 11.2 Asset depreciation

Normally, firms sell their goods or services for more than they cost to produce – revenues exceed costs. This is called profit and it increases the net assets of the business, but not necessarily cash. The income statement therefore tells you how all the assets of the business are growing through trading.

Profit is not an exact figure since it involves elements of judgement, for example in the calculation of depreciation or an estimated liability. An owner-manager can also charge whatever they want for their services, whether that is above or below any 'market rate'. Profit can therefore be manipulated.

Finally, it is worth pointing out that the income statement on its own does not tell you how well you are doing. If you make a profit of $5,000 from a capital investment of $250,000 you are making a return of only 2% ($5,000 divided by $250,000) and would probably be better off putting your money in a bank. So it does not tell you about capital investment – for that you have to go to the balance sheet.

Understanding the balance sheet

The balance sheet is a snapshot at a point of time that shows two things:

> The assets the business has – cash, debtors or receivables (amounts you are owed from sales), stock or inventory (raw materials, work-in-progress and finished goods stocks) and fixed assets (things the business means to keep over a number of years such as equipment, machinery, vehicles, premises etc.).
> Where the 'money' or 'funds' for these assets came from – overdraft, loans, creditors or payables (amounts you owe suppliers of goods and services), share capital invested in the business and the accumulated or retained profits of the business. (Remember, profit measures how *all* the assets of the business have increased through trading activities.) These are often referred to simply as liabilities and capital.

There are two sides to the balance sheet and, as depicted in Figure 11.3, they always balance. This is an ancient method of financial control called '**double-entry**' bookkeeping. As long as you have a record of 'money' coming in and going out of the business – the transactions taking place – you should therefore know the assets that the business should have. If any assets 'go missing', the balance sheet will not balance and you know something is wrong.

Let us look at a series of simple transactions to see how this works. If you drew up a balance sheet when you invest $10,000 capital in a new venture (as a company) it would show two things:

Figure 11.3 The balance sheet

cash $10,000 and share capital $10,000. If you went on to purchase assets with the $10,000 of cash, those assets would be listed together with their purchase price, and the other side of the balance sheet would remain the same, showing where the funds of $10,000 for these assets came from. If you can secure more funds or credit, this would be shown in the balance sheet as a liability, with the assets purchased on the other side of the balance sheet as assets. In this way, stock (or inventory) purchased on credit for $5,000 would be shown on one side of the balance sheet as a creditor (or payable), with the stock (or inventory) shown on the other side as an asset:

Assets	$10,000
Stock (inventory)	$ 5,000
	$15,000
Creditors (payables)	$ 5,000
Share capital	$10,000
	$15,000

Once the business starts trading and making a profit by charging a higher price for the product than the cost of production, the assets of the business will start to grow. If it sold this stock for $10,000 (on credit rather than for cash), making a (accumulated) profit of $5,000, the balance sheet would change, but it would still balance:

Assets	$10,000
Stock (inventory)	0
Debtors (receivables)	$10,000
	$20,000
Creditors/payables	$ 5,000
Share capital	$10,000
Accumulated profit	$ 5,000
	$20,000

Understanding cash flow

It is important to remember that profit is not the same as cash. You can be profitable but short of cash, just as you can have cash but be unprofitable. Cash pays the wages and other bills. It ensures your survival. Cash flow is about how quickly you can convert the 'money' in the cycle in

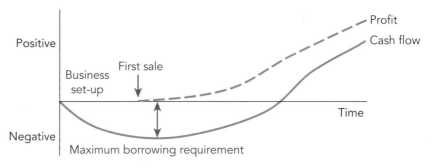

Figure 11.4 Death Valley

Ensure you are realistic about the amount of time it will take to become financially viable.

Angie Coates, founder, Monkey Music, *The Sunday Times*, 30 November 2014

Figure 11.1 into cash. Cash flow is the lifeblood of a business. Cash flow in any period is measured by how much cash you receive from your sales minus the cash expenditures you make against your costs and capital expenditures.

A new venture might spend cash on premises, equipment, stock or inventory and so on before the first customer even walks through the door. The first sale might even be on credit and it can take time before debts are collected. During this time the business will have a negative cash flow – a Death Valley that can be difficult to survive, shown in Figure 11.4. Without external finance, the company would be unable to pay its creditors. The length and depth of the valley depends on how quickly you pay out and collect cash and determines how much you need to borrow and for how long. Generally, cash coming in will lag behind your cash expenditures, but by getting debtors (receivables) to pay quickly and paying creditors (payables) more slowly you can speed up the flow of 'money' and minimize Death Valley. But your ability to influence this can vary from industry to industry and the negotiating power of your debtors or creditors. So, for example, supermarkets are notorious for securing generous payment terms from suppliers, while often receiving cash from customers before payment for the goods is due. It can also be affected by the economic cycle as credit customers delay payment.

However, knowing that you've passed through Death Valley after the event is of little use. You need to plot Death Valley's course and plan how to navigate it in advance – and that means preparing a cash flow forecast. Only this will tell you how much finance you might need to launch your business. By altering the assumptions on which your cash-flow model is based, you can see the effects on Death Valley. A good model should allow you to understand how you might reduce the depth and length of Death Valley.

The faster your growth, the deeper and longer Death Valley is likely to be. Profitable businesses – particularly ones that experience rapid growth – can still run into difficulty and ultimately have to cease trading because they run out of cash. It is called **overtrading**. So, be warned – many firms do not survive to come through Death Valley. You need to plan and monitor your cash flow.

Preparing financial forecasts

Just as you can have historic financial statements that show how a business actually performed, you can also have predicted financial statements or financial forecasts. These need to go into a business plan. Financial forecasts in a business plan are typically for at least a three-year period – five years for larger projects where significant commercialization risks, particular to the project, have not been resolved. Forecasting the financial results of a start-up can be tricky, but essentially they are nothing more than a 'best guess'. However, they will be used, just like actual results, to evaluate the (forecast) performance of the business.

Forecasting sales or turnover

Financial forecasts can either start one of two ways:

> By forecasting sales or turnover and the costs needed to generate them – the result is your profit (this is the most usual approach);
> By calculating the costs needed to set up the business and then working back to a level of sales that you need to generate a target profit level.

Either way, a number of iterations – altering price, volumes and/or costs – will probably be necessary before a satisfactory profit target is calculated. Monthly sales forecasts will be needed for the first year – perhaps for longer where these significant commercialization risks remain unresolved.

Realistic, achievable sales forecasts are the starting point for the rest of the financial forecasts, so it is important that they are more than just aspirations. However, as we observed in Chapter 4, the more radical the product/service innovation and/or market innovation you are introducing in your new venture, the more difficult it will be to forecast sales. Market research is unlikely to yield an insight into demand for this kind of new product/service or market because customers do not understand it. Often the only sure way of knowing whether the idea will make a lucrative business is to try it out – launch the business but minimize your risks of doing so (lean start-up). That means calculating the minimum costs needed to set up the business and then working back to the level of sales needed to generate a target profit level. After that it is about taking the leap of faith that Henry Ford and Steve Jobs did, but if you need financial backers you will need a persuasive argument and very attractive profit targets.

For more incremental innovations in products/services or markets your sales forecasts need to be justified by demonstrating that:

> **There is sufficient market demand** – You might be able to do this by market research that demonstrates that there is a market need that is, as yet, unmet (Chapter 5). This can take many forms but must be underpinned by a convincing understanding of customers, competitors and differential advantage. For example you might be able to demonstrate from desk research that there are relatively few competitors within a certain geographic area, compared to market demand, and you might establish the total size of the market size and should certainly be able to show market growth. Alternatively, if you can identify potential customers you might decide to contact them directly to establish whether they might be willing to at least try your product or service. And if you want to open a new shop in a certain area you might decide to measure footfall in that area yourself by field research. Another approach is to demonstrate that the market share you are aiming for in a particular market is so small that you are highly likely to achieve it. In this case the definition of this market needs careful attention. While you may not be able to prove there *certainly* is sufficient market demand, you should be able to establish that there *probably* is.

> **Targets are achievable, within the operating and cost parameters of the business** – Your forecasts need to be internally consistent. There is no point in convincingly forecasting sufficient demand if you have not built in sufficient costs to meet the sales you forecast. It is important to make clear the assumptions upon which your sales forecasts are based. That means clearly stating selling prices and volumes and ensuring that the volumes predicted are consistent with costs. Some costs that need to be incurred to set up the business are fixed costs and will not change significantly if your sales forecast is inaccurate, for example, property lease/rental costs or fixed salaries. These forecasts can only be 'reasonable estimates'. Some costs are variable costs that vary with sales volumes, for example, materials or piecework labour costs. Every time an additional unit is produced and sold, an additional cost is incurred. These costs vary with your sales forecast, and can be calculated on a percentage-of-sales based upon your detailed costings.

Investors will typically pay great attention to the assumptions underpinning the financial forecasts of a new venture, and if they feel they are unrealistic it may severely dent the credibility of the entire plan. They will often apply a range of pragmatic, common sense tests. For example, predicted sales for a retail business could be divided by the selling space taken up. This can often be compared to industry norms. Alternatively, forecast sales per day might be calculated, divided by the expected average spend per customer to arrive at a figure for buyers per day which can then be compared to footfall and buyer conversion rates. In a bar or restaurant you might look at the number of covers and the average spend per cover to see whether sales estimates are realistic. However you show it, investors will certainly want to know the volumes and price assumptions that underpin these estimates.

Forecast income statement

Once you have estimates of your sales and costs, you can prepare your forecast of profit. This is simply a case of slotting the estimates into an accepted format for an income statement, such as the one shown in the Case insight. The amount of detail you enter into is a matter of judgement, but the larger the start-up the greater the detail that will be expected.

Financial statements generally highlight the gross profit of a business. From this the operating costs (such as selling, marketing, administrative costs etc.) are deducted to arrive at the operating profit, and from this financing costs (interest) are deducted to arrive at net profit (before taxes and dividends).

Gross profit	=	Turnover – cost of goods sold (e.g. materials, labour etc.)
Operating profit	=	Gross profit – operating costs
Net profit	=	Operating profit – interest

The cost of goods sold is exactly what the words imply. However, these costs can comprise both variable and fixed costs. For a shop these costs represent the cost of the items sold – which indeed is a variable cost. For a service business, such as a consultancy, most costs, like salaries, will be fixed and very few costs will be variable. For a manufacturing business, in addition to the cost of the raw materials there will also be labour costs involved in adding value to the goods. If workers are paid by the volume they produce – called piecework – then this is a variable cost. However, most employees now expect to be paid a regular weekly wage – which is fixed. However, if volumes change beyond certain levels new employees might have to be recruited or existing employees made redundant. The cost of sales will also represent other fixed factory overheads such as the depreciation cost of machinery and equipment used in the process. Cost of sales for a manufacturing business therefore might comprise material costs (variable), labour costs (variable and/or fixed) and factory overheads (fixed). To work out the cost of goods sold (and the value of the goods you hold in stock) you need to know the cost of each manufactured good. That means undertaking a costing exercise so that the fixed costs can be spread over the volume of goods *produced* – not necessarily the same as goods sold (for an example see Xtreme SnoBoards (1) Case insight on page 90). This is the basis for what is called cost+ pricing (Chapter 7). If a manufacturing business fails to sell everything it produces, the cost of the extra it produces is reflected in the valuation of the unsold stock or inventory. To summarize, the cost of sales is a variable cost for a shop, probably fixed for a service business (up to a certain level of output) and comprises of both variable and fixed costs for a manufacturing business.

Forecast cash flow statement

The cash flow forecast lists the expected cash receipts and payments for the business in the period they are expected to come in or go out. It can be prepared on a daily or weekly basis, but normally for a business plan it is prepared on a monthly basis. It is a vital part of a start-up business plan as it shows your liquidity and borrowing requirements. You start with your monthly sales and cost estimates and convert these into cash receipts and payments. For example, if your terms of a credit sale are payment within one month, you might show the cash receipt coming in one month after the sales estimate. Similarly, if you purchase assets on credit, you might expect to pay cash after, say, one month.

Total cash receipts for the month are netted off against total cash payments and the resulting balance (negative or positive) is carried forward to the next month. Remember that depreciation is not a cash expenditure. The process is repeated each month until the total for the year end is arrived at. This cash balance should agree with the amount shown in the balance sheet. A format for a cash flow forecast is shown in the Case insight. As with sales, it is important that the assumptions on which it is based are clearly listed.

Forecast balance sheet

The balance sheet lists the assets the business owns alongside its liabilities and capital. A format is shown in the Case insight. It will show:

> All assets, whether paid for or not, alongside outstanding liabilities or shareholders capital;
> The net 'value' of fixed assets, after depreciation has been charged to the income statement;
> The profit for the period that will be added to any retained or accumulated profit from previous periods.

Understanding break-even

The break-even point is an important piece of financial information. It is the point where a business stops making a loss and starts making a profit – where sales revenues are equal to the total costs. Some costs, often called **overhead costs**, are **fixed costs** – they do not change with the volume of activity or sales (at least up to a certain level of output) – for example, property lease/rental costs or fixed wages and salaries. These fixed costs are represented by the dotted horizontal line AB in Figure 11.5. Producing the product or delivering the service will mean incurring additional **variable costs** – costs that vary with volume like materials and direct, piecework labour costs. Every time an additional unit is produced and sold, an additional cost is incurred. Line AC therefore represents the total cost of producing the product or delivering the service – the fixed cost plus the variable cost. Over large volumes, this line may curve downwards as the effects of economies of scale are felt. Line LM represents the revenue generated by sales – sales volume multiplied by unit price, often called **turnover**. At volume X all costs are covered by revenue. This is the break-even point. If your target sales volume is Y, this will generate the profit represented by the distance between lines LM and AC (total sales – total costs).

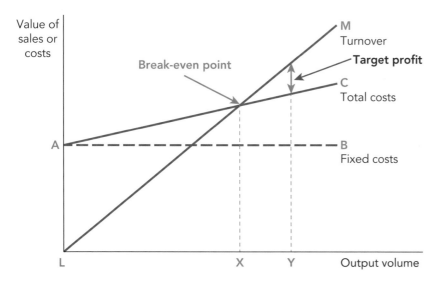

Figure 11.5 Break-even point

The higher your break-even point, the more sales you have to achieve before you start to make a profit and therefore the higher the risk you face. The lower the break-even point, the less risk you face. Indeed, if the break-even point cannot, reasonably, be expected to be achieved then a venture is probably not viable.

The break-even point can be easily calculated without a diagram using the formula:

$$\text{Break-even point (expressed in \$ turnover)} = \frac{\text{Fixed costs}}{\text{Contribution margin}}$$

Contribution per unit is the difference between the sales price and the *variable* cost of each unit you sell. **Total contribution** is the difference between turnover and your *total variable* costs. **Contribution margin** = contribution per unit ÷ sales price (*or* total contribution ÷ turnover). Usually this is expressed as a percentage. Where you are selling a range of products/services with different margins the calculation using total sales and variable costs is easier.

For example (assuming target sales of 1,000 units per week):

Sales price per unit	$10	Turnover (per week)		$10,000
Variable cost per unit	6	Total variable costs		6,000
Contribution per unit	4	Total contribution		4,000
Contribution margin	0.40 *or* 40%	Contribution margin		0.40 *or* 40%

If your fixed costs are $2,000 per week, your total profit will be $2,000 ($4,000 − $2,000).

$$\text{Break-even point} = \frac{\$2,000}{0.40} = \$5,000 \text{ per week (or 500 units @ \$10 each)}$$

You can check this calculation:

Break-even point	500 units @ $10	=	$5000
Total variable costs	500 units @ $6	=	$3000
Total contribution		=	$2000
Total fixed costs		=	$2000
Profit			nil

Once above the break-even point, each $1 of sales contributes $0.40 (40%) to profits. If you start with a profit rather than a sales target you can use the break-even point to work out the level of sales you need to achieve this. Dividing your profit target by your contribution margin tells you how much above the break-even point you need to be. So for example, if your target profit is $4,000 per week, then your sales target would have to be:

$$\frac{\$4000}{0.40} = \$10,000, \textit{ above break-even} = \$15,000 \ (\$10,000 + \$5,000)$$

You can check this calculation:

Sales	=	$15,000
Total contribution @ 40%	=	$ 6,000
Total fixed costs	=	$ 2,000
Profit	=	$ 4,000

Even if you keep your fixed costs low at start-up, they are bound to creep up as your business grows. As they increase, your break-even point will also drift up and what is really important about the break-even point is its position in relation to turnover – how much your turnover must drop before you arrive at your break-even point. This is measured by the margin of safety. It tells you the percentage reduction in sales needed to get down to your break-even point.

$$\text{Margin of safety (normally expressed as \%)} = \frac{\text{Turnover} - \text{Break-even}}{\text{Turnonver}}$$

The higher the margin of safety, the better, because the firm is safer in terms of maintaining its profitability should sales suddenly decline. This reflects a number of factors: level of sales, contribution margin and fixed costs. It is therefore a simple but powerful piece of information that can be used to control a business as it grows. If the margin of safety can be maintained (or increased) as a business grows, despite the increase in fixed costs, it shows that the financial risks of the business are under control.

Case insight   Xtreme SnoBoards (2)

Building financial forecasts

Purestock/ Punchstock/ Getty Images

Xtreme SnoBoards is a company set up by two young snowboarding enthusiasts to manufacture a specialist snowboard that they have perfected after two years of development. We looked at the company's costs and how it set prices in the Case insight on page 90. The boards have been tested and used by professionals in competition and proved to be particularly responsive. So much so that a number of retailers have contacted the company to enquire about placing orders. There are three variations of board, designed for different conditions. The pair have researched their market and lined up two national retail chains and one overseas distributor who have placed advanced orders for the board at the price of £135 per board, net of delivery costs. The initial sales estimates for the boards in the first year are shown below. These figures represent total boards. 60% of these sales will go through the two major retailers and the overseas distributor. The sales estimates are highly seasonal, with sales mainly in the winter months.

The founders intend to establish their small manufacturing facility in September and start manufacturing in October. These will be sent out to shops as demonstration models but, by agreement, they will not be invoiced as sales until January. They expect to have produced some 400 boards by then. These will be counted as starting stock in January and the sales invoices will be issued in the same month. They estimate that their maximum production capability in any month is some 320 boards, and this will be reached by March. This means that they will be unable to meet the initial sales estimates for March. Consequently they have revised their sales forecasts. Unlike sales, production levels have to be kept constant, although production is lower in August and December because of holidays. Forecast total production is therefore 3,780 boards (3,380 + 400), forecast sales is 3,140 boards, leaving 640 (3,780 – 3,140) boards in stock at the end of the year.

Initial sales forecast	Jan	Feb	March	April	May	June	July	Aug	Sept	Oct	Nov	Dec	Total
Units	400	400	440	280	100	100	80	80	200	360	360	440	3,240
Production													
Start stocks	400*	180	20	0	40	260	480	720	800	920	880	840	
+prodn	180	240	320	320	320	320	320	160	320	320	320	240	3,380
− sales	400	400	340**	280	100	100	80	80	200	360	360	440	3,140
End stocks	180	20	0	40	260	480	720	800	920	880	840	640	

*pre-January production

**unable to meet sales estimate

Continued...

Continued from previous page...

The revised sales forecast is shown below. The sales price of £135 (trade price) is net of delivery costs and represents the average of the three boards, since the best guess at the moment is that the boards will sell in equal proportions.

Revised sales forecast	Jan	Feb	March	April	May	June	July	Aug	Sept	Oct	Nov	Dec	Total
Units	400	400	340	280	100	100	80	80	200	360	360	440	3,140
£ value @ £135 per unit	54,000	54,000	45,900	37,800	13,500	13,500	10,800	10,800	27,000	48,600	48,600	59,400	423,900

Forecast income statement and break-even

The founders need a range of machinery to produce their boards. They estimate that the total cost of this machinery will be £55,680 and that it will last some 8 years before needing replacement. Depreciation is therefore calculated at £6,960 per year (£8,700 in the first period of 15 months). They have also found a suitable unit that can be used as a factory. The annual lease cost for this is £11,520, including rates (£960 per month or £14,400 for the first 15 months). The founders intend to employ two factory workers immediately in October. They will be paid a fixed monthly wage – a total of £3,000 per month. An extra member of staff will be taken on in March, when production gets up to its maximum level. They will be paid £1,300 per month. The founders will also work in the factory and intend to pay themselves a fixed monthly wage – £2,000 per month, each – in the first year, starting in January. The estimated wages bill during the first 15 months (October to December) is therefore £106,000.

The founders undertook a detailed costing exercise that showed that the average material costs for each board was £32 and the average variable factory overhead was £5 per board (consumables, electricity etc.). Total variable costs are therefore £37 per board. The average costs of producing a board is shown below based on target production of 3,780 units:

Variable costs:		
Direct materials		£32.00
Direct factory costs		£ 5.00
		£37.00
Fixed costs:		
Direct labour	£106,000	
Factory overhead	– depreciation	£ 8,700
	– factory lease	£ 14,400
	£129,100 ÷ 3,780 =	£34.15
Total average cost of producing each board		£71.15

The founders therefore estimate that they should make an average profit of £63.85 (47.3%) on each board, before other running costs.

They intend to spend £10,000 on promotional material in October. After that they estimate that their marketing and other general costs will be £3,000 per month (£45,000 in the first 15 months) and professional fees, paid at the end of the year, will be £3,000. These are all fixed costs.

The founders work out their break-even point for this first 15-month period of trading by adding these to the fixed production costs and dividing by the contribution margin:

Contribution (Sales price – variable costs)	=	£135 – £37 = £98 per unit
Contribution margin	=	£98 ÷ £135 = 0.726 or 72.6%
Fixed production costs (15 months)	=	£129,100
Other fixed costs (15 months)	=	£ 58,000
Total fixed costs (15 months)		£187,000
Break-even point = £187,000 ÷ 0.726	=	£257,576
Margin of safety = (£423,900 – £257,576) ÷ £257,576 × 100	=	64.6%

Continued...

Continued from previous page...

The founders are very pleased that they have such a high contribution margin and, combined with keeping their fixed costs low, they have such a low break-even point compared to their forecast sales. They feel that with such a high margin of safety in their first year, combined with a high level of advanced orders for their snowboards, that they are really onto a winning business idea.

They go on to estimate their income for the 15-month period on sales of 3,140 units:

Sales	3,140 × £135	=	£423,900	
Cost of sales	3,140 × £71.154	=	£223,422	
Gross profit			£200,478	(47.3%)
Marketing and general costs	£55,000			
Professional fees	£ 3,000	=	£ 58,000	
Net profit			£142,477	(33.6%)

Forecast cash flow statement

The founders are convinced that their snowboards present a highly attractive opportunity, but they need to know how the opportunity can be financed, so they decide to prepare an initial cash flow forecast. There estimates are based on the following assumptions:

1   Sales receipts are lagged by 2 months.
2   Purchases for materials and other direct factory costs (£37 per unit) can be matched directly to production, which means at maximum production of 320 units purchases are £11,840 (320 × £37). Payments are lagged by 2 months, but payments related to the pre-January production of 400 units must be paid for in December (400 × £37 = £14,800).
3   Wages are paid monthly.
4   The £10,000 promotion expenditure will be paid in November. Other marketing and general costs are spread equally over the period.
5   Professional fees are paid in December.
6   Machinery purchased in September for £55,680 will be paid for in the following November.
7   Lease costs and rates are paid annually, in advance in October (£11,520).

£	Oct	Nov	Dec	Jan	Feb	March	April	May	June	July	Aug	Sept	Oct	Nov	Dec	Total
Receipts																
Sales						54,000	54,000	45,900	37,800	13,500	13,500	10,800	10,800	27,000	48,600	315,900
Payments																
Materials			14,800			6,660	8,880	11,840	11,840	11,840	11,840	11,840	5,920	11,840	11,840	119,140
Wages	3,000	3,000	3,000	7,000	7,000	8,300	8,300	8,300	8,300	8,300	8,300	8,300	8,300	8,300	8,300	106,000
Marketing	3,000	13,000	3,000	3,000	3,000	3,000	3,000	3,000	3,000	3,000	3,000	3,000	3,000	3,000	3,000	55,000
Prof. fees															3,000	3,000
Machinery		55,680														55,680
Lease	11,520												11,520			23,040
Net cash flow	−17,520	−71,680	−20,800	−10,000	−10,000	+36,040	+33,820	+22,760	+14,660	−9,640	−9,640	−12,340	−17,940	+3,860	+22,460	−45,960
Cash B/F	0	−17,520	−89,200	−110,000	−120,000	−130,000	−93,960	−60,140	−37,380	−22,720	−32,360	−42,000	−54,340	−72,280	−68,420	
Cash C/F	−17,520	−89,200	−110,000	−120,000	−130,000	−93,960	−60,140	−37,380	−22,720	−32,360	−42,000	−54,340	−72,280	−68,420	−45,960	

When the founders review this, they see that, despite the profitability of the company, there is a cash deficit in every month, with a maximum of £130,000 in February. The overall deficit for the year is £45,960. They also observe that the deficit is reducing by the end of the year, just as the primetime for sales (and cash receipts from sales) is approaching, and speculate that the deficit might be corrected in the following year. Because they do not want to share ownership of such a profitable business, they decide to put in £42,000 of their own capital – £30,000 in share

Continued...

Continued from previous page...

capital and £12,000 by way of a two-year interest-free loan. They decide to seek bank finance – probably overdraft – for the balance of their funding. The revised cash flow forecast is shown below. It shows the maximum overdraft requirement is £88,000 in February but thereafter the requirement reduces rapidly. Nevertheless, they are aware that this is just a forecast and things can go wrong, so they decide to ask the bank for an overdraft facility of £120,000.

£	Oct	Nov	Dec	Jan	Feb	March	April	May	June	July	Aug	Sept	Oct	Nov	Dec	Total
Net cash flow	−17,520	−71,680	−20,800	−10,000	−10,000	+36,040	+33,820	+22,760	+14,660	−9,640	−9,640	−12,340	−17,940	+3,860	+22,460	
Capital	+42,000															
Cash B/F	0	+24,480	−47,200	−68,000	−78,000	−88,000	−51,960	−18,140	+4,620	+19,280	+9,640	0	−12,340	−30,280	−26,420	
Cash C/F	+24,480	−47,200	−68,000	−78,000	−88,000	−51,960	−18,140	+4,620	+19,280	+9,640	0	−12,340	−30,280	−26,420	−3,960	

Forecast balance sheet

The founders are now in a position to draw up a balance sheet for Xtreme at the end of the first 15 months of trading. They realize that they have assets that comprise machinery, stock of snowboards, money they are owed for sales (called debtors or receivables) and lease costs they have paid in advance (called prepayments). They also realize they owe money for the purchase of materials (called creditors or payables) and an overdraft.

Machinery	Cost – depreciation	=	£55,680 – £8,700	=	£ 46,980
Stock	Number of boards × average cost	=	640 × £71.154	=	£ 45,538
Debtors	November + December sales	=	£48,600 + £59,400	=	£108,000
Prepayments	9 months lease costs	=	£960 × 9	=	£ 8,640
Total Assets					£209,158
Creditors	November + December purchases	=	(320 + 240 boards) × £37	=	£ 20,720
Overdraft	from Cash Flow Forecast				£ 3,960
Founders' loan capital					£ 12,000
Founders' share capital					£ 30,000
Profit for the year					£142,478
Capital and liabilities					£209,158

QUESTIONS:

1 Work through all the financial projections of Xtreme SnoBoards, making sure you understand how they were constructed and where the information came from.

2 Do you think the assumptions on which they are based are realistic? If not, assess the effect of any changes you would make.

3 Going forward, do these projections alert you to any potential issues facing the company?

Using financial information for decision-making

It is important that you know your contribution margin. You can use this simple piece of information to help you make decisions and even estimate the profit (or loss) you are making.

Should I incur additional expenditure?

It can help you make business decisions about whether to incur additional expenditure by telling you how much additional sales you need to generate to pay for, and hence justify, a fixed-cost expenditure. It will not make the decision for you but it does provide you with valuable information to help you make a judgement.

$$\text{The extra sales needed} = \frac{\text{Increase in fixed costs}}{\text{Contribution margin}}$$

So for example, if you are considering an increase in advertising expenditure of $10,000 and your contribution margin is 40%, the extra sales needed to justify the expenditure are:

$$\frac{\$10,000}{0.40} = \$25,000$$

What happens if I change prices?

Contribution analysis can also be used to help you make pricing decisions. Suppose that a competitor to a business selling skateboards wholesale at $20 each (retail is $50–$60) starts price-cutting, selling equivalent boards at just $16 wholesale. The question is to decide whether to match the price reduction or to seek a more profitable alternative strategy. Look at the calculation below. Column 2 shows the effect on profits if prices are maintained with the result that there is a one-third fall in sales. Column 3 shows the effect on profits if prices are reduced in order to maintain the level of sales.

	1 Current position	2 Competitor lowers price but we hold it	3 Competitor lowers price & we follow
Price per board	$20	$20	$16
Variable cost per board	$12	$12	$12
Contribution per board	$8	$8	$4
Sales volume per month (units)	3,000	2,000	3,000
Total contribution	$24,000	$16,000	$12,000
Fixed costs per month	$16,000	$16,000	$16,000
Profit/(loss) per month	$8,000	nil	$(4,000)

As we see from column 3, the business will actually lose money ($4,000 per month) if it follows the price lead of the competitor. If it maintains its prices, the position is rather better, although it will still not make a profit (column 2). However, there may also be the opportunity in this situation to reduce overheads to reflect the lower sales, or even to spend more on advertising to persuade customers that the board is better and worth more than $20. Despite the evidence that an analysis of this kind can reveal, many companies automatically cut prices as a 'knee-jerk' reaction to competitive pressures, without evaluating the alternatives.

Which are the most profitable product lines?

For any business producing more than one product or service, the question as to which is the more profitable, and therefore the one which is to have its sales 'pushed' hardest, is an interesting one, and one to which the answer is not as straightforward as you might think. However, it is a fundamental question in deciding upon the mix of sales.

Suppose our skateboard company can produce three versions: 'Standard', 'All-terrain' and 'Freestyle'. As shown on the next page, the Freestyle board has the highest £ contribution, but the Standard board has the best contribution margin (%). So which is the one that the firm should encourage the sales of most? The answer depends on the market that the different products are selling to. Where the products or markets are independent, that is if the Freestyle board is sold to one customer, the Standard to another and the All-terrain to a third, *and selling one does not reduce the budget available for the others*, then you should 'push' sales of the board with the highest $

contribution: Freestyle first, All-terrain second and finally Standard. This will generate the highest profit. However, if the total $ budget to purchase these boards is fixed (for example because you are selling to one customer) and increasing the $ sales of one simply reduces the $ sales of the others by the same amount, then you should 'push' the sales of the Standard board. As can be seen below, for every $1,000 spent, the company will make a higher profit than from any other board.

	Standard	All-terrain	Freestyle
Price per board	$25	$32	$50
Variable cost per board	$10	$16	$30
Contribution per board	$15	$16	$20
Contribution margin (%)	60%	50%	40%
Contribution per £1,000 of sales	$600	$500	$400

Where should I focus my limited resources?

In the case of the customer with a limited budget, the firm has to take account of a limiting factor – the amount of money available to buy their products. In fact, many start-ups face some type of internal limiting factor, such as a lack of skilled labour, limited machine capacity, shortage of raw materials, lack of management expertise, or shortage of money. This approach can be applied to making decisions about which product to 'push' in these circumstances. Retailers often regard available shelf space as being their main limiting factor, while for a fast-growing manufacturing business the limiting factor may well be the availability of cash to finance their working capital needs. Where a limiting factor exists, then a business will maximize its profits by making the best use of the limiting resource. For example, retailers need to make the best use of their available shelf space. And in these circumstances they should always 'push' the sales of the product making the highest £ contribution per limiting resource.

Assume that our skateboard company has a shortage of machinery which reflects itself in availability of machine hours. It needs to decide how to use the machine hours available to maximize its profits. As can be seen below, the contribution per machine hour is highest for the All-terrain board. It should therefore 'push' sales of the All-terrain board, followed by Standard and finally Freestyle.

	Standard	All-terrain	Freestyle
Price per board	$25	$32	$50
Variable cost per board	$10	$16	$30
Contribution per board	$15	$16	$20
Machine hours needed to produce 100 boards	1.0	0.5	2.0
Contribution per machine hour	$1,500	$3,200	$1,000

As always, the real world doesn't behave quite like a mathematical formula. If a supermarket filled its shelves entirely with small, high-margin items it might find it had a lot of dissatisfied customers unable to find bread, sugar and washing powder. Similarly, a manufacturer may prefer to sell to reliable large customers rather than to take greater risks selling to small traders, even though the contribution per sale may be higher in the latter case. A technique called ABC analysis can give you an insight into this decision. This will be covered in Chapter 13.

What does break-even mean when I have a portfolio of products?

One practical problem for a company with a portfolio of products, each with different contribution margins, is to interpret just what the break-even calculation means in terms of the mix of sales. If you use the contribution margin calculation based on total sales and variable costs, the resulting break-even point represents an identical mix of sales. Using our skateboard company as an example again, if annual sales were $1,900,000 with the mix shown below, producing an average contribution margin of 50% (based on total sales and costs), we could go on to calculate the break-even point using the usual formula.

	Standard	All-terrain	Freestyle	Total $'000	
Sales volume (units)	8,000	2,000	4,000		
Price per board	$25	$32	$50	Turnover	464
Variable cost per board	$10	$16	$30	Variable costs	232
Contribution per board	$15	$16	$20		
Total contribution	$120,000	$32,000	$80,000		232 (50%)
Contribution margin (%)	60%	50%	40%	Fixed costs	190
				Total profit	42

$$\text{Break-even point} = \frac{\$190.000}{0.50} = \$380,000 \text{ per annum}$$

The problem is that this break-even point only holds if the mix of sales always remains the same; that is, for every eight Standard boards sold, we always sell two All-terrain boards and four Freestyle boards. Should the mix change, then the break-even point will change and a new calculation becomes necessary. Notwithstanding this, an understanding of which products, customers or markets generate the best contributions, and of the optimal way to utilize limited resources, can make a significant difference to the overall profitability of the business. You will be in a much better position to optimize the sales mix if you know which products are most profitable. It is also essential to know the break-even point, together with its limitations, and manage it in the appropriate way.

How well is the business doing?

Finally, this powerful decision-making tool can also be used to help you estimate your profitability, without having to wait for the financial results each month or each year. Once you are above your break-even point, your fixed costs are covered and all the contribution you make is profit. The formula for this is:

Profit = (Actual sales – Break-even sales) × Contribution margin

Using our skateboard example again, if annual sales were $5 million, the profit would be $600,000, but only if the mix of sales remained the same as it is above.

Profit = ($5,000,000 − $3,800,000) × 0.5 = $600,000

Using financial information to monitor performance

All businesses use financial information to monitor and control performance. The normal way this is done is by comparing actual performance against the forecasts you have made. These forecasts provide a framework against which the performance of the firm can be judged. By comparing actual financial results to the forecast on a timely basis you can 'manage by exception', only intervening when performance deviates from your forecasts. This can free up time to concentrate on strategy or dealing with real business problems.

My own businesses have always been very tightly controlled. I was able to sell my (first) business because the books were very clean, we had grown steadily, we never lost money and I knew where all the figures were month by month, if not day by day.

Mark Mason, serial entrepreneur and business angel, *The Sunday Times*, 2 June 2013

Digital Vision

Computer-based accounting systems provide the financial information you need to monitor your performance, normally on a monthly basis. However, sometimes they can provide so much financial information that you can become 'numbers-blind' – unable to see the important pieces of information because of the detail provided. In fact, most firms can be controlled by monitoring just six pieces of information that tell you different, but vital, information on the performance of the business. These are called **financial drivers**. They are like the instruments on a car dashboard. They tell you different things about the engine of the business. Different pieces of information are important at different times and in different circumstances. On a road with a speed restriction you watch your speedometer. When changing gear at speed you watch your rev counter. When low on petrol your eye never strays from the fuel gauge.

The financial drivers tell you all you need to know about driving the business. They can be reproduced on a single piece of paper and provide the headline information on how the business is doing. If they disclose a problem, more information will be needed to accurately diagnose the cause and decide on the appropriate corrective action. There are six financial drivers:

> **Cash**

Knowing your cash balance and monitoring cash flow is fundamental for survival. Early in the life of a business you will probably need to monitor this on a weekly basis. But if you are really short of cash you may have to monitor it on a daily basis.

> **Sales/turnover**

Sales information tells you about the volume of work going through the business. It drives all the other financial results. Early in the life of a business you will probably need to monitor this on a weekly, possibly even a daily, basis. If you are ahead of your forecasts, do you have the resources to meet the increased demand? If you behind your forecasts, are there sufficient sales in the pipeline, or do you have to cut back on expenditure?

> **Profit margins**

By monitoring your profit margins you know whether your costs are in line with your sales. Your target margins will only be achieved if the sales volume targets are met, at the appropriate prices, and costs are under control. The operating profit margin, gross margin and contribution margin each give you different information. They probably need to be monitored only monthly.

Image Source \ Image Source/Michael Gross

> **Margin of safety**

The margin of safety tells you about the operating risk of the business. A deteriorating margin of safety should sound warning bells. It means you are approaching break-even point. That could mean sales volumes are going down, contribution margins are not being maintained (prices are being discounted, or variable costs are increasing) or fixed costs are out of control. If the deteriorating margin of safety is due to falling sales, then you might try to reduce fixed costs – particularly the ones that you have some discretionary control over. This is therefore a powerful piece of information and should be monitored monthly.

> **Productivity**

For most firms the single largest and most important expense they face is their wage costs. It therefore needs to be controlled carefully. Wages are therefore best measured in relation to the productivity that they generate, and for many firms this is most easily measured by the simple percentage of wages to sales. Often there are industry norms to compare this to. For example, in the UK licensed trade wages of bar staff should be about 20% of sales. If higher, the bar is overstaffed, if lower, it is understaffed – a crude but simple and effective measure that needs to be checked at least monthly. Of course, to achieve this benchmark, staff need to work shifts, being brought in at peak periods.

> **Debtor (receivables) and/or stock (inventory) turnover**
Most firms will have one important current asset on their balance sheet that represents over 50% of their total assets. For a service business this will probably be debtors (receivables), for a retail business stocks (inventory) and for a manufacturing business it is likely to be both. You can use debtors and stock turnover ratios to monitor this investment, again on a monthly basis. These ratios should be kept as high as possible.

$$\text{Debtor (receivables) turnover (expressed as a number)} = \frac{\text{Sales or turnover}}{\text{Debtors (receivables)}}$$

$$\text{Stock (inventory) turnover (expressed as a number)} = \frac{\text{Sales or turnover}}{\text{Stock (inventory)}}$$

Cash is king – everybody says that, but fulfilling orders so you can raise invoices and collect the cash are the most important things you can do.

Elizabeth Gooch, founder, **eg** solutions, *Launch Lab* (www.launchlab.co.uk), 13 January 2009

 Practice insight 3 tips for controlling debtors (receivables)

Debtor control is often neglected in SMEs and can be a major cause of illiquidity. You can speed up the collection of debts by:

1 Choosing customers carefully to start with and invoicing them immediately upon sale. In choosing credit customers always ask for, and check up on, trade references: ask for a bank reference, make credit checks with other suppliers, check any published information (such as accounts) about the customer and, if possible, visit their premises.

2 Setting appropriate credit limits and making payment terms clear. Once the customer's references are checked they can be set a credit ceiling that must be kept. This minimizes exposure to any bad debts. Bad debts are expensive. If you are making a 20% margin, you need to increase sales by £4 to recover each £1 of bad debt.

3 Taking the right measures to speed up payments. These include sending statements, following up outstanding debts by telephone – it could be that there is a problem with the delivery, offering discounts for prompt payment or charging interest on overdue accounts, withholding supplies, threatening to reclaim your goods, taking legal action or using debt collectors when all else fails.

Using financial information for control

Forecasting is not just for start-ups. You should continue to prepare financial forecasts as the firm grows because they help you control the business. Forecasts for an established firm are called budgets. They can be prepared at the department as well as company level, consistent with how you structure the business. You can use budgets to help you delegate responsibility to your management team and then monitor their performance, consistent with your leadership style. The budgeting process can then be used as a process for communicating and coordinating the activities of your management team. It can become a systematic tool for establishing standards of performance, providing motivation and assessing the results your managers achieve.

An essential element in this process of making managers accountable is that each knows exactly what they are held responsible for, and each does indeed control this aspect of the firm's operations. Responsibility cannot be assigned without authority. A clear management structure is a fundamental necessity alongside this. The principle is to make every manager responsible for the costs and revenues they control, even if they, in turn, delegate responsibility down the line.

Of course, if managers are going to be held responsible for the costs and revenues they control, they are going to want to be involved in the budgeting process. This is consistent with a dispersed leadership style where you want to involve them in developing strategies for the business. Indeed, as the business grows, they should come to know more about the area they are responsible for than you. So involving managers in setting their own budgets means that they should remain realistic. If budgets are to motivate staff generally, they have to 'buy into' them and believe that they are realistic and achievable. Once they accept the standards of performance against which they are to be judged, they will normally try hard to achieve them. Imposing budgets from above normally causes resentment and leads to a lack of commitment.

Having effective monitoring and control processes in place for your venture will help you manage it. They will help you delegate and control. They will help you achieve your targets. And they add value to your business.

Case insight   The Pub (2)

Using financial drivers to monitor performance

The founder of The Pub* was always hoping to establish a small chain of pubs and to sell them as a going concern to another pub chain or a brewery within 10 years. Once he proved that his formula for filling the pub throughout the day really worked (see Case insight on page 161), his attention shifted to finding new, large city-centre sites. But he also realized that to sell on to any chain he would have to prove that it was profitable and that it had good financial control – something that was often absent in the licence trade. He believed that rigorous, centrally applied financial controls were the key to profitable operation and a successful sell-on. One of the first things he did was appoint a finance director to provide the board with in-house financial management skills.

As part of the emphasis on control, the company ensured the five key financial drivers were monitored on a regular and timely basis. The first four drivers were linked to targets for individual pub managers and tied into their bonus scheme:

> **Cash** – Daily checks on cash takings and banking, carried out by telephone and direct computer input to the company's bank account.
> **Sales and profit margins** – Weekly sales and profit performance measured within 16 hours of each week ending. Results were reviewed immediately by management and priorities for action identified.
> **Stocks** – Weekly stocktaking to ensure there were no stock losses and gross margin targets were attained.
> **Productivity** – Labour costs, as a percentage of sales, monitored through monthly management accounts, mailed to all affected parties no later than 10 working days after each period.
> **Break-even point and the margin of safety** – The founder believed that any growing business needs to monitor these two important drivers. He monitored this data monthly. Above his desk he kept a graph showing sales against break-even point (i.e. the margin of safety). It made interesting reading, showing the gradual improvement in the margin of safety because of the high margins and low fixed costs as The Pub concept was rolled out across new sites.

Within 10 years of being set up, The Pub chain of licensed houses was sold to a brewer for an eight-figure sum!

QUESTIONS:

1 Why are strong financial controls important for a pub chain?

2 Why do strong financial controls add value to a business?

*The Pub is a real company but the name is fictitious.

All photos courtesy of Tiger company

Open book management

The next chapter will look at the balance between control and autonomy that there needs to be within a growing entrepreneurial firm. Burns (2013) is one of many who have advocated 'loose control but tight accountability'. Morris and Kuratko (2002) advocate a 'no-surprises' approach – one that 'generates adequate information on a timely basis for all who need to know'. They believe that 'open book' management, where there is transparency of information, is important. Control mechanisms should produce indicators or early warning signals of problems before they occur – consistent with the 'financial drivers' outlined earlier.

A by-product of such a system is that it also conveys a sense of trust. Employees are trusted to get on with the job but the outcomes, rather than the processes, are monitored. Morris and Kuratko envisage the control system becoming 'a vehicle for managing uncertainty, promoting risk tolerance, encouraging focused experimentation, and empowering employees'. For them, giving up control is also about greater accountability and a greater sense of staff responsibility:

> Where there is an elaborate system of control measures, the employee can be secure in the knowledge that, if the control system has been complied with, then his or her accountability is absolved, that his or her responsibility has been fulfilled. He or she need not take any further responsibility for outcomes or the implications of personal behavior for company performance. However, by giving up control to the employee, there is a much deeper sense of responsibility not only for accomplishing a task or behaving in a certain manner but also for the quality of task performance and the impact it has on the organization ... to give up control is to empower.

Open book management focuses on the outcomes – the bottom line – rather than the processes. It gives people autonomy but focuses on the outcomes of their actions. It is built around free flows of information and seeks to motivate employees to improve the performance of the organization by thinking outside their narrow job definition and focusing on the consequences of their action. It encourages them to take ownership of and responsibility their actions. Equally it encourages employees to think the way owner-managers would think about their own business. Case (1997) says it is built around six principles:

1 Free access to all financial information that is critical to tracking the firm's performance.
2 A continuous and overt attempt to present this information to employees.
3 Training processes that encourage understanding of this information.
4 Employees learning that part of their job is to improve the financial result in whatever way they can.
5 Empowering people to make decisions in their jobs based on what they know.
6 Giving employees a stake in the organization's success or failure.

The system of financial control that an organization has is important. Not only does is control its resources, it also provides valuable information to help manage it. It therefore needs to be accurate and provided on a timely basis. However, the way it is used can also affect the culture within it and there needs to be a careful balance here between control and accountability.

 Practice insight reminder Characteristics of a good business idea – 11 & 12

11 Low fixed costs – low fixed costs mean lower risk, should volume reduce. It gives you flexibility. A combination of high profit margin and low fixed costs (high profit, low risk) is always very attractive.

12 Controllable – putting in robust operating and financial controls increase your chances of survival and success, and ultimately will add value to the firm. The major imperative in the early years is to monitor and manage cash flow.

⟳ Summary

› For a new venture to survive and grow it needs to be financially viable. This means it needs to be profitable and efficient, sufficiently liquid to pay its bills, while minimizing the risk that it faces.

› Profit is measured by sales or turnover minus total costs. It is represented by the growth in all the assets owned by a company.

› Profit is not the same as cash flow. You can be profitable but illiquid, without cash to pay your bills. If you cannot pay your bills you risk going bankrupt. A new venture therefore needs to plan and monitor cash flow carefully as it moves through 'Death Valley'.

› The balance sheet is a snapshot at a point of time that shows the assets the business has and where the funds for these assets came from.

› The business plan can provide information on these things by including forecast income statements (including break-even projections) and balance sheets for three years (five years for larger projects). Your cash flow forecast will indicate the funding you need to launch the business.

› Monthly sales forecasts should be provided for at least the first year of a business plan (longer where there are

substantial commercialization risks) and the detailed assumptions on which your sales and costs are based should be listed.

› The break-even point is an important benchmark that tells you about the operating risk you face. The higher it is the higher the risks you face.

› Margin of safety measures how far above break-even you are.

› It is important that you know your contribution margin. You can use this simple piece of information to help you make decisions and even estimate the profit you are making.

› Financial drivers are headline measures of the financial performance of a business: cash, sales, profit margins, margin of safety, productivity and debtor (receivables) and/or stock (inventory) control. They are quick and easy to calculate and monitor.

› Actual performance is normally compared to forecasted performance – called budgets. As the business grows, the preparation and monitoring of budgets on a decentralized basis can encourage delegation and help control the performance of managers.

✓ Activities

1 Prepare a sales forecast for your first year of business. List the assumptions on which this is based.

2 Estimate the costs associated with this level of sales and draw up a forecast income statement.

3 Estimate the break-even point and margin of safety for your business.

4 Prepare a monthly cash flow forecast for your first year of business. List the assumptions on which it is based.

5 Prepare the forecast balance sheet at the end of the first year of business.

💬 Group discussion topics

1 Why is cash not the same as profit?
2 What would you do to make sure you get through Death Valley?
3 Profit is something that an accountant can manipulate. It is not objective and therefore means nothing. Discuss.
4 Can you really forecast sales? How might you go about doing it?
5 How important are the assumptions on which sales forecasts are based? Why is this? What can you do to test them?
6 Are fixed costs really fixed?
7 Are wages a fixed or a variable cost?
8 How easy is it to calculate contribution margin?

9 What are the limitations of break-even analysis?
10 If you have a portfolio of products with different contribution margins, break-even is a meaningless concept. Discuss.
11 Entrepreneurs make decisions based on instinct, not by using financial analysis. Discuss.
12 Can you really control a business by monitoring only six financial drivers?
13 What would you do to maintain tight control of debtors?
14 How can budgets help you delegate?
15 Behind every successful entrepreneur there is an accountant. Discuss.

☛ References

Burns, P. (2013) *Corporate Entrepreneurship: Innovation and Strategy in Large Organizations*, Basingstoke: Palgrave MacMillan.

Case, J. (1997) 'Opening the Books', *Harvard Business Review*, 75, March/April.

Gates, B. (1999) *Business @ the Speed of Thought*, New York: Time Warner.

Morris, M.H. and Kuratko, D.F. (2002) *Corporate Entrepreneurship*, Fort Worth: Harcourt College Publishers.

⊕ www.palgrave.com/Burns-Entrepreneurship-And-Small-Business-4e

Go online to access additional teaching and learning resources for this chapter on the companion website. Click here in the ebook to complete a multiple choice revision quiz for this chapter.

Part 2: Start-up

With their business ideas developed, our entrepreneurs now face the challenges of launching, as their start-ups take their first steps. Watch the videos, by clicking on the play buttons in the ebook to find out how they added values to their business idea, found their first customers, refined their marketing mix, and managed their cash-flow.

AJ Asver

Cassandra Stavrou

John Loughton

Ross Beerman

Sandra Wanduragala and
Selyna Peiris

Scott Cupit

Stefan Botha

Questions

> What lessons do you learn about finding customers and securing repeat business?
> How strong are each of the brands?
> For John, what were the advantages and disadvantages of the legal form of business that he chose?
> How important have partnerships and relationships been in launching these businesses?
> What were the operational challenges that the entrepreneurs faced?
> For Stefan, how important was managing cash flow? How did he achieve this?

The full videos of each entrepreneur's story are available on the companion website.

PART 1 ENTREPRENEURSHIP

PART 2 START-UP

PART 3 GROWTH

Click on the play button in the ebook to watch a video of Paul Burns highlighting key issues faced by entrepreneurs in growing their business.

PART 4 MATURITY

12 | GROWTH: BUILDING THE FOUNDATIONS

Contents

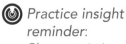

Practice insight: Benchmarking performance

Practice insight reminder: Characteristics of a good business idea

ImageSource

Learning outcomes

When you have read this chapter and undertaken the related activities you will be able to:

> Explain the implications of the stage models of growth for the entrepreneur and how they develop and cope with change;
> Understand the issues affecting how a business might be structured given its size, the tasks to be undertaken and the environment in which it operates;
> Understand the issues determining the balance between the degree of control and autonomy of staff in an organization;
> Understand how strategy is developed in SMEs;
> Undertake a strategic review;
> Describe the issues facing a social enterprise at different stages in its growth and understand how social capital can be built up;
> Undertake a SWOT analysis;
> Use financial ratios to analyse the performance of a firm;
> Understand the broad strategies that are most likely to lead to successful growth.

 Case insights

Google (2)	audioBoom
Adrenaline Alley (2)	Xtreme SnoBoards (3)
American Giant	

The challenges of growth

Given the high failure rate for start-ups, survival can be a real badge of success. Lifestyle and salary substitute businesses may be able to survive on a day-to-day basis with an informal, tactical orientation; but as a business grows and more staff are recruited, systems and process are likely to become more formalized. For some businesses – the gazelles we looked at in Chapters 1 and 2 – the real challenge is dealing with growth. And the skills and capabilities of the entrepreneurs leading them need to change.

Greiner (1972) was one of the earliest academics to point to the changing skills needed by the entrepreneur as the business grows, in particular the shift to becoming a manager and leader, rather than a 'doer'. Churchill and Lewis (1983) expanded on this to emphasize the shift from operational to strategic capabilities. These are called 'stage models' of growth. Greiner's model offers a framework for considering the development of a business, but more particularly the managerial challenges facing the founder as they recruit more staff. Each phase of growth is followed by a crisis that necessitates a change in the way the founder manages the business. If the crisis cannot be overcome, then the business risks failure. The length of time it takes to go through each phase depends on the industry in which the company operates. In fast-growing industries, growth periods are relatively short; in slower-growth industries they tend to be longer. Each evolutionary phase requires a particular management style or emphasis to achieve growth. The model predicts four crises, shown in Figure 12.1:

1   **Leadership** – Growth initially comes through creative opportunity-seeking. However, this growth leads to a crisis of leadership as staff, financiers and even customers increasingly fail to understand the focus of the business – where it is going, what it is selling – and resources become spread too thinly to follow through effectively on any single commercial opportunity. The challenge is to give direction by effective leadership.

2   **Autonomy** – Entrepreneurs have a strong internal locus of control, which means that there is a danger they will try to do everything themselves. Not only do they delay recruiting staff, partly because they are careful in managing cash flow, but when they do, they find it difficult to delegate. The challenge is to develop an effective management team, and delegate to them.

3   **Control** – There is a danger that delegation becomes an abdication of responsibility and there is a loss of proper control. As we shall see later in this chapter, there is a balance to

> *Managing a hyper-growth company is like putting a rocket into space: if you are off by inches at launch, you will be off by miles in orbit.*
>
> **Jeff Weiner**, CEO, LinkedIn, *The Sunday Times*, 14 July 2013

> *You delegate but you obviously have got to have that hands-on approach for a while, and then you develop people that will eventually take over from you*
>
> **Divine Ndhlukula**, founder, SECURICO, Zimbabwe, *BBC News Business*, 6 July 2012

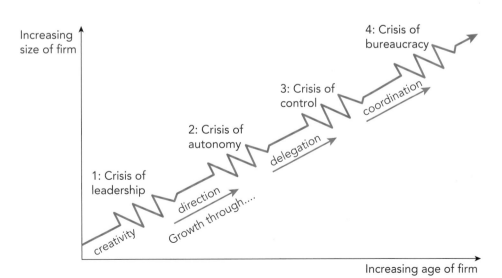

Figure 12.1 Greiner's stage model of growth

Source: Greiner, L.E. (1972) 'Evolution and Revolution as Organizations Grow', *Harvard Business Review*, July/August. Reproduced with permission of Harvard Business Publishing.

be achieved between autonomy and control. The challenge is to coordinate decision-making through appropriate organizational structures and culture that balance autonomy and control and encourage collaboration.

4   **Bureaucracy** – As the organization becomes larger, the danger is that it might lose its entrepreneurial drive. The challenge is to facilitate collaboration – making people work together through a sense of mission or purpose rather than by reference to a rule book – and to develop an organization that balances the need for autonomy and control, avoiding too much bureaucracy.

The Churchill and Lewis (op. cit.) model emphasizes the link between management style, organizational structure, formality and the strategic imperatives as the business grows. The strategic imperatives are shown alongside each of the five stages in Figure 12.2. In this model all firms go through stages 1 (existence) – with simple organization, direct supervision and the owner lending a hand at most things – and 2 (survival) – when the business must demonstrate that it has enough customers to be viable. However, most do not go beyond stage 3 (success: disengagement), where the strategic imperative is maintaining a profitable status quo. This is the typical lifestyle or salary substitute business described in Chapter 1. For the 'gazelles', stages 1 and 2 prove the success of their business model and stage 3 (success: growth) becomes a platform for further growth into stages 4

	Stage 1 Existence	Stage 2 Survival	Stage 3 Success: Growth / Stage 3 Success: Disengagement	Stage 4 Take-off	Stage 5 Maturity
Management style	Direct supervision	Supervised supervision	Functional	Divisional	Line and staff
Organization	Simple	Growing	Growing	Growing	Sophisticated
Formality of systems	Minimal	Minimal	Developing / Basic	Maturing	Extensive

Owner's attributes

	Stage 1	Stage 2	Stage 3	Stage 4	Stage 5
Own goals	☆☆☆☆	☆	☆☆☆☆	☆☆☆☆	☆☆
Operational ability	☆☆☆☆	☆☆☆☆	☆☆	☆☆	☆
Management ability	☆	☆☆	☆☆	☆☆☆☆	☆☆
Strategic ability	☆	☆☆	☆☆☆☆	☆☆☆☆	☆☆☆☆

Resources

	Stage 1	Stage 2	Stage 3	Stage 4	Stage 5
Financial	☆☆☆☆	☆☆☆☆	☆☆	☆☆☆☆	☆☆
Personal	☆	☆	☆☆	☆☆☆☆	☆☆
Systems	☆	☆☆	☆☆☆☆	☆☆☆☆	☆☆
Business	☆☆☆☆☆	☆☆☆☆	☆☆	☆☆	☆

Key: ☆☆☆☆ critical   ☆☆ important but manageable   ☆ not very important

Figure 12.2 Churchill and Lewis growth model

Source: N.C. Churchill and V.L. Lewis (1983) 'The Five Stages of Small Business Growth', *Harvard Business Review*, May/June.

(take-off) and 5 (maturity). Stage 3 is crucial. It is when they must consolidate and start assembling the resources – human and financial – that they will need for growth.

This model is also useful in identifying the key attributes needed by entrepreneurs and the importance of key resources at each of the different stages for those. The important point here is the move from the entrepreneur's operational ability to their strategic ability as the business grows – one of the key skills for leaders. Another point worth noting is the increasing importance of personnel and systems resources at stage 4 (take-off). Having the right management in place at this stage is vital.

There have been a number of growth models, each focusing on the different business imperatives at different stages a business goes through (e.g. Burns, 1996; Scott and Bruce, 1987). However, while they provide a useful checklist of these imperatives, they cannot be applied mechanistically, particularly in relation to sequence and timing. Many firms do not survive beyond the first stage. Those that do can face many other crises along these paths which make their sequence and timing unpredictable. Nevertheless, these models provide a valuable narrative for the journey facing an entrepreneur as they start up and grow their business.

DigitalVision/ Punchstock

Building the organizational structure

Spider's web structure

How organizations are structured is a key issue, but probably only as the business starts to grow. Entrepreneurs tend to manage staff through their strong personal relationships, rather than through hierarchy and structure. They prefer informal organization structures and the power of influence rather than rigid rules and job definitions. They often persuade and cajole staff, showing them how to do things on a one-to-one basis rather than having prescribed tasks. This reflects itself in the culture in the organization. The most typical organization structure seen in a small scale start-up is the spider's web, shown in Figure 12.3. The founder sits at the centre of the web with each new member of staff reporting to them.

This is a very efficient structure that can respond quickly and flexibly to change. The uncertainty and rapid pace of change in a start-up probably means that rigid rules and structures would

> " Business is like a relay race and I am very, very good at the first leg and I am very, very good at the last leg, and I'm really not the best person to do the second and third legs … At that point I start to lose focus and so that's when you need to recognize what your strengths and weaknesses are and then you come back in to sell the business. It's not that you disengage completely during the second and third legs, but you certainly pass the responsibility over to somebody who is more capable than you.
>
> **Shaa Wasmund**, founder, Mykindaplace and Brightstone Ventures, *Management Today* (www.managementtoday.co.uk), 18 July 2008 "

Figure 12.3 Spider's web organizational structure

2 people: 2 interactions

3 people: 3 interactions

4 people: 6 interactions

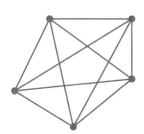

5 people: 10 interactions

Figure 12.4 People and interactions

be out of date quickly. What is more, in a small firm everybody has to be prepared to do other people's jobs because there is no cover, no slack in the system if, for example, someone goes off sick. The web is perfectly flat and therefore efficient – overheads are reduced. It is responsive – communication times are minimized. It works quite well up to about 20 employees. There are two reasons for this. Firstly, communication becomes more complicated, with greater opportunity for misunderstanding and conflict, as the number of people interacting increases. Figure 12.4 shows the number of interactions possible with groups of two, three, four and five people. The number of interactions is represented by the mathematical formula:

$$n \times \left[\frac{n-1}{2} \right]$$ where n represents the number of people.

Thus, 5 people generate 10 interactions, 10 people generate 45 and 15 people generate 105. Postulated by Northcote Parkinson, 'Parkinson's Coefficient of Inefficiency' proposes that the optimum *inefficient* number for a group is 21, at which point group interaction becomes impossible.

The second reason is to do with the character of the entrepreneur themselves. Their high internal locus of control means that they tend to want to meddle and do things themselves. Even when they try to delegate and introduce new staff who report to existing members of staff, entrepreneurs tend to meddle and the new employees soon find an informal reporting line to the entrepreneur, short circuiting the manager or supervisor they are supposed to report to, as in Figure 12.5. It is no wonder that this creates frustration, resentment and an unwillingness to accept responsibility in the manager. Why should they take responsibility when their decisions are likely to be questioned or reversed, or when staff supposedly reporting to them are constantly being checked up on by the entrepreneur?

Hierarchical structure

The larger an organization, the greater the need for hierarchical structure. It creates order and allows coordination of complex tasks. Hierarchy is the fundamental feature of organizational structure, not only for humans, but for all complex systems. It gives managers confidence that they have the authority to manage and allows coordination, cooperation and specialization. Figure 12.6 shows a simple five-person hierarchical structure with four interactions. This can be contrasted to a self-organizing structure without hierarchy in Figure 12.4, where there are 10 interactions. Simple hierarchy offers fewer interactions and relationships to manage. However, while this may be efficient it says nothing about the quality of the interactions and the hierarchy structure can discourage collaboration and sharing of knowledge.

- - - - - Informal reporting lines

Figure 12.5 A growing web structure

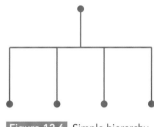

Figure 12.6 Simple hierarchy

As an organization grows further, more structure can be put in place. However, there is no one 'best' structure. Figure 12.7 shows a classic hierarchical structure. Functional groups, such as marketing, production and accounting, might be formed into hierarchical departments, coordinated through central control. This fosters stability and encourages efficient, rule-driven operation. It shows individuals that there is a career path within their department. When a business grows beyond a certain size there is a tendency for it to adopt a divisional structure – representing different product or market groupings. Each division might then have its own departmental structure within it. Divisions might be legally separate companies.

An issue with any hierarchy is the span of control within them. Some hierarchies have 'tall' structures, with more managers each having a narrower span of control (fewer people reporting to them). Others have 'flat' structures, with fewer layers of management each having a wider span of control (more people reporting to them). The taller the structure and narrower the span of control, the more managers are required. The tendency over recent years has been to delayer – to flatten structures and increase their span of control. Technology, in particular the internet, has made this easier. Some Japanese manufacturing companies have only four layers of management; top, plant, departmental and section management. You need to decide on the structure of your start-up and that, primarily, will depend on the number of people you want to employ.

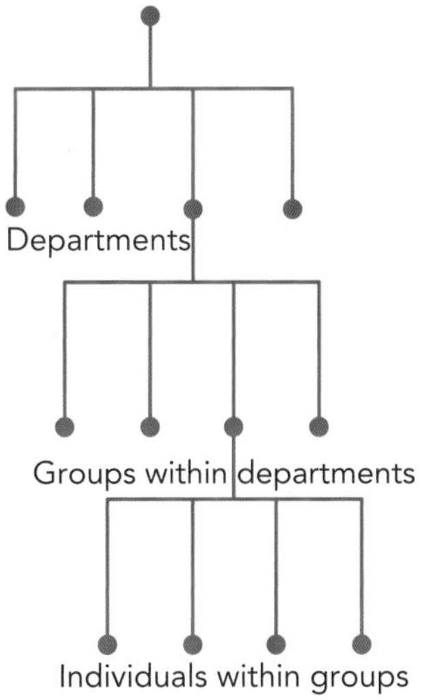

Departments

Groups within departments

Individuals within groups

Figure 12.7 Hierarchical structure

Matrix structure

A business that has multiple products, functions or geographic locations still needs to coordinate activities across all these dimensions. The organizational structure used to aid this is the matrix structure, shown in Figure 12.8. People have multiple reporting lines – to their functional manager (e.g. accounting) and their geographic or product manager. This was popular among large organizations in the 1960s and 1970s but has become far less popular as their excessive complexity and slow responsiveness to change became apparent. Nevertheless, Starbucks still uses a matrix structure, combining functional and product-based divisions, with employees reporting to two managers.

Team-working structure

The matrix blueprint in Figure 12.8 is also the basis for bringing together informal self-organizing project teams from different departments, divisions or geographic parts of an organization. It is

Geographic/product reporting lines

Functional
reporting
lines

Figure 12.8 Matrix structure

I believe in as flat a management structure as possible …
in leading without title … I
most certainly try to lead by
example and I'm very much
a big believer in making my
mistakes public so that other
people feel confident and
comfortable to be able to air
their own mistakes.

Shaa Wasmund, founder,
Mykindaplace and
Brightstone Ventures,
Management Today
(www.managementtoday.co.uk),
18 July 2008

used extensively in businesses that seek to encourage creativity and innovation, particularly in technology-based firms like Apple and Google. They bring together different functional disciplines, foster communication and interaction and can be highly flexible. Teams are also used to allow informal coordination within the formal structures, for example, within multinational companies that need to maintain functional consistency between geographic locations. One company that makes extensive use of project-based team structures with a minimum of top-down direction is Gore, the manufacturer of the famous hi-tech Gore-Tex fabric. Employees (called Associates) apply to or are asked by other team members to join particular teams. They elect team leaders, decide upon their own goals and manage themselves.

One of the characteristics of less hierarchical organizational forms such as teams is that they rely on coordination by mutual adjustment rather than control through hierarchy. They are therefore more flexible and quicker to respond to changing situations. Individuals within them often have multiple roles. We have already seen in Chapter 7 that values can add value for customers. Shared values can also help align goals within a growing organization. And, as we shall see in Chapter 18, the culture of an organization can be just as effective a mechanism for coordination and control as structure. We also saw in Chapter 11 how financial information can be used systematically to control an organization, a topic we shall return to later in this chapter. The important thing is to ensure that structures, systems and organizational culture are consistent and working to reinforce each other, rather than pull the organization in different directions.

Controlling people

A key issue highlighted by Greiner's stage model is the issue of control vs autonomy for staff. The more staff you employ, the greater the need for formalizing the control you have over them. Most organizational control systems are aimed at minimizing risk and uncertainty and promoting efficiency and effectiveness. The degree of control you exert on the people in your business should reflect not only your own philosophy, but also the core value proposition on which your business is based. If yours is a low-cost/price business model, then you may need to be highly efficient and controls may need to be tight. By definition, a highly efficient organization has no slack. Everything is tightly controlled, every penny accounted for, all jobs are defined and individuals made to conform. This environment leads to high degrees of efficiency.

However, the degree of control you exert also depends on two other factors: task complexity and the environment in which the business operates. The simpler and more repetitive the task,

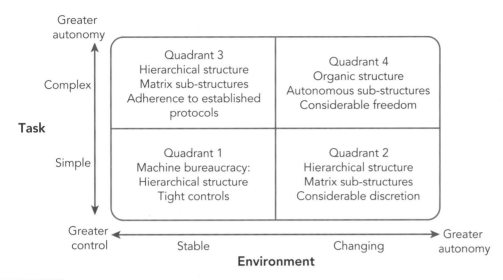

Figure 12.9   Structure, change and task complexity

Source: Burns, P. (2013)

the easier it is to impose control and the less the need for initiative. Similarly, the more stable the environment, the less the need for initiative. But rigid control stifles initiative and inhibits entrepreneurship and therefore the more complex the task, the greater the need for autonomy. Similarly, the more change in the environment, the greater the need for autonomy. This is shown in Figure 12.9.

Quadrant 1 – A machine bureaucracy is one with hierarchical structures and tight controls. It is most appropriate where the organization is tackling simple tasks with extensive standardization, in stable environments, and/or where security is important and where plans and programmes need to be followed carefully. Well-developed information systems reporting on the production/processing activity need to exist for it to be effective. Power is centralized. It is more concerned with production than marketing and is good at producing high volumes and achieving the efficiency in production and distribution needed for the low cost value discipline outlined in Chapter 6. It is appropriate for continuous and line production typologies outlined in Chapter 10.

Quadrant 2 – As the environment becomes more changeable, standardization becomes less viable and responsibility for coping with unexpected changes needs to be pushed down the hierarchy. Staff are usually given more autonomy, although within guidelines. The structure needs to be responsive to change – although hierarchical, relatively flat with few middle-management positions. A matrix sub-structure (teams) can be used to tackle unexpected projects. Culture is important because the workforce needs to be motivated to make frequent changes to their work practices. It is appropriate for jobbing and batch production typologies outlined in Chapter 10.

Quadrant 3 – Complex tasks performed in stable environments mean that it becomes worthwhile to develop standard skills to tackle the complexities. The matrix can be an effective sub-structure within a hierarchical organization. The matrix team can work on their complex tasks within set protocols – as they do, for example, in a surgical operation. In a changing environment the matrix team must have a higher degree of autonomy because established protocols may be inappropriate to the changing circumstances, even for the simple tasks they face. It is appropriate for jobbing and batch production typologies outlined in Chapter 10.

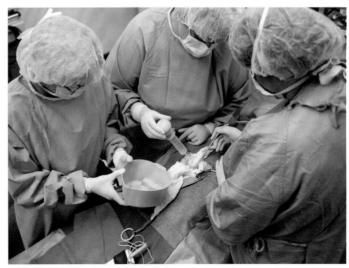

Quadrant 4 – In a changing environment where there is high task complexity an innovative, flexible, decentralized structure is needed, often involving structures within structures. Authority for decision-making needs to be delegated and team working is likely to be the norm, with matrix-type structures somehow built into the organization. Staff autonomy becomes far greater. Clear job definitions should never lead to a narrowing of responsibilities so that people ignore the new tasks that emerge. This is often called an 'organic structure' – one with a highly flexible, even changing structure with limited hierarchy; one which places greater emphasis on personal relationships and interactions than on structures; one in which power is decentralized and authority is linked to expertise, with few bureaucratic rules or standard procedures. In many ways, far more important than the formal organization structure for a firm of this sort is the culture that tells people what needs to be done and motivates them to do it – a truly entrepreneurial firm. It is appropriate for project production typologies outlined in Chapter 10.

While these principles may seem straightforward, their application in practice can be difficult, particularly in the context of a growing business. As with most areas of management, there are no set rules and their application involves judgement. However, the less stable and predictable the environment you operate in and the more complex the tasks you face, the greater the autonomy you should give your staff and the more important is organizational culture, rather than structure, in giving them direction.

Autonomy and motivation

Balancing the degree of control with the need for autonomy in a start-up facing a changing, uncertain environment ultimately boils down to finding the appropriate 'balance' for different members of staff. However, entrepreneurial firms generally need looser control (or staff with greater autonomy), with tighter accountability for meeting targets and objectives. As you grow, you can then afford to establish operating divisions or subsidiaries with different structures, different degrees of control and different cultures.

Pink (2011) highlighted autonomy as a major motivational influence on individuals undertaking cognitive (compared to mechanical) tasks involving complexity or creativity. He argued that self-direction and autonomy is an important motivator if you want people to be innovative, engaged with their tasks and proactive rather than just compliant. Creative people like autonomy. They are also motivated by 'purpose' – a reason for doing something based not upon monetary remuneration but upon a wider vision of what the organization can achieve – and 'mastery' – the challenge of completing a complex or creative task.

So if autonomy is a motivator, the dilemma is the amount of autonomy to give. Too much, and anarchy or worse might result. Too little, and creativity, initiative and entrepreneurship will be stifled. The answer provided by Julian Birkinshaw (2003) was 'balance'. He outlined the model used by BP to help guide and control entrepreneurial action: direction, space or slack, boundaries and support. All four need to be in balance. If they are too tight they constrain the business, but if too slack they might result in chaos. This is shown in Figure 12.10.

Direction – This is the company's broad strategy and goals. Managers should have scope to develop the strategy for their own operating unit, in line with the company's general direction, values and mission. Pink agrees, saying creative people need a strong sense of 'purpose' in their work, which is not just about making profit. Birkinshaw gave two pieces of advice on getting this balance right:

> Set broad direction and re-evaluate periodically as markets and the environment change;
> Let the company's strategy inform that of the unit and the unit's inform that of the company.

Space or slack – Space or slack is to do with the degree of looseness in resource availability – monetary budgets, physical space and supervision of time. In a tightly run, highly efficient organization there is no time or other resources to think, experiment and innovate. Creative organizations require a degree of space or slack to allow experimentation. 3M allow researchers to spend 15% of their time on their own projects. Google allows 20%. However, if employees

> "Employees today should be encouraged to think for themselves. They should be cultivated to have an entrepreneurial, innovative spirit, and not just to implement orders."

Zhang Ruimin, CEO, Haier Group, *Strategy + Business*, Issue 77, Winter, 2014

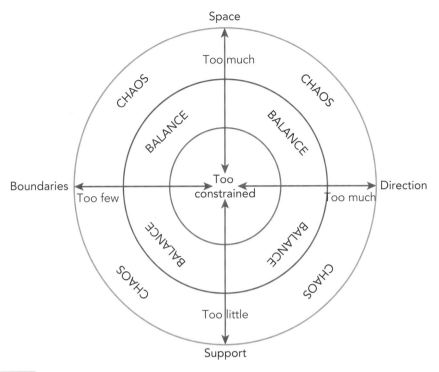

Figure 12.10 Control vs. autonomy

are given too much space they run the risk of losing focus on the day-to-day detail of the job and it can be wasteful. Birkinshaw's advice was:

> Goal setting should be carefully managed, clear and specific, but individuals should be given freedom in how the goals are to be achieved;
> Individuals should be allowed to learn from their own mistakes.

Boundaries – These are the legal, regulatory and moral limits within which the company operates. But rigid rules that are not shared beg to be circumvented. Boundaries should come from your values – which are shared by your staff. Not having boundaries courts extreme danger, particularly if breaking them might lead to the failure of the organization. Birkinshaw's advice was:

> Identify critical boundaries that, if crossed, threaten the survival of the organization and control them rigorously;
> Manage other boundaries in a non-invasive way through training, induction, codes of conduct and so on.

Support – This refers to the knowledge transfer systems and training and development programmes you provide to help managers do their job. Systems should encourage knowledge sharing and collaboration. Training and career planning should be top-down. Both should, however, be discretionary. The danger here is that knowledge will not be shared and there will be little collaboration, encouraging managers to go their own way. On the other hand, if there is too much support the manager will be 'spoon-fed' and initiative stifled. Birkinshaw's advice was:

> Put in place enough support systems to help managers and ensure they know where to go for help;
> Systems should encourage collaboration.

The broad conclusions are therefore that the greater the complexity of tasks and the more staff have to use their cognitive abilities to undertake these tasks within the context of a changing environment, then the greater the need for autonomy. Autonomy is, however, not enough on its own. It needs to be combined with a sense of 'purpose' and the challenge of 'mastery' of that task. It can be influenced through giving individuals direction, slack, boundaries and support. And finally it needs to be combined with a strong accountability. Getting the balance right is a major challenge for any entrepreneur – a challenge that will determine how effective they are as leaders. We return to this issue in Chapters 18 and 19.

 Case insight   Google (2)

Team working

Google operates in a fast-moving commercial environment that values innovation and swift action. It has a flat, decentralized organizational structure with lean hierarchies and is highly democratic and tightly interconnected. Each manager has about 20 people reporting to them. It also has an informal culture with low job specialization, emphasizing principles rather than rules and horizontal communication. Staff are allowed 20% of their time to work on new projects.

All of the staff involved in product development work in small teams of three or four people. Larger teams get broken down into smaller sub-teams, each working on specific aspects of the bigger project. Each team has a leader that rotates depending on the changing project requirements. Most staff operate in more than one team.

QUESTION:

1 List the advantages of working in this way at Google.

The challenges facing social enterprise

The challenges for a successful, growing social enterprise can be even more complicated. A social enterprise usually combines some form of income-generating activity with a social goal. When it comes to reviewing operations and strategies it therefore has to review both sets of activities – commercial and social – and how it binds these together operationally. Leadbeater (1997) argued that entrepreneurial social organizations that grow can run into a range of problems that can stunt their growth or even lead to failure. He proposed the three-stage model shown in Figure 12.11. At each stage there are different imperatives and a need for different skills.

Stage 1

This sees the enterprise trying to establish itself. The key issue was to set the appropriate mission. But as the enterprise grows, this may have to be revisited as the scope of its activities expands. This needs to be handled sensitively with all the stakeholders. There is always the danger that one group of stakeholders may hijack the mission and revise it to meet its own ends, thus alienating others. This can be a risk for an enterprise that is short of funds and the funders therefore are able to set conditions that affect the mission. At the other extreme, too much influence by consumers may result in low prices and financial problems for the enterprise, and this can threaten its survival. These are issues of governance, which become more complex as the social enterprise grows.

Stage 2

As a social enterprise grows, it may have to change the products or services it offers because of changing social need. New products or services may displace existing ones and, without clear

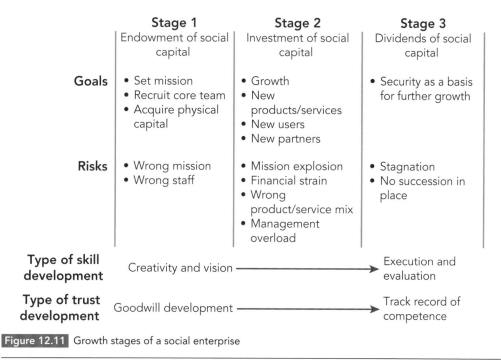

	Stage 1 Endowment of social capital	Stage 2 Investment of social capital	Stage 3 Dividends of social capital
Goals	• Set mission • Recruit core team • Acquire physical capital	• Growth • New products/services • New users • New partners	• Security as a basis for further growth
Risks	• Wrong mission • Wrong staff	• Mission explosion • Financial strain • Wrong product/service mix • Management overload	• Stagnation • No succession in place
Type of skill development	Creativity and vision ———————→		Execution and evaluation
Type of trust development	Goodwill development ———————→		Track record of competence

Figure 12.11   Growth stages of a social enterprise

Source: C. Leadbeater (1997) *The Rise of the Social Entrepreneur*, London: Demos. Reproduced with permission.

criteria for making these decisions, such as profit, the process can become political. This means that the enterprise needs to become very adept at evaluating the success of its work – developing appropriate measures of accountability is a significant issue in a not-for-profit organization. At the same time, it needs to become more professional and to develop, and the social entrepreneur needs to develop their entrepreneurial leadership skills (Chapter 18). Effective, efficient delivery becomes increasingly important. The organization needs to build a reputation based on its track record – in the commercial world it would be called 'developing a brand' (Chapter 7).

Stage 3

By this stage, if it is to survive, the enterprise needs to be firmly established in its commercial and social environment. The final challenge is the same as for its commercial counterpart – how to manage succession (Chapter 17). However, unlike its commercial counterpart, many social enterprises have a number of stakeholders who can have a range of different, and often changing, priorities. It is not uncommon for a social enterprise to cease trading despite being successful because an important backer, such as the government, has pulled out because of a change in its policy priorities.

Leadbeater placed great store on the development of social capital during the life of the social enterprise. He called this the 'virtuous circle', shown in Figure 12.12. It starts with an endowment of social capital – 'a network of relationships and contracts, which are tied together by shared values and interests.' The trick for the social entrepreneur is to lever this up to gain access to more resources – firstly, physical capital such as buildings, and then financial capital to start the wheel turning and then human resources to start delivering the project. Organizational capital is then generated as the project starts delivering its objectives and further resources are attracted, but this will only be achieved with greater formalization in structures and financial controls and a stronger set of relationships with partners. Finally the project starts to pay dividends, such as the creation of permanent physical infrastructure that can be used by the community – new community centres, hospices or sports facilities. And the increased trust and cooperation generated by a successful project can lead to a fresh injection of social capital as the network of relationships and contacts expands.

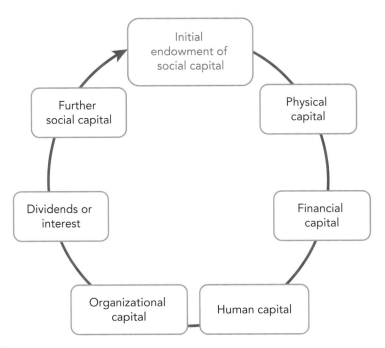

Figure 12.12 The virtuous circle of social capital development

Source: C. Leadbeater (1997) *The Rise of the Social Entrepreneur*, London: Demos. Reproduced with permission.

Crises and strategy development

Previous chapters have outlined how strategies might be developed for a new venture in a systematic way and have encouraged you to underpin this with a formal, written business plan. But do successful entrepreneurs actually approach strategy development in this way – particularly when faced with the reoccurring crises highlighted by Greiner and shown in Figure 12.1? Once their business is established, entrepreneurs seem to approach strategy development differently. They are seen as being intuitive, almost whimsical, in their decision-making and they can seem to lurch from one crisis to another in an unplanned way. Economists find it difficult to understand and to model their approach. It certainly does not fit well into 'logical' economic models such as discounted cash flow. In fact, the 'science of muddling through' (Lindblom, 1959) is as old as strategy itself. The reason entrepreneurs take this approach lies at the heart of any entrepreneurial venture – the greater degree of risk and uncertainty it faces. The result is a different approach to developing strategy and making decisions that is just as logical but little understood.

For many entrepreneurs, strategies evolve on a step-by-step basis. If one step works, then the second is taken. At the same time, they will keep as many options open as possible, because they realize that the outcome of any action is very uncertain. It was Mintzberg (1978) who first coined the phrase 'emergent' strategy development to describe this where: 'the strategy-making process is characterized by reactive solutions to existing problems … The adaptive organization makes its decisions in incremental, serial steps.' This is inherent in the approach called effectual reasoning, outlined in Chapter 6, where the goals of entrepreneurs are broad and evolve over time depending on their resources (Sarasvathy, 2001).

Mintzberg contrasted emergent strategy with the more systematic approach which he called 'deliberate'. However, in a study of growing firms, McCarthy and Leavy (2000) showed that strategy development in SMEs was *both* deliberate and emergent: changing from emergent to deliberate as the firm went through recurrent crises followed by periods of consolidation – a process highlighted in Greiner's stage model of growth. These crises force the entrepreneur to change their preconceptions and 'unlearn' bad habits or routines ahead of learning new ones (Cope, 2005). Therefore, rather than having only one style of strategy development, entrepreneurs would seem to adopt both, depending on circumstances. And the reoccurring crises precipitate

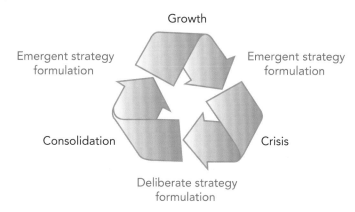

Figure 12.13 Strategy formulation cycle

this switch in approach. In this way, the well-documented process of growth to crisis to consolidation parallels a process of emergent to deliberate and back to emergent strategy formulation, shown in Figure 12.13. It also helps explain why their decision-making can seem incremental and short-term – they are always anticipating yet another crisis.

There is a wonderful old Chinese proverb that underlines the need for a consistent, coherent strategy to ensure success:

> *Tactics without strategy is the noise before defeat.*

It also makes the point that without a coherent strategy miscellaneous tactics (or reactions to situations) will just cause 'noise' – arguments among stakeholders about what to do and why they should be doing it.

Coping with crises

Coping with the successive reoccurring crises is not easy. As the company passes through each crisis, the entrepreneur encounters a roller coaster of human emotions as they find themselves facing a different role with new demands. The classic change/denial curve is based on a model originally developed in the 1960s by Swiss psychiatrist Elisabeth Kübler-Ross to explain the grieving process (Kübler-Ross, 1969). Since then it has been widely used as a method of helping managers understand their reactions to significant changes or crises (e.g. Kakabadse, 1983). It gives us an insight into the attitude of the entrepreneur at as they try to cope with one of these reoccurring crises. Figure 12.14 shows the process of change broken down into three phases. The process will have been triggered by some sort of crisis. The company will be facing problems. Things will be going wrong. The entrepreneur must adopt new ways of doing things and change to overcome these problems. Most likely they will need to learn new managerial skills to enable them to become more effective.

Phase 1

As each new crisis hits, the entrepreneur risks being immobilized with shock. They will be anxious and uncertain about their changing role and the contribution they might make. After all, they may not have the necessary skills to do things differently. Consequently, their effectiveness is likely to drop. They need to understand the new circumstances facing the business and adapt. However, entrepreneurs are tenacious and they might just reapply their old skills to the crisis with greater vigour, and in the short term their effectiveness might improve. However, they are in denial and not really dealing with the changed circumstances they face and the need to do things differently or acquire new skills.

The biggest problem in the business was me ... Staff were saying they were not clear where the business was going, they didn't know what I wanted and they didn't get a chance to voice their opinions ... The way I operated was to shout at people ... I thought you got results out of people by putting them under pressure. It was a ruthless kind of culture where if you performed well you were in, and if you didn't perform well you were out.

Gary Redman, founder, Now Recruitment, *The Sunday Times*, 8 August 2004

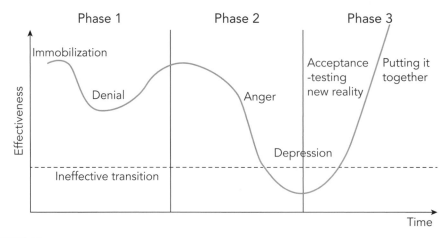

Source: Kakabadse, A. (1983) *The Politics of Management*, London: Gower. With permission of A. Kakabadse.

Phase 2

Eventually this becomes apparent as their effectiveness drops once more. They experience stress as they realize that they do have to develop new skills to keep up with the demands of their changing role. The first reaction is likely to be anger and tendency to blame someone or something. A period of anxiety and depression follows. This makes them even less effective and they may believe that they can no longer cope. In fact, this low point in their emotions indicates that they are beginning to realize that they have to change and learn new skills. At some point, they abandon the past – the old way of doing things – and accept that they have to change how they do things and acquire new skills. This can be a daunting prospect and it is the most dangerous point in the change cycle, as the entrepreneur is least effective, feels depressed and may be tempted to just give up.

Phase 3

Eventually the entrepreneur should start to change and acquire and implement these new skills. This testing period can be as frustrating as it can be rewarding. Mistakes may cause further depression, but, as the newly learned skills are brought into play more effectively, performance starts to improve. However, this transition is not inevitable and many entrepreneurs do not make it from one cycle to the next.

Strategic frameworks

Turning back to the issue of strategy development, there is nothing wrong with strategy that is emergent, incremental and adaptive. Indeed, it is an approach that resonates in complexity theory which attempts to describe how to navigate complex, unpredictable systems that are affected by multiple independent actions – a good description for today's turbulent, interconnected global marketplace. Burns (2014) observes that:

> *Successful entrepreneurs have a strong* **vision** *and this helps them build a* **strategic intent** *for the organization that allows them to reconcile where they are with where they want to be, even when the path to achieve this vision is not clear. They continually* **strategize** *[develop strategy] and that means that strategy will often be seen as* **emergent**. *However, there are always* **strategic options** *that they have thought through and developed. Decision-making is then incremental, based upon opportunistic circumstances at the time.*

So, while entrepreneurs may not always want to write a formal business plan they will still need to strategize – to think about the future, analyse their options and develop strategies – and strategic frameworks like the New Venture Creation Framework outlined in Chapter 6 help to do this. They give your thoughts structure and focus. They help you to make the right decision consistently. And they ought to make common sense. They are not in the nature of a scientific discovery. They are, to quote a colleague, 'a glimpse of the blindingly obvious' – something you knew all along but were never quite able to express in that simple way. As Kay (1998) explains:

> An organizational framework can never be right, or wrong, only helpful or unhelpful. A good organizational framework is minimalist – it is as simple as is consistent with illuminating the issue under discussion – and is memorable … [It] provides the link from judgement through experience to learning. A valid framework is one which focuses sharply on what the skilled manager, at least instinctively, already knows. He is constantly alive to strengths, weaknesses, opportunities, threats which confront him … A successful framework formalizes and extends their existing knowledge. For the less practised, an effective framework is one which organizes and develops what would otherwise be disjointed experiences.

There is nothing here to contradict what Sarasvathy called the 'effectual process' outlined in Chapter 6 (Sarasvathy, op. cit.), which tends to eschew calculative logic. Strategic frameworks simply provide structure for thought and replicate good practice. They provide a set of techniques and processes that can help with strategizing, not least because they generate a common language and mechanism for communication – something that can be valuable as the firm grows and you try to encourage other staff to strategize.

> Think big, act small.
>
> **Elizabeth Gooch**, founder, **eg** solutions, Launch Lab (www.launchlab.co.uk), 13 January 2009

Case insight   Adrenaline Alley (2)

Sustainable social enterprise

Based in Corby in Northamptonshire in the UK, Adrenaline Alley is the Europe's biggest urban sports park. Although it is run as a commercial business, it is a charitable social enterprise (see Chapter 9) and a Company Limited by Guarantee. It opened its doors in 2003 thanks to the efforts of Mandy Young, who, at the time, was an apprentice hairdresser. The spark that caused her to set up the social enterprise was a violent incident involving her terminally ill son. Mandy's son John, then aged 13, had struggled through childhood because of an undiagnosed brain tumour, which resulted in major surgery, radiotherapy and chemotherapy. In his teens he made friends with a group of local skateboarders who he felt less vulnerable with, enjoying the sport and companionship. However, in 2001 Mandy found out that he had been attacked by some of those who knew about his health issues, taunting him with his illness as they attacked him. Mandy and her family were devastated, but were determined to turn the experience into a positive one. Talking with John and his friends it was apparent that not only was intimidation a major national problem for those undertaking 'extreme sports' but also there was a woeful lack of facilities. Mandy decided to try to do something about both problems.

In 2002 she set up the Corby Wheels Project and approached Ashley Pover, ex-CEO of Rockingham Motor Speedway, who donated land and the resources to build an outdoor park until an indoor facility became feasible. Corby Borough Council supported the venture with £15,000 of funding for equipment, and the Community Safety Partnership donated funds to help young people access the park with their own transport. In 2003 Adrenaline Alley opened, attracting some 13,000 visitors in the first 20 months. But Mandy was not happy with just this. She organized events and training at the park as well as continuing to fundraise. However, it became clear that renting a building for an indoor facility and sustaining the project would be difficult without further funding. Never daunted, in 2006 Mandy persuaded Bee Bee Developments to donate a building to the project, albeit a former chicken processing factory, and with the help of score of local helpers and £125,000 of partner funding Adrenaline Alley opened Building 1 – one of the biggest indoor ramp parks in the UK. Then Mandy secured funding to install the UK's only 'Resi Jump' box, a foam pit and bowl, followed by an extension housing rooms for outreach work, a cafe and other services such as equipment hire facilities and Europe's only 76 ft × 14 ft 'Resi/Vert' ramp.

In 2010 Mandy secured further funding from a range of local and national sources that allowed them to refurbish some offices, install new indoor ramps, outdoor dirt jumps and develop a new skate only area as well as adapting many facilities to enable disabled participation.

Continued…

Continued from previous page...

In 2013 Bee Bee Developments donated another two adjacent buildings, and Mandy secured further funding from a range of public and private sources enabling them to open Building 2 as a performance and event arena, and Building 3 as a scooter park, making Adrenaline Alley the biggest park in Europe. It also extended the range of youth work undertaken by opening a photography and media suite for those interested in acting, filming, script writing, directing, camerawork, lighting etc.

Adrenaline Alley has grown through the hard work of Mandy Young and the team she has drawn around her. While the project has grown incrementally, Mandy has always had a wider vision and cajoled people to push this through. It prides itself on being a safe environment with a warm and welcoming atmosphere. It also makes a point of partnering with other public and private, local and national organizations to help it achieve its ultimate goal, which is: 'to improve the lives of young people in Corby and Northamptonshire giving them a facility they have ownership over and can be proud of'. It charges for many of the services and facilities offered, but as a social enterprise, all the generated income is ploughed into the organization.

Mandy's son, John, died in 2010 at the age of 24 years. Adrenaline Alley is her legacy from John to the local community.

Repeated from Chapter 7, here are the vision, mission and values of Adrenaline Alley.

Vision

To expand our thriving centre for urban sports and community use bringing change that makes a real difference to people's lives, and provide opportunities for other communities to develop social enterprises in the same way.

Mission

To provide safe, secure and manageable facilities addressing the needs of local communities and to be recognized as a leading provider of urban sports using a range of partnerships to become a sustainable social enterprise.

Values

Delivering our mission as a team, we strive to be:

> Approachable and honest – always willing to listen and learn;

> People focused – operating for the benefit of our community and participants;

> Accessible – willing to go the extra mile to ensure everyone can participate;

> Affordable – always striving to reduce costs;

> Versatile! – adapting the business to the needs of our customers.

❑ Visit the website: www.adrenalinealley.co.uk

Watch a video about it: www.youtube.com/watch?v=Hyprd ACG0Ac#t=340

QUESTIONS:

1 How important was Mandy Young to this project? Could it have worked without her?

2 Why is it a social enterprise? Is this the best form for the venture?

3 How important are partnerships to this venture?

4 How has strategy been developed?

5 Has Adrenaline Alley remained true to its vision, mission and values?

6 Which growth stage has Adrenaline Alley reached?

Reviewing strategy

Strategies do not last forever, and launch strategies, particularly those for disruptive innovations, need to be reviewed shortly after start-up once customer and competitor reaction can be gauged. The needs of customers or the market might have changed since start-up, or the reaction of competitors might not have been accurately predicted and the original business model needs to be modified. In the USA changing your strategy is called '**pivoting**' and many successful businesses have done it. Twitter, Instagram and WhatsApp all changed their start-up business model. New market opportunities or competitive threats may emerge. The social needs that a social enterprise was set up to serve may change. Growing a business is dangerous, and without a clear understanding of what has made the business successful there is no sound foundation for the move forwards.

Some entrepreneurs understand what they are doing, what works and what does not, as they do it, sometimes almost instinctively. Others are more reflective and need time to analyse the situation. Getting the right people and putting the right systems in place can take time, so operational problems can complicate the analysis. Once entrepreneurs understand the basis for their

No plan survives first contact with customers

Steve Blank, serial entrepreneur, *http.//steveblank. com/2010/04/08/l*

successful survival – so far – they can start to plan their take-off, the growth that will eventually make them leaders of the very small number of high-growth businesses upon which whole economies are so dependent for their growth. This is the point where the gazelles start to emerge.

The strategic frameworks identified so far can easily be adapted to apply to a new or changed environment or new product/service launch. However, it is about *competitive* or *business strategy* – how the organization competes – and the strategy literature makes the distinction between this and *corporate strategy* that determines the scope and structure of the organization. In a multi-business organization, competitive strategy is determined at the divisional or subsidiary level and corporate strategy at the head office or holding company level. For SMEs this distinction is irrelevant – it is all about strategy. But we do need to modify the model to incorporate this broader concept of strategy for an established business. A review of strategy for a social enterprise needs to ensure that it is developing the cycle shown in Figure 12.12 and generating the expected dividends of social capital.

The process of strategic review is shown in Figure 12.15. Central to this is strategic analysis – the process of developing strategy by reviewing the business and the environment it operates in to determine the optimum 'fit' that will be explained in greater detail in the next section. The review starts by looking at your vision and mission statements. The question is whether they are all still appropriate. Read et al. (2011) point out that many entrepreneurs do not have a vision when they launch the business. Visions evolve as opportunities emerge and you define your own vision and measures of success. Are there new, more attractive, opportunities? Have the values and beliefs on which the business is based changed? Has the mission changed, perhaps because of new opportunities or, in the case of a social enterprise, changing social needs? The strategic analysis might therefore modify both your vision and mission (shown as feedback loops). However, its main function is to generate strategic options and to inform strategy formulation. This then feeds into strategy implementation and entrepreneurial decision-making.

One of the areas that is likely to need review as a business grows is its involvement in corporate social responsibility (CSR) and philanthropy. This may have been undertaken in the early years for a myriad of reasons, from purely altruistic to commercial. However, as we saw in Chapter 7, if looked at strategically, CSR can be used to enhance both – bringing social and economic goals into alignment and leveraging capabilities and relationships in support of charitable causes (Porter and Kramer, 2002, 2006). Nevertheless, these activities may grow to such an extent that they need to be separated from the business so as to form a separate social enterprise. This allows objectives to be separated and may help resolve conflicts.

The way entrepreneurs approach decision-making is often seen as incremental, almost tentative (Burns and Whitehouse, 1995a, 1995b). It is, in fact, part of this entrepreneurial approach to

Most businesses aren't overnight successes … Spending the early years perfecting systems and developing competitive advantage is critical. At the same time ensuring the business is lean is a vital prerequisite to future growth. Once the building blocks are in place, you can take the next step.

Adam Schwab, founder, Aussie Commerce Group, *Business Review Australia* (issuu.com), July 2014

Have a clear strategy and don't get side tracked by activities that don't enable you to achieve this. Review your strategy constantly to ensure you are meeting market demands.

Elizabeth Gooch, founder, **eg** solutions, *Launch Lab* (www.launchlab.co.uk), 13 January 2009

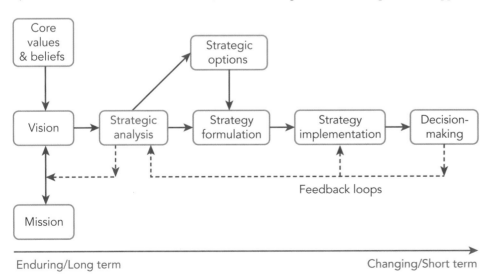

Figure 12.15 A framework for strategy review

> It's important to be intuitive, but not at the expense of facts. Without the right data to back it up, emotion-based decision-making during difficult times will inevitably lead a company into greater danger.
>
> **Michael Dell**, founder, Dell Corporation (1999) *Direct from Dell: Strategies that Revolutionized an Industry*, New York: Harper Business

strategy development and risk mitigation. It is a contingent approach that uses information to modify strategies to reflect the reality of uncertain situations – shown by the feedback loops in Figure 12.15 – and mitigate risk. It is part of the process of strategizing and developing emergent strategies. For example, successful entrepreneurs tend to keep capital investment and fixed costs as low as possible, often by subcontracting some activities. They tend to commit costs only after the opportunity has proved to be real, which may be prudent and reflect their resource limits, but then they run the risk of losing first-mover advantage in the marketplace – a difficult judgement call. Frequently, therefore, they will experiment with a 'limited' launch – what Ries (2011) called a lean start-up – into the market and learn from this. They also view an asset as a liability rather than just an asset in the balance-sheet sense, meaning that it may limit the flexibility that they need and commit them to a course of action that may prove unsound. Successful entrepreneurs find ways of reconciling these issues – ways of developing strategy without over committing to one course of action and ways of minimizing their investment in resources. They start with the resources they can afford to lose and then move forwards (Sarasvathy, op. cit.). The feedback loops in Figure 12.15 signify that strategies can be changed quickly to accommodate changing circumstances that reflect the uncertain world of entrepreneurial business. They signify the way strategies can switch from deliberate to emergent as circumstances change.

Case insight   American Giant

Sticking to your principles

Established in 2012 and only 18 months into business and everything was going according to plan for the online clothes retailer American Giant. The San Francisco–based company was founded by Bayard Winthrop and sells better-quality sweatshirts and other items of clothing produced in the USA from US cotton. With limited resources, the company had relied upon word-of-mouth marketing and had estimated it would take at least two years before growth really started. It had built this into its business plan. It only took pre-orders on its most popular styles, like the zipped hooded sweatshirt, while recognizing that it was not possible to restock the other less popular styles quickly. It bought and stocked prudently so as to manage its cash flow.

But growth does not always go according to plan, and unplanned success can cause as many problems as failure. It was December 2012 and the firm was actually a little overstocked when the online magazine Slate ran an article saying that the company's hooded sweatshirt was 'the greatest hoodie ever made.' Within two days the company received over half a million dollars of extra orders, clearing out the stocks of hoodies. The company had neither the manpower nor the materials to meet demand. Because the company's supply chain went all the way back to cotton fields in the USA, with fabric specially woven and dyed for American Giant, it could not simply pick up a phone and order more material. At the same time, the factory was

Courtesy of American Giant

set up to make hundreds of sweatshirts – not thousands. Since the company was not willing to change some of the founding principles on which it was based and source elsewhere, all it could do was to apologize to customers and hope they would be patient and wait for orders to be fulfilled – not the ideal situation for a company relying on quality of product and service and repeat sales.

Some customers agreed to wait but many did not. Nevertheless, the open and honest way the company dealt with the problem was appreciated by customers. And running out of stock proved to be further good PR – everybody likes to have something others cannot. So American Giant survived the crisis and sales continued to increase, although they never peaked in the same way again:

'Commitment to quality comes first ... we're going to ask our customers to be patient because we believe in the quality and the pay-off is worth it ... it's an acceptable thing for a customer to fall out of the queue.' (BBC News Business, 10 March 2013)

QUESTION:

1 What lessons do you learn from American Giant?

Strategic analysis

The process of strategic analysis starts with a thorough understanding of your strengths and weaknesses. It then goes on to contrast this with the opportunities and threats that you face in the environment. This is the classic **SWOT analysis** (strengths, weaknesses, opportunities and threats). It seeks to identify an overlap between the business environment and a firm's resources. In other words, a match between the firm's strategic or core competencies, capabilities and resources and market opportunities. This match, as such, may not identify *sustainable* competitive advantage because it may be copied by competitors or may change over time. Kay (op. cit.) identified three capabilities that he said formed the basis for sustainable competitive advantage:

> **Reputation**
> This is often encapsulated in brand identity but equally can be communicated through the relationships.

> **The way the organization innovates**
> This is one of the defining characteristics of an entrepreneurial organization. Ideally you want innovation to be able to take place again and again and again.

> **The organization's strategic assets**
> These are the unique ones that competitors do not have access to, the most valuable of which are likely to be the two capabilities detailed above.

The process therefore starts with the identification of this unique set of competencies and capabilities. This portfolio of resources can be combined in various ways to meet opportunities or threats. If you go back to your original business idea and your value proposition, it will be based upon your own competencies and capabilities. As the business grows, these should intensify but also change. They could, for example, allow a firm to expand into new markets by re-applying and reconfiguring what it does best. The chief proponents of this approach were Prahalad and Hamel (1990). They saw core competency as the 'collective learning of the organization, especially how to coordinate diverse production skills and integrate multiple streams of technology … [through] … communication, involvement, and a deep commitment to work across organizational boundaries … Competencies are the glue that binds existing businesses. They are also the engine for new business development.' They suggested that there were three tests which can be applied to identify core competencies:

1   They provide potential access to a wide variety of markets rather than generating competitive advantage only in one.
2   They make 'a significant contribution to the perceived customer benefits of the end-product' – they add value.
3   They are difficult for competitors to copy. Products are easier to copy than processes.

The SWOT analysis is also the basis for undertaking customer analysis and deciding on market segmentation. It informs marketing strategy but equally must be interpreted in the context of a particular market, taking into account both customers and competitors. Strengths can be transformed into weaknesses in a different market and vice versa. The market context is crucial. Thus a SWOT analysis on the fast-food chain McDonald's in the context of the US market would yield completely different results from one undertaken in the context of the market in a developing country. In a developing economy it will still be a novel product in high demand. Most opportunities also carry associated threats. Threats are part of the risks a business faces. They may be classified according to their seriousness and probability of occurrence. A view of the overall attractiveness of a market is based upon the opportunities it offers balanced by the threats that it poses. In making this judgement it is important to remember your critical success factors and understand your degree of control over them.

One of the outcomes of this analysis is that it may get you to question your original value proposition and its match to target markets because you see your core competencies as of more value to different markets. This can lead you to question your mission and, in particular, your domain of operation (the market/industry you operate in). For example, Dell originally sold computers. It claims that one of its core competencies is its direct relationship with customers that allows them to configure their own computers. If this competency is of higher value than its product/market offering, why should it not sell other digital consumer electronics and office automation equipment directly rather than just computers – something it has already started doing. And why should it not subcontract more of its assembly, focusing rather on the core strength that the customer values – the direct relationship? This raises many questions about the scope of Dell's activities and the nature of its business domain. But this is nothing new. As we shall see in the next chapter, Amazon moved from the virtual sale of physical products produced by other people (books, CDs, DVDs etc.) to the virtual sale of virtual items (e-Books and music downloads), often now using its own brand of tablet computer or e-reader. All of which reminds us of Ohmae's word 'kosoryoku' (Chapter 7) and that we need to be quite open minded about the business domain we are in, particularly during the early life of a business.

The whole process of strategic analysis is an art rather than a science. There is no prescriptive approach. To undertake a SWOT analysis brutal honesty is required. That means not pretending that something is a core competency when really it is not. And it means listening to people with different opinions and judging what is the prevailing wisdom in the organization. There are tools that can help you do this, some of which we have already covered. These are summarized in Table 12.1.

Table 12.1 Tools for a SWOT analysis

Internal appraisal (strengths, weaknesses)	External appraisal (opportunities, threats)
> Financial performance analysis and benchmarking (next section)	> PESTEL analysis and other idea-generating techniques about the future (Chapter 4 and 5)
> Value chain analysis (Chapter 5)	> Market research (Chapter 5)
> Life cycle analysis (Chapters 5 and 13)	> Porter's Five Forces analysis (Chapter 5)
> Product portfolio analysis (Chapter 13)	> Value disciplines or generic business models (Chapter 6)
> Value disciplines or generic business models (Chapter 6)	

 ## Case insight   audioBoom

Changing the business model

 audioBoom is the audio equivalent of Netflix. The business was launched in 2009 in the UK and already has over four million listeners. It is also quoted on the London stock exchange after a reverse takeover of One Delta, an AIM (Alternative Investment Market – see Chapter 14) listed shell company in 2014. Later the same year, the company raised £8 million in a share placing with a number of blue-chip institutional investors, valuing it at over £73 million. The company is still based in London, where most of its users remain, but it has recently opened offices in New York, San Francisco and Sydney – key markets for expansion. The reason audioBoom has attracted so much attention is because so many analysts believe it has tremendous potential for future growth, particularly outside the UK in markets like the USA, Australia and India. audioBoom's strategy and business model have changed a number of times since its launch:

Stage 1: Amateur users were allowed to record, post and share audio clips – spoken word, not music – for free. Because there was no music, audioBoom did not have to pay performance royalties. This phase attracted many celebrity users and generated a loyal listening. The problem was that audioBoom had not yet worked out how to generate income.

Stage 2: This was to approach professional organizations to make audio content such as news, reviews and

Continued...

Continued from previous page...

interviews available on the site. By the end of 2014 it had developed some 2,000 commercial partners such as the BBC, Sky Sports, talkSport, Premier League and many newspapers and magazines. At the same time, it started developing a new business model that would allow it to generate income, but to enable this to happen it also had to develop a new software platform and it was this that much of the financial investment was used for.

Stage 3: The next stage, in late 2014, was to re-launch, allowing for content embeds on the user's own website, Twitter, Facebook or Tumblr feed. It allows users to create their own personalized feed by downloading content that interested them. Content ranges across sport, news, financial markets and entertainment. Users can select the content they wish to receive and this can be downloaded automatically at times they select – a system called 'content curation'. In this way, a sports fan can download up-to-date selected content and listen to it as the news breaks or store it to listen on the way to work. At the same time, the original idea of allowing users to post their own audio clips via mobile devices was made easier. Just as YouTube does not pay for content, audioBoom does not pay for most audio clips and generates income by selling and inserting advertising before and after a clip.

❑ Visit the website: www.audioBoom.com

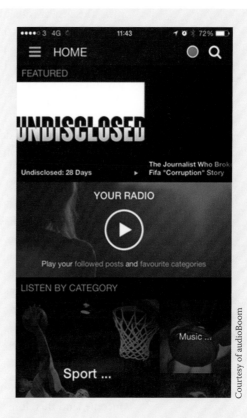

Courtesy of audioBoom

QUESTION

1 What lessons do you learn from audioBoom about changing your business model?

Financial performance analysis

No SWOT analysis would be complete without an analysis of your financial performance using a technique called **ratio analysis**. As we have seen, a business needs to be profitable and efficient and for it to survive it needs to be sufficiently liquid to enable it to pay its bills. Ratio analysis is a technique that enables you to evaluate your performance. It can be applied to either historic financial statements or financial forecasts, depending whether you want to look backwards or forwards.

Let us start with the principle that investors, including you as a founder/owner, will want to maximize the return they get on their investment. If you invest $100 and receive $10, you get a 10% return which you can then compare to other investment opportunities. Similarly, owners (shareholders), who own the assets of the business, will normally want to maximize the return they receive on their investment. The critical performance ratio, that shareholders expect to be kept as high as possible, is therefore return to shareholders.

$$\text{Return to shareholders} = \frac{\text{Net profit}}{\substack{\text{Shareholders' funds} \\ (\text{total assets} - \text{total liabilities})}} \qquad (\text{expressed as \%})$$

To maximize this, operating profit should be as high as possible, interest should be as low as possible and shareholders' funds should also be as low as possible. And here lies the dilemma. One way of keeping shareholders' funds low is to borrow (shareholders' funds = total assets − liabilities), but this increases interest payments and reduces net profit. So the question is, how much to borrow? The answer is that it pays to borrow as much as you can, as long as you can obtain a return on those borrowed funds that is higher than the interest rate.

For example, you put $5,000 into the business and then obtain a bank loan of $5,000 with an interest rate of 10%. If the return on this $10,000 investment is 25%, you will make $2,500 but only pay interest of $500 ($5,000 × 10%), giving you a net profit of $2,000 – equal to a return to the shareholders of 40% ($2,000 ÷ $5,000 × 100). You earned an extra 15% on the bank loan – a total of $750 ($5,000 × 15%). This goes directly to you, on top of the $1,250 ($5,000 × 25%) from your own investment. The downside of this is that the financial risk of the business increases with the higher level of borrowing. The business is obliged to pay interest of $500 whatever profit it makes and, if it were only able to make a 5% return on the $10,000, then all the money would go to pay interest ($10,000 × 5% = $500), leaving nothing for you, despite the fact you had invested $5,000. The appropriate level of borrowing is the classic risk/return trade-off decision – it is a question of judgement. Bankers have some benchmark ratios to inform their lending decisions, as we shall see later in this section.

The return to the shareholder therefore measures both the operating performance of the business and its gearing/leverage. The critical performance ratio measuring operating performance only – your efficiency or productivity – is return on total assets. This should be kept as high as possible.

$$\text{Return on total assets} = \frac{\text{Operating profit}}{\substack{\text{Shareholders' funds} + \text{loan capital} \\ (\text{total assets} - \text{current liabilities})}} \qquad (\text{expressed as \%})$$

However, be aware that founders take a salary, which is deducted in arriving at operating income, and therefore the ratio (and return to shareholders) can be distorted if your salaries are unrealistically low or high.

In seeking to be as efficient as possible, a company will look to do two things: maximize its operating profit and minimize its total assets, minus current liabilities. Ratio analysis can help with an understanding of this by looking separately at profit management and asset management.

Profit management

Profits normally increase as turnover increases. Therefore, looking at profit in isolation tells you nothing about the operating efficiency of a business. The first profit ratio measures overall profitability compared to sales or turnover. It reflects the price you are able to charge, compared to the costs you face. The ratio should be as high as possible.

$$\text{Operating profit margin} = \frac{\text{Operating profit}}{\text{Sales or turnover}} \qquad (\text{expressed as \%})$$

The next ratio explains how the direct costs of the product/service sold – the cost of goods sold – are controlled. It should be as high as possible.

$$\text{Gross profit margin} = \frac{\text{Gross profit}}{\text{Sales or turnover}} \qquad (\text{expressed as \%})$$

Gross profit margin is different to contribution margin – which reflects your control of variable costs. Companies often break this ratio down further by looking at ratios of key direct costs such as materials or labour, compared to turnover/sales.

Asset management

Assets also normally increase as sales increase. Therefore, looking at asset levels in isolation tells you nothing about the operating efficiency of a business. The key ratios below measure the efficiency of asset usage compared to sales/turnover. They should be as high as possible.

$$\text{Total asset turnover} = \frac{\text{Sales or turnover}}{\text{Total assets}} \qquad \text{(expressed as a number)}$$

$$\text{Debtor (receivables) turnover} = \frac{\text{Sales or turnover}}{\text{Debtors (receivables)}} \qquad \text{(expressed as a number)}$$

$$\text{Stock (inventory) turnover} = \frac{\text{Sales or turnover}}{\text{Stock (inventory)}} \qquad \text{(expressed as a number)}$$

Liquidity

There are also a number of ratios that measure the liquidity of a business. The first two are of particular interest to those offering credit because they measure the firm's ability to repay the debt. These ratios are all expressed as numbers.

$$\text{Current ratio} = \frac{\text{Current assets}}{\text{Current liability}}$$

This is expected to be greater than 1, indicating that current assets exceed current liabilities.

$$\text{Quick ratio} = \frac{\text{Current assets, excluding stock/inventory}}{\text{Current liabilities}}$$

This is expected to be near to 1, perhaps as low as 0.8.

Break-even

As already explained, break-even is a very important measure of riskiness of a business. It measures fixed costs in relation to contribution margin. It is the point where a business stops making a loss and starts making a profit. The break-even point should be as low as possible.

$$\text{Break-even point} = \frac{\text{Fixed costs}}{\text{Contribution margin}} \qquad \text{(expressed in \$ turnover)}$$

However, this is an absolute measure and, as a business grows, the break-even point is almost certain to rise. A better measure of risk is where break-even is in relation to sales. This is measured by the margin of safety. The margin of safety should be as high as possible.

$$\text{Margin of safety} = \frac{\text{Turnover} - \text{Break-even}}{\text{Turnover}} \qquad \text{(normally expressed as \%)}$$

Financial gearing/leverage

The level of borrowing is called financial gearing or leverage. Ratios that measure this are of particular interest to bankers. High gearing or leverage is risky.

$$\text{Gearing/leverage} = \frac{\text{All loans} + \text{overdraft}}{\text{Shareholders' funds}} \qquad \text{(expressed as \%)}$$

Bankers like this ratio to be under 100%, indicating that shareholders have invested more money than the banks. Frequently for growing firms this is not the case. Above 400% is considered very high risk – the business is likely to fail. However, some management buy-outs have had gearing levels even above this. Often bankers will also look at the proportion of all the loans that are short-term (due within one year). They are also interested in how secure are their interest payments.

$$\text{Interest cover} = \frac{\text{Operating profit}}{\text{Interest}} \qquad \text{(expressed as a number)}$$

This measures how many times interest is covered by profit. From the bankers' perspective, the higher this number, the better.

Ratios allow you to evaluate performance and are a basis for valuing the business. They are useful because they measure one number against another – they therefore allow for growth. So, for example, debtors/receivables are bound to increase as the business grows and sales increase, but what is important is not the absolute value of debtors/receivables but rather its relationship to sales, measured by debtor turnover. Similarly, there is no way of knowing whether a $2 million profit in one company is better than a $1 million profit in another unless you know how much was invested in each to achieve it. To obtain a high return to the shareholder, a firm needs effective profit management and efficient asset management. Put crudely, margins need to be as high as possible and assets should be kept as low as possible – a point made in Chapter 11.

The exception to this rule may of course be the social enterprise, where maximizing the financial return to the shareholders – or stakeholders – may not be the main objective of the undertaking. Here the financial return may be set at some 'satisfactory' level. The problem with this is that it becomes very difficult to benchmark performance and efficiency, particularly against pure commercial organizations. As we saw in Chapter 9, this is one reason why organizations with social objectives are often divided in legal terms into a commercial company, with profit maximizing objectives, and a social or charitable organization, with social objectives. The problem then remains how to measure attainment of the social objectives. It may be easy to measure the accumulation of financial capital, but it is almost impossible to measure the accumulation of social capital.

 Practice insight Benchmarking performance

Systematic calculation of performance ratios can give you clues about how profit might be increased and where assets might be reduced. Of course, to do this you need some benchmarks. One fundamental benchmark is the rate of interest. The return on total assets should never fall below this – otherwise you are better off closing the company and putting the money in the bank. All the other measures are a question of judgement, but you can judge them against:

> **Forecasts** – Ratios can be calculated both on forecast and actual financial information. Comparing actual to forecast financial performance is part of effective financial control.

> **Trends over time** – Ratios do change over time and trends can give both good and bad news.

> **Industry norms** – Industry-based ratios, often based on published financial statements, are produced by a number of organizations (e.g. in the UK, Centre for Interfirm Comparison and ICC Business Ratios). These are important benchmarks against which to judge the realism of projections. If your margins are higher than industry norms, how can you justify this? Founders and investors often use these norms and ratios to validate a set of financial projections.

Formulating strategy

A strategy is just a linked pattern of actions. An organization is likely to have a range of strategies linking the development of products/markets with its capabilities. You decide upon an appropriate strategy by:

> Matching the firm's strategic or core competencies, capabilities and resources to market opportunities. The resulting actions can lead you into developing new growth strategies, including new product and market developments.

> Using the firm's strategic or core competencies, capabilities and resources to repair any organizational weaknesses that have appeared. The resulting actions should be prioritized. This will also help identify any critical success factors – things you need to get right to ensure your survival and success.

> Using the firm's strategic or core competencies, capabilities and resources to combat any threats. This should also generate a series of critical success factors.

The process of developing strategy starts with your vision. As the firm grows, this should develop and it will become an important tool to help you lead your organization. Successful entrepreneurs develop a strong vision of what they want their business to become – unconstrained by uncertainty or lack of resources. Although they do not always know how they will achieve their vision, they always have strong 'strategic intent'. This is accompanied by a loose or flexible strategy underpinned by continuous strategizing – assessing the options about how to make the most of opportunities or avoid risks as they arise. By creating more strategic options they improve their chances of successfully pursuing at least one opportunity and avoiding most risks. They keep as many options open as long as possible. The greater the number of strategic options, the safer they are in an uncertain environment. Make no mistake; successful entrepreneurs to a large extent create their own luck.

Many, if not most, entrepreneurs will not approach strategy development in this systematic way. And when we look at the progress of these ventures it is likely to be characterized as a series of muddled, haphazard incremental decisions and rescheduling of activities with little coherence. Without any strategy to give them structure, these ventures are blown in different directions and are constantly reacting to different opportunities or threats from their commercial and social environment. While their actions may be described as 'emergent', there is no strategic underpinning. For these ventures, luck plays a large part and their progress reflects the complex interaction of the entrepreneur with their environment and society as a whole.

Using your business model to strategize

The New Venture Creation Framework outlined in Chapter 6 and shown in Figure 6.1 was a simple seven-stage model around which start-up planning could be facilitated in the sequential manner indicated by the arrows (Burns, 2014). It can be used for strategizing in an informal, holistic way, using drawings or Post-it™ notes. Figure 12.16 shows how the business model of the low-cost airline easyJet might be shown in note form. The framework can also be used to examine the consequences of changing environments or new product/service launches and how your business model might adapt. The simple framework encourages you to experiment with different business models and ask the 'what-if?' question, working through the likely consequences without necessarily preparing a formal business plan.

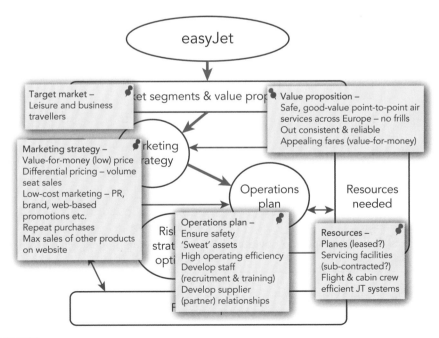

Figure 12.16 The New Venture Creation Framework

As a start-up your core leadership qualities need to be adaptability and flexibility – you need to be continually looking at the business and responding and enhancing thing until you get to an operating model that works for you.

David Peckham, co-founder, Samba Swirl, *The Times*, 25 February 2014

Using the New Venture Creation Framework in this way as a pictorial framework can help you develop new business ideas and modify target markets, value propositions and your marketing strategy. It should lead to a series of strategic options, each option contingent upon different environmental circumstances, using information to modify strategies to reflect the reality of these uncertain situations. The more options that you can identify, the more flexibility you have in formulating, or indeed changing, your strategy. However, it is important that not all these options are constrained by your resources or your current competitive position. Sometimes your vision might generate options that transcend these constraints, but may or may not be realistically attainable at the moment. The great entrepreneurs of our time never felt constrained by resources when they set up their businesses.

Chapter 6 pointed out that this approach mirrored that of Osterwalder and Pigneur (2010). Their 'Business Model Canvas' has been used as a model for consultants and trainers across the world, albeit mainly in larger companies. It is based around the nine blocks shown in Figure 12.17 and can be used in the same way as the New Venture Creation Framework, using drawings or Post-it™ notes, to explore the effects of changes to the business model. The left side of the canvas is driven by efficiency and the right side by value to customers. The idea is that you can use the canvas to sketch out (literally) and develop your business model. Their innovatively designed book certainly provides a stimulating pictorial structure for better understanding and developing business models as well as numerous examples of real business models for companies and/or products that translate onto the Canvas (e.g. Apple, Google, Skype and Amazon).

Osterwalder and Pigneur (op. cit.) encourage you to challenge conventional business models using six techniques:

> **Generating new ideas** – encouraging you not always to accept the 'dominant logic' of how to do things in a particular industry;
> **Prototype development** – encouraging you to explore alternative business models that might add value for customers;

Key partnerships:	Key activities:	Value proposition:	Customer relations:	Customer segments:
The network of suppliers and partners that make the business model work	The most important things you need to do to make the business model work	The product/service bundle that creates value for each customer segment	The types of relationships you aim to have with each customer segment	The different groups of people or organizations you aim to reach
	Key resources:		Channels:	
	The most important assets required to make the business model work		How you communicate with and reach each customer segment	
Cost structures:			Revenue streams:	
All the costs that you will incur to operate your business model			The cash generated from each customer segment	

Figure 12.17 The Business Model Canvas

Source: A. Osterwalder and Y. Pigneur (2010), *Business Model Generation: A Handbook for Visionaries, Game Changers and Challengers*, New Jersey: John Wiley & Sons. With permission granted via Copyright Clearance Center.

> Storytelling – encouraging you to be able to articulate the concept behind the product/service and how it creates value for customers;
> Customer insights – encouraging you to develop a deep understanding of customer needs, even if they are not always derived directly from the customers themselves;
> Scenario development – building on customer insights and development in the competitive environment to make future possibilities more tangible;
> Visual thinking – encouraging you to draw or sketch out the business model on the Canvas and use Post-it™ notes to explain it, thereby making abstract concepts more concrete.

Business models underpin business plans. You need to develop your business model before you can draw up a business plan. The techniques outlined here allows you to 'tinker' with your business model and explore alternative scenarios and develop strategic options. They are strategic frameworks that encourage strategizing. You need to do this before you commit too much time in writing a formal business plan.

Strategies that work

Nothing is certain in business and some economists would suggest that empirical evidence about the causes of business growth (and failure) remains unexplained (Storey and Greene, 2010). But the strategy a firm selects will greatly affect its business model (Casadesus-Masanell and Ricart, 2010; Zott and Amit, 2010). And research does give us a clue about which competitive strategies are *most likely* to deliver sustainable competitive advantage and growth:

Differentiation and focus

As we saw when we developed our business model in Chapter 6, Porter (1985) wanted us to select cost leadership, differentiation or focus. Treacy and Wiersema (1995) called them operational excellence, product leadership or customer intimacy. Which theory do you choose? The answer is that investors believe a business should try to match its core competencies and strategic assets to create competitive advantage (Lusch et al., 2010; Macmillan and Seldon, 2008), and all the evidence points to differentiation having a greater potential than low cost for producing sustainable competitive advantage (Grant, 2012). Differentiation takes more time to copy. For example, just one element of differentiation, quality, has been shown by many studies to be more likely to lead to growth than competing simply on price (Burns, 1994; Harrison and Taylor 1996; Ray and Hutchinson, 1983; Storey et al., 1989). Often differentiation is coupled with market focus to develop a market niche. Strategy should therefore emphasize something that makes the firm as unique and difficult to copy as possible and delivers as much value to the customer as possible today and, more importantly, tomorrow (Harrison et al., 2010; Lusch et al. op. cit.; Newbert, 2008; Wu, 2010).

Speed of market dominance

Speed of execution is also important, particularly in new and technology-based markets (Markides and Geroski, 2005). A 'window of opportunity' can be very small. Delay can attract unwelcome competitors. However, first-mover advantage can disappear rapidly if the product/market offering proves too unattractive or too many elements of the market offering prove inappropriate and there is good case for delaying until the market needs are clearer, called active waiting (Sull, 2005). But while there may be a 'just right' time for a product launch (Figure 12.18), many surveys show that rapid domination of a market niche is the real key to success and is likely to lead to sustainable growth (3i European Enterprise Centre, 1993; Birley and Westhead, 1990; Harrison and Taylor op. cit.; Macrae, 1991; Siegel et al., 1993; Solem and Steiner, 1989; Storey et al., op. cit.). There is also a strong relationship between market share and financial return (Boston Consulting Group, 1968, 1972; Buzzell et al., 1974; Buzzell and Gale, 1987; Yelle, 1979).

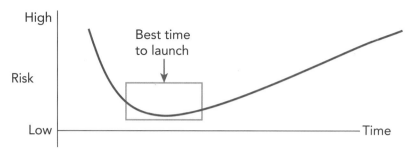

Figure 12.18 Best time to launch

Continuous innovation

Frequent product or service innovation is also seen as important by many researchers, particularly for manufacturing and technology-based businesses (Calvo, 2006; Dunkelberg et al., 1987; Freel, 2000; Geroski and Machin, 1992; Roper, 1999; Solem and Steiner, op. cit.; Storey and Greene, op. cit.; Woo et al., 1989; Wynarczyk et al., 1993).

Flawless execution

Nohria and Joyce (2003) provide a postscript. They reported the results of a 10-year study of 160 companies and their use of some 200 different management techniques. They concluded what we all know: that it does not really matter so much which technique you apply but it matters very much more that you execute it flawlessly. They claim flawless execution is something too many management theorists have forgotten. Attention to detail is important.

The conclusions, therefore, are obvious. While nothing in this world is guaranteed, the strategy with the best chance of generating sustainable growth and the highest profits is to differentiate with the aim of dominating your market as quickly as possible, and to continue to innovate around that differential advantage. Gaining rapid market dominance is important. It can come from internal growth but, as we shall see in the next chapter, might also involve acquisition of competitors.

 Case insight   Xtreme SnoBoards (3)

Evaluating a financial forecast

In the Case insights in Chapters 7 and 11 we saw how a couple of snowboard enthusiasts set up a company called Xtreme SnoBoards, designing and building three types of boards. They drew up a set of financial forecasts. Using the ratios outlined in this chapter, they now decided to evaluate the forecasted performance of their business in its first 15 months of trading.

$$\text{Return on total assets} = \frac{\text{Net profit}}{\text{Shareholder' funds}}$$
$$= \frac{£142,478}{£184,478} = 77.2\%$$

$$\text{Operating profit margin} = \frac{\text{Operating profit}}{\text{Turnover}}$$
$$= \frac{£142,478}{£423,900} = 33.6\%$$

$$\text{Gross profit margin} = \frac{\text{Gross profit}}{\text{Turnover}}$$
$$= \frac{£200,478}{£423,900} = 47.3\%$$

$$\text{Contribution margin} = \frac{\text{Contribution per unit}}{\text{Sales price per unit}}$$
$$= \frac{£98}{£135} = 72.6\%$$

$$\text{Margin of safety} = \frac{\text{Turnover} - \text{Break-even point}}{\text{Turnover}}$$
$$= \frac{£423,000 - 257,576}{£423,900} = 39.2\%$$

$$\text{Total asset turnover} = \frac{\text{Turnover}}{\text{Total assets}} = \frac{£423,900}{£209,158} = 2.0$$

Continued...

Continued from previous page...

$$\text{Debtor turnover} = \frac{\text{Turnover}}{\text{Debtors (receivables)}}$$
$$= \frac{£423,00}{£108,000} = 3.9$$

$$\text{Stock turnover} = \frac{\text{Turnover}}{\text{Stock (inventory)}} = \frac{£423,000}{£45,538} = 9.3$$

Although the founders do not have any industry norms and there are no trends to observe in the first period of trading, they feel that this is an exceptional level of performance by any standards, reflecting a high profit margin and strict cost control. However, they are aware that they have accepted a lower salary than they wish (estimated as an additional £20,000) and provided an interest-free loan for the company (estimated as an interest cost of £2,000). They calculate that if these costs had been charged, the return on total assets would be reduced to 65% and the operating profit margin to 29% – still very good. The debtors turnover reflects the 2-months credit terms they require from shops, and the high stock turnover reflects both the high value added reflected in the board price and the minimal stocking policy they are trying to adhere to.

The high margin of safety leads them to believe that this is a relatively low-risk venture. The pair do intend to pay themselves more in the second year of trading; however, a quick calculation shows them that they could double their salaries and still make over 50% return on total assets at this level of profitability. This gives them confidence that, if all goes according to plan, they should look forward to expanding the business in its second year.

$$\text{Current ratio} = \frac{\text{Current assets}}{\text{Current liabilities}} = \frac{£162,178}{£24,680} = 6.6$$

$$\text{Quick ratio} = \frac{\text{Current assets, excl.stock}}{\text{Current liabilities}} = \frac{£116,640}{£24,680} = 4.7$$

Despite the early need for cash, the business looks highly liquid by the end of the first period because of the high value of debtors, compared to creditors, again reflecting the high value added in the board price. The pair are, however, very aware that earlier in the year, when the actual overdraft was far higher, these ratios would have been much lower.

$$\text{Gearing} = \frac{\text{All loans + overdraft}}{\text{Shareholders' funds}} = \frac{£15,960}{£184,478} = 8.7\%$$

Not only is this gearing level low, the outstanding interest-free loan is from the founders and not from an external borrower. This encourages them to think that not only might the company repay their loan early next year, but it also should be in a very strong position to borrow money to expand. The founders conclude that these financial forecasts look very encouraging. However, being inherently cautious, they are aware that they are just forecasts and the pair will have to work hard to turn them into reality.

QUESTION:

1 Do you agree with the founders about the projected performance of the company? What reservations might you have?

 Practice insight reminder Characteristics of a good business idea – 13 & 14

13 **Management skill that can be leveraged** – you need to have the appropriate management skills, and if you do not, you need to acquire them or recruit or partner with others with the appropriate skills.

14 **Scalable** – small projects can usually get off the ground easily but bigger projects can be problematic because they are just 'too big'. In which case, you need to see whether the project can be broken down into smaller projects that can be implemented when the original idea is proved – scalability. The idea is to avoid as much risk as possible for as long as possible – but to make sure you do not miss the window of opportunity completely. This is all a question of judgement and changing market conditions, so you need to remain flexible and think through how you might scale-up the project when it proves successful.

⊃ Summary

> Stage models of growth tell us about the different problems and organizational imperatives at different stages in the development of a commercial or social enterprise. These often mean that the entrepreneur must learn new skills at different stages.

> Structures create order but there is no single 'best' structure. This depends on task complexity and environmental turbulence.

> The greater the complexity of tasks and the more staff have to use their cognitive abilities to undertake these tasks within the context of a changing environment, then the greater the need for autonomy. Autonomy is, however, not enough on its own. It needs to be combined a sense of 'purpose' and the challenge of 'mastery' of that task. It can be influenced through giving individuals direction, slack, boundaries and support. And finally, it needs to be combined with a strong accountability.

> The first step in growing the business is to understand how it has survived so far – what has worked and what has not, how the original launch strategies have been adapted to suite unanticipated changes to the competitive environment.

> A social enterprise needs to review both its commercial and social activities. The virtuous circle that generates social capital can lead to growth and the building of capacity.

> Most growing organizations go through a reoccurring process of growth, followed by crisis, followed by a period of consolidation. This parallels a process of emergent to deliberate and back to emergent strategy formulation.

> These constantly reoccurring crises can cause the entrepreneur to endure an emotional roller coaster of a journey, diminishing their effectiveness.

> A framework for developing strategy is useful but a good one should be minimalist. Effective strategy is rooted in the distinctive capabilities of the firm.

> Entrepreneurs develop a strong vision for what the organization might become, but more particularly, they develop a strong 'strategic intent', accompanied by a loose or flexible strategy underpinned by continuous strategizing from which they create multiple strategic options.

> Strategy development in most growing small firms is likely to be incremental and adaptive – emergent rather than deliberate – with strategic intent giving direction. However, small firms do adopt both types of strategy development, depending upon circumstances, with shifts from one mode to another precipitated by some form of crisis.

> Figure 12.15 outlines a process for a strategic review. This involves questioning all aspects of the business, including your fundamental vision for it, and builds on the information continuously being gained from the competitive environment.

> Strategic analysis involves undertaking a SWOT analysis and highlighting the core competencies of the organization. However, there are a number of other tools that can also help. The main ones are summarized in Table 12.1.

> Financial ratio analysis is an important tool in a SWOT analysis. It allows you to assess your financial performance. Based on the premise that shareholders want to maximize the return they make on their investment, it provides information on how profit might be increased and assets reduced. It also provides information about risk, liquidity and gearing (or leverage).

> Ratio analysis can be based both on forecast and actual financial information. Ratios can be compared to industry norms or used to assess trends over time.

> Strategy formulation involves identifying, evaluating and selecting strategic options. The New Venture Creation Framework and the Business Model Canvas can be used to 'tinker' with your business model and explore alternative scenarios and develop strategic options. They are strategic frameworks that encourage strategizing.

> Research indicates that the strategy with the best chance of generating sustainable growth and the highest profits is to differentiate with the aim of dominating your market as quickly as possible, and to continue to innovate around that differential advantage. Gaining rapid market dominance may come from internal growth but may also involve acquisition of competitors. So the advice is: differentiate, dominate and innovate.

✓ Activities

1 List the questions you would ask an entrepreneur in order to explore the crises they have faced in managing a growing business. Based on these questions, interview a successful entrepreneur and use this as the basis for an essay describing the challenges they faced as the business grew and how they coped.

2 Prepare a SWOT analysis on your course, college, university or university department.

3 Undertake a financial ratio analysis on the financial statements of a SME (or social enterprise).

4 Prepare a SWOT analysis on a SME (or social enterprise).

5 Undertake a full strategic review of a SME (or social enterprise).

6 Outline your launch strategy using either the New Venture Creation Framework or the Business Model Canvas. Use the framework to explore alternative scenarios and develop your strategic options.

💬 Group discussion topics

1 How does the role of and the skills needed by the founder change as the business grows?

2 Is Greiner's model an accurate predictor of the growth process?

3 Is operational capability more important than strategy at start-up?

4 How are the reoccurring crises facing the growing firm likely to affect the entrepreneur and what might be the consequences?

5 How do you determine the degree of control you should exercise over staff?

6 Why and in what circumstances is autonomy important?

7 How will a social enterprise know if it is successful?

8 What are the effects of a social enterprise being over-reliant on an external stakeholder such as government?

9 What are the differences between the accumulation of social capital and financial capital?

10 Can you undertake a financial ratio analysis on a social enterprise? What would it tell you?

11 What should happen when a social enterprise meets and fulfils its social objectives?

12 How do entrepreneurs develop strategy? Explain and give examples.

13 What are the advantages of using strategic frameworks like the New Venture Creation Framework or the Business Model Canvas?

14 If your business model is constantly changing to suit changing circumstances, when (if ever) should you write a business plan?

15 What might cause you to change your core values and beliefs?

16 How can you review the effectiveness of strategy if you do not know what might have happened if it had been different?

17 How can you make a SWOT analysis as objective as possible?

18 What are competencies and capabilities? Explain and give examples.

19 How would you go about undertaking a SWOT analysis on an established SME?

20 In different contexts strengths can be weaknesses and opportunities can be threats. Discuss.

21 You cannot determine profit in a SME because there are just too many ways the owner-manager can manipulate it. Therefore, any form of financial analysis will not work. Discuss.

22 In a global marketplace, how can you ever dominate a market?

23 How important is 'first-mover advantage'?

24 Everything can be copied, therefore competitive advantage can never be sustained. Discuss.

👉 References

3i European Enterprise Centre (1993) *Britain's Superleague Companies*, Report 9, August.

Birley, S. and Westhead, P. (1990) 'Growth and Performance Contrasts between Types of Small Firms', *Strategic Management Journal*, II.

Birkinshaw, J. (2003) 'The Paradox of Corporate Entrepreneurship', *Strategy and Business*, 30.

Boston Consulting Group (1968) *Perspectives on Experience*, Boston, MA: Boston Consulting Group.

Boston Consulting Group (1972) *Perspectives on Experience*, Boston, MA: Boston Consulting Group.

Burns, P. (1994) *Winners and Losers in the 1990s*, 3i European Enterprise Centre, Report 12, April.

Burns, P. (1996) 'Growth' in P. Burns and J. Dewhurst (eds), *Small Business and Entrepreneurship*, London: Macmillan.

Burns, P. (2013) *Corporate Entrepreneurship: Innovation and Strategy in Large Organizations*, Basingstoke: Palgrave Macmillan.

Burns, P. (2014) *New Venture Creation: A Framework for Entrepreneurial Start-ups*, Basingstoke: Palgrave.

Burns, P. and Whitehouse, O. (1995a) *Investment Criteria in Europe*, 3i European Enterprise Centre, Report 16, July.

Burns, P. and Whitehouse, O. (1995b) *Financing Enterprise in Europe*, 3i European Enterprise Centre, Report 17, October.

Buzzell, R.D., Heany, D.F. and Schoeffer, S. (1974) 'Impact of Strategic Planning on Profit Performance', *Harvard Business Review*, 52/2.

Buzzell, R.D. and Gale, B.T. (1987) *The PIMS Principles – Linking Strategy to Performance*, New York: Free Press.

Calvo, J.E. (2006) 'Testing Gibrat's Law for Small, Young and Innovating Firms', *Small Business Economics*, 26(2).

Casadesus-Masanell, R. and Ricart, J.E, (2010) 'From Strategy to Business Models and into Tactics', *Long Range Planning*, 43(2/3).

Cope, J. (2005) 'Toward a Dynamic Learning Perspective of Entrepreneurship', *Entrepreneurship Theory and Practice*, 29(4).

Churchill, N.C. and Lewis, V.L. (1983) 'The Five Stages of Small Business Growth', *Harvard Business Review*, May/June.

Dell, M. (1999) *Direct from Dell: Strategies that Revolutionized an Industry*, New York: Harper Business.

Dunkelberg, W.G., Cooper, A.C., Woo, C. and Dennis, W.J. (1987) 'New Firm Growth and Performance', in J. Harrison and B. Taylor (eds), (1996) *Supergrowth Companies: Entrepreneurs in Action*, Oxford: Butterworth-Heinemann.

Freel, M.S. (2000) 'Do Small Innovating Firms Outperform Non-innovators?', *Small Business Economics*, 14(3).

Geroski, P. and Machin S. (1992) 'Do Innovating Firms Outperform Non-Innovators?', *Business Strategy Review*, Summer.

Grant, R.M. (2012) *Contemporary Strategic Analysis*, 8th edn, Chichester: John Wiley.

Greiner, L.E. (1972) 'Evolution and Revolution as Organizations Grow', *Harvard Business Review*, July/August.

Harrison, J. and Taylor, B. (1996) *Supergrowth Companies: Entrepreneurs in Action*, Oxford: Butterworth-Heineman.

Harrison, J.S., Bosse, D.A. and Phillips, R.A. (2010) 'Managing Shareholder Utility Functions and Competitive Advantage', *Strategic Management Journal*, 31(1).

Kay, J. (1998) *Foundations of Corporate Success*, Oxford: Oxford University Press.

Kakabadse, A. (1983) *The Politics of Management*, London: Gower.

Kübler-Ross, E. (1969) *On Death and Dying*, Abingdon: Routledge.

Leadbeater, C. (1997) *The Rise of the Social Entrepreneur*, London: Demos.

Lindblom, L.E. (1959) 'The Science of Muddling Through', *Public Administration Review*, 19, Spring.

Lusch, R.F., Vargo, S.L. and Tanniru, M. (2010) 'Service, Value Networks and Learning,' *Journal of the Academy of Marketing Science*, 38(1).

Macmillan, I.C. and Seldon, L. (2008) 'The Incumbent's Advantage', *Harvard Business Review*, 86(1).

Macrae, D.J.R. (1991) 'Characteristics of High and Low Growth Small and Medium Sized Businesses', *21st European Small Business Seminar*, Barcelona, Spain.

Markides, C. and Geroski, P.A. (2005) *Fast Second*, San Francisco: Jossey-Bass.

McCarthy, B. and Leavy, B. (2000) 'Strategy Formation in Irish SMEs: A Phase Model of Process', *British Academy of Management Annual Conference*, Edinburgh.

Mintzberg, H. (1978) 'Patterns in Strategy Formation', *Management Science*.

Newbert, S.L. (2008) 'Value, Rareness, Competitive Advantage and Performance: A Conceptual Level Empirical Investigation of the Resource-Based View of the Firm', *Strategic Management Journal*, 29(7).

Nohria, N. and Joyce, W. (2003) 'What Really Works', *Harvard Business Review*, July/August.

Osterwalder, A. and Pigneur, Y. (2010), *Business Model Generation: A Handbook for Visionaries, Game Changers and Challengers*, New Jersey: John Wiley & Sons.

Pink, D. (2011) *Drive: The Surprising Truth about What Motivates Us*, New York: Riverhead.

Porter, M.E. (1985) *Competitive Advantage: Creating and Sustaining Superior Performance*, New York: The Free Press.

Porter, M.E. and Kramer, M.R. (2002) 'The Competitive Advantage of Corporate Philanthropy', *Harvard Business Review*, December.

Porter, M.E. and Kramer, M.R. (2006) 'Strategy and Society: The Link between Competitive Advantage and Corporate Social Responsibility', *Harvard Business Review*, 12.

Prahalad, C.K. and Hamel, G (1990) 'The Core Competence of the Corporation', *Harvard Business Review*, 68(3), May/June.

Ray, G.H. and Hutchinson, P.J. (1983) *The Financing and Financial Control of Small Enterprise Development*, London: Gower.

Read, S., Sarasvathy, S., Dew, N., Wiltbank, R. and Ohisson, A-V. (2011) *Effectual Entrepreneurship*, London: Routledge.

Ries, E. (2011) *The Lean Start-up: How Today's Entrepreneurs Use Continuous Innovation to Create Radically Successful Businesses*, New York: Crown Publishing.

Roper, S. (1999) 'Modelling Small Business Growth and Profitability', *Small Business Economics*, 13(3).

Sarasvathy, S.D. (2001) 'Causation and Effectuation: Towards a Theoretical Shift Economic Inevitability to Entrepreneneurial Contingency', *Academy of Management Review*, 26(2).

Scott, M. and Bruce, R. (1987) 'Five Stages of Growth in Small Business', *Long Range Planning*, 20(3).

Siegel, R., Siegel, E. and MacMillan, I.C. (1993) 'Characteristics Distinguishing High Growth Ventures, *Journal of Business Venturing*, 8.

Solem, O. and Steiner, M.P. (1989) 'Factors for Success in Small Manufacturing Firms – and with Special Emphasis on Growing firms', *Conference on SMEs and the Challenges of 1992*, Mikkeli, Finland.

Storey, D.J. and Greene, F.J. (2010) *Small Business and Entrepreneurship*, Harlow: Pearson Education.

Storey, D.J., Watson, R. and Wynarczyk, P. (1989) *Fast Growth Small Business: Case Studies of 40 Small Firms in Northern Ireland*, Department of Employment, Research Paper No 67.

Sull, D. (2005) 'Strategy as Active Waiting', *Harvard Business Review*, September.

Treacy, M. and Wiersema, F. (1995) *The Discipline of Market Leaders*, Reading, MA: Addison-Wesley.

Woo, C.Y., Cooper, A.C., Dunkelberg, W.C., Daellenbach, U. and Dennis, W.J. (1989) 'Determinants of Growth for Small and Large Entrepreneurial Start-Ups', *Babson Entrepreneurship Conference*.

Wynarczyk, P., Watson, R., Storey, D.J., Short, H. and Keasey, K. (1993) *The Managerial Labour Market in Small and Medium-Sized Enterprises*, London: Routledge.

Wu, L.Y. (2010) 'Applicability of the Resource-Based and Dynamic Capability Views Under Environmental Volatility', *Journal of Business Research*, 63(1).

Yelle, L.E. (1979) 'The Learning Curve: Historical Review and Comprehensive Survey', *Decision Sciences*, 10.

Zott, C. and Amit, R. (2010) 'Business Model Design: An Activity System Perspective', *Long Range Planning*, 43(2/3).

www.palgrave.com/Burns-Entrepreneurship-And-Small-Business-4e

Go online to access additional teaching and learning resources for this chapter on the companion website. Click here in the ebook to complete a multiple choice revision quiz for this chapter.

13 | STRATEGIES FOR GROWTH

Contents

© Woody Pictures/Corbis

Learning outcomes

When you have read this chapter and undertaken the related activities you will be able to:

> Critically evaluate the strategic options for growth and understand the implications for a start-up;
> Understand how to go about selling into new markets;
> Understand what is involved in product development;
> Critically evaluate the effects of product life cycles on marketing strategy and how the life cycle can be lengthened through product expansion and extension;
> Use the Growth Share Matrix to communicate marketing strategies for a portfolio of products;
> Show advanced knowledge of the effects of the product portfolio on cash flow and how the product portfolio can be managed;
> Critically evaluate the use of acquisition as part of a growth strategy and the advantages and disadvantages of diversification.

 *Practice insight*: Help and advice on exporting

 *Practice insight reminder*: Characteristics of a good business idea

 Case insights

Fat Face	AussieCommerce Group (2)
Zoobug	Brompton Bicycle (3)
B&Q China	Reliance Industries
Levi's jeans	Amazon
Crocs	

Growth options

Initially start-ups grow by increasing sales of their product or service in the target market(s) they have identified. This is called **penetrating the market(s)**. Businesses start by penetrating their existing market with their existing product or service as quickly as possible. They will probably have started to move from a selective distribution network to a more intensive network that gets them to more of their target market and probably a broader geographic base. At the same time, they may already be adopting a more aggressive promotion and pricing strategy that encourages further market penetration ahead of the emerging competition. Alongside this, they will be building the brand as a vital part of their promotional message. The question that arises is how to achieve further growth once the original market has been successfully penetrated and its limits reached. Investors are always looking at the scalability potential of a business. Once the initial idea has been proved in the market, where will future growth come from? Unless we are talking about a lifestyle business with limited growth potential, some consideration must be given to this in the business plan, even for a start-up. The extent of planning depends on the time scale and degree of certainty for this growth.

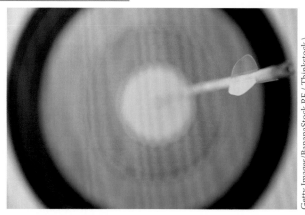

Getty Images/BananaStock RF / Thinkstock \ BananaStock

Once the original market has been successfully penetrated there are three growth options:

1   Market development – selling the existing product or service into new markets.
2   Product or service development – developing the original business idea into new products or services that can be sold into existing markets.
3   Diversification – selling new products or services into new markets. Often this option is pursued through mergers or acquisitions.

Figure 13.1 presents a simple framework for looking at these options in a systematic way. We shall discuss each in turn.

Market development

Market development is the natural extension of market penetration. Instead of just selling more of the same to your existing customers, you go out and find new customers and new markets for those products or services. There are four reasons for selecting market development as a route for expansion:

1   To achieve economies of scale of production. This is particularly important if cost leadership is your core value proposition and is dependent upon achieving these economies.

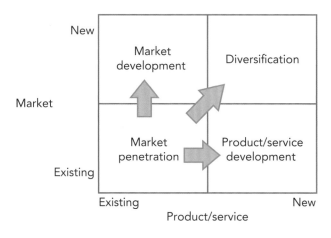

Figure 13.1 Growth options

After you've launched your business, while you are still privately-owned … what you have to do is grow very fast, so that some day when you have to really drop a lot of dollars to the bottom line, you've laid in a base that can still grow at maybe 10% or 20% a year … Five years into being a public company, you can never do that again.

Kevin Surace, founder, Serious Materials, *BBC News Business*, 20 June 2010

We have always very carefully managed growth against profitability. Cash is king.

Eileen Gittins, founder, Blurb, *BBC News Business*, 11 December 2012

When expanding into different territories or creating new products, having a brand uniting them all under one roof is one of the best advantages a business can have.

Richard Branson, founder, Virgin Group, *The Guardian, Media Planet*, May 2015

2   Your key competency lies with your product, for example with technology-based products in which you have some intellectual property (IP) and you need to exploit your IP by finding new markets to sell the product into within a limited window of opportunity. Most technology-based companies follow this strategy – opening up new overseas markets as existing markets become saturated – because of the high cost of developing new products. By way of contrast, many service businesses such as consultancies have been pulled into overseas markets because their clients operate there. A large-scale survey of EU manufacturing businesses (Hauser and Wagner, 2010) found that innovation activity had a significant impact on export intensity.

3   The product is nearing the end of its life cycle in the existing market and you need to develop new markets, if you can find them, to continue to grow.

4   To reduce the risk of overdependency on one market. This is particularly the case for geographic markets that might face similar economic cycles.

Any growing firm will have to find new customers, and the key to doing so is to understand the customers it already has – who they are and why they buy – and then try to find more customers with similar profiles. Many firms start out by selling locally and gradually expand their geographic base by selling regionally and then nationally. However, it is one thing to find new customers in a market that you are familiar with, but it is quite another to enter completely new markets, even when you are selling existing products or services that you are familiar with. Nevertheless, if you want to grow you will have to do so. These new markets might be new market segments – the ones you originally identified but did not have the resources to target. They might be new geographical areas – often foreign markets. The low-risk option is to seek out segments in the countries that are similar to the ones already sold to.

Trying to sell the same product or service to new market segments usually involves reconfiguring the marketing mix in some way so as to 'fine-tune' your value proposition. Sometimes market development and product development might go hand in hand, since the move into a new market segment may involve the development of variants to the existing product offering by altering the marketing mix or making minor changes to the product range. However, we are talking about incremental and minor changes rather than brand-new products.

As we saw in Chapter 5, the structure of any new market – its customers, suppliers, competitors – and the potential substitutes and barriers to entry determine the degree of competition and therefore the profitability you are likely to achieve. Porter's Five Forces analysis is a valuable tool that can equally be applied to help assess the potential of a new market.

 ## Case insight   Fat Face

Market development

Tim Slade and Julian Leaver began selling their own printed t-shirts in a shop in the ski resort of Méribel, France, in 1988. They were skiers, but had run out of money and sold their belongings, including a Volkswagen camper van, to purchase plain T-shirts on which to print logos. The whole idea was to finance their lifestyle as 'ski-bums'. The first Fat Face store was opened in the UK in 1993. Fat Face has now become an up-market brand for all sorts of casual leisurewear, selling through an international network of shops.

In 2000 Julian Leaver explained what they were trying to achieve:

'When you buy a Fat Face product, you are not just buying the fleece, you are buying the experience – the chat in the shop about the snow in Val d'Isère – or surfing in Cowes. Staff are selected because they are passionate about the lifestyle.'

In 2000 the company raised £5 million expansion capital from Friends Ivory & Sime Private Equity to finance their expansion but they were careful to manage the brand as they expanded. Julian Leaver explained once more:

'We could easily wholesale the hell out of it and be in every ski and surf shop and department store inside

Continued...

Continued from previous page...

a year. Within two years, we would have trashed the brand.' (*The Sunday Times*, 27 February 2000)

Slow, planned expansion came through increasing the range of leisurewear products and increasing the number of shops in Britain and Europe and eventually the rest of the world, making certain that the right sort of staff, with the right sort of personality, were recruited. Initially Fat Face entered new markets based upon intuition and on an experimental basis, and later they undertook more professional market research. Across all their markets their typical customer is a well-off professional in their mid 30–40s who enjoys skiing or water sports. And they tried to keep close to their customers by getting feedback by email and having regular face-to-face focus meetings. They have a loyal customer following. The key to their successful expansion has been good brand management. All Fat Face shops have the same 'fun' feel with enthusiastic young staff. And while the product range has been expanded into shoes, bags and jewellery, they all have the same lifestyle, sporty image. The company is also very good at stock management. They have regular, but limited, sales and rotate unsold stock around their network of stores for these events. This maintains the interest of their loyal customers and encourages them to visit the store to browse through the sale items.

In 2005 Tim and Julian sold their major shareholding in the company to Advent for £100 million. Advent in turn sold it on to Bridgepoint Capital in 2007 for £360 million. Tim and Julian are millionaires and retain a minor stake in the company. They both still enjoy skiing.

❑ Visit the website at: www.fatface.com

QUESTIONS:

1 What are the advantages and disadvantages of a systematic market development?

2 What sort of businesses might prefer a different approach?

Internationalization

At some point, rather than just finding new customers, a growing company will need to look for new markets. This is called market expansion. For many businesses this involves internationalization. As SMEs grow in size they are more likely to be involved in international markets (Selassie et al., 2004). We have already noted that there appears to be a significant relationship between internationalization and financial performance (Chelliah et al., 2010), although others (Lu and Beamish, 2001) have noted that this might be preceded by a decline for a short period as resources are invested in developing the new market. What is more, Zahra et al. (2009) suggested that having a wider international market scope can enhance future product innovation by exposing SMEs to a 'rich network of information'. We also noted that Kuhlmeier and Knight (2010) linked four dimensions of internationalization to performance, particularly in export markets: relationship quality, cooperation, trust and commitment. Cooperation and commitment were significant drivers of performance and trust underpinned commitment, and communication drives cooperation, trust and commitment.

So how do SMEs approach the move into foreign markets? While some businesses are international from birth (Anderson et al., 2004), the stage model of growth suggests most start selling in their home markets and progress incrementally to overseas markets. There are two stage models of internationalization. The first is the **Product Life Cycle Theory** (Vernon, 1966, 1971, 1979) which proposed that firms first introduce new products into their home market, followed by exporting as overseas demand grows and the product ages in its home market. Many manufacturing businesses sell overseas because their key competence lies in the product they produce and they need to open up new markets as their existing ones become saturated. Most capital goods companies follow this strategy. Finally, these companies start producing overseas as the product nears the end of its life cycle and cost reduction becomes important. Eventually these foreign producers may start to export themselves as price becomes the driving competitive force. By way of contrast, many service businesses such as accounting, advertising, consulting etc. are 'pulled' into overseas markets because their clients operate there. Vernon admitted that this model had lost much of its explanatory power as technological developments accelerated, but he still proposed it as offering a guide to behaviour of some firms (Vernon, 1979).

The second, more widely used model, based upon a study of Swedish manufacturing firms, is called the **Uppsala Internationalization Model** (Johanson and Wiedersheim-Paul, 1975; Johanson and Vahlne, 1977, 1990, 2006). This placed learning and knowledge acquisition at the centre of the process by proposing that firms increase their knowledge about foreign markets before expanding abroad. They target psychically close markets – ones that they feel mentally comfortable with – initially using market entry methods that require limited commitment, such as exporting. As they gain knowledge and experience from their market involvement over time, so they increase their commitment. This process is repeated from market to market. This form of creeping incremental internationalization is called '**graduated entry**'. Small firms start with low-cost, low-risk entry modes and then, if the experience is rewarded, they move to more complex, often higher-risk, modes – a sort of international lean start-up.

Leonidou and Katsikeas (1996) characterized this as having three phases – pre-engagement, initial and advanced. The pre-engagement phase is when the firm is active in its domestic market but not in an export market. The initial phase is when it has sporadic or exploratory export activity. The advanced phase is when it is actively and consistently involved in exporting and internationalization of its activities. If these phases are successful the firm builds confidence, eventually embedding internationalization into the mainstream of its activities – the advanced phase. However, should it experience failure then it can retrench and re-evaluate its growth options without endangering its core markets and activities.

The Uppsala Model is appealing, not least because of its inherent risk-minimizing logic. It also mirrors the way entrepreneurs 'learn by doing'. In addition, the stepwise progression towards internationalization mirrors the incremental approach entrepreneurs have towards business development and decision-making. It is also conditionally compatible with the 'resource-based' view of internationalization. As the firm develops its resource base over time, so too will it develop its export capability.

However, the model has been criticized (Leonidou and Katsikeas, op. cit.). While firms seem to fit into different stages of the model at any point of time (using cross-sectional data), there is no empirical evidence of dynamic progression based upon longitudinal studies over time. Indeed, the existence of international start-ups (Chapter 6) suggests that this model is but one of a number of approaches to internationalization, and it has been suggested that firms may skip or compress different stages to the point where the model becomes meaningless (Sullivan and Bauerschmidt, 1990; Welch and Loustarinen, 1988). From a logical viewpoint, graduated entry can also be criticized because it fails to recognize first-mover advantage and the competitive reaction to the failure to exploit it. That is not to say that the model was not a meaningful generalization when it was proposed. However, the world continues to change rapidly and once-distant markets now seem altogether closer – which is causing management attitudes to shift and first-mover advantage to take on a shorter time frame.

Selling into foreign markets

These stage models highlight the process that a SME might go through in developing its overseas markets, each stage requiring a greater degree of resource commitment and risk:

Exporting

There are many ways to enter a foreign market. If your competitive advantage is based on resources located in your home country, then the form this takes should be exporting. Exporting is also often a low-cost, low-risk way of finding out about a market. It can take the form of spot sales – one-off sales to individual customers. As we saw with the Figleaves Case insight on page 154, this is now much easier with the advent of the internet. However, exporting can also bring risks. It is, for example, far more difficult to recover bad debts from overseas customers. To overcome this, governments often sponsor insurance schemes that cover bad debts, like the Export Credit

Guarantee Scheme in the UK. Also, if you are selling into an overseas market in local currency, there is the risk of currency fluctuations that mean the value of the transaction in your currency is not guaranteed. The answer to this is to price in your currency – something often done for small value transactions – or to 'forward-purchase' the local currency, thus guaranteeing the amount you receive. This service is offered by most banks.

Sales agent

PhotoDisc/Getty Images

However, if you need to achieve market presence in foreign distribution channels you will probably need a local sales agent. A good agent should have valuable local knowledge and might suggest changes to the product or other elements of the marketing mix to better suit local needs. They might expect you to finance or contribute to advertising and promotion – and with no certainty of a profitable return. Finding an agent can be difficult enough but if, for whatever reason, they do not meet your sales targets then there is little you can do other than change your agent, if you can terminate the contract. Then the only alternative may be to set up a sales outlet of your own in the country – and that can be both expensive and risky. Sales agents can also bring the same risks as exporting – bad debt and currency fluctuations.

However, the relationship is not all one-sided. The sales agents – often themselves small firms – also face risks. Firstly, they are likely to be paid on a commission-only basis – no sales, no commission. They may have an exclusive contract but it will relate to a specified geographic area, so they cannot expand without the agreement of the exporter. Nor are they likely to be able to sell competing products. What is more, the contract will be time-limited so that if they are too successful, exporters may be tempted to distribute the product themselves and save paying the commission. Agents may be expected to finance advertising and promotion themselves but they are likely to be dependent on the exporter for a range of sales and promotional information and materials. All of these things will be set out in the contract, and when the contract comes to an end, its terms can be renegotiated. Finally, the agent is completely dependent on the exporter for product and product range development. If the exporter does not invest in this, the agent may have difficulties, no matter how good their sales skills. There are inherent dangers in having an agent, particularly when there is information asymmetry (one party having more knowledge than another) that can make the relationship unbalanced and unstable. If the balance of power or dependency shifts too far from one party to the other, the relationship may be threatened. There must be trust based upon a mutuality of interest for any agency agreement to work effectively. We shall look at this in Chapter 14 when we consider agency theory in the context of the provision of finance.

Licence and franchise

Another approach to entering foreign markets is to offer a local firm a licence to produce your product or offer your service. This allows the licensee to capitalize on their local knowledge but requires them also to take on many of the business risks. Their local market knowledge and dedication is vital if the market is to be effectively penetrated. For a service business, the equivalent is to appoint a Head Franchisee who will be responsible for the franchise roll-out in their country (Chapter 9). They might operate some franchises themselves and also offer it to others. Franchises offer a fairly standard format to the particular market in which they operate. If the franchise roll-out is successful, the Head Franchisee shares in the success. As with an agent, to be effective, the firm and their franchisee or distributor must have a symbiotic relationship, one based upon mutual trust but with effective incentives and legal safeguards to ensure success. The Body Shop's rapid growth over 30 years owes much to its successful global roll-out using a franchise format. In most countries a Head Franchisee was granted exclusive rights as distributor and user of the trademark, and, after an initial trial of running a few shops themselves, the right to subfranchise. In this way, The Body Shop built upon local market knowledge and minimized its risks. The model was not successful in every country; for example, The Body Shop had to take back control of the franchise in France because the Head Franchisee was not delivering the volume of sales expected.

Strategic alliance, partnership and joint venture

The next stage in involvement in a foreign market is to form a strategic alliance, partnership or joint venture, whereby the partner brings different resources to the joint venture and shares the profits as well as the risks (see Chapter 9). Lu and Beamish (op. cit.) found that an alliance with partners with local knowledge was an effective strategy to overcome the deficiencies SMEs face in resources and capabilities. They can be vital in providing insights into effective market entry and competitive strategies (Coviello and Munro, 1995). In some developing economies, the only way to enter the market may be through a joint venture with a local firm. Used properly, strategic alliances, partnerships and joint ventures can leverage up the capabilities of the firm (Laanti et al., 2007).

Direct investment

The final stage is direct investment. This involves the setting up of a wholly-owned subsidiary which may involve simply marketing and distribution or be fully integrated into the operations of your company. Clearly this is an expensive option, normally only taken by larger companies. These different degrees of involvement in foreign markets and the increasing risk associated with them are shown in Figure 13.2. There is no prescriptive 'best' approach to internationalization and often the degree of involvement in the foreign market increases with the success of the product or service.

It is important to undertake a thorough market and country analysis before deciding to get involved in a foreign market with any degree of investment (anything beyond a sales agent). You are assessing the opportunities there but also the risks you will face. You need to undertake an economic analysis of the environment of the country – domestic demand, local laws and regulations, government policies, exchange rates, related and supporting industries etc. Try using the PESTEL analysis from Chapter 4. You can use Porter's Five Forces analysis to assess profit potential but, in addition to entry barriers, you should also consider the exit barriers you face. Exit barriers can arise from legal constraints and/or high costs associated with exit. Just as high entry barriers increase profit potential (because they discourage new competitors), high exit barriers increase the risks you face because, if you do not find the market profitable, exiting it might be expensive or even prohibited.

Every country needs to be evaluated in its own right – and not just using strict economic criteria. Cultural differences can greatly affect consumer preferences. Some of the most economically attractive countries can prove the most difficult to penetrate. For example, China is proving

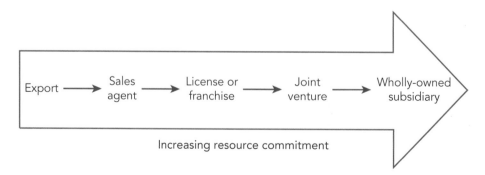

Figure 13.2 Degree of involvement in foreign markets

particularly difficult for Western retailers to penetrate. In 2013 the UK's largest supermarket, Tesco, announced that 80% of its Chinese operation would be bought by the state-run China Resources Enterprise Ltd., the country's second largest supermarket chain. Earlier that year, Germany's Metro AG announced it was pulling out of consumer electronics, and in 2012 the US Home Depot Inc. announced the closure of a number of stores across China.

 Practice insight Help and advice on exporting

Brand X Pictures

Governments across the world are keen to encourage SMEs to export. They offer a range of help and advice, including market intelligence about particular countries, much of which is free. They organize seminars, trade fairs and missions. Because they have their own network of contacts, government agencies can often put you in touch with potential partners or agents. In the UK, the government offers financial support for exporters that can guarantee against bad debts. It also has a register of business opportunities. Here are some useful first-stop websites:

UK

UK export website: https://www.gov.uk/government/organisations/uk-trade-investment
For online advice: http://www.bestbusinessoffers.co.uk/UKTI
The Institute of Export: http://www.export.org.uk/
HMRC provides information about taxes and tariffs: http://customs.hmrc.gov.uk/channelsPortalWebApp/channelsPortalWebApp.portal

Europe

EU export help-desk: http://www.exporthelp.europa.eu

USA

US export website: http://export.gov/

Case insight Zoobug

Exporting

Julie Diem Le was a successful 29-year-old eye surgeon with the NHS and a member of the Royal College of Ophthalmologists when she decided to start up her own business. It started when she tried to buy a pair of sunglasses for her young niece. She regularly saw young eyes damaged by bright sunshine and yet could not find a pair that provided maximum protection from the harmful rays of the sun. She also realized that few were also both fashionable and comfortable to wear. The idea therefore formed to produce an up-market, fashionable but ophthalmologically correct range of sunglasses for children. Having attended a government-funded start-up course in Birmingham, Julie wrote a business plan and, on the back of the plan, obtained a £35,000 loan from NatWest Bank. She found an Italian designer to help create the first spectacles for children aged 7 to 16. A month later in 2006 she launched her company,

Zoobug, at the Premier Kids trade exhibition in Birmingham, offering the Flexibug range of sunglasses.

Within a year she was selling more than 2,000 pairs of sunglasses a month through up-market opticians and stores like Selfridges. But things rarely go according to plan and she had to adjust both her prices and target age range downwards as she discovered what the market actually wanted. Also, two summers of poor weather in the UK convinced her that she needed to sell the sunglasses overseas if she was to do well. She funded this with another £60,000 loan. In 2008 she added a range of optical frames for children aged 2 to 12 to her product portfolio, launching them at an exhibition in Milan. The sunglasses are made in Italy and the Far East. By 2009, sales of optical frames outstripped those of sunglasses and Julie was selling sunglasses and optical frames in 20 countries, eight through official distributors. France was her biggest market, ahead of the UK.

Continued...

Continued from previous page...

'It was helpful that I started with sunglasses because it meant I had to look overseas for new business because there wasn't any sun in Britain. So I already had distributors in place overseas when the recession began. If we just relied on the British market, we wouldn't exist ... It is really hard work. When you first approach it, it is fun and you don't really know what is involved so you go in there with a lot of bravado. When you get down to the nitty-gritty, this industry is all about building relationships, and you have to fulfil your promise every time in stock, distribution and supply ... I'm glad I did it. The experience has taught me a lot about business which I could never learn in a book.' (*The Sunday Times*, 24 May 2009)

By 2014 the company had six staff based in its north London offices. Its website now generates 10% of sales but the company also sells in the UK through stores like Selfridges, Harrods and Igloo as well as 300 British opticians. Zoobug continues to sell strongly overseas and plans to expand its overseas presence into China, South Korea and Australia.

❏ **Visit the website: www.zoobug.co.uk**

QUESTIONS:

1 What are the advantages and disadvantages of exporting for Zoobug?

2 What are the problems it brings?

 ## Case insight   B&Q China

Moving into overseas markets

British retailers have a history of failure in overseas ventures and the experience of B&Q, the UK do-it-yourself (DIY) store chain, in setting up in China is interesting. B&Q opened its first store in China in 1999. Up until 2005, when China joined the World Trade Organization, foreign retailers were prevented from opening more than three stores in any one city and some towns were completely off limits. What is more, they had to work with Chinese partners. B&Q did deals with a number of Chinese organizations, normally giving them a 35% stake in the business, but making it very clear that B&Q intended to buy them out at soon as it could – which it typically did in 2005. Also in 2005, it acquired 13 stores of OBI (a German DIY retailer) in China for an undisclosed sum, all of which have been converted to the B&Q format.

The stores were initially a huge success and the Beijing store boasted the highest average customer spend of any of its stores in the world (over £50). But it is the cultural similarities and differences and how they affected the retailer that are really interesting. The stores looked very similar to those in the UK, although they were usually considerably bigger. At 20,000 sq ft, the Beijing Golden Four Season store was the largest of its kind in the world. Like their UK counterparts, staff wore orange overalls. The products offered were also very similar, although the space devoted to garden products was considerably smaller and the Chinese B&Q also sold soft furnishings.

But the big difference is that Chinese customers do not want to 'do-it' themselves at all, they prefer to get others to do it for them. The Chinese customers were typically middle class and wealthy. They came to the store to select what they wanted and get it installed by a professional. The reasons for this are partly cultural and partly economic. Labour is significantly cheaper than in the West, but also things like decorating are regarded as a major DIY job in China. What is more, if you buy one of the thousands of apartments being built in Beijing you buy a concrete shell – with no garden – and customers will then purchase everything else they need – plumbing, lighting, kitchens, bathrooms and furnishings – from one store. B&Q therefore started to offer more services to customers – designers and contractors to install its products. The Beijing store had a room full of designers working at computer terminals, ready to design the customer's living room, kitchen or bathroom. Teams of workers then delivered and install the products. Of all B&Q sales in China, 25% involved some kind of B&Q service.

In 2008/09, sales at B&Q China fell dramatically and continued to fall into 2013. Local press comments indicated local price competition was a major factor in this decline, although high costs and a decline in housebuilding also contributed. The ensuing losses resulted in B&Q closing almost one-third of its stores and reducing floor space in others so as to stabilize losses at £6 million by 2014. Nevertheless, with 39 stores employing over 3,000 staff, B&Q remained one of the largest Western retailers in China. Yet, in 2014 it announced that it had sold a controlling 70% stake in the business for £140 million to Beijing-based Wumei Holding, which operates about 650 supermarkets and 10 department stores in China, owning brands such as Wumart, Jingbei Shopping Mall and Merrymart. B&Q said it planned to use the cash to invest in its core European market.

❏ **Visit the website: www.kingfisher.com**

QUESTION:

1 What lessons do you learn from the experience of B&Q in China?

Product life cycles

Product/service development is a characteristic of successful growth companies. Before we look at this, however, it is useful to review the concept of the product or service life cycle, introduced in Chapter 5, because this has implications for marketing strategies generally and how your value proposition and target market(s) might change as the product ages. Products and services age, and increasingly rapid changes in technology can mean that their viable market life can be short. Life cycles can vary in length from short for fashion products such as clothing and other consumables, to long for more durable products like cars. Often the life cycle can be extended by a variety of marketing initiatives. Figure 13.3 shows a four-stage product life cycle with the implications for

	Completely new & emergent	Growth	Maturity	Decline
Sales	Low	Increasing	High	Declining
Growth	Low growth	High growth	Static growth	Retrenchment
Profit	Low – high costs	Increasing	High & focus on cost reduction	Declining
Competition	Low level	Emerging & intensifying	High levels	Exiting the market

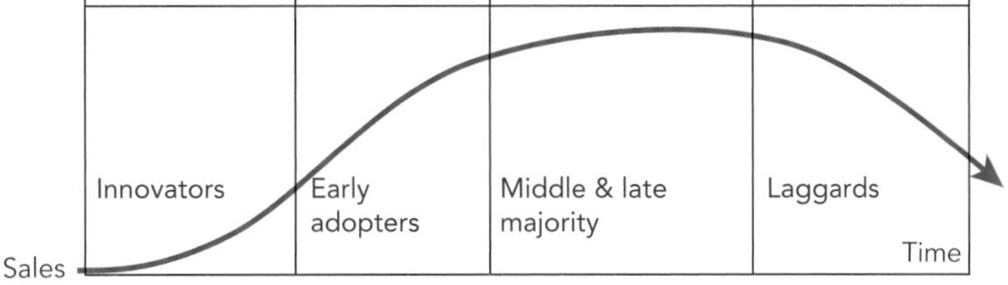

	Innovators	Early adopters	Middle & late majority	Laggards

Sales / Time

Characteristics of marketing strategy

Product	Basic product	Product modification & expansion	Product expansion, extension (eventually slowing) & new product development	Completely new product development

Weak products dropped & range narrowed |
| Customer relationship | Need to encourage customer trial & monitor customer evaluation | Need to promote and maintain loyalty | Need to encourage and maintain loyalty & monitor changes in customer needs | Need to encourage and maintain loyalty for surviving products |
| Pricing | Low price to encourage trial or repeat purchase

or

High price because of novelty or uniqueness | Penetrate market

Price competitively to combat competition | Price defensively to meet competition

Selective marketing based around special offers and promotions | Low price to dispose of stock at end of life

or

High price if reducing competition means demand remains high |
| Promotion & branding | Develop brand | Heavy promotion

Differentiate & build brand | Heavy promotion

Differentiate & build brand | Minimum promotion to maintain loyalty |
| Distribution | Selective distribution | Wide distribution | Intensive push on distribution, including trade discounts | Selective distribution

Look for overseas markets |

Figure 13.3 The product life cycle

marketing strategy at the different stages. The simplicity of the model has much to recommend it. However, these broad generalizations must be treated with caution because all products are different, as are different market segments and the customers that compose them.

At the completely new and emergent stage your objective should be to make potential customers aware of the product and to get them to try it. The benefits need to be explained and the relevance to the customer needs to be underlined. Strategies to do this were outlined in Chapter 8. Early customers are likely to be 'innovators' – that is, people who think for themselves and try things. These are likely to be a small percentage of the target market (under 5%), although, with fashions or fads the proportion can be higher. Entrepreneurial firms launching innovative new products are particularly interested in this phase, and where novelty or uniqueness is high, as it was with the iPad, prices charged can be high.

At the growth stage your objective should be to grab market share as quickly as possible because competitors will be entering the market. This means that prices will have to be competitive, depending on the uniqueness of the product and how well it can be differentiated. The promotion emphasis should shift to one of promoting the brand and why it is better than that of competitors. By this stage, 'early adopters' will be buying the product. These tend to be people with status in their market segment and opinion leaders. They adopt successful products, making them acceptable and respectable. At this stage the market is likely to have multiplied in size to, say 10–15% of your target market. The product range should start to be developed at this stage so as to give customers more choice and gain advantage over competitors.

The 'middle and late majority' next start buying the product and take it into the mature stage of its life cycle. The middle majority (comprising some 30–40%) are more conservative, have slightly higher status and are more deliberate purchasers. They only adopt the product after it has become acceptable. The late majority (also comprising some 30–40%) are typically below average status, are sceptical and adopt the product much later. In this phase, competitors are becoming established as some companies fall by the wayside. In order to maintain market share, pricing tends to be defensive at, or around, the level of competitors. There should be an emphasis on cost reduction so that profits are as high as possible. As we noted in Chapter 5, it is at this point that products tend to get revamped – by changing designs, colours, packaging and so on – in order to extend their life cycle and product innovation may start to emerge. Towards the end of this period, price reductions may be hidden by offering extra elements to the product for the same price. Cars, for example, often get this treatment with limited edition models offering many extras for the same price.

'Laggards' (comprising some 10–20%) tend to view life through the rearview mirror and will continue buying products because of habit. The interesting thing about the decline stage of the life cycle is that there may still be the opportunity to charge high prices and make good profits, at least in the short term, because competitors may be exiting the market quicker than demand is tailing off. It is therefore a matter of careful judgement exactly when to exit from a market. This is the point where less-developed international markets may become important. As we noted in Chapter 5, it is also the point where radical product /service innovation may be taking place.

The problem with the product life cycle concept is trying to establish where a product might actually be. Firms plotting their own product sales are not recording the product's life but their ability to manage it. Bad management can lead to an early downturn in sales which is not necessarily the mature phase of the life cycle, and vice versa. What is more, products can be at the mature phase of their life cycle in one market but at the introductory phase in another. You only have to see the queues and check the prices for McDonald's hamburgers in many emerging markets to realize that the product still has novelty value, despite its ageing status in mature Western markets. Not only can the length of the life cycle vary from country to country, product to product and new technology to new technology, but the length of each phase can also vary. The take-off phase is generally becoming shorter and shorter. Good ideas now move into the early adopters phase very quickly. In 2003 Tellis et al. studied 137 new product launches across 10 consumer durable categories in 16 European countries and found that there were considerable differences.

They concluded that cultural factors partly explain the differences. In particular, the probability of rapid take-off increased in countries that were placed high on an index of achievement and industriousness and low on uncertainty avoidance. Economic factors were found not to be strong explanatory variables. They also found that the probability of take-off in one country increased with successful prior take-offs in other countries. The authors therefore recommend a 'waterfall' strategy for product introduction, putting them first into the countries that are likely to have the shortest 'time-to-take-off'.

Product development

It is in the late growth and mature phases of the life cycle that product/service innovation generally takes place. This can take four forms, reflecting increasing degrees of innovation:

Product modification

This involves the modification of existing products where the changes are small and evolutionary. They might be modified in terms of quality, function or style so as to address any weaknesses or to suit local markets. Service levels might be improved. This is usually necessary when competition increases as the middle and late adopters start to buy the product/service and other firms start to produce 'better' products. This can be a particular problem if you are pioneering a product in a market with low barriers to entry, especially if the product is developing into a commodity. However, even successful products such as the iPhone need constant modification to keep up with the competition.

Product expansion

This involves developing product variations that meet the needs of different market segments. Most business will start to offer a range of products or services quickly after launch as they spot new market opportunities. So, for example, a car manufacturer might start offering sports, estate or fuel-efficient variants of a model. A soft drinks manufacturer might start to offer 'light' variants or new flavours for a successful brand. A tablet-computer manufacturer might offer 7 inch and 11 inch screens.

Product extension

This is where a successful brand is extended to similar but different products or services that might be purchased by the same customers. For example, a number of chocolate bar manufacturers have successfully extended their brand into ice cream. The key to success here is having a strong brand, one that actually means something to customers, with values that can be extended to the other products. Thus Timberland, a company well-known for producing durable outdoor footwear, extended its product range to include durable outdoor clothing. Virgin and Saga are good examples of brands that have been applied to a wide range of diverse products, mainly successfully, linking customers and their lifestyle aspirations. Virgin, however, rarely undertakes 'production', relying instead on partners with existing expertise. On the other hand, Mercedes-Benz is a brand that has a strong association with quality, and the company has capitalized on this by producing an ever wider range of vehicles, always being able to charge a premium price for its product. This has allowed it to move into new and different segments of the vehicle market.

Completely new products

Although normally associated with the end of a product life cycle, you might introduce completely new products simply because you spot new market opportunities. They might be innovative products to either replace or sell alongside your existing product range. This is most successful when you have built up a loyal customer base and you have a close relationship with customers – a customer focus – and a good reputation for quality or delivery that can be built upon. A customer-focused firm will have an advantage in developing new products because, if it understands how its customers' needs are changing, it ought to be able to develop new products that meet them. What is more, if there is a relationship of trust, customers are more likely to try your new product, provided of course they perceive a need for it. The key to this strategy, therefore, is building good customer relationships, often associated with effective branding. For example, Apple started with computers but moved into tablets and smartphones as mobile technology became increasingly important. They are now introducing smart-watches.

One advantage of product development over market development is that it might be more cost-effective to increase the volume of business with existing customers than it is to go out looking for new ones. What is more, good relationships often result in customers becoming product advocates, bringing in new customers and even being willing to help with product development. However, developing new products, even for existing customers, can be expensive and risky. Developing a prototype is a process of experimentation, where numerous iterations of an idea are created and tested to see whether it provides the desired results. Prototyping used to be complicated, but now can be done early and inexpensively by using computer simulations. There are even low-cost tools available like Google's SketchUp. Eventually, however, a physical prototype will have to be built. For example, cars are now designed and developed on computers and prototype development is left increasingly to later stages. However, concept cars still represent an important part of product development – an opportunity to test out ideas, not just in terms of mechanical feasibility, but also in terms of market acceptability. And often only by seeing, touching and using the product can the potential consumer make judgements about it. Product development must be grounded firmly in the needs of the existing market. Even then, if done too rapidly, it can mean resources are spread too thinly across an unbalanced portfolio.

 ## Case insight   Levi's jeans

The disorderly product development process

The development of Levi's jeans was neither linear nor orderly. The tailor Levi Strauss started out making hard-wearing work overalls. These were so popular that he ran out of the brown canvas sailcloth from which they were made so he decided to switch to a sturdy twill fabric called serge that was made in Nîme in France. The material was named 'serge de Nîme', but this soon became shortened to denim. It proved very popular. The next development

came when a Nevadan tailor called Jacob David suggested to Strauss that he insert metal rivets at points of stress, typically pocket corners and the base of the fly, to make the trousers even sturdier. The pair patented the idea. The final element was added by a rival tailor, H.D. Lee, who introduced a novelty to replace the button fly, called the Whizit. We know this today as the zip or zipper.

QUESTION:

1   What are the differences between innovation and product development?

Developing a product portfolio

As we have seen, products require different marketing strategies at different stages of their life cycle. So, for example, McDonald's may have a different marketing mix for its products in developing countries, where it is at the introductory phase of its life cycle, compared to the USA, where it is a mature product. The added complexity of having a portfolio of product/market offerings, each at a different stage of its life, can be handled using a technique adapted from the Growth Share Matrix. This is also known as the 'Boston matrix' after the Boston Consulting Group that developed it, and is shown in Figure 13.4. The vertical axis measures market attractiveness – the growth and profit potential of the market. The horizontal axis measures the strength of your product/

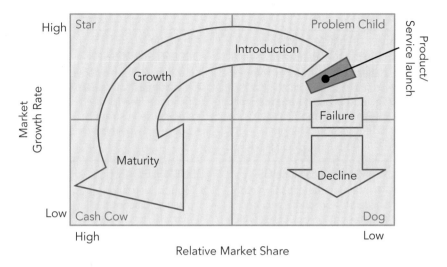

Figure 13.4 Growth Share Matrix

Source: Adapted from *The BCG Portfolio Matrix* from the *Product Portfolio Matrix*, The Boston Consulting Group, 1970. With permission.

service in the market – its sales, relative market share etc. You launch a product/service into an attractive market (otherwise why do it?), but you are likely to be weak in the market. This is called a 'Problem Child'. Sometimes the market proves to be unattractive – then its life is very short as it becomes a 'Dog'. More often, if the market continues to be attractive, sales will grow and your market position will strengthen. This is called a 'Star'. Eventually, however, the market will mature, becoming less attractive, and your product/service will become a 'Cash Cow' – market leaders with a lot of stability but little additional growth because they are at the end of their life cycles.

Different business skills are valued at different points in the matrix. Entrepreneurial skills are of most value in the Problem Child phase. Once the product is in its mature phase it needs to be managed as a Cash Cow – milked for all the cash flow it can generate. That means high levels of efficiency are needed, probably achieved through a high degree of control and direction. The Cash Cow is likely to be best managed by an accountant. And, if we are to characterize the management discipline needed to manage the Star, it would probably be marketing. In other words, as the product works its way around the matrix the imperatives of management change. In a one-product company this presents a challenging but manageable problem. In a multi-product firm the problem is more complex.

There are a number of measurement issues with the framework. How do you define your market so that you can measure market share or market growth? You might use just one factor on each axis or a number of them weighted in some way. Nevertheless, the problem of measurement remains. The Boston matrix is therefore probably best used as a loose conceptual framework that helps clarify complexity. Anything that simplifies complexity and therefore helps our understanding must be of value.

Marketing strategy and product portfolios

The Growth Share Matrix allows us to make some broad generalizations about marketing strategy for product/service offerings in the different quadrants. These are shown in Figure 13.5. If you can place the product/market offering within its life cycle on the matrix, these would be the elements of marketing strategy you would, a priori, expect to see. But remember that while this framework reflects product life cycles, it does not reflect the value disciplines or generic marketing strategies outlined in Chapter 6, which need to be superimposed on them. Nevertheless, as a product nears the end of its life and becomes a Cash Cow, it is more likely to be on its way to becoming a commodity and therefore having to sell on price.

	Star	Problem Child
	INVEST FOR GROWTH • Penetrate market • Accept moderate short-term profits • Sell and promote aggressively • Expand geographically • Extend product range • Differentiate product/service	**DEVELOP OPPORTUNITIES** • Be critical of prospects • Invest heavily in selective products/services • Specialise in strengths • Shore up weaknesses
	MANAGE FOR EARNINGS • Maintain market position with successful products/services • Differentiate products/services to keep share of key segments • Prune less successful products/services • Stabilise prices, except where a temporarily agressive stance is required to deter competitors	**GENERATE CASH** • Monitor carefully – judge when to discontinue • Live with low growth • Improve productivity • Reduce costs • Look for 'easy' growth segments
	Cash Cow	Dog

Figure 13.5 Strategy implications of the Growth Share Matrix

The Growth Share Matrix also allows us to present complex information more understandably, particularly when linked to forecasting future market positions and strategies involved in getting there. For example, Figure 13.6 represents a hypothetical three-product portfolio. The size of each circle is proportionate to the turnover each achieves. The lighter circles represent the present product positions, and the darker circles represent the positions projected in three years' time. The portfolio looks balanced as long as product C continues on its upward trajectory and the diagram can be used to explain the strategies that are in place to move the products to where they are planned to be (including the possibility of eliminating product C if the launch fails). Again, one essential added complexity is the generic marketing strategies. If products A and B are commodities, selling mainly on price, with low margin under intense pressure, it has implications not only for strategy but also for the cash flow available to invest in product C, particularly if this is a niche market product needing heavy investment. This might mean that rather than succeed, this product might fail and have to be killed off.

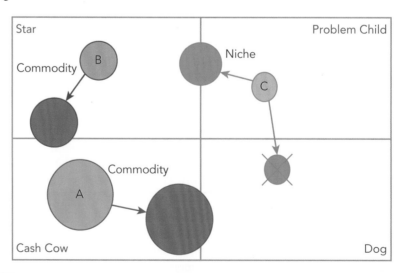

Figure 13.6 Presenting strategy using the Growth Share Matrix

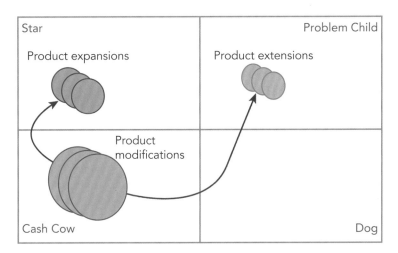

Figure 13.7   Product development options shown on the Growth Share Matrix

Product modification, extension and expansion opportunities can also be represented in the Boston matrix. An example of this is shown in Figure 13.7. The range of products represented as Cash Cows might be expanded or used as a basis for developing product extensions. Again, this can be a useful visual aid to understanding strategy options.

 Case insight   Crocs™

Niche product life cycles

The ubiquitous Croc can be found in over 125 countries, having sold more than 150 million pairs by 2011. And that means that about 1 person in every 500 on the entire planet has bought a pair. The Colorado-based company was founded only in 2002 by George Brian Boedecker Jr. and two friends to produce and distribute a plastic clog-like shoe, now available in all the colours of the rainbow, at a relatively cheap price. It was an instant success at the Florida Boat Show, where it was launched. It sold 76,000 pairs in its first year and 649,000 in its second year. The brightly-coloured Crocs are made from Croslite, a durable, soft, lightweight, non-marking and odour-resistant material originally manufactured by Foam Creations, a Canadian company that Crocs purchased in 2004. Crocs are now manufactured in Mexico, Italy, Romania and China, having closed its Canadian facility in 2008.

Crocs was a 'fairy-tale' entrepreneurial story, if the press were anything to go by in the early days. *Business 2.0* magazine (3 November 2006) summarized the story: 'Three pals from Boulder, Colorado, go sailing in the Caribbean, where a foam clog one had bought in Canada inspires them to build a business around it. Despite a lack of venture capital funding and the derision of foot fashionistas, the multicolored Crocs with their Swiss-cheese perforations, soft and comfortable soles, and odor-preventing material become a global smash. Celebrities adopt them. Young

people adore them. The company goes from $1 million in revenue in 2003 to a projected $322 million this year [2006]. Crocs Inc.'s IPO [Initial Public Offering] in February was the richest in footwear history, and the company has a market cap of more than $1 billion.'

The company went public in 2006 with a hugely successful $200 million stock market float (the biggest float in shoe history). Its initial strategy can be summarized as selling a relatively cheap product to as many people as possible, as quickly as possible. The company used the money to diversify and acquire new businesses, such as Jibbitz, which made charms designed to fit Crocs' ventilating holes, and Fury Hockey, which used Croslite to make sports gear. It built manufacturing plants in Mexico and China, opened distribution centres in the Netherlands and Japan, and expanded into the global marketplace. A foray into Croslite clothing in 2007 fell flat and was quickly scaled back. The company liquidated Fury Hockey in 2008.

And herein lies the paradox. Popularity breeds contempt in the fashion business. Arguably, the backlash started in 2006, almost as soon as the company went public, with a *Washington Post* article that said: 'Nor is the fashion world enamored of Crocs. Though their maker touts their "ultra-hip Italian styling", lots of folks find them hideous.' A blog named 'I Hate Crocs.com' followed Croc opponents. The shoes and those who wear them – from US ex-President George W. Bush to Michelle Obama and stars such as Al

Continued...

Continued from previous page...

Pacino, Steven Tyler (Aerosmith) and Faith Hill – became objects of satire on US television shows, and by 2009 over 1.4 million people had joined a Facebook group which had the sole purpose of eliminating the shoes. The site even featured a ritual Croc-burning.

Nevertheless, in 2008 Crocs was ranked by the NPD Market Research Group as the number-one casual brand in the athletic specialty sporting goods channel for men, women and children. However, having had a bumper year in 2007, the company incurred a $185 million (£113 million) loss in 2008 and had to cut 2,000 jobs. It suddenly began to look very fragile. In late 2008 the company replaced chief executive Ron Snyder, who had been at college with the company's founders, with John Duerden, an industry veteran who ran a consulting firm focused on brand renewal. He believed there was life yet in Crocs and what the company needed was new products to which he could extend the brand.

By 2009 the company was stuck with a surplus of shoes it could not sell and a mountain of expensive debt. The new business lines it had purchased – often at a premium – failed to prosper. As a result, the share price plummeted. By this time the company produced a range of different products, mainly plastic clogs and sandals but also a range called 'Bite', aimed at the golf market. The problem was that Crocs were hitting saturation point and the company had failed to successfully diversify. With a nearly indestructible product and about 1 in every 500 people owning a pair, how many more can the company sell? And the company had invested enormous amounts into meeting a demand for a product that then seemed endless but now seems ridiculous, as the shoe's ubiquity put off even the most ardent Crocophile. In May 2010, *Time* magazine rated Crocs as one of the world's 50 worst inventions.

But behind the scenes the company brought in Italian designers and started producing a new range of attractive Crocs, albeit at much higher prices than the original clogs, that celebrities such as Brad Pitt, Ryan Reynolds and Halle Berry, once more, started wearing. These new shoes and sandals played to the strengths of the Croslite material from which the sole was made and targeted mainly beach and boat wear ('so light, they float' – 'vents let air and water flow through' – 'grooved rubber outsole improves grip'). As well as diversifying their range of shoes, Crocs diversified into retailing by opening their own branded stores. And just to prove that the fashion business can be fickle, in 2011 Crocs sold $1 billion (£630 million) worth of shoes, with one-third of the revenue coming from sales of the original clogs. The 'I Hate Crocs.com' blog gave up and closed in that year. Pondering the turnaround and the ugliness of the original Crocs, *The Sunday Times* (22 April 2012) said: 'In the history of retail, has a brand ever thrived so well on adversity? It seems the more the loathers loath them, fans go wild. While for under-10s (a core market) they're a straightforward sell, grown-up clog wearers appear torn between love and hate.' It seems that having an ugly product polarizes opinion and this can give a brand its uniqueness.

❏ Visit the website: www.crocs.eu

QUESTIONS:

1 Who is the target market and what is the value proposition for Crocs?

2 Where is the original Crocs clog now in its life cycle? How reliable are future sales?

3 How did Crocs grow its sales?

4 What went wrong at Crocs and how was it put right?

5 What is the company's current strategy? What do you think of it?

Cash flow and product portfolios

The structure of the product portfolio has implications for your cash flow. The Problem Child consumes cash for development and promotional costs at a rate of knots, without generating much cash by way of revenues. The Star might start to generate revenues but will still be facing high costs, particularly in marketing to establish its market position against new entry competitors. It is therefore likely to be cash neutral. Only as a Cash Cow are revenues likely to outstrip costs and cash flow likely to be positive. There are two kinds of Dogs. One is a cash dog that covers its costs and might be worth keeping, for example if it brings in customers for other products or services or it shares overheads. The other is the genuine dog which is losing money – both in cash flow and profit terms – and should be scrapped. It is from this model that phrases like 'shoot the dog', 'invest in stars' and 'milk the cow' came. These implications are shown in Figure 13.8.

Ideally you should have a balanced portfolio of product/ service offerings so that the surplus cash from Cash Cows can be used to invest in the Problem Children. However, that situation may take many years to achieve. These surplus funds can be used almost as venture capital to invest, selectively, in new products and services. This ideal firm – if it exists – is self-financing. The

Star		Problem Child	
Revenue	+ + +	Revenue	+
Expenditure	– – –	Expenditure	– – –
Cash flow	neutral	Cash flow	– –
Cash Cow		Dog	
Revenue	+ + + +	Revenue	+
Expenditure	– –	Expenditure	–
Cash flow	+ +	Cash flow	neutral

Figure 13.8 Cash flow implications of the Growth Share Matrix

problem that arises with an unbalanced portfolio is that there is either a surplus of cash (no new products) or a deficit (too many new products). If you have too many Problem Children and Stars in your portfolio (too many good, new ideas), then you will require cash flow injections which will only be forthcoming if you can either borrow the capital or raise more equity finance.

Profit and product portfolios

Remember, however, that cash flow is not the same as profit. The analysis above explains the cash flow implications of different product/market offerings. Their success might normally be measured in terms of overall profitability, and for that you would look to a technique called **ABC Analysis**. This measures success in terms of the total contribution a product makes towards your fixed costs (see Chapter 7) in relation to its sales value within the context of your overall product portfolio. An example is shown in Figure 13.9. The vertical axis represents sales value and the horizontal axis represents contribution value. The diagonal line from bottom left to top right should represent your average contribution margin and therefore the margin achieved by your

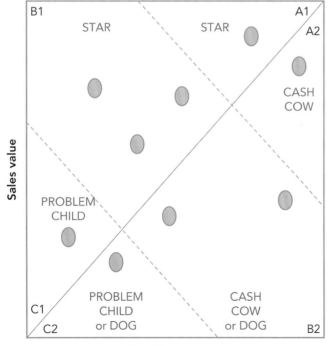

Figure 13.9 ABC Analysis

various product/market offerings should fall either side. The dots on Figure 13.9 represent these product/market offerings, which are then grouped into ABC clusters according to where they fall.

Your 'A' products (top right) are important because of the high value of sales they generate, with A1 products generating a higher contribution than A2. Your 'C' products (bottom left) are of least importance in terms of sales value, but C1 products generate a higher contribution than C2. For example, you may have a product with sales of $10,000, which makes a contribution of $4,000 (40%) and another with sales of only $1,000, which makes a contribution of $600 (60%). The average contribution margin is 42% ($4,600 ÷ $11,000). The first product might therefore be classified as an A2 product, while the second as a C1 product, depending on the rest of the product portfolio.

The analysis can be combined with the Growth Share Matrix to give an insight into how your portfolio might affect profitability:

> **A1 products**, combining high sales and high contribution, are really successful and are vitally important to the business. These should be your Stars, but may be moving towards becoming Cash Cows.
> **A2 products** are probably your Cash Cows. They are important because of the value of sales they generate, despite their lower contribution. If you were to stop producing them your fixed overheads would have to be spread over fewer products.
> **B1 products** should also be your Stars, with high sales generating both profit and cash, and should have further growth potential. However, they might become Cash Cows if sales do not increase.
> **B2 products** are probably Stars that have waned, with sales and contribution lower than other products. If they are not Cash Cows, then they are Dogs.
> **C1 products** are probably Problem Children that could become Stars in the future, unless the increase in expected sales does not materialize.
> **C2 products** are either Problem Children or Dogs and, unless there are sound commercial reasons for keeping them, are candidates for axing.

This analysis highlights attractive products – where contribution and sales are high – but it can also be used to identify attractive or vulnerable customers or markets. If sales are low but contribution is high, it shows where a sales push, even if margins are eroded, would yield the greatest reward. Similarly, it identifies product/markets where sales are high but contribution is low. These may be products where profits could be increased by increasing price, despite the resulting reduction in sales volume. However, they may be products where a higher price cannot be charged and are vulnerable to price competition. Their survival is justified by the cash flow they generate and this will need to be continually monitored.

Case insight   AusssieCommerce Group (2)

Growth strategies in e-commerce

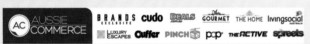

Courtesy of AussieCommerce Group

Founded by Adam Schwab and Jeremy Same in 2010, the AussieCommerce Group is now one of the largest e-commerce businesses in Australia. Based in Melbourne and Sydney, it has a turnover of more than AUD 200 million annually and employs almost 400 staff. Websites in the AussieCommerce portfolio include:

> **Luxury Escapes** – offering a small number of specially selected luxury trips, holidays, tours and cruises as well as featuring a travel magazine;
> **Brands Exclusive** – offering premium brand, designer fashion items as well as featuring regular fashion editorials;

Continued...

Continued from previous page...

> **TheHome** – offering premium home and lifestyle brands of designer furniture and homewares, often with flash sales as well as featuring an online magazine;
> **LivingSocial** – offering locally-based 'experiences' from restaurants to travel and holiday as well as shopping deals on a wide range of products;
> **Cudo** – offering deals on restaurants and bars, hotels, spas, salons, theatre tickets, tours, gadgets, décor and fashion;
> **DEALS.com.au** – offering daily deals in cities throughout Australia from massages to restaurant meals and from gifts to everyday household items;
> **Pop** – offering designer fashions, home décor and gadgets to a younger market looking for novel ideas;
> **The Gourmet** – offering 'gourmet', quality food such as meat, seafood, vegetables, wine and hampers, mainly sourced from Australia;
> **Ouffer** – offering 'lifestyle inspirations' including 'experiences' like hot-air ballooning or driving a sports car, premium holidays and high-end restaurant dining, all offered on a limited-time sale basis;
> **The Active** – offering flash sales of products and events targeted at sport, fitness and outdoor adventure enthusiasts;
> **Spreets** – offering a marketplace of restaurant, travel, shopping and pamper deals in cities across Australia;
> **Dailydo (New Zealand)** – offering beauty services, restaurants, leisure activities, family entertainment and vacations as well as everyday essentials;
> **PINCHme** – providing manufacturers with access to a targeted membership database of consumers (based on AussieCommerce's own customers) who can sample and provide feedback on their products. Members can also purchase the products through the site. PINCHme has become Australia's leading product sample distributor, with clients including Procter & Gamble, Nestlé and Reckitt Benckiser.

The original DEALS.com.au website, based on the US daily deals site Groupon, has consistently been a profitable business – a difficult feat in the group buying sector which has seen thousands of similar businesses across the globe collapse. Schwab credits the Group's 'retail savvy' and 'lean culture' to its success.

'It's a difficult business in that a lot of e-commerce businesses don't make much money. So what we've always found is you have to be really lean and hire some good people. Essentially it's a people business and you need to stay true to being a good retailer but with a strong tech-bent. Get your product right, your team right and *then start looking for customers and they will come to you.'* (Smartcompany.com.au, 8 April 2015)

While e-commerce is a relatively fast-growing sector in Australia, competition still looms from global giants like Amazon, Alibaba and eBay, as well as omni-channel retailers like UK-based John Lewis and US giants like Macy's and TJ Maxx. According to research house Telsyte, online retail sales are expected to exceed AUD 30 billion in 2016 – twice the level recorded in 2011. Flash retailers like the AussieCommerce group are the main drivers of this growth.

AussieCommerce has been able to compete through a combination of organic growth and shrewd acquisitions – not unexpected given Adam Schwab's background as a lawyer specializing in mergers and acquisitions and executive director Josh David's background in venture capital (see Case insight (1), page 66).

'We tend to be pretty adept at identifying good opportunities when they come up. We won't make an acquisition unless we know we can integrate quickly and effectively. We would never purchase a business purely for scale. It's always about profitability and return on equity.' (Australian Anthill, anthillonline.com.au, 22 October 2013)

Schwab notes that the Group remains focused on profit rather than revenue and insists that the acquisition route has not been followed simply for the sake of growth itself. Businesses are acquired as cheaply as possible and then rigorous cost controls applied before looking at ways sales can be grown through synergies. One of the AussieCommerce Group's greatest successes has been the website TheHome .com.au. Purchased in 2012 for AUD 300,000, the business, then known as Dalani, was losing over AUD 200,000 each month. Aussie Commerce rescued the business after it had been shuttered and re-hired 18 staff. Less than three years later, AussieCommerce's homewares division was turning over more than AUD 2 million each month and was highly profitable.

There is a synergistic logic to the portfolio of sites. Excluding PINCHme, they have a number of common characteristics:

> Although many products are 'premium' or 'luxury' and often branded, they are all offered at a 'discount', and flash sales – that is, the offers are only available for a short time (usually less than a week) to both maintain urgency and protect clients' brands;
> The sites offer 'overlapping' products that can be sold on more than one site, allowing sites to target different markets but offering economies of scale;
> Because many of the sites are membership sites,

Continued...

Continued from previous page...

customer data can be used to provide a better user experience, also offering economies of scope.

Schwab says that there is always something different about each site that sets it out from competitors. Often this is about offering premium brands, but always at a discounted price. The Group is quick to follow a market trend or develop a business idea that others have pioneered and proved successful, rather than developing completely new product ideas. AussieCommerce will look to change the product offering incrementally, thus minimizing risks, but doing so quickly and decisively.

'When we were looking to expand our travel business, we didn't set out to create a new travel category. Instead, we looked to improve on what other brilliant businesses were already doing. We knew there was no point taking on established marketplaces at their own game, so we developed a slightly different model. Instead of listing every hotel possible, our in-house team of travel experts curate luxury properties from around the world, but with a focus on south-east Asia, the Pacific and Australia. Our LuxuryEscapes team visits properties, films reviews, writes blogs and negotiates promotions with hotels, resorts and cruise liners. Instead of 29,000 offerings, LuxuryEscapes will usually feature less than ten at one time.' (BRW.com .au, 29 July 2014)

'While it might take a new player a year and AUD 300,000 to setup a fully customised website, they can do it in less than a month for a fraction of the cost.' (Australian Anthill, anthillonline.com.au, 22 October 2013)

However, following a strategy of growth through acquisition can be risky. Schwab described the first few years of AussieCommerce's existence as 'an extended near-death experience', saying the closest the business came to the failing was in 2012 after it acquired Ouffer and TheHome in the space of two weeks:

'Both businesses were heavily indebted and not yet at scale, and it took a period of approximately eight months to fully integrate the businesses. There was a period of several months where our cash flows came under strain until we were able to fully synergize the businesses and deliver strong profit growth. Three years later, we have a handful of competitors still remaining and we've become the largest player in the space by maintaining really close cost control and expanding into new areas of e-commerce.' (Smartcompany.com.au, 17 September 2014)

Another characteristic of the business is its lack of reliance on outside capital. This lack of outside interference allows it to make quick decisions. Almost all the earnings have been ploughed back into the business, often paying for acquisitions. It is currently developing its mobile platforms and investing heavily in native mobile applications for both iOS and Android.

'The beauty of being shareholder-owned and run with no outside capital is that we can make quick decisions ... We were able to make the decision to buy TheHome within a few days and complete the transaction in a couple of weeks.' (Management Today, July 2014)

AussieCommerce has grown rapidly in a new market that has seen many companies come and go quickly. Establishing yourself in such a competitive market is not easy. Sustaining yourself is just as difficult. Will the company itself fall prey to acquisition by a larger rival? Only time will tell.

❏ Visit the website:
http://www.aussiecommerce.com.au/index.html

QUESTIONS:

1 What are the strategies that have allowed the company to grow and why have they been successful?

2 What are the strengths and weaknesses of the company and the major threats and opportunities it faces?

3 What changes to strategies might you suggest for the future?

4 What are the advantages and disadvantages of the company floating on the stock exchange?

Diversification

Diversification involves moving away from core areas of activity into completely new and unrelated product/market areas. While it is central to the process of corporate evolution, it is only something to be undertaken after very careful consideration, because it is high risk. Developing either new products or new markets is always risky. Developing both at once is even riskier – akin to another start-up.

A focus on core business at corporate level was emphasized in the 1980s by researchers (e.g. Abell, 1980). A firm's core business is the one in which it has a distinct advantage by adding the greatest value for its customers and shareholders. Many studies have showed that firms that are more focused on their core business perform better than diversified ones (e.g. Wernerfelt and

Montgomery, 1986). This was popularized by Peters and Waterman (1982) as 'sticking to the knitting'. Although some studies were subsequently disputed (e.g. Luffman and Reed, 1984; Michel and Shaked, 1984; Park, 2002), Peters and Waterman (op. cit.) concluded: 'Organizations that do branch out but stick to their knitting outperform the others. The most successful are those that diversified around a single skill … The second group in descending order, comprise those companies that branch out into related fields … The least successful are those companies that diversify into a wide variety of fields. Acquisitions especially among this group tend to wither on the vine.'

Nevertheless, several studies have found that diversification is associated with improved performance up to a point, after which continued diversification is associated with declining performance (e.g. Palich et al., 2000). Grant (2010) suggests that diversification has probably caused more value destruction than any other type of strategic decision. He describes diversification as being 'like sex: its attractions are obvious, often irresistible. Yet the experience is often disappointing. For top management it is a mine field.'

Developments in financial theory in the 1970s, in particular the Capital Asset Pricing Model (CAPM), also showed that **conglomerates** – diversified companies with interests in a range of different industries – did not create shareholder value in stock markets by reducing risk (Levy and Sarnat, 1970; Mason and Goudzwaard, 1976; Weston et al., 1972). This is because diversification does not reduce **systematic risk** – that part of risk associated with how the share price performs compared to the overall market (measured by the company's beta coefficient). Shareholders can simply buy shares in undiversified companies representing the diversified interests of the conglomerate. This spreads their risk, probably with lower transaction costs. Therefore, at the corporate level diversification does not create shareholder value. Indeed, conglomerates often trade at a discount on the value of their component parts because of their complexity.

Why growing firms diversify

Nevertheless, growing firms often seem to 'diversify', so the question is why? The answer probably lies in two parts:

Market dominance

One of the two main reasons growing firms diversify is to gain market dominance in newly emerging markets or industries. They do this as a way of gaining market dominance quickly by moving into related areas, often through acquisitions – simultaneously developing new products and markets. Most importantly, it is a way of defining and redefining the scope of any newly emerging industry, for example in technology. It is therefore worth considering if your start-up involves disruptive innovation, market paradigm shift or new-to-the-world industries (quadrants 4, 5 and 6 in Figure 4.4 on page 95). The risks associated with it can be reduced if it is done in incremental moves, constantly bundling new products and services while extending the newly developing market.

This incremental diversification is therefore generally into related areas, where you have some product or market knowledge and/or expertise. Related diversification is therefore less risky than unrelated diversification. However, the distinction between related and unrelated areas is not always clear, shading into grey particularly in the areas of rapidly developing new technologies in which new markets are being created where none existed before. There are three types of related diversification. When companies move into complementary or competitive areas, as above, it is called **horizontal integration**. When companies move into their supply chain, for example to become a manufacturer, it is called **backwards vertical integration**. When they move into their distribution chain, for example to become a retailer, it is called **forwards vertical integration**.

However, it is the speed of this simultaneous product and market development that is significant. As we saw in the Case insight in Chapter 5, five of the most successful entrepreneurial companies since 2000 – Apple, Amazon, Facebook, Google and Microsoft – have adopted strategies of rapid related diversification that are probably starting to redefine their business scope – linking hardware, software and internet services. This is happening through a combination of

Capital needs to be deployed into areas where you are able to reap the highest returns. If a business segment isn't successful you need to be able to quickly divert valuable capital … There is no point in purchasing a business if you lower your return on equity.

Adam Schwab, founder, Aussie Commerce Group, *Business Review Australia*, issuu.com, July 2014

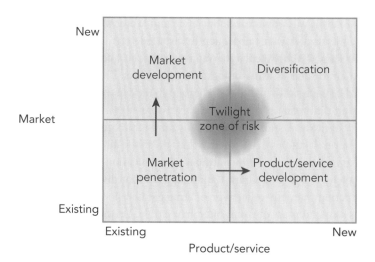

Figure 13.10 The twilight zone of risk

organic market development, internal product/service development and external acquisitions. Their moves into new areas have been incremental, bundling additional services to sell to existing customers, finding out about market acceptance of their new products experimentally – a form of market testing. Often they have used acquisition to buy new customers as well as new services. Incremental, related diversification means lower risks. It is also a way of mitigating the risks of introducing disruptive innovation by using an incremental approach to test markets and obtain product/service and market information.

Typically the product/market matrix in Figure 13.1 has been used to show increasing risk as a business moves away from its core business of existing products and markets. However, there is an area in the centre of the product/market matrix where many growing entrepreneurial businesses may have a competitive advantage – facing lower risks than larger, more bureaucratic competitors because they are able to handle continuous market-related changes. This is shown above in Figure 13.10 as the twilight zone of risk. It is often the way new industries or markets are created – by bundling new combinations of products with markets. This is where a good understanding of customer needs, combined with mechanisms for market testing, mitigates what might otherwise be called risky diversification.

 ## Case insight   Brompton Bicycle (3)

Growth strategies

Despite a slow start, Brompton Bicycle (Case insights, Chapters 3 and 7) has grown rapidly since the arrival of Will Butler-Adams as Managing Director in 2002. By 2014 it had become the UK's largest cycle-maker, producing over 40,000 cycles a year and employing some 190 people. And, as shown in the matrix below, it has used all of the strategies outlined in this chapter.

Courtesy of Brompton Bicycle. Photograph by Anna Batchelor

Continued...

Continued from previous page...

	Market development	Diversification
New	By 2014 Brompton exported some 80% of its bikes to 44 countries. In the UK, USA, Canada and Ireland, it sells through bicycle retailers. In other territories, it sells to distributors who operate their own dealer networks.	By opening its own stores, Brompton has undertaken forward vertical diversification. It opened its first UK store in Covent Garden, London in 2013, adding to sites in Kobe, Shanghai, Hamburg and Amsterdam. Its launch in 2014 of a bike rental scheme in 20 UK locations is an example of horizontal diversification.
	Market penetration	Product development
Existing	Originally Brompton sold bikes direct to the UK public, but it quickly realized that it needed to develop a network of retail outlets that stocked the bike to penetrate the market further. It supplied these shops directly. It still sells direct through its website.	There was only one original Brompton bicycle, but by 2014 the company offered seven basic models at prices ranging from almost £800 to over £2000. Each one could then be customized to suit personal requirements.

Market (vertical axis label)

Existing   New
Product/Service

❏ Visit the website: www.brompton.com

QUESTIONS:

1 What options does Brompton now have to achieve further growth?

2 Evaluate these options in terms of likely risks and returns.

Risk reduction in privately owned businesses

The second main reason for diversification is to reduce risk in privately owned businesses. By having business interests in a range of different markets or industries you spread the risk of a business downturn in any one. However, this only works in companies that are owned by individuals or families where the main wealth of the individual or family is tied up in the business. If the company is quoted on a stock market and owned by the general public, the public can simply spread their risk by buying shares in a range of companies in different markets or industries. They do not value diversification, because it does not reduce their risk. It only adds to the complexity of managing the business.

Diversification and the formation of conglomerates therefore remains a powerful driver of strategy for private, unquoted companies. For example, the Virgin Group is a private conglomerate whose scope of business reaches into markets across the world and covers different industries from transport (airlines, trains and buses) to media (TV, radio, mobile phones and internet), from health and lifestyle (health programmes to gyms) to financial services (credit cards, pension and insurance products and banking). Richard Branson withdrew Virgin from the stock market some years ago, buying back its shares.

However, publicly quoted conglomerates do continue to exist and prosper, particularly in developing economies (see Case insight on Reliance Industries, page 352). This may be because of local stock market inefficiencies such as high share-transaction costs and consequent low level of trading, but is more likely to do with the high concentration of share ownership in family hands. When a private company is the main store of wealth for a family it makes good sense to diversify the risks associated with doing business.

Case insight   Reliance Industries

Family-owned conglomerates

Reliance Industries is the largest publicly traded company in India (by market capitalization). It is a family-run conglomerate and was started by Dhirubhai Ambani, the son of a poor Gujarati school teacher who began work at a Shell petrol station in Aden. To make extra money he traded commodities and, at one time, even melted down Yemeni Rial coins so as to sell the silver for more than the currency's face value. He returned to India and started a yarn trading company in 1959 which, by the end of the 1990s, had become an integrated textiles, petrochemicals and oil conglomerate that then diversified into telecommunications and broadband, power, biotechnology, retail business and even financial services. Initially the business grew primarily through exploiting contacts with Indian politicians and bureaucrats, but in the wake of the changes caused by economic liberalization in the early 1990s, it started to do things differently – it built production sites that were competitive in global markets.

Dhirubhai also popularized share ownership in India – which is where financial services comes in – and the two holding companies now have over 3.5 million shareholders.

Dhirubhai died in 2002 and the business is now run by his two sons Mukesh and Anil. Both have MBAs from the USA and have been involved with the business for some 20 years, managing the company increasingly since their father had his first stroke in 1986 and having a strong role in forging it into the world-class company that it is today. Although little known outside its native country, Reliance has high brand recognition in India. According to a 2010 survey conducted by Brand Finance and *The Economic Times*, Reliance is the second most valuable brand in India and the 2011 Brand Trust Report ranked it the sixth most trusted brand in India.

QUESTIONS:

1 Why is Reliance such a diversified company?

2 Is this likely to change in the future?

Using acquisition for market and product development

Obtaining rapid market dominance can be very important for certain types of new venture. And sometimes acquiring rivals – just as Zipcar bought Streetcar (see Case insight on page 113) – is a way of consolidating your market position at home and buying market share in foreign markets. One of the reasons for the early success of Lastminute.com was its aggressive acquisition strategy in European markets after its launch in 1995. It purchased similar online businesses as well as a wide range of related travel and holiday firms such as Lastminute.de in Germany, Dégrif-tour in France, Destination Holdings Group, Med Hotels, First Option and Gemstone. These acquisitions helped it to gain international market dominance as well quickly as scale in both product categories and geographic markets was important. In this way it consolidated its brand across Europe very quickly.

Clearly a growth strategy based on acquisition requires access to funds – acquiring another successful new venture in another country can be expensive. It is really, therefore, only an option for high-growth businesses that have proved their business model and where economies of scale or scope are vital. 'Economies of scope' is the term used when less of a resource is used because it is spread across multiple activities – also called 'synergy'. This can arise when an intangible asset like a brand can be extended across more than one product (brand or product extension). This is the claim made by Virgin. It can also arise when organizational capabilities such as sales or technological management and their related fixed costs can be extended across more products or services. Many technology-based firms such as Amazon have used an acquisitions strategy extensively to expand both their product/service offering and customer base (see Case insight below).

When large companies 'buy-in' product development by acquiring smaller companies it is called 'corporate venturing'. It happens in a wide range of sectors from telecommunications to consumer goods to engineering, and is particularly common in the pharmaceutical industry and in the USA, where it represents a very significant proportion of venture capital investment. The reason for mentioning it at this point is because in the future this may be a way of realizing your investment by selling on your business.

Generally, a strategy of using acquisition for market and product development should be approached with caution – it is expensive and very risky. Acquisitions have a high failure rate. The larger the acquisition compared to the acquiring company, the riskier it is because the acquired business will be more difficult to integrate. It should only be used where there is a newly emerging market and it is the only way to gain rapid market dominance in what otherwise might become a fragmented industry. An alternative to acquisition is strategic alliances and joint ventures (Chapter 9). These do not require funding and keep the management of the businesses separate. Although you have to share the profits with your partner, you also share the associated risks. And for the founder it can mean that they do not have to spread themselves too thinly.

 ## Case insight   Amazon

Growth through acquisition

Amazon is one of the great entrepreneurial start-ups of this generation. It changed the way we shop, popularizing online shopping, and even changed the high streets in which real shops are based. Jeff Bezos first registered a company called Cadabra in 1994, but too many people thought it was called 'Cadaver', so he quickly changed its name to Amazon (because it started with an 'A' and sounded exotic). He launched Amazon onto the internet in 1995. Amazon started life selling books online but now sells almost everything, not to mention the gadgets you buy them on as well as the mechanisms you use to pay for the things you buy. Its journey is one of both internal organic growth and external growth, often through acquisition and investments (* denotes a minority investment in the list below). Although the full extent of Amazon's acquisitions is not public, it appears to have made over 80 within the first 20 years of its existence – an extraordinary average of one every three months.

1995 – Amazon started life selling books online, mainly titles that were difficult to find in normal book stores. A high proportion of sales went to US military personnel based overseas.

1996 – Sales increased when Amazon introduced an 8% referral commission to sites that directed customers to it. However, orders doubled overnight and increased 30–40% per month after the *Wall Street Journal* featured a front page interview with Bezos under the headline: 'How Wall Street whiz finds niche selling books on the internet'.

1997 – Amazon announced its stock market launch. Shares were offered at $18 and raised $54 million. Much of the cash was invested in improving its logistics infrastructure. Sales were now approaching $60 million per annum, having grown some 900% from the previous year.

1998 – Funded by its stock market launch, Amazon's acquisition trail started this year. It purchased **Bookpages** and **Telebook**, respectively the largest UK and German online book retailers. Both became part of

Amazon and, at a stroke, it gained a dominant market position in both countries. It went on to purchase **PlanetAll** (an address book, calendar and reminder service), **Junglee** (a data mining service for shoppers) and **Internet Movie Database**.

1999 – Bezos was named *Time* magazine's 'person of the year', announcing on its front cover 'E-commerce is changing the way we shop'. Acquisitions and investments accelerated sharply in this year with: **Drustore.com**, **Geoworks*** (owner of wireless communications patents), **Pets.com**, **LiveBid.com** (live internet auctions), **Exchange.com** (developing internet marketplaces), **Bibliofind.com** (then the world's largest inventory of books), **Musicfile.com** (a music site), **Accept.com** (a financial services company), **Alexa Internet** (web databases), **HomeGrocer.com***, **Gear.com**, **Tool Crib of the North** (the online division selling tools), **Convergence Corp.** (software connecting the internet with mobile devices), **MindCorps** (web applications), **Della.com*** (gift registry), **Back to Basics Toys** (a catalogue toy store), **Ashford.com*** (luxury goods retailers), **Leep Technology Inc.** (online database query tools developer).

2000 – This was the year that the dot.com bubble burst and Amazon's share price tumbled. However, Amazon fought back by diversifying the range of products it sold online as well as launching Amazon Marketplace, allowing businesses to sell their products directly on Amazon. Investments continued, but with only minority stakes, in: **Greenlight.com*** (online car retailer), **Greg Manning Auctions*** (collectible auctions), **Basis Technology*** (internationalization technology developer), **Kozmo.com*** (company offering free delivery of products from DVDs to Starbucks coffee), **WineShopper.com***, **Audible.com*** (content based spoken audio device).

2001 – Amazon retrenched, laying off 1,500 staff and closing its Seattle call centre. It also made its first quarterly profit ($5 million). Amazon joined with Borders to launch **Borders.com** using Amazon technology. It bought bankrupt electronic online retailer **Egghead.com** and also

Continued...

Continued from previous page...

invested in **CatalogueCity.com** and signed a commercial agreement with this group of catalogue merchants.

2002 – Amazon renegotiated its shipping contract with UPS and launched free shipping on higher value orders.

2003 – Amazon announced first full-year profits of $35.3 million. It took over the defunct CDNow website (CDs and records) to fulfil orders.

2004 – Diversification of online products continued. Amazon bought **Joyo.com**, the largest online retailer of books, music and videos in China. It also bought **A9.com**, a company researching and developing innovative technology and **Lab126**, developers of integrated consumer electronics such as the then yet to be produced Kindle.

2005 – Acquisitions restarted with **BookSurge LLC** (inventory-free, on-demand book printing), the French company **Mobipocket.com** (e-books for mobile devices), **CustonFlix** (film and CD downloads) and **Smallparts.com** (industrial component supplier).

2006 – Amazon head office relocated to Kent, Washington, USA. It acquired **Shopbop.com** (women's fashion online retailer) and **Wikia Inc.*** (software development for wiki sites).

2007 – Amazon entered the hardware market and introduced the first Kindle e-book reader (production was subcontracted). Initial stocks were sold out in five hours. Acquisitions continued with the **dpreview.com** (the Digital Photography Review was the largest independent publisher of audiobooks in the USA), **Brilliance Audio Inc.** (then the largest independent US publisher of audio books), **Endless.com** (internet shoe retailer) and **Amie Street*** (music store and social network site).

2008 – Acquisitions and investments surged with **AbeBooks.com** (a rival online book site specializing in used books and collating online sales for independent bookstores), **TextBuyIt** (a phone-texting, shopping and price-comparison service), **Lovefilm.com** (online CDs and DVDs), **Box Office Mojo** (box office tracking data), **Audible.com** (online spoken-word audio provider), **Without A Box** (film promoter), **Animoto*** (video creation technology), **Fabric.com** (online fabric store), **Engine Yard Inc.*** (cloud-based web applications), **Elastra Corp.*** (cloud-based software development), **Shefari** (a global community of book lovers) and **Reflexive Entertainment Inc.** (video game development).

2009 – Acquisitions and investments continued: **Stanza** (manufacturer of a rival e-book reader to Kindle), **Zappos** (online shoe retailer), **SnapTell** (image matching software), **Yieldex*** (online ad targeting), **Lexcycle** (electronic book reading application for iPhone and iPod), **Booktours*** (author profiles), **Foodista*** (cooking encyclopaedia and wiki), **Talk Market* Inc.** (which allows the uploading of videos etc. to assist online shopping) and **Snaptell** (mobile image recognition software).

2010 – Acquisitions and investments continued: **Touchco** (touchscreen manufacturer, bought to produce the next generation of Kindle e-readers), **Toby Press** (publisher), **LivingSocial*** (local deal website), **Woot** (US internet retailer), **Quidsi** (US online baby product retailer) and **BuyVIP** (online fashion retailer).

2011 – Amazon moved into online video streaming, available to members of Amazon Prime. It also announced a digital partnership with DC Comics. Acquisitions and investments included **The Book Depository** (a UK online book-seller with a large catalogue), **Yap** (voice-to-text software) and **Pushbutton** (UK digital agency developing interacting TV).

2012 – Amazon launched the second generation of e-book readers – the colour touchscreen Kindle Fire, usefully preloaded with your Amazon account details. It comes with social networking that connects you to others who purchase the same books and films. Amazon also launched a 'free' digital book lending library for members of Amazon Prime. Acquisitions and investments included **Kiva Systems** (manufacturer of robotic fulfilment systems), **Teachstreet*** (a local student website) and **Evi** (voice guided search software).

2013 – Acquisitions and investments included **IVONA Software** (voice recognition software), **Goodreads** (social reading website) and **Liquavista** (digital currency).

2014 – Acquisitions and investments included **Double Helix Games** (video game development) and **comiXology** (digital comic book store). The Amazon Fire TV set-top box launched. It also launched Kindle Unlimited – a subscription-based service offering e-books and audio books. By this date Amazon also has its own app store, online payment system and cloud computing facility.

Many of the retail websites bought by Amazon were closed down or consolidated into its main activities but some survive as 'independent' operations. Some acquisitions have become subsidiaries. Some acquisitions and investments were resold.

QUESTIONS:

1 What is the difference between an investment and an acquisition? Why has Amazon made both?

2 Categorize the acquisitions and investments Amazon has made.

3 From this categorization, can you see any strategic logic in this long list of acquisitions? What part do they play in the growth of Amazon?

4 What industry/market did Amazon start out in? What industry/market is it now in?

Practice insight reminder Characteristics of a good business idea – 14

14 **Scalable** – small projects can usually get off the ground easily, but bigger projects can be problematic because they are just 'too big'. In which case, you need to see whether the project can be broken down into smaller projects that can be implemented when the original idea is proved – scalability. The idea is to avoid as much risk as possible for as long as possible – but to make sure you do not miss the window of opportunity completely. This is all a question of judgement and changing market conditions, so you need to remain flexible and think through how you might scale up the project when it proves successful.

⊃ Summary

> Growth comes from market penetration, market and product/service development and/or a combination of both – diversification.

> Market development is about finding new markets. This can be geographic – going from local to regional to national and on to global. It might also be going on to sell to different market segments.

> One reason for finding new markets is to achieve economies of scale of production. Another is that your key competency lies with the product, for example with technology-based products, and therefore the continued exploitation of the product by market development is the preferred route for expansion. A final reason might be that the product is nearing the end of its life cycle in the existing market.

> The Uppsala Internationalization Model proposes that SMEs target psychically close markets – ones that they feel mentally comfortable with – initially using market entry methods that require limited commitment, such as exporting. As they gain knowledge and experience from their market involvement over time, so they increase their commitment. This process is repeated from market to market.

> Porter's Five Forces is a useful tool to help assess competitiveness in new markets. It can be used to assess foreign markets but the risks associated with exit barriers also need to be considered.

> There are a number of ways to enter a foreign market, each one increasing your degree of commitment and investment: to export, to appoint an agent, to license/ franchise, to set up a joint venture or to set up or acquire a wholly-owned subsidiary.

> Product development might include product modification, extension and expansion, leading to the development of completely new products.

> The Growth Share matrix is a loose conceptual framework that helps clarify the complexity of managing a portfolio of products. It has implications for the appropriate marketing strategy for each product/market and the cash flow and profit it generates.

> Diversification involves moving from core areas of activity into completely new and unrelated product/ market areas. It is central to the process of corporate evolution as new markets and industries are created.

> Diversification is high risk, but if done incrementally by constantly bundling new products and services together while extending the newly developing market, the risks can be reduced.

> Acquisitions can be used to help companies gain rapid market dominance early in the life of a product. They can also help develop a more comprehensive offering to customers.

> Diversification does not reduce risk in a publicly quoted company, and hence does not increase shareholder value – unless new markets or industries are being created. It does, however, reduce risk for the individual or family owning an unquoted company by spreading risk across different sectors.

> Any strategy of using acquisition for market and product development should be approached with caution – it is expensive and very risky. It should only be used where there is a newly emerging market and it is the only way to gain rapid market dominance in what otherwise might become a fragmented industry.

✓ Activities

1 Using Figure 13.1, list the strategies your university might use to grow your university department and the time scales involved. Explain your strategies and the reasons for selecting them.

2 Repeat this exercise for your business.

3 Lists the activities you need to undertake to the options in activity 2. Using the risk index developed in Chapter 10, assign an attractiveness classification to these options (i.e. identifying those options that have high impact, high probability and are highly controllable).

4 Identify the critical success factors coming out of the previous activity and determine what would be the relevant milestones.

5 Map the course portfolio of your university department onto the Growth Share matrix in Figure 13.4. What are the strategic implications of this product portfolio?

6 Map Apple's product portfolio onto the Growth Share matrix in Figure 13.4. Research the strategies adopted by Apple to launch and roll out the iPad since 2010. Have the strategies been effective? If so, why? Chart its move in the Growth Share matrix. Where is the product now in its life cycle?

7 Map the product/service developments you might consider as your business grows onto the Growth Share matrix in Figure 13.4. Note down the marketing and cash flow implications of this product portfolio.

🗨 Group discussion topics

1 Penetrating your existing market is a low-risk option and should therefore always be the strategy you pursue first. Discuss.

2 Selling internationally is risky but not selling internationally may be more risky. In what circumstances might this be true?

3 Exporting is expensive and risky. It is therefore not an attractive option. Discuss.

4 How can you minimize your risk of exposure to currency fluctuations?

5 Some products – basic necessities like food and drink – do not have life cycles. Discuss.

6 In what circumstances might product development be a lower-risk strategy than market development, and vice versa?

7 In practical terms it is impossible to find out where a product is in its life cycle. Discuss.

8 How useful is the Growth Share matrix?

9 How might you go about creating a scale for the Growth Share matrix? Give practical examples.

10 In what circumstances might you want to 'shoot a dog'?

11 Give examples of product expansions and extensions.

12 Can a 'Problem Child' be profitable? Explain with examples.

13 You never diversify. Discuss.

14 Why might you want to own a diversified company?

15 Why might you decide to pay a premium to acquire other companies rather than to grow organically?

16 What is synergy and how can it be achieved?

☛ References

Abell, D.F. (1980) *Defining the Business*, Hemel Hempstead: Prentice Hall.

Anderson, S., Gabrielsson, J. and Wictor, I. (2004), 'International Activities in Small Firms: Examining Factors Influencing the Internationalization and Export Growth of Small Firms', *Canadian Journal of Administrative Sciences*, 21(1).

Chelliah, S., Sulaiman, M. and Yusoff, Y.M. (2010) 'Internationalization and Performance: Small and Medium Enterprises (SMEs) in Malaysia International', *Journal of Business and Management*, 5(6).

Coviello, N.E. and Munro, H.J. (1995) 'Growing the Entrepreneurial Firm: Networking for International Market Development', *European Journal of Marketing*, 29(7).

Grant, R.M. (2010) *Contemporary Strategic Analysis*, 7th edn, Chichester: John Wiley.

Hauser, C. and Wagner, K. (2010) 'Innovation as a Pre-condition for Export Activities of SMEs – Evidence from the European Union', *International Council for Small Business (ICSB)*. World Conference Proceedings.

Johanson, J. and Vahlne, J.-E. (1977) 'The Internationalization Process of the Firm – A Model of Knowledge Development and Increasing Foreign Market Commitment', *Journal of International Business Studies*, 8(1).

Johanson, J. and Vahlne, J.-E. (1990) 'The Mechanism of Internationalization', *International Marketing Review*, 7(4).

Johanson, J. and Vahlne, J.-E. (2006) 'Commitment and Opportunity Development in the Internationalization Process: A Note on the Uppsala Internationalization Process Model', *Management International Review*, 46(2).

Johanson, J. and Wiedersheim-Paul, F. (1975) 'The Internationalization of the Firm: Four Swedish Cases', *Journal of Management Studies*, 12(3).

Kuhlmeier, D.B. and Knight, G. (2010) 'The Critical Role of Relationship Quality in Small- and Medium-Sized Enterprise Internationalization', *Journal of Global Marketing*, 23(1).

Laanti. R, Gabrielsson, M. and Gabrielsson, P. (2007) 'The Globalization Strategies of Business-to-Business Technology Industry', *Industrial Marketing Management*, 36.

Leonidou, L.C. and Katsikeas, C.S. (1996) 'The Export Development Process: An Integrative Review of Empirical Models', *Journal of International Business Studies*, 27 (Third Quarter).

Levy, H. and Sarnat, M. (1970) 'Diversification, Portfolio Analysis and the Uneasy Case for Conglomerate Mergers', *Journal of Finance*, 25.

Lu, J.W. and Beamish, P.W. (2001) 'The Internationalization and Performance of SMEs', *Strategic Management Journal*, 22(6).

Luffman, G.A. and Reed, R. (1984) *The Strategy and Performance of British Industry*, London: Macmillan.

Mason, R.H. and Goudzwaard, M.B. (1976) 'Performance of Conglomerate Firms: A Portfolio Approach', *Journal of Finance*, 31.

Michel, A. and Shaked, I. (1984) 'Does Business Diversification Affect Performance?', *Financial Management*, 13(4).

Palich, L.E., Cardinal, L.B. and Miller, C.C. (2000) 'Curvi-linearity in the Diversification-Performance Linkage: An Examination of Over Three Decades of Research', *Strategic Management Journal*, 22.

Park, C. (2002) 'The Effect of Prior Performance on the Choice between Related and Unrelated Acquisitions', *Journal of Management Studies*, 39.

Peters, T.J. and Waterman, R.H. (1982) *In Search of Excellence*, London: Harper & Row.

Selassie, H., Mathews, B., Lloyd-Reason, T. and Mughan, T. (2004) 'Internationalization Factors and Firm Size: An Empirical Study of the East of England', in F. McDonald, M. Mayer and T. Buck (eds), *The Process of Internationalization: Strategic, Cultural and Policy Perspectives*, Basingstoke: Palgrave Macmillan.

Sullivan, D. and Bauerschmidt, A. (1990) 'Incremental Internationalization: A Test of Johanson and Vahlne's Thesis', *Management International Review*, 30 (January).

Tellis, G.J., Stremersch, S. and Yin, E. (2003) 'The International Take-off of New Products: The Role of Economics, Culture, and Country Innovativeness', *Marketing Science*, 22(2).

Vernon, R. (1966) 'International Investment and International Trade in the Product Cycle', *Quarterly Journal of Economics*, 80(2).

Vernon, R. (1971) *Sovereignty at Bay: The Multinational Spread of US Enterprises*, New York: Basic Books.

Vernon, R. (1979) 'The Product Life Cycle Hypothesis in a New International Environment', *Oxford Bulletin of Economics and Statistics*, 41(4).

Welch, L. and Loustarinen, R. (1988) 'Internationalization: Evolution of a Concept', *Journal of General Management*, 14(2).

Wernerfelt, B. and Montgomery, C.A. (1986) 'What is an Attractive Industry?', *Management Science*, 32.

Weston, J.F., Smith, K.V. and Shrieves, R.E. (1972) 'Conglomerate Performance Using the Capital Asset Pricing Model', *Review of Economics and Statistics*, 54.

Zahra S.A., Ucbasaran, D, and Newey, L.R. (2009) 'Social Knowledge and SMEs' Innovative Gains from Internationalization', *European Management Review*, 6(2).

Go online to access additional teaching and learning resources for this chapter on the companion website. Click here in the ebook to complete a multiple choice revision quiz for this chapter.

14 | FINANCING THE BUSINESS

Contents

- Practice insight: Government loans, grants and support

- Practice insight: What banks look for

- Practice insight: 7 signs that worry banks

- Practice insight: What equity investors look for

- Practice insight reminder: Characteristics of a good business idea

ImageSource

Learning outcomes

When you have read this chapter and undertaken the related activities you will be able to:

> Understand the principles of prudent financing;
> Describe the sources of finance available to small firms and evaluate which are appropriate for different needs;
> Understand how banks assess lending to start-ups and small firms and how they monitor the performance;
> Understand how business angels and venture capitalists assess investments in start-ups and small firms and how they might work with the founder;
> Make a preliminary assessment of the finance needed for your business.

Case insights

Softcat	FarmDrop
Hotel Chocolat	Kickstarter
Lingo24	Hamijoo
Purplle.com	TransferWise
Lontra	Mears Group
Zopa	Alibaba (2)
inSpiral Visionary Products	

Selecting the right sort of finance

Many new ventures require finance to get started. The more fixed assets you need, the higher your stock-holding, and the longer debtors take to pay, the greater your need for finance. And while a cash flow forecast will tell you how much you require and for how long (we deal with this in the next chapter), it will not tell you what sort of finance you require.

The first thing to realize is that not all money is the same. Different sorts of money ought to be used for different purposes and not all types of money are available to all new ventures. In fact, many entrepreneurs, particularly at start-up, try to avoid using money at all by borrowing or using other people's assets wherever possible – 'bootstrapping'. They also use their personal credit cards, often repaying and recycling balances month-by-month. Where this fails, they might borrow money from friends or relatives. Friends and relatives can be flexible, perhaps agreeing to lend at a low or zero interest rate and without any guarantees because they know and trust you. They might even help with running the firm and bring valuable experience with them. However, rather than relying on informal agreements, most advisors would recommend that more formal loan agreements are drawn up so as to avoid misunderstandings and arguments later. Inevitably, however, most firms will need to obtain some form of external finance at some point in their life.

Table 14.1 summarizes the major forms of finance and how they *ought* to be used – in theory. The principle is that the term duration of the source of finance should be matched to the term duration of the use to which it is put. Fixed or permanent assets, including the permanent element of working capital (stock and debtors, net of creditors) should be financed by long- or medium-term sources of finance, and only fluctuations in working capital should be financed by short-term finance, such as overdraft.

For a limited company the money that you put into the venture can take two forms – equity or loans. Equity takes the form of share capital. Over time the shareholders' equity grows with profitable trading. But if the venture fails then the shareholder risks losing everything, including the share capital they have put into the venture. For profitable, fast-growing businesses with a good management team there may be the opportunity to attract further equity investment from crowdfunding, business angels or venture capital organizations. These are covered in more detail later in this chapter.

Loans can come from many sources, but most firms will have to turn to the banks for finance at some point. Loans are serviced by regular interest payments and the capital will,

> To succeed in business you should never chase money. If you achieve success money will chase you. If you get too attached to the money you never reinvest. You have to treat the money in the business like it's not yours.

John Elliott, founder, Ebac, *The Sunday Times*, 10 March 2013

> We wanted to raise £250,000 to get the company off the ground and there were relatively few people who were interested in investing in three young guys without a track record and a product that was new to the UK. Equity was really the only alternative option. As the three founders were young, they had not built up a capital base and so debt was not a viable route as there was nothing to secure it on.

James Davenport, Finance Director, Innocent, *The Guardian*, 23 October 2014

Table 14.1 Matching sources and uses of finance

Duration of finance	Source of finance	Use of finance

Long- & medium-term	> Equity
	  > Personal, family & friends investment
	  > Angel finance
	  > Venture finance
	> Long- & medium-term loans
	  > Personal, family & friends
	  > Bank
	> Lease & hire purchase
	> Crowdfunding (equity or loan)
		> Fixed assets: land, buildings, machinery, plant, equipment, vehicles, furniture etc.
		> Permanent working capital: stock, debtors (net creditors)

Short-term	> Bank overdraft
	> Short-term loans
	  > Personal, family & friends
	  > Bank
		> Seasonal fluctuations in working capital: stock, debtors (net creditors)

> We did look at securing [a conventional loan] but we quickly ended up where we are – invoice discounting … A lot of friends run small businesses, and banks are not being generous to say the least. They're very careful – which is why they prefer to offer invoice discounting, because it's safe for them.
>
> **Tim Ewington**, co-founder, Shortlist Media, *The Daily Telegraph*, 5 July 2013

ultimately, have to be repaid, depending on the duration: short (under one year), medium (up to five years) or long-term (over five years). Interest may vary with base rate or be fixed for the term of the loan. Agreeing to a fixed rate may involve a certain amount of crystal-ball gazing, but it does ensure that a small firm knows what its financing costs will be for some time to come.

As we shall see in the next section, bankers are likely to look for the security of assets to act as **collateral** against any loan, and if they cannot get this, they may ask you for **personal guarantees**. Personal guarantees can come from you or family or friends. Many countries have government loan schemes that offer lower rates of interest to small firms and/or guarantee provisions to replace or supplement personal guarantees. Some countries have credit mutual schemes for small firms that offer similar advantages.

There are two other ways of financing the purchase of fixed assets:

> **Lease** – This allows the firm to use the asset without owning it by making regular lease payments;
> **Hire purchase** – This allows the firm to purchase the asset over a period of time, again, by making regular payments with the asset acting as security in the event of default.

The main practical difference between the two methods is their tax treatment. Interest rates on lease and hire purchase schemes may be higher than on loans, but for a firm with little security to offer a banker they might be the only way to secure finance.

Once you start trading, other sources of finance become available. Most suppliers of goods and services offer trade credit terms (e.g. payment in 30 days), although they might insist on taking credit references and might also undertake a credit check. They will also place credit limits on accounts. Start-ups may have to establish a payment history to be offered credit and only gradually will the credit limit be extended. Trade credit is an important source of finance for most established firms – and it is free. It is also worth mentioning **factoring** and **invoice discounting** which is, again, only available once you establish a trading history. These are ways of obtaining finance against the invoices you issue (typically 75–80% of the value). You pay interest on the cash advanced, until the invoice is paid. It can be expensive and there are many restrictions, but it can be a lifeline to undercapitalized, rapidly growing businesses. Your bank will put you in touch with organizations offering these facilities.

 Case insight   Softcat

Factoring

Peter Kelly never finished his university degree. Instead he travelled the world before returning to the UK. He worked for Rank Xerox in Sales and Training for seven years before starting Software Catalogue, a mail-order software business, in 1993. This became Softcat Limited and is now based in Marlow, UK. Peter is still chair. Softcat employs over 200 people and has a turnover in excess of £100 million. It has become a leading supplier of software licensing, hardware, security solutions and related IT services to companies.

Success brought unexpected problems early in Softcat's life. Initially Peter drew up a business plan, put in £35,000 of his own money and found two external investors willing to each put in a further £10,000. The mail-order software

market was virtually untapped at the time and it was the firm's success that caused the problem. Within a year it had run out of cash and had reached the end of its ever-increasing overdraft limit as debtors/receivables were increasing at an alarming rate. The firm was overtrading – trading beyond its financial resources. Peter's response was to factor his debts – relying on the one asset in his balance sheet for security. It might have been more expensive than overdraft finance, but it helped the company to survive, grow and become the success it is today.

❏ Visit the website: www.softcat.com

QUESTION:

1 What are the advantages and disadvantages to Softcat of using factoring?

Finally, it goes without question that if there are grants or 'soft-loans' available then they should be considered. Grants are 'free money', although they can involve bureaucracy and take time to come through. They vary enormously between countries and even regions, changing frequently to reflect national and regional priorities. There are often special schemes for start-ups, particularly social enterprises and often for younger people.

Most new ventures will struggle to find finance appropriate for their needs. It is rarely easy. The flowchart in Figure 14.1 attempts to at least guide you through the process of deciding what form of finance is most appropriate and available to you. Of course, actually persuading somebody to offer you the equity or loan finance will be more difficult.

All providers of funds rely on legal contracts to give them security over their loan or investment. Developing countries like China, where formal legal mechanisms tend to be less important than relationships (Allen et al., 2005), are therefore at a disadvantage when it comes to the provision of funds. Weak property rights add to this problem. SMEs in these countries can face significant constraints in accessing all the forms of finance discussed here and, as a result, often make greater use of informal sources of financing.

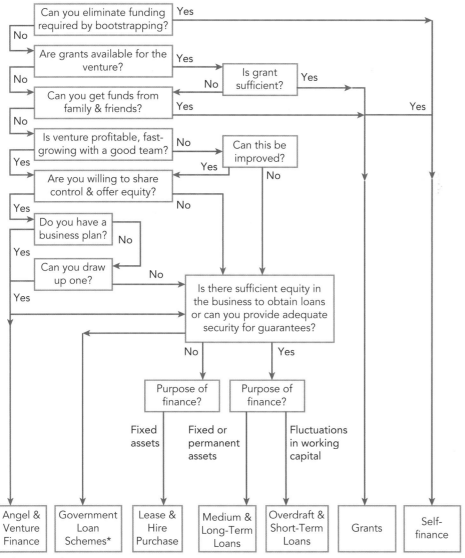

*These vary from country to country

Figure 14.1 Selecting the appropriate sort of finance for a new venture

Source: Adapted from DTI (1997) *Financing Your Business: A Guide to Sources of Finance and Advice*, and updated. Contains public sector information licensed under the Open Government Licence v3.0.

Case insight   Hotel Chocolat

Raising funds from customers

Hotel Chocolat is a luxury choco- late maker and retailer set up in the 1990s by Angus Thirlwell and Peter Harris. Over the years it developed a loyal customer base that opened up interesting funding opportuni- ties for business later in their lives. In 2010 it raised £3.7 million by offering 100,000 members of its 'tasting club' £2,000 or £4,000 annual bonds with the inter- est paid in monthly deliveries of a chocolate tasting box:

'This was prompted by our customers asking how they could get more involved with the company. We found a way of inviting them to invest in our development plans in exchange for a return paid in chocolate. And we have been bowled over by their response. We are now in a strong position to grow the business further using funds provided directly from our customers.' (Angus Thirlwell, The Independent, 14 July 2010)

The bonds fell due for repayment in 2013 and the company re-offered the bonds to their customers on similar terms. Of these customers, 97% signed up for another three years.

❏ Visit the website: www.hotelchocolat.com

QUESTION:

1   What sort of businesses can raise funds from customers? Give examples.

Courtesy of Hotel Chocolat

Sources of finance in the UK

Start-up sources of finance conform to a 'pecking order', with internal finance from the entrepreneur's personal savings used before external finance principally in the form of bank debt followed by equity from business angels and venture capitalists. Based upon a random sample of 160 UK start-ups (under two years old) interviewed in 2008, Fraser (2009a) found 85% used internal finance, of which 91% used personal savings, 13% loans or gifts from family or friends, 4% home mortgages and 4% personal credit cards (businesses use more than one source). Only 13% used external finance, of which 94% used bank loans and 7% used grants or subsidies.

The same study looked at a random sample of 2,500 established small firms (under 250 employees) and found that they all used some sort of external finance. It found 54% still used credit cards, 43% used overdrafts, 37% (free) trade credit, 21% asset finance (lease and/or hire purchase), 16% term loans, 9% loans from family or friends but only 3% used equity (which mainly came from the owner or family or friends) and 2% used factoring, invoice discounting or stock finance (again, businesses use more than one source). Citing supporting evidence from the Bank of England, Wright and Fraser (2014) conclude that bank finance remains the dominant element of external start-up and SME finance in the UK.

Two other interesting points emerge from these studies. Firstly, the continuing but increasing use of credit card finance, where balances might be paid off and recycled month-to-month. Secondly, the low use of equity finance, particularly from external sources. Indeed, only 1.7% of the firms used business angels and less than 1% used venture capitalists.

 ## Case insight　Lingo24

The funding dilemma

Lingo24 is an Edinburgh-based online translation business started by Christian Arno in 2002 while still at university. Today it has a turnover of over £7 million and over 200 staff and has won many awards for the translation services it offers, which range from 'budget' to 'professional, fully proof read translations which adhere to on-brand messaging'. Surprisingly, this growth has been entirely self-funded. That is, until 2013 when Christian wanted to introduce a new automated translation platform that would cost substantially more cash than the business had available. Christian considered selling an equity stake in the business but was reluctant to give away equity. So, he has hired corporate finance advisors to help him select the right option:

'I've been nervous and kept costs low at every turn to avoid the needs for funds. But now It's a pace thing. We need to move ahead quickly … If a bank could give us a £3 million loan, I'd love it – but they'll never do that with a business like ours because of the type of assets we have. We only have our debtor book and that won't facilitate that level of borrowing … Someone I know had a very bad experience with outside investors. You hear horror stories of people losing control and losing the value they've built up. But with the level of ambition we have and the dynamic of the marketplace at the moment, we need those funds'. (The Daily Telegraph, 5 July 2013)

In April 2014 Lingo24 announced a seven-figure investment by a consortium led by Paul Gregory, who became chair. In the same year it went on to be named Scottish Exporter of the Year and International Trade Best Professional Service Advisor.

❏ Visit the website: www.lingo24.com

QUESTION:

1 What was the dilemma facing Lingo24? Is there a 'right answer'?

Social investment

There are no legal reasons why most social enterprises should be unable to apply for commercial sources of finance. Indeed, many use bank loans or lease assets on a day-to-day basis. However, being set up primarily to achieve social aims, you might think they will struggle to attract equity investors. But, as we shall see, you would be wrong. Social enterprises also have access to a number of sources of finance available exclusively to them.

The UK government set up Big Society Capital as a wholesale investor for social investment, investing in intermediaries who are willing to invest in social enterprises rather than the enterprises themselves. 'Front-line' social investors include the Social Investment Business (www.sibgroup.org.uk) which manages over £400 million of funds. It provides loans, grants and other financial products to charities, social enterprises and community organizations. One of these is the Social Enterprise Investment Fund, which was set up in 2007 by the Department of Health to help social enterprises provide health and social care services in England. Many of the financing deals offered by government departments are structured as 'social impact bonds', whereby the department repays the capital loaned with a return of 7%–10% if agreed social targets are met.

UnLtd provides advice, training and support as well as funding for social enterprise (https://unltd.org.uk/). Established in 2000 through a partnership with several leading UK non-profit organizations, the foundation provides grants to individuals with projects to improve their communities and access to a range of funding for social enterprises for start-ups and growth enterprises, from small amounts up to £500,000.

There are also ethical banks such as Charity Bank (www.charitybank.org), which lends only to registered charities, social enterprises and community organizations, and Triodos Bank (www.triodos.co.uk), which finances organizations ranging from organic food and farming to recycling and nature conservation. Both banks offer savings accounts to the general public. Commercial organizations also invest in social enterprises, using funds invested by the general public for that specific purpose. For example, Threadneedle Investment, in partnership with the Big Issue's investment arm, has a fund that invests in businesses that deliver both a certain financial return and a 'positive social outcome'. They invest in the bonds of organizations operating in sectors such as affordable housing, community services and health and social care.

Indeed, there are a growing number of schemes that enable people to give financial (and other) backing to community owned and run projects – anything from cafes to post offices and solar cooperatives to hydroelectric schemes. Investors usually have local links and are sympathetic to the cause. They invest by buying shares or loan-stock in the organization, often using crowdfunding websites. There is usually a minimum investment and there can be enormous variations in the promised return. For example, the Halton Lune hydroelectric scheme is the biggest community-owned hydroelectric project in England and expects to raise £976,000 by 2014 to build a 200KW scheme on the River Lune at Halton (Lancashire). It expects to pay 5% interest once the scheme becomes operational. The point is that the opportunities for funding a social enterprise are many, but the principles behind doing so remain pretty well the same as for any organization.

 Practice insight Government loans, grants and support

Government loans, grants and other support schemes vary from country to country. In the UK, they can vary from region to region and from sector to sector. They also change regularly. The Business Finance Bank provides an online Business Finance Guide at http://british-business-bank.co.uk/bfg/. To access an interactive tool that tells you what grants, loans and other support might be available to your business in the UK go to www.gov.uk/business-finance-support-finder. Details of the UK Enterprise Finance Guarantee scheme can be found at www.gov.uk/government/publications/enterprise-finance-guarantee.

Details of loans, grants and other support schemes in the USA is available at www.sba.gov (click on 'Loans & Grants').

Loan finance: banks

Banks are the main source of loan finance to small firms. And so long as the return you make on the total assets in the business (see Chapter 15) exceeds the current rate of interest, then you benefit by getting an extra return on the bank's money. However, if your return drops below the rate of interest then the loan will drain money out of the firm.

Banks can be reluctant to lend to small firms and new ventures in particular, because they view them as risky propositions. And it is worth understanding why this is the case. Banks lend a sum of money in return for agreed interest payments and the repayment of the sum borrowed. They do not share in the profits of the business, and if a firm fails, they stand to lose their capital. That bad debt is expensive to recoup. For example, if banks make a 4% margin on a loan (the difference between the rate they can borrow at and the rate they can lend at), then every $100 lost as a bad debt will need a further $2,500 to be lent for the sum to be recovered ($2,500 × 4% = $100). Put another way, the bank has to make a further 25 loans to cover this one bad debt. Not surprisingly, therefore, banks are risk averse and will do all they can to avoid a bad debt. Since they are all too aware of the failure statistics for business start-ups, entrepreneurs have an uphill task convincing banks of the viability of their project and obtaining a loan or even an overdraft facility.

Entrepreneurs seem naturally drawn to overdraft finance – surveys show it to be the major source of finance for small firms. After all, it is flexible: once agreed you can dip into it when

The banks are very supportive but they either lend you twice what you need, or half what you need.

John Elliott, founder, Ebac, *The Sunday Times*, 10 March 2013

you need it and you will only pay interest when you use it. However, it is repayable immediately should the bank demand it and it can be expensive if you are in permanent overdraft because the rate of interest charged is usually higher than on term loans. Term loans (short, medium or long) are loans for a fixed period of time. They are usually not repayable on bank demand (but do check terms). The capital repayments are fixed and known in advance. The interest rate can vary or be fixed and is usually lower than for an overdraft.

Banks expect higher rates of return from loans that they perceive to be higher risk. New ventures are therefore likely to face higher rates of interest than larger businesses with an established track record. They are also likely to face a demand for collateral against the loan. **Collateral** is the additional security demanded in case there is a default on a loan. It can take many forms and is normally specified by some form of charge or guarantee in the legal loan agreement. Collateral might come from business assets, but if these are insufficient then the entrepreneur (or their family or friends) may well be asked to provide personal collateral or guarantees for the loan. This can mean that the separation between your finances and those of your limited liability company is little more than theoretical.

In valuing business collateral the bank assumes that the assets will be sold on a second-hand market and this typically leads to far lower values being put on assets than you might expect. Table 14.2 gives a guide to what you might expect. Given these asset security values, it is clear that the full cost of new fixed assets will never filter down to the collateral base of your business – an incentive to use lease or hire purchase.

Table 14.2 Asset security values

Asset	Typical % value that can be borrowed in the UK	
Freehold land and buildings	70	
Long leasehold	60	
Specialist plant and machinery	5–10	100% can be obtained through leasing
Non-specialist plant and machinery	30	100% can be obtained through leasing
Debtors	30–50	Depends on age of debts and 'quality'
Stock	25	Depends on age of stock and 'quality'; in the event of business failure, raw materials will be worth more than work-in-progress or finished goods stocks

DTI (1997) *Financing Your Business: A Guide to Sources of Finance and Advice.* Contains public sector information licensed under the Open Government Licence v3.0.

 Practice insight What banks look for

Banks are in business to make as much money as possible with the least risk. Bank managers are employees, work in a highly regulated environment, and have very limited discretion. Lending decisions are heavily influenced by bank lending policies and procedures. Some banks use computer-based credit scoring systems to produce lending recommendations for managers. Lending decisions can reflect general economic conditions and the balance of the bank's lending portfolio as much as the lending proposition itself. One bank can turn down an applicant that another will accept.

For a bank, the starting point for agreeing to any loan is its **purpose**. Is this consistent with bank policy? Is it legal? Is it in the best interest of the business? Next, the bank needs to assess whether the **amount** is appropriate. Have all associated costs for the project been included? Has the borrower put money in themselves? Is there a contingency? The bank also wants to ensure that interest is paid and the loan capital repaid on the due date. So is cash flow adequate? Are the **repayment** terms realistic? To make this judgement the bank will want to understand the fundamentals

Continued...

Continued from previous page...

Image Source \ Image Source/Alexander Porter C

of the business – whether it is viable – and will ask for financial information. In short, the bank will normally ask for a business plan.

Within the business plan, banks are particularly keen to scrutinize the **cash flow forecast** because it shows whether interest payments can be afforded and what 'slack' there might be to allow for uncertainties. They expect interest to be paid first, and that may mean delaying capital expenditures and reducing or delaying personal drawings. They are also keen to look at a range of ratios detailed in Chapter 12, in particular the **break-even point** and the **margin of safety** – this tells them about the operating risk of the business in terms of the overheads it faces and the margin it is able to command. These are vital pieces of information in judging a loan to a start-up. Banks may also look at the projected future **gearing** ratios (particularly for larger-scale start-ups), to see whether the business might become over-borrowed. Banks are also keen to see good financial controls are in place since this should lead to strong cash flow.

However, banks understand that most small firms are dominated by the owner-manager and usually seek to establish a good understanding of the person they lend to. They are interested in your **personal character**. Honesty and integrity are difficult to judge, but most bankers still think lending is a very personal thing and making a judgement on your character is vital. Your business track record and personal credit history are important. They will also make a judgement about your **personal ability**. How likely are you to turn this business plan into a successful business? Do you have a good management team behind you? Banks usually judge your personal character and ability by looking at your credit history, education and training, relevant business experience and proven track record. Unfortunately, with all these personal judgements, one person's objectivity might just be another's prejudice.

Agency theory and information asymmetry

Agency theory is about the behaviour of different parties to an agreement who have different goals and different divisions of labour. Its origins lie in financial theory and are generally credited to Jensen and Meckling (1976). Agency theory is relevant when there is an arm's-length relationship between a principal (such as a bank or an equity investor) and an agent (such as a borrower or small firm). It seeks to identify the mechanisms and costs that the principal has to put in place to ensure that the agent conforms to some legal agreement – such as a loan agreement. Information asymmetry is where these two parties do not have the same information on which to base their decisions.

This is relevant to how providers of finance approach new ventures. By definition, a new venture has no track record, and the provider of finance has little information on which to base their financing decision. What they have may not be reliable or relevant to this specific financing decision. This is when **asymmetric information** favours the entrepreneur, who should have more or better information than the provider of finance. This means that the provider of finance must incur extra costs in obtaining and checking the information they need to make and then monitor their decision. Many of these costs are fixed, whatever the size of the deal or the return made by the small firm. The conclusion is that providers of finance are naturally reluctant to lend or invest in start-ups or smaller ventures. This is less of a problem with larger firms because they have a track record and there is so much more public information about them, with many independent analysts reviewing this information for investment purposes.

Agency theory suggests that the natural response of a bank to these problems is to charge higher rates of interest, to impose conditions in the loan agreement (e.g. on use of funds or the provision of information) and/or to ask for business or personal collateral. Where sufficient collateral can be made available, the bank may feel that less information is required because the debt is more likely to be recovered in the event of default. Indeed, the bank may also feel that the provision of collateral gives the entrepreneur a strong incentive to see the business succeed. Agency theory also explains why the bank will want to be kept up to date on the progress of the business.

Similarly, the response of an equity investor is to look for higher rates of return. However, they will also expect the entrepreneur to maintain a controlling interest in the business so that, in the event of failure, they have more to lose than the other investors. This might impose a funding limit. The investor is also likely to want a greater involvement in the business so they can monitor their investment. Because of the fixed costs involved, many larger providers of equity finance will not get involved in small-scale start-ups because the return they can obtain does not cover their costs.

Banking relationship

Even after the loan is granted banks will continue to monitor the financial performance of the business – using many of the ratios outlined in Chapter 12. They expect to see annual audited accounts and sometimes budgets for the next year. What is more, they will also monitor the bank account itself, looking out for irregularities and checking that throughput is in line with expectations. And their expectations will be based upon your cash flow forecasts.

Despite increasing centralization and the declining importance of local banking, you still need to have a good working relationship with your local bank manager. A close relationship has the potential to provide them with the information they need about your firm and thus avoid the problem of information asymmetry. Like any relationship, this must be based on two elements: trust (that both parties will honour the terms of the loan) and respect (that both parties are good at what they do). These elements are personal and developed by keeping in regular contact. Bankers must ultimately trust and respect you, not just the business. That means visits and the provision of information. Bankers like to make regular visits. They like to feel they know the business and the individuals in it. However, bankers, more than anything, do not like surprises.

 Practice insight 7 signs that worry banks

Here are seven signs that start to make banks worry that all is not well in a firm:

1   **Frequent excesses on the bank account beyond the agreed overdraft facility:** This makes the bank start to think cash flow is not being properly controlled.
2   **Development of hard-core borrowing on an overdraft facility:** This makes the bank believe that a term loan would be more appropriate.
3   **Lack of financial information:** If the accounts and other information do not arrive regularly, they worry about the firm's ability to produce control information and, in extremis, can become suspicious that all is not well.
4   **Your unavailability:** If you are never available for a meeting or even a telephone conversation, the bank will start to believe something is wrong. Most people do not want to give bad news and avoidance is one way of not having to.
5   **Inability to meet forecasts:** The bank will eventually start to question the credibility of your forecasts and your ability and understanding of the market.
6   **Continuing losses, declining margins and rapidly diminishing or even increasing turnover:** At the end of the day the bank is really only interested in your ability to service its loan.
7   **Overreliance on too few customers or suppliers:** The loss of just one customer or supplier can create a disproportionate problem for small firms.

Is there gender discrimination in lending?

An issue often raised about finance is that bankers discriminate against certain sections of society in their lending decisions. Research shows that there is a strong relationship between start-up funding strategies and business performance (Brush et al., 2006; Greene et al., 2003; Jennings and Cash, 2006; Watson et al., 2009). So is there any evidence of prejudice and discrimination causing financing gaps for groups within society? It is true that women-owned businesses tend to attract less outside funding than men-owned businesses. Studies have repeatedly found that

Getty

women-owned businesses not only are reluctant to apply for finance but start with significantly less financial capital (typically only one-third) than men-owned start-ups (Carter and Rosa, 1998; Coleman, 2000; Hisrich and Brush, 1984). Women entrepreneurs prefer to use their own savings or to borrow money from their families, relatives or friends at start-up (Brush et al., op. cit., Ufuk and Ozgen, 2001). They borrow less and rarely gain access to venture funding (Greene et al., 1999; Marlow and Patton, 2003). The question of whether there is active discrimination against women in the provision of finance or the existence of a supply-side finance gap therefore needs to be addressed.

As noted in Chapter 3, using financial measures of performance, women entrepreneurs seem to underperform compared to their male counterparts (Department for Business Enterprise & Regulatory Reform, 2008), clustering in the retail and traditional service sectors. Access to all forms of capital – social, human as well as financial – tends to be poorer for women, and the female self-employed are much more likely to be part-time (Brush, 2006; Fairlie and Robb, 2009; Parker, 2009). Those who are self-employed are more likely to have family care responsibilities and to work shorter hours than males (Carree and Verheul, 2009; Verheul et al.,2009). There may be many sound personal and cultural reasons for all this; however, all these factors, especially financial performance, impact lending and investment decisions.

While research in the UK and USA has found differences in bank loan rejection rates by gender (in the UK: Fraser, 2006; in the USA: Treichel and Scott, 2006), it has failed to unearth evidence of a supply-side finance gap for women (in the UK: Fraser, op. cit.; in the USA: Levenson and Willard, 2000). Similarly, a Canadian study found no evidence of discrimination in capital availability (Orser et al., 2006). These studies could not find evidence of actual discrimination of any form by financial institutions. This suggests that other demand-side factors related to the personal and social circumstances of women are at play. Although not conclusive, other researchers broadly concur.

So why do women entrepreneurs seem to avoid external funding? Studies indicate the reasons are many and varied, ranging from risk aversion (Leitch, Hill and Harrison, 2006) to perceived obstacles (Henry et al., 2006; Leitch et al., 2006; Neergaard et al., 2006; Watson et al., op. cit.) and from lack of social capital, skills and a growth orientation (Greene et al., op. cit.) to an aversion to potential loss of control (Watson et al., 2006). It would seem that, for whatever reasons, women entrepreneurs choose not to make full use of the external funding that is available.

Is there ethnic discrimination in lending?

Turning to ethnic minority businesses, in the USA Cavalluzzo and Wolken (2005) found striking differences between ethnic groups in terms of loan rejection rates. In the UK, with the exception of black African and black Caribbean businesses, there appears to be no difference between ethnic and white businesses in their dependence on bank finance (Bank of England, 1999). Black African and black Caribbean businesses have lower levels of bank finance. Specialist banks have grown up to cater for the needs of different ethnic groups; for example, there are specialist Islamic banks which allow Muslim businesses to bank according to their principles and faith. There is also evidence of a strong preference for informal sources of finance by ethnic minorities (Ram et. al., 2002). This study found the reliance on informal finance was most significant in South Asian–owned businesses. These informal sources are usually accessed from a wide network of family, friends and others within the ethnic community, thus combining social with financial capital. Many of these sources are not available to white entrepreneurs.

Although there is a strong feeling of prejudice towards ethnic minorities by traditional banks, the Bank of England (op. cit.) could find no evidence of this in the UK, citing sectoral

> I don't think there is any lack of talent among female entrepreneurs, quite the opposite, it's just that they often have a different mentality to men … when they have constructed a successful business from scratch, in general they remain faithful to the business rather than sell up and move on. It would be great to see more women found and run fast-growth businesses that turn into large companies but it's easier to do that when you have several bites at the cherry.

Duncan Bannatyne, serial entrepreneur, *The Daily Telegraph*, 17 June 2009

concentration, failure rates and lack of business planning for rejection rates. It concluded the same about women entrepreneurs. A large-scale study of ethnic minority business and their access to finance broadly supported this conclusion (Ram et al., op. cit.) noting, however, that the issue was 'complex'. It did find evidence of diversity of experience from bank manager to bank manager and between different ethnic minority groups, confirming the existence of particular problems for Africans and Caribbean people. Not surprisingly, it found that best practice was where the bank manager had built up trust with their local minority community through close contact and stable relationships.

More recently, Fraser (2009b) used econometric analysis on a large-scale survey of UK small business finance to look for evidence of ethnic discrimination (loan rejection, interest rates and discouragement). He concluded firstly that there were large differences across ethnic groups. He also noted that many from the ethnic minorities felt they were discriminated against. Black and Bangladeshi businesses experienced high loan-rejection rates compared to white and Indian businesses. From the finance provider's perspective, black African firms were significantly more likely to miss loan repayments or exceed their agreed overdraft limit. However, he concluded very firmly that this was largely explained by a lack of collateral and poor credit histories and that there was no evidence of discrimination. He felt that many in these groups needed to tackle fundamentals like a lack of financial skills, lack of financial advice and poor levels of financial performance rather than just addressing cultural differences and the effects they might have.

Looking at gender and ethic discrimination in lending using the quarterly SME Finance Monitor statistics, Carter and Mwaura (2014) came to similar conclusions, that the lending outcomes were: 'largely, but not entirely, a consequence of underlying structural factors that lead women-owned and black and minority ethnic businesses to present a particular set of characteristics … coupled with the marked gender and ethnic dimensions to financial track records which inform risk ratings'. In conclusion, we can say that academic studies cannot uncover any systematic discrimination on grounds of ethnicity or gender.

Equity finance: business angels and venture capitalists

For a company with real growth potential, there may also be the opportunity to get private individuals (called 'business angels') or a venture capital institution to invest equity in the business. Equity funding is not available to sole traders or partnerships. Equity investment involves giving up a percentage of the ownership of the business, and potentially some of the control, in exchange for cash. That means giving up some of the future wealth the business will create. Investors are paid dividends, which are only paid at the discretion of the company. While the capital invested can be sold on in the form of shares, it is unlikely to be repaid by the business unless it ceases to trade and only then if other creditors are paid in full. It is therefore long-term, risk finance.

Both angel and venture financiers might expect dividends, but more importantly they hope to see the value of their shares increase if the firm does well and they will probably expect to realize their investment at some time in the future (normally 5–10 years) by selling on their shares in the business. Often an angel investment helps take the investee business to a point at which it is attractive for a venture capital firm.

Business angels invest smaller amounts of money than venture capital institutions (£10,000–£1 million) and operate in less formal ways. They are usually 'high net worth individuals', often with a successful entrepreneurial background themselves. They are looking to back start-up and early-stage ventures. The typical UK angel makes only one or two investments a year. Many have preferences about sectors or stages of investment based on their personal knowledge. Many also expect to exercise some degree of directorial control over the business. Most prefer local investments, in companies within, say, 100 miles from where they live or work. Most also prefer to stay anonymous.

Since angels are mainly locally based, angel networks can now be found from Cambridge in England to Mumbai in India One of the largest networks in Europe is located in London (http://

I want to know whether it will be attractive to buyers. The only way someone like me can make money is if someone will buy me out.

Ajith Jayawickrema, business angel, *The Sunday Times*, 2 June 2013

If your business is demanding of capital you've got to have a very clear business plan … because people will only lend you money to make money. They'll want a three times return on their investment within a three to four year window.

Will King, founder, King of Shaves, *RealBusiness*, 1 July 2009

> I always back the jockeys because they can ride any horse. That's fundamental. I think 'If things get difficult, will they still be there?'
>
> **Ajith Jayawickrema**, business angel, *The Sunday Times*, 2 June 2013

www.lbangels.co.uk/). These networks circulate business plans among the angels ahead of a physical pitch or presentation to the angels. If any angels are interested in investing, then a period of investigation and negotiation will take place before funds are committed. Often a fee is charged to the business seeking investment and some networks take a stake in the company if a deal is successfully negotiated. Some of the networks can also provide help in raising finance from other sources and in preparing a business plan for an additional fee.

In the UK many business angels belong to the UK Business Angel Association (http://www.ukbusinessangelsassociation.org.uk/). It has a code of conduct for its members, and a directory of members is available on its website. Local Investment Network Company (LINC) Scotland is the national association for business angels in Scotland. In the USA, angel groups are also locally based. Your local Chamber of Commerce or Small Business Development Centre should be able to put you in touch with your local group.

 ## Case insight   Purplle.com

Early stage finance

Manish Taneja and Rahul Dash left professional jobs to set up Purplle.com, a website selling beauty and grooming products, in Mumbai, India, in 2012. Within a year they employed 25 people, based in a tiny office and warehouse in the north of Mumbai:

> 'We realized that beauty and grooming was at an inflexion point in India and we knew that it would take off.'

Initially they used their own savings to set up the business and establish the website, but they then approached family and friends for loans and equity as well as used trade credit to finance their products. Once the business model proved successful, they decided they needed more equity

and approached a group of 15 business angels in Mumbai where they pitched their business model. They were successful and the investors brought not only capital but also website expertise and a network of contacts. Time will tell if the business succeeds.

❏ **Visit the website: https://purplle.com**

QUESTIONS

1 Softcat used factoring to raise finance, Hotel Chocolat used customer bonds, and Purplle used business angels. Under what circumstances are these different forms of finance best used?

2 Are any appropriate for your business? If so, why and at what stage?

Venture capital institutions are well established in the West. Typically, they invest larger amounts than business angels (usually over £2 million), mainly investing in established businesses (often buying out angel investments), **management buy-outs** (the management of a firm buying it) and **management buy-ins** (external managers buying a firm and normally replacing the management), although they can invest in larger start-ups. Because venture capitalists rely on financial contracts and the ability to mitigate agency problems through contracting, the most successful venture capital investments tend to be seen in countries with strong legal systems (Cumming and Johan, 2013), placing developing countries at a disadvantage. Investment decisions are usually made using sound financial criteria (see Practice insight on next page), but entrepreneurs will usually be asked to present their business plan if the fundamentals are sound. Based upon a 'laboratory experiment' and a field study, Chen et al. (2009) concluded that venture capitalists' investment decisions were based very much on the entrepreneur's preparedness rather than the passion of their presentation.

Neither business angels nor venture capitalists want to take control of the business away from the entrepreneur and therefore usually limit their investment to less than 50% of the share capital. However, because venture capitalists invest larger amounts, they often put together funding deals that involve ordinary shares, preference shares[1] and loan finance. In the past some of the management buy-out and buy-in deals they have structured have been notable for their high

---

[1]Preference shares are non-voting, with dividends at a fixed percentage of face value and with preference over ordinary shareholders in the event of liquidation.

leverage or gearing. The British Venture Capital Association (BVCA) produces a free Directory of Members, which gives a full list of venture capital institutions and their investment criteria (http://www.bvca.co.uk/). A similar organisation for Europe is called Invest Europe (http://www. investeurope.eu/).

 ## Case insight   Lontra

Funding new technology

UK Government grants were used to prove that Steve Lindsey's compact, low-maintenance, low-energy blade compressor technology design actually worked. However, to get it to prototype stage he required equity investment and, to get it beyond that – to a stage ready for market – would probably require further investment. Having been told that business angels do not like multiple investment stages, Lindsey decided to approach institutional investors and venture capitalists.

'We had two options: institutional investors, or a large group of business angels. We went for the first ... even though the valuation was slightly lower, because we realised the company would need multiple stages of funding.' (The Sunday Times, 4 May 2014)

Imperial Innovations and Nikko (a Japanese bank) agreed to back the new company, Lontra, but when it came to the second-stage financing round in 2009, both companies pulled out (for different reasons, unrelated to Lontra) and the company had to find new venture capital. With only a month to go before funding ran out, Midven, a Midlands firm, decided to invest.

Lontra is now a successful business. It sells its intellectual property rather than building compressors, reasoning that was where its competitive advantage lay. This technology can be used to replace traditional pistons and cylinders that form the basis of compressors in factories, fridges, air conditioners or even vacuum pumps in medical environments. In 2013 its design won it and the water utility, Seven Trent, the Water Industry Achievements Award for the most innovative new technology category. In 2014 turnover was some £1.2 million.

❏ Visit the website: www.lontra.co.uk

QUESTION:

1 What are the issues surrounding the funding of new technology and how did Lontra overcome them?

 ## Practice insight What equity investors look for

While business angels and venture capital institutions may look at the same range of criteria as a banker, their perspective is very different since, unlike the banker, they are sharing in the risk of the business. If it fails, they stand to lose everything. Consequently, they are interested primarily in two things:

1 **Return and risk:** Most investors are interested in the return they will make on their investment rather than the security they can obtain from the entrepreneur. The return on one investment must compensate for the loss on another. However, they are primarily interested in the capital gain on the sale of their investment rather than the dividends they might receive. Typically, they will be looking for an annual return on their investment of between 30–60%, depending on the perceived risk. Start-ups will usually be at the top end of that spectrum, but the final deal always requires negotiation. So for example, in the UK an investment of £100,000 might be expected to yield £400,000–£800,000 in five years' time – a multiple of four to eight times the original investment. And, while some may achieve this return,

others will not and the investor will be lucky to exit with their money intact. The business plan for a start-up is very important to an investor – they do not take guarantees and there is no track record to rely on. They will be particularly interested to see an identified and accessible market with strong growth potential. If yours is a technology-based start-up, the technology must be market ready. They also pay far greater attention to the quality of management – your experience and that of your management team. This is the only track record they have. And they expect this experience and expertise to be reflected in the quality of the business plan. When looking at the financial projections they will apply the full range of performance criteria, profitability and risk ratios outlined in Chapter 12. They will also pay great attention to your detailed assessment of the business risks and how they might be overcome.

2 **Exit route (liquidity event):** They will also want to be assured that they can sell on their investment at some time in the future and realize their profit – called the exit route in the UK or liquidity event in the USA. Most

Continued...

Continued from previous page...

business angels will want to realize their investment within a timeframe of 5 years. Venture capitalists may take a longer-term view, perhaps up to 10 years. For a start-up, that may be a problem because there may not be an established market for their shares within this time frame. So who might buy the shares? One option could be that you will want to **buy back** the shares and regain 100% control of your business. A **management 'buy-out'** or **'buy-in'** might be another option. Angels might sell on their shares to venture capitalists. Another option for both angels and venture capitalists is to sell on their share in the business (and perhaps those of the founder) to another company, often in the same industry, by way of a **'trade sale'**. They might also seek to obtain an **initial public offering** (IPO) or stock market floatation – a listing on a stock market – so that they can sell their shares to other institutional investors or the public. This can be expensive (a trade sale is far cheaper) and means that the business will have to comply with a whole range of regulations and disclosure requirements designed to make trading in their shares fairer. It also means that the firm needs a track record of solid profitability and good growth potential. There are two 'junior' markets in the UK that ultimately lead to a full listing on the Stock Exchange Main Market. These are called the **Off Exchange** (OFEX) and the **Alternative Investment Market** (AIM) and offer limited trading. However, many entrepreneurs (like Richard Branson) do not like the public accountability and loss of control implied by 'going public' on the stock market.

Both angels and venture capitalists will also undertake a thorough investigation of both the founder(s) and the business. Assessing all this will, inevitably, take longer than arranging a bank loan. Investors will want to be represented as a non-executive director on the board. This is their response to the issues raised through agency theory and information asymmetry, mentioned earlier. Business angels, particularly, may also expect a more 'hands-on', day-to-day involvement in the business. As with bank managers, it is important to develop a close personal relationship. Ultimately they invest in people rather than businesses and, since they face more risk than the banker, they need to be convinced that the entrepreneur and the management team can make the business plan actually happen. Trust and respect are important. Since they only make money if the firm succeeds, they are highly committed to helping the growing firm through the inevitable problems it will face. They can be an invaluable sounding board for sharing both problems and ideas. Many have valuable business experience, sometimes in the same business sector, and they can provide a strategic overview that helps you see through the day-to-day problems of business. They may also bring with them a wealth of business contacts. In short, used properly they can be a valuable asset to the firm – as Kirsty Henshaw realized when she selected the investors in her business (Case insight on page 264).

Crowdfunding and peer-to-peer lending

The recession of 2008 saw bank lending contract as banks tried to recapitalize and consolidate their balance sheets. The first victims of this were those 'riskier' loans to start-ups and small businesses. However, the growth of the internet has spawned the development of a new form of funding called crowdfunding. Crowdfunding is a form of peer-to-peer (P2P) funding which connects companies looking for finance directly with potential private lenders and equity investors. The connection is made through internet platforms which act as a sort of eBay for lenders and borrowers. In the UK, sites like Zopa, Funding Circle, RateSetter and Market Invoice have targeted P2P lending, while sites like Crowdcube and Seedrs have targeted equity finance. Registered lenders and investors can browse through lending opportunities posted by businesses and decide whether they wish to lend or invest.

P2P lending offers advantages to both lenders and borrowers. Lenders generally earn far more than they would if they put the money in a savings account – an average of over 9%. Borrowers who may not necessarily be approved for a bank loan might find it easier to borrow, albeit at a higher interest rate if their credit rating is low. The intermediary charges the borrower a percentage of the funds raised. This is how they make money. As with bank borrowing, borrowers and lenders will be party to a legal loan agreement which, among other things, will specify interest rates and capital repayment. These are organized by the intermediary.

See if you can sweat more cash out of the business plan, particularly using things like cash (invoice) discounting invoice factoring, to try and reduce the need for external cash; or look at alternative methods of raising cash, particularly peer-to-peer lending.

James Davenport, Finance Director, Innocent, *The Guardian*, 23 October 2014

Case insight   Zopa

Peer-to-peer lender start-up

Courtesy of Zopa, photo by Vickicouchman.com.

Giles Andrews

Giles Andrews had been a car salesman and had already built and sold a business that acquired failing firms in the motor industry and turned them around, when he got together with James Alexander, Richard Duvall and David Nicholson to think through the idea of a business that helped people lend to each other on the web, cutting out the middlemen. In 2005 they got the backing of some leading venture capital firms to launch Zopa, the first peer-to-peer lending website in the UK. It earns money by taking a margin on each lending transaction. The business was slow to take off until the credit crisis of 2008, which caused people and businesses to seek alternatives to banks. And during this time an attempt to start a similar business in the USA failed, despite the fact they raised £9 million for the launch.

'We launched with a large amount of noise but attracted no business. It took a long time to gain any traction … We had a British company that wasn't growing and an American business that was doing nothing and investors were frustrated.' (*The Sunday Times*, 10 August 2014)

But Zopa was eventually a success and is now the UK's largest peer-to-peer lender. It has facilitated loans of some £600 million, and revenues in 2013 were £5.3 million. Based in London, it employs 62 people. The other founding partners are no longer involved with the company and Andrews is chief executive. However, he and the founders own 14% and the rest of the management team 13% of Zopa.

❏ Visit the website: www.zopa.com

QUESTIONS:

1 How risky was this business to start up? Explain.
2 How risky was it to finance? Explain.

Some crowdfunding platforms offer equity funding opportunities, again usually charging the business a percentage of the funds raised (typically 5–7.5%). Some platforms also accept a slice of the equity rather than a flat fee. These sites have seen a huge increase in activity since they were set up. The first equity deal in the UK using crowdfunding was agreed in 2013, using an intermediary called Crowdcube. By the end of that year these equity crowdfunding platforms had raised approximately £28 million (*The Sunday Times*, 14 September 2014).

Typically each crowdfunding investor purchases only a very small percentage of the company. Rewards-based sites are popular. These are where the investor accepts 'gifts' from the company rather than equity. Being web-based, videos are used extensively to demonstrate products or services and, perhaps more importantly, the owner-managers seeking the finance. However, it is still vital to have a business plan that investors will expect to see. Crowdfunding is not an easy shortcut to raising finance. Crowdcube estimates that 30% of the offerings on their site do not achieve their target funding. The Seedrs site puts this estimate higher at two-thirds (*The Sunday Times*, 14 September 2014). Nevertheless, some offerings seem to create a momentum of their own, leading to questions about crowdfunding creating an 'auction mentality' that encourages bidding.

In many ways crowdfunding is the logical extension of the business angel networks discussed in the previous section; however, equity investment is inherently riskier than loans, and crowdfunding investors probably have less expertise than business angels in making this sort of investment. What is more, the issue about how and when their investment will be realized in the form of a capital gain remains even more up in the air. All of which makes this sort of investment very risky, which is why each investor will only ever contribute a small proportion of the funds raised and why the success of this source of finance – for both parties – is yet to be proved. So far, it has mainly been successful for 'quirkier' or niche businesses often with quasi-social objectives where investors might be less interested in risk and return than supporting the objectives of the venture (see Hamijoo Case insight on page 375).

Strangers will not invest in zero. If you can't raise 10–20% from your mates and your family first, that speaks volumes

Julia Groves, Chair, UK Crowdfunding Association, *The Sunday Times*, 14 September 2014

If you expect to post your pitch and have people throw money at it, you're in for a disappointment. The more momentum there is the more others will join in; nobody wants to walk into an empty bar.

Jeff Lynn, founder, crowdfunding site Seedrs, *The Sunday Times*, 14 September 2014

Case insights   inSpiral Visionary Products

Crowdfunding

Dominik Schnell and Bella Willink founded inSpiral Visionary Products in 2010. Starting life in a vegan cafe near Camden Market in London, the company sells organic products, including crisps made from dried kale that originally sold for £3.49 a packet. In 2013 inSpiral became the first company to raise equity rather than loan finance from crowdfunding. Using Crowdcube, the company raised £250,000 from 120 investors, handing over 10% of their equity – valuing the company at £2.5 million. inSpiral paid Crowdcube a fee of 5% of the money raised.

inSpiral has used the money raised to redesign its packaging and to sell its products online through Graze.com and through other retail outlets. It also now produces own-label products for a number of major high street stores. Increasing production allowed it to spread its overheads and bring down its sales prices significantly. For example, the price of kale crisps came down to £2.19 per pack, and that opened up more retail opportunities.

❏ Visit the website: www.inspiral.co

QUESTION:

1 What are the risks of investing in inSpiral using crowdfunding like this?

Case insights   FarmDrop

Crowdfunding

Ben Pugh also used Crowdcube to raise funds for FarmDrop, a London-based company he started in 2012 which by 2014 had nine staff. FarmDrop is a website that allows users to 'click and collect' local produce. He had a target of £400,000 to raise, but already had offline 'commitments' of £100,000. He hit his target within eight days. Indeed, he was so successful that he went on to raise £750,000 from 360 investors in the next 20 days. He parted with 27% of the company and paid Crowdcube a fee of £40,000.

'We now have hundreds of advocates for FarmDrop dotted around the country in the form of our investors.' (The Sunday Times 14 September 2014)

Both inSpiral and FarmDrop use Exeter-based Crowdcube, a platform set up in 2011 by Darren Westlake and Luke Lang. Crowdcube has a database of over 90,000 registered investors and has raised approximately £37 million in loan and equity finance since it was launched in 2011. In 2014 it raised £1.2 million on its own site. Balderton, a venture capital firm, also invested £3.8 million.

❏ Visit the website: www.farmdrop.co.uk

QUESTION:

1 What are the risks of investing in FarmDrop using crowdfunding like this? Is it any different than inSpiral?

I'm not sure we're ready to declare victory on Britain being the fintech capital of the world. It is still early days. But there is a disproportionate number of really interesting fintech companies emerging. The market potential of some of these companies is limitless.

Neil Rimer, co-founder, Index Ventures, *The Sunday Times*, 16 November 2014

The crowdfunding industry, sometimes called 'fintech' (short for financial technology), is in its infancy internationally but it is growing quickly and the UK has a strong foothold in it. The first British crowdfunding company was Zopa, started in 2005. By 2014 there were some 100 'fintech' start-ups housed in 'Level39', an accelerator located within One Canada Square at Canary Warf in London. In 2012 it was estimated that about €735 million was raised from all forms of crowdfunding in Europe, and the predicted figure for 2013 is about €1 billion (Massolution, 2013). This compares to an estimated bank lending of €6 billion in 2011 (EBF, 2012), business angel investments of €660 million in 2010 (CSES, 2012) and venture capital investments of €7 billion in 2012 (EVCA, 2012).

The crowdfunding industry is currently unregulated, but industry bodies are now beginning to be set up. In the UK there is the UK Crowdfunding Association (UKCFA) with 38 members, which collectively has some nine million investors (www.ukcfa.org.uk), and in the USA there is the National Crowdfunding Association (NLCFA) (http://www.nlcfa.org/main.html. A European Equity Crowdfunding Association (EECA) is being set up. With confidence in banks falling, many people are predicting P2P lending and investing will grow and could change the way we invest and borrow our money.

Some intermediaries allow you to browse through small-scale projects posted by social and not-for-profit organizations and donate funds (e.g. Global Giving). Other platforms specialize in certain types of investments (e.g. Abundance and the Trillion Fund, which specialize in renewable energy projects). There are also platforms that facilitate crowdfunding of loans managed by microcredit organizations in developing countries (e.g. Kiva).

Case insight   Kickstarter

Niche crowdfunding

Crowdfunding is proving itself particularly attractive to SMEs in general, but in particular to specialist, niche businesses that might have difficulties raising mainstream finance. Kickstarter was launched in 2009 by Perry Chen, Yancey Strickler and Charles Adler. It is an online crowdfunding site that focuses on creative projects – films, music, stage shows, comics, journalism, video games, technology and food-related projects. Originally based in New York, USA, it started accepting projects based in the UK in 2012, Canada in 2013, Australia and New Zealand in 2013 and Denmark, Ireland, Norway and Sweden in 2014. It is open to backers from around the world.

Projects posted on Kickstarter must have a set deadline to achieve a minimum funding target. If the goal is not met by the deadline, any funds offered are not collected. Funds pledged by donors are collected through Amazon Payments. Kickstarter charges a 5% fee on the total amount of funds raised and Amazon Payments charges an additional 3–5% fee.

By 2015, Kickstarter had reportedly received more than $1.5 billion in pledges from 7.8 million backers to fund 200,000 creative projects, several of which have gone on to receive critical acclaim. These include documentary films, contemporary art projects and music albums.

❏ Visit the website: https://www.kickstarter.com/

QUESTION:

1 Why has Kickstarter been so successful?

Case insight   Hamijoo

Niche crowdfunding

Hamijoo.com is a crowdfunding site for Iranian artistic and film projects that is similar to Kickstarter. Because of sanctions, in 2015 Iran's banking system remained cut off from the rest of the world and start-ups were starved of funding, not least because they could not attract funding from outside the country, even through crowdfunding. Hamijoo was founded by Mohammed Noresi, a 28-year-old biomedical engineering graduate who had previously worked on a number of tech start-ups that failed. Despite the problems of doing business in Iran (see Case insight about the Iranian internet market on page 134), within two months of start-up Hamijoo had employed three staff. By 2015 some 160 people had used the site to fund artistic projects such as a documentary film by award-winning independent Iranian film-maker Mehrdad Oskouei and a music album by Meysam Azad.

QUESTION:

1 Compare and contrast the opportunities and threats facing Kickstarter and Hamijoo. Can Hamijoo survive in the longer term?

The funding ladder

You have to hang on to that initial money like it is gold. Look after every pound because it will allow you to get your idea right and prove it. Nobody will give you money until you can prove your idea is a winner … There's lots of money out there but only for proven concepts.

John Elliott, founder, Coffee Nation, *The Sunday Times*, 23 May 2004

For any start-up, deciding what assets are needed, when to acquire them and how this is to be financed are important strategic decisions. Generally, you are best advised to minimize the resources you need at each stage of the business. Remember, you do not necessarily have to own an asset to use it – you can bootstrap or partner with others. Although inevitable if you want to maximize the potential of your business, once you start to use external funds you start to limit your flexibility and lose control. Deciding on the form of this funding is therefore every bit as important a decision as anything else that goes into the business plan.

 ## Case insight   TransferWise

The funding ladder

Taavet Hinrikus left his job at Skype in 2008 to join Kristo Käärmann, a financial consultant, and set up a new venture called TransferWise, an online money transfer service. The pair are Estonians and had first-hand experience of sending money back home and losing about 5% in transfer and currency conversion charges. They thought they could cut costs by using technology to match currency transfers – a form of peer-to-peer currency exchange that allows customers to wire money to one another cheaply, bypassing banks – and their commission charges. They raised about £21 million in venture finance from investors like Index Ventures and Kima Ventures and, more recently, Richard Branson. TransferWise went live in 2011. By 2014 it had transferred some £1 billion of cash and had 180 staff based in London, with technical staff in Estonia. TransferWise is cheaper than traditional

fund-transfer mechanisms, charging a fee of 0.5% or a flat fee of £1 if the amount is less than £200. Such is the success of the firm that US venture capital firm Sequoia Capital is looking to make a $50 million investment, valuing the company at about $1 billion (£640 million).

'It comes down to doing one thing and being the best at it ... Faith in the banking system dropped significantly after the financial crisis ... customer expectations changed and the time was right for financial technology.' (*The Sunday Times*, 16 November 2014)

❏ Visit the website: www.transferewise.com

QUESTION:

1 What are the advantages and disadvantages of using venture capital in this way?

 ## Case insight   Mears Group

The funding ladder

Mears Group started life as a small, private building contractor in 1988. It is now a leading UK PLC. In 1992 Mears was awarded its first multidisciplinary maintenance and repairs contract from a local authority. Since then it has grown to become the leading social housing repairs and maintenance provider in the UK. In 1996, with a turnover of £12 million and 83 employees, its Chair and Chief Executive Bob Holt floated the company on AIM, raising £950,000 with a market capitalization of £3.6 million. Over the following years it grew partly through organic growth and partly through acquisition, moving into the domiciliary care market. In

2008 it moved to the Main Market of the London Stock Exchange, with a turnover of £420 million and over 8,000 employees. In 2009 Mears Group won the PLC Award for New Company of the Year on the London Stock Exchange Main Market. Mears is listed on the FTSE4Good Index in recognition of its Community and Social Responsibility activity.

❏ Visit the website: www.mearsgroup.co.uk

QUESTION:

1 What are the advantages and disadvantages of having a stock market quotation?

Most firms use a range of finance to suit their differing needs and circumstances. The advantages and disadvantages of these different methods of financing your business are summarized in Table 14.3. Getting started on the funding ladder can be difficult, particularly in today's depressed trading environment. Many sources may not appear to be open to you as a start-up. Getting that first tranche of funding requires you to persuade financiers that you can make your business dream come true. They need to believe in you. You need to have credibility and to gain their trust and respect. However, a good business idea will always eventually find backing, particularly if you have a good business plan to explain it. And a good plan will help give you credibility and help you gain their trust and respect.

Table 14.3 Advantages and disadvantages of different sources of finance

Source	Advantages	Disadvantages
Equity Personal, family and friends investment	> Good, secure long-term finance > No interest or capital repayment > Can be used to lever further loan finance	> Dividends may be expected > Selling shares to outsiders dilutes your stake in the business and may lead to loss of control > Outsiders providing equity may want to interfere in the business
Equity Angel finance	> Good, secure long-term finance > Can be used to lever further loan finance > Small amounts of equity available > Investment based on business plan rather than security > Investment usually made for 5 to 10 years > Often offers hands-on expertise	> Only really available to businesses with growth prospects > A significant proportion of the profits and capital growth of the business will go to the angels > Dividends may be expected > Angels will want to sell on their stake in the business at some point in the future to realize their profit > Hands-on expertise may be seen as interference in the business
Equity Venture finance	> Good, secure long-term finance > Larger amounts of equity available – often used as second stage finance rather than at start-up > Investment based on business plan rather than security > Investment usually made for 5 to 10 years > Can offer longer-term strategic advice > Not normally involved in day-to-day running of business > Should be able to arrange loans to go with equity investment, if required > No interest or capital repayments, unless loans are part of the package	> Only really available to businesses with very significant growth prospects and with a view to stock market floatation > A significant proportion of the profits and capital growth of the business will go to the investor > Dividends may be expected > Investors will want to sell on their stake in the business at some point in the future to realize their profit usually through a stock market floatation > Will require very detailed information about the company > Takes time to arrange
Equity Crowdfunding	> Good, secure long-term finance > Can be used to lever further loan finance > Small amounts of equity available > Investment based on business plan rather than security	> Investors will need to see an exit route (liquidity event) – how they can dispose of their equity investment > Dividends may be expected > Crowdfunding website will expect a fee based on funds raised
Term Loans Personal, family and friends	> Security unlikely to be required > Loans may be 'informal' – capital repaid as and when cash flow improves > Interest payments may not be required or may be deferred	> Interest payments may be required > Can strain relationships if repayments are not made as expected > If business fails, family and friends may suffer > Family and friends may interfere in the business
Term Loans Bank and crowdfunding	> Term of loan is fixed – usually not repayable on bank demand (but do check terms) > Capital repayments fixed and known in advance > Interest rate can vary or be fixed and is usually lower than for an overdraft	> Usually secured against business or personal assets > Can be refused because of lack of security > Requires good cash flow to pay interest and meet capital repayments > Crowdfunding website will expect a fee based on funds raised
Lease and Hire Purchase	> Guarantees not required – security is on assets purchased	> Expensive compared to rates of interest charged on loans > Requires adequate cash flow to meet regular payments
Bank Overdraft	> Flexible – once agreed, available on demand > Can be cheap if you dip into and out of it – you only pay interest when you use it > Good solution to short-term financing needs	> Repayable on bank demand > Interest rate is variable > Can be expensive if you are in permanent overdraft, because the rate of interest charged is usually higher than on term loans > Usually secured against business assets and can be refused because of lack of security > Personal guarantee may then be required

Case insight   Alibaba (2)

Company valuation for an IPO

As we shall see in Chapter 16, company valuation is difficult enough, but if you are valuing a Chinese internet company for an IPO on the New York Stock Exchange it can be really tricky. Value it too high and the underwriters are left with unwanted shares, too low and you know the company could have increased its funding. To make matters even more complicated, the IPO of Alibaba was not for actual shares in the group, since China forbids foreign ownership, but rather just shares in a Cayman Islands shell corporation. Nevertheless, Alibaba's IPO in September 2014 was set to raise $21.8 billion, but strong demand sent shares surging 38%, prompting the underwriters to exercise an option to sell an additional 48 million shares sourced from Alibaba, Yahoo and founders Jack Ma and Joe Tsai. Alibaba's final IPO now ranks as the world's biggest at $25 billion. Underwriters netted fees and commissions of more than $300 million.

But if the IPO seemed to undervalue the share, the share price in subsequent months showed how volatile that can

be. Initially priced at $68, the share price rose 38% to $94 on listing and soared a further 27% to $119 by November 2014. It then fell back to below $80 by early 2015, after it purchased a number of US internet companies including the messaging app Snapchat, and amid concerns about slowing economic growth in China. However, the price bounced back to over $90 in May 2015 on the announcement that its revenue rose 45% to 17.4 billion yuan ($2.8 billion; £1.8 billion) in the three months to March 2015. The company said that the number of active annual users had risen by 3% to 350 million. It also announced that Daniel Zhang, Alibaba's chief operating officer and one of the founders, would take over as chief executive from Jonathan Lu, who would remain as vice chair. By the end of 2015 the share price had slipped back to below $90.

QUESTIONS:

1 What factors are likely to make Alibaba's share price volatile?

2 How might this affect company strategies?

Is there a financing gap for small firms in the UK?

If you ask any business person in the current recession whether there is a shortage of finance for business they would answer, 'yes, of course', and look at you as if you had just landed on the planet. The issue of funding gaps, in the provision of debt and equity finance, as constraints on the development of SMEs is not new. In the UK, the MacMillan (1931), Bolton (1971) and Wilson Committees (1979) all identified gaps in provision, and more recently the Cruickshank (2000), and Breedon (2012) reports have drawn attention to shortcomings in the provision of financial support for growth companies.

Because banks are by far and away the major source of external finance for small firms, most of the focus for this debate has fallen on them. The supply of this has been restricted since the financial crisis of 2008, partly due to the banks' need to consolidate their balance sheets, increased risk aversion, increased uncertainty about risk and higher funding costs. Whatever the reasons, and despite various policy measures in the UK to alleviate the situation, Fraser et al. (2013) observed that there has not been a rise in *net* lending to SMEs. However, they also observed that 'while there has been a tightening in the supply of entrepreneurial finance across debt and equity sources due to the financial crisis – particularly affecting start-ups, high growth and other higher risk businesses – there has also been a significant fall in the demand for finance.' What is more, the paradox also exists that large companies are sitting on increasingly large cash mountains. They do not need to borrow, but refuse to invest. Could it be that the problem is lack of consumer demand rather than lack of finance supply that is to blame?

Both loan application and acceptance rates have fallen since the financial crisis of 2008. Before the recession, one survey covering the early part of this century showed 89% of UK loan applications were successful (Fraser, 2005). In the USA it was 72% (Cavalluzzo and Wolken, 2005). However, evidence in the UK shows that while bank funding certainly reduced since the 2008 recession, as did the proportion of small firms using it, loan acceptance rates remained high – dropping from 92.6% in 2004 to only 83.7% in 2008 (Fraser, 2009a). Put another way, 16.3% of applications were rejected. What has happened is that small firms have been 'discouraged' from applying in the first place, and if you add those in, Fraser estimates you get to about 25% being rejected. More up-to-date statistics from Eurostat (2011) show the UK loan rejection rate at 20.8%, which is higher than Germany (8.2%), France (7%), Sweden (6.1%), Italy (4.9%) and Spain (13.2%) but smaller than the Netherlands (22.5%) and Ireland (26.6%). The fact remains that UK loan rejection rates remain high by international comparison.

Notwithstanding the 2008 recession, the question remains as to whether there is a long-term financing gap for small firms – defined as an unwillingness on the part of financiers to supply finance on terms that owner-managers need. Owner-managers who are unsuccessful in obtaining finance will always say there is. Survey after survey of owner-managers will reveal this to be a major 'barrier to growth'. Almost inevitably, lack of appropriately priced finance will be cited as a major constraint, particularly for fast-growing and newer firms. However, this proves nothing – perception is one thing and reality another. Even if accurate, the lack of appropriately priced finance for certain projects may actually indicate that the market is working perfectly well. However, just because the owner-manager might want finance – on specific terms – does not necessarily mean that it should be provided – for the good of the owner-manager, the financier or the economy as a whole.

Economists would criticize the use of the word 'gap' and prefer to use the term 'market failure' or 'credit rationing' because there may be a 'gap' even in a perfect market simply because, for example, an owner-manager is unwilling to pay higher rates of interest or investors judge a project to be too risky. 'Gaps' can easily arise, largely as a result of information asymmetry, the fixed costs of providing small amounts of capital, in terms of assessing the project and monitoring the investment, and the requirement of bankers for small firms or owner-managers to provide collateral. Also, there is the inherent reluctance of the owner-manager to share equity in their business. The question is, however, whether there is evidence that the gap actually exists.

The fact is that numerous surveys in the UK have been unable to establish objectively that a 'gap' exists in any systematic way. In the early 1990s a survey of small, albeit mainly innovative, growing firms (Aston Business School, 1991) about growth constraints concluded that 'small firms in Great Britain apparently face few difficulties in raising finance for their innovation and investment proposals'. Most authors in the years that followed agreed. For example, Cosh and Hughes (1994) concluded that it was 'difficult to argue that there were financial constraints on business formations as a whole in the 1980s or that there is a more pervasive market failure for small firms in the availability of funds at least in quantitative terms'. Similarly, in his review of the literature, Storey (1998) concluded that 'the major empirical studies of the UK small business sector do not suggest the existence either of market failure or credit rationing on a major scale'. He added that 'although there are instances where small firms are unable to obtain finance in the quantities and at the price they would like, the financial institutions in the provision of both loan and equity capital have increased their involvement with the small firm sector over the last ten years'. Reviewing the evidence over a decade later, Storey and Greene (2010) came to broadly the same conclusion: 'for much of the period from the early 1990s until recent times, small businesses in the UK were able to draw upon an increasingly diverse source of funds. However, the 2008 recession abruptly halted the trend, to the extent that perhaps one in four UK small businesses were unable to access the funding they required'. The recession has certainly changed the financing environment – for businesses of any size.

 Practice insight reminder Characteristics of a good business idea – 15

15 Financeable – if you do not have sufficient resources
  yourself, the project needs to be able to attract finance.

↻ Summary

> Before using external sources of finance you should minimize your use of assets (bootlegging resources), partner with others, use your own money and borrow money from family and friends.

> Deciding on the nature and source of finance for a start-up is an important strategic decision. To be prudent you should match the term-duration of the source of finance with the use to which it is put. Fixed or permanent assets should be financed with equity, medium- and long-term bank finance or lease/hire-purchase. Working capital can be financed by short-term loans and factoring, with fluctuations financed by overdraft.

> Table 14.3 summarizes the advantages and disadvantages of different sources of finance.

> Banks are very risk averse. They do not share in the success of the business but stand to lose all their capital if the business fails, and therefore they will do all they can to avoid a bad debt. Small firms present a riskier lending proposition than larger firms.

> Banks are likely to seek personal or business collateral for a loan which will offer them security in the event of default. Since the asset base of a start-up is unlikely to be able to provide this, bankers often ask for personal collateral or guarantees.

> Bankers look at a range of financial indicators in arriving at their lending decisions, but they are particularly interested in the cash flow forecast because this shows the ability of the firm to make its interest payments and repay capital.

> It is important that you establish a good working relationship with your banker. This is based upon mutual trust and respect.

> Equity finance can be obtained from family, friends, business angels and venture capitalists. Equity investors share in the success or failure of the business, and consequently they can be expected to scrutinize your business plan very closely.

> Angels and venture capitalists expect an annualized return of 30–50%, normally as a capital gain. They also normally expect to realize their investment within 5 to 10 years. They will expect a seat on the board of directors, and many angels will expect a closer involvement in the management of the business. They might realize their investment through a trade sale, management buy-out or buy-in or stock market floatation. These are also opportunities for the founder to realize all or part of their investment.

> Internet-based crowdfunding has emerged in recent years as a way of matching lenders and investors with small firms in need of finance. It is too early to evaluate its success, but 'quirkier' businesses, often with a social aim, have found it a useful mechanism.

> Despite the current recession and surveys that suggest the supply of finance is a major constraint on growth, it has been impossible to objectively establish that there is a long-term, systematic financing gap for small firms.

✓ Activities

1 List (and quantify if possible) the different sorts of capital you have access to: social, human and financial.

2 List (and quantify if possible) the different sorts of capital you will need to launch your new business: social, human and financial.

3 Compare the results and consider how you might bridge any gap.

💬 Group discussion topics

1 Is there sufficient provision of finance for SMEs?
2 How can banks improve the services they offer SMEs?
3 Since it costs so much to recover a bad debt, it is little wonder that banks are reluctant to lend without collateral or a good knowledge of the loan applicant. Discuss.
4 If you were a bank manager, what would you be looking for in a loan applicant?
5 What sources of start-up finance most attract you? Why?

6 There is no such thing as limited liability for an owner-manager. Discuss.
7 Is there discrimination in lending?
8 Lending is about discriminating between 'good' and 'bad' borrowers. Discuss.
9 Why do so many women not want to seek external finance and, if they do, then seek so little compared to men?

10 Should peer-to-peer funding and crowdsourcing be regulated?

11 What are business angels looking for in an investment?

12 If you were a business angel, what would you be looking for in an investment?

13 What are the advantages and disadvantages of having a business angel invest in a firm?

14 Where might the interests of the owner-managers and external investors conflict?

15 Why do so many entrepreneurs (like Richard Branson) that float their companies on the stock market subsequently buy them back and delist them?

16 Does the financing gap exist?

17 If there is a financing gap it is the fault of the SMEs. Discuss.

18 Why might owner-managers not go to banks to seek finance?

☞ References

Allen, F., Qian, J. and Qian, M. (2005) 'Law, Finance and Economic Growth in China', *Journal of Financial Economics*, 77(1).

Aston Business School (1991) *Constraints on Growth of Small Firms*, Department of Trade and Industry, London: HMSO.

Bank of England (1999) *The Financing of Ethnic Minority Firms in the UK: A Special Report*, London: Bank of England.

Bolton Committee (1971) *Report of the Committee on Small Firms*, Cmnd. 4811, London: HMSO.

Breedon, T. (2012) *Boosting Finance Options for Business*. Department for Business Innovation and Skills.

Brush, C.G. (2006) 'Woman Entrepreneurs: A Research Overview', in M. Casson, B. Yeung, A. Basu and N. Wadeson (eds), *The Oxford Handbook of Entrepreneurship*, Oxford: Oxford University Press.

Brush, C., Carter, N.M., Gatewood, E.J., Greene P.G. and Hart M.M. (2006) 'Women's Entrepreneurship In the United States', in B. Candida, N.M. Carter, E.J. Gatewood, P.G. Greene and M.M. Hart (eds), *Growth Oriented Women Entrepreneurs and Their Business*, Cheltenham: Edward Elgar.

Carree, M. and Verheu, I. (2009) 'Time Allocation by the Self-employed: The Determinants of the Number of Working Hours in Start-ups', *Applied Economics Letters*, 16.

Carter, S. and Rosa, P. (1998) 'The Financing of Male and Female Owned Businesses', *Entrepreneurship and Regional Development*, 8.

Carter, S. and Mwaura, S. (2014) *The Financing of Diverse Enterprises: Evidence from the SME Finance Monitor*, ERC Research Paper 18, available online at http://enterpriseresearch.ac.uk/publications/erc-research-papers/.

Cavalluzzo, K. and Wolken, J. (2005) 'Small Business Loan Turndowns, Personal Wealth, and Discrimination', *Journal of Business*, 78.

Chen, X-P., Yao, X. and Kotha, S. (2009) 'Entrepreneur Passion and Preparedness in Business Plan Presentations: A Persuasion Analysis of Venture Capitalists' Funding Decisions', *Academy of Management Journal*, 52(1).

Coleman, S. (2000) 'Access to Capital and Terms of Credit: A Comparison of Men and Women-owned Small Businesses', *Journal of Small Business Management*, 38(3).

Cosh, A. and Hughes, A. (1994) 'Size, Financial Structure and Profitability: UK Companies in the 1980s', in A. Hughes and D.J. Storey (eds), *Finance and the Small Firm*, London: Routledge.

Cruickshank, D. (2000) *Competition in UK Banking: A Report to the Chancellor of the Exchequer*, London: HM Treasury.

CSES (2012) *Evaluation of EU Member States' Business Angel Markets and Policies Final Report*, Brussels: EU.

Cumming, D.J. and Johan S.A. (2013) *Venture Capital and Private Equity Contracting: An International Perspective*, 2nd edn, London: Elsevier Science Academic Press.

Department for Business Enterprise & Regulatory Reform (2008) *High Growth Firms in the UK: Lessons from an Analysis of Comparative UK Performance*. BERR Economics Paper No 3, available online at http://www.berr.gov.uk/files/file49042.pdf.

EBF (2012) *European Banking Federation Facts and Figures 2012*, available online at http://www.ebf-fbe.eu/uploads/FF2012.pdf.

Eurostat (2011) *Access to Finance Statistics: Data from September 2011*, Eurostat Statistics Explained, available online at: http://epp.eurostat.ec.europa.eu/statistics_explained/index.php/Access_to_finance_statistics.

EVCA (2012) *European Venture Capital Association Yearbook 2012*, available online at http://www.evca.eu/uploadedfiles/home/press_room/Yearbook_2012_Presentation_all.pdf.

Fairlie, R. and Robb, A. (2009) 'Gender Differences in Business Performance: Evidence from the Characteristics of Business Owners Survey', *Small Business Economics*, 33(4).

Fraser, S. (2005) *Finance for Small and Medium-sized Enterprises*, London: Bank of England.

Fraser, S. (2006) *Finance for Small and Medium-sized Enterprises: A Report on the 2004 UK Survey of SME Finances*, Warwick Business School, Centre for Small and Medium-sized Enterprises, Coventry.

Fraser, S. (2009a) 'How Have SME Finances Been Affected by the Credit Crisis?' *BERR/ESRC Seminar*, March.

Fraser, S. (2009b) 'Is there Ethnic Discrimination in the UK Market for Small Business Credit', *International Small Business Journal*, 27(5).

Fraser, S., Bhaumik, S. and Wright, M. (2013) *What Do We Know about the Relationship between Entrepreneurial Finance and Growth?*, ERC White Paper No.4, April.

Greene, P., Brush, C., Hart, M. and Saparito, P. (1999) 'Exploration of the Venture Capital Industry: Is Gender an Issue?', *Frontiers of Entrepreneurial Research Series*, Wellesly, MA: Babson College.

Greene, P.G., Hart, M.M., Gatewood, E.J., Brush C.G. and Carter N.M. (2003) 'Women Entrepreneurs: Moving Front and Center: An Overview of Research and Theory', *Women Entrepreneurs: Moving Front and Center*, available online at http://usasbe.org/knowledge/whitepapers/greene2003.pdf.

Henry, C., Johnson, K. and Hamouda, A. (2006) 'Access To Finance for Women Entrepreneurs in Ireland: A Supply Side Perspective,' in B. Candida, N.M. Carter, E.J. Gatewood, P.G. Greene and M.M. Hart (eds), *Growth Oriented Women Entrepreneurs and Their Business*, Cheltenham: Edward Elgar.

Hisrich, R. and Brush, C.G. (1984) 'The Woman Entrepreneur: Management Skills and Business Problems', *Journal of Small Business Management*, 22(1).

Jensen, M.C., and Meckling, W.H. (1976) 'Theory of the Firm, Managerial Behavior, Agency Costs, and Ownership Structure', *Journal of Financial Economics*, 3.

Jennings, E.J. and M.P Cash (2006) 'Women's Entrepreneurship In Canada: Progress, Puzzles and Priorities,' in B. Candida, N.M. Carter, E.J. Gatewood, P.G. Greene and M.M. Hart (eds), *Growth Oriented Women Entrepreneurs and Their Business*, Cheltenham: Edward Elgar.

Leitch, C.M., Hill, F. and Harrison, R.T. (2006) 'The Supply of Finance to Women Led Ventures: The Northern Ireland Experience,' in B. Candida, N.M. Carter, E.J. Gatewood, P.G. Greene and M.M. Hart (eds), *Growth Oriented Women Entrepreneurs and Their Business*, Cheltenham: Edward Elgar.

Levenson, A.R. and Willard, K.L. (2000) 'Do Firms Get the Financing They Want? Measuring Credit Rationing Experienced by Small Businesses in the USA', *Small Business Economics*, 14(2).

MacMillan Committee (1931) *Report on the Committee on Finance and Industry*, Cmnd. 3897, London: HMSO.

Marlow, S. and Patton, D. (2003) 'The Financing of Small Business – Female Experiences', in M. Davies and S. Fielden (eds), *International Handbook of Women and Small Business Entrepreneurship,* Cheltenham: Edward Elgar.

Massolution (2013) *Crowdfunding Industry Report 2012*, available online at http://www.crowdsourcing.org/research.

Neergaard, H., Nielsen, K.T. and Kjeldsen, I.J. (2006) 'State of the Art of Women's Entrepreneurship, Access to Financing and Financing Strategies in Denmark', in B. Candida, N.M. Carter, E.J. Gatewood, P.G. Greene and M.M. Hart (eds), *Growth Oriented Women Entrepreneurs and Their Business*, Cheltenham: Edward Elgar.

Orser, B.J., Riding, A.L. and Manley, K. (2006) 'Women Entrepreneurs and Financial Capital', *Entrepreneurship: Theory and Practice*, 30(5).

Parker, S.C. (2009) *The Economics of Entrepreneurship*, Cambridge University Press.

Ram, M., Smallbone, D. and Deakins, D. (2002) *Ethnic Minority Business in the UK: Access to Finance and Business Support*, London: British Bankers' Association.

Storey, D.J. (1998) *Understanding the Small Business Sector*, London: International Thompson Business Press.

Storey, D.J. and Greene, F.J. (2010) *Small Business and Entrepreneurship*, Harlow: Pearson.

Treichel, M.Z. and Scott, J.A. (2006) 'Women-owned Business and Access to Bank Credit: Evidence from Three Surveys since 1987', *Venture Capital: An International Journal of Entrepreneurial Finance*, 8(1).

Ufuk, H. and Ozgen, O. (2001) 'Interaction Between the Business and Family Lives of Women Entrepreneurs in Turkey', *Journal Of Business Ethics*, 31.

Verheul, I., Carree, M. and Thurik, R. (2009) 'Allocation and Productivity of Time in New Ventures of Female and Male Entrepreneurs', *Small Business Economics*, 33(3).

Watson, J., Newby, R. and Mahuka, A. (2006) 'Comparing The Growth and External Funding of Male and Female Controlled SME's in Australia,' in B. Candida, N.M. Carter, E.J. Gatewood, P.G. Greene and M.M. Hart (eds), *Growth Oriented Women Entrepreneurs and Their Business*, Cheltenham: Edward Elgar.

Wilson Committee (1979) *The Financing of Small Firms, Interim Report of the Committee to Review the Functioning of the Financial Institutions*, Cmnd. 7503, London: HMSO.

Wright, M. and Fraser, S. (2014) 'Financing Growth', *ERC Insights*, June 2014.

 www.palgrave.com/Burns-Entrepreneurship-And-Small-Business-4e

Go online to access additional teaching and learning resources for this chapter on the companion website. Click here in the ebook to complete a multiple choice revision quiz for this chapter.

FROM BUSINESS MODEL TO BUSINESS PLAN

15

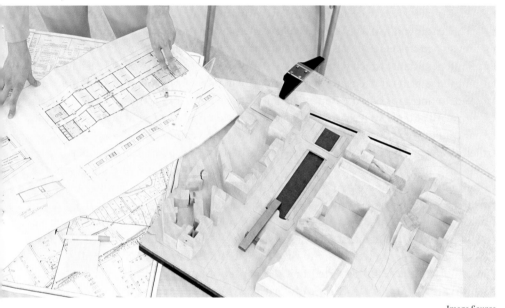

Image Source

Contents

- Why you need a business plan
- Purpose of a business plan
- Structure and content of a business plan
- A social enterprise plan
- Using the business plan to obtain loan or equity finance
- Summary

Learning outcomes

When you have read this chapter and undertaken the related activities you will be able to:

> Explain the purpose, structure and content of a business plan;
> Draw up a business plan for your new venture;
> Recognize the information needs of bankers, equity investors and other stakeholders;
> Present the plan convincingly.

Case insights

One Day

- *Practice insight*: 5 tips for preparing a business plan

- *Practice insight*: Presenting a case for finance

- *Practice insight reminder*: 15 characteristics of a good business idea

Why you need a business plan

Your business model underpins your business plan. Chapters 6 and 12 showed you how to develop your business model and then modify it to reflect the changing circumstances you will inevitably face after launch. You need to develop a business model before you can draw up a business plan. Some start-ups need a business plan prior to launch, probably because they need external finance to enable this; others may be able to wait until after launch when the business idea has been proved and the model modified to reflect the realities of the market. Developing your business model and writing a business plan allows you to crystallize your business idea and to think systematically through the challenges you will face before you have to deal with them. The process allows you to develop strategies and strategic options that should improve your chances of success. It allows you to set key milestones against which to monitor your performance. And the greater detail involved in writing a business plan often ensures that the document faces greater scrutiny and things are not overlooked. But perhaps of more immediate importance, it can also act as a vehicle to attract external finance. All of these things can mean that the development of a sound business plan can improve your confidence in launching into what is an uncertain venture.

Nevertheless, evidence about the positive effect of business plans can be mixed, particularly for early stage businesses where the product may still not be well defined and the market uncertain. While Sarasvathy (2001) observed that entrepreneurs do not like extensive formal research and planning, Timmons (1999) claimed that the vast majority of *INC.* magazine's annually produced 500 fastest growing US companies had business plans at the outset. However, another study claimed that this figure was only 28% of a 'sample' of these companies (Bhidé, 2000), and this figure was closer to the 31% in another survey of 600 US SMEs (Wells Fargo, 2006). Burke et al. (2010) asserted that the impact of business plans depends on their purpose, observing that in the UK firms with formal, written plans reported superior employment growth.

Entrepreneurs may not like formal plans, but they do seem to produce them, especially when they are needed to obtain finance. And this, perhaps, is the link. Formal plans are needed to convince others to invest in their ventures. As Bygrave et al. (2007) argued: 'unless a would-be entrepreneur needs to raise substantial start-up capital from institutional investors or business angels, there is no compelling reason to write a detailed business plan before opening a new business.' Notice the words 'detailed business plan'. There is no point in formalizing frameworks and documenting plans unless they help in the planning process or are needed to help communicate those plans to your wider group of stakeholders. It is both a question of scale of the venture and nature of the stakeholders you wish to communicate with. Small-scale ventures may not need detailed or formal plans, but many providers of finance expect them. Notice also the phrase 'before opening a new venture'. As businesses grow and the need is to communicate with more people, such as investors, suppliers, partners and prospective employees, the need to formalize and document the process increases. Even Sarasvathy (op. cit.) conceded this increasing formalization as she observed that entrepreneurs became both 'causal' as well as 'effectual' thinkers as their business grew.

So, the conclusion is that any business plan should be tailored for the scale of start-up and for the audience it is aimed at. The business plan can be as formal or informal as it needs to be, depending on its purpose. It does not have to be long and elaborate. Internal Plans for internal use can be brief, informal working documents that can be amended as circumstances change. The smaller the scale of start-up, the briefer the document. However, when you need a business plan to secure a significant investment it needs to become a more elaborate 'selling document'. This chapter is about how to produce that more elaborate, formal document – usually for external use – although the structure can give you a framework for a briefer, more informal version. However, the process of thinking through how to go about setting up the business and the development of a business model that can be used to strategize is far more important than any formal business plan document.

"Entrepreneurs treat a business plan, once written as a final collection of facts. Once completed you don't often hear about people rewriting their plan. Instead it is treated as the culmination of everything they know and believe. It's static. In contrast, a business model is designed to be rapidly changed to reflect what you find outside the building in talking to customers. It's dynamic.

Steve Blank, serial entrepreneur, *http://steveblank.com/2010/04/08/*

We are constantly reviewing our business plan. It is a fluid, live document … A business plan is not set in stone. It shouldn't become something that you are measured or beaten up with … A plan makes you think about what you are doing and what your goals are. If things happen along the way that will help you reach those goals faster then the business plan should change.

Alex Reilley, founder, Loungers, *The Sunday Times*, 20 April 2014`

Social enterprises often need to draw up a business plan before they launch. This is because of the large and varied number of stakeholders often involved in a social enterprise. Some stakeholders may be quite bureaucratic in their procedures – such as government or local authority agencies – and are required to deal with formal documents because they use taxpayer resources. Indeed, if the enterprise is applying for grant funding it is almost certain that a formal business plan will be required – and probably much additional 'form-filling'. And, while the entrepreneurial and commercial side to the plan is important, the social objectives of any social enterprise are probably paramount, and therefore need emphasizing.

Purpose of a business plan

The business plan is a formal written document. It should set out what your venture seeks to achieve and how it will achieve it. There are no set rules that can be used to create a 'perfect' business plan. While the next section sets out a general pro-forma plan, each plan is particular to its business and will be different to others. Plans also differ, depending on the audience they are aimed at and the purpose they will be used for. Sections might be expanded or contracted and it may well be appropriate to omit or add complete sections to suit different circumstances. For a social enterprise, great attention needs to be spent on how it will achieve its social as well as commercial objectives. Because each business is unique, every business plan will be different, at least in the detail it contains. Nevertheless, any business plan needs to be succinct, professional and well presented.

The complexity and length of the plan will vary with the scale of the start-up and the purpose and audience for which the plan was written. If it is simply for you, to help you organize the venture systematically, then it might be brief and functional, almost an 'aide-memoire' or summary plan, running to a few pages. And if assumptions and circumstances change, then you may have to look again at your business model and start altering these plans. A business plan should be sufficiently detailed to give you direction but should never be so rigid as to blind you to new opportunities or threats.

If the plan is intended for external use, for example to help you raise finance, then it will need to be thorough, better presented and, inevitably, longer. After all, it is a document that should be 'selling' your venture to a financier, supplier or business partner. A full business plan of this sort could easily run to 20 pages, with financial projections and other details going into the appendices. If it is intended to help you raise finance, the more money you are trying to raise, the more thorough it will need to be. Indeed, if you are trying to raise equity finance it will need to be extremely thorough and well presented. Although you might keep to approximately the same length of plan, the appendices might run to 30 pages and be placed in a separate document. Having said that, keep the plan as succinct as possible. Do not pad it out unnecessarily. Different providers of finance are interested in slightly different things, so plans need to be tailored to provide them with the information they particularly need. Investors seem to prefer to evaluate a business idea first

You need focus and commitment. Keep your goals simple and communicate them to your team.

Martin Ephson, co-founder, Fermoie ,*The Sunday Times*, 7 December 2014

What is the right plan? It's the one that helps you identify what you need to ensure success. It's the one that rallies your employees around a few common goals – and motivates them to achieve them. It's the one that involves your customers' goals and suppliers' goals and brings them all together in a unified focus.

Michael Dell, founder, Dell Corporation (1999) *Direct from Dell: Strategies that Revolutionized an Industry*, New York: Harper Business

by looking through a business plan – or at least the executive summary – before they are willing to meet the founders and commit more time and effort (Mullins and Komisar, 2011). Some plans for large-scale start-ups can take the form of professionally produced brochures. However, there is always a fine balance between including sufficient detail in the plan to convince the reader that you know what you are talking about, but not so much that they lose interest. Indeed, too much focus on the operations may convince equity investors that you are product- rather than market-focused – and that will definitely turn them off.

If you are developing a completely new product or service, your business plan will need to explain what stage the development is at, and what further development is needed to take it to market. Basic ideas are unlikely to find funding. Even when there is a prototype, finding finance might prove difficult. The earlier the stage in its development, the more difficult this will prove. There is no guarantee the product will work and there is no guarantee that there will be customers for it. Even if it works, will you be able to stop competitors from copying it?

Structure and content of a business plan

The structure and content of a full commercial business plan intended for external use is shown in Table 15.1. How this might be adapted for a social enterprise is discussed in the next section. This is a general pro-forma plan and, as already stated, it may be appropriate to omit or add complete sections to suit different circumstances, and the contents of each section needs to be adapted to suit your venture. For example, location is a vital part of a business plan for a retail start-up, web functionality for an internet start-up. Your plan should read like a professional business report – succinct and to the point and full of vital information. It must be convincing. Table 15.1 shows the structure of a typical business plan. The contents of each section is explained in greater detail below. The indicative page extent (in brackets) is based upon a typical 20-page plan – anything more should go into the appendices.

Table 15.1 Business plan structure

Business plan structure
> Cover
> Table of contents
> Executive summary
> Business details
> Industry and market analysis
> Customers and value proposition
> Marketing strategy
> Operations plan
> Management team and company structure
> Resources
> Financing
> Financial projections
> Risks and strategic options
> Key milestones
> Appendices

Cover

The cover should include the business name and contact details. You should consider whether the plan needs to be marked 'confidential'.

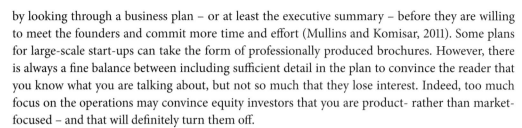

I see business plans so complicated that you need to set aside a week to read them but it's the ability to identify a simple solution that continues to set apart the best entrepreneurs.

Duncan Bannatyne, serial entrepreneur, *Sunday Telegraph*, 30 July 2009

I receive business plans of 20 to 40 spread-sheets. It makes my head spin. If it's all too technical, then it will alienate investors.

Luke Johnson, Chair, Risk Capital Partners, *The Sunday Times*, 20 April 2014

Table of contents

This is a list of sections and subsections, with page numbers.

Executive summary (1–2 pages)

If you are seeking external finance, this is probably the most important section of the plan. Many equity investors will only read the full plan if they find the summary attractive. It should only be written after the full plan is complete, and then it should be written with the reader and purpose of the plan in mind. If it is to be used to attract funding, it should state what is requested from the lender or investor and how they will benefit by providing the funds. It must be a summary of the plan – not an introduction. It should highlight the nature of your product/service, target customers, value proposition and competitive advantage. It should appeal to the reader by highlighting the distinctive capabilities and potential of the business, including the financial return. If the plan is written to attract an equity investor it should state what deal you are offering. For example, '20% of the business in exchange for £100,000'.

Above all, the executive summary must be focused and succinct – no more than one or two pages long.

Business details (1–2 pages)

This section covers basic information such as business name, address, legal form and ownership. It should include:

> A description of your product/service;
> Your mission and vision statement;
> Your aims and objectives.

If this is an existing business, you should include a brief business history.

In a well-thought-out business plan, it should be made clear that a company is attacking a big enough market and that there is an experienced team.

Darren Westlake, founder, Crowdcube, *The Sunday Times*, 14 September 2014

Industry and market analysis (2–3 pages)

This section provides background information on your industry sector and the market segments within it. It should take the form of a narrative informed by academic models such as a PESTEL analysis and Porter's Five Forces. You should review your competitors and their strengths and weaknesses. The more you know about an industry and market, and the competitors you face, the more confidence your readers will have in your ability to compete within it. This section should include:

> Industry size, growth, structure (macro and micro/local level);
> Industry and market trends (macro and micro/local level);
> Market segments and reasons for target market(s) selection;
> Buyer behaviour across segments;
> Competitor analysis (strengths and weaknesses);
> For an existing business, market share.

In most industries there are some key success factors that industry players have to be competent in to compete. These need to be highlighted, but judgement is required about what is important for your particular venture.

Customers and value proposition (2–3 pages)

This is the section where you outline your target market segment(s) and the value proposition(s) for your product/service. It is essential that your 'unique selling proposition' is clearly and simply articulated. In doing this you should highlight your differential advantage over competitors. The more the points of difference and the stronger and more sustainable these differences, the better. This is where you also set out your sales targets. If you have firm orders for the product or service, be sure to mention this.

Marketing strategy (3–4 pages)

This section provides the details about how you propose to achieve those sales targets – not only the details of your marketing mix but also the details of your sales tactics (how the product or service will actually be sold). As well as the launch strategy, this should also highlight the growth potential through market and product development, your competitive reaction and strategy for establishing your brand. It should include:

> Price, promotions, distribution etc.;
> Launch strategy;
> Sales tactics;
> Brand development;
> Competitive reaction;
> Product and market development;
> Growth potential;

Investors are always particularly interested in pricing strategy because this is a prime determinant of the profitability of the business.

Operations plan (2–3 pages)

This section outlines how your business will be run and how your product/service will be produced. What goes into the operations plan varies depending on the nature of the venture. However, what is important is that the key activities for your venture are highlighted. It must convince the reader that you understand the operation of the business – how to do whatever needs to be done to deliver your product/service. So, issues of business control, if critical to the business, need to be covered. Also, the prospect of scalability – should the business prove to be even more successful than planned – can be addressed in this section. What are your strategic options? The content of this section is difficult to predict but might include:

> Key operating activities (e.g. manufacturing processes, business model etc.);
> Partnerships;
> Business controls;
> IP issues;
> Scalability.

Management team and company structure (1–3 pages)

This section outlines all the people involved in the venture – details of their background and experience – as well as the organizational structure you are adopting. A new venture team with an established track record in the industry or with relevant experience will certainly add credibility to any start-up. Remember that investors ultimately invest in people, not products. An experienced board of directors can achieve the same result. Brief CVs can go in the appendices. For larger start-ups, an organization chart can go in this section. This section should include:

> Key people, their functions and background;
> Business organization or structure;
> Directors, advisors and other key partners;
> Skills gaps and plans for filling them.

Resources (1–2 pages)

This section describes what the business needs to operate. It should include:

> Premises and facilities;
> Machinery and equipment;
> Staff.

Investors are backing the people behind the idea as well as the idea itself.

Peter Jones, serial entrepreneur, *The Guardian, Media Planet*, May 2015

Financing (1–2 pages)

This section highlights the finance you need to launch your business. External funders will expect you to contribute some capital. Lenders will be interested in the risks they face and the security they can obtain. Equity investors will be interested in the overall return they might make and how this might be realized. This section should include:

> Founders' contribution;
> Loan and/or equity finance requirements;
> Gearing/leverage;
> Timescale and exit routes for equity investors.

Financial projections (1 page summary, plus appendices)

Typically financial projections for three years are expected by funders, with a monthly cash flow forecast for the first year. A very small-scale start-up might only provide financial projections for the first year. Five-years forecasts might be expected for larger projects where significant commercialization risks have not been resolved. You should provide a one-page financial summary and place the detailed projections in the appendices.

Financial details going into your appendices should be as long as it takes to provide all the information required. These should include:

> Income projections;
> Cash flow projections;
> Balance sheet projections;
> Key ratios;
> The assumptions on which your financial projections are based, particularly the basis for your sales projections.

Risks and strategic options (1 page)

This section should identify the key risks you face and explain how they will be monitored and mitigated. You need to identify your critical success factors and the strategic options you face should these risks materialize. Strategic options are valuable because circumstances can, and do, change. They give you flexibility in a changing environment. This section should include:

> Identified risks;
> Risk monitoring and mitigation;
> Critical success factors;
> Strategic options.

Key milestones (1 page)

These milestones, often incorporating critical success factors, highlight the progress needed to launch and grow the business. They might include prototype completion, formalization of partnerships, obtaining finance, securing of key customers etc. This section gives an overview of the sequence and timing of important events.

Appendices

Any information that is vital but might impede the flow of the plan should go into the appendix. One key piece of information is the assumptions upon which the financial projections are based, in particular the sales projections. These need to be made explicit and you can expect an investor to scrutinize them closely. This section might include:

> Detailed financial projections;
> Financial assumptions (start-up costs, basis for sales projections, fixed/variable costs, profit margins);

Setting some milestones for you and your team to work towards will keep you motivated and driven

Richard Branson, founder, Virgin Group, *The Guardian*, *Media Planet*, May 2015

> Background information (CVs) on key people;
> Location information (maps, layouts etc.);
> Operations information (Gantt charts etc.)
> Details of market research;
> Details of IP protection;
> Website screen shots;
> For an existing business, historic financial statements, brochures etc.

If used for external purposes, the business plan must convince the reader that you understand the industry, market and business you want to establish. It must convince them of the viability of the business – that you have a good product/service and value proposition, and that you know how to combat the competition. It must enhance your creditability and make them trust your judgement. They need to believe that you can turn your business idea into reality. So, when you have written the plan, try getting friends or relatives to read it and give you honest feedback.

> I see some [business plans] where the CV is so vague as to be useless. Give me dates, give me details. Be honest about things that have gone wrong. Talk about the setbacks and mistakes and explain how you fixed them.
>
> **Luke Johnson**, serial entrepreneur and business angel, *The Sunday Times*, 2 June 2013

A social enterprise plan

A social enterprise is established primarily to achieve social objectives, usually using entrepreneurial approaches and commercial mechanisms. Your business plan needs to reflect this. And that means that your plan needs to be commercially realistic while demonstrating how your social objectives will be met. This can mean that your plan will be longer than a normal commercial plan; however, that does depend very much on the purpose of the plan and for whom it is written. Indeed, this will determine much of the emphasis, if not the content, of the plan. For example, grant funding may be dependent on your ability to demonstrate an *innovative* approach to meeting a social need by tapping into as yet unused private-sector resources. To attract grant (or loan) funding for a social enterprise, you will need to emphasize your social rather than commercial objectives and how this grant will be used to enable these to be met. You will certainly have to demonstrate that commercial profits will be directed towards these social objectives and/or ploughed back into the enterprise.

It is sometimes easier to write two separate business plans for a social enterprise – one commercial, the other social – and then integrate them. The commercial business model should demonstrate commercial viability – and the plan content from the previous section should do this. But there are some important additions or changes that are needed for a social enterprise:

> **Executive summary** – This should emphasize the achievement of social rather commercial objectives;
> **Industry and market analysis** – This also needs to demonstrate the gap in social provision for your social enterprise. However, remember you are not usually competing against other providers so much as complementing their provision;
> **Customer and value proposition** – This needs to cover those who will benefit from the provision you are offering. What is their need? Why is your provision unique or how does it 'add value' to existing provision?
> **Marketing strategy** – Social provision rarely needs to be 'marketed', certainly not in the same way as commercial products, but target markets still need to be communicated with and a convincing communications plan outlined;
> **Operations plan** – This needs to show how your social objectives will be met. The contents outlined previously can be applied to both commercial and social operations;
> **Financing** – This needs to be tailored to the funders being approached; however, they are rarely involved in a social enterprise for commercial gain. More normally they will want to see their money being put to good (and efficient) social use and not for simple commercial gain;
> **Financial projections** – These still need to demonstrate commercial viability; however, stakeholders will not have a profit-maximization objective. It is far more likely that what you need to demonstrate is commercial sustainability beyond the initial period of subsidy. Surpluses should go towards meeting your social objectives and/or be ploughed back into the enterprise.

Practice insight 5 tips for preparing a business plan

1 Keep the plan as short and simple as possible. Do not pad it out. The plan should be sufficiently long to cover the project adequately but short enough to maintain interest. To do this you need to be able to prioritize and focus on the important things for your business. If you overcomplicate your plan you risk losing that focus and the interest of the reader.

2 Keep it as realistic as possible. Are sales targets, costs, milestone deadlines and so on realistic? If your claims are unrealistic you will never gain the trust of lenders and investors. It is better to under-estimate and over-deliver than vice versa.

3 Make it clear, specific and unambiguous. Are market segments clearly identified? Are objectives concrete and measurable? Are targets and deadlines clear? Lack of clarity is often taken to indicate a lack of knowledge or willingness to be committed.

4 Check your spelling, grammar, punctuation and, most important of all, financial accuracy. Errors will damage your credibility and, if noticed at a presentation, can put you off your stride. Computers have grammar and spelling checks – use them. Using a spreadsheet package for your cash flow forecast can ensure arithmetic accuracy.

5 If you are not confident about putting the financial projections together yourself, seek professional advice, but be sure you understand how they were arrived at.

The UK government provides information on writing a business plan, examples for different sectors and a free pro-forma download at www.gov.uk/write-business-plan.

In the USA the Small Business Administration provides information about how to write a business plan at www.sba.gov.

Using the business plan to obtain loan or equity finance

Your initial cash flow forecasts show you how much finance you need, and the previous chapter should have helped you decide on the appropriate type of external finance. External funders will expect you to have contributed some capital yourself. They will expect to see a business plan, and while both lenders and investors might look at the same elements of information from the plan, each places a different importance upon these elements. However, the reality is that both banks and equity investors ultimately invest in individuals, not in businesses or plans. The plan is just one way, albeit a very important one, of communicating with them. It must therefore reinforce the perceptions the banker or investor has of you and your venture team.

Before letting anybody see your business plan you need to consider whether they should be asked to sign a non-disclosure agreement, which binds the reader to confidentiality. If you are invited then to meet with the lender or investor, you need to be clear whether you are expected to present your plan or simply discuss it. If you are asked to present the plan, you need to know how long you have and then prepare a professional presentation. However, first it is worth recalling what banks and investors are looking for.

They're backing you. You've got to convince your investors that you won't give up. You've got to create a vision for the backers.

Martyn Dawes, founder, Coffee Nation, *The Sunday Times*, 23 May 2004

Banks

Banks are in the business of lending money; in that respect they are just like any other supplier of a commodity – and there are many banks you can approach. The thing to remember about banks is that they are not in the risk business. They are looking to obtain a certain rate of interest over a specified period of time and see their capital repaid. They do not share in the extra profits a firm might make, so they do not expect to lose money if there are problems. What is more, the manager stands to lose a lot if he lends to a business that subsequently fails. The plan therefore needs to demonstrate how the interest on the loan can be paid, even in the worst possible set of circumstances, and how the capital can be repaid on the due date. In this respect, the cash flow forecast is something that the bank manager will be particularly interested in. Where a long-term loan for product development or capital expenditure is being sought and there is little prospect of loan repayment in the short term, the plan must emphasize the cash-generating capacity of the business and take a perspective longer than one year. In addition, banks are also particularly interested in the break-even and gearing ratios. In an ideal world, they would like both of these to be as low as possible.

Bank managers represent a set of values and practices that are alien to many entrepreneurs. They are employees, not independent professionals, and lend only within very strict, centrally dictated, guidelines. They often talk 'a different language' and are subject to numerous rules and regulations that an entrepreneur would probably find very tedious. Since they trade in money, they often cannot make decisions on their own without getting approval from 'up the line'. In these circumstances the business plan is an essential weapon in helping them get authorization for a loan. Any manager will only be able to lend within the bank's own policies, at acceptable levels of risk and with adequate security to cover the loan. However, each of these three constraints requires the exercise of judgement and can therefore be influenced, not only through the style and content of the business plan but also the credibility and track record of the founder and their team.

Bank managers are trained to examine business plans critically. So expect to be questioned. They will ask about risks. They will always ask questions about some of the claims in the plan and the assumptions on which they are based, so you must always be able to back them up. Avoid any tendency to generalize in order to disguise a weakness in your knowledge. Your plan should seek to identify and then reassure the bank manager about the risks the business faces. They tend to dislike plans that they see as overly ambitious, since they do not share in the success and see this as an unnecessary risk.

However good the business plan, bankers are still likely to ask for a personal guarantee. After all, if they don't ask, they certainly won't get it. And it does make any loan more secure from their perspective. But be prepared to haggle and shop around. A bank may turn you down for internal reasons unconnected with your business. Indeed, the same bank may offer you a loan one month and turn you down on another. And remember, this is just a sales negotiation like any other and the banker is really trying to 'sell' you a loan, albeit at a certain price and with certain conditions.

Equity investors

Prospective equity investors will normally expect to see a business plan before meeting you. And while most entrepreneurs will submit business plans to more than one investor for consideration, most investors are inundated with business plans seeking finance. Less than 1 in 20 will ever lead to a face-to-face meeting. To a large extent, therefore, the decision whether to proceed beyond an initial reading of the plan will depend crucially on its quality. The business plan is the first, and often the best, chance that an entrepreneur has to impress prospective investors with the quality of their investment proposal. A good executive summary is, therefore, vital – many investors do not read beyond it.

Business plans written with the aim of raising funds from equity investors tend to be longer than those for banks. They are more comprehensive, offering greater detail, and are better presented. After all, equity investors share the risk of failure and, as we saw in the previous chapter, they want to know about the return they will make and when they will make it (the exit route). They need to be convinced that the founder and their team are as good as the business idea and they are the right people to trust an investment with. This requires a careful balance between making the proposal sufficiently attractive and realistically addressing the many risks inherent in the proposal, in particular how rapid growth will be handled. To do this the plan needs to emphasize the strengths of the business, particularly compared to the competition. Behind all plans there are people, and investors, like bank managers, need to be convinced that you and the venture team can deliver what you are promising. It is often said that the single most important element in the investment decision is the credibility and quality of the firm's management.

The most difficult aspect of any deal is deciding on the split of equity between the various partners. The simple answer is that there is no set of rules, and the final result will depend on the attractiveness of the proposal and the negotiating skills of the individuals concerned. Investors will not normally want control of the business (over 50% of the shareholding) as this might affect your motivation, but they will want a sufficiently large say to influence important decisions. Key managers on your team might also want a share in the business, so you need to think through the final shareholding you will be left with. You will not want to surrender control, so you need to think through how much equity

Change your [business] plan and see if you can take a longer and slower pace to build credibility and some capital. Proving the case reduces the risks to any potential investors and hence makes the cost of equity cheaper.

James Davenport, Finance Director, Innocent, *The Guardian*, 23 October 2014

you want to keep, not just at this point but also after the equity investor has sold off their shareholding. You also need to think about who might buy their shares and whether they are an equity partner that you are happy with.

You need to find out how the investor operates. Some investors prefer a 'hands-on' approach to managing their investment whereby they have a non-executive director on the board, visit the firm monthly and keep in regular phone contact. As we saw in the Kirsty's Case insight on page 264, business angels can bring considerable experience and a network of contacts to the business, so do your homework on the background of your angel. Other, mainly institutional, investors have a more 'hands-off' approach, preferring not to interfere once they have invested, perhaps meeting once a year to review the progress of the business.

Image Source

As explained in the previous chapter, business angels and venture capitalists expect an annualized return of 30–50%, normally as a capital gain. They also normally expect to realize their investment within 5 – 10 years (an exit route or liquidity event). They will expect a seat on the board of directors, and many angels will expect a closer involvement in the management of the business. You need to find out how your investor wants to take income from their investment – through dividends or a capital gain (they have very different tax implications). You should not be afraid to ask about the timescale they have for realizing their investment – it is important that you both understand each other's expectations. They may also have views about who they might sell their stake to. This may be an opportunity for you to increase your stake in the business by buying out the investor, as happened with Mark Constantine and Lush (Case insight – on page 192). Alternatively, it may be an opportunity for you to dilute your share of the business or exit completely, by encouraging a merger with, or buy-out by, another company.

Remember, whereas a bank loan will probably take weeks to arrange, an equity investment will take months. It will involve numerous meetings, interviews and presentations. The investors, or their accountants, will undertake their own investigations into the business (called '**due diligence**') and the production of the legal documentation will involve lengthy, detailed work. You will need professional advice.

Finally, business plans should never be 'set in concrete'. As the organization and the environment within which it operates changes, so too will your plans for how to deal with it – from detailed cash flow projections to broader details of marketing strategy. Never stop strategizing, and even if you do not write a formal business plan, the exercise of systematically going through a strategic review, as outlined in Chapter 12, should prove invaluable.

> Writing a business plan was a vital first step that helped me focus on the task ahead and apply a professional approach. But after a few months things had changed so much that those initial projections looked laughably naïve … What they don't tell you is that this doesn't really matter. Ditching the old plan and writing a new one just shows how adaptable you are in the face of all those "unforeseen challenges".
>
> **Lara Kelly,** co-creator, Hum Flowerpots, *The Guardian*, 12 May 2015

 Practice insight Presenting a case for finance

At some point you might be asked to 'present' your business plan to financiers. Part of the reason for this will be to support and elaborate on details contained in the business plan, but part of it will be to allow the potential backer to form judgements about you, and possibly your venture team. They will be looking for motivation, enthusiasm and integrity but most of all the managerial ability to make the plan actually happen.

'Presentations' can take a number of forms. A bank might just expect an informal meeting to discuss the business plan, perhaps coming back to discuss issues that might arise. Investors are likely to require a number of meetings. The first meeting might involve a 15- to 20- minute formal presentation of the plan, using dedicated presentation software such as Microsoft PowerPoint or Prezi, followed by questions which could easily go on for twice as long. If this is successful you will be invited back for a second meeting to sort out details about an investment.

The first thing to do is to follow instructions. If you are asked to make a 15-minute presentation, keep it to 15 minutes – and that means about 10 slides. Make sure there is a computer and projector available. If there is not, you need to make your own arrangements – a large tablet computer can be useful if there is only one investor because it breaks down the 'us and them' feel of using a projector. Remember that what you really want is to engage in a discussion – to start forming a relationship – and you need to work to break down

Continued...

Continued from previous page...

barriers. It is always good to bring in samples or examples of the product, service website etc., so that the audience can see and/or touch it. You need to grab their attention.

Slides should be clear and uncluttered, focusing on the main points of the topic and inviting the audience to engage and ask questions because the topic interests them. Do not put too much detailed information on them. Remember to 'brand' every slide with your business name. Highlights to be covered on individual slides include:

> **Why you are there, the financing you are seeking and the deal you are offering** – Remember that in doing this you are placing a value on the business. You will inevitably be asked what you intend to spend the money on.

> **The product/service offering and the value proposition to customers** – You need to explain and/or demonstrate your product or service, the problem customers currently have and how this will solve it for them.

> **Target market and opportunity** – You need to be able to describe the prospective customers (better still, name names) and explain how you will get to them. If you already have orders for the product or service this will add enormously to your credibility.

> **The competition (they will expect you to name names), your competitive advantage and how you will react to them when they respond** – If you have any intellectual property (IP), this is the point to highlight it.

> **Marketing strategy** – This is where you can sketch out how you will achieve your sales targets over the planning period. They will be interested in your sales processes and your distribution channels. Primary market research information can add to the credibility of your plans.

> **Your management team (including board of directors)** – What is important is your background and experience. If you have skill gaps, explain how they will be filled.

> **Financial highlights (not financial details) sales and profit, when profitability is achieved, capital investment, cash flow implications and break-even** – They will

ask about the details, in particular how your sales projections and costs were arrived at, so you might want to prepare some additional slides to go back to. Remember, they will be thinking about what their share of this will be and how it might convert into business valuation.

If you have or are looking to find prospective partners then this will need to be highlighted in the presentation. If there are particular issues of control related to your industry, these may also need to be covered, albeit briefly.

The presentation is an opportunity to demonstrate your personal qualities and start to develop a relationship. First impressions are important, but an in-depth knowledge of the key areas in the business plan will go a long way towards generating the confidence that is needed. There are ways of enhancing a presentation. It is important to rehearse it thoroughly. Always stress the market and the firm's competitive advantage, rather than the product features. Stress the competencies of the management team. In terms of style, it is important to demonstrate the product and, in Western culture, to make frequent eye-to-eye contact. You should manage the presentation with respect to any co-presenters. Finally, never try to weasel your way out of questions to which you do not know the answers. The best advice is to say you do not know but will get back with the answer in a few days.

An experienced investor once admitted that, while discussions with the entrepreneur might centre on the business plan, the final decision whether or not to invest was really the result of 'gut feel' – a personal 'chemistry' between them and the entrepreneur. At the end of the day, that chemistry must lay the foundation for a long-term relationship based, as always, on trust and respect. However, remember the work of Chen et al. (2009) mentioned in Chapter 14. Based upon a 'laboratory experiment' and a field study, they concluded that venture capitalists' investment decisions were consistently based on the entrepreneur's preparedness for the business plan presentation rather than the 'passion' of their presentation.

Case insight   One Day – Bridal Wear & Accessories

Business Plan

This is an actual business plan, although some details have been changed. It is not intended as an example of either good or bad practice.

© Royalty-Free/Corbis

One Day – Bridal Wear & Accessories

Business Plan

Contents

Executive Summary

One Day is a bridal wear retailer that will offer brides an opportunity to select and purchase their wedding gown for their special day, from a limited range of quality wedding dress designers. The business will operate on a strategy of differentiation, achieved through the quality and design of gowns on offer; the look, feel and layout of the store and fitting area; and from a focus on an attentive personal customer service. It will also offer a range of bridal underwear, accessories and bridesmaid gowns to complement the main product offering in-store, creating opportunities to supplement revenue.

The target market for One Day is middle-class females, aged 25–40. The retail outlet will be based in a rural location in the county of Hertfordshire, UK, a region where this target market is well represented. The target market are fashion conscious and have high levels of disposable income available to spend on luxury items, such as wedding gowns. The communications strategy for One Day will focus on wedding exhibitions, both local and regional, and engagement with local business and industry press.

Projected first year profits are £34,300 based on sales of £200,000. This comprises eight wedding gowns and accessories a month. Profits will rise to £70,500 from year two on sales of £264,100 (12 gowns). The business will be funded by personal capital investment and a bank overdraft facility.

Business Details

Business name: One Day   Address: 33 Confetti Crescent, Hitchin, Hertfordshire
This business is a bridal wear and accessories retailer. It will be operated as a sole trader and offer the following products: bridal gowns, bridal underwear, bridal shoes, jewellery, bridal headdresses, bridesmaid dresses, bridesmaid shoes, handbags and purses.

Mission and values

To provide customers and their bridal party with quality bridal wear and accessories through a valued, quality personal customer service experience, ensuring that their appearance at their special event reflects the confidence and beauty of each individual.

Aims and objectives

> To provide quality bridal wear products to our customers;
> To provide a quality personal service to our customers and their bridal party;
> To ensure that each lady making a purchase feels confident and happy with their appearance in the product.

Industry and Market Analysis

The UK wedding industry is currently worth £10 billion with over 250,000 weddings every year. The average amount spent on a bridal outfit is £1,194. The average cost of a bridal gown has risen almost 15% over the last five years. This increase is forecasted to continue at a similar rate over the next five years. There are around 3,500 bridal wear retailers in the UK. One Day will be based in Hertfordshire, where there are currently around 82 retailers. Generally, brides use the internet to search for their bridal gown and bridal wear retailer, so a web presence will be an imperative for the business.

> The power of buyers – The target customers for One Day are brides-to-be from a middle-class socio-economic group, in the age range of 25–40, as this group will have disposable income to spend on bridal wear. The population of women in the Eastern region of the UK is around 3 million, with around 30% in the target demographic. Buyers have a choice of nearly 100 other bridal wear retailers in the Hertfordshire region with similar products, product mixes and price points. Differentiation arises mainly from the design ranges that retailers offer, as well as the quality of the customer

Continued...

Continued from previous page...

service experience. The importance of word-of-mouth reviews and recommendations can impact a bridal retail business, both positively and negatively. The increased communication through the internet and social media has increased the level and power of impact of this type of feedback.

> The power of suppliers – Wedding dress designers tend to operate on a national scale. They have individual agreements with retailers based on guaranteed number of purchases of sample gowns per season, guaranteed retail price/price range and geographical exclusivity. There is evidence that designers sell their bridal wear ranges direct to the public, but this tends to be limited to the local area where the designer is based. Designers do not tend to offer their products direct to customers online. Customers are, instead, directed to stockists available regionally/ nationally.

> Threat of new entrants – New entrants to the bridal wear retail sector are common. Retailers are not required to buy large amounts of stock to begin selling to customers, as most gowns are purchased on a 'per order' basis. This means that it can be a relatively easy and low-cost business to set up. The number of bridal retailers is greater than the number of bridal wear designers available in the market. This means that there are high levels of competition for supplier agreements and design ranges offered to customers.

> Threat of substitutes – The culture of weddings in the UK is one heavily embedded in tradition. While there has been a rise in destination weddings abroad, these events do still retain many of the traditional elements of a UK wedding, for example the wedding dress. While the market may fluctuate a little in response to economic pressures and changes in fashion, the wedding gown remains a traditional product with very few significant changes to either the type of gown produced by the market or the price points at which they are offered. The target customers for One Day are willing to pay a higher price to purchase their chosen wedding gown, as evidenced by the year-on-year price increases in the sector. Consequently, this market is not as exposed to substitutes and changes in technology like other consumer categories.

> Competitive rivalry in the industry – With a high number of bridal wear retailers in the Hertfordshire area, differentiation from competitors is vital. As mentioned previously significant differentiation in customer experience of the retail service offered, as well as variety in designs and price points, is important. This includes look and design of the retail unit, the experience and service from staff, and the efficiency, consistency and reliability of the fitting and delivery process, as well as the overall quality of the product.

Competitors

There are numerous bridal retailers in Hertfordshire, with others in the surrounding counties of Bedfordshire, Buckinghamshire and Cambridgeshire. Retailers in these areas offer a variety of products; from cheaper wedding gowns, priced under £1,000, which tend to be manufactured in the cheaper global regions (e.g. China), through to high-end designer gowns that can sell anywhere up to £4,000. See Appendix A for research on competitors. Of the competitors reviewed, all stores emphasize the personal and committed aspect of their customer service.

The unique aspect of the bridal wear retail trade is that competitors grouped close together can be mutually beneficial. Brides-to-be are often willing to travel to an area to search for their gown. If there are many bridal retailers concentrated in a particular area, this can encourage customers to visit as they feel that they will be able to reduce the overall time needed for their dress search by visiting many stores in one shopping trip.

Continued...

Continued from previous page...

Based on this analysis it is more important for One Day to focus on competing with its local competitors, rather than county wide.

Customers and the value proposition

The target customers for One Day are brides-to-be from a middle-class socio-economic group, in the age range of 25–40, with high disposable income. They are looking for a product that makes them look and feel beautiful and special for their wedding day. The service provided to them by the staff during the selecting of gowns can impact on how they feel about the product.

Each customer will want a look that suits their self-image and physical body shape, so it is important to carry a variety of sample wedding gowns with different shapes and styles that will suite a variety of female body shapes. The emphasis in the customer experience will be of 'what is right for the customer'. It would damage the reputation of the store to force a sale of an inappropriate product on a customer. The focus will be to help the customer to find the wedding dress that suits their body shape and the image that they wish to project on their wedding day.

This customer service experience will be augmented through careful planning and consideration of the layout and fitting of the retail store, and through a well communicated knowledge of One Day's products, with sensitivity and empathy towards the customer, pro-actively helping them to achieve their desired image. The store will have a relaxed, approachable style to the main retail area. This will include the use of soft inviting colours in the interior décor, as well as the ornamental features and furniture details that will evoke the feel of a ladies dressing room in a home. The range of products will be displayed in sections defined by designer and overall dress shape. The management of product displays in this way will help the customer focus their search when they enter the store. The relaxed, approachable style of the store will be continued into the separate fitting area towards the rear of the store. This area will have a large space for the customer to try and view wedding gowns, and a relaxed seating area for the friends/relatives to sit in comfort while the customer tries the gowns.

One Day will offer customers a guarantee 'buy-back' service for their wedding gowns, thus providing an added benefit to the customer in the form of a solution of what to do with their wedding gown after the wedding.

One Day will also offer bridesmaid dresses and bridal accessories to include underwear, shoes, headdresses and jewellery. Offering bridesmaid gowns and bridal accessories will allow the customer to select items to match their wedding gown at the same time as selecting the dress. For customers who are busy planning a big event, the opportunity to purchase all they need for their outfit in one store is a definite benefit. Also, it is not common to find a bridal wear retailer who stocks bridal underwear, and as this is a key decision choice related to the wedding gown, it would provide an opportunity for One Day to differentiate itself from competitors. One Day will offer an exclusive distribution channel for a start-up underwear designer, at the same time as offering other established products.

Marketing Strategy

The marketing strategy for One Day will have the following key activities:

> Attendance at local and regional wedding exhibitions, around 3–4 per year
> Advertisements in local press and regional sector press 4–5 times per year (e.g. *Your Herts & Beds Wedding Magazine*)
> A photo shoot of products to provide images to use in promotional material, both for the launch and moving forward with the business
> A vibrant website – to include videos and photos of products on offer

Continued...

Continued from previous page...

Price and promotions

One Day will offer wedding gowns at the mid-price point, between £1,300 and £2,500. There will be a 100% mark-up on wholesale/trade prices of the gowns. The regional market for bridal wear in Hertfordshire indicates that this mark-up is realistic. It will also offer accessories priced between £15 and £100, and bridesmaid dresses priced between £120 and £300.

One Day aims to sell eight wedding gowns per month in the first year, with 50% of these sales converting to include accessories and bridesmaid outfits. As wedding dresses can typically run on a 6-month lead time, peak sales periods are expected to be around September/October for brides wishing to marry in the popular summer months. Low periods, therefore, are expected to be from June to August, as many brides will have already purchased their gowns by this time. Lower sales may also be expected in December and January, as people have less disposable income due to the Christmas shopping period.

One Day will offer a guarantee 'buy-back' service for wedding gowns. Customers will be offered a guaranteed resale price of between 35%–40% of the original retail price of the gown. One Day can then offer the gown as pre-owned with an additional mark-up of 5%–20%. Many customers will not actually use this facility but it does allow them sell on their dress without the inconvenience of going through channels like eBay. It would also generate additional revenue for the business from the same stock item. This 'buy-back' offer will be made available to customers with a time limit, so as to increase the chance that the style of the dress will still be in keeping with current fashion trends, and prevent the opportunity for 'dead stock' that is unsaleable.

In line with other retailers in the sector, One Day will periodically offer gowns for sale at reduced prices of around 50%– 70% of the retail price as part of a 'sample sale' offer. This will be an opportunity for the business to reduce stock levels from previous seasons and stimulate sales at low season.

Launch strategy

The launch of One Day will be focused on a launch event in-store with a fashion show of the products on offer. Guests will be invited from local media, regional sector press and people who are active in social media locally (Hitchin has a good example of local social media publicizing and promoting local businesses). Press releases will be sent to media outlets to help publicize the event and the business, both before and after. Images and videos from the launch fashion show will be used in supporting print and online marketing campaigns in regional publications and websites, to showcase the products available. These images will also be used on the One Day website and in promotional material to be used at exhibitions.

Sales tactics

The layout of the store and display of the products in categories of design and overall dress shape will provide an opportunity for staff to engage with the customer as they enter. Staff will be able engage the customer in a conversation about the type and style of gown they are searching for to assist them to focus on the more relevant product lines within the store. This opportunity for establishing a relationship between the customer and the staff member can be then carried through to the fitting area, where the honesty and interpersonal skills of the staff member will assist the customer in selecting the most appropriate gown for them. The guaranteed 'buy-back' service will also incentivize customers to purchase as this will provide a solution for them of what to do with the product once it has served its purpose. Offering accessories and bridesmaid dresses in-store will provide an opportunity for generation of additional revenue, as customers will be encouraged to seek all bridal party products in one place.

Continued...

Continued from previous page...

Brand development

The development of the One Day brand will be most reliant on its reputation among customers. In order to ensure a reliable reputation, the importance of maintaining quality customer service in-store is significant. While it is necessary to ensure that sales are secured, pressuring customers into purchasing a gown that is not appropriate, and does not satisfy the requirement of the customers' self-image, could damage the brand over the long term through poor recommendation and negative customer feedback. Assisting customers to select gowns that truly reflect their self-image, give them confidence and make them look good will work to the benefit of the One Day brand. Word-of-mouth reviews, particularly in a regionally focused industry such as bridal wear, can have high positive impact in generating future sales. The importance of communication and inter-personal skills of the staff members must be emphasized and developed accordingly. The key values for the One Day brand reflect those of the business as a whole: offering quality products, offering a quality customer service, ensuring the confidence and satisfaction of each customer in their purchase.

Competitive reaction

The aspects of One Day's differentiation, offering underwear products and a guaranteed 'buy-back' scheme, can be copied by rival retailers. However, One Day will only benefit from being first to market with these features. It will rely on the quality of its products, customer service and reputation to remain competitive.

Product and market development & growth strategies

The bridal retail industry is one that centres on a very traditional concept of the main product. Wedding gowns vary little in overall design, and apart from developments in new fabrics and manufacturing techniques, are subject to little in terms of product innovation. Product and market development for One Day will focus on discovering and collaborating with new bridal wear designers. This will provide One Day with the opportunity to expand the product lines offered in-store. Research has indicated that other bridal retailers have moved into designing their own products to sell in-store and this could be a future development possibility.

One Day will look to scale up the retail business by entering into collaborations with other wedding product/service suppliers to offer other services such as beauty/spa treatments, hair styling, bridal make-up services, specialist cake services, catering, photography, entertainment and full wedding planning services. With this anticipated scalability, One Day will be looking to exploit its rural location, where there would be the possibility for availability of supplementary retail units through conversion of existing buildings/premises, or availability of land for construction of additional units/space. This offers the opportunity to become a one-stop-shop wedding retail and service provider.

Operations Plan

To begin with, designers and product lines will be selected by attending the national trade shows to make connections with the bridal wear designers. Many designers host 'trunk shows' to exhibit their latest bridal collections, and national shows showcase many designers at one event (e.g. the British Bridal Exhibition in Harrogate). Direct contacts with individual designers, e.g. Blue Bridal, will also be made. Designers usually release their new collections in the spring of each year. They normally request bridal retailers to purchase anywhere between 6 and 10 sample designs from each collection.

Continued...

Continued from previous page...

One Day anticipates making sample design purchases from two or three individual bridal designers. It will focus on selecting styles that match and flatter the predominant body shape of women from the target market segment found in the locale of the business. This product selection would allow sufficient product diversity in-store for customers to select their individual gown, while not overwhelming the customer with too much choice, or by presenting opportunities for the business to be left with surplus 'dead stock' at the end of the fashion season.

One Day will sell dresses to customers with a six-month lead time. Customers will be asked to pay a 50% deposit on their chosen gown, with the remaining 50% paid when the gown arrives in-store. One Day will initially look to rent a rural retail premises with a floor space of 450– 700 sq ft. The rural location will enable the business to rent a unit for a lower amount than would be required for a retail unit in a town centre location. One Day will lease the unit on a five-year lease, with a three-year break clause. This style of lease is common and the break clause would offer an opportunity to exit the lease agreement early if the business success does not proceed as anticipated.

One Day will start up with two members of staff – the business owner and another family member. Neither will draw a salary from the business initially. If target sales are able to be increased by 25% after the first year, one additional staff member would be employed on a casual contract for two 8-hour days per week, at a cost of £8,000 per year. This employee would assist customers in-store over the weekend, as this would be the anticipated busiest time for customers dropping into the store and attending pre-booked appointments.

One Day will collaborate with one or two seamstresses in the local area to offer an alteration service to its customers. It will provide the seamstresses with access to its customer base, as well as a space for the fittings to take place in-store, in return for being able to publicize the gown/garment alteration service in-store as part of the product offering to customers. Alteration services will be priced separately, per section of garment to be altered.

One Day will offer 'Sample Sale' promotions before new collections arrive in-store and to supplement sales in the low season around December and January. These promotional periods will offer One Day the opportunity to clear 'dead' and 'sample' stock from its inventory, as well as clear physical space in-store to make way for the new designs coming in each year. This will also allow for a reinvigoration of the store's product offering, and additional opportunities for mini-launch evens of the new season stock to generate and maintain market interest.

Management Team and Company Structure

The business will be owner-managed by RC. RC has a MBA and some retail experience, but not in the bridal industry, although she has recently participated in the bridal wear sector as a customer. RC will be assisted in day-to-day operations by ST, who has experience of dress-making.

RT will act as adviser to the business. With two successful business start-ups, RT has demonstrated a risk management approach to businesses, ensuring that they have the margins to allow for expansion and growth. Both businesses offer services to the commercial energy sector, with one business operating globally within the Middle East and Europe.

Seamstress skills will be required. One Day will collaborate with one or two seamstresses based in the local area to provide an in-store alteration service to its customers.

Continued...

Continued from previous page...

Resources

One Day will require the following resources:

> Retail premises based in a rural location with a floor space of 450–700 sq ft.
> Initial capital of £50,000 to cover the businesses initial fixed costs in the first year consisting of: premises rental and rates, purchase of initial sample stock, fitting of retail unit, marketing campaign and strategy costs.
> Seamstress skills from a collaboration with one or two seamstresses based in the local area.
> A website to establish an online presence and assistance with initial web design – it is thought that initially this could be achieved by the owner-manager alone.

Financing

One Day will be financed by personal investment, with the possibility of seeking additional funding from a bank in the form of an overdraft for contingency and in order to assist in the management of the cash flow of the business. The initial investment will be £50,000, to cover property rental and rates costs; fixtures, fittings, and decoration of the interior of the retail space; initial stock inventory; and marketing activities. Fixed costs are detailed in the financial projections section below. The lease on the retail unit will be for five years, with a three-year break clause, to allow for exit from the business in the event of failure to reach anticipated sales and revenue targets. In the event of early exit from the business, any remaining stock assets would be saleable to release cash to any remaining creditors.

Financial Projections
Forecast Income Statement (3 years)

£	Year 1		Year 2		Year 3	
Sales	£1900 × 103	195,700	£1900 × 139	264,100	£1900 × 139	264,100
Cost of Sales	£950 × 103	97,850	£950 × 139	132,050	£950 × 139	132,050
Gross Profit		**97,850**		**132,050**		**132,050**
Wages	0		8,000		8,000	
Property Rental	10,000		10,000		10,000	
Property Rates & Utilities	8,000		8,000		8,000	
Shop Fittings & Decorating	6,000		1,000		1,000	
Marketing & Exhibition	5,000		5,000		5,000	
Write Down Of Sample Stock (50% pa)	14,775		14,770		14,770	
Total Fixed Costs		43,775		46,770		46,770
Net profit		**54,075**		**85,280**		**85,280**
Tax @ 20%		**10,815**		**17,056**		**17,056**
Retained earnings		**43,260**		**68,224**		**68,224**

Forecast Contribution & Breakeven (Year 1)

Contribution per gown   £1900 − £950 = £950
Contribution margin   £950 ÷ £1900 = 50% (0.5)
Fixed costs   £43,775
Breakeven   £43,775 ÷ 0.5 = £87,550 (equal to 46 gowns a year or less than one per week)
Margin of safety   (£195,700 − £87,550) ÷ £195,700 × 100 = 55%

Continued...

Continued from previous page...

Forecast Monthly Cash Flow (Year 1)

£	Start-up	1	2	3	4	5	6	7	8	9	10	11	12	Total
Receipts:														
Sales Deposits	0	8,550	8,550	7,600	7,600	7,600	8,550	8,550	8,550	7,600	7,600	8,550	8,550	97,850
Sales Balance								8,550	8,550	7,600	7,600	7,600	8,550	48,450
Payments:														
Property Rental Costs	−5,000	−834	−834	−834	−834	−834	−834	−834	−834	−834	−834	−834	−826	−15,000
Property Rates & Utilities Costs	−667	−667	−667	−667	−667	−667	−667	−667	−667	−667	−667	−663	−667	−8,667
Shop Fittings & Decorating Costs	−6,000	0	0	0	0	0	0	0	0	0	0	0	−1,000	−7,000
Sample Stock Purchase Costs	−29,550	0	0	0	0	0	0	0	0	0	0	0	0	−29,550
Marketing & Exhibition Costs	−1,300	−1,500	0	−500	0	0	−1,000	0	0	−500	0	−200	0	−5,000
Inventory		−8,550	−8,550	−7,600	−7,600	−7,600	−8,550	−8,550	−8,550	−7,600	−7,600	−8,550	−8,550	−97,850
Net Cash Flow	−42,517	−3,001	−1,501	−2,001	−1,501	−1,501	−2,501	7,049	7,049	5,599	6,099	5,903	6,057	−16,767
Capital	50,000	–	–	–	–	–	–	–	–	–	–	–	–	50,000
Cash B/F	0	7,483	4,482	2,981	980	−521	−2,022	−4,523	2,526	9,575	15,174	21,273	27,176	
Cash C/F	7,483	4,482	2,981	980	−521	−2,022	-4,523	2,526	9,575	15,174	21,273	27,176	33,233	33,233

Forecast Balance Sheet (Year 1)

£	At start-up	Year 1
ASSETS		
Current Assets		
Stocks/Inventories	29,550	14,775
Debtors/Receivables	0	49,400
Property Deposit	5,000	5,000
Prepaid Property Rates	667	667
Prepaid Marketing	1,300	0
Prepaid Fixtures & Fittings	6,000	1,000
Cash	7,483	33,233
Total Assets	**50,000**	**104,075**

EQUITY & LIABILITIES		
Capital	50,000	50,000
Retained Earnings	0	43,260
Current Liabilities		
Borrowings (Overdraft)	0	0
Trade Payables	0	0
Taxation (@ 20%)	0	10,815
Total Equity & Liabilities	**50,000**	**104,075**

Continued...

Continued from previous page...

Forecast Key Ratios (Year 1)

Return on total assets	Operating profit margin	Gross profit margin
$\frac{54,075}{104,075}$ = 52%	$\frac{54,075}{195,700}$ = 28%	$\frac{97,850}{195,700}$ = 50.0%

Total asset turnover	Debtor turnover	Stock turnover
$\frac{195,700}{104,075}$ = 1.9 pa	$\frac{195,700}{49,400}$ = 4.0 pa	$\frac{195,700}{14,775}$ = 13 pa

Current ratio	Quickratio	
$\frac{104,075}{10,815}$ = 9.6	$\frac{89,300}{10,815}$ = 8.3	

Refer to Appendix B for details on financial projections.

Risks and Strategic Options

Identified risks

Risks for One Day include:

> The management of cash flow and trade receivables to ensure long-term survival and success of the business.
> The long-term commitment to the lease of a property with the possibility of the need close the business before the lease terms expires.
> The management of sample product stock, to ensure the minimal opportunity for dead stock.

Risk monitoring and mitigation

> Cash flow will be forecast and monitored on a monthly basis. Access to a bank overdraft facility will provide a margin of safety for the business in relation to its cash flow, particularly if the business experiences problems with poor debtors from customers.
> The lease for the retail unit will include a three-year break clause which will allow sufficient time for the business to operate past the point at which the Death Valley curve should have impact. This three-year break will allow an opportunity for the performance of the business to be reviewed and for the business to be closed with minimal costs in relation to the lease agreement, if necessary.
> The implementation of 'sample sale' promotions should reduce the risk around the business maintaining a store of dead stock. This will help to ensure revenue can be realized from sample stock inventory.

Critical success factors

The success factors for One Day include:

> Maintenance of positive cash flow and profit accounts.
> Ensuring target sales are met, and/or exceeded on a monthly basis.
> Positive feedback from customers, both from word-of-mouth recommendations and through online social media.
> The elimination of the need for a bank overdraft facility after month 8 of trading.

Strategic options

> The strategic options for One Day are either to price the product lines low, or offer differentiation in their service and products to the target customer group.

Continued...

Continued from previous page...

> Research and experience indicates that there is difficulty in achieving delivery of quality products to customers at low price points within the bridal wear retail industry. In light of this, One Day will focus on a strategy of differentiation, through both its product offerings in-store and high quality, personal customer service experience.

> If the business suffers negative impacts from the risks associated with poor cash flow management and surplus of 'dead stock', then a price reduction strategy could be implemented in the short term to liquidize money from the businesses holdings of inventory. The high mark-up on wedding gowns allow for a price reduction to be made by almost 50% before the business will suffer a loss on the original purchase price of the product.

Key Milestones

Key milestones for One Day for end of year 1:

> Locating an appropriate retail unit in a rural location.
> Negotiating agreements with 2–3 wedding gown designers, e.g. Blu, for the supply and stock of a range of 10 products per designer in-store.
> Negotiating agreements with underwear, accessory and bridesmaid gown suppliers to supply and stock a range of products in-store.
> Negotiating an overdraft facility with the bank to assist in the management on cash flow for the business in the first year.
> To meet target monthly sales of eight gowns.
> To reach positive cash flow, thereby eliminating the need for use of the bank overdraft on an ongoing basis.
> To receive 30% of customers as referrals from word-of-mouth and social media recommendations (to be measured via in-store survey).

Key milestone for One Day for end of year 2:

> To meet a 25% target increase in monthly sales.

Appendix A – Competitors – Bridal Retail, Hertfordshire

Competitor	Location	Type of Bridal Wear	Designers	Accessories	Opening Hours	Appointments	Price Points
A	Hitchin	Made to standard sizing	Cymbeline; Augusta Jones; Suzanne Neville; Anouska G; Maggie Sottero; Allure; Jesus Peiro; Annasul Y; Eliza Jane Howell	Head dress; jewellery	Mon-Fri – 10-5; Sat – 9-5	Mon-Fri – 10-15.45; Sat – 9-15.45	<1,000–2,000
B	Tring	Made to standard sizing	Atelier Diagonal; Amanda Wyatt; Charlotte Balbier; Paloma Blanca; Ellis	Bridesmaids; head dress	Mon-Sat – 10-5	No information	No information
C	St Albans	Made to measure; Made to standard sizing	Shanna Melville; White One; Johanna Hehir; Lusan Mandongus; Ebony Rose; Annasul Y; Lazaro; Jim Hjelm	Bridesmaids; full range of accessories; evening wear	No information	No information	750–2,000
D	Hertford	Made to measure; Made to standard sizing	Sophia Tolli; Marylise; JLM Couture; Annette Carey Couture	Bridesmaids; collaborations with other services, e.g. hair & make-up	Mon & Sun – closed; Tues, Wed & Fri – 10-4; Thurs – 1-7; Sat – 9-5	No information	No information
E	Stevenage	Made to standard sizing	Alfred Angelo; Benjamin Roberts; Mori Lee; Ronald Joyce	Bridesmaids; full range of accessories; evening wear; menswear	Mon-Fri – 10-5; Sat – 9-5	Sun – 11-3	No information

Continued...

Continued from previous page...

Appendix B – Financial Projection Details

Sales Forecast (Years 1 & 2)

The business plan includes a target increase in sales of 25% after the first year. The sales forecast, therefore, has been produced for the first two years of the business in order to demonstrate the effect of this increase.

Year 1, month	1	2	3	4	5	6	7	8	9	10	11	12	Total
No. of units sold	9	9	8	8	8	9	9	9	8	8	9	9	103
£ value of units sold (@ average unit price of £1900)	17,100	17,100	15,200	15,200	15,200	17,100	17,100	17,100	15,200	15,200	17,100	17,100	195,700

Year 2, month	1	2	3	4	5	6	7	8	9	10	11	12	Total
No. of units sold	12	12	11	11	11	12	12	12	11	11	12	12	139
£ value of units sold (@ average unit price of £1900)	22,800	22,800	20,900	20,900	20,900	22,800	22,800	22,800	20,900	20,900	22,800	22,800	264,100

Assumptions

All forecasts are based on the following assumptions:

1 Unit sale price of £1,900 is an average price from the range of wedding gown products priced between £1,300 and £2,500. Cost is 50%.
2 Sales targets include up-selling 50% of customers per month to include a purchase of accessories and/or bridesmaid gowns, at the same time as purchasing a wedding gown. To enable the supplementary product line sales to be included in forecast calculations, and for simplicity, the value of these supplementary product line sales has been equated to one additional wedding gown sale per month.
3 Sales of all gowns and accessories are charged at a deposit of 50% at the time of purchase, with the remaining 50% paid upon collection of the gown six months later.
4 Property rental fees and rates will be paid monthly, assuming a six-month deposit on rental property at the beginning of the lease (£5,000).
5 Sample Stock Purchase Costs include sample product lines for wedding and bridesmaid gowns (30 sample wedding gowns @ £950; 15 sample bridesmaid gowns @ £70). These costs are written off over two years (50% pa).
6 Initially stock/inventory purchases are paid in month of purchase. Extended terms will be negotiated in due course.
7 Initial start-up costs will be funded by a personal capital investment of £50,000. Additional funding in the form of a bank overdraft facility to the value of around £10,000 would be negotiated for the first year.
8 The owner will take no salary from the business, but will take dividends on any profits from the business.

 Practice insight reminder 15 characteristics of a good business idea

Remember the 15 characteristics of a good business idea:

1 Identified market need or gap.
2 No or few existing competitors.
3 Growing market.
4 Identified customers and a viable business model.
5 Low funding requirements.
6 Sustainable.
7 High profit margins.
8 Effective communications strategy.

9 Not easily copied.
10 Identifiable risks that can be monitored and mitigated.
11 Low fixed costs.
12 Controllable.
13 Management skill that can be leveraged.
14 Scalable.
15 Financeable.

Does your business plan satisfy all these characteristics? Can it be improved in any way?

Summary

> A business plan describes what your new venture seeks to achieve and how it will do this. It can be used for internal purposes, as a management 'aide-memoire', or for external purposes, particularly to raise finance.

> Plans for external purposes are generally longer and more formal than those for internal use. The larger the start-up and more finance being sought, the longer and more detailed the plan is likely to be. Plans for equity investors are likely to be the longest and best presented.

> Although there is no set format, a typical structure of a typical business plan for external use is set out in Table 15.1.

> The plan for a social enterprise needs to be commercially realistic while demonstrating how its social objectives will be met. To attract grant funding, you will need to emphasize these social objectives and how the grant will be used to enable them to be met. You will have to demonstrate that commercial profits will be directed towards these social objectives and/or ploughed back into the enterprise.

> A business plan presented to a bank needs to demonstrate how interest on the loan can be paid and the capital repaid on the due date, with minimum risk. Particular attention, therefore, needs to be paid to the cash flow forecast. To obtain a loan you need to gain the trust of the bank manager and develop their respect in your business ability. Personal credibility is vital.

> A business plan developed for an equity investor needs to demonstrate that a business opportunity exists that can earn a high return – typically from 30 to 50% per annum – that can be realized in a 5 to 10-year time frame. It also needs to convince the reader that the management team is capable of exploiting the opportunity. Investors place great reliance on the managerial credibility of the founder and their team.

> A business plan presentation needs to be just as good as the plan itself – focusing on the highlights of the plan and well executed. You are trying to interest and engage with the audience and invite them to enter into a discussion about your venture. You want to gain their trust and respect.

✓ Activities

1 List the contents of a business plan that is drawn up:
   a)   For planning purposes within the firm;
   b)   For raising external finance.
   How are they different?
2 Draw up a business plan for your business idea based upon the business model you have developed through the activities in this book.
3 An 'elevator pitch' is where you have only three minutes to explain your start-up idea to a potential investor/lender and persuade them to see you again to find out more. (It is called this because you might be trapped in the elevator with them for three minutes.) It requires you to know exactly what is unique about your product or service and what the investor/lender is interested in. Pair up with other students and practice your pitch. Give each other scores out of 10 but, more importantly, be prepared to explain your score. You should improve with practice.

4 Draw up a report for your superior in a bank outlining the criteria you recommend the bank to use in making a loan to:
   a) A start-up business;
   b) An established firm.
   How are they different? How much of the information you need to make a loan can come from the business plan?
5 Visit any of the websites that contain specimen business plans, select a plan and critically evaluate the business proposition.

💬 Group discussion topics

1 What is the difference between a business model and a business plan?
2 What are the advantages and disadvantages of following pre-prepared business plan formats?
3 How can computer-based systems help develop a business plan? What advantages do they offer? Are there any drawbacks?
4 What form do you think a business plan should take for your own, internal use?
5 The best business plan is a short business plan. Discuss.
6 For what purposes might a social enterprise prepare a business plan? How would this affect the content?
7 If you were a bank manager, what would persuade you to lend to a social enterprise?

8   Preparing a business plan for a social enterprise is more difficult than preparing one for a commercial enterprise. Discuss.

9   What different things do lenders and investors look for in a business plan? How does this affect the contents?

10 Lenders and investors put their money with people, not plans. Discuss.

11 In a rapidly changing world, is planning really of any use?

12 Are entrepreneurs congenitally incapable of planning?

13 Every business graduate can produce a good business plan, but not even 1% can become entrepreneurs. Discuss.

14 What does an elevator pitch teach you? Why is this important?

☞ References

Bhidé, A. (2000) *The Origin and Evolution of New Businesses*, Oxford: Oxford University Press.

Burke, A., Fraser, S. and Greene, F.J. (2010) 'Multiple Effects of Business Plans on New Ventures', *Journal of Management Studies*, 47(3).

Bygrave, W.D., Lange, J.E., Mollow, A., Pearlmutter, M. and Singh, S. (2007) 'Pre-Start-up Formal Business Plans and Post-Start-up Performance: A Study of 116 New Ventures', *Venture Capital*, 9(4).

Chen, X-P., Yao, X. and Kotha, S. (2009) 'Entrepreneur Passion and Preparedness in Business Plan Presentations: A Persuasion Analysis of Venture Capitalists' Funding Decisions', *Academy of Management Journal*, 52(1).

Dell, M. (1999) *Direct from Dell: Strategies that Revolutionized an Industry*, New York: Harper Business.

Mullins, J. and Komisar, R. (2011) 'Measuring Up: Dashboarding for Innovators', *Business Strategy Review*, 22(1).

Sarasvathy, S.D. (2001) 'Causation and Effectuation: Toward a Theoretical Shift from Economic Inevitability to Entrepreneurial Contingency', *Academy of Management Review*, 26(2).

Timmons, J.A. (1999) *New Venture Creation: Entrepreneurship for the 21st Century*, Singapore: McGraw-Hill International.

Wells Fargo (2006) 'How Much Money Does it Take to Start a Business?', Wells Fargo/Gallup Small Business Index, August 15.

🌐 www.palgrave.com/Burns-Entrepreneurship-And-Small-Business-4e

Go online to access additional teaching and learning resources for this chapter on the companion website. Click here in the ebook to complete a multiple choice revision quiz for this chapter.

Meet the Entrepreneurs

Part 3: Growth

To sustain the initial success they experienced with their start-ups, the entrepreneurs had to think about how they could grow their businesses. Click on the play buttons in the ebook to learn about the different strategies they used, from increasing their workforce, making their business scalable, diversifying their product portfolio, or securing investment. They also reflect on mistakes they made along the way.

AJ Asver

Cassandra Stavrou

John Loughton

Ross Beerman

Selyna Peiris

Scott Cupit

Stefan Botha

Questions

> What strategies for growth can you identify being used by each of these businesses?
> What other potential growth avenues do you think these businesses could explore?
> What advice does Ross give about securing investment?
> What lessons do you learn about scalability and the importance of people?

The full videos of each entrepreneur's story are available on the companion website.

PART	1	ENTREPRENEURSHIP
PART	2	START-UP
PART	3	GROWTH
PART	4	MATURITY

Click the play button in the ebook to watch
Paul Burns discuss the challenges of
businesses in maturity.

16 | MATURITY – THE EXIT

Contents

Getty

Learning outcomes

When you have read this chapter and undertaken the related activities you will be able to:

> Understand the reasons why businesses cease trading;
> Understand and recognize the causes of business failure, the influences on them and how they interact;
> Understand the emotional impact of business failure upon the entrepreneur;
> Explain what options are open to a sole trader, partnership or company that is insolvent;
> Explain how the value of a business might be realized for the owner-manager;
> Explain how company valuations are arrived at.

○ Case insights

SportsBase	Vivid Imaginations
The English Grocer	**eg** solutions
ZedZed.com	AO World plc
Sponge	Xtreme SnoBoards (4)
Cobra Beer	The Body Shop
Moonpig	Titus Salt
Playfish	Cotton On Foundation

Exit routes

Most small firms are born to stagnate or die. As we saw in Chapter 1, in the UK most do not grow to any size – almost two-thirds of businesses comprise only one or two people, and often the second person is the spouse. Some 95% of firms employ fewer than 10 employees and 99% fewer than 50 employees. From the VAT statistics we see that half of businesses cease trading within three years of being set up, although, as pointed out, this does not necessarily mean that the closure has left creditors unpaid, and it can be viewed in a positive light as part of the dynamism of the sector as it responds to changing opportunities in the marketplace. What is more, when the number of start-ups increases, the number of businesses ceasing to trade tends to do so as well. The pattern is broadly similar internationally. The younger and smaller the business, the more likely it is to cease trading – a conclusion supported by a review of 34 business closure studies from around the world (Storey and Greene, 2010). A cynical observer might conclude that, in such a turbulent environment, mere survival is a badge of success.

Many entrepreneurs start a business without thinking about their exit route – whatever that might turn out to be (King, 2002) – and a survey of fast-growing, privately held companies showed that almost half of those who expect to leave their company in the next 10 years had not undertaken any exit planning (Dahl, 2005). There are many reasons why an entrepreneur might leave the firm they founded. It could be that they see other better, more lucrative, commercial opportunities, or their personal or family circumstances change and they decide to wind down the business. Perhaps they can sell the assets or the entire business as a '**going concern**' (one that functions without the threat of liquidation for the foreseeable future) and reap the harvest of their years of investment in the business. Based on a literature review, Levie et al. (2011) say that as many as half of firms that 'disappear' from the market are voluntary closures. Indeed, studies suggest that many firms are profitable at the point of closure as these owners have a planned exit or sale strategy (Bates, 2005; Headd, 2003; Storey and Greene, 2010). But, even with a sale, definitions are not straightforward because it could be that the sale was prompted by the business making continuing losses which could ultimately have led to failure. Nevertheless, even this form of 'distress sale' might still yield a capital gain for the entrepreneur.

However, ceasing to trade may involve the business failing because it no longer is profitable or because it has run out of cash. Insolvency is the term used when an individual or company cannot pay its debts. However, as we shall see later in this chapter, there are a number of ways even this might be resolved. Insolvency, at its worst, might lead to the personal bankruptcy of a sole trader or partnership (which can only be discharged by a court of law) as creditors pursue their debts by claiming the personal assets of the entrepreneurs. Only a tiny number of business closures involve bankruptcy. It might lead to the liquidation of a limited company, when a liquidator is appointed to dispose of the assets of the business, with their value going to the creditors. For statistical purposes, total insolvencies are defined narrowly as the total of personal bankruptcies plus corporate liquidations.

Even with this definition there are problems of interpretation. It is not uncommon for a bank to foreclose on its debt, forcing a company into liquidation, knowing that it will secure repayment of its preferential debt at the expense of other creditors, and then to provide support for a 'new' company set up by the owner-manager undertaking exactly the same type of business. Is this a business failure? The liquidation of a company, in itself, may be a natural way of bringing the business to an end. This is called a voluntary liquidation. If there are surplus assets, then the company is not insolvent and the owner-manager may make a capital gain after creditors are paid.

So ceasing to trade is not necessarily something to mourn, so long as the entrepreneur is not left out-of-pocket and creditors left unpaid. It is when this happens that failure might be viewed as a bad thing – and even here there may be positive consequences (not least because the entrepreneur ought to learn from that experience). In the USA, business failure can be seen as a worthwhile experience for entrepreneurs provided they are seen to learn from it (as we shall see later in this

If you're an entrepreneur, you're trying to create things that have never been created before, you're trying to do it better than anybody else has done it, you're trying to make sure that you protect the downside, so that if it all goes wrong it's not going to bring everything else you've created crashing down.

Richard Branson, founder, Virgin Group, *The Observer*, 14 September 2014

chapter, this is a view that is questioned by researchers). In the UK there is still a stigma attached to it. Being associated with a failed company can lead to problems when it comes to raising cash for another start-up. Bankers, in particular, still need some convincing to persuade them to give an entrepreneur a second chance – particularly if they lost money on the first attempt.

 ## Case insight   SportsBase

From failure to success

In 2006 former school friends and graduates Nick Kenton and Rob Taub set up SportsBase, an online directory of UK sports clubs and personal trainers. Both were only 23 years old. Their idea was that access to the site would be free and they would earn revenue from advertisers. They put in £12,500 of their own savings and obtained an unsecured loan of the same amount from Barclays Bank. It took them seven months to set up the business, supporting themselves by Nick working in a pub and Rob giving tennis lessons. They launched the site with 70 different sports across the UK, using 35,000 pages of information, and employed an agency to sell advertising on the site. They hoped to break even by the end of the first year and make a profit by the end of 2007.

However, things did not go according to plan. Four months after the launch, Nick decided to leave the business for personal reasons. The business struggled to find advertising revenue. In 2008 Rob found two partners, Global E-Network, a technology company, and Mediarun, an online advertising agency. Together they promised to invest resources worth £80,000 in return for a 50% share of the business. The idea was to upgrade the website to incorporate an internet telephone service that would allow sports clubs to offer members free calls and texting. But the new service was never offered because in December 2008 Global E-Network went into administration. At the same time, visitors to the site continued to decline, and with them advertising revenue. An insolvency practitioner advised Rob that the business could not survive without an injection of cash. Rob's parents came to the rescue, setting up another company to buy the assets of SportsBase for £12,000, leaving Rob as director although he returned to his previous job as a tennis coach to help with cash flow. But Rob did not give up and by 2015 SportsBase had some 10,000 members covering 250 sports and activities and 40,000 sport clubs.

❏ Visit the website: www.sportsbase.co.uk

QUESTIONS:

1   Was the initial failure of SportsBase down to bad luck or other factors?

2   How would you judge SportsBase to be a success?

Reasons for business failure

The conclusion that younger and smaller businesses are more likely to cease trading than their older, larger counterparts is of little use to entrepreneurs. They are more likely to want to know why this occurs and, therefore, how it can be avoided. Figure 16.1 shows the influences that can cause business failure – some external, others internal – gleaned from numerous academic studies of firm closure. These influences interact. Individually they are present in many firms, often manifesting themselves as personal or business weaknesses, but it is only when they combine and

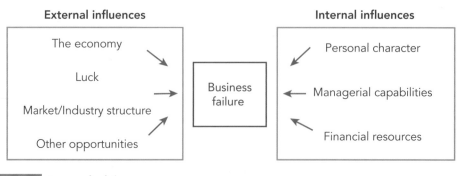

Figure 16.1   Reasons for failure

interact that the potential for failure is realized. So, timing and luck play their part. The similarities with the influences on success and growth are obvious and, as with this, while the ingredients may be clear, the precise recipe is not.

This model gives us an insight into the process of failure. It also reinforces many of the lessons of success. What makes the small firm different from the large one is the disproportionate importance of the influence of the entrepreneur. Many bad business decisions stem from a lack of managerial capabilities, but they also originate from the entrepreneurial character. Business weaknesses often stem from the bad business decisions, which in turn may originate from the entrepreneurial character. However, the crisis that triggers the decline into failure is often brought about by some external factor such as an unexpected change in the economy or the marketplace. This may lead to further bad decisions being made by the entrepreneur, for example a decision to overtrade or borrow too much. Again this might originate from the inherent optimism of the entrepreneur – part of the reason they started up in the first place. These decisions, in turn, result in symptoms of failure such as running short of cash or declining profitability. The paradox is that the asset of the entrepreneurial character can become a liability in certain circumstances.

External influences on failure

The economy

SMEs have less financial 'fat' than larger firms and have to cope with an ever-changing market and economy, over which they have little control. It's little wonder then that the general economy is a major influence on closure (e.g. Berryman, 1983). Baldwin et al. (1997) found this to be *the* major external influence on closure. Everett and Watson (2004) estimated that external economic factors are associated with between 30% and 50% of SME failures. Changes in overall consumer demand, interest rates and inflation can have a disproportionate effect on smaller firms. Many dot.com start-ups that received first-round finance in 1999 failed to obtain second-round finance in 2000 because the market had changed so dramatically, forcing them to cease trading. The recession of 2008, caused by the reckless lending of Western banks, saw many smaller companies cease trading because of the combination of a downturn in trade and a drying up of finance to support them. Many start-ups could not obtain the finance they needed. The banks were so big that they could not be allowed to fail. Small firms were not in the same position.

A recession is essentially a time for rebalancing ... If you've got a business with either a great product or great brand or offering a great service, all that happens is a lot of things come to challenge you ... but if your business has momentum it can help.

Will King, founder, King of Shaves, *RealBusiness*, 1 July 2009

Luck

Some external influences are clearly due to sheer bad luck – 'acts of God' like a strike, fire or the loss of the major customer. A larger company might weather such events, but the smaller firm with fewer resources cannot. You can add to this the impact of random personal events such as sickness and ill-health that impact disproportionately on an owner-manager. But sometimes entrepreneurs make their own luck and find themselves in the wrong place at the wrong time because they decided to pursue an obviously risky course of action. Luck can have a disproportionate effect on smaller firms. Economists have suggested that these external influences can be likened to a game of chance – an approach called '**gambler's ruin**' (Cressy, 2006) – with the entrepreneur as the roulette-wheel gambler betting resources on the outcome of each business decision they make. This model stresses 'luck' as the key determinant of the outcome, together with resource levels – the gambler with the least resources is least likely to weather a period of bad luck. This approach offers an explanation for why younger, smaller businesses are more likely to fail – they simply have less

PhotoDisc/ Getty Images

resources. It dismisses the influence of the gambler or entrepreneur and their skills and abilities on the final outcome – success or failure.

Market or industry structure

In reality the effect of the environment depends upon the time period, geographic area and market sector in which the firm operates. Perhaps the most significant influence on SMEs is the structure of the market or industry in which they operate, called the '**population ecology**' – an approach originally developed by Hannan and Freeman (1977). For example, the degree of competition within an industry is influenced by what Porter calls 'Five Forces' (Chapter 5). This influences not only profitability but also, in extremis, the likelihood of failure. A small firm operating in a highly competitive market is more likely to fail than one operating in a market with low levels of competition. In Baldwin et al.'s study (op. cit.) 'competition' was the second biggest influence on closure after 'economic downturn' and just ahead of 'customer difficulties'. Berryman (op. cit.) also cited competition. Like gamblers' ruin, this approach would also offer an explanation for why younger, smaller businesses are more likely to fail, but again minimizes the influence of the entrepreneur.

Other opportunities

The personal circumstances and aspirations of individuals change and other opportunities offering an attractive income, either from employment or from another business opportunity, can also persuade the entrepreneur to close the business they are currently running. This means that it may not always be the least profitable businesses that close. Closure is influenced by personal factors such as the enjoyment the individual might get from self-employment, their minimum income 'threshold' and the alternatives available to them (Gimeno et al., 1997) and is therefore difficult to predict at the individual level. However, it will be influenced by the general economy and elements of luck.

> You feel a lot of shame. I had 200 staff. You feel you've let them down.
>
> **Mark Constantine**, founder, Lush, on the bankruptcy of his *Cosmetics to Go* business, *RealBusiness*, 26 May 2009

 ## Case insight   The English Grocer

Reasons for failure

In 2006 Peter Durose decided to leave his £250,000 a year job running the fresh produce section at the supermarket chain Tesco. He was fed up with the early starts and long days and wanted to spend more time with his wife and two young daughters. The mortgage was almost repaid so he felt he could indulge his dream and open a gourmet corner shop in the village of Buntingford. He invested £100,000 of his savings in the venture, called The English Grocer, which opened its doors to business early in 2007.

The English Grocer stocked high-quality, traditional food targeted at up-market customers – good breads, hams, cheese from Neal's Yard dairy, pickles, teas, coffee, olive oils etc. Sales grew steadily, and at the Christmas of 2007 one of its most popular lines was its luxury £100 Christmas hamper. But starting up a business was harder than either Peter or his wife believed. Because planning to open the shop took time and they needed the money, Peter started a small consultancy with a friend advising growers on how to find the best market for their produce. That continued once

the shop was opened, leaving his wife, Marion, to work in the store.

'I found it difficult to organise my time. I quickly found I was doing seven days a week again. It's easy to lose that balance and you have to stop and think – remember what you are doing here.'

Things only got worse when Marion became pregnant with their third child. As she observed:

'We both did a lot of work in the evening. We would put the kids to bed and then at 8.00 pm we would be sat with our laptops.'

In 2008 the recession hit. At first, sales remained buoyant, but by November, just as Marion gave birth to a son, sales started to decline as families economized. Peter tried leafleting but with little effect. Customers bought £30 hampers in place of the £100 hampers they had bought the year before. In January 2009 Peter was forced to inject more cash into the business. He even persuaded his landlord to accept a 25% cut in the shop rent. But things did not improve.

Continued...

Continued from previous page...

'I kept thinking that maybe trade would pick up when the weather got better. But it didn't get better – it snowed in March.'

The final blow came when the Council started work in the high street, erecting bollards and restricting parking. The high street was closed for three weeks and when it reopened the browsers did not reappear. In April, Peter and Marion decided to close the business. They reassigned the shop lease to a coffee shop within three weeks and sold off the remaining stock. Peter is philosophical:

'I don't regret any of it, not at all … We had a lot of fun setting up the shop. I learnt more in the past three years than in the previous ten. There is something all-encompassing about starting a business … The hardest part, I guess, was that we could have carried on. It wasn't just a commercial decision – it was an emotional decision. There may be green shoots [of recovery] out there, but I am not sure anyone agrees … We found we were consistently talking about the year after next year – and for a small business that is a heck of a gamble. In our hearts we don't think the English Grocer is over for ever. Maybe, another time, another place.' (The Sunday Times, 26 April 2009)

QUESTIONS:

1 Did the English Grocer fail?
2 What part did luck play in its closure?

Internal influences on failure

Personal character

Referring back to Chapter 3, we recall that certain of the character traits of entrepreneurs can have very negative effects. For example, the strong internal locus of control can lead to 'control freak' behaviour such as meddling, an inability to delegate, a mistrust of subordinates or an unwillingness to part with equity in the business. Similarly, the strong need for public achievement might lead to unwise overspending on the trappings of corporate life, or the 'big project' that is too risky. The strong self-confidence can, in extremis, become 'delusional' behaviour evidenced by an excessive optimism, an exaggerated opinion of their business competence and an unwillingness to listen to advice or seek help. Excessive optimism is a frequently cited personal characteristic associated with failure (Berryman et al., op. cit.; Larsen and Clute, 1979). On top of this can be layered the problems associated with family firms – such as nepotism (cited by Berryman, op. cit., as a cause of failure) – that we shall look at in the next chapter. These combine to produce a potent set of behavioural ingredients which might become underlying causes of failure.

Beaver and Jennings (2005) found evidence of 'non-rational' behaviour contributing to business failure. Larson and Clute (op. cit.) listed the personal characteristics they found in owner-managers of failed firms. It is interesting how many of these factors are the negative sides of the character traits of entrepreneurs that we have already noted. The characteristics were:

> Exaggerated opinion of business competency based upon knowledge of some skill;
> Use of own personal tastes and opinions as the standard to follow;
> Decisions based upon intuition, emotion and non-objective factors;
> Past (not future) orientation, inflexibility and not being sufficiently innovative;
> Limited formal education and reading in literature associated with the business;
> Resistance to advice from qualified sources but, paradoxically, accepts it from the less-qualified.

Managerial capabilities

Much of the literature suggests that it is a lack of management competency in entrepreneurs that underpins business failures (Baldwin et al., op. cit.; Kiggundu, 2002; Knotts et al., 2003; Larson and Clute, op. cit.). In his review of some 50 articles and five books on the subject of small business failure, Berryman (op. cit.) listed a number of management deficiencies such as inability to delegate, reluctance to seek help, unawareness of the environment, inability to adapt to change and thinness of management talent, excessive drawings and pure negligence as reasons for failure.

Lack of management capability and bad decisions are closely related, like chicken and egg. And bad and untimely business decisions have also been frequently shown to contribute to business failure (Gaskill et al., 1993; Stokes and Blackburn, 2002). A bad decision about location can be a frequent contributory reason for failure, particularly for a retail business. Many bad decisions lead to weaknesses in the business but stem from the character traits of entrepreneur. For example, the decision to undertake the risky 'big project' that eventually brings the company down may have been influenced by the entrepreneur's need to demonstrate achievement and receive public applause and recognition. The same company's high gearing – a frequently cited symptom of vulnerability – may be because the entrepreneur wants to retain control of the business and does not want to dilute their ownership by selling equity.

Bad decisions can also stem from poor information caused by inadequate systems or an unwillingness or inability to understand the information. For example, bad marketing decisions feature regularly in the literature on causes of failure and these often stem from a lack of understanding of what customers are really buying (benefits), who customers are (market segmentation) and why they do not buy from competitors (competitive advantage).

The frequently cited managerial deficiencies and/or business weaknesses do not seem to have changed much over the years despite the advent of the internet. They include:

> **Poor financial control** – Poor, infrequent financial information, lax debtor and/or stock control and an inability to manage cash flow are frequently cited causes of closure (Baldwin et al., op. cit.; Berryman, op. cit.; Haswell and Holmes, 1989; Watkins, 1982; Wichmann, 1983). Poor financial control inevitably leads to the reappearance of Death Valley and a cash-flow crisis. If you couple that with poor cash-flow planning, then you have the potential for failure.

> **Poor marketing** – The marketing problems cited are many and various, including a lack of understanding of customer needs, failure to identify target customers, and poor selling skills (Baldwin et al., op. cit.; Berryman, op. cit.; Larson and Clute, op. cit.; Watkins, op. cit.). A major weakness cited by a number of studies is the typical overdependence of small firms on a small number of customers for too high a proportion of their sales (Cosh and Hughes, 1998). Another angle on this is the size of the product range. Some studies have shown that the wider the range, the lower the likelihood of failure (Reid, 1991). It would be interesting to know more about the availability of websites and internet marketing generally in this context.

> **Lack of planning** – Business failure has been blamed on poor planning and inappropriate strategies (Larson and Clute, op. cit.). Delmar and Shane (2003) showed that those Swedish businesses that prepared business plans were more likely to survive than those that did not. Saridakis et al. (2008) and Stearns et al. (1995) highlighted the importance of business strategy in the UK and USA, respectively; in particular, they showed that an over-reliance on inappropriate strategies such as price competitiveness was more likely to lead to closure.

An interesting related issue is what (if anything) an entrepreneur learns from the bad decisions they make. You might expect that if they make sufficient mistakes they might realize or 'learn' that they have insufficient knowledge and skill to run their own business successfully and they decide to close it. And you might expect that they would learn from these mistakes if they go on to start another venture. Metzger (2007) found that, while German entrepreneurs who went bankrupt were just as likely to start up again in business as those who had voluntarily closed their business, they were then more likely to face closure again. It was not 'failure' as such but how they failed that was significant. Indeed, in a review of the literature, Storey and Greene (op. cit.) concluded that the empirical evidence that entrepreneurs learn from failure was weak, possibly being submerged

One of the first things I learned though was that there was a relationship between screwing up and learning: the more mistakes I made, the faster I learned.

Michael Dell, founder, Dell Corporation (1999) *Direct from Dell: Strategies that Revolutionized an Industry*, New York: Harper Business

by their over-optimism. The reason for this may lay in the emotions generated by failure and in particular the grieving process which can interfere with the learning process (Shepherd, 2003; Shepherd and Kuratko, 2009).

Financial resources

Almost by definition a failing firm is bound to have inadequate finance. Cash flow will be poor and further funding may be unavailable. However, this is usually simply a symptom of the problem rather than a root cause. The cause is more likely to be undercapitalization at start-up and subsequent overtrading (too-rapid expansion). And the root cause of this may well be the lack of management capability of the entrepreneur.

 ## Case insight   ZedZed.com

A personal view of failure: 'Don't pity the pioneers – envy us for our experience'

'This is a story with an unhappy ending about my dot. com company ZedZed.com, a site for independent travellers, which went into liquidation in 2000. ZedZed. com was meant to be called ZigZag.com but that name had already gone. We raised £800,000, which was no mean achievement, but it wasn't enough. In February we encountered dot.com envy from our friends. In March we were winning awards and being asked to speak at conferences in Paris. In June we achieved 1800 user reviews per week. In August we were calling in the liquidators. Mistakes are always easier to see with the benefit of hindsight, and our worst error was to believe that internet businesses should be valued by the number of subscribers rather than the transactions that they make … Today you have to be profitable or else you are not going to get funded again. They say that internet speed is fast but three months is a short period of time to reverse your whole raison d'être. I think we did a lot right too. We built a site in six weeks on a very complicated back-end platform. We chose a content management system that would make us a serious force in the market, and we successfully leveraged that asset with larger organisations who might otherwise have ignored us. We devised a very

successful low-cost user subscription campaign without the help of an expensive marketing agency like so many dot.coms. We kept our non-essential expenditure to a minimum, which allowed us to return 20 per cent of the initial subscription to investors.

We employed 19 people on low salaries who genuinely loved their daily work. Being a chartered accountant, I knew where our financial position was on a daily basis and knew when the time had come to close the door. Setting up a dot.com business has been the most exciting, rewarding experience of my life, and of the lives of the team that I had around me. We did something new, different and useful to other people. Sadly for us and our investors, the capital markets have changed to such a degree that we have had to end our quest early. In doing so we are showing that there is sanity amid the madness. Don't pity the pioneers – envy us for our experience. Oh, and pay us well for them too!'

Edward Johnstone, co-founder of ZedZed.com,
Daily Telegraph, 17 August 2000

QUESTIONS:

1 What personal qualities do you need to see through the closure of your own business?

2 How would you feel if your business failed?

Predicting failure

It is one thing to understand what influences failure, but it is quite another to try to predict it. Nevertheless, this has been of considerable interest to academics over the last 50 years, albeit with limited success. Beaver (1966), Altman (1968) and Taffler (1982) were pioneers in this area of study, mainly using financial ratios as relevant variables. Today, forecasts of business distress or difficulty are widely used for a range of purposes, including the monitoring of business solvency, assessment of loan security, and going concern evaluations by auditors. Most studies have looked at large public companies because of the ready availability of this information. However, forecasting failure is fraught with dangers, particularly for SMEs.

Financial information in SMEs tends to be less reliable, with the profit figure more easy to manipulate, less complete, since they do not have to disclose the same amount of information as public companies, and less timely, since they do not face stock market pressures. However, it has been argued (Keasey and Watson, 1991) that, because of these factors, if predictive models could be developed they would be extremely valuable, not only in terms of their predictive ability but also in terms of their information value or usefulness. This is not surprising, given the problems of information asymmetry facing bankers in particular. For this reason trying to predict failure in SMEs using models that employ publicly available information has attracted just as much interest as trying to predict success.

Most of these studies use a statistical technique called step-wise multiple discriminant analysis. This uses a sample of failed and non-failed firms to select financial ratios that best discriminate between the two groups and then combine them into a simple number, or 'Z score', which indicates the likelihood of failure. Companies are usually matched by industry and size. Most studies then go on to test the predictive ability of the 'Z score' on a hold-out sample which includes failed and non-failed firms. Studies have used the full range of ratios discussed in Chapter 11 – performance, profitability, asset efficiency, liquidity, gearing and risk – in an attempt to see which best predict failure.

Most published studies look at large, publicly quoted companies but a study by Love and D'Silva (2001) looked at SMEs in the construction and civil engineering sector. It tested 25 ratios, and the final calculated 'Z score' is shown below:

$$Z = -0.143 + 1.608a + 0.001b + 0.461c + 0.352d - 0.007e$$

where: a = net profit margin
b = debtor days
c = profit before tax divided by shareholders' funds
d = profit before tax divided by current liabilities from the previous year
e = total sales over working capital from the previous year

Companies scoring below 0.36 were deemed as having a high probability of failure. However, in this study 72.9% of the predictive ability came from the simple net profit margin ratio, so you might question the value of the other information.

Studies like these have been criticized on many counts, not least because they look at symptoms rather than root causes of failure. In this respect the major practical problem with them is their timeliness. It is quite probable that by the time these symptoms manifest themselves in published accounts, the company will already have filed for bankruptcy. What is more, the effect of the external environment, particularly for SMEs, is likely to be very high. For example, profit margins are likely to decline in most firms at times of recession and therefore any bank using this as a predictive tool might be tempted to foreclose on a large number of loans, thus creating a self-fulfilling prophecy. One major UK clearing bank tested 'Z scores' extensively in the 1980s and decided not to use them.

Banks, of course, have a major piece of information at their fingertips that gives them an immediate insight into what is happening within the firm. This is the firm's bank account. From this, banks can monitor cash inflows and outflows as well as balances, and this can give them invaluable information about current performance long before it finds its way into published financial information. Banks look for the other symptoms of distress outlined in Chapter 14. Notwithstanding this, two major UK clearing banks started using a computer-based expert system in the 1990s to help them make lending decisions and monitor loans. This combined 'hard' financial data with 'soft' judgemental data using weightings that could be adjusted to produce a lending 'recommendation'. The 'hard' financial data included a range of historic as well as projected financial ratios. The 'soft' data included a range of judgements about the management of the firm as well as its competitive advantage within its industry. In many ways the system simply attempted to make lending decisions more rational and consistent. The danger with such a system is that it masks the areas of judgement that are inevitably involved and focuses attention on the simple, final lending recommendation.

Case insight   Sponge

Dealing with failure

Courtesy of Alex Meisl

Alex Meisl

Alex Meisl's first company, Taotalk, a telecoms business that offered a real-time internet chat and voice messaging service, failed after a potential investor had a last-minute change of mind. Alex lost half a million pounds of his own money, but found the hardest part was telling his 12 employees that they would be made redundant and would not be paid their month's salary. He felt guilty – a very common emotion.

'I felt a huge guilt towards the staff. They had trusted me because I said it would be all right. They missed out on their last month's salary and they didn't get any redundancy other than the statutory minimum.'

When a business fails, many people feel depressed and embarrassed and just want to get away from everything and everyone. However, Alex felt it was important to tell all creditors – customers and suppliers, as well as employees – what was happening, personally, either face-to-face or by phone. He was trying to maintain a personal relationship with creditors and keep at least some of their trust and respect and scotch any unfounded gossip that might develop in the industry.

Alex set up his second business, Sponge, a year later in 2002. Sponge offers voice and mobile applications for agencies and their brands and media groups using a platform called TG³ which allows integration of mobile, web and email in a digital campaign. This time Alex approached things differently. Firstly, instead of going it alone as with Taotalk, he set up Sponge with an experienced business partner, Dan Parker. Secondly, they wrote a business plan together and approached every business deal more systematically. This more considered approach seems to have worked. Sponge became the UK market – leading full-service mobile marketing agency, claiming to be able to reach almost two million mobile shoppers. The company had offices in London, Nairobi and Lagos, with clients such as Autotrader, IPC, News International, Vodafone and over 50 agencies such as Ogilvy and BBH. Sponge was responsible for Europe's largest mobile campaign for Walkers crisps. Sponge was sold in 2014, allowing Alex and his partner to focus on their new business, Wi-Fi marketing company Wiforia. The experience of failure changed Alex:

'It hardened me and it made me slightly more cynical, in a constructive way. If someone comes through the door and says I am sure we have got a deal with company X, I don't believe it until I have seen the signature on the bottom of the document.' (*The Sunday Times*, 17 February 2008)

❑ Visit the website: www.spongegroup.com

QUESTIONS:

1 How do you think Alex dealt with the first failure? Explain.

2 How valuable do you think is the experience of failure?

Personal insolvency

Insolvency is the term used when an individual or company cannot pay its debts. In the UK if a trade creditor is owed more than £750 and can demonstrate to a court that an invoice has remained unpaid for 21 days, they have the legal right to petition the court for bankruptcy proceedings, although whether they chose to do so is quite another matter. Similarly if the balance sheet of a business shows its liabilities to be greater than its assets, then it is deemed to be insolvent, although by the time this is produced the business is likely to be long-dead.

For an individual struggling to pay their debts – as a sole trader or a partner or as a director of a limited company who has personally guaranteed the company's debts – there are a number of courses of action open to you in England and Wales (Scotland has different rules). Most other

> You can get more information and advice on insolvency in the UK online:
> https://www.gov.uk/government/organisations/insolvency-service
> https://www.gov.uk/government/organisations/companies-house

countries have similar legal arrangements, but these should be checked. In all cases it is essential that the advice of a professional accountant or lawyer is sought before proceeding. If you cannot pay your business debts when they fall due, or if your business assets are less than your debts, your business is technically insolvent and this may lead to your business being wound up, with the assets sold off to pay its debts, and you personally being declared 'bankrupt'. If you face this danger, you have several options.

Informal 'family' arrangements

This is where family or friends agree to provide funds on a short-term basis and creditors agree not to take action. However, getting other members of the family involved in the business may present other problems (see the next chapter).

Formal voluntary arrangements

This is where all the creditors agree to a proposal you and your advisors (which must include a licensed insolvency practitioner) put forward. This proposal will typically specify the amount (or proportion) of debt to be repaid and the timescale. If accepted, the creditors are bound by the proposal.

Partnership voluntary arrangements

Partnerships can propose this arrangement. It is similar to the individual arrangement above, but to remove the individual partners' joint and several liability to meet the partnership debts, the partners will either have to pay off the whole partnership debt or propose an individual voluntary arrangement.

Bankruptcy

If you are unable to pay your debts you can be made personally bankrupt. You or your creditors can apply to the courts for this to happen. The court will appoint an official receiver to take over your affairs (an insolvency practitioner may later take over) and sell off any assets – both your own personal assets and those within the business – so as to discharge your debts as soon as possible. Until the debts are discharged, the receiver will manage all your affairs and there are restrictions on the financial arrangements you might enter into. As a sole trader or partner your business will normally be closed down and the assets sold off. Until you are discharged as bankrupt you cannot be a director of a company. Unless you are seen as not cooperating with the receiver, you will usually be discharged from bankruptcy within a year; however, you may not regain full control of your own finances straight away. A major consequence of bankruptcy is that your personal credit rating will be badly affected for some years to come, which means that obtaining credit will become more difficult and more costly. Most individuals seek to avoid bankruptcy.

Company insolvency

For a limited liability company struggling to pay its debts and facing possible failure, there are a number of courses of action open in England and Wales (again, Scotland has different rules). Most other countries have similar legal arrangements, but these should be checked. In all cases it is essential that the advice of a professional accountant or lawyer is sought before proceeding. The company has several options.

Refinancing

This involves bringing in new debt and/or equity finance to support the business. This may mean that the owner-manager will lose some of their equity in the business and may lose control.

Refinancing will usually require the company to be restructured and may involve a pre-packaged sale of the business. Sources of finance were discussed in Chapter 14.

A pre-packaged sale

This allows the profitable part of the business to restart without being weighed down by the company's existing debts. Pre-packaged sale, or 'pre-pack', is the name given to the process of buying the assets of a business from the old failing company. Typically a new company owned by the existing management will take over some or all of the assets of the business but not the debts. This structure allows a new business to rise from the remains of the old, often referred to as 'phoenix-like', with the effect that the business and jobs are saved. Once the transaction has taken place, the old company is placed into liquidation. We discuss company valuation later in this chapter.

Company voluntary arrangement (CVA)

This course of action is best suited to companies which are fundamentally profitable, or which have the potential to be profitable, but which have serious cash-flow problems. The existing company continues but is given protection from its creditors. For a CVA all creditors must agree to either accept a longer payment term or a reduced amount, or both. A typical CVA may defer payments for between two and four years and, in England, must be administered by a licensed insolvency practitioner who will report to the court.

Administration

This is appropriate for companies that urgently need protection from creditors. Unlike with a CVA, a company can be placed into administration almost immediately by the court, if the court considers it appropriate. The approval of creditors is not needed. A company placed into administration is instantly protected from its creditors and, probably most importantly, from any pending legal action. In England, the company will be administered by a licensed insolvency practitioner, although this is often delegated to the existing management. The administration process is designed to provide protection for a limited period of time while the business is restructured and rescued.

Creditors voluntary liquidation (CVL)

A CVL takes place if the directors and shareholders decide to liquidate the company. In the UK a licensed insolvency practitioner is appointed by the directors. He then sells the assets of the company and pays the remaining funds to the creditors. The process is regulated by the court. CVL can be a relatively quick process and can provide an effective way to shield directors from the pressures of a failing company.

Compulsory liquidation

This is the final option. It is a process begun by the court at the request of a creditor. In England the creditor applies to the court for the company to be wound up, and if the court approves this it will appoint a liquidator. Compulsory liquidation is most commonly a result of action taken by government agencies to recover taxes (VAT or PAYE), although it can be initiated by any creditor. A court-appointed liquidator, which may sometimes be the official receiver, will look very closely at the actions of the officers of the company and in some circumstances, such as in mishandling of tax payments, the directors may become personally liable and may face legal consequences. The company will then be sold off, in whole or in part, as a going concern, or the assets of the company will be sold off, often at a discount, to pay the creditors as soon as possible. Most companies would seek to avoid compulsory liquidation.

Case insight   Cobra Beer

Company voluntary arrangements

Cobra Beer was set up in 1990 by Karan Bilimoria, the son of an Indian army general and a former accountant, to sell a different type of beer to Indian restaurants.

'I entered the most competitive beer market in the world against long established brands. The product itself was innovative – an extra smooth, less gassy lager that complements all cuisine and appeals to ale drinkers and lager drinkers alike ... Deciding to import the beer in a 650ml bottle was important in positioning the product within the market and raising the profile among restaurant owners. It also promoted a new, shared way of drinking ... The brand's point-of-sale items, such as unique and different glasses, were another effective way of establishing brand awareness ... Also [the glass] is embossed with six icons telling the story of Cobra beer, from concept and production to growth and development, and this is the first time in the world that, to our knowledge, the brand has incorporated its story directly into its packaging.' (The Times, 23 May 2004)

By 2009 the company had sales of £177 million, but there was one problem. It had yet to make a profit. Indeed, in the year to July 2007, the last year for which accounts are publicly available, Cobra lost £13 million. Instead of tracking profits, Cobra had focused on sales growth, spending £40 million on marketing since its launch. Sales growth had indeed been spectacular, showing 20% year-on-year growth in a falling market.

Unfortunately, the 2008 recession took its toll. While growth stalled, the banking crisis made it impossible to secure fresh funding. In the autumn of 2008 Bilimoria tried to find a buyer for the business, but the big brewers were not interested and the credit squeeze prevented a sale to a private equity firm. He cut costs. Four directors stood down and staff numbers were cut from 150 to 50.

Bilimoria called in the accountants Pricewaterhouse-Coopers in the spring of 2009 to work on a company voluntary arrangement (CVA). This would have given all creditors some money back, but one creditor, Wells & Young's, which brewed Cobra under licence in Bedford, vetoed the proposal. Bilimoria therefore decided to restructure Cobra in what is called 'pre-packaged sale'. In this arrangement the business was acquired by a joint venture company

comprising Molson Coors, the US brewer of Carling lager, and the former owner, Bilimoria. Molson paid £14 million for its 50.1% share. Karan Bilimoria kept 49.9% and remained as director.

Unfortunately, the nature of this form of administration in the UK means that, while the secured creditors, largely banks, who were owed some £20 million were paid back in full, unsecured creditors, who were owed almost £70 million, got nothing. These debts included £57 million to investors, £6 million to the government in taxes and £6 million to 330 small unsecured trade creditors. These included many small businesses such as Spark Promotions UK, owed £62,018 for developing a beer pump for Cobra, Pop Displays, owed £31,129 for producing printing and packaging for Cobra promotions and MicroMatic, another pump maker, which was owed £60,143. They were not happy:

'[Bilimoria] has risen from the ashes like a phoenix while people like us, the creditors, have been burnt alive.' (Brian Flanagan, MD Spark Promotions UK, The Sunday Times, 2 August 2009)

'How can someone dump all their debts on creditors and then the next day walk into what is, effectively, the same business with a 49% stake?' (Chris Hall, MD Pop Displays, The Sunday Times, 2 August 2009)

While the unsecured creditors may have lost out, observers suggest Molson Coors have landed a 'fantastic' deal. Bilimoria, who was made a Lord in 2007, said he lost the £20 million he invested in the firm and insists he is committed to repaying as many debts as possible:

'We had no choice but to go down this route. I feel terrible about that. I feel gutted that the unsecured creditors aren't going to be paid.' (The Sunday Times, 31 May 2009)

❏ Visit the website on: www.cobrabeer.com.

QUESTIONS:

1 What was Cobra's business model and what were the key elements of competitive advantage in its value proposition up to 2009?

2 Was Cobra successful up until this point? Was its strategy prudent?

3 Who has paid for the growth of Cobra? Is this fair? If not, what are the alternatives?

Harvesting your investment

Business success usually brings with it wealth. It also presents the opportunity to either sell the business, harvesting the investment you have made in its growth and development, or pass it on within the family, forming the foundation for the family's wealth in the future. We shall deal with family succession in the next chapter. Some entrepreneurs set up their business so that they can sell it on quickly once it proves successful, making a swift capital gain and possibly going on to start another. They might realize that they are at their best as serial entrepreneurs, starting rather than growing a business. And harvesting your investment can happen earlier than you might expect. Only a small percentage of growth firms reach maturity with the founder in place (Haveman and Khaire, 2004). Research by Nesta (National Endowment for Science, Technology and the Arts) showed that the average time from first-round funding to exit through IPO (initial public offering) internationally for technology start-ups was around seven years in 2009, up from an incredibly short three years at the time of the dot. com boom (1998–2002). In the UK, the period was around six years in 2008, and the number of exits, either through IPOs or acquisition, has been decreasing each year since the peak in 2006 (Pierrakis, 2010). But not all entrepreneurs want to leave the business quickly. Increasing numbers want to take money out when the firm gets its second or third round of funding, only exiting some years later when the capital gain is maximized. They want to share in the success of the firm as it grows, without taking capital out and thus endangering its growth, by relinquishing some ownership and even control.

For the entrepreneur to be able to harvest their investment, the business must be of value to somebody else. That means it must have good potential and a good financial track record that demonstrates success so far. If the entrepreneur intends to leave the business, then they must be able to demonstrate that it can function effectively without them. That means it must have good control systems and a good management team. The departure of the founder may infuse a firm with cash and/or new resources, including new management and renewed energy. Conversely it may have negative affects – disrupting routines, interrupting lines of command, increasing employee insecurity and generally leading to declining performance (Haveman and Khaire, 2004).

DeTienn (2010) argued that the exit from the business is just as much of the entrepreneurial process as the start-up and that founders of entrepreneurial firms are more likely to develop an exit strategy than founders of lifestyle or income substitute firms (defined in Chapter 1). This is simply because they are more likely to develop strategy generally. This propensity depends upon their equity ownership and their psychological commitment to the firm as well as a number of other external influences. He goes on to develop a profile of entrepreneurs likely to exit in the firm's infancy, adolescence and mature phases and the circumstances that might contribute to this.

The timing of any sale can make an enormous difference to the price paid for the business. Normally the better the general economic prospects, the higher the price paid. But there are also circumstances that are particular to the founder or their company – and luck can play a part in all this. It might also be just the right time to get a very good deal, for example because of consolidation in the industry. It might simply be that the business has become less attractive or more risky than when the founder set it up and there are better new opportunities they want to pursue elsewhere.

> "You start the business as a dream, you make it your passion for a while and then you get experienced managers to run it because it's not as much fun as starting.
>
> **Stelios Haji-Ioannou**, founder, easyJet, *The Sunday Times*, 29 October 2000

> Many entrepreneurs nowadays start with a view to selling. The holy-grail is capital gain. That is largely encouraged by the British tax structure, which taxes you at 45% on income but 10% on capital gain … in Britain we have an entrepreneurial culture that doesn't have too much pride. Most realize that selling is a good thing.
>
> **Howard Leigh**, Cavendish Corporate Finance, *The Sunday Times*, 17 February 2015"

Harvest options

If an entrepreneur wants to harvest their investment they have a number of options:

Trade sale

The most attractive harvest option is probably to find a trade buyer – another company in the industry that understands the business and wants to run it as a going concern or simply consolidate its own market share. They are likely to place a higher value on the business than others because they can see ways of 'adding value' through the purchase, perhaps by synergy. This is particularly the case with 'high-growth' and technology start-ups, where the smaller business offers innovation and the bigger company offers resources to take the innovation to a mass, global market much more quickly than the smaller business might be able to. It has been estimated that over a third of 'high-growth' firms can expect to be acquired, many by larger firms (Department for Business Enterprise & Regulatory Reform, 2008). This is an important option which allows high-growth firms to access finance and support infrastructures which enable further growth. The larger firm is simply buying innovation. In many cases it might be willing to pay cash or shares to the founder, so they can walk away from the firm on the day of sale. Cash may be attractive if it is needed for retirement or other family reasons. However, if you already have other equity investors like business angels or venture capitalists it is probable that they will have to agree to the sale. Indeed they are likely to be able to help with it.

 ## Case insight   Moonpig

Harvesting your investment

In 2011 Nick Jenkins sold Moonpig, the personalized greeting card business he had started 12 years earlier, for £120 million to the French online photo album business PhotoBox. He started the business with £160,000 of his own money, but had attracted other private investors including a neighbour and two friends of friends who had experience of greeting cards. When he sold the business he still owned 34% himself:

'When you have investors they want an exit. Floating the business did not make sense. It just wasn't big enough.'

Nick had prepared well in advance for the sell-off. He had employed an experienced managing director four years earlier and had gradually handed over the reins to him.

Nick's father was a director at the engineering and building firm Alfred McAlpine. He studied Russian at Birmingham University before getting jobs working in Russia at the time the Soviet Union collapsed. It was working here where he made the money to start up Moonpig, but he came up with the idea while doing a MBA at Cranfield. While doing the course he worked on five business ideas: growing exotic mushrooms, running company gyms, running internet incubators, teaching English to Japanese businessmen online but eventually decided on Moonpig. Moonpig allows you to select a greeting card and write a personalized message on it, all online. The physical card is delivered to you within 24 hours:

'I used to buy cards, Tip-Ex out the caption and write my own – I just thought if I could use the internet to do that, I could make a better product.'

It also proved to be a unique product, with no competition so no price pressure and high barriers to market entry once established. When he sold the company it claimed 90% of the British online card market and made profits of £11 million on a turnover of £32 million with just 100 employees. But starting a business that sold personalized physical cards seemed quite a risk in 1999, when most competitors thought e-cards would be what customers wanted. Nick's MBA taught him the important things needed to lead a business.

'My job is just to keep the business on track, the right people doing the right jobs, and the strategy sound ... It's a fun environment. I'm a firm believer that the culture of a company comes from the top. You can have an HR department saying "we have a collaborative culture", but if the guy at the top is a total arse, it's not going to happen ... I'm a firm believer in creating enough spare time to get a bit bored to think up new things. If you're fire fighting you don't do that.' (The Sunday Times, 31 July 2011)

QUESTIONS:

1 Why would a larger company want to purchase a smaller one in the same industry?
2 Why might Photobox be willing to pay a premium to purchase it?
3 If you were to sell on your business, after how many years would this be and what would you need to do to prepare for it?

 ## Case insight   Playfish

Risks in buying an entrepreneurial company

The UK firm Playfish was set up in 2007 by Kristian Segerstråle, Sebastien de Halleux, Sami Lababidi and Shukri Shammas. Segerstråle is from Finland but chose to set the business up in the UK after studying at Cambridge and the London School of Economics. He is a serial entrepreneur, having already sold another mobile games start-up called Macrospace in 2005. Playfish developed a series of games for social network sites such as Facebook. The company's

Continued...

Continued from previous page...

first hit game was *Who has the Biggest Brain?* It was one of the first Facebook games to attract millions of daily players, and allowed the company to raise the funds necessary to produce other hit games like *Pet Society* (with 21 million monthly users). The company also made money by selling virtual goods inside its games.

In 2009 Playfish was sold for $400 million to Electronic Arts, the US firm behind *The Sims* – $275 million cash, $25 million in equity and $100 million in performance-related

bonuses. In February 2013, all four of the original founders left the company, with Lababidi and Shammas starting a new learning games development company called Mindshapes and Segerstråle returning to games start-ups. Within seven months all of the Playfish-developed games were retired.

QUESTIONS:

1 What does this tell you about the risks of buying a company that is so dependent on key entrepreneurs?

Management buy-out (MBO)

If there is a strong management team in the firm they might be interested in bidding for the firm if they can arrange funding. Although managers are unlikely to have the necessary capital, many venture capitalists look very favourably on management buy-outs and are keen to provide funds for them, provided the terms are right. However, managers are likely to know as much about the firm as the founder and can negotiate a tough deal. Indeed some management buy-outs fail because managers know the business too well and are unwilling to meet the asking price. What is more, it is possible that the owner might have to wait several years before the full balance of the sale price is paid.

Management buy-in (MBI)

An external management team, often with experience in the industry, might be persuaded to bid for the firm, again as a going concern. It is difficult to know where to turn to find managers interested in this sort of option. However, some accountants keep confidential registers of just such managers.

Finding a buyer, valuing the business and negotiating its sale are a daunting series of tasks that really should not be undertaken without professional advice and help. Many larger firms of accountants can help find buyers, just as they can help find companies to purchase, and they can act as a confidential 'front' in the search process. They are also likely to take a more objective view on company valuation than the entrepreneur and are essential in sorting out the details of the deal, including the inevitable warranties and indemnities that will be requested by the purchaser. Finally there is the important consideration of taxation, where planning can considerably increase the money actually pocketed by the entrepreneur.

 Case insight   Vivid Imaginations

Harvesting your investment

Courtesy of Vivid

Vivid Imaginations specializes in producing toys related to TV or cinema series by purchasing the franchise rights. Its portfolio over the past 20 years has included high-profile toy and games brands like Crayola, Moshi Monsters, Disney, Toy Story, Peter Rabbit, Roary the Racing Car, Care Bears, Bratz, Thunderbirds Are Go, Cayla, Logo Game and many others. It was originally set up by Nick Austin and Alan Bennie in the 1992 with £300,000 obtained by pooling their severance pay from their old jobs and re-mortgaging their houses and a rolling bank overdraft for the same amount.

By 1998 Vivid had become one of the fastest growing private companies in the UK, and Austin and Bennie decided to realize their investment and sell off the business

Continued...

Continued from previous page...

to Jordan Group, an American venture capital company for £27 million – a deal that generated almost £20 million each for them. This included an agreement for the pair to stay with the company for the next five years. But when the time to go arrived they could not bring themselves to leave the business they had set up. Instead, with the help of Phoenix Equity Partners, a British private equity firm, they staged a management buy-out, buying back the company for £32 million, sharing ownership with employees and retaining 4% each for themselves. Vivid Imaginations remains Britain's biggest independent toy company.

❏ Visit the website: www.vividimaginations.co.uk

QUESTION:

1 Why might Jordan Group have agreed to the management buy-out of Vivid?

You need to allow plenty of time, not just to find the right buyer, but to consider the implications of the sale … Do your research and plan to sell in a market that's rising but hasn't yet peaked … Get professional advice, but compare quotes carefully and remember you know more about your business than anybody else.

Julian Harley, founder, Harley West Training, www.businesslink.gov.uk

Running a company that is listed on the Stock Exchange is different from building up and running a private company. The history of the City is littered with entrepreneurs who hold onto their creations for too long, failing to recognize the changing needs of the company. I am a serial entrepreneur … It is all part of growing up. I've built something and now it is time to move on.

Stelios Haji-Ioannou, founder, easyJet, *The Times*, 19 April 2002

Floating the company and selling shares

Owner-managers of sizeable companies can unlock personal liquidity and raise additional capital by selling shares. The most obvious way to do this is by 'going public' – floating the company on a stock market and selling shares. There are two 'junior' markets in the UK that offer limited trading - **Off Exchange** (OFEX) and the **Alternative Investment Market** (AIM). Listing on these ultimately leads to a full listing on the **Stock Exchange Main Market**. For a company new to the stock market this is called making an **Initial Public Offering** (IPO). However, this option can be problematic if the entrepreneur wishes to retire because the stock market's assessment of IPOs centres on the future potential of the firm, and if the float is simply intended to provide an exit for the entrepreneur it is unlikely to be popular. The same applies if the business already has a stock market quotation. If the entrepreneur is looking to sell up completely or relinquish operational control the share price is likely to drop. This option is therefore probably best for the entrepreneur who wants to take some money out of the firm but wishes to continue running it and seeing it grow. However, many entrepreneurs – like Richard Branson – do not like the public accountability and loss of control that goes with a publicly quoted company. As we shall see in the next chapter, this can also be problematic if the entrepreneur wants the business to stay in family hands. As an alternative, selling some of the shares to a venture capital company as part of a refinancing deal can be a way of realizing part of the entrepreneur's investment in the firm at the same time as raising additional funds for growth without necessarily losing control.

These options can become more complicated if there are other shareholders in the company. However, the fundamental problem of ensuring the continuing success of the business after the founder's departure remains. Few entrepreneurs plan properly how or when to sell-on their business so as to maximize its value at the point of sale. Most rely instead on their instincts for sorting out an opportunistic deal at the last minute. And yet they are far more likely to achieve the best price for their business by planning ahead and building into the business plan any steps that are needed to help them exit with minimum disruption and reap the best possible harvest from their investment. That almost certainly involves bringing in effective management and implementing proper business controls so the business can survive after the entrepreneur has left. It also probably involves taking professional advice sooner rather than later.

 **Case insight   eg solutions**

Floating a company

Elizabeth Gooch is founder and CEO of **eg** solutions plc, a company selling workforce management software for complex processing teams that helps clients to generate improvements in operational performance. **eg**'s clients include major names like Nationwide, Lloyds, Barclays, Aviva and Santander. The company's software captures work from all sources, i.e. phone calls, documents and emails, and then allocates and distributes work to staff based on their skills, wherever they

Continued...

Continued from previous page...

Courtesy of **eg** solutions

Elizabeth Gooch

intelligent operations management

are in the world. It then provides monitoring and performance management information in real time. **eg** prides itself on implementing its programmes on a fixed-cost, fixed-timescale basis. It is the only company that guarantees return on investment (between 20–40%), and its sales receipts are based on the results delivered. Typically, implementation will usually pay for itself within six months.

Elizabeth started work for Midland Bank (now HSBC) aged 18 as part of a performance improvement team. Eight years later, in 1988, she started her own business, **eg** consulting ltd (named using her initials). **eg** consulting initially offered consultancy and training in operations management to financial services companies. In its first year turnover reached £600,000. However, the repeated requirement of collecting the information needed to advise on improving efficiency led Elizabeth to develop software to help with the task. After initially providing the software on a free-of-charge basis, in 1993 **eg operational intelligence®** suite was launched as a product in its own right. It enabled data to be collected in real time, permitting all departments of a company to monitor its production processes. At that point the business had six employees, several contract workers and a turnover of £1 million.

It was not until Elizabeth met Rodney Baker-Bates, then CEO of Prudential Financial Services, that things changed dramatically. He believed she was not making enough of the business and said she should focus on the software rather than the consultancy work. The company changed its name to **eg** solutions ltd and he became chair, engaging the services of a strategic planning consultant to help them develop the business in a focused way. The strategy worked, increasing turnover by 28% a year. By 2005 turnover was £4.2 million and the business needed more capital to meet some ambitious growth targets. Elizabeth decided to float the company on the Alternative Investment Market (AIM) rather than going for venture capital because she wanted the input of more than one shareholder.

'We had two options really – venture capital or floatation. I liked the float model where you had several institutional investors with a range of views and advice rather than a single venture capital investor with a large stake in the business.'

The float was successful, but the problem with the stock market is that it expects the company to deliver good results year after year. Getting contracts with big financial institutions takes long enough, but implementing them can take even longer – there's a sales cycle of up to two years and extra investment is also usually needed upfront. Deals can, therefore, be lumpy, which can make forecasting more difficult. Unfortunately in 2006 **eg** solutions plc failed to make its sales targets by £700,000. Worse still, in 2007 it posted losses of £800,000. The analysts and shareholders were damning.

'I had really personal attacks from analysts and shareholders alike. They told me they had never seen anything so bad and that the business would never recover.'

Elizabeth's reaction was to cut costs by £1.2 million, returning the business to profit by 2008, admitting that she took her eye off the UK market as she looked overseas for business opportunities that would help her achieve her ambitious growth targets.

'Flotation gives a public face to your business and access to finance that is so often key to development. But there needs to be a lot more attention to strategy. I do not believe in failure. I have needed sheer determination – although my shareholders would probably describe it as stubbornness.' (Sunday Times, 23 November 2008)

By 2009 the company was back on track. Cutting costs ahead of the recession stood them in good stead, and the recession was actually helping the recovery because companies were looking to improve their efficiency. In 2010 **eg** bought XTAQ and its 3D business performance measurement software to enhance its own offering. However, results were still uneven. By 2012, it was turning a small profit on revenues of £5 million.

Over the period from flotation in 2005 to 2012 **eg** was undergoing a major transformation. At the time of the IPO it was still a consulting business with a software solution. Revenues were 70% services and 30% software licences, not the typical profile of a software business. The company made the bold decision to switch from services to software, improving gross margins and its future potential. The acquisition of XTAQ also bought large clients who had undertaken pilots of the XTAQ product. Those were converted to **eg**'s software and expanded globally. The fundamentals for growth were firmly in place and the company needed some experience of growing software businesses on its board of directors.

Continued...

Continued from previous page...

In 2013 there was a major boardroom battle when 'industry heavyweight' John O'Connell was brought in as chair. He was brought in to lead the growth strategy, but wanted rapid share-price growth and tried to oust Elizabeth Gooch from her (or any) role within the company, becoming CEO himself, despite the fact she had invented the product and secured most of the contracts. But he lasted barely six months on the **eg** board of directors and only eight weeks as CEO when majority shareholders turned on him, bringing in a new chair and reinstating Elizabeth as CEO. As a result of O'Connell's bearing, 2013 saw losses mount to £1.4 million.

Yet again the company appears to have been brought back on track by Elizabeth. After winning 10 new contracts, turnover leaped by 70% to £7.5 million in the six months in the financial year to 31 January 2015, generating a pre-tax profit of £621,000, as well as £1.7 million of cash from operations. Perhaps most significantly, after investing in a number of pilot schemes and spending on staff training (which contributed to a small portion of the loss in 2013), **eg** now has a partnership agreement with US customer engagement company Aspect Software to sell its products worldwide.

Elizabeth now only owns 23% of **eg** and the company is valued at £16 million – surprisingly, the same as the value of its order book.

QUESTIONS:

1 What are the advantages and disadvantages of gaining a stock market listing?

2 How would you feel if you were in Elizabeth's situation in 2013/14?

3 What would you advise Elizabeth to do now?

Valuing the business

Valuing an established business can be difficult. Valuing a start-up is even more so because of the uncertainties involved and the lack of any track record on which to evaluate forecasts of future income. However, if you are seeking equity investment or offering the business for sale, then the investor will try to place a value on the business before making you an offer. It is therefore worthwhile trying to value it yourself before going to an outsider. So, for example, if you are only looking to sell a part stake in the business – say 20% – then a $250,000 valuation of the company would raise $50,000 ($250,000 × 0.20). Put it the other way around and, should an investor offer $50,000 for a 20% stake, they are valuing the business at $250,000 ($50,000 ÷ 0.20). If you wish to part with a smaller percentage or you judge that the amount of equity being demanded by an investor for a given investment to be too high, you are, in effect, putting a higher value on the business. If you wanted to part with only 10% of the business but needed to raise £50,000, you are valuing it at $500,000 ($50,000 ÷ 0.10).

The value of the business determines how much equity you might need to dispose of to raise a certain amount of money – and company valuation is not a science. It is based primarily on expectations about the future, and those are uncertain. So for example, information asymmetry (Chapter 14) might lead to investors being unaware of some information you have and therefore placing a lower value on the business. There are two widely used ways of valuing a business:

1   **Market value of assets** – Businesses that are asset-rich, such as farms or freehold retail premises, are often valued in this way. Tangible assets such as debtors/receivables, stocks/inventory, equipment, fixtures and fittings and particularly property are valued at their market rate, although even this is not objective and uncertain. For certain kinds of businesses this might give a higher value than the second approach, but for any business the asset value provides a minimum valuation.

2   **Multiple of profits** – Many firms, particularly those with few tangible assets, are valued based upon some multiple of net profit. For example, if an appropriate multiple of profits were 5, a company making $100,000 per year would be valued at $500,000. If the multiple were 20, its value would be $2 million. If you look in the financial press (e.g. *The Financial Times*), every

public company has its price-earnings or **PE ratio** quoted. This is the multiple of net profits (from the previous year) and the current share price represents.

Companies can also be valued using a mix of both methods. Where there are tangible assets, such as property, these might be valued at market rates and then an element of 'goodwill' added based upon a multiple of profits. Often this is based upon the popularity or resonance a brand has with customers and, as we shall see in the next chapter, long-established and successful family businesses can often command a premium for this. The often-used term 'goodwill' is therefore a loosely defined concept that describes the difference between asset values (often taken as the net asset value from the balance sheet) and the perceived or stock market value of a business.

While the PE ratio in the financial press is based on actual reported profits, start-ups only have forecast profits to work on. This is not an issue in principle because buyers of shares are interested in the future profits of the business and only use actual profits as a proxy measure. However, one factor that influences the size of multiple is the 'quality' of earnings. The longer the firm's track record of profitable trading, the higher the multiple is likely to be. So start-ups, with no track record, tend to command a lower multiple than established firms. Other factors can increase the size of the multiple because they make the forecast of profit more credible, for example the experience of the management team or the existence of substantial pre-launch orders. Different industry sectors tend to have different multiples that reflect the risk they are perceived as facing. The lower the perceived risk, the higher the multiple. So, the higher the risks an investor perceives your venture as facing, the lower the multiple they will apply. However, despite the risks they face, start-ups involved in disruptive innovations or new technologies can sometimes command a very high multiple if it is believed that there may achieve substantial first-mover-advantage by creating a whole new industry (for example, Facebook or Twitter). It has to be said that these valuations often prove to be unfounded.

The key question, then, is: what multiple of profits to use? There is no straightforward answer to this. It is all a matter of judgement. Just like the price of any product or service, it requires a willing buyer and a willing seller – and a company can be 'marketed' in the same way as any product or service. In any given industry, the longer the business has been in existence and able to demonstrate consistency of earnings, the higher the multiple is likely to be. However, for a start-up:

> Risks are high;
> There is no track record;
> If the buyer wishes to sell their shares, there is no established market to sell them on (unlike for a public company).

These factors mean that multiples in single figures are currently quite normal for a start-up. However, if your venture is involved in disruptive innovation (a new industry), or has an established brand and market share with a proven track record, as is often the case for a family business, the multiple could be very much higher. Another factor may be the quality of the management the owner will be leaving behind to continue running the firm. Can they do it without the owner-manager? Different industry sectors tend to have different multiples that reflect the risk they are perceived as facing. The higher the perceived risk, the lower the multiple. Small, privately held firms typically command a lower multiple than public companies in the same industry because there is a market for shares in a public company. Multiples in single figures are usual for small firms but at the end of the day it depends how much the buyer wants the firm. And if you decide to sell the business, the multiple can be very high if a larger company perceives it as strategically important for some reason. For example, when Avis bought Zipcar in 2013 it paid $500 million – a multiple of 34 times net profits of $14.6 million (see Case insight on page 113).

Case insight   AO World plc

Company valuation for an IPO

John Roberts wanted to quit his job as a kitchen salesman and his friend Alan Latchford bet him that he would not dare to start his own business. Fourteen years later, in 2014, the company he founded with his friend was floated on the stock exchange. The IPO made Roberts £86 million on his sale of 10% of the company. This left him with 28.6% of the company, worth at the time over £400 million. The finance director, Steve Caunce, owned 13.6% and other directors 17.1%, meaning that the directors retained control of the company. The company raised £41 million from the share sale and said this would be used to fund its expansion into Europe, in particular to set up a warehouse and a delivery network in Germany

Starting life as Appliances Online in 2000, the company changed its name in 2013 to AO.com (the name it keeps for its website) and became AO World plc when it was floated on the stock exchange. It sells white goods like fridges, freezers, washing machines, tumble dryers and other household appliances online. Roberts hadn't heard of the internet when he started the company, but Latchford had and recognized the potential of e-commerce. He was tasked with building the website that has been much praised by industry observers. The quality of service has also been praised. Call centre staff have the autonomy to despatch a new product on the day that a customer calls and any customer with a complaint can be sent a bunch of flowers without seeking a supervisor's approval. However, the industry is known for stiff competition from established retail chains and slim margins.

The shares, which floated in February 2014 at £2.85, soared above £4.00 before closing on the day at £3.78, valuing the business at nearly £1.6 billion. This worked out at 5.8 times AO's annual sales of £275 million and an amazing 220 times its profits of less than £7 million. However, this valuation could not last and the share price quickly fell. By June 2015 the share price was down to £1.55 on sales of £476 million and an operating loss of £2.52 million in 2014/15.

QUESTIONS:

1 Was the company wise to make its IPO in February 2014?

2 What was the basis for the share price of £2.85 in 2014 and the subsequent rise to £4.00? What is the basis for the share price of £1.55 in 2015?

3 How will this reduction in the stock market value of the business affect it?

4 Compare and contrast this IPO to that of Alibaba (Case insight, page 378).

External factors outside of your control are also important in company valuations. The recession of 2008 saw private company valuations plunge as forecasts of economic activity were cut back. As economies emerge out of recession, valuations should improve. Another factor is the rate of interest. High interest rates usually mean lower multiples and therefore lower valuations, since an investment in a company is competing against that market rate of interest. Since the purchase of a business often necessitates a buyer borrowing funds, the gearing of the purchased firm, in its final form, can be a factor. If borrowings are high, as they often are in management buy-outs, the company is vulnerable to changes in profitability as it will have high, fixed interest charges. If the return on total assets falls below the rate of interest, it can be in trouble, and the higher the borrowing, the greater the trouble. This is what happened to the heavily borrowed small firms in the early 1990s when interest rates soared at the same time as profits tumbled. Interest rates are currently very low, so, as interest rates increase, valuations should also decrease. Nevertheless, the net effect is likely to be that company valuations will improve in the future. Accountants experienced in raising equity funding can provide advice on the 'going-rate' for multiples is in particular sectors.

One way of dealing with the problem of early valuation – particularly for fast, high-growth businesses – is to delay valuation but set out the details of how it will be determined at some point in the future. The initial investor then receives equity based on a discount of that future valuation. This is particularly effective when equity funding is to be sought in tranches and valuation is easier at these later stages. For example, a new venture receives equity funding of $100,000 on the understanding that the valuation will be based on a 50% discount on the next investor's valuation, when $200,000 is needed in one years' time. If this valuation turns out to be $2 million and the investor receives 10% of the equity, then the original investor will also receive 10%, reflecting the 50% discount.

Case insight   Xtreme SnoBoards (4)

Valuing a private business

In the Case Insights in Chapters 7, 11 and 12 we saw how a couple of snowboard enthusiasts set up a company called Xtreme SnoBoards, designing and building three types of boards. They drew up a set of financial forecasts and they undertook an evaluation of the projected performance using ratio analysis. They were very pleased with the results and, although they were not thinking of selling the business so early, they were curious about how much it might be worth if they achieved their targets.

Starting with basics, they would have put £42,000 of their own money into Xtreme and built a company with approximately £184,000 of capital or net assets (although almost £50,000 of this would be represented by machinery that may or may not have this market value). Against this, they would have liked a higher salary and did not take interest on the loan to the business. This would have reduced profit and assets by approximately £22,000. Still, if they could realize or sell the assets for £184,000 that would make the venture worthwhile.

However, they had learned that a thriving business was normally valued as a multiple of its profits, and with net profits of approximately £142,000 (or £120,000 after their additional salary and interest) they tried to find out what that multiple might be. The problem was that nobody would give them a firm indication of what that might be. On the one hand they were told that the business probably had great future potential, but on the other hand it had no track record and the stock market was generally depressed because of the recession. They multiples they were given ranged from 20 to 3, although most thought at this stage the multiple was probably in single digits. This wide range valued the company at anything between £426,000 and £1.7 million (or £360,000 and £1.4 million after their additional salary and interest) – quite a lot more than the net assets.

The founders were astounded. Taking the net asset value and the lowest multiple of income the company would be worth something between £184,000 and £426,000 (£162,000 and £360,000 taking the additional salary and interest into account). Not bad for a £42,000 investment and a lot of hard work over 15 months. Whichever way they looked at it, if the forecast was achieved, the business would be highly successful, and that made them even more determined than ever.

QUESTION:

1 Is the valuation of the company realistic?

Planning for an exit

Planning is the key to a successful harvest. Selling at the right time can have a significant impact on the value of the business. The business will be worth most when profits are at their highest and can be seen to be growing. You need to consider the impact of the business cycle upon sales, profits and the order book. The general state of the economy – and in particular the sector the business is in – can have an effect on valuation. It is easier to find a trade buyer when a sector is doing well and interest rates are low with bankers willing to lend. Other factors – like strong internal controls and an effective management team – need to be in place. Consideration needs to be given to the legal, tax and pension consequences of the sale. Most entrepreneurs will need advice on this and help in finding buyers. And finally, as we shall see in the next chapter, even if the entrepreneur is hoping to pass on the business to other members of the family, this is also likely to need careful planning and advice. All this means that the exit of the founder needs to be planned at least three to five years ahead.

The never-ending cycle of start-up and exit is part of the dynamic of the small firm sector as firms respond to the ever-changing marketplace. It is one of the reasons why governments all over the world now recognize that small firms have a vital and increasingly important part to play in the economy of the 21st century. In this environment survival is a badge of success. And behind every success, and indeed failure, there is a person and a human interest story to tell. Successfully managing growth is a Herculean task. Is it any wonder that so few owner-managers decide to try it? Those who do and succeed really are the superheroes of the modern world. But at this point are they really willing to retire quietly from the business they have founded and live off the wealth they have acquired?

Case insight   The Body Shop

From start-up to harvest

Perhaps the best known complete cycle from start-up to exit is The Body Shop, which was set up by Anita Roddick in 1976. It obtained a listing on the Unlisted Securities Market in the UK in 1984 and a full stock market listing in 1986. The Roddicks remained as directors and retained significant ownership. In 1996 an attempted re-privatization by the Roddicks was abandoned because of the gearing implications. By the late 1990s the Roddicks were taking a back seat. The Body Shop was attracting more competition from both newcomers and established retailers introducing 'natural' products. In 1998 a new Chief Executive was recruited, with the Roddicks becoming co-chairs. In 2000 both Anita and Gordon Roddick both resigned from The Body Shop as multimillionaires, but retained a majority shareholding. In 2001 an abortive bid from Mark Constantine, a former supplier and owner of competitor Lush, was turned down with some acrimony. In 2006 The Body Shop was sold to L'Oreal, part of the Nestlé group, for £652 million. With the Roddick's stake in the company then estimated at 18%,

they made about £130 million. Anita Roddick, famed for her good causes, was made a Dame. She died in 2007 after suffering a brain haemorrhage, aged 64.

Mark Constantine said:

'Anita's legacy is the creation and establishment of a small brand that reshaped cosmetic retailing, firstly in the UK and then globally. The Body Shop offered fun, novelty and excitement. It became the forerunner of responsible and ethical trading and, through Anita, gained and developed a voice heard not only in the beauty columns and glossy magazines but all the way to the City, major business and financial institutions around the world after the flotation in 1984. Her reputation as a fearless and challenging businesswoman grew alongside The Body Shop.' (The Daily Telegraph, 12 September 2007)

QUESTION:

1 What issues are relevant in a decision whether or not to sell-on a business?

I think every business needs a leader that does not forget the massive impact business can have on the world. All business leaders should be thinking 'how can I be a force for good?' What I see is demand from our people to be a business that is good, makes a profit, but also does something for the planet and humanity.

Richard Branson, founder, Virgin Group, www.hrmagazine.co.uk, 13 July 2010

Beyond business – entrepreneurial philanthropy

Entrepreneurs are hardly likely to be the kind of people who will enjoy doing nothing, even if they are about to retire from the business they have founded. One of the things that many entrepreneurs have turned to is philanthropy. Andrew Carnegie, founder of the Carnegie Steel Company which became the U.S. Steel Corporation, gave away to charities and foundations almost 90% of his wealth – about $350 million. His 1889 article advocating 'The Gospel of Wealth' called on the rich to use their wealth to improve society, and it stimulated a wave of philanthropy. Many entrepreneurs turn to philanthropy before they retire. But entrepreneurial philanthropy tends to be something altogether more powerful than just charitable giving. The distinction between charitable giving and entrepreneurial philanthropy is the difference between giving people food to alleviate hunger and giving them the training and the means to produce the food themselves. It involves sustainable entrepreneurship (see Chapter 1) and corporate social responsibility (CSR) may, but does not always, involve entrepreneurial philanthropy.

Case insight   Titus Salt

Entrepreneurial philanthropy

Entrepreneurial philanthropy has a long history. Titus Salt (1803–1876) made his fortune in the Bradford textile industry manufacturing woollen fabrics and became one of the greatest Victorian philanthropists, donating liberally to local and national good causes. However, today he is probably

best known for the model village he built, called Saltaire, which became a UNESCO World Heritage site in 2001.

Because of the employment offered by the wool mills, Bradford attracted workers from all over the country – but it was not a good place to live or work. Working conditions in the mills were bad and Bradford itself was insanitary and overcrowded with poor housing conditions. Salt decided

Continued...

Continued from previous page...

to relocate his mill and his employees to a site outside Bradford on the banks of the river Aire alongside the Leeds Liverpool Canal and the railway so that he could distribute his products quickly and cheaply. But he also wanted his workers to be healthier, happier – and more productive.

He employed local architects Henry Lockwood and Richard Mawson to build the mill and village. Work started in 1851 and continued until 1876. When the Salts Mill opened in 1853 it was the biggest factory in the world, employing some 3,000 workers on 1,200 looms, producing 30,000 yards of fabric every day. The village grew alongside it, designed in the classical style and inspired by the Italian Renaissance, importantly located upwind of the smoke and pollution coming from the factory chimneys. Allotments, where workers could grow their own food, separated the factory from the town, heralding the zoning approach to town planning used today. The housing was laid out in a grid fashion and, although close together, was of the highest quality. Each house had water supply, separate living and cooking spaces and several bedrooms and a garden, varying in size depending on the status of the worker, foreman or executive. Green spaces were dotted around the village, something normally found only in the most affluent of Victorian towns. The finest building was the Saltaire United Reform Church, now a Grade 1 listed building. The village also had its own well-equipped factory school and a Victoria Hall that housed a library, dance hall and lecture hall, meeting rooms, billiard room and gymnasium. Salt also provided rent-free Almshouses for the elderly or infirm 'of good moral character' which overlooked a small green and

Victoria Hall, Saltaire

came with a pension, some 40 years before the first state pension in the UK.

The UK textile industry was in steep decline by the late 20th century and the mill finally closed in 1986. Rescued by Jonathan Silver, it today houses an art gallery exhibiting the work of Bradford-born artist David Hockney, as well as shops and the 'Salts Diner'. Saltaire influenced town planning around the world and is one of the earliest, largest and best preserved Victorian model villages anywhere in the world.

❏ Visit the website: www.saltsmill.org.uk

QUESTION:

1 Was Titus Salt an entrepreneurial philanthropist? Explain.

For the entrepreneur, philanthropy may be a way to do something socially or environmentally useful with their time and the wealth they have accumulated that may have a longevity after their death. It provides an opportunity to bring their skills to bear in a more productive way than simply giving money to a cause. Entrepreneurs such as Bill Gates (Microsoft), Richard Branson (Virgin), Steve Case (AOL) and Jeff Skoll and Pierre Omidyar (eBay) have helped recalibrate what exactly philanthropy can mean. They bring a practical, entrepreneurial approach, a network of contacts and sometimes near-celebrity status to a project that can open doors at the highest levels of government. Entrepreneurial philanthropy is about bringing cash, passion, creativity and leadership to the cause. It is about having a large-scale, real impact that changes people's lives and that is sustainable. Of course, social and civic entrepreneurs can bring these things too, but they often give time instead of money – and that can make a difference to what is possible by leveraging up other funding.

Alto (2013) proposes a six-step approach to entrepreneurial philanthropy that you may say can be applied to most social enterprise projects:

1   Research social issues and decide on underlying causes of a problem.
2   Decide upon the nature of your involvement (time, money etc.).
3   Assess the time needed to make an impact and whether this is acceptable.
4   Decide on the tipping points when making timely and targeted philanthropic interventions, which can have an outsized impact beyond traditional giving methods.

5 Decide on and assemble resources.

6 Track progress.

One of the popular forms this has taken is the establishment of separate trusts or foundations (see Case insight below). There are often tax advantages to these separate legal entities (see Chapter 9). These trusts or foundations can work hand in hand with the founder's business to raise resources for their cause and, as we saw in Chapter 7, having a strong CSR and philanthropic base to the business can also make commercial sense, creating a win-win situation for both the business and the philanthropic cause.

 ## Case insight   Cotton On Foundation

 ### Entrepreneurial philanthropy

Nigel Austin started selling acid-wash denim jackets from the boot of his car at the markets in Geelong, Australia in 1991. This led him to start his own business, Cotton On Group, which today has a turnover of AUD 1.51 billion and over 1,300 stores around the world (see Case insight on page 249). Nigel set up the Cotton On Foundation after the birth of his first son in 2007. The foundation raises money and organizes charitable work for communities in southern Uganda, where it sponsors some 1,500 children. It organizes work for its staff and raises money from events, selling cloth bags, bottled water, mints, coffee etc. in the Cotton On Group shops. So far it has raised approximately AUD 35 million.

The Foundation's projects are based on four pillars derived from the United Nations Millennium Development Goals: health (targeting the reduction of child mortality and HIV prevention), education (providing primary and secondary education and school meals), sustainability (encouraging and funding community projects) and infrastructure (building schools, dams, wells, health centres etc.). They form the basis of every project undertaken by the Foundation. The purpose, vision, mission and values of the Foundation are set out on its website:

Purpose: We take action to inspire lasting positive change with limitless possibilities.

Vision: To empower youth, mobilize communities and build futures.

Mission: To develop 20,000 educational places in Southern Uganda by 2020.

Values:

> **Engaged** We give everyone the opportunity to participate in different ways: big or small, from our global team members to our customers. We roll up our sleeves, get our hands dirty and help out our mates. Together, we make big things happen.

> **Ethical** We go beyond doing the right thing. It's our shared belief that we can build sustainable communities, create measurable change and enrich people's lives, through responsible and compassionate decision-making.

> **Family** We are part of one big family that extends across the globe. Our relationships are built on deep trust and mutual respect with our communities, customers, partners and team members.

> **Fun** Our job is to empower people and the communities in which we operate. We genuinely love what we do and we have fun doing it!

> **Entrepreneurial** We do not just take the easy road. We are visionary, passionate and fearless. We are determined to achieve our mission, to continue to do things differently and to never give up.

> **Keeping it real** We are an optimistic and resourceful bunch. We're realistic about our impact, but are unwavering in our efforts to change the world.

The Foundation is part of the culture of Cotton On Group. Hundreds of photos of Cotton On staff building schools and digging bores in Uganda adorn the office walls and are displayed in stores to raise the profile with consumers.

❏ Visit the website: http://www.cottononfoundation.org/

QUESTION:

1 Is the Cotton On Foundation just an example of philanthropy or does it make any commercial sense? Explain.

↻ Summary

> Most firms are born to stagnate or die and not to grow to any size. A business might cease to trade for many reasons, not all of them bad. However, when the sole trader, partners or company are insolvent then there are unpaid creditors.

> The main factors influencing the statistical likelihood of failure are age and size of business. The younger and smaller the business the more likely it is to cease trading.

> The causes of failure involve a coincidence of external and internal influences that might occur simultaneously.

External influences include:

- The general economy, which SMEs cannot influence but has a large influence on them;

- Luck (and resource levels), which likens failure or success to a game of chance;

- Market/Industry structure, where the degree of competition can have a large influence;

- Other opportunities that face individuals, rather than just the state of their business, can influence decisions.

Internal influences include:

- Personal character flaws of the entrepreneur, particularly a tendency to be overly optimistic;

- Lack of managerial capabilities of the entrepreneur, which can lead to poor financial control and marketing and a lack of planning;

- Financial resources, which can lead to cash-flow problems often arising through over-trading.

> There are a number of courses of action for individuals or companies that are insolvent. They may involve refinancing, some form of compromise with the creditors and/or sale of all or part of the business. Sometimes this involves compromising the position of creditors so that the business can survive as a going concern. Ignoring the reality of the situation and not planning to cope can only lessen the chances of survival.

> Harvesting your investment involves selling the business as a going concern either to a trade buyer or through a management buy-out or management buy-in. All these options need careful planning and professional advice. Another option may be selling shares – 'going public' – but the entrepreneur may then find it difficult to leave the business in the short term.

> Company valuation is not a science. It depends on how important the purchase is to the buyer, and therefore what they are willing to pay. Companies can be valued based upon their assets or a multiple of earnings or net profits (or both). There is, however, no set formula for judging what that multiple should be. Multiples depend on the quality of earnings, the quality of management, the industry sector and the general economic climate. Few private companies command a multiple into double figures.

> Rather than valuing a business straight away, another approach, particularly suitable for fast, high-growth businesses, is to delay valuation but set out the details of how it will be determined at some time in the future. The initial investor then receives equity based on a discount of that future valuation.

> Timing of the sale is important and therefore careful planning is essential. To maximize the value of the business, profits need to be high and rising, the sector needs to be booming with interest rates low, and good controls and an effective management team need to be in place.

> Entrepreneurial philanthropy is more than just charitable giving. The distinction between charitable giving and entrepreneurial philanthropy is the difference between giving people food to alleviate hunger and giving them the training and the means to produce the food themselves. It involves sustainable entrepreneurship. CSR may, but does not always, involve entrepreneurial philanthropy.

✓ Activities

1 Find a business that has recently failed and try to fit the circumstances of its failure into the framework of the failure model shown in Figure 16.1.

2 Using desk research, write a case study on a failed business.

💬 Group discussion topics

1 Why do most small firms stagnate or die?
2 Is it good that so many small firms cease trading?
3 What constitutes failure in business?
4 What do you think of the observation that young and smaller SMEs are most likely to fail than their older, larger counterparts?
5 How do you distinguish between causes and symptoms in business failure?
6 What is involved in bankruptcy? What are its consequences?
7 What is compulsory liquidation? What are its consequences?
8 How is a CVA different to administration?
9 How is a CVL different to liquidation?
10 Is a pre-packaged sale fair?
11 If you are trying to predict failure does it matter if you measure symptoms rather than causes?
12 If luck plays such an important part in determining failure, do entrepreneurs really make their own luck? If so, how?
13 The entrepreneurial character is as much a liability as an asset. Discuss.
14 You cannot distinguish between bad business decisions and managerial or business weaknesses. Discuss.
15 What do you think would be your emotions if the business you set up faced failure? What do you think of the insights by Edward Johnstone (ZedZed.com) and Peter Durose (The English Grocer) regarding their business failures?
16 How might planning to sell your business affect your plans and strategies?
17 There is no such thing as company valuation, only a willing buyer and a willing seller negotiating a price. Discuss.
18 How are SMEs different from large firms when it comes to facing possible failure?
19 Why do you think business failure is more of a stigma in the UK than in the USA?
20 What are the reasons, other than just money, that you might want to sell a business that you have founded?
21 If you were buying a business founded by an entrepreneur, what safeguards might you want to put in place?
22 An entrepreneur could never relinquish control of the company they founded, whether to private or stock market investors. Discuss.
23 What personal issues might an entrepreneur encounter in facing retirement?
24 Why should an entrepreneur consider setting up a charitable foundation?

☛ References

Altman, E.J. (1968) 'Financial Ratios, Discriminant Analysis and the Prediction of Corporate Bankruptcy', *Journal of Finance*, 23(4), September.

Alto, P. (2013) 'Entrepreneurial Philanthropy', *Stanford Social Innovation Review*, 28, January, available online at www.ssireview.org/blog/entry/entrepreneurial_philanthropy.

Baldwin, J., Gray, T., Johnson, J., Proctor, J., Rafiquzzaman, M. and Sabourin, D. (1997) *Failing Concerns: Business Bankruptcy in Canada*, Ottawa: Ministry of Industry.

Bates, T. (2005) 'Analysis of Young, Small Firms that Have Closed: Delineating Successful from Unsuccessful Closures', *Journal of Business Venturing*, 20(3).

Beaver, W.H. (1966) 'Financial Ratios as Predictors of Failure', *Journal of Accounting Research*, Supplement on Empirical Research in Accounting, pp. 71–111.

Beaver, G. and Jennings, P. (2005) 'Competitive Advantage and Entrepreneurial Power: The Dark Side of Entrepreneurship', *Journal of Small Business and Enterprise Development*, 12(1).

Berryman, J. (1983) 'Small Business Failure and Bankruptcy: A Survey of the Literature', *European Small Business Journal*, 1(4).

Cosh, A. and Hughes, A. (eds) (1998) *Enterprise Britain: Growth Innovation and Public Policy in the Small and Medium Sized Enterprise Sector 1994–97*, Cambridge: ESRC Centre for Business Research.

Cressy, R. (2006) 'Determinants of Small Firm Survival and Growth', in M. Casson, B. Yeung, A. Basu and N. Wadeson (eds), *The Oxford Handbook of Entrepreneurship*, Oxford: Oxford University Press.

Dahl, D. (2005) 'A New Study Says Most Small Biz CEOs Lack Succession Plans', *Inc. Magazine*, available online at www.inc.com?criticalnews/articles/200502/exit.html.

Dell, M. (1999) *Direct from Dell: Strategies that Revolutionized an Industry*, New York: Harper Business.

Delmar, F. and Shane, S. (2003) 'Does Business Planning Facilitate the Development of New Ventures?', *Strategic Management Journal*, 24(12).

Department for Business Enterprise & Regulatory Reform (2008) *High Growth Firms in the UK: Lessons from an Analysis of Comparative UK Performance*. BERR Economics Paper No 3, available online at http://www.berr.gov.uk/files/file49042.pdf.

DeTienn, D.R. (2010) 'Entrepreneurial Exit as a Critical Component of the Entrepreneurial Process: Theoretical Development', *Journal of Business Venturing*, 25(2).

Everett, J. and Watson, J. (2004) 'Small Business Failure and External Risk Factors', *Small Business Economics*, 11(4).

Gaskill, L.A.R., Van Auken, H.E. and Manning, R.A. (1993) 'A Factoral Analytic Study of the Perceived Causes of Small Business Failure', *Journal of Small Business Management*, 31(4).

Gimeno, J., Folta, T.B., Cooper, A.C. and Woo, C.Y. (1997) 'Survival of the Fittest? Entrepreneurial Human Capital and the Persistence of Underperforming Business', *Administrative Science Quarterly*, 42(4).

Hannan, M.T. and Freeman, J. (1977) 'Population Ecology of Organizations', *American Journal of Sociology*, 82(5).

Haswell, S. and Holmes, S. (1989) 'Estimating the Small Business Failure Rate: A Reappraisal', *Journal of Small Business Management*, 27.

Haveman, H.A. and Khaire, M.V. (2004) 'Survival Beyond Succession? The Contingent Impact of Founder Succession on Organizational Failure', *Journal of Business Venturing*, 19(3).

Headd, B. (2003), 'Redefining Business Success: Distinguishing between Closure and Failure', *Small Business Economics*, 29(4).

Keasey, K. and Watson, R. (1991) 'The State of the Art of Small Firm Failure Prediction: Achievements and Prognosis', *International Small Business Journal*, 9.

Kiggundu, M.N. (2002), 'Entrepreneurs and Entrepreneurship in Africa: What Is Known and What Needs to Be Done', *Journal of Developmental Entrepreneurship*, 7(3).

King, N. (2002) *Exit Strategies*, Oxford: Capstone.

Knotts, T.L., Jones, S.C. and Udell, G.G. (2003), 'Small Business Failure: The Role of Management Practices and Product Characteristics', *Journal of Business and Entrepreneurship*, October.

Larson, C. and Clute, R. (1979) 'The Failure Syndrome', *American Journal of Small Business*, IV(2), October.

Levie, J., Don, G. and Leleux, B. (2011) 'The New Venture Mortality Myth', in K. Hindle and K. Klyver (eds), *Handbook of Research on New Venture Creation*, Cheltenham: Edward Elgar.

Love, N. and D'Silva, K. (2001) 'A Model for Predicting Business Performance in SMEs: Theory and Empirical Evidence', *British Accounting Association Conference*, 26–27 March, University of Exeter, England.

Metzger, G. (2007) *Personal Experience: A Most Vicious and Limited Circle!? On the Role of Entrepreneurial Experience for Firm Survival*, Discussion Paper 07-046, Baden-Württemberg Centre for European Economic Research.

Pierrakis, Y. (2010) *Venture Capital: Now and After the Dotcom Crash*, London: Nesta Research Report, July 2010.

Reid, G.C. (1991) 'Staying in Business', *International Journal of Industrial Organisation*, 9.

Saridakis, G., Mole, K.F. and Storey, D.J. (2008) 'New Small Firm Survival in England', *Empirica*, 35.

Shepherd, D.A. (2003) 'Learning from Business Failure: Propositions of Grief Recovery for the Self-Employed', *Academy of Management Review*, 28(2).

Shepherd, D.A. and Kuratko, D.F. (2009) 'The Death of an Innovative Project: How Grief Recovery Enhances Learning', *Business Horizons*, 52(5).

Stearns, T.M., Carter, N.M., Reynolds, P.D. and Williams, M.L. (1995) 'New Firm Survival: Industry, Strategy and Location', *Journal of Business Venturing*, 10(1).

Stokes, D. and Blackburn, R. (2002) 'Learning the Hard Way: The Lessons of Owner-Managers who have Closed their Businesses', *Journal of Small Business and Enterprise Development*, 9(1).

Storey, D.J. and Greene, F.J. (2010) *Small Business and Entrepreneurship*, Harlow: Pearson Education.

Taffler, R.J. (1982) 'Forecasting Company Failure in the UK using Discriminant Analysis and Failure Ratio Data', *Journal of Royal Statistical Society*, 145, part 3.

Watkins, D. (1982) 'Management Development and the Owner-manager', in T. Webb, T. Quince and D. Watkins (eds), *Small Business Research*, Aldershot: Gower.

Wichmann, H. (1983), 'Accounting and Marketing – Key Small Business Problems', *American Journal of Small Business*, 7.

www.palgrave.com/Burns-Entrepreneurship-And-Small-Business-4e

Go online to access additional teaching and learning resources for this chapter on the companion website. Click here in the ebook to complete a multiple choice revision quiz for this chapter.

17 | FAMILY BUSINESS

Contents

Photodisc/ Getty Images

Learning outcomes

When you have read this chapter and undertaken the related activities you will be able to:

> Explain the significance of family firms in the business world;
> Explain the advantages and disadvantages of being part of a family firm;
> Describe and explain the conflict of cultures between family and business;
> Identify the points of conflict within the family firm and understand the mechanisms that might resolve them;
> Identify and explain the dangers of generational succession and use a framework for planning succession;
> Describe what goes into a family constitution and how it might be developed.

 *Practice insight*: Genograms

 *Practice insight*: Family constitution checklist

 Case insights

Kongō Gumi	Mars Inc.
Wilkin & Sons	Alex Ramsay
JCB	J&B Wilde and Sons Littlewoods
Adidas vs Puma	Everards Brewery
Fisherman's Friend	Wates Group
Ferrero	Timberland

The importance of family business

Defined – at this stage – simply as an organization in which decision-making is influenced by multiple generations of a family, family businesses are the oldest and most common form of any business organization. Rather than starting a business from scratch, many entrepreneurs will join a family business and eventually take over the leadership of it. In the UK it is estimated that family firms account for two in three private sector enterprises (some three million firms), almost half of all mid-sized businesses (£20–50 million turnover), provide two jobs in five in the private sector (employing 9.2 million people) and generate almost a quarter of UK GDP (£1.1 trillion) (Institute for Family Business, 2011). Their importance is estimated to be even greater across the EU and the USA. What is more, the stereotypical image of the family living above the shop does not do the sector credit. They are not all small, lifestyle firms. Family-owned companies account for a substantial proportion of the value of the stock market. In the USA, family firms – where family members own more than a quarter of the shares – represent more than a third of the *Fortune* 500 (Clark, 2014). In Europe the pattern is similar. But most family firms – of any size – are privately owned or family controlled and the family have a strong hand in influencing management decision-making.

 ## Case insight   Kongō Gumi

The oldest firm in the world

Up until its takeover in 2006, Kongō Gumi could probably have claimed to be the oldest continuously operating firm in the world. Founded in 578 by a carpenter brought to Japan from Baekje (now Korea) by Prince Shotoku to build a Buddhist temple, the Kongō family built some of the most famous buildings in Japan, including many temples and Osaka Castle. In fact, temple construction had until recently been a reliable mainstay of the business, contributing 80% of Kongō Gumi's $67.6 million turnover in 2004. The family owned and managed the business for over 40 generations. Its last president, Masakazu Kongō, was the 40th member of the family to lead the company. He has cited the company's flexibility in selecting leaders as a key factor in its longevity – rather than always handing reins to the oldest son, the son or daughter who best exhibited the 'health, responsibility, and talent for the job' was selected. Indeed, the common Japanese practice of sons-in-law taking the family name allowed the company to continue under the same name, even when there were no sons in a given generation.

In the year of its takeover it still had a turnover of $70 million and some 100 employees – despite falling sales and redundancies. However, a high level of debt ($343 million), brought about by heavy investment in property or real estate, and an unfavourable business climate, which saw a decline in the building of temples, contributed to the company's decline. It now operates as a wholly owned subsidiary of Takamatsu and the Kongō family are still carpenters.

QUESTIONS:

1 What are the lessons from Kongō's longevity?
2 What are the lessons from Kongō's decline?
3 What are the advantages and disadvantages of the age of a business?

Family firms have some of the strongest brands in business today. In the USA, Walmart, Mars, Gap and Levi Strauss & Co (to name but a few) are global brands and remain family controlled companies. In India there is the Tata Group (now owner of Jaguar/Rover); in Taiwan, Foxcon; in Korea, Samsung; in Germany, Porsche; and in Denmark, LEGO® (probably the best-known toy brand in the world which we shall look at in Chapter 19). In the UK the pattern is repeated – JCB (the third largest manufacturer of construction equipment in the world), R. Griggs Group (maker of the famous Doc Martens boots, founded 1901, which we shall look at later in this Chapter), J. Barbour & Sons (maker of the very British waxed jackets, founded in 1894), Wilkin & Sons (maker of the famous Tiptree jams, founded 1885, see below), Morgan Motor Company (maker of Morgan sports cars, founded 1909 and the world's oldest privately owned car manufacturer, Chapter 6) and Quad Electroacoustics (maker of distinctive hi-fi equipment, founded 1936, Chapter 6). Family-owned businesses account for over 30% of companies and have sales of over $1 billion

(Katchaner et al., 2012). Not only have these firms been around for a long time, but also the values and beliefs on which they were established are well known and respected. Familial brands build consumer trust over long periods and can be very valuable assets.

 Case insight   Wilkin & Sons

Family values

Wilkin & Sons was founded in 1885 and is still a family business. It is best known for its luxury Tiptree jams which sell to over 50 countries. The more esoteric jams such as 'Little Scarlet Strawberry' have attained almost a cult status among jam lovers. The company is committed to sharing success with its workforce. At the company's 450-hectare estate at Tiptree in Essex, managers and directors grow fruit, test products as well as man the production lines when required. Many members of the workforce live in houses owned by the firm. It was one of the early businesses, over a century ago, to introduce a form of pension scheme for employees. The firm has also created a trust which gives employees ownership of the business, with a current shareholding of just under 50%. The firm strives to be remarkable in its activities and is focused on the three guiding principles of quality, integrity and independence.

❑ Visit the website: www.tiptree.com

QUESTION:

1 How are family values different from personal values?

Courtesy of Wilkin & Sons

Indeed, many of the best known brands today started out as family firms before becoming public companies. For example, the H.J. Heinz Company was in family hands until 1946, when it went public. It was founded in 1888, although Henry J. Heinz started producing bottled condiments from 1869. Many companies still have links with the founding family. For example, the Ford Motor Company was launched by Henry Ford in a converted wagon factory in Detroit in 1903. His great grandson, William Ford Jr, was appointed chair in 1998 and the family still own some 40% of the company. The Disney Corporation is the largest entertainment conglomerate in the world. Roy E. Disney, a descendant of the original Disney family and the principal shareholder, was vice chair until 2003 and is now consultant and vice chair director emeritus.

The family firm has been the backbone of many continental European economies for decades. None more so than in Italy where names like Agnelli, Pirelli and De Benedetti have long controlled large parts of Italy's industry. Because of the historically strong family networks, Italian owner-managers have been loath to surrender even part of the equity capital of their firms to investors, and non-family managers have rarely received shares or share options. And in Germany family firms make up the majority of the Mittlelstand that contribute so much to employment, exports and GDP.

However, most family firms – like most businesses generally – are small, and traditionally they are characterized as less innovative than non-family firms (McCann et al., 2001), although more recent studies link innovation with the more established family firms (Craig and Moores, 2006). Traditionally, family businesses have been important in many primary sectors, such as farming. They also tend to thrive in areas such as hotels and restaurants, where high levels of personal service are required. The retail sector – butchers, bakers, florists, corner stores and so on – also boasts a large number of family firms, with members of the family helping to staff the shop. Family firms are also to be found in the cash generating food-processing industry. Finally, there are many in the supply industries like transport and distributorships, especially in the motor sector.

Case insight   JCB

The importance of family firms

Stories of successful entrepreneurs always make good reading. And successful entrepreneurs have been with us for many, many years in Britain. Joseph Cyril Bamford gave his initials to the ubiquitous yellow hydraulic excavator and digger seen on just about every building site or road works – the JCB. In fact, JCB became one of the few post-war British industrial success stories. By the time of Joseph Bamford's death in 2001 the company employed over 4,500 people across three continents and had a turnover of £833 million. Over 70% of JCB production is for overseas markets.

Joseph Bamford came from a Staffordshire engineering family which had been making agricultural equipment since mid-Victorian times. When he returned to civilian life after the Second World War he decided to start up on his own doing what he knew best. Starting his business with only a welding set he bought for £1, he began producing tipping farm trailers from a garage in Uttoxeter, using wartime scrap. These sold well, but in 1948 he decided to branch out into hydraulic equipment and, in 1953, invented the famous backhoe loader that combined the two functions of excavator and shovel and became the visual embodiment of the initials JCB.

Joseph Bamford was a paternalistic employer, who provided a social club and a fishing lake next to his factory in Rocester. He ran a 'tight ship' but rewarded effort. He also knew how to get PR. In 1964, when he famously paid his workers £250,000 in bonuses because the company's turnover had topped £8 million, he personally handed out the bonus to each employee, standing on the first farm tractor he had designed in 1945. Joseph Bamford helped turn JCB into one of the most successful privately owned companies in Britain. Eventually the company diversified from his central control into a group of several operating companies. He retired and gave up his position as chair of the group in 1975, handing it over to his eldest son, Anthony, now Lord Bamford.

When Anthony Bamford took over as chair the company had just one factory in Rocester, Staffordshire. Under his leadership, JCB now has 22 plants: 12 in the UK and others in the USA, China, Brazil and India, employing more than 12,000 people. Today the company is the third-biggest maker of construction equipment, manufactures around 70,000 machines a year for construction, agricultural and industrial markets and achieves annual sales in excess of £2.5 billion. The company sells its products in 150 countries through 1,500 dealer depot locations. It remains a family business.

❏ Visit the website: www.jcb.com

QUESTIONS:

1 JCB is no longer a 'gazelle'. It is a large family-owned company. What are the differences between a large family-owned company and a large publicly owned company?

2 How might these differences impact on public policy?

Reproduced with kind permission of J C Bamford Excavators Limited ™

Defining a family business

All this begs the question: what precisely constitutes a family business? We defined it at the beginning of the chapter simply as an organization in which decision-making is influenced by multiple generations of a family. However, much of the academic literature is concerned with defining this more precisely. Essentially, a family business is one that is owned or controlled by one family, related by blood or marriage, although researchers have suggested many more precise definitions, for example:

> An owner-managed enterprise with family members predominantly involved in its administration, operations and the determination of its destiny. Family members may include parents, children and grand-children; spouses; brothers, sisters and cousins (Poutziouris, 1994).

> A company in which majority ownership (in terms of shares) or control lies in a single family and in which two or more family members are, or at some time were, directly involved in the business (Rosenblatt et al., 1985).

> For a quoted company, one in which 25% of voting shares are controlled by the family (Nelton, 1986).

A widely used definition is provided by Chua et al. (1999) as 'a business governed and/or managed with the intention to shape and pursue the vision of the business held by a dominant coalition controlled by members of the same family or a small number of families in a manner that is potentially sustainable across generations of the family or families.' This then begs the question of what constitutes 'a dominant coalition'. The authors say it is the 'powerful actors in an organization who control the overall organizational agenda', but that begs the question of how do you judge 'power' and 'control'. Gersick et al. (1997) suggested this could consist of a single individual, as is often the case in a founder-controlled family business, or many individuals, as might be the case in sibling partnerships or cousin consortiums. But then this means all sole traders might be classified as family businesses. Chua et al.'s definition is significant because it introduces the issue of the family influencing the vision and therefore the strategic direction of the business. Astrachan et al. (2002) attempted to address this issue by developing an instrument called the Family Influence on Power, Experience, and Culture (F-PEC) scale for assessing the extent of family influence in the three dimensions of power, experience, and culture. However, the resulting scale is a continuous one and therefore provides a subtle answer rather than a simple yes/no as to whether an enterprise is a family business or not.

The problem is that family firms are heterogeneous – each one seems different in so many ways – and the search for a precise definition could be endless and rather fruitless. Westhead and Howarth (2007) distinguished between first- and multiple-generation firms, professional family firms, average family firms, diluted family firms, open family firms and transitional family firms. Probably the real answer is to ask the family. If family members are involved in the firm and feel a responsibility for it, then that is a good indication that it is a family business. They will probably say it is anyway. One of the overriding characteristics of the family business is the atmosphere of belonging and common purpose. Just as the personality of the owner-manager is imprinted on the small firm they own and manage, so the culture of the family is imprinted on the family firm. Rather than 'two arms, two legs and a giant ego', you have many arms, legs and egos. It is no wonder that *Spectator* magazine once described the family business sector as 'an endless soap opera of patriarchs and matriarchs, black sheep and prodigal sons, hubris and nemesis'. And there you have the problem.

 Case insight   Adidas vs Puma

Family rivalry

On 21 September 2009, two football teams came together in the town of Herzogenaurach in Bavaria, Germany, to play a game of football. The game was preceded by what was described as a 'historic handshake' in support of the Peace One Day organization, which was celebrating its annual day of non-violence. The teams were from the footwear companies Adidas and Puma – whose commercial rivalry is famous – and the story behind the game is a remarkable tale of how family businesses can break up and, in this case, split a town in two.

Continued...

Continued from previous page...

For over 60 years Herzogenaurach has been a town split into two factions, separated by a river and two major employers – Adidas and Puma. Townsfolk were either 'Adidas' or 'Puma' people, even if they did not work for either firm. Stores and tradespeople proclaimed their loyalty to one brand or the other. Two soccer teams emerged – ASV Herzogenaurach and FC Herzogenaurach – each sponsored by one of the firms. Rival gangs fought each other and intermarriage was out of the question. This curious split in the town can be traced to a family squabble in the 1940s between two local shoemakers – brothers Adolf and Rudolf Dassler. They had made shoes together since the 1920s, starting in their mother's kitchen, and had set up a family business called the Dassler Brothers Shoe Factory. For some reason that has melted into the mists of time, the pair fell out and set up rival companies on either side of the town's river. Rudolf set up Puma, and Adolf renamed the company Adidas. It was this falling out that spawned decades of fierce business rivalry, split a town in two, and led to the establishment of two of the best-recognized sporting brands in the world. Once the Dassler brothers died in the 1970s and the companies gradually fell out of the control of the founding families, the tensions between the two firms started to ease. However, the handshake on 21 September 2009 was important for Herzogenaurach residents, whose psyche has been shaped for years by their choice of footwear and its consequences.

QUESTION:

1 Is this form of rivalry good for the company? Explain.

The advantages of family

Starting up a business on your own can be a stressful, lonely way to make money. Many people start up a business with friends – they are known and trusted and may well possess complementary skills. So why not start up a business with the family? Trust is something that there is in abundance – particularly between husband and wife – and if all the family's income depends on the success of the venture then there is no doubting that the motivation to succeed will be strong, although this should be tempered with the recognition of the risk of depending on only one source of family income. What is more, getting the whole family to help with the work brings an added resource to the firm – and one that may not have to be paid a wage. Davis et al. (2010) talk about the 'stewardship culture' in family firms and how it encourages pro-organizational behaviour from all family members. Leach (1996) suggests that family firms have a number of advantages over others:

1 **Commitment.** Family enthusiasm and family ties can develop added commitment and loyalty;

2 **Knowledge.** Special ways of doing things in the business can be coveted and protected within the family;

3 **Flexibility in time, work and money.** Putting work and time into the business when necessary and taking money out when the business can afford it rather than according to the dictate of a contract;

4 **Long-range planning.** Because the firm is seen as the family's main store of value, something to be passed on to the next generation, family firms are better than others at taking a long-term view, although this may not involve formal planning processes;

5 **A stable culture.** Relationships in family firms have had a long time to develop and the company's ethics and working practices are therefore stable and well established;

6 **Speedy decision-making.** Like owner-managed companies, family firms can make decisions quickly because of the short lines of responsibility;

7 **Reliability and pride.** Because of the commitment and the stability of their culture, family firms can be very solid and reliable structures that, over time, build up good reputations with customers, reputations that the family guard with fierce pride.

Many family firms started out as or remain husband and wife teams – for example Mark and Mo Constantine who established Lush Cosmetics (Chapter 7), Anita and Gordon Roddick

Inevitably when you are talking about family businesses there is a sense of generation. There has to be something to hand down, which is the greater shareholder argument of the long-term view. Other sorts of business may have different time horizons.

Adrian Cadbury, former family owner, Cadbury, *The Times*, 8 July 2000

We are a family-owned, private business. We do what's right for the business. We do not have to prove anything to anybody.

Gary Grant, founder, The Entertainer, *The Guardian*, 7 April 2015

who established the original The Body Shop chain (Chapter 9) or Doug and Mary Perkins who established Specsavers (Chapter 9). There is the added advantage for husband and wife of giving each other support and friendship, and working long hours may not be such a grind when with your partner. For some couples, being together all the time can help in their personal as well as business relationship. However, for others it might be a recipe for divorce and business failure. As with many issues relating to the family firm, there are few hard and fast rules. Conflict is most likely to arise in making decisions, and here clear role definition and a separation between work and home are important. Based upon interviews with husband and wife teams in the USA, Nelton (op. cit.) suggested that the successful husband and wife teams shared the following characteristics:

> Marriage and children came first;
> The partners had enormous respect for each other;
> There was close communication between partners;
> Partners' talents and attitudes were complementary;
> Partners defined their individual responsibilities carefully;
> Partners competed with other companies, not each other;
> Partners kept their egos in check.

Family firms can be characterized as having both economic and non-economic goals, and there is no theoretical justification for or clear evidence that family firms actually outperform non-family firms. However, one meta-analysis by van Essen et al. (2015) showed that publicly traded family firms outperformed non-family firms, although an earlier study suggests this is explained by the influence of the founder rather than the family (Miller et al., 2007). Katchaner et al. (op. cit.) studied 149 publicly traded, family-controlled businesses with revenues greater than $1 billion, based in the USA, Canada, France, Spain, Portugal, Italy and Mexico, during the period from 1997 to 2009 – a period when economies across the world moved from expansion to recession. They made some interesting observations. Compared to their peer groups throughout this period, these large family businesses:

1   Had leaner cost structures. Consequently, they entered the recession with lower fixed costs and were therefore better able to survive;
2   Had a higher cut-off for capital expenditures. Consequently, they missed out on some profitable investments opportunities that their peers might have invested in and therefore underperformed during periods of expansion, but this worked to their advantage in recession;
3   Had lower levels of gearing. Consequently, they were better able to survive the recession;
4   Made fewer (and smaller) company acquisitions. They preferred organic growth and often pursued partnerships or joint ventures instead of acquisitions;
5   Were more highly diversified. Companies such as Cargill, Koch Industries, Tata and LG were far more diversified than the average corporation – 46% of family businesses were highly diversified, compared to only 20% of the comparison group;
6   Were more international. They generated more sales from abroad than their comparison group but they achieved this foreign growth organically or through small local acquisition, without big cash outlays.
7   Had lower staff turnover. They focused on 'creating a culture of commitment and purpose, avoiding layoffs during downturns, promoting from within, and investing in people'.

Katchaner et al. observed that in times of economic boom these large family businesses under-performed financially and in times of recession they over-performed, compared to their peers, and concluded that these businesses were taking a longer-term view focusing on financial resilience rather than performance, thus increasing their chances of survival during recession: 'A CEO of a family-controlled firm may have financial incentives similar to those of chief executives of nonfamily firms, but the familial obligation he or she feels will lead to very different strategic choices. Executives of family businesses often invest with a 10- or 20-year horizon, concentrating on what they can do now to benefit the next generation.'

Case insight   Fisherman's Friend

Family firms

Back in 1865 a pharmacist called James Lofthouse, who lived in the fishing village of Fleetwood in Lancashire, England, made a few jottings in his recipe book for a lozenge that cleared the nose and throat when blocked with mucus from colds and flu. For the next 100 years the lozenge was sold to the fishing community in Fleetwood and it was the fishermen that coined the name 'Fisherman's Friend'. But when Doreen Lofthouse married into the family things started to change. She was the driving force behind Fisherman's Friend, now a global brand worth £165 million and selling over five billion lozenges a year in more than 120 countries. Almost all (97%) of production is exported and the firm has won the Queen's Award for Export Achievement three times. Still based in Lancashire, in 2013 profits were £1.9 million on turnover of £43.4 million and the company employed some 280 staff.

The lozenge's strong distinctive taste comes from its blend of liquorice, menthol and eucalyptus oil. The 'inventor', James, never made much of the lozenge and the book of recipes passed to his son, Charles, and then to Charles's son, James, who married Frances, daughter of a Yorkshire miner. Tony was their only child. The family ran a small pharmacy in Lord Street in Fleetwood, and in the summer they would open a seafront gift shop for the visitors from nearby Blackpool. It was here that the lozenges became popular, so much so that people would write to the shop ordering more. These were sent off by Frances Lofthouse,

Tony's mother, complete with a hand-typed label. Tony was working in the gift shop when he met Doreen. It was Doreen who, seeing that so many people went to the trouble of ordering the lozenges by post, realized that there was an untapped market beyond the town. She went to the nearby towns and persuaded shops to stock it. The breakthrough came when Doreen persuaded Boots, the high-street pharmacy chain, to stock the lozenges. It was actually Doreen that registered the name 'Fisherman's Friend', although the family had been using it for some time.

These days the lozenge comes in eleven flavours, from blackcurrant to mandarin (popular in the Far East) as well as the distinctive original, although only seven can be found in the UK. The company remains a family firm with all the shares held by the Lofthouse family. Doreen is chair and shares an office with her husband, Tony, who is joint managing director and supervises production. (Doreen's first husband was Tony's uncle.) Doreen's son, Duncan, is financial director, and his wife, Linda, runs the accounts department. Duncan is the youngest of the Lofthouse family and, like Tony, has no heir. What will happen to the famous brand when the family retire remains an unanswered question.

❏ Visit the website: www.fishermansfriend.com

QUESTION:

1 What are the advantages and disadvantages of Fisherman's Friend remaining a family-owned business?

The conflict between family and business cultures

There are also some disadvantages associated with family business. At the heart of the family firm are its distinctive values and beliefs – its culture. Often the family culture can strengthen the business. For example, many successful family firms were originally built around strong religious ethics whereby the success of the firm was shared with the workforce. In many ways the workforce becomes an extended family, and relationships are cemented with trust and respect for the founding family. Families can display their values and beliefs in all sorts of quirky ways in the family firm. Sometimes these are good for the firm. They can bring clear values, beliefs and a focused direction. However, they can also bring a lack of professionalism, nepotism rather than meritocracy, rigidity and family conflict or feuding into the workplace. Any consultant who has worked with family firms realizes how important it is to understand the family politics if they are to understand how the business operates.

So, family culture can be a tremendous asset for the firm. However, if it is not aligned with the values, beliefs and culture of the business it can also create friction and the potential for conflict.

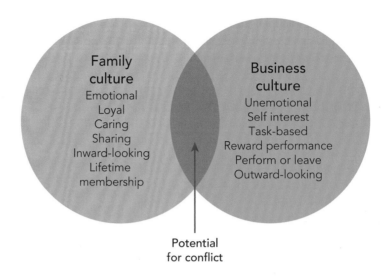

Figure 17.1 Family vs business cultures

The problem can arise because families exist primarily to take care of and to nurture family members. They value emotional capital. Business exist to profitably generate goods and services. As shown in Figure 17.1, the family culture is based on emotion emphasizing loyalty, caring and sharing. It is inward-looking and lasts a lifetime. In contrast, business culture is unemotional, task-orientated and based on self-interest. It is outward-looking, rewarding performance and penalizing lack of performance. Conflict between the two cultures is unlikely at start-up, but, as the firm grows and time passes, the potential for conflict increases.

Gomez-Mejia et al. (2011) have argued that the **socioemotional wealth** (SEW) of the family affects decision-making within it. SEW characterizes the emotional value associated with a family firm. It serves to meet the family's affective needs like identity, influence and perpetuation of the family dynasty, and means that decisions can be made for seemingly irrational, specifically non-economic, reasons which are not always in the best interests of the business. On the one hand, high levels of SEW in a family firm might be universally beneficial, for example by prompting the firm to act in philanthropic ways or by showing high levels of CSR. However, it could also become a driver of selfish and self-serving behaviour by the family. The point is that these decisions might reflect the politics of the family and a non-family firm might make different ones.

SEW is used to explain why and how business and family identities can be closely linked. At its best this can work to the benefit of both the family and the business. The business can become not only a source of income for the family but also a framework for family activity and an embodiment of the family's pride and identity (Zellweger et al., 2013). The family's values and identity can benefit the company by becoming part of its brand and culture. The point is that it is important that there is a close identity fit between the identity and culture of the family and the firm, and in particular the family's reputation and that of the company.

Kets de Vries et al. (2007) take this further by pointing out that there can be a conflict between the values and beliefs of the owners and the managers within a business. Owners tend to be interested in financial capital: business performance, dividends and wealth creation. Managers are employees and tend to be concerned with strategy, social capital (professional reputation) and emotional capital (career opportunities, bonuses, fairness) – not the SEW that interests family members. Kets de Vries et al. propose what they call the three circle model of authority within the firm: family, owners and management. In this model, roles can overlap and cause conflict between individuals. Only the founder or senior family member may hold all three roles, in which case they must resolve the conflicts within themselves (see Figure 17.2).

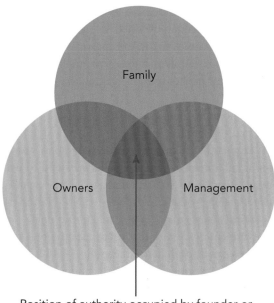

Position of authority occupied by founder or
senior family member involved in the firm

Figure 17.2 Three circle model of authority

 ## Case insight   Ferrero

Values and beliefs

In 2015 Italy's richest man, Michele Ferrero, head of the Ferrero family whose fortune was estimated by *Forbes* magazine to be £14.9 billion, died at the age of 89 in his Monaco home. Not only was he head of the family, he was also head of the Ferrero Group. The company was founded by Pietro Ferrero and his wife Piera in the Italian Alba region in Piedmont in the immediate post-war years. They produced a chocolate bar which included nougat and hazelnuts and called it *pasta gianduja*. The same basic recipe is used today for its famous Nutella chocolate spread, to which Michele added liqueur to make the famous Ferrero Rocher chocolate. Other brands owned by the company include Kinder and Mon Cheri.

The company is the fifth-largest sweet maker in the world, with over 22,000 workers and a turnover in excess of €8 billion. It is registered in Amsterdam but employs 22,000 workers in 11 factories around the world. The family has lived in Brussels now for over 30 years. They are obsessively secretive and Michele has been described as an autocrat with a paternalistic management style. It has never held a press conference and does not allow media visits to its plants. Ferrero's products are made with machines designed by an in-house engineering department

The company follows a number of core principles outlined on its website, which include 'loyalty and trust', 'respect and responsibility' and 'integrity and sobriety'. Every 29 June, Ferrero executives attend church in San Domenico to honour the day the company was founded. Every three years Ferrero organizes a pilgrimage to Lourdes for all its 22,000 workers. How the company might change after Michele's death is still unclear.

❏ Visit the website: www.ferrero.com

QUESTION:

1 What factors influence a family in deciding whether or not to sell off a family business when the head of the family and its business dies?

The emotion-based family culture operates at a subconscious level. There are deep emotional ties that create love, trust and loyalty; but equally there can be disruptive influences like divorce, rivalry between siblings or conflict between a parent and son or daughter. While families are based on permanence and stability, entrepreneurial firms are based on opportunity and change. Even the positive influences of the family may be bad for the business, for example, when parental pride and loyalty gets in the way of objectivity and a son or daughter is appointed to a management

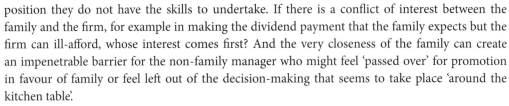

position they do not have the skills to undertake. If there is a conflict of interest between the family and the firm, for example in making the dividend payment that the family expects but the firm can ill-afford, whose interest comes first? And the very closeness of the family can create an impenetrable barrier for the non-family manager who might feel 'passed over' for promotion in favour of family or feel left out of the decision-making that seems to take place 'around the kitchen table'.

Family culture even influences the management style within a family firm. Research by Ram and Holliday (1993) suggested that family firms tend to adopt a style of 'negotiated paternalism', although Alderson (2011) argued that it changes as one generation succeeds another. Because of the relationships between family members, family businesses tend to use fewer formal management techniques. Family influence acts to dilute managerial power and discretion, with family members often able to negotiate their duties. In the researchers' opinion this can constrain operating efficiency and lead to management practices that are 'sub-optimal'.

So, while generally it is the family culture that influences the business (Denison et al., 2004; Fletcher et al., 2012), business can also influence the culture within the family. Indeed, business can exact a toll on family life. The separation between the two can become very blurred in a family firm. Building a successful business can become an obsessive, single-minded occupation that drives family life into the shadows, creating tensions at home as well as at work. Married couples working together may feel unable ever to 'get away from the shop' and let the stress and tension of growing a business damage their personal relationship. Conflict at work – and there will be conflict in any growing business – may continue at home, feeding on itself and intensifying. A husband and wife team that divorce will find it difficult to continue working together. To survive, a family must learn to separate family and business life. Business and family issues need to be addressed directly, but in an open and balanced way that allows the business to be run properly while not disrupting family harmony. This is not always easy.

Case insight   Mars Inc.

Family and business values

Mars is the seventh-largest private company in the USA. The company is home to global food brands such as Mars, Milky Way, Snickers, Twix and M&Ms as well as Whiskas, Pedigree and Uncle Ben's. It is a second- (arguably third-) generation family firm – a family that is one of the richest in the world. Founded by Forrest Mars Sr, who died in 1999, it is now governed by a board of directors made up of Mars family members and advisors and run by a global management team led by President and CEO Paul S. Michaels. Forrest Mars Sr was born into a confectionery-making family in 1904. His father, Frank, ran a modestly successful business in Minnesota where he made buttercream candies overnight and his wife, Ethel, sold them from a trolley the next day. They had two main products, the Mar-O-Bar and

Victoria Butter Creams, which became successful in 1923 when Woolworths started distributing them.

Forrest Mars Sr claimed that the idea for the family's first really successful product, the Milky Way, came to him while sitting drinking a chocolate malt drink in a cafe and he suggested to his father that he should put it into a chocolate bar. Some time later, his father did just that, putting caramel on top and chocolate around it. Milky Way was a huge success with sales of $800,000 in its first year. The family moved to Chicago and Frank built a mansion in Wisconsin. However, relations between father and son deteriorated as Forrest wanted further growth and expansion but Frank wanted to settle for an easy life.

In 1932 Forrest left to set up a one-room chocolate business in Slough, England. He quickly produced a similar

Continued...

Continued from previous page...

product to Milky Way, calling it a Mars Bar, using creamier milk chocolate and a sweeter toffee filling. The Mars Bar is a very British product, unknown in the USA. The company returned to the USA in the late 1930s with the hugely successful M&Ms, the candy-coated chocolate 'that melts in your mouth, not in your hand'. Also in this period the company made the first moves into the European pet food industry by combining modern manufacturing techniques with nutritional science. In 1946 it applied modern manufacturing techniques to parboil rice and launched Uncle Ben's rice.

Mars Inc. is committed to remaining under private ownership. It is also a very secretive company. The founder, Forrest Mars Sr, was a recluse and his sons shun public life. They also live and work with a frugality that is in stark contrast to many modern firms. There are no company perks such as cars, reserved parking or executive toilets. Indeed, no one even has a private office. Memos are against company policy. Meetings take place 'as needed'. Elaborate presentations are seen as a waste of time. All employees must do their own photocopying, make their own telephone calls and travel economy class on planes. John and Forrest Jr even share a secretary with their sister, Jacqueline. All employees are known as 'associates' and are on first name terms. Everyone from the top to the bottom has to punch their timecards daily and receives a 10% bonus for punctuality.

A visit to the company website gives an impression of the strong culture within the organization. Words like 'ethical', 'honest', trust', 'pride', 'passion', and 'support' abound, as do phrases like 'we like being the best at what we do', 'we are passionate about how we do things and about quality' and 'I know that as a Mars associate I am ethical and have high standards'. The company is run according to a 24-page booklet which codifies Forrest Sr's management philosophy. These are called 'The five principles of Mars':

1   Quality – 'The consumer is our boss, quality is our work and value for money is our goal.'
2   Responsibility – 'As individuals, we demand total responsibility from ourselves; as associates we support the responsibility of others.'
3   Mutuality – 'A mutual benefit is a shared benefit; a shared benefit will endure.'
4   Efficiency – 'We use resources to the full, waste nothing and do only what we do best.'
5   Freedom. – 'We need freedom to shape our future; we need profit to remain free.'

❏ Visit the website: www.mars.com

QUESTIONS:

1   What are the benefits of the Mars philosophy to both the company and to its employees?
2   In your opinion, does the Mars philosophy replicate itself in its retail brand?
3   Mars is a US company but its products are sold in over 100 countries. Does the Mars philosophy resonate in your country? Explain why or why not.
4   How important is the Mars family in generating this philosophy? If Mars were to move out of family control, would its philosophy have to change?

Generational succession

Another problem for a family business is the issue of generational transition – the mechanisms by which business leadership, ownership and knowledge are passed from one generation to another. Most owner-managers in Europe want to keep their business in the family – 57% in Germany, 62% in Italy and 74% in Spain, according to a large-scale survey by Burns and Whitehouse (1996) – although this figure dropped to 32% in the UK where owner-managers preferred to sell the business, usually to a trade buyer, in order to make a capital gain. It also showed that most owner-managers who had inherited their business wanted to pass it on to their children. Once the business is passed on to the next generation there seems to be a strong emotional attachment to it. This is confirmed by another large-scale survey in the USA which showed that 88% of family-owned businesses believed the same family would control the business in five years (Family Business Institute, 2007).

However, there seems to be a mismatch between aspiration and reality. There is an old adage: 'from clogs to clogs in three generations' – meaning you might find wealth but

Bananastock

you can easily lose it all in three generations, and this is definitely true in relation to family firms. And despite the desire of many owner-managers to keep their business in the family with the passing of each successive generation, the chances of surviving the transition diminish. It has been estimated that both in the USA and UK less than a third of family businesses survive into the second generation, about 10% survive into the third generation and less than 5% into the fourth generation (Family Business Institute, 2014; Poutziouris and Chittenden, 1996). Succession is becoming an increasingly important issue in Asia because so many of the businesses there are relatively young and the issue is arising for the first time. Indeed, a large-scale study of 200 transfers of power in family-controlled companies listed on the Hong Kong, Singapore and Taiwan stock exchanges showed that these companies lost, on average, some 60% of their market value during the transition from one generation to another (Bennedsen and Fan, 2014).

De Massis et al. (2008) suggested that there is a chain of causation that results in an abortive succession attempt. They undertook an extensive literature search and listed the factors in Table 17.1 as most likely to prevent succession. These issues are many and various, and not always restricted to what we might call a family business.

Table 17.1 Factors likely to cause unsuccessful succession in a family business

> Low ability of potential successor(s)

> Dissatisfaction/lack of motivation of potential successor(s)

> Unexpected loss of potential successor(s)

> Personal sense of attachment of the incumbent with the business

> Unexpected, premature loss of the incumbent

> Incumbent's unforeseen remarriage, divorce, or birth of new children

> Conflicts/rivalries/competition in parent–child relationship

> Conflicts/rivalries/competition among family members

> Perils related to high "consensus sensitiveness" of the family business

> Lack of trust in the potential successor(s) by family members

> Lack of commitment to the potential successor(s) by family members

> Conflicts between incumbent/potential successor(s) and non-family members

> Lack of trust in the potential successor(s) by non-family members

> Lack of commitment to the potential successor(s) by non-family members

> Inability to sustain the tax burden related to succession

> Inability to find financial resources to liquidate the possible exit of heir(s)

> Inadequate financial resources to absorb the costs of hiring professional managers

> Change in the business performance

> Decrease in the scale of the business

> Loss of customers or suppliers/decline of the relationship between the potential successor(s) and customers or suppliers

> Not clearly defining the roles of the incumbent and the successor(s)

> Not communicating and sharing the decisions related to the succession process with family members and other stakeholders

> Incorrectly evaluating the gaps between needs and potential successor's abilities

> Late or insufficiently exposing potential successor(s) to the business

> Not giving the potential successor(s) sufficient feedback about the succession progress

> Not formalizing rational and objective criteria for selection

> Not defining the composition of the team in charge for the assessment of potential successor(s)

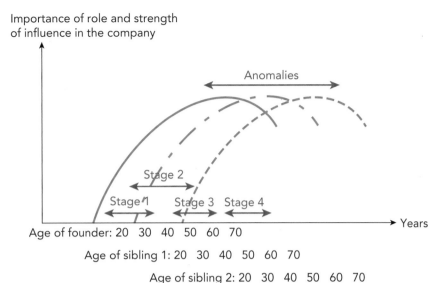

Importance of role and strength
of influence in the company

Figure 17.3 The family business life cycle

Source: Churchill, N. and Hatten, K. (1997), 'Non-Market-Based Transfers of Wealth and Power: A Research Framework for Family Business', *Family Business Review*, 10: 53-67. With permission from SAGE publications

Churchill and Hatten (1997) developed a four-stage model that shows generational succession over three generations (Figure 17.3). This provides a framework that shows the family dynamics during the process of succession and transfer of power from one generation to another. It suggests that changes in management, strategy and control can be planned and executed over the four stages, but are shaped by family relationships and driven by the inexorable human life cycle. In the model the life cycle of three generations is expressed as the level of influence a family member has on the strategic orientation and operations of the business, during the phases of family business development.

Stage 1: Owner-managed business
This is the early stage, beyond start-up, when the founder is in control but a son or daughter is introduced into the business on a permanent basis.

Stage 2: Training and development of the new generation
This is the stage where decisions are made, although not always formally, about passing the business on to the son or daughter and a process of training and development should be taking place to groom them for their role.

Stage 3: Partnership
This is the stage when the son or daughter shows sufficient business acumen and expertise that the founder starts to loosen the reins of control, delegates authority and starts to share responsibility with them.

Stage 4: Power transfer
This is the phase when strategic planning, management control and operational responsibility shifts from one generation to another. The succession process accelerates as the founder begins the retirement process and reduces their active participation in the business.

This four-stage model repeats, with increasing complexity as new generations join the firm. The problems arise as one generation hands over to another – the areas marked as 'anomalies' in Figure 17.3. It is here that there is conflict within the family and here that there is the greatest danger facing the business. Alderson (op. cit.) reports that decision-making within the firm changes as each generation succeeds another. The founder makes decisions themselves. The second generation tends to be more consultative. And by the third generation, decision-making is more consensual, with other members of the family influencing the outcome.

It's an Asian way of working. We are all focused on what we are doing and we are working for succession. It's all in the family. We are not growing the business for an exit route.

Bharat Sha, founder, Sigma Pharmaceuticals, *Kenyan Jewel* (www.alusainc.wordpress.com)

You have to prove yourself more when it's a family business. You have to show that you are serious about your job and about your career. You only get respect by working alongside people and not being just the boss's daughter.

Zeeat Noon, daughter of the founder Noon Products, *Family Business*, The Story Centre for Family Business, 8(1), 20

I know a lot about the mistakes that my father made with me. I'm not going to make [them] with my children. He was always extremely worried that I'd make a mistake so he never really gave me any authority. Until I did have a lot of authority – when, if you made mistakes, you make big ones. So with my daughters, I've given them authority in the areas they control. They have the respect of the people in the company.

Rocco Forte, founder, Rocco Forte Hotels, *The Sunday Times*, 30 November 2014

Relationships with siblings

The succession from one generation to the next is the most likely point of conflict in the family business. And although daughters are being brought increasingly into the family business, the most common form of succession is still from father to son. Many father–son relationships can work extremely well, but psychologists tell us that this relationship has a unique potential for conflict. If you revisit the personal qualities likely to be present in the entrepreneurial founder, detailed in Chapter 3, you will realise that an entrepreneur is likely to have a very close emotional link with the business. A male entrepreneur is likely to see it as an extension of himself, a symbol of his achievement, even an extension of his masculinity. He may guard power jealously and have problems with delegation. He may want to facilitate his son's succession but he may also want to control it. Subconsciously he may feel the need to be stronger than, and in control of, his son, and succession may be seen as a 'threat' to his masculinity. This can result in rivalry between father and son, each trying to be the dominant character.

From the son's perspective things are different. We are told that rebellion is natural in youth but, although it is tolerated and sometimes encouraged at home, at work it is something that is normally repressed. Even in its mildest form, this natural tendency will show itself in an increasing drive for independence from father. But if father is also the boss, there is potential for conflict, particularly if father is himself having problems delegating control. So the scene is set with a rebellious son, pressing for more power within the firm, seemingly opposed by a father who, at the same time, is saying that he wants to pass the business on to the son. To the son, the father may appear to be hanging on to power and he may begin to doubt whether father really will retire. In fact, he may even begin to distrust his father, and that is the start of the end of the relationship. At the very least, the contradictory signals from the father are likely to lead to frustration in the son. What is more, for the son the option of leaving the business is problematic as it might be seen as disloyalty to the family.

Levinson (1983) described how fathers often try to avoid conflict. For example, they might cultivate an atmosphere of ambiguity in decision-making where rules and boundaries are unclear and they can 'meddle' – in this way avoiding any overt conflict. Alternatively, they may defer decisions until the last possible moment, continually putting off the time for conflict. The father seeks to avoid the business conflict because he does not want to harm his family relationship with his son. However, conflict is rarely best handled through avoidance, and putting off an important business decision is usually a very bad idea.

Leach (op. cit.) claimed that father–daughter relationships are less problematic. Fathers seem more able to accept advice about the business and some criticism from daughters, and they often say that they would react to sons saying the same thing as if it were a personal attack. He observes that fathers do not feel threatened by daughters, and daughters are more accommodating, being brought up to be more nurturing, attuned to emotional needs and giving priority to family harmony. Perhaps that is changing.

Despite the growing importance of women in business, there is little research into mother–son relationships in the family firm, and even less mother–daughter relationships. We know next to nothing about the influences of an extended family (except in the context of ethnicity) or the development of new forms of families, such as those based upon gay relationships. Indeed, the assumed relationship in most of the literature is that of a patriarchal hierarchy. Perhaps the future will see a redefinition of the term 'family business'.

There can be yet another layer of complexity to the problems facing the family firm, this time caused by sibling

IMAGESOURCE

rivalry. Sibling rivalry is normal, but some parents actively encourage it, particularly in the context of the family firm. If a number of sons and/or daughters work in the firm, there may be rivalry between them as they vie for favour in the eyes of the father or mother. The custom of favouring elder sons with respect to inheritance, although in decline, still shows itself when it comes to succession in the family firm. Elder sons may be favoured at the expense of daughters or younger sons who may be more able. This can lead to the best talent leaving the family business or the brothers or sisters trying to carve out niches for themselves in the business to establish their independence. Even if the business is split equally between the children, there is the danger of sibling rivalry becoming institutionalized in the firm.

 ## Case insight   Alex Ramsay

Working with the family

In 1965 Alex Ramsay invited his three sons to work for the manufacturing firm he had set up in Sussex. He gave them and his three daughters large shareholdings in the business. But Alex did not find sharing control easy and the eldest son, William, left in frustration. Alex died in 1988. At this point William returned, insisting that, as the eldest son, he should become managing director. The others reluctantly complied, but his management style and free spending ways soon brought conflict. And when evidence of 'sharp business practice' came to light, his brothers used their shareholdings to suspend him. One of the other brothers, Charles, explained what happened next:

'William decided that if he wasn't to run the company, then nobody would. My elder sister sided with William and they demanded to be bought out – in cash – assuming that the business would have to be sold or split up as a result. But we re-mortgaged the company's property, sold some assets and managed to save the company … It's sad. There were lots of things we could have done to stop the tensions becoming so damaging. We just got it badly wrong.' (*The Sunday Times*, 25 May 2003)

Since then the business has recovered but the two sides of the family are still not speaking.

QUESTION:
1 Do families and business really mix? Explain.

Relationships across the family

All businesses must adapt and change to meet the demands of a changing marketplace, but there is a danger that family firms will become moribund and unable or unwilling to respond with each succeeding generation. Many firms do, of course, adapt. However, some become increasingly introverted – becoming inward-looking, unresponsive to messages from the marketplace and unreceptive to new ideas. They might even become unwilling to recruit managers from outside the firm or, worse still, from outside the family. How does this come about?

It is not surprising that, as the size of the family increases with each succeeding generation, the tensions and the complexity of the problems that the family business faces can increase. Families can become distracted from business for a number of reasons. Disagreement between family members might paralyse decision-making within the firm. Avoidance behaviour in the extreme might lead to important business issues not being addressed. Damage done to the firm and relationships within it by the traumatic succession from one generation to another might leave it weak and, like the rabbit caught in the headlights of the car, traumatized. The past success of the firm which has led to increased prosperity for the family might itself cause problems. The family might start to regard the firm as their main store of wealth, demanding regular dividends when the firm can ill-afford them, imposing restrictions on commercial decisions that reflect their risk aversion or vetoing capital investment decisions because it would drain cash flow. The family might also start to view the firm as a cash cow, draining the cash away through expense accounts, pensions, cars and other perks or 'jobs for the family'. Borrowings might be vetoed because the family do not want their main store of wealth and source of income to be exposed to any form of risk or the possibility that they might lose control. All of these things damage the business and can mean that it is not doing what it is supposed to do, that is, profitably generate goods and services.

Case insight   J&B Wilde and Sons

Adapting to change

The family business of J&B Wilde and Sons has had a stall in Manchester's New Smithfield Fish Market for 100 years. However, it has had to adapt and change in order to stay in business. Originally, it sold British white fish, made popular with the growth of fish and chip shops. Today British white fish is hard to find, fish and chip shops are in decline and the family has had to develop new products and find new customers just to survive. Many years ago it started selling chicken, mainly to Indian restaurants in the area. It still sells fish, but most fish is now foreign, flown in from around the world, and it is now sold filleted. J&B Wilde has also developed a reputation for stocking a wide variety of 'exotic' fish which are sold mainly to Chinese restaurants. Fish has now become a food that is susceptible to fashions and fads, and the family have to keep on top of market trends.

QUESTION:

1 Why has have J&B Wilde survived for so long?

The interests of the family are often seen as coming first in the family firm. However, what those interests might be can differ from one member of the family to another, and the larger the family, the greater the potential for different views. How these views might influence the business – both formally and informally – depends on the relationships within the family but, as we shall see in the next section, there are ways that these conflicts can be resolved in a more pragmatic and objective fashion than just relying on family politicking and in-fighting.

The problems facing the family firm can be compounded by a sense of alienation felt by non-family members as they see cash being squandered and no decisions or bad decisions being made. The continuous politicking and family in-fighting may make them feel uneasy and unsure about the future direction of the firm. They may feel forced to take sides when they do not wish to. They may feel that they are not part of the decision-making at all or that family considerations are always paramount. They may feel passed over for promotion in favour of less able family members. They might feel that there is no system for adequately rewarding them for the good work they do, for example, by taking some equity in the firm, because the family would not countenance losing control. Indeed, the family might actively discourage or prohibit the employment of non-family managers.

Many of these issues come down to the business no longer having clear leadership. Second-generation firms might have a board comprising three brothers or sisters each with equal shareholdings and none with clear control. Perhaps none of them possess the entrepreneurial spirit of the founder. They may even all hate each other and be unable to agree on anything. To compound the problem, shareholding might be diluted and distributed wider across an extended family. To avoid this catastrophe, family firms need ways of managing succession and resolving family conflict. The focus needs to shift from what the business can do for the family to what the family can do for the business, and two important questions need to be answered. Firstly, what special contribution can each member of the family make to the business? A family might have assets that can be leveraged to help the business. Apart from the personal qualities of family members, these might include strong family values or personal and business networks. Secondly, how can the business make best use of these contributions? By leveraging these family assets, the value of the business will be increased, as will the family store of wealth.

Case insight   Littlewoods

Family squabbles

The one-time UK national retail chain and pools operator Littlewoods was set up by Sir John Moores and his brother, Cecil, in Liverpool in the 1920s. Sir John died in 1993. By then the Moores family had multiplied and, now into the third generation, there were some 40 family shareholders. After his death, bitter arguments broke out within the family which are credited with damaging the expansion of the business. In 1996, family relationships deteriorated so much that an external chair and chief executive was brought in to try to save the business. The rows finally came to an end in 2002 when the business was sold off to the Barclay brothers for £750 million. In 2005 it was sold off again and broken up. Today the name no longer exists on UK high streets.

QUESTION:

1 Why do tensions exist within families? How is this different from tensions within a business?

Bennedsen and Fan (2014) suggest that the importance of these family assets (e.g. personal qualities, values, networks etc.) and the barriers to using them (e.g. degree of family conflict, size of family legal constraints etc.) are key drivers of what *should* be the extent of family involvement in the business and its ownership structure. Figure 17.4 is based upon their work. It suggests that where the assets are important and the barriers low, then the firm can remain closely held with a strong involvement by the family in its day-to-day running. Even where the barriers are high, the family might still be involved in the management of the firm, even if it does not have control, for example because it has 'gone public' at some point. However, where the importance of the family asset is low and the barriers to ownership are high, then there is a strong incentive for the family to sell or dilute its ownership. Even where the barriers are low there will be an incentive to dilute ownership or, at the least, bring in external management.

In addition, how external management reacts to the complexity of the family firm is also a factor. Where the importance of the family asset is high, the role of external management may well be diminished and in any family firm the process of conflict resolution is likely to be political, with the external manager feeling that they are not part of the family decision-making. Non-family members can feel marginalized and undervalued. There is therefore the need to evaluate the performance of all staff objectively and reward and promote family employees strictly in line

	Low	**High**
High	External management and/or ownership	Family management but diluted ownership
Low	Family ownership but external management	Family ownership and management

Barriers to use (degree of family conflict, size of family legal constraints etc.)

Importance of family assets (personal qualities, values, networks etc.)

Figure 17.4 Influences on the family business

with their contribution to the firm. Being a member of the family should not be part of the criteria for promotion or appointment and delegation outside the family should be taking place regularly for sound commercial reasons. In other words, the culture of the family business needs to firmly emphasize business.

Case insight   Everards Brewery

The family constitution

Everards Brewery is a family company that was founded in Leicestershire in 1849. It brews beers such as Tiger Best Bitter, Beacon Bitter and Original from its Castle Acre site near Leicester, and has a pub estate of over 170 units. The fifth-generation chair is Richard Everard. He sees himself as the 'custodian' of the family assets in the business. The family objectives are the driving force behind the philosophy and resulting strategy of the firm. When Richard became chair he sat down with the family, outlined the objectives and set about changing the business strategy to reflect them. Now the emphasis is on property and brewing accounts for only 30% of turnover.

'After five generations, 90 per cent of the shares are held by only two family members ... There is a rule

that only one family member can have an executive position on the board in any one generation ... We do not offer share options to attract senior people. That would be against our philosophy ... I see my custodianship lasting another twenty years, but should anything happen to me I have left clear instructions on how the next generation should be trained for the position. This would include at least four years of external training.' (*Family Business*, The Story Centre for Family Business, 7(3), 1999)

❑ Visit the website: www.everards.co.uk

QUESTIONS:

1 How much of Everards' longevity might be because it has only two principle shareholders? Explain.

Family businesses have a high potential for conflict, and the ability to highlight where this may arise, its causes and how it might be resolved is important. Indeed, many consultancies offer related specialist services to family firms. One of the techniques used to highlight points of conflict and their causes is the **genogram** (see Practice insight). Chapter 18 gives you an insight into how people can behave in situations involving conflict.

 Practice insight Genograms

The genogram to the right is an organizational chart of a family that shows not only the hereditary links but also the relationships (close, conflicting etc.) as well as personal details of individuals (medical history, addictions etc.). It is used alongside the family tree to show hereditary patterns and psychological factors that might influence family dynamics that might influence family social and emotional relationships and behaviours. It can often highlight points of conflict. Using its own set of symbols and with related genealogy software, it is a useful tool often used by family therapists and consultants for understanding relationship patterns within the family, particularly when trying to resolve dysfunctional or problematic behaviour. Genograms were first developed by Monica McGoldrick and Randy Gerson in 1985 (*Genograms in Family Assessment*).

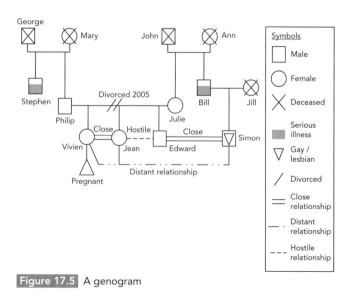

Figure 17.5 A genogram

Resolving conflict: the family constitution

Arguably, the only real way to resolve conflict in the family firm is to resolve conflict in the family itself– a very tall order indeed. However, restricting ourselves to business, the key to conflict resolution is communication and, as we shall see in Chapter 18 when we look at the Thomas–Kilmann conflict modes framework (page 479), the appropriate style is one of 'collaboration' or 'compromise'. Admitting and, most importantly, understanding the nature and cause of the problem is a good first step – and the genogram should help with this. Understanding that many of the problems come from our genetic make-up should help to defuse the situation and make it less personal. Understanding how individuals naturally react to conflict – using the Thomas–Kilman framework – can help to explain why arguments happen. With a will, behaviours can be modified. With particularly difficult situations a third-party facilitator – a friend or family therapist or mediator – might help. However, the British are known for avoiding sensitive personal and family issues and difficulties.

Kets de Vries et al. (op. cit.) say that the family needs to identify the issues they face, develop strategies to deal with them and create narratives or family stories that explain their emotional dimensions. Leach (op. cit.) advocates the development of a family strategic plan which should be articulated in a written constitution that sets out the family's values and policies in relation to the business. He advocates a four-stage process:

1   Addressing the critical issues relating to family involvement in the business. This involves looking at the business and the family and how they relate to each other. How are conflicts between family and business interests to be resolved?
2   Establishing a family council to provide a forum in which members can air their views and participate in policy-making. The council should develop ground rules as to how it should operate.
3   Drawing up a family constitution. This is a written statement of the family's values and beliefs and its policies and objectives in relation to the business. Does the family have any shared values and beliefs in relation to the business? What does the family want from the business? What is the involvement of the family to be? Does the family wish to retain control of the firm? What should be the criteria for family entry into the firm? What is the management succession policy? Should family members who are active in the business be treated differently from those who are not? Who might own shares in the business and how might shares be disposed of? What should the dividend policy be?
4   Monitoring the family's progress and maintaining communication within the family through regular council meetings. If there is disagreement or conflict, the family constitution can be used to help resolve it.

 Practice insight Family constitution checklist

A family constitution is a written document that sets out the family's values and policies in relation to the business. It should cover these eight areas:

1   Family values, beliefs and philosophy;
2   Family objectives in relation to the business;
3   Family involvement in the business – share ownership and disposal, voting and control;
4   Family involvement in the business – board membership, voting;
5   Family involvement in the business – selection of chair and managing director;
6   Family involvement in the business – jobs and remuneration;
7   Family council meetings;
8   Procedures for changing the family constitution.

Leach also advocates giving sons or daughters managerial autonomy within part of the business to help them grow and mature, separating out roles for other members of the family so as to minimize sibling rivalry. Many writers advocate the use of non-executive directors on the boards of family companies (see Chapter 9). They can be the insurance against a company becoming too introverted. They can bring balance to boardroom discussions and should be relied on to put the firm, not the family, first. In that sense they bring independence to meetings and can help resolve family squabbles. Alongside this they bring their own particular expertise and a new network of contacts.

 ## Case insight   Wates Group

Developing a family constitution

Wates Group (WG), based in Leatherhead, Surrey, is a fourth-generation family construction and land-trading business that was established in 1897 by Edward and Arthur Wates. In 2013 it had a turnover of almost £1 billion with net income of over £16 million and over 2,000 employees. The company can boast of both commercial success and longevity as a family business. This longevity is based upon a well thought-out and well-structured approach to family governance. This includes a family charter that forms the basis of the relationship between the voting shareholders and regular meetings of a family forum. As Andrew explains:

> 'Our success has been achieved by the ability to get an alignment between the professional management and the family. We have been in business for 110 years and have developed a family strategy as well as a business strategy.' (This Money, 10 June 2007, www.thismoney. co.uk)

WG is now owned by Wates Family Holdings (WFH), having recently bought back 40% of the shares in WG from two branches of the family. There is a clear legal separation between the two companies, and WFH also has some business interests other than WG. The WG board comprises seven members, including two family members and three non-executives. It is chaired by a non-family member, Paul Drechsler, who is chief executive and joined WG in 2004. The WFH board comprises six family members, two non-executive members and the director of the Wates Family Office. Five of the six family members also have roles with WG:

> Timothy Wates – Chair of WFH
> Andrew Wates – former Chair of WFH and WG
> James Wates – Deputy Chair of WG
> Jonathan Wates – Marketing Director and board member of WG
> Andy Wates – Managing Director of Wates Interiors
> Charlie Wates – Joint Managing Director of Needspace, a WG-managed workspace business

To achieve these structures, the family went through a strategy development process, spread over six months, involving all family members and professionally facilitated. The results started with a vision: 'Wates will be a world-class, family-owned and professionally managed enterprise, generating long-term stakeholder value.' To achieve this vision, the family focused on four things – the interface with WG, finance, co-investment and the family 'modus operandi'. At the heart of this was the need to diversify the wealth and income of the family away from WG and at the same time insulate WG from the worst influences of the family. The family tackled the issue of effective family governance structures by setting up a family council that meets regularly, a shareholder management committee that operates through WFH, and a charter that governs the family's relations with its trading activities through WFH. Succession planning is based upon encouraging the best of the next generation to succeed within WG. Progression is based on psychometrics, team building, personal development and coaching, supported by outside advisors.

> 'The family ... have grappled with their changing role from owner-managers to just owners – they have invested an enormous amount of time and effort into defining their roles and getting the transition just right. Through shunning the easy options they have developed a prescriptive governance model, which makes it easier for all parties to understand and execute their roles. We behave as a plc. Our governance structure looks and feels like that of a plc, with independent non-executive directors, an established audit, remuneration, nominations and risk committees. Although there is no legal or regulatory reason for organising ourselves in this way, it underpins our focus on growing shareholder value.' (Huw Davies, chief financial officer of WG, JP Morgan Family Business Honours Award for Overall Excellence, 2006.)

❑ Visit the website: www.wates.co.uk.

QUESTIONS:

1 Why has the family separated ownership and management of WG by setting up WFH?

2 What areas of dispute within the family might you anticipate?

3 Will WG always be effectively insulated from these disputes? If not, how might they be handled?

Succession planning

The usual approach to managing succession in a family business is to ignore the issue and do nothing. It is almost as if owner-managers, particularly founders, are in denial about ever leaving the firm. It is a blind spot that they do not wish to discuss – a little like death. They are reluctant to relinquish power and control; they fear that doing so will somehow reflect on them, diminishing their status, identity and masculinity. Sometimes planning involves making unwelcome decisions that might upset the family, particularly if it means selecting a successor from members of the family. Founders often fear retirement – the lack of activity, purpose, status, independence – and often typical entrepreneurs are so single-minded that they do not have other outside interests. However, if succession is not planned and managed it can be a traumatic and stressful event which might threaten the very existence of the firm.

Figure 17.3 provided a framework for considering the appropriate models for ownership and management of a family business – and therefore planning for succession. Actually keeping the business within the family is just one of the options open to the founder or family. If external management and ownership is appropriate, then the options – outlined in detail in Chapter 16 – are:

> **Floating the business on a stock market ('going public') or selling existing shares.** This can be problematic, especially if there is no established leadership within the firm, and it requires careful succession planning to ensure that the company continues to operate successfully after the float. What is more, once the firm has gone public there is the issue of how the family might protect its own interests and the values of the firm from those of institutional investors, particularly hedge funds. This was particularly the case in the controversial hostile takeover by the US food giant Kraft of the UK chocolate maker Cadbury – a company that had been in family hands for over 180 years. However, once a company has gone public, there may be a ready market for its shares and a divided family might be tempted to dilute its ownership even further.

> **Trade sale.** This may be attractive if cash is needed for retirement or other family reasons. It might also be just the right time to get a very good deal, for example because of consolidation in the industry. It might simply be that the business has become less attractive or more risky than when the founder set it up and there are better new opportunities for children.

> **Management buy-out.** If there is a strong management team in the firm they might be interested in bidding for the firm if they can arrange funding.

> **Management buy-in.** An external management team might be persuaded to bid for the firm, again as a going concern. There is little research on family firm buy-outs and buy-ins, but Wright and Kellermanns (2011) report that there is anecdotal evidence that these often fail because of the loss of family's tacit knowledge.

> **Liquidate.** In extremis, it may be impossible to find a buyer. Liquidation is usually the least attractive option as the price for the assets will not reflect any goodwill.

If external management is to be sought but ownership retained in the family, then there are two options:

> **Appoint a professional manager.** With this option the family remains as shareholders and probably non-executive directors, receiving dividends and hoping to see the value of the business grow.

> **Appoint a caretaker manager.** If the founder or family wishes to pass on the firm but the son or daughter is too young or inexperienced, they may appoint a caretaker manager to see the firm through until such time as the next generation is ready to take on the role.

In both cases there must be mechanisms in place to resolve family conflict and provide the professional manager with sufficient autonomy to manage the business effectively.

If the business is to be maintained within the family, then succession will need careful planning. Who should be the successor? Do they possess the necessary skills and temperament? If not, can they be developed through training and experience within the available time frame? What is the role of the rest of the family? What are the financial, tax and pension consequences? The issues that need to be addressed may seem endless. To help approach the task systematically, Leach (op. cit.) made eight recommendations:

1 **Start planning early.** The most successful successions are those that involve the next generation early in the process so as to allow them to grow into the role rather than coming as an unexpected 'event'.

2 **Encourage inter-generational teamwork.** It is important that all issues surrounding the succession are addressed and agreed by all the next generation, not just the chosen successor.

3 **Develop a written succession plan.** This is an action plan setting down what has to be done, by whom and when. It will include details of the founder's reducing involvement and the successor's expanding role and responsibilities. It should also address the structure of the management team.

4 **Involve the family and colleagues in your thinking and, when complete, show them the succession plan.** This is about communication and getting commitment everyone to the plan.

5 **Take advantage of outside help.** Succession has important financial, tax and pension consequences for the founder and the family. Consulting the firm's accountant and lawyer early in the process is vital.

6 **Establish a training process.** The plan should lay out how the successor is expected to develop the skills needed to take over the firm and over what time frame. This might involve education and training as well as job or work experience.

7 **Plan for retirement.** The owner-manager needs to be prepared financially and emotionally for retirement. Retirement will bring lots of free time and entrepreneurs, particularly, like to keep on the go.

8 **Make retirement timely and unequivocal.** When the timetable for succession is set, it is important to stick to it and not hang on in the job. The longer the founder has run their business, the greater the likelihood that they will want a role after transition. Sonnenfield (1988) characterized the founder as typically having four exit styles, the last two having a more positive effect on the business:

> *Monarchs*: who do not leave the business until they are forced out through ill-health, death or a palace revolt;

> *Generals*: who leave the business, but plot a return and quickly do so 'to save the business';

> *Ambassadors*: who leave the business quickly and gracefully, frequently to serve as post-retirement mentors;

> *Governors*: who rule for a limited term and then turn to other activities to gain fulfilment.

Despite their current importance, it could be that the future will see a decline in the number of family businesses passing down from one generation to the next. The breakdown of family networks, increasing demands for capital that families cannot supply, booming stock markets which makes obtaining a stock market listing attractive – all these factors may mean that more and more companies are sold-on rather than passed-on. However, even today the high proportion of owner-managers still wishing to pass-on their business to the next generation contrasts strongly with the proportion actually succeeding in doing so.

 ## Case insight   Timberland

Selling-on

Started in Abington, Massachusetts, USA, in 1952 by the Swartz family as a boot manufacturer, until 2011 Timberland was a third-generation family firm. Timberland is a strong retail brand that has extended its product range from durable outdoor footwear to include outdoor clothing and it also has opened a number of prominently-sited retail outlets selling its boots and other branded products. But the business was also famously based on strong ethical

Continued...

Continued from previous page...

foundations. It had a strong commitment to CSR which it said was 'grounded in the values that define our community: humanity, humility, integrity and excellence'.

Until 2011 Jeff Swartz was president and chief executive, and his father Sidney was still in post as chair. Like his family, Swartz is an orthodox Jew and the values of the business reflected those of the family and its religion. It had a motto: 'Doing good by doing well', stating that 'community has been synonymous with the ethic of service – the desire to share our strength for the common good. Our approach to building and sustaining strong communities includes civic engagement, environmental stewardship and global human rights.' As Swartz said:

'Investment in the community is important to me because this is a family company. It's not just because my grandfather and my father grew up on the factory floor but because I did too. Workers' health and safety, for instance, isn't just an ideal. It's as visceral to me as the missing fingers on my grandfather's hand.' (The Times, 29 May 2004)

'I have faith in the entrepreneurial system, we will innovate or perish … There are health and safety standards, those too have costs. And you know what? Business has figured out a way to make profits while respecting that social policy. The same is true about the cost of carbon … you can hide behind an economic crisis and say that business can't afford any more pressure but first of all it's not true, second it's disingenuous.' (The Sunday Times, 22 November 2009)

Timberland cared about its employees. They got one week of paid volunteer time a year, and enjoyed such perks as a $3,000 subsidy to buy a hybrid car. *Fortune* magazine has long recognized the company as one of best companies to work for. Timberland believed that these values reinforced the brand, because customers care about the same things as the company.

However, the company faced increasingly competitive markets and rising materials costs at a time of recession, and, with its operating margins falling to just 9% in 2010, it reported a 30% drop in first-quarter profits in 2011 and the share price started to tumble. In 2011 Timberland was sold to VF Corporation for $2 billion in cash – a 40% premium on the share price. VF owns a range of well-known brands such as Wrangler, The North Face, Vans, Reef, Jansport and Eastpak. And, unusually, the share price of VF rose by 10% when the deal was announced, so the stock market seemed to think that the deal was a good one.

We still do not know all the reasons for the family deciding to sell its shares in Timberland, but it is interesting that Swartz did not negotiate a contract to stay on either as CEO or as an advisor. VF says it intends to grow sales and make the company more efficient (VF's operating margin is about 20%). By 2013 turnover had risen to $1.6 billion. As to whether the strong ethical policy and commitment to CSR will continue, that remains to be seen.

❑ Visit the website: www.timberland.com

QUESTIONS:

1 Why might a family have decided to sell the business it had run for three generations?

2 What are the potential synergies that the stock market might have identified in this acquisition?

3 Why might VF decide to maintain or to change Timberland's ethical policy and commitment to CSR?

⊃ Summary

> Family business is the oldest and most common form of any business organization in the world. Although there are a number of legal definitions, they might be defined simply as an organization in which decision-making is influenced by multiple generations of a family. Many of today's best-known public companies started life as family firms and still have relationships with the founding family. Familial brands build consumer loyalty over long periods which can be a very valuable asset to the family and the firm.

> Starting up as a family business can be attractive because of the emotional support and helping hands that may not expect to be paid. As they grow, family firms can foster loyalty, responsibility, long-term commitment – not least to ethical standards, and a pride in 'the family tradition'. These virtues are often welded into a desire to transfer the business from one generation to the next and to preserve it in difficult financial times.

> At the heart of the family firm is the family culture – its values and beliefs. These can be based upon strong ethical or religious beliefs, but they can also be quite quirky. The family culture influences the culture of the business and can affect how it is managed.

> There is the potential for conflict here because family culture is essentially based on emotion – loyalty, caring and sharing – whereas business culture is unemotional – task-orientated and based on self-interest. The emotion-based family culture operates subconsciously and can get in the way of business.

❭ Family conflict and politics can result in the firm being neglected or business decisions being made for other than commercial reasons – the introvert firm which tries to ignore commercial reality. It can also mean that the firm is used as a cash cow for the family and loses its commercial edge.

❭ Succession in the family firm is often problematic and can itself lead to conflict. Founders tend to ignore succession until the last minute. Many of the problems stem from the entrepreneurial characteristics of the founder that include a reluctance to relinquish control of the business. Added to this there may be father–son rivalry as the son rebels or strives for independence within the firm. If there are more sons or daughters, then sibling rivalry can intensify the problem.

❭ Resolving conflict in a family business is often difficult. It requires accommodation or compromise. A genogram can help to understand the nature and underlying causes of the conflict. Ultimately, the best approach is to develop a family constitution and a family council to monitor it.

❭ Succession can be managed. Planning needs to start early and needs to be inter-generational, building in consultation with the firm's accountants and lawyers. A written succession plan should be developed which shows how the founder will exit and how the new generation will take over. It will detail any training and development needed and help the founder plan for retirement. Finally, when it is time to go, go!

✓ Activities

1 List the questions you would ask members of the family working in a family firm in order to highlight the advantages and problems of working there. Based upon these questions, interview members of the family and write an essay highlighting the advantages and problems of working in the family firm.

2 List the questions you would ask the manager of a second- or third-generation family firm in order to highlight the problems they encountered in taking over the firm. Based upon these questions, interview the manager and write an essay highlighting the problems they encountered.

3 Write a specimen family constitution.

4 Investigate the tax problems associated with succession in the family firm and how they might they be mitigated.

💬 Group discussion topics

1 What are the advantages and disadvantages of starting up a business with your partner or spouse?

2 What are the advantages and disadvantages of being part of a family firm?

3 How can the family contribute to making a start-up successful?

4 Familial brands build consumer trust over long periods and can be very valuable assets. Discuss.

5 Family firms are more common in most continental European countries than in Britain. Why do you think this might be?

6 How does national culture affect the desire to pass on a business as a going concern?

7 In the future, family firms will decline in importance. Discuss.

8 Does it matter how you define a family firm?

9 How might family and business cultures clash?

10 Why are there so many examples of successful family firms which are based on strong religious or ethical beliefs?

11 What are the problems you might face in being a non-family member running a family business?

12 What are the problems you might face in being a non-family employee in a family business?

13 What are the problems you might face in being the son or daughter of the founder employed in the family business?

14 How would you get on if you were working for your mother or father?

15 What are some of the underlying causes of conflict in a family and how might these show themselves in a family firm?

16 The family business sector is an endless soap opera of patriarchs and matriarchs, black sheep and prodigal sons, hubris and nemesis. Discuss.

17 What is an introvert firm? How might a business avoid becoming one?

18 How can succession be managed?

19 What do you think would be a good training programme for a son or daughter intending to take over the running of the family business?

20 From what you have read in this book about the gender of entrepreneurs, how might issues around gender affect succession?

21 In what circumstances might it be wise not to pass on the firm to a member of the family?

22 What should go into a family constitution? What are the advantages of having one?

☛ References

Alderson, K. (2011) *Understanding the Family Business*, New York: Business Expert Press.

Astrachan, J.H., Klein, S.B. and Smyrnios, K.X. (2002) 'The F-PEC Scale of Family Influence: A Proposal for Solving the Family Business Definition Problem', *Family Business Review*, 15(1).

Bennedsen, M. and Fan, J.P.H. (2014) *The Family Business Map: Assets and Roadblocks in Long Term Planning*, Basingstoke: Palgrave Macmillan.

Burns, P. and Whitehouse, O. (1996) *Family Ties*, 3i European Enterprise Centre, Special Report no. 10.

Chua, J.H., Chrisman, J. J. and Sharma, P. (1999) 'Defining the Family Business by Behavior', *Entrepreneurship Theory and Practice*, 23(4).

Churchill, N. and Hatten, K. (1997), 'Non-Market-Based Transfers of Wealth and Power: A Research Framework for Family Business', *Family Business Review*, 10: 53–67.

Clark, T. (2014) 'The Biggest Myth About Family Business', *Forbes*, available online at http://www.forbes.com/groupthink/2014/05/20the-biggest-myth-about-family-business/.

Craig, J. and Moores, K. (2006) 'A 10-Year Longitudinal Investigation of Strategy, Systems, and Environment on Innovation in Family Firms', *Family Business Review*, 19(1).

Davis, J.H., Allen, M.R. and Heyes, H.D. (2010) 'Is Blood Thicker than Water? A Study of Stewardship Perceptions in Family Business', *Entrepreneurship Theory and Practice*, 34(6).

De Massis, A., Chua, J.H. and Chrisman, J.J. (2008) 'Factors Preventing Intra-Family Succession', *Family Business Review*, 21.

Denison, D., Lief, C. and John, L. (2004) 'Ward Culture in Family-Owned Enterprises: Recognizing and Leveraging Unique Strengths' *Family Business Review*, 17(1).

Family Business Institute (2007) *Family Business in Transition: Data and Analysis*, Raleigh: Family Business Institute.

Family Business Institute (2014) *Succession Planning*, available online at http://www.familybusinessinstitute.com/index.php/Succession-Planning/.

Fletcher, D., Melin, L. and Gimeno, A. (2012) 'Culture and Values in Family Business – A Review and Suggestions for Future Research', *Journal of Family Business Strategy*, 3(3).

Gersick, K., Davis, J., Hampton, M.M. and Lansberg, I. (1997) *Generation to Generation*, Boston, MA: Harvard Business School Press.

Gomez-Mejia, L.R., Cruz, C., Berrone, P. and De Castro, J. (2011) 'The Bind that Ties: Socioemotional Wealth Preservation in Family Firms', *Academy of Management Annals*, 5(1).

Katchaner, N., Stalk, G. and Bloch, A. (2012) 'What You Can Learn from Family Business', *Harvard Business Review*, November.

Institute for Family Business (2011), *The UK Family Business Sector: Working to Grow the UK Economy*, Oxford Economics, November.

Kets de Vries, M., Carlock, R.S. and Florent-Treacy, E. (2007) *Family Business on the Couch: A Psychological Perspective Hardcover*, Chichester: John Wiley & Sons.

Leach, P. (1996) *The BDO Stoy Hayward Guide to the Family Business*, London: Kogan Page.

Levinson, H. (1983) 'Consulting with Family Business: What to Look For', *Organizational Dynamics*, Summer.

McCann, J.E., Leon-Guerrero, A.Y. and Haley, J.D. (2001) 'Strategic Goals and Practices of Innovative Family Businesses', *Journal of Small Business Management*, 39(1).

McGoldrick, M. and Gerson, R. (1985) *Genograms in Family Assessment*, New York: W.W. Norton.

Miller, D., Le Breton-Miller, I., Lester, R,H. and Cannella, A.A. (2007) 'Are Family Firms Really Superior Performers?', *Journal of Corporate Finance*, 13(5).

Nelton, S. (1986) *In Love and in Business*, New York: John Wiley & Sons.

Poutziouris, P. (1994) 'The Development of the Familia Business', in A. Gibb and M. Rebernick (eds), *Small Business Management in New Europe,* Proceedings of 24th ESBS – September, Slovenia, in *New Europe.*

Poutziouris, P. and Chittenden, F. (1996) *Family Businesses or Business Families*, Institute for Small Business Affairs and National Westminster Bank Monograph 1.

Ram, M. and Holliday, R. (1993) 'Relative Merits: Family Culture and Kinship in Small Firms', *Sociology*, 27(4).

Rosenblatt, P.C., de Mik, L., Anderson, R.M. and Johnson, P.A. (1985) *The Real World of the Small Business Owner*, San Francisco: Jossey-Bass.

Sonnenfield, J. (1988) *The Hero's Farewell: What Happens when CEOs Retire*, New York: Oxford University Press.

van Essen, M., Carney, M., Gedajlovic, E. and Heugens, P., (2015) 'How does Family Control Influence Firm Strategy and Performance? A Meta-Analysis of US Publicly Listed Firms', *Corporate Governance: An International Review*, 23(1).

Westhead, P. and Howarth, C. (2007) 'Types of Private Family Firm: An Exploratory Conceptual and Empirical Analysis', *Entrepreneurship and Regional Development*, 9.

Wright, M. and Kellermanns, F.W. (2011) 'Family Firms: A Research Agenda and Publications Guide', *Journal of Family Business Strategy*, 2.

Zellweger, T.M., Nason, R.S., Nordqvist, M. and Brush, C.G. (2013) 'Why do Family Firms Strive for Non-Finacial Goals? An Organizational Identity Perspective', Entrepreneurial Theory and Practice, 37(2).

 www.palgrave.com/Burns-Entrepreneurship-And-Small-Business-4e

Go online to access additional teaching and learning resources for this chapter on the companion website. Click here in the ebook to complete a multiple choice revision quiz for this chapter.

18 | FROM ENTREPRENEUR TO ENTREPRENEURIAL LEADER

Contents

- ⦿ *Practice insight*: 7 principles of communicating a vision

- ⦿ *Practice insight*: 5 ways to destroy a rich culture

- ⦿ *Practice insight*: Dealing with conflict situations

- ⦿ *Practice insight*: Are you a visionary leader?

- ⦿ *Practice insight reminder*: Characteristics of a good business idea

© Stockbyte Royalty Free Photos

Learning outcomes

When you have read this chapter and undertaken the related activities you will be able to:

> Understand the characteristics of how entrepreneurs manage;
> Describe the difference between management and leadership;
> Explain what the job of leader involves;
> Understand how culture can be created and influenced in an organization;
> Critically analyse the theories of leadership that have been proposed and their contribution to an understanding of how to lead an entrepreneurial organization;
> Understand and explain how leadership style can be tailored to different circumstances, and evaluate your preferred leadership style;
> Understand how conflict can be handled and evaluate how you handle it;
> Understand what is involved in entrepreneurial leadership.

 **Case insights**

| AirAsia (2) | Steve Jobs and Apple |

Differences between leadership and management

Studies on the personality traits of entrepreneurs have focused on their propensity to start and maintain a business successfully. Increasingly, however, the debate on entrepreneurship is moving to consider not only what the entrepreneur 'is' but what they actually 'do'. And successful entrepreneurs have a number of characteristic approaches to management, particularly as the business grows and becomes more complex. They face a constant struggle if they wish their business to continue to be entrepreneurial and they need to constantly adapt and change – not an easy task. But whilst they need to develop their managerial skills as the business grows, ultimately they need to metamorphose from an entrepreneur into an entrepreneurial leader. At the same time the business needs to operate in certain ways, adapting its structures and cultures as it grows to become more formalized but without becoming more bureaucratic. This chapter will highlight how entrepreneurs can become entrepreneurial leaders – extending the longevity of their organization. Chapter 19 will highlight how they might then ignite the spark of entrepreneurship within the organizations that they lead.

Leadership and management are different and distinct terms, although the skills and competencies associated with each are complementary. As we saw in Chapter 10, management is concerned with handling complexity in organizational processes and the execution of work. It is concerned with detailed planning, organizing, commanding, coordinating and controlling. It is about detail and logic, efficiency and effectiveness. It is linked to the authority given to managers within a hierarchy.

Leadership on the other hand is concerned with setting direction, communicating and motivating. It is about broad principles and emotion and less detail. If management is the head, leadership is the heart of an organization. It is therefore quite possible for an organization to be over-managed but under-led, or vice versa. An organization needs both good leadership and good management. In a start-up good leadership is essential, while effective management quickly becomes increasingly important to get things done. But good leadership is situation-specific.

Blank (1995) argues that leadership is an 'event' – a 'discrete interaction each time a leader and a follower join … Leadership can appear continuous if a leader manifests multiple leadership events.' However, some leaders are good in one situation but not others. Leaders can therefore have rollercoaster careers as they exhibit successful leadership characteristics at certain discrete times, in certain circumstances, with particular people, but these characteristics do not work when things change. They fail to adapt. Winston Churchill was widely acknowledged as a great war-time leader but a poor peace-time leader. Therefore, entrepreneurs might be good leaders at start-up but poor leaders as the business grows – unless they adapt and change their leadership style.

The one certain characteristic that separates leaders from other people is the obvious one that they have willing followers. Why is this? What is it about them that persuades others to follow them? The characteristics and personality traits of good leaders tell us a limited amount about good leadership. Leadership is not about who you are, it is more about what you do with who you are and how you form relationships with your followers. It is also group-, task- and situation- or context-specific. And, as we see later in this chapter, leadership style can be crafted to meet these changing circumstances. However, while it is too simplistic just to say that leaders have certain enduring character traits, some individuals can and do seem to emerge as leaders across a variety of situations and tasks. And this gives us some indications of the leadership characteristics and *behaviours* needed to lead an entrepreneurial organization. What is more, we are beginning to better understand the importance of a leader's personal cognitive abilities, motives, social skills, expertise and problem-solving skills. What emerges is a complex interaction of many factors that underlines that effective leadership is an art rather than a science – and it is very dependent upon the context. While we can isolate the main factors that influence it and point to good practice in particular contexts, there is no magic formula.

Defining the role of leader

Our traditional view of leaders is that they are special people – often charismatic 'heroes' like Churchill – who set direction, make key decisions and motivate staff, often prevailing against the odds at times of crisis. They have vision – something most entrepreneurs have aplenty. They are strategic thinkers and are effective communicators while still being able to monitor and control performance. Above all, they create the appropriate culture within the organization to reflect their priorities. Indeed, leadership is more about guiding vision, culture and identity than it is about decision-making. If there were ever a job description for a leader, therefore, it would probably include five elements:

Having a vision for the organization

This gives people a clear focus on the direction of the organization, the values it stands for and the key issues and concerns it faces in achieving its goals. Visions are underpinned by the values of the organization and the values are reflected in the culture of the organization. These issues were covered in Chapter 7. Having a strong vision, mission and values for an organization goes a long way towards developing a valuable brand as well as underpinning strong leadership.

Being able to develop strategy

It is one thing to know where you want to go, it is quite another to know how to get there. The heart of leadership is about being able to chart a course for future development that steers the organization towards the leader's vision. This is what strategy is about – linking various actions and tactics in a consistent way that forms a coherent plan. Your business plan gives you the strategy for how you will achieve your vision for this business. As we saw in Chapter 12, entrepreneurs have a different approach to strategy development. The reason for this lies at the heart of any entrepreneurial venture – the greater degree of risk and uncertainty it faces. To summarize their approach, it involves developing a strong vision but more particularly a strong 'strategic intent', accompanied by a loose or flexible strategy underpinned by continuous strategizing from which they create multiple strategic options.

Entrepreneurs go on to make decisions differently. In the same way as they develop strategy, they adopt an incremental approach to decision-making, despite their strong long-term vision. This is also part of their wide-ranging approach to risk mitigation. For example, they tend to keep capital investment and fixed costs as low as possible, often by subcontracting some activities. They tend to commit costs only after the opportunity has proved to be real, which may be prudent and reflect their resource limits but then they run the risk of losing first-mover advantage in the market place – a difficult judgement call. Frequently, therefore, they will experiment with a 'limited' launch into the market and learn from this. Successful entrepreneurs find ways of reconciling these issues – ways of developing strategy without overcommitting to one course of action and ways of minimizing their investment in resources.

Getty Images Thinkstock Images \ Digital Vision

Being able to communicate effectively (particularly the vision)

There is no point in having a vision for the organization unless you can communicate it effectively and it inspires and motivates staff. Staff need to understand how the vision will be achieved, and believe that they can achieve it, particularly in an uncertain world. They need to understand where the organization is going and the strategies that are being adopted to take it there. To be an effective leader, the entrepreneur needs to develop their interpersonal skills, although their ability to develop strong personal relationships indicates this is probably playing to one of their strengths. We shall return to this later in this chapter.

Creating an appropriate culture in the organization

The culture of an organization is the cement that binds it together. It influences how people think and how they act. Creating an appropriate culture for an entrepreneurial organization is probably the single most important thing a leader has to do and, although it is not an easy task, there are ways of building the culture of an organization and we shall return to this later in the chapter.

Managing and monitoring performance

Leaders still have to manage. You need to be a good leader *and* a good manager. You need to see the big picture *as well as* deal with the detail. These may be routine tasks but the leader is still expected to have a grasp of them.

As we highlighted in Chapter 8, entrepreneurs are good at developing relationship with customers, staff, suppliers and all the stakeholders in the business. They tend to manage their staff by developing strong personal relationships rather than relying on formal structures and hierarchies. Formality reduces flexibility, so they manage informally, setting an example by their behaviour. As we highlighted in Chapter 12, this reflects itself in the 'spider's web' organization structure often seen in SMEs. This ability to form strong personal relationships also helps them develop the external partnerships and networks that are part of the social capital they create. Relationships are based upon trust and respect and this takes time to build up. In order to develop these strong relationships entrepreneurs need strong interpersonal skills.

Underlying their approach to strategy development and management is how entrepreneurs approach risk. As we saw in Chapter 10, while entrepreneurs are prepared to take measured risks, they always want to keep them to a minimum. Typically, entrepreneurs adopt a number of approaches to mitigate risk. Primarily they do this through knowledge and information, often coming from the network of close personal relationships they have developed. They can also use this network to form partnerships that help them spread the risk of a venture, as well as leveraging the strategic skills of the partnership. They commit only limited resources – the resources they can afford to lose – to a new venture at any time and take an incremental approach to decision-making, assessing information and risks at each decision point. Finally, entrepreneurs are adept at compartmentalizing risk, for example by separating out business ventures into separate legal entities, so that the failure of one does not endanger the survival of the others.

This approach to risk management – using relationships to deliver information on which strategic and day-to-day decision are based while generally dealing with risk on a planned but incremental basis – is at the heart of entrepreneurs' approach to management and leadership.

Building a shared vision

So, the first task of leadership is to have vision, and building that shared vision is vital for an organization striving to succeed in a changing, uncertain world. It gives a sense of direction and helps develop organizational confidence. As Bartlett and Ghoshal (1994) explained:

> *Traditionally top-level managers have tried to engage employees intellectually through the persuasive logic of strategic analysis. But clinically framed and contractually based relationships do not inspire the extraordinary effort and sustained commitment required to deliver consistently superior performance . . . Senior managers must convert the contractual employees of an economic entity into committed members of a purposeful organization.*

In other words, vision is not just an antiseptic, logical concept. It is a vibrant, inspirational one. Good visions motivate. Two strong motivations for people are fear and aspiration. Fear is probably the strongest motivation, galvanizing action and forcing people to change, but it tends to have a limited life. It worked well for Winston Churchill in the Second World War, but not thereafter. However, aspiration – what we might become – has greater longevity and is altogether a more positive motivator. It is the one that underpins most entrepreneurial organizations. It emphasizes striving – a continuous journey of improvement.

Where there is shared ownership in a business it is important that the partners share and commit to the vision for the organization. As we noted in Chapter 8, the considerable research into what makes a successful partnership group has repeatedly shown the importance of cohesion and 'shared cognitions' – a shared vision but also effective communication and transfer of knowledge between partners. Shared cognition improves the quality of decision-making and the general performance of the business (Burgers et al., 2009; Smith et al., 2005; West III, 2007). However, conflict can arise because each member of the partnership team may have a tendency to select goals that optimize performance indicators defined by their respective professions, while imposing unfavourable effects on other partners' areas of responsibility (Jehn and Bendersky, 2003). This underlines the importance of partner selection, since building this shared cognition after launching the business can be difficult and is likely to take time. Indeed, resolving the almost inevitable conflict that is likely to arise between partners as major decisions are made can be a challenge that we return to later in the chapter.

Visions are living things that evolve over time. Developing the vision is a continuous process. It involves continually checking with staff to ensure that the vision has a resonance with them – modifying it little by little, if appropriate. Some entrepreneurial leaders can find this difficult and frustrating as they are more used to setting goals and seeking compliance. But to succeed as the organization grows leaders need to develop their listening as well as influencing skills.

Successful entrepreneurs have a strong vision for their start-up. However, having your own individual vision is relatively easy. Building that shared vision with staff as the organization grows is altogether more difficult. It is not simply about going off and writing a vision statement that you circulate to staff. Senge (1992) observed:

> Building a shared vision is important early on because it fosters a long-term orientation and an imperative for learning . . . Crafting a larger story is one of the oldest domains of leadership . . . leaders may start by pursuing their own vision, but as they learn to listen carefully to others' visions they begin to see that their own personal vision is part of something larger. This does not diminish any leader's sense of responsibility for the vision – if anything it deepens it.

One important way a leader can build a shared vision is by becoming a storyteller. Gardner (1995) maintained this was *the* key leadership skill. This storytelling skill can be either verbal or written, however, leaders must 'walk the talk' – model the behaviour they expect from others (Kouzes and Posner, 2007) – otherwise they have no credibility and are not believed. Gardner maintains that the most successful stories are simple ones that hit an emotional resonance with the audience, addressing questions of identity and providing answers to questions concerning personal, social and moral choices. Is it any wonder that entrepreneurs skilled at developing personal relationships can also become powerful leaders?

Senge (op. cit.) highlighted the creative tension this storytelling must create by contrasting the shared vision with a constantly updated view of current reality:

> The leader's story, sense of purpose, values and vision, establish the direction and target. His relentless commitment to the truth, and to inquiry into the forces underlying current reality continually highlight the gaps between reality and the vision. Leaders generate and manage this creative tension – not just themselves but in an entire organization. This is how they energize an organization. That is their basic job. That is why they exist.

This creative tension therefore acts as a motivator. Too little tension produces inertia but too much can create chaos. Get it right and you create the 'strategic intent' or *kosryoku* discussed in Chapter 7. It can be used for achieving ambitious goals by energizing the organization into learning how to achieve them.

Senge went on to underline how this tension can create within an entire organization the sense of internal locus of control that is part of the character traits of an entrepreneur – emphasizing the belief in control over destiny: 'Mastering creative tension throughout an organization leads to a profoundly different view of reality. People literally start to see more and more aspects of reality as something that they, collectively, can influence.' And this is one important psychological way that individuals within the entrepreneurial organization deal with the uncertainty they face. You might also recognize it as one aspect of 'empowerment' – a motivation for people to do 'the right thing' – whatever that might be – to resolve a problem or secure an opportunity for the good of the organization, even if it is not in their job description.

Leaders often inspire their followers to high levels of achievement by showing them how their work contributes to worthwhile ends – the sense of 'purpose' highlighted by Pink (2011) in Chapter 12. It is an emotional appeal to some of the most fundamental of human needs – the need to be important, to make a difference, to feel useful, to be part of a successful and worthwhile enterprise. And when the organization is successful it appeals to that third motivating sense – that of 'achievement'. All of which is amplified if the followers believe they have made a real contribution because of the 'autonomy' they have within the organization.

But entrepreneurial leadership that is to perpetuate itself is more than just charismatic leadership. Charismatic leaders deal in visions and crises, but little in between. Entrepreneurial leadership is about systematic and purposeful development of leadership skills and techniques within an organization – which can take a long time. It is about developing enduring relationships, commitment and loyalty. It is about creating long-term sustainable competitive advantage. And most of all it is about making the organization systematically entrepreneurial.

If there is a spark of genius in the leadership function at all, it must lie in the transcending ability, a kind of magic, to assemble … out of a variety of images, signals, forecasts and alternatives … a clearly articulated vision of the future that is simple, clearly understood, clearly desirable, and energizing.

Warren Bennis and Burt Nanus (1985), *Leaders: The Strategies for Taking Charge*, New York: Harper & Row.

 Practice insight 7 principles of communicating a vision

John Kotter (1996) said that there were seven principles of communicating a vision:

1   **Keep it simple** – Keep the message focused and jargon-free.
2   **Use metaphors, analogies and examples** – Engage the imagination.
3   **Use many different forums** – The same message should come from as many different directions as possible.
4   **Repeat the message** – The same message should be repeated again, and again, and again.
5   **Lead by example** – Walk the talk.
6   **Address small inconsistencies** – Small changes can have big effects if their symbolism is important to staff.
7   **Listen and be listened to** – Work hard to listen, it pays dividends.

Creating culture

Organizational culture is about the unspoken, prevalent norms, basic beliefs and assumptions about the 'right' way to behave in an organization. It can be more important for a start-up than any formal structure it adopts because it manifests itself in the way people are inclined and likely to behave rather than the way they are supposed to behave. As the founder of your venture, you profoundly influence its culture – either consciously or unconsciously. It is grounded in your basic beliefs and values, and these ought to underpin your mission and vision (Chapter 7).

Johnson (1992) talked about the cultural paradigm – how it is around here – as comprising stories, symbols, control systems, rituals and routines, power and organizational structures, that together both help to describe and contribute to the culture of an organization. This underlines

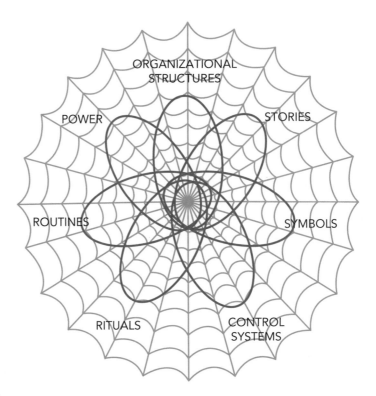

Figure 18.1 The cultural web

the fact that culture is self-reinforcing. And taken together these factors form an interlinking cultural web for an organization, as shown in Figure 18.1.

We shall talk about what an entrepreneurial culture looks like in the next chapter. The first thing to understand is how you go about constructing or affecting the culture of an organization. Organizational culture can be influenced using cognitive processes, organizational processes and behaviours (Figure 18.2).

Cognitive processes

These are the beliefs, assumptions and attitudes that staff hold in common and take for granted. They are embedded and emanate from the firm's philosophy, values, morality and creed. They generate norms of behaviour – rules or authoritative standards. They are strongly

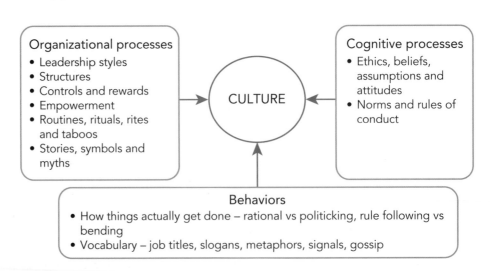

Figure 18.2 Influences on organizational culture

influenced by what the founder of the organization really pays attention to and what they actually do – not just what they say. But the important point is that they take time to frame. They do not happen overnight.

Organizational processes

These can be deliberate or just emerge, evolving organically, perhaps in an unintended way. There are many influences on this:

> **Leadership styles** – These send signals about appropriate behaviour. How you treat people, react to situations, even allocate your time, sends powerful signals about priorities.
> **Organizational structures** – Hierarchical organizations can discourage initiative. Functional specialization can create parochial attitudes and send signals about which skills might be valued. Flat, organic structures with broader spans of control and frequent use of teams encourage creativity, innovation and entrepreneurship.
> **Controls and rewards** – People take notice of which behaviours get rewarded (as well as which get punished) and behave accordingly. If salaries are based mainly on sales bonuses and there is a monthly league table of the best sales people, what does this tell you about the firm, its values and its goals? Criteria used for recruitment, selection, promotion and retirement are all important. Status, praise and public recognition are powerful motivators.
> **Empowerment** – The power to make (or not make) decisions sends defining signals. Flat, decentralized structures with delegated decision-making send signals about encouraging local decision-making, although sometimes informal power can lie outside formal hierarchies. The reaction to failure is an important message in this.
> **Routines, rituals, rites and taboos** – These form the unquestioned fabric of everyday life, and say a lot about the organization. 'Guarded' or 'open' management offices, reserved or unreserved parking spaces, dress codes and normal methods of communication all influence culture.
> **Stories and symbols** – Who are the heroes, villains and mavericks in the firm? What do staff talk about at lunch? Are there symbols of status that are important such as car or office size? How do staff talk about customers, other key managers and even you? These stories and symbols perpetuate a culture.

Getty Images/iStockphoto Thinkstock Images \ g_studio

Behaviours

This is what actually happens in an organization. It decides whether outcomes are rational, transparent or the result of politicking. It influences whether the organization does actually follow rules, or is about bending them in the appropriate circumstances. Behaviour is also about vocabulary – job titles, slogans, metaphors, signals, even gossip. Language is laden with value judgements that we do not realize most of the time – but they subconsciously influence the culture of the organization. To cement an organizational culture, behaviours must be congruent with the other influences and consistent with your organizational structures and your leadership style.

In Chapter 3 we looked at the work of Hofstede in relation to the effect of national cultures on individuals. Hofstede et al. (1990) also looked at the different dimensions of organizational culture in an attempt to discriminate between entrepreneurial and what they called 'administrative' (or bureaucratic) organizations. These were not so much dimensions as descriptors of what an entrepreneurial culture might look like compared to an administrative or bureaucratic one. These descriptors are shown in Table 18.1. Most small firms start life with a 'task culture' – an orientation

Table 18.1 Entrepreneurial vs administrative cultures

Entrepreneurial		Administrative
Results orientated	vs	Process orientated
Job orientated	vs	Employee orientated
Parochial interest	vs	Professional interest
Open system	vs	Closed system
Loose control	vs	Tight control
Pragmatic orientation	vs	Normative orientation

towards getting the job done and results achieved. If the entrepreneur finds it difficult to delegate that may turn into a 'power culture' – where people vie to have power and influence over the entrepreneur. As this sort of firm grows, especially if the delegated authority is not genuine, there is a danger of developing a 'role culture' whereby job titles become too important. These cultures are not conducive to success and are to be avoided. We shall look at how you might construct an entrepreneurial culture in the next chapter.

Even if you do not actively try to create a culture, one will emerge anyway. If it is the wrong one you have nobody else to blame. However, having the 'right' culture can help you manage the business and achieve success. Having the 'wrong' culture can spell disaster and can lead to conflict within the partner team (Gelfand et al., 2008). So, what culture do you want to create in your business and what are the behaviours you wish to encourage that will reinforce this?

Case insight   AirAsia (2)

Creating a culture

Courtesy of AirAsia

Tony Fernandes

Tony Fernandes set up AirAsia in 2001 (see Case insight on page 11). An article in *The Economist* ('Cheap, but Not Nasty', March 2009) made a number of observations about his management style and its effect on the company's culture, saying that 'he came to the industry with no preconceptions but found it rigidly compartmentalized and dysfunctional. He wanted AirAsia to reflect his own unstuffy, open and cheerful personality. He is rarely seen without a baseball cap, open-neck shirt and jeans, and he is proud that the firm's lack of hierarchy (very unusual in Asia) means anyone can rise to do anyone else's job. AirAsia employs pilots who started out as baggage handlers and stewards; for his part, Mr. Fernandes also practices what he preaches. Every month he spends a day as a baggage handler, every two months as a cabin crew, every three months as a check-in clerk. He even established a "culture department" to "pass the message and hold parties".'

Tony puts the success of AirAsia down to 'culture, focus and discipline'. His comments on his management style include:

'*If you sit up in your ivory tower and just look at financial reports, you're going to make some big mistakes ... Employees come number one, customers come number two. If you have a happy workforce they'll look after your customers anyway ... You can have all the money you want in the world, and you can have all the brilliant ideas but if you don't have the people, forget it ... I look for people who have drive, who have ambition, who are humble. I've hired many people at very strange places ... Good leadership is to know when to go and you only succeed as a good leader if you've transported someone else in and the company gets stronger. Then you've succeeded as leader.*' (BBC News Business, 1 November 2010)

QUESTION:

1 In commenting on AirAsia's success, what does Tony mean by 'culture, focus and discipline'? How has each of these contributed?

Practice insight 5 ways to destroy a rich culture

Mintzberg et al. (1998) said there were five certain ways to destroy a rich organizational culture:

1 Manage the bottom line – as if you manage money to make money.
2 Make a plan for every action – no spontaneity or learning necessary.

3 Move managers around so as to be certain they never get to know anything but management – and kick the boss upstairs as they might know too much about the real business.
4 Always be objective – which means treating people like objects that you can buy and sell.
5 Do everything in five easy steps.

Personal attributes of leaders

A key mind-shift for a leader is to become a strategic thinker. They move away from operational detail to a broad, strategic, organizational perspective – an ability to rise above day-to-day crises and see the bigger picture. It involves taking a longer-term, holistic view of the organization. Strategy sets a framework within which short-term actions can be judged, and the frameworks outlined in Chapter 12 should help you do this. Leaders understand where they have come from – knowledge of the past – and how it affects the current situation, where they are going to and how to get there. They are also engaged in perpetually 'scanning' the environment, both for opportunities and risks. They therefore become strategic learners. This learning may involve looking at the big picture, trying to find patterns over time and looking for complex interactions so as to understand the underlying causes. The discovery skills needed to find your original business idea is essentially a process of 'scanning' (Chapter 4).

Based on this information, leaders can then envision a new and desirable future which they reframe in the context of the organization. This is their vision and strategic intent. During the process they engage in synthesis as well as analysis. However, leadership is also about then persuading people to follow you towards this new future. This requires high levels of 'emotional intelligence'. George (2003) outlined the skills and personal attributes this requires:

> **Self-awareness** – the ability to understand themselves, their strengths, weaknesses and emotions;
> **Self-management** – an ability to adapt their behaviour to meet different circumstances; this requires control, integrity, initiative and conscientiousness;
> **Social awareness** – an appreciation of different circumstances – both people and the environment or context in which they find themselves; this requires empathy, sensing other people's emotions;
> **Social skills** – an ability to relate to people and collaborate with them and, above all, build relationships with them.

A key skill for this whole process is honest reflection, and that requires time. It also means that you need to check that your perception of yourself or of different circumstances corresponds with that of others. Is it real? This involves a degree of mature judgement that is not easily taught, but develops over time and can be much enhanced by having a supportive network of people around you that you are able to talk with.

 You have to be self-critical and constantly aware of how you translate yourself to your staff.

Alex Head, founder, Social Pantry, *The Times*, 25 February 2014

Authentic leadership

Trust and respect underpin the relationship that a leader needs to establish with those they wish to lead. Indeed, if these factors underpin the relationship between founding partners of a business, research shows that there will be less overall conflict within the organization (Martinez and Aldrich, 2011). Followers need to want the new future that the leader envisions and buy into the strategies that will make it happen. But they also need to trust that the leader can and will deliver it and it is easier to trust someone who has high moral characteristics or ethical values. These are the leaders who really command our respect and loyalty. They generate more commitment from staff. However, ethics are not an 'add-on'. It is not easy to adopt personal attributes that do not represent the person you really are. Eventually your guard will slip and your followers will see through the image you portray. To sustain your leadership, you need to be 'authentic' – you need to believe in and act out these ethical underpinnings. Trust and respect come not just from words but also from actions – 'walking the talk'.

Reflecting on interviews with 125 of today's top leaders, George and Sims (2007) talked about 'authentic leadership' coming from those individuals who follow their real values and beliefs – their 'internal compass'. Authentic leaders build a support team of people with whom they have a close relationship (spouses, family members, mentors etc.) and they have a network of professional contacts to provide counsel and guidance. These are people with whom they can reflect honestly on the issues they face.

Authentic leaders also have strong values and beliefs that they practice at work and at home – 'pursuing purpose with passion'. They have ethical foundations and boundaries and lead with their hearts as well as their heads. They establish enduring relations with staff because they listen to them and demonstrate that they care. George and Sims argue that, in this way, authentic leaders not only inspire those around them but also empower people to lead. But they only do this by always being true to their own principles, values and beliefs. They are authentic. And that cannot be faked.

Brubaker (2005) gave us an insight into what staff might consider ethical foundations. When asked in a survey what values they looked for in ethical leaders, respondents listed nine major attributes:

1   Truth and honesty.
2   Integrity and alignment of words and actions.
3   The keeping of promises.
4   Loyalty to the organization and the people in it.
5   Fairness between staff.
6   Concern and respect for others.
7   Law abiding.
8   Pursuit of excellence.
9   Personal accountability, taking responsibility, admitting mistakes and sharing success.

Leadership style and contingency theory

Leadership style is a complex thing. It is dependent upon the interactions and interconnections between the leader, the task, the group being led and the situation or context. The appropriate style to adopt depends upon how these factors interact. This is called situational or contingency theory. Three broad styles of leadership have been popularized (Figure 18.3). Each style involves different degrees of freedom or control for the employees.

> **Authoritarian** – This style focuses decision-making powers in the leader. It is most appropriate in times of crisis but usually fails to win 'hearts and minds'.

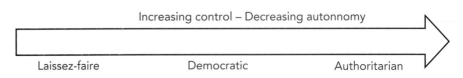

Figure 18.3 Leadership styles and control

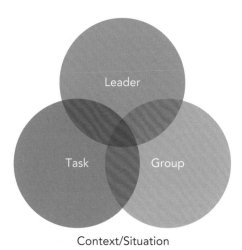

Figure 18.4 Leadership style

> **Democratic** – This style favours group decision-making and consensus-building. It is more appropriate in circumstances other than crisis.
> **Laissez-faire** – This style allows a high degree of autonomy for followers. However, a leader adopting this style is often perceived as weak.

In reality there are many permutations of these three extremes, and contingency theory states that the leader should adapt their style to suit different situations or contexts. It emphasizes that there is no one 'best' way of managing or leading. This depends on the interaction of all the factors in Figure 18.4 – leader, group, task and situation or context. A leader may personally prefer an informal, non-directional style, but faced with an inexperienced apprentice working a dangerous lathe they might be forgiven for reverting to a fairly formal, directive style with heavy supervision. In that situation the change in style is appropriate. Try the same style with a group of senior creative marketing consultants and there would be problems. Many different styles may be effective, with different tasks, different groups and in different contexts. Remember there is no evidence of any single leadership style characterizing successful businesses. What is more, the ability of leaders to change and adapt their styles may vary enormously. By picking off the individual elements of these four factors we can understand what style is best suited to different circumstances.

Leader and task

Leaders have to work through others to complete tasks. The degree of concern for the people they are leading, compared to the task in hand, will, in part, determine the style they adopt. The leadership grid shown in Figure 18.5 shows style as dependent upon the leader's concern for task compared to the concern for people. Entrepreneurs are usually more concerned with completing the task but, as the firm grows, you must become more concerned with people if the tasks are to be accomplished. Task leadership – getting on with the job – may be appropriate in certain situations, for example emergencies. However, concern for people must surface at some point if effective, trusting relationships are to develop. Low concern for both people and task is hardly leadership at all. High concern for people at the expense of the task – the country club style – is rare in business but can be appropriate in community groups, small charities or social clubs where good relationships and high morale might be the dominant objectives.

PhotoDisc/Getty Images

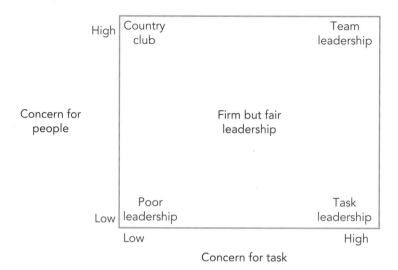

You can find your preferred style on this grid by answering the leadership questionnaire in Activity 4 at the end of this chapter and mapping your results on the scoring grid. The questionnaire is also available on the website accompanying this book.

Leader and group

Successful leaders are likely to adopt different styles with different groups approaching the same task. Leadership style also depends on the relationship of the leader with the group they are leading. Figure 18.6 shows this in relation to the leader's degree of authority and the group's autonomy in decision-making. If a leader has high authority but the group has low autonomy, they will tend to adopt an autocratic style, simply instructing people what to do. If they have low authority (for example because of past failure) they will tend to adopt a paternalistic style, cajoling the group into doing things, picking off individuals and offering grace and favour in exchange for performance. If the leader has low authority and the group has high autonomy, then they will tend to adopt a participative style, involving the whole group in decision-making and moving forward with consensus. If the leader has high authority, then they will seek opinions but make the decision themselves using a consultative style.

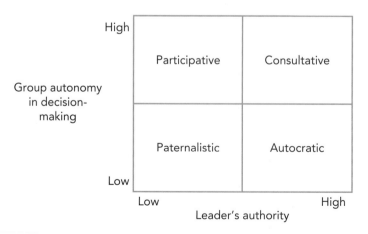

Figure 18.6 Leader and group

Leader and context or situation

The weight the leader should put on these different influences depends on the situation or context. However, obtaining an objective view of any context is always problematic as we view life through our own biased lens. As already observed, a leader's judgement about context might be faulty. What is more, they might be tempted to 'construct' social contexts that legitimize their intended actions, rather than viewing them objectively. And most leaders have a preferred style that they are predisposed to use.

Entrepreneurial firms face an environment that is uncertain, ambiguous and constantly changing, which can often lead to conflict as they try to get people to do different things or things differently. Conflict between the partners of a business is almost inevitable but can be particularly damaging and effect performance, even survival. As we noted in Chapter 8, conflict generally takes two forms – relationship conflict and task conflict (De Dreu and Weingart, 2003; Jehn and Bendersky, op. cit.). While conflicts over task can sometimes be productive and beneficial, relationship conflicts are rarely beneficial and may erode cohesion within the team, negatively effecting performance (Gelfand et al., op. cit.; Marks et al., 2001). Relationship conflict is mainly about personal taste, political preferences, and interpersonal style (De Dreu and Weingart, op. cit.). Shared cognition has been shown to cut down on this conflict and positively effect performance (Burgers et al., op. cit.). Not only does it improve collective understanding within a group, it also helps individuals with different functional backgrounds to reach consensus. However, conflict situations between partners as well as other staff are almost certain to arise and will need to be resolved.

> You can't avoid conflict. As well as rewarding people you need to be able to say "that won't do".

Alex Head, founder, Social Pantry, *The Times*, 25 February 2014

◎ Practice insight Dealing with conflict situations

Based on research by Kenneth Thomas and Ralph Kilmann, the Thomas-Kilmann Conflict Modes Instrument shows how a person's behaviour in situations involving conflict can be classified in two dimensions:

> Assertiveness – the extent to which individuals attempt to satisfy their own needs.

> Cooperativeness – the extent they attempt to satisfy the needs of others.

These two dimensions lead the authors to identify five behavioural classifications which the questionnaire can identify in individuals.

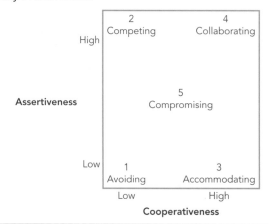

1 **Avoiding** is both unassertive and uncooperative. It may involve sidestepping an issue or withdrawing from the conflict altogether. In this mode any conflict may not be even addressed.

2 **Competing** is assertive and uncooperative. Individuals are concerned for themselves and pursue their own agenda forcefully, using power, rank or ability to argue in order to win the conflict. This can be seen as bullying with less forceful individuals or, when others use the same mode, it can lead to heated, possibly unresolved, arguments.

3 **Accommodating** is unassertive and cooperative, the opposite of competing. Individuals want to see the concerns of others satisfied. They might do so as an act of 'selfless generosity' or just because they are 'obeying orders'; either way they run the risk of not making their own views heard.

4 **Collaborating** is both assertive and cooperative, the opposite of avoiding. Issues get addressed but individuals are willing to work with others to resolve the conflict, perhaps finding alternatives that meet everybody's concerns. This is the most constructive approach to conflict for a group as a whole.

5 **Compromising** is the 'in between' route, the diplomatic, expedient solution to conflict which partially satisfies everyone. It may involve making concessions.

Continued...

Continued from previous page...

This gives us an insight into how conflict might be handled. Each style of handling conflict has its advantages and disadvantages and can be effective in certain situations. However, top management teams or boards of directors, if they are to get the most from each member over a longer period of time, work best when all members adopt the collaborating or compromising modes. A team made up of just competitors would find it difficult to get on and, indeed, to survive. A team made up of just accommodators would lack assertiveness and drive.

The Thomas-Kilmann Conflict Modes Instrument is available at http://www.kilmanndiagnostics.com/catalog/thomas-kilmann-conflict-mode-instrument.

Leadership style and national cultures

Contingency theory explains why there is no one 'best' leadership style. Context or situation is everything. And many studies have shown significant national and gender differences in management and leadership styles. For example, using Hofstede's dimensions of culture that we looked at in Chapter 3, Torrington (1994) highlighted some of the differences in manager–subordinate relationships in six countries – Britain, USA, France, Germany, Japan and in a number of Arab countries:

> British managers were willing to 'listen' to subordinates (low uncertainty avoidance) and liked 'old boy networks' (high masculinity);
> US managers had a 'tough', results-orientated style in dealing with subordinates (high individualism and high masculinity);
> French managers liked formality (high power distance) and 'intellectualism' (high individualism);
> German managers liked routines and procedures and close control of apprentices (high uncertainty avoidance);
> The Japanese were high on both masculinity and collectivism, producing a 'nurturing father' style of management;
> Arab countries valued loyalty and the avoidance of interpersonal conflict (high power distance).

This tells us that leadership styles do need to be modified to reflect (or counteract) national cultures. So what sort of leadership style do you adopt in order to help achieve an entrepreneurial culture? Do you simply adopt a style that reflects your values or what you think might be entrepreneurial values, even if the national culture finds this alien? Morden (1995) supports the view that it is unrealistic to take a 'one style suits all' approach to the principles and practice of leadership as they are applied from one country to another. What works well in one country may be entirely inappropriate in another. He advocates adapting to suit local circumstances and that means remembering two things:

> Leadership is the art of the achievable and it may be impossible to achieve the 'ideal' organizational culture within some national cultures. That means a suboptimal solution – 'not quite an entrepreneurial culture' – may be appropriate. On the other hand, however, there is no theoretical guarantee that this solution will be effective in delivering entrepreneurial activity.
> It is one thing knowing where you want to get to but quite another thing getting there. Leadership style can be adapted and changed gradually over time to suit circumstances so that it moves towards a more entrepreneurial style. There is a lot of evidence that it takes quite some time to change inherent cultures, whether we are talking about the impact of national cultures or changing the cultures of existing organizations.

The problem of reconciling the different leadership styles and cultures in different contexts – not just related to geography but also to different organizational tasks – is one reason pushing companies to fundamentally rethink many of their organization structures so as to allow greater diversity (Chapter 12).

Leadership paradigms

The academic literature provides many leadership paradigms that describe different leadership styles. Each is appropriate to different situations.

Transactional leadership

This style of leadership is about setting goals, putting in place systems and controls to achieve them and rewarding individuals when they meet the goals. It is about efficiency and incremental change, reinforcing rather than challenging organizational learning. It is associated with closed cultures, rigid systems, formal procedures and bureaucratic organization structures. Bass (1985, 1998) contrasts this to transformational leadership.

Transformational leadership

This is more emotional and is about inspiration, excitement and intellectual stimulation. It is a style best suited to highly turbulent and uncertain environments where crises, anxiety and high risk are prevalent (Vera and Crossan, 2004) – which tends to describe the entrepreneurial context. Not surprisingly, this style of leadership is associated with open cultures, organic structures, adaptable systems and flexible procedures. Transformational leaders are often seen as being charismatic, inspirational, intellectually stimulating and individually considerate (Avolio et al., 1999) and having empathy and self-confidence (Egri and Herman, 2000). They inspire and motivate people with a vision, create excitement with their enthusiasm and get people to question the tried-and-tested ways of doing things and 'reframe' the future (Bass and Avolio, 1990).

Visionary leadership

Sashkin (1996) characterized this style as providing clear, visionary leadership which focuses people on goals that are part of a vision and on key issues and concerns. The visionary leader has good interpersonal and communication skills. They get everyone to understand the focus for the business and to work together towards common goals. They act consistently over time to develop trust and care and respect others, making them self-confident, while having an inner self-confidence themselves. Finally, they provide creative opportunities that others can buy into and 'own' – empowering opportunities that involve people in making the right things their own priorities.

 Practice insight Are you a visionary leader?

The Visionary Leader Behaviour Questionnaire by Marshal Sashkin measures the 'three core elements of true visionary leadership':

1 Your use of visionary leadership behaviours.
2 The degree to which you possess the personal characteristics of visionary leaders.
3 The extent of the positive impact you are having on your organization.

When completed by three to six colleagues, the questionnaire provides a more accurate 360 degree assessment,

rather than just reflecting your own perceptions. It consists of 50 questions that measure leadership in 10 dimensions and provide feedback on these three 'core elements'. The ten dimensions of leadership are:

> **Focus** – your ability to focus people's attention on key issues.

> **Communication** – the effectiveness of your communication skills, including 'active listening'.

> **Trust** – the consistency of your views and behaviour and how you develop trust.

Continued...

Continued from previous page...

> **Respect for self and others** – whether you give others respect and unconditional, positive regard.

> **Risk** – your willingness to engage in rational risk-taking.

> **Bottom-line orientation** – belief in your impact on the profitability of the organisation.

> **Empowerment** – your use of power and influence to empower others.

> **Length of vision span** – your ability to think clearly over relatively long spans of time.

> **Organisational leadership** – your ability to have a positive impact on helping the organisation adapt to change.

> **Cultural leadership** – your ability to develop the values that will enhance how the organisational functions.

The questionnaire is available on: http://www.mlruk.com/the-visionary-leader-self-questionnaire

The notion of the leader as a heroic decision maker is untenable. Leaders must be recast as social-systems architects who enable innovation … Leaders will no-longer be seen as grand visionaries, all-wise decision makers, and iron-fisted disciplinarians. Instead they will need to become social architects, constitution writers, and entrepreneurs of meaning. In this new world, the leader's job is to create an environment where every employee has the chance to collaborate, innovate, and excel.

Gary Hamel, 'Moon Shots for Management', *Harvard Business Review*, February 2009

Image 100

Dispersed leadership

This style draws on models of dispersed or distributed leadership which focus on leadership across all levels of an organization and in different forms (Bradford and Cohen, 1998; Chaleff, 1995; Mintzberg, 2009). It is based on the realization that organizations are networks of individuals, all exercising some form of leadership and with no one person in total control, but with everyone open to influence through patterns of relationship (Raelin, 2003; Rost, 1991). It emphasizes the importance of 'emotional intelligence' in the leader and their ability to listen, empathize and communicate with those they lead (Goleman, 1996) – social skills essential to building effective relationships. As already mentioned, it emphasizes 'authenticity' (George, op. cit.; George and Sims, op. cit.) – leaders being true to their own beliefs (having an ethical underpinning) so that trust and respect can be built. The literature also emphasizes leaders as 'servants' of their workforce, acknowledging that self-interest is part of any relationship (Greenleaf, 1970) as well as 'educators' that develop organizational learning (Heifetz, 1994).

Entrepreneurial leadership

An entrepreneur may already have many of the leadership skills and attributes outlined so far. However, to be a leader of an entrepreneurial organization they will need to transform not only themselves but also the organization so that the organization itself demonstrates these qualities.

So, being an entrepreneurial leader is subtly different, as Collins and Porras (1994) eloquently explained:

> *Imagine you met a remarkable person who could look at the sun or stars at any time of day or night and state the exact time and date. … This person would be an amazing time teller, and we'd probably revere that person for the ability to tell the time. But wouldn't that person be even more amazing if, instead of telling the time, he or she built a clock that could tell time forever, even after he or she was dead and gone.*

Being just a transformational, charismatic or visionary leader is 'time telling'. Being an entrepreneurial leader is about building an organization that can prosper far beyond the single leader, through multiple product life cycles – it is 'clock building'. So, entrepreneurial leaders are builders of organizations that are both visionary and transformational. They are clock builders, not the time tellers.

This applies equally if there is a founding team of partners. What is not needed is for them all to be vying for leadership. This is destructive. They need to be seen to be working together. As already noted, they need to exhibit 'shared cognition' – to be cohesive and work together effectively towards agreed goals. Cohesive partnership teams improve job satisfaction and their businesses demonstrate superior performance (Ensley et al., 2002; Lechler, 2001; Mach et al., 2010; Thye et al., 2002).

Context is everything in leadership and the entrepreneurial context of leadership is one characterized by uncertainty, rapid change and risk-taking. To become a leader of an entrepreneurial organization you need to build an organization that is fundamentally entrepreneurial, one that embodies the entrepreneurial character traits or DNA outlined in Chapter 3, as well as the entrepreneurial approach to management – building relationships, developing strategy and dealing with risk. You do this by building structures and a culture and developing strategies that combine with your leadership style to create an **organizational architecture** that is entrepreneurial – an approach that will be explained in the next chapter. And instead of concentrating just on acquiring the individual characteristics of a strategic and authentic leader, you should take an architectural approach – building these leadership characteristics into the organization and spreading them throughout it.

However, even an entrepreneurial leader needs to remain flexible and modify their style to suit changing circumstances. In this way, the entrepreneurial leader may modify their leadership style as an organization cycles through periods of rapid change (transformational leadership) followed by consolidation (transactional leadership), all the time having a strategic intent based upon their vision for the organization (visionary leadership) and spreading elements of leadership throughout it (dispersed leadership). A truly entrepreneurial leader has the opportunity to build an entrepreneurial organization through this architecture that is self-sustaining – one that will continue to thrive in its changing, competitive environment even after their departure. By building this architecture they create value that they can capitalize on should they decide to sell-on. This combination of influences is shown in Figure 18.7.

Kirby (2003) likened the entrepreneurial leader to the leader of a jazz band. They decide on the musicians to play in the band and the music to be played but then allow the band to improvise and use their creativity to create the required music. In the process the band has fun as the leader brings out the best in them. The leader's authority comes from their expertise and values rather than their position. Leaders of jazz bands lead by example, often playing an instrument themselves. They empower their teams and nurture parallel leaders at all levels – encouraging solo performances.

This chapter has underlined the the personal leadership skills you will need to grow your business. It has emphasized the need for the leader of an entrepreneurial organization to be a good strategic thinker and learner – and all that entails from vision to execution. It has emphasized the need to have strong emotional intelligence – good interpersonal and team-working skills, alongside good conflict resolution skills – but, more than anything, strong influencing skills to manage through informal structures and culture. These attributes, skills and behaviours are summarized in Table 18.2 (taken from Burns, 2013). They are all focused towards taking the organization with you by consensus and agreement rather than by dictate. However, they will always need to be 'fine-tuned' to suit specific audiences, undertaking specific tasks in different contexts. There is an ancient Chinese proverb that still rings true:

The wicked leader is he who the people despise. The good leader is the one who the people revere. But the great leader is he who the people say 'we did it ourselves'.

I believe in as flat a management structure as possible … in leading without title … I most certainly try to lead by example and I'm very much a big believer in making my mistakes public so that other people feel confident and comfortable to be able to air their own mistakes.

Shaa Wasmund, founder Mykindaplace and Brightstone Ventures, *Management Today* (www.managementtoday.co.uk), 18 July 2008

Making an enduring company is far harder and far more important than making a great product.

Steve Jobs, founder of Apple, *The Real Leadership Lessons of Steve Jobs*, Walter Isaacson, HBR April 2012

Leader's characteristics
Strategic leaders
• strategic thinkers
• reflectors
• strategic learners
Authentic leaders
• emotional intelligence
• self-awareness
• self-management

Contingency/ Situational Theory

Leadership paradigms
• Transformational/ Transactional leadership
• Visionary leadership
• Dispersed leadership

Entrepreneurial leadership

Figure 18.7 Entrepreneurial leadership

Table 18.2 Attributes, skills and behaviours of entrepreneurial leaders

Attributes, skills and behaviours of entrepreneurial leaders

1 **Visionary** – the essential bedrock of leadership. The vision should give clear direction and be underpinned with values. It should, however, be grounded in reality.

2 **Good communicator/motivator** – the vision should be shared by all the staff in the organization and motivate them to achieve it. Motivation should be underpinned by loyalty to both the leader and the organization.

3 **Strategic thinker and learner** – the vision should be supplemented with an understanding of how to achieve it and what the strategic options for direction might be.

4 **Emotionally intelligent with strong interpersonal skills** – able to listen, to influence rather than direct, to resolve conflict and to manage 'with a light touch'. They should 'walk the talk': model the behaviour they expect from others.

5 **Relationship builder** – able to build a cohesive, open and trusting management team. This comes about by acting consistently over time based upon a dominant set of values so as to generate trust (firm but fair) and is underpinned by care and respect for staff.

6 **Team player** – willing to share information and delegate to the team. This is based upon an understanding of how teams work.

7 **Builder of confidence** – encouraging organizational self-confidence and self-efficacy in the face of uncertainty and risk-taking. They should inspire others to share their visions and dreams.

8 **Builder of an open organization that shares information** – fostering the sharing of knowledge, information and ideas, and the willingness to question the status quo and to experiment and take measured risks.

9 **Clarifier of ambiguity and uncertainty** – so as to give a clear focus on the key issues and concerns facing the organization in the face of rapid change. This focus should be effectively communicated.

10 **Builder of empowering opportunities** – so that staff make 'the right thing' for the organization their own enthusiastic priority. In other words, spreading entrepreneurship and leadership throughout the organization.

 ## Case insight   Steve Jobs and Apple

Entrepreneurial leadership

Steve Jobs died of pancreatic cancer on October 5, 2011, aged 56. He was the epitome of an entrepreneurial leader and revolutionized three industries – computing, music sales and cinema animations. With Steve Wozniak, he co-founded Apple in 1976. Apple revolutionized the computer industry through its innovative designs: the Macintosh with its computer mouse, the iPod with its click wheel and the iPhone with its 'user interface'. Apple also revolutionized how digital content, in particular music, could be sold rather than pirated. Through Jobs' animation studio, Pixar, films such as *Toy Story* (1995) completely changed our ideas about how films could use computer generated animations. And yet he was not an inventor. He was the bridge between the business idea and the marketplace – the entrepreneur who built an organization to deliver his vision. Not only did he start up Apple, he was also forced out of it in 1985 after an acrimonious boardroom battle. He returned to it in

1997 to turn it around from near bankruptcy and, by 2011, created the second most valuable company in the world, measured by market capitalization, with a cash mountain of approximately $80 billion.

The story of Steve Jobs is the story of a Silicon Valley hero. Born to a Syrian father and an American mother in San Francisco, he was the adopted child of a blue-collar couple and grew up in Mountain View, a suburb of San Francisco close to what is now known as Silicon Valley. The fact that he was put up for adoption by his birth parents was said to have left a deep scar. While at high school, he met Steve Wozniak working on a summer job with Hewlett-Packard in Palo Alto. He left high school reluctantly going to Reed, a liberal arts college in Portland, Oregon, but failed to attend his required classes and dropped out after one term. He grew his hair and did the sorts of things that drop-outs at the time did, including visiting a guru in India. His engagement with Zen Buddhism was to become ingrained in his personality with a focus on stark, minimalist aesthetics and

Continued...

Continued from previous page...

a belief in intuition. However, he never achieved the inner peace associated with Zen Buddhism, rather always being driven by the particular challenges facing him at the time.

But it was his friend Steve Wozniak who had the talent for electronics and designing circuits with the minimum number of chips, and he built the first Apple computer. At the time, Wozniak was working for Hewlett-Packard and Jobs for Atari. Apple I was a hobbyist machine assembled by hand in Steve Jobs' parents' home and housed in a wooden box. The couple sold many of their personal possessions to get the start-up finance that was needed. Jobs' role was that of the businessman, the salesman who persuaded the local computer store to order 50, then persuading the local electrical store to give him 30 days credit on the parts to build them. He also eventually persuaded Mike Markkula, a former Intel employee, to invest in the company and become its first chief executive. What followed was the beautifully designed, classic Apple II with its built-in colour graphics, easily accessible expansion slots and ability to connect to a TV set. Its simple design, understandable instruction manual and consumer friendly advertising guaranteed it success until the launch of the IBM PC. Apple went public in 1980 with a market valuation of $1.8 billion only four years after being launched.

Steve Wozniak retired from Apple one year later, following a serious plane accident. Jobs took over the development of the Apple II's successor, the Apple Macintosh. The Mac was intended to be the first mass-market, closed-box computer based on the now ubiquitous mouse and a graphic user interface. These ideas were not new. They were developed by scientists at Xerox Palo Alto Research Centre (PARC) and had been tried out in high-priced computers (Xerox Star and Apple Lisa), without commercial success. The launch of the Mac was the start of what became the signature Steve Jobs product launch. He appeared on stage with Bill Gates promising Mac versions of Word, Excel and PowerPoint. There were 20-page advertisements in major US magazines. But it was the TV commercial that had the biggest impact. Shown in the USA during the 1984 Super Bowl, it associated IBM with the character Big Brother from George Orwell's *1984*. Despite the dramatic launch, the Mac failed to sell in the expected volumes, signalling the start of Apple's decline. In 1985 it closed three of its six factories, laying off 1,200 employees. In the same year, Steve Jobs was forced to leave Apple, and by 1987 the Mac II was launched as a conventional three-piece computer system.

Jobs resented being thrown out of Apple, particularly by someone he had recruited two years earlier to the job of chief executive officer – John Sculley, former president of PepsiCo. He took several Apple employees with him and set up another company called NeXT to produce a powerful Unix workstation targeted at business and universities. It was very expensive and flopped, so the company switched to selling the operating systems, again without much success.

Steve Jobs bought what became Pixar in 1986 from Lucasfilm. Initially, the company produced expensive computer hardware. The core product was the Pixar Image Computer, a system primarily sold to government agencies and the medical market, but this never sold particularly well. The company struggled for years and, in an effort to demonstrate its capabilities, Pixar began producing computer-animated commercials. This led to a deal in 1991 with the Walt Disney Corporation to produce three computer-animated films, the first of which was the groundbreaking *Toy Story*. Until this point Pixar had been in decline, having already sold off its hardware operations. Released in 1995, *Toy Story* was an outstanding box-office success, which was just as well because as late as 1994 Jobs had considered selling off Pixar. After a series of highly successful, award-winning films such as *A Bug's Life* (1998), *Toy Story 2* (1999), *Monsters Inc.* (2001), *Finding Nemo* (2003) and *The Incredibles* (2004), the Walt Disney Company eventually bought Pixar in 2006 at a valuation of $7.4 billion, making Jobs the largest shareholder in Disney.

Meanwhile the PC market was again transformed in 1995 by the launch of Microsoft Windows 95, which really popularized the mouse and the graphic user interface. Apple was struggling to survive and the new Mac OS software development was not working. It was managed by committees and had lost its innovative flair. Apple knew it needed to buy in a new operating system, and fast, so it turned to Steve Jobs and paid a much inflated price to buy NeXT. In reality this turned out to be a reverse takeover and Jobs took over as 'interim CEO' in 1997.

Jobs killed off weak products and simplified the product lines. He adapted NeXT's NextStep operating system to become the Mac OS X operating system. He also started the process of creating the distinctive eye-catching Apple designs with the teardrop-shaped iMac, followed by the portable iBook. Explaining himself to the 1997 meeting of the Apple Worldwide Developers Association, Jobs said:

'Focusing is about saying no ... and the result of that focus is going to be some really great products where the total is much greater than the sum of the parts ... One of the things I've always found is that you've got to start with the customer experience and work backwards to the technology and try to figure out where you are going to try to sell it. I've made this mistake probably more than anyone else in this room, and I've got the scar tissue to prove it, and I know that it's the case.'

But Apple's fortunes were really transformed when Jobs completely changed directions and launched the iPod in 2001 and the iTunes music store in 2003. This transformed

Continued...

Continued from previous page...

the music industry which was facing a decline in CD sales as more and more music was being pirated through online sites like Napster, by allowing music to be easily downloaded, but at a price. Apple started on its growth path, which was reinforced in 2007 by its launch of the iPhone – a clever but expensive combination of cell phone, iPod and internet device. This was followed in 2010 by the iPad – a tablet computer without a physical keyboard. By 2011 the iPad was outselling the Macintosh.

Jobs was, of course, in the right place at the right time to capitalize on developments in computing and the change from analogue to digital technologies. But he shaped these developments to appeal to customers. The distinctive feature about Apple products was never the innovation – that normally came from elsewhere – but rather the application of an innovation to make the product easier and simpler to use, whether it be the physical product design or applications such as iTunes. All Apple products also enjoy a distinctive, eye-catching design. And they are never cheap. They were also supported by massive marketing campaigns with Jobs, dressed in black turtleneck, jeans and trainers, launching products himself with carefully choreographed, pseudo-religious stage presentations (known as 'Stevenotes') that attracted adoring fans and received massive worldwide press coverage. In many people's eyes Jobs enjoyed the status of a rock star. At the same time, the Apple brand had become iconic.

However, many of Jobs' personal character traits did not endear him to others in business. He was a perfectionist who was highly secretive and had, at the very least, what might be described as a hard-driving management style. In 1993 *Fortune* magazine placed him on the list of America's Toughest Bosses for his time at NeXT, quoting co-founder Daniel Lewin as saying: 'The highs were unbelievable ... but the lows were unimaginable' (October 18, 1993). Fourteen years later it called him 'one of Silicon Valley's leading egomaniacs' (March 19, 2007). He was notorious for micromanaging things, from the design of new products to the chips they used. In his obituary, *The Telegraph* (6 October 2011) claimed he was 'almost pathologically controlling' when it came to dealing with news reporters and the press, actively trying to stifle any reports that might seem critical of him or Apple. It went on to reveal some elements of his dark side:

> *He oozed arrogance, was vicious about business rivals, and in contrast to, say, Bill Gates, refused to have any truck with notions of corporate responsibility. He habitually parked his car in the disabled slot at Apple headquarters and one of the first acts on returning to the company in 1997 was to terminate all of its corporate philanthropy programs ... He ruled Apple with a combination of foulmouthed tantrums and charm, withering scorn and flattery ... and those in his regular orbit found he could flip*

> *with no warning from one category to the other ... Yet members of Job's inner circle, many of whom came with him from NeXT, found working for him an exhilarating experience. To keep them on the board, Jobs eliminated most cash bonuses from executive compensation and started handing out stock options instead.'*

The Sunday Times (30 October 2011) was just as scathing about his personality, giving examples of his bad-tempered, often rude, tantrums with staff and suppliers. He had a propensity for tears and the article cited the example of him throwing a tantrum and crying when he was assigned No. 2 on the Apple payroll when Wozniak was assigned No. 1. Jobs insisted on being 'number zero'. It cited examples of him often claiming the ideas of other Apple employees as his own and described him as 'selfish, rude, aggressive, lachrymose, unpredictable ... a good candidate for the boss from hell.' It described Apple as 'a cultish, paranoid, joyless organization where public humiliations were a regular occurrence and cut-throat competition among the ranks was encouraged' (*The Sunday Times*, 29 January 2012). And yet it also observed that Jobs could inspire incredible loyalty, albeit in the people he had helped to make rich.

Jobs' personal life was equally murky. Before starting up Apple, he famously paid his partner Steve Wozniak only $300 for a job he was paid $5,000 for by Atari, when the agreement with Wozniak was for a 50:50 split. At a point in his life where he was already wealthy, he denied paternity of a daughter, leaving the mother on welfare, even swearing an affidavit that he was not the father because, in effect, he was 'sterile and infertile'. He eventually acknowledged paternity. Jobs went on to marry Laurene Powell and have three more children, living in an unassuming family home in Palo Alto, on the San Francisco Bay.

Writing after Jobs' death, Adam Lashinsky (2012) gives us a rare insight into the effects this must have had in generating an organizational culture at Apple. As he says: 'you're expected to check your ego at the door' because there really is only room for one – that of Jobs, who he says exhibits 'narcissism, whimsy and disregard for the feelings of others'. Jobs emerges as a short-tempered, authoritarian dictator ruthlessly pushing, even bullying, staff to complete assigned tasks. On a somewhat more positive note Jobs is described as 'a visionary risk taker with a burning desire to change the world ... charismatic leader willing to do whatever it takes to win and who couldn't give a fig about being liked.'

Central to Apple's culture is product excellence – a cult of product – where employees do not want to let the company down by being the weakest link. And if they do, they can become collateral damage because of the aggressive, competitive environment. It is work-orientated and definitely not play-orientated, and long hours, missed holidays and tight deadlines are expected and encouraged. However,

Continued...

Continued from previous page...

Lashinsky admits that 'by and large, Apple is a collaborative and cooperative environment, devoid of overt politicking … but it isn't usually nice, and it's almost never relaxed'. In his view, unquestioning collaboration and cooperation were necessary to ensure instructions were communicated and followed in this command-and-control structure. He believes that employee happiness was never a top priority for Steve Jobs. But on the other hand, employees derived pride from Apple's products and in working for Jobs' vision. Jobs appeared omnipresent, or at least visible, around the campus, despite the fact that very few people had access to his office suite.

Secrecy, mistrust and paranoia seem to underpin the Apple culture. Apple emerges as a cultish, joyless organization, built on fear and mistrust, where competition and aggressive in-fighting between staff was encouraged and public humiliation was regular. According to Lashinsky:

'Apple is secretive … Far from being empowered, its people operate within narrow bands of responsibility … employees are expected to follow orders, not offer opinions … Apple's CEO was a micromanager … and to an amazingly low level … Apple isn't even a nice place to work … Job's brutality in dealing with subordinates legitimized a frighteningly harsh, bullying, and demanding culture … a culture of fear and intimidation found roots.'

Apple's organization structure encouraged secrecy – it did not have organization charts, although Lashinsky's attempt to draw one showed Jobs in the middle of a spider's web. He describes Apple's organization as 'unconventional', with 15 senior vice presidents and vice presidents reporting directly to Jobs 'at the centre'. Staff were frequently organized into small project teams, isolated from each other and operating under strict secrecy rules – 'siloes within siloes'. Staff only knew about the elements of new product development that they needed to know about. The fact there were no conventional organization charts limited the people employees knew outside their immediate environment – a cell-like structure.

Just like all entrepreneurs, Jobs' personality was integral to his leadership style. And he built an organization structure and culture to match his leadership style. However, it was almost the direct opposite of most successful high-tech businesses in Silicon Valley – Lashinsky frequently contrasted Apple with Google. And, at the time of Jobs' death, many commentators observed that this organization was so based upon one man, that they questioned how long it would prosper without him.

Nevertheless, Jobs had many admirers and he certainly achieved enormous things in his life. Walter Isaacson (2012) believes that you should not 'fixate too much on the rough edges of his personality'. He said of Jobs that:

'He acted as if the normal rules didn't apply to him, and the passion, intensity, and extreme emotionalism he brought to everyday life were things he also poured into the products he made. His petulance and impatience were part and parcel of his perfectionism.'

Isaacson said there were 14 keys to his success:

1 **Focus** – Jobs was always able to focus and spend time on what he considered important, often to the frustration of others trying to get him to consider other things. As he explained to the 1997 meeting of the Apple Worldwide Developers Association: 'Focusing is about saying no … and the result of that focus is going to be some really great products where the total is much greater than the sum of the parts.'

2 **Simplify** – Jobs admired simplicity, and simplicity of use was a key design feature of all Apple's products: 'It takes a lot of hard work to make something simple, to truly understand the underlying challenges and come up with elegant solutions.'

3 **Take responsibility end-to-end** – In his quest for simplicity, Jobs took end-to-end responsibility for the user experience, integrating hardware, software and peripherals – part of his controlling nature and drive for perfection.

4 **When behind, leapfrog** – Rather than copying competitors, Jobs would always try to create something better and different.

5 **Push for perfection** – Jobs was a perfectionist and would delay production until he thought the product was 100% right.

6 **Put products before profits** – Because he was a perfectionist he also wanted his products to be the best, whatever the price. He believed that if the product was great, profits would follow.

7 **Don't be a slave to focus groups** – Because Apple's products were so innovative, Jobs never trusted focus groups and market research, preferring his own instincts: 'Customers don't know what they want until we show them.'

8 **Bend reality** – Jobs' famous 'reality distortion field' persuaded people that his vision of the future would prevail. Some called it bullying and lying, others called it effective communication of strategic intent.

9 **Impute** – Jobs used the design of products and even its packaging to 'impute' signals to customers, signals that underpinned the brand identity.

10 **Tolerate only 'A' players** – Jobs' passion for perfection extended to employees and, perhaps, explains his rudeness to people who did not perform as he expected.

11 **Engage face-to-face** – Jobs was a believer in face-to-face meetings. His executive team met once a week, without an agenda, to 'kick around ideas'.

Continued...

Continued from previous page...

12 **Know both the big picture and the detail** – Jobs had both vision and a grasp of detail, or at least the detail he thought important.

13 **Combine humanities and sciences** – Jobs was able to connect ideas from different disciplines to create features in his products that customers valued (a creativity 'Discovery Skill').

14 **Stay hungry, stay foolish** – Jobs never wanted to lose the drive he had in his youth and always wanted Apple to keep the culture of a start-up.

So was Steve Jobs a great entrepreneurial leader? He certainly was a great entrepreneur. And under his leadership Apple certainly was extremely successful. But has he created an organization that is entrepreneurial and that can succeed and prosper without him? Only time will tell.

QUESTIONS:

1 What entrepreneurial qualities or characteristics did Jobs exhibit?

2 Why was he so successful? How much of this success was just good luck?

3 How would you describe Jobs' leadership style?

4 How did the structure and culture within Apple reflect Jobs' leadership style?

5 How many of the attributes, skills and behaviours listed in Table 18.1 did Jobs exhibit? How would you reconcile any differences?

6 Was Jobs a great entrepreneurial leader? Explain and justify.

7 Do you have to be a likeable character to be a great entrepreneurial leader? Explain and justify.

 Practice insight reminder Characteristics of a good business idea – 13

13 **Management skills that can be leveraged** – you need to have the appropriate management skills, and if you do not, you need to acquire them or recruit or partner with others with the appropriate skills.

↻ Summary

> Management and leadership are different and distinct terms, although the skills and competences associated with each are complementary. Management is concerned with handling complexity in organizational processes and the execution of work. It is about detail and logic, efficiency and effectiveness. Leadership, on the other hand, is concerned with setting direction, communicating and motivating. It is about broad principles and emotion. It is particularly concerned with change.

> A leader's role means they have to be able to:
> - Develop a vision for the organization;
> - Be an effective communicator, particularly of that vision;
> - Be able to develop a strategy to deliver the vision;
> - Create a culture to support their leadership style and the strategy;
> - Manage the organization, particularly through the development of close relationships, and monitor performance within it.

> The ability to influence and build relationships – a key characteristic of entrepreneurial leaders – requires certain characteristics: emotional intelligence, self-awareness and self-management.

> Leaders also need to be able to be strategic thinkers and learners and be able to reflect realistically and honestly on situations and personalities.

> Contingency theory tells us that the leadership style appropriate for one situation may be inappropriate for another. The appropriate leadership style depends on the leader, the group, the task and situation or context facing the leader.

> The entrepreneurial context of leadership is one characterized by uncertainty, rapid change and risk-taking. There are various other leadership paradigms that inform us about leadership in this context – transactional leadership, transformational leadership, visionary leadership and dispersed leadership.

> The attributes, skills and behaviours needed for effective leadership of an entrepreneurial organization are summarized in Table 18.2. In line with contingency theory, however, these may need to be 'fine-tuned' for specific contexts.

› Leadership styles, organizational cultures and structures are linked. If any one is inappropriate for the other two, then the organization will not function as well as it should.

The task of the entrepreneurial leader is to construct an organizational architecture that is consistent and where one reinforces the other.

✓ Activities

1 List the questions you would ask an entrepreneur who had successfully grown their business, with the aim of exploring their leadership style. Based on these questions, interview an entrepreneur and prepare a report on their leadership style.

2 Jot down words that describe the culture you would like to establish in your business. Then list the actions (behaviours, organizational and cognitive processes) you need to undertake or establish to achieve this culture.

3 Answer the questions in the Thomas-Kilmann Conflict Mode Instrument and prepare a report on how you handle conflict.

4 If you already operate in a leadership role complete the Leadership Style questionnaire below. For each of the following statements, tick the 'Yes' box if you tend to agree or the 'No' box if you disagree. Try to relate the answers to your actual recent behaviour as a manager. There are no right and wrong answers. When you have completed the test, score yourself with the answers at the end of this chapter. What does this tell you about your leadership style?

		Yes	No
1.	I encourage overtime work	☐	☐
2.	I allow staff complete freedom in their work	☐	☐
3.	I encourage the use of standard procedures	☐	☐
4.	I allow staff to use their own judgement in solving problems	☐	☐
5.	I stress being better than other firms	☐	☐
6.	I urge staff to greater effort	☐	☐
7.	I try out my ideas with others in the firm	☐	☐
8.	I let my staff work in the way they think best	☐	☐
9.	I keep work moving at a rapid pace	☐	☐
10.	I turn staff loose on a job and let them get on with it	☐	☐
11.	I settle conflicts when they happen	☐	☐
12.	I get swamped by detail	☐	☐
13.	I always represent the 'firm view' at meetings with outsiders	☐	☐
14.	I am reluctant to allow staff freedom of action	☐	☐
15.	I decide what should be done and who should do it	☐	☐
16.	I push for improved quality	☐	☐
17.	I let some staff have authority I could keep	☐	☐
18.	Things usually turn out as I predict	☐	☐
19.	I allow staff a high degree of initiative	☐	☐
20.	I assign staff to particular tasks	☐	☐
21.	I am willing to make changes	☐	☐
22.	I ask staff to work harder	☐	☐
23.	I trust staff to exercise good judgement	☐	☐
24.	I schedule the work to be done	☐	☐
25.	I refuse to explain my actions	☐	☐
26.	I persuade others that my ideas are to their advantage	☐	☐
27.	I permit the staff to set their own pace for change	☐	☐
28.	I urge staff to beat previous targets	☐	☐
29.	I act without consulting staff	☐	☐
30.	I ask staff follow standard rules and procedures	☐	☐

Adapted from Pfeiffer, J. and Jones, J. (eds) (1974) *A Handbook of Structured Experiences from Human Relations Training*, vol. 1 (rev.), San Diego, CA: University Associates.

Scoring for Activity 1: Leadership style questionnaire

To obtain your leadership orientation rating, score 1 point for the appropriate response under each heading, then total your scores. If your response is inappropriate you do not score. As a guide, a score of 5 or less is low and 12 or more is high.

Concern for PEOPLE score (maximum score 15)
'Yes' for questions 2, 4, 8, 10, 17, 19, 21, 23, 27.
'No' for questions 6, 13, 14, 25, 29, 30.
Concern for TASK score (maximum score 15)
'Yes' for questions 1, 3, 5, 7, 9, 11, 15, 16, 18, 20, 22, 24, 26, 28.
'No' for question 12.

Next plot your position on the Leadership Grid below.

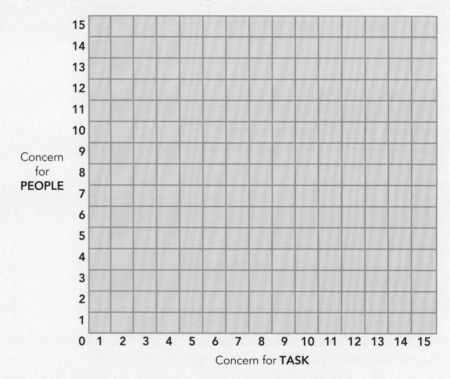

🗫 Group discussion topics

1 How does the role of leader differ from that of manager?
2 How does the role of leader differ from that of entrepreneur? Are there any similarities?
3 Leaders are born, not made. Discuss.
4 Explain what the job of leader involves.
5 What personal qualities do leaders need? Explain.
6 How do you build trust as a leader?
7 What is culture and how can it be created or developed in an organization?
8 Culture is the cement that holds the organization together. Discuss.

9 Why is organizational culture important?
10 What is the contingency theory of leadership?
11 Why is the ability to handle conflict important for an entrepreneur?
12 How do the leadership paradigms discussed in this chapter reconcile with contingency theory?
13 What is entrepreneurial leadership? How is it distinctive or different?
14 Is an entrepreneurial leader the same as entrepreneurial leadership? Explain the difference.

☞ References

Avolio, B.J., Bass, B.M. and Jung, D.I. (1999) 'Re-examining the Components of Transformational and Transactional Leadership using the Multifactor Leadership Questionnaire', *Journal of Occupational and Organisational Psychology*, 72.

Bartlett, C.A. and Ghoshal, S (1994) 'Changing the Role of Top Management; Beyond Strategy to Purpose', *Harvard Business Review*, November/December.

Bass, B.M. (1985) *Leadership and Performance Beyond Expectations*, New York: Free Press.

Bass, B.M. (1998) *Transformational Leadership: Industry, Military and Educational Impact*, Mahwah, NJ: Lawrence Erlbaum Associates.

Bass, B.M and Avolio, B.J. (1990) 'The Implications of Transactional and Transformational Leadership for Individual, Team and Organizational Development', *Research in Organizational Change and Development*, 4.

Bennis, W. and Nanus, B. (1985) *Leaders: The Strategies for Taking Charge*, New York: Harper & Row.

Blake, R. and Mouton, J. (1978) *The New Managerial Grid*, Houston: Gulf Publishing Co.

Blank, W. (1995) *The Nine Laws of Leadership*, New York: AMACOM.

Bradford, D.L. and Cohen, A.R. (1998) *Power Up: Transforming Organizations Through Shared Leadership*, New York: John Wiley.

Brubaker, D.L. (2005) 'The Power of Vision', in D.L. Brubaker and L.D. Colbe (eds), *The Hidden Leader*, Thousand Oaks, CA: Corwin Press.

Burgers, J.H., Jansen, J.J.P., Van den Bosch, F.A.J. and Volberda, H.W. (2009) 'Structural Differentiation and Corporate Venturing: The Moderating Role of Formal and Informal Integration Mechanisms', *Journal of Business Venturing*, 24(3).

Burns, P. (2013) *Corporate Entrepreneurship: Innovation and Strategy in Large Organizations*, Basingstoke: Palgrave Macmillan.

Chaleff, I. (1995) *The Courageous Follower: Standing Up, To and For Our Leaders*, San Francisco: Bennet-Koehler.

Collins, J.C. and Porras, J.I. (1994) *Built to Last: Successful Habits of Visionary Companies*, New York: Harper Business.

De Dreu, C.K.W. and Weingart, L.R. (2003) 'Task versus Relationship Conflict, Team Performance, and Team Member Satisfaction: A Meta-analysis', *Journal of Applied Psychology*, 88.

Egri, C.P. and Herman, S. (2000) 'Leadership in the North American Environmental Sector: Values, Leadership Styles and Contexts of Environmental Leaders and their Organizations', *Academy of Management Journal*, 43.

Ensley, M.D., Pearson, A.W. and Amason, A.C. (2002) 'Understanding the Dynamics of New Venture Top Management Teams: Cohesion, Conflict, and New Venture Performance', *Journal of Business Venturing*, 17.

Gardner, H. (1995) *Leading Minds: An Anatomy of Leadership*, New York: John Wiley & Sons.

Gelfand, M.J., Leslie, L.M. and Keller, K.M. (2008) 'On the Etiology of Conflict Cultures', *Research in Organizational Behavior*, 28.

George, B. (2003) *Authentic Leadership: Rediscovering the Secrets to Creating Lasting Value*, San Francisco: Jossey-Bass.

George, B. with Sims, P.E. (2007) *True North: Discover your Authentic Leadership*, San Francisco: Jossey- Bass.

Goleman, D. (1996) *Emotional Intelligence: Why It Can Matter More Than IQ*, London: Bloomsbury.

Greenleaf, R.F. (1970) *The Servant as Leader*, Mahwah, NJ: Paulist.

Hamel, G. (2009) 'Moon Shots for Management', *Harvard Business Review*, February 2009.

Heifetz, R.A. (1994) *Leadership Without Easy Answers*, Cambridge, MA: Harvard University Press.

Hofstede, G., Neuijen B., Ohayv, D.D. and Sanders, G. (1990) 'Measuring Organizational Cultures: A Qualitative and Quantitative Study across Twenty Cases', *Administrative Sciences Quarterly*, 35.

Isaacson, W. (2012) 'The Real Leadership Lessons of Steve Jobs', *Harvard Business Review*, April.

Jehn, K.A. and Bendersky, C. (2003) 'Intragroup Conflict in Organizations: A Contingency Perspective on the Conflict-outcome Relationship', *Research in Organizational Behavior*, 25.

Johnson, G. (1992) 'Managing Strategic Change: Strategy, Culture and Action', *Long Range Planning*, 25(1).

Kirby, D. (2003) *Entrepreneurship*, London: McGraw-Hill.

Kotter, J.P. (1996) *Leading Change*, Boston: Harvard Business School Press.

Kouzes, J.M. and Posner, B.Z. (2007) *The Leadership Challenge*, San Francisco: Jossey-Bass.

Lashinsky, A. (2012) *Inside Apple: The Secrets Behind the Past and Future Success of Steve Jobs's Iconic Brand*, London: John Murray.

Lechler, T. (2001), 'Social Interaction: A Determinant of Entrepreneurial Team Venture Success', *Small Business Economics*, 16.

Mach, M., Dolan, S. and Tzafrir, S. (2010) 'The Differential Effect of Team Members' Trust on Team Performance: The Mediation Role of Team Cohesion', *Journal of Occupational and Organizational Psychology*, 83(3).

Marks, M.A., Mathieu, J.E. and Zaccaro, S.J. (2001), 'A Temporally Based Framework and Taxonomy of Team Processes', *Academy of Management Review*, 26.

Martinez, M.A. and Aldrich, H.E. (2011), 'Networking Strategies for Entrepreneurs: Balancing Cohesion and Diversity', *International Journal of Entrepreneurial Behaviour and Research*, 17(1).

Mintzberg, H., Ahlstrand, B. and Lampel, J. (1998) *Strategy Safari*, New York: The Free Press.

Mintzberg, H. (2009) *Managing*, London: FT Prentice Hall.

Morden, T. (1995) 'International Culture and Management', *Management Decision*, 33(2).

Pink, D. (2011) *Drive: The Surprising Truth about What Motivates Us*, New York: Riverhead.

Raelin, J.A. (2003) *Leading Organizations: How to Bring Out Leadership in Everyone*, San Francisco: Barrett-Koehler.

Rost, J.C. (1991) *Leadership in the Twenty-first Century*, Westport, CT: Praeger.

Sashkin, M. (1996) *Becoming a Visionary Leader*, Amherst, MA: HRD Press.

Senge, P.M. (1992) *The Fifth Discipline*, London: Century Business.

Smith, K.G., Collins, C.J. and Clark, K.D. (2005) 'Existing Knowledge, Knowledge Creation Capability, and the Rate of New Product Introduction in High-technology Firms', *Academy of Management Journal*, 48(2).

Torrington, D. (1994) *International Human Resource Management*, Hemel Hempstead: Prentice Hall.

Thye, S.R., Yoon, J. and Lawler, E.J. (2002) 'The Theory of Relational Cohesion: Review of a Research Program', *Advances in Group Processes: Group Cohesion, Trust and Solidarity*, 19.

Vera, D. and Crossan, M. (2004) 'Strategic Leadership and Organizational Learning', *Academy of Management Review*, 29(2).

West III, G.P. (2007) 'Collective Cognition: When Entrepreneurial Teams, Not Individuals, Make Decisions', *Entrepreneurship: Theory and Practice*, 31(1).

www.palgrave.com/Burns-Entrepreneurship-And-Small-Business-4e

Go online to access additional teaching and learning resources for this chapter on the companion website. Click here in the ebook to complete a multiple choice revision quiz for this chapter.

CORPORATE ENTREPRENEURSHIP

19

Getty Images/iStockphoto Thinkstock Images \ Robert Churchill

Contents

Learning outcomes

When you have read this chapter and undertaken the related activities you will be able to:

> Explain what is meant by the term 'corporate entrepreneurship' and terminology used around it;

> Explain what is meant by the term 'organizational architecture' and in particular the term 'entrepreneurial architecture' and how it might be shaped through leadership, culture, structure and strategies so as to develop sustainable competitive advantage in the appropriate environment;

> Explain what is meant by the term 'learning organization' and how it underpins the entrepreneurial architecture in a larger firm;

> Understand the role intrapreneurs and venture teams have in developing innovations and how they might be encouraged and facilitated;

> Describe the options for organizing new venture developments and explain which are best in different circumstances;

> Explain why large organizations undertake corporate venturing and what is needed to make such a strategy successful.

Practice insight: Measuring organizational culture

Practice insight: 13 commandments for intrapreneurs

Practice insight: Corporate entrepreneurship audit

Case insights

Haier Group	Boeing
LEGO®	Google (3)

The challenge facing large firms

Corporate entrepreneurship is the term used to describe entrepreneurial behaviour in an established, larger organization. The objective of this is to gain competitive advantage by encouraging innovation at all levels in the organization – corporation, division, business unit, functional and project team. Morris and Kuratko (2002) use innovation and entrepreneurship interchangeably to demonstrate the concept of entrepreneurial and/or innovative intensity, shown in Figure 19.1 (and first introduced in Figure 2.1, on page 36). The scale of an entrepreneurial or innovative endeavour can range from incremental to radical and from infrequent to continuous. Entrepreneurial firms are constantly trying to push out the envelope of entrepreneurial intensity, increasing both the degree or scale of entrepreneurship and/or innovation and its frequency. Corporate entrepreneurship is the overarching term used to describe the mechanisms and processes they use to achieve this.

Big companies ought to be good at innovation. After all, they have more resources, more experience – more of everything to throw at the challenge. But the reality is that it is often newer, smaller businesses that come up with innovations, particularly radical ones. And, as the pace of change accelerates, they seem more able to cope. The core of the problem is that traditional management focuses on efficiency and effectiveness rather than creativity and innovation – control rather than empowerment. They look for cost savings through scale efficiencies rather than differentiation through economies of small scale. They look for uniformity rather than diversity and stress discipline rather than motivation. And they often discourage what they see as the risk-taking associated with a market opportunity without the information to evaluate it, by which time the opportunity will have been seized by a small firm.

Larger companies have some significant advantages such as financial resources, credibility with stakeholders, established routes to market, trusted brands and, most valuable of all, large workforces. Indeed, up to the middle of the last century they were thought of as the route to economic plenty. The challenge is to find ways of transforming them so that they can bring their resources

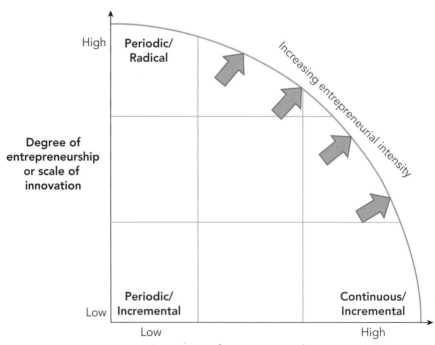

Figure 19.1 Entrepreneurial intensity

to bear on the challenges of the 21st century. Corporate entrepreneurship is now seen as a vital part of the strategies needed to rejuvenate these larger companies, maintaining their ability to innovate quickly through entrepreneurial activities (Antoncic, 2006; Burns, 2005; Brizek, 2014; Kuratko et al., 2013).

Defining corporate entrepreneurship

Although there is a large amount of literature on the general phenomenon stretching back over 30 years, even as late as the 1980s some academics still believed it was difficult, if not impossible, for entrepreneurial activity to take place in larger organizations (Morse, 1986). Indeed, there was no real consensus on what the term 'corporate entrepreneurship' meant. Shama and Chrisman (1999) identified a number of terms used to describe entrepreneurial efforts within organizations, mainly under the headings of strategic renewal and corporate venturing, and in many ways corporate venturing can be viewed simply as a series of approaches or techniques that can help bring about or maintain strategic renewal and encourage innovation. As Zahra (1996) said: 'Corporate entrepreneurship is seen as the sum of a company's innovation, strategic renewal and venturing efforts.' Figure 19.2 shows a hierarchy of the often confusing terminology used in corporate entrepreneurship.

The premise behind the overarching approach to corporate entrepreneurship is that large firms need to adapt to an ever-changing environment if they are to survive, and to do so they need to adapt their strategies, structures and cultures so as to encourage entrepreneurial activity in individual employees (Ghoshal and Bartlett, 1997; Kanter, 1989; Peters and Waterman, 1982; Sharma and Chrisman, op. cit.; Tushman and O'Reilly, 1996). It is about adapting or changing an organization so as to be more entrepreneurial and better able to cope with change and innovation. This process has been called **strategic renewal** (Sharma and Chrisman, op. cit.), **entrepreneurial transformation** (Birkinshaw, 2003) and/or **strategic entrepreneurship** (Kuratko and Audretsch, 2009; Morris et al., 2008). Organizations involved in these processes have been said to exhibit a sustained pattern of entrepreneurial behaviour over time. This has been called an **entrepreneurial orientation** (EO). There is some debate about how this pattern of behaviour might be defined (Covin and Wales, 2012), but most conceptualizations include three elements – innovativeness, risk-taking and pro-activeness (Dess et al., 1996; Rauch et al., 2009; Wales et al., 2013). A further

> "
> There is a real need for corporate entrepreneurs at the moment. For too long the prevailing consensus has been if it ain't broke, don't fix it but entrepreneurs recognize that action and change are crucial for maximizing potential and taking advantage of opportunities. You have to be tough and outgoing and not afraid of leaving calm waters to ride the waves of a storm.
>
> **Diane Thompson**, chief executive, Camelot, *The Sunday Times*, 17 March 2002
> "

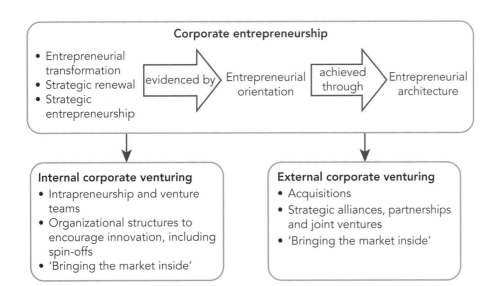

Figure 19.2 Hierarchy of terminology used in corporate entrepreneurship

two dimensions – competitive aggressiveness and internal autonomy – have also been shown to have validity (Covin and Wales, op. cit.; Lumpkin and Dess, 1996). EO has received much attention from academics and has been shown to be a strong predictor of firm performance, confirmed by a meta-analysis by Rauch et al. (2009). Covin and Slevin (1989) developed a simple nine-item psychometric scale to measure EO across the original three dimensions of innovativeness, risk-taking and pro-activeness (http://www.entrepreneurialorientation.com/measures.html). Rauch et al. (op. cit.) showed this to be the most frequently used method of measuring EO, producing similar results to other variants. However, it can be argued that the innovativeness scale used to measure EO measures the results of entrepreneurial behaviour rather than the causes of it, and that entrepreneurial behaviour in large firms is caused by an organizational infrastructure or *architecture* that encourages and facilitates it. This in turn leads to entrepreneurial behaviour that results in, and is evidenced by, greater innovativeness, measured in both scale and frequency. The architecture needed to encourage this entrepreneurial behaviour comprises four elements – leadership, culture, structures (including systems) and strategies – and has been called **entrepreneurial architecture** (Burns, 2005). This architecture can be measured using an audit tool covering 100 characteristics of an entrepreneurial organization in the four dimensions of organizational architecture (http://www.palgrave.com/companion/Burns-Corporate-Entrepreneurship/student-zone/Corporate-entrepreneurship-audit/).

In the overarching view of corporate entrepreneurship, the activity of corporate venturing is just one of the tools that can be used to achieve this strategic renewal or corporate transformation. It is one of the structures that can be used in the entrepreneurial architecture and can be used in two contexts:

> **Internal corporate venturing** is concerned with the **organizational structures** larger businesses need to encourage new businesses to develop internally while aligning them to the company's existing activities (Burgelman, 1983; Drucker, 1985; Galbraith, 1982). It is also concerned with how companies can manage the sort of **disruptive innovation** discussed in the context of new venture typologies and shown in Figure 4.4 (on page 95) (Christensen, 1997). A significant strand of the literature in its own right is concerned with **intrapreneurship**. This is concerned with individual employees and how they might be encouraged to act in an entrepreneurial way within a larger organization (Chapter 1). The term was introduced and popularized by Pinchot (1985) building on the earlier work of Kanter (1982). Rarely the inventor of the product, intrapreneurs usually work with teams – called **venture teams** – to cut through the bureaucracy of the organization to develop the product for the marketplace as quickly as possible. Intrapreneurs share many of the characteristics of the entrepreneur (page 77) and may ultimately become the managing director of a company set up by its larger parent to exploit the idea, but they are a hybrid of entrepreneur and 'company-man'. The associated literature looks at their character and personality and the systems, structures and cultures that inhibit this activity and how they might be circumvented.

> **External corporate venturing** is concerned with investment and acquisitions by larger firms in strategically important smaller firms and the corporate venturing units needed to undertake this role (Chesbrough, 2002). The reasons for doing this rarely involve short-term financial gain but more normally relate to issues of strategic foresight, innovation and market dominance (Chapter 13). It happens when new industries are emerging because of technological advances (see Amazon, Apple, Facebook, Google and Microsoft Case insight, in Chapter 5. Small firms are often good at innovation and larger firms therefore have to buy them out to capitalize on their 'first-mover advantage' in a critical area of new technology development. This happens frequently in the pharmaceutical industry where large companies simply buy out the smaller companies making new drug discoveries. It also happens more in the USA than in the UK with technology firms like Amazon being particularly active (see Case insight, page 353).

The formation of strategic alliances, partnerships and joint ventures (Chapter 9) is also a feature of corporate entrepreneurship that might be classified under this heading. As we saw, these can be an effective way of sustaining competitive advantage and can be particularly important in relation to innovation. There are often explicit strategic and operational motives for alliances such as gaining access to new markets. Some firms have based their international expansion strategy almost entirely on foreign alliances. Similarly, acquiring new technologies, enhancing new product development capabilities or leveraging on economies of scale or scope may all be reasons for strategic alliances.

One strand of the literature in both internal and external corporate venturing might be called **'bringing the market inside'** (Birkinshaw, op. cit.). This focuses mainly on the structural changes needed to encourage entrepreneurial behaviour and argues for a market approach to resource allocation and people management systems using market-based techniques such as **spin-offs** and venture capital operations (Foster and Kaplan, 2001; Hamel, 1999). For example, just as many firms use venture capital teams to search out strategic investments or acquisitions in smaller firms; Monsanto, Apple, 3M and Xerox use independent venture capital conduits to finance their spin-outs from in-house research (internal corporate venturing).

To understand how entrepreneurial transformation or strategic renewal – central themes to corporate entrepreneurship – can be achieved, we need to first understand the term entrepreneurial architecture.

Entrepreneurial architecture

Organizational architecture is a metaphor used to describe the infrastructure an organization needs in order to build business processes that deliver its vision – human resources, structures, culture and strategies. The term first appeared in a book by Nadler et al. (1992). It is built on four pillars of leadership, culture, structure and strategies. An entrepreneurial architecture is one that embeds entrepreneurial characteristics – the DNA of the entrepreneur – into the organization, allowing it to adapt and compete in a changing environment. It is one that encourages an entrepreneurial orientation (EO) – facilitating innovation, pro-activeness, risk-taking, competitive aggressiveness and internal autonomy. This entrepreneurial architecture creates within the organization the knowledge and routines that allow it to respond flexibly to change and opportunity in the way the entrepreneur does. It is better suited to survive in the age of uncertainty. It is a very real and valuable asset. It creates competitive advantage in its own right and is sustainable. As explained below, this architecture is based upon relationships, but it is built on the four pillars shown in Figure 19.3.

Complexity theory lends support to both the concept of organizational architecture and the structure of an entrepreneurial architecture that can facilitate change. Complex adaptive systems – the result of multiple independent actions – are unpredictable. Small actions at one level can have large-scale unexpected consequences elsewhere. Here we think of the increasingly interconnected global marketplace of today and the turbulent environment it generates. Complexity theory hints that there are no stable equilibria in these situations. But we also realize that small actions within an organization can have a big effect, particularly if they can be marshalled. At the same time, complex social systems have a capacity to self-organize, changing and creating new structures and systems without being directed to do so. It is the capacity to self-organize that can give direction

Entrepreneurship is based on the same principles, whether the entrepreneur is an existing large institution or an individual starting his or her new venture single-handed. It makes little or no difference whether the entrepreneur is a business or a non-business public-service organization. The rules are pretty much the same.

Peter Drucker, *Innovation and Entrepreneurship: Practice and Principles*, London: Heinemann, 1985

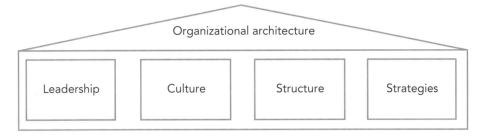

Figure 19.3 Four pillars of organizational architecture

to the changes. The three main requirements for self-organization according to Grant (2010) are: '*identity* that permits a common sense-making process within the organization, *information* that provides the possibility of synchronized behaviour and *relationships* that are the pathways through which the information is transformed into intelligent, coordinated action' (my emphasis added). And here we start to see the entrepreneurial architecture that we are trying to build: based on relationships, knowledge and information, with a strong dominant logic that aids understanding and provides strategic intent.

Complexity theory also gives us an intellectual basis for the apparent dilemma of whether to encourage incremental or radical change within an entrepreneurial architecture. The two are not mutually exclusive and systems that have the capability of making *both* small-scale adaptations as well as large-scale revolution are most likely to thrive in a turbulent environment. They exist at the 'edge of chaos', adapting all the time but able to make the occasional radical leap. The theory also provides intellectual support to the 'emergent' school of strategy development in contrast to the 'deliberate' school with its linearity of approach, since it would support the view that the complex, interconnected world of today is inherently unpredictable. As Grant (op. cit.) said:

> *Not only is it impossible to forecast the business environment but managers cannot predict with any certainty what the outcome of their actions will be. The concept of the CEO as the peak decision-maker and strategy architect is not only unrealistic – it is undesirable. Managers must rely on the self-organizing properties of their companies. The critical issues are how can they select structures, systems and management styles that will allow these self-organizing properties to generate the best outcomes?* (My emphasis added)

To which I would add organizational culture.

And this brings us to how we build and shape organizational architecture to become entrepreneurial. What does it look like and how can it be shaped? The arrows in Figure 19.4 show how architecture can be shaped and influenced through its four pillars. While one of the key strategies of the organization can be to create an entrepreneurial architecture, once in place that architecture will start to influence strategy. All of this is within the context of the environment and an entrepreneurial architecture is only really appropriate to certain environments. We shall return to this later.

As we have seen, leadership styles, organizational cultures and structures are linked, with one reinforcing the other. To be effective, all three elements of architecture must be congruent. As we saw in Chapter 18, certain leadership styles are appropriate for different sorts of tasks, different groups of people and different situations or environments. Handy (1995) popularized four leadership typologies – based upon Greek mythology – and the cultures and structures for which they are most appropriate. These are summarized in Table 19.1.

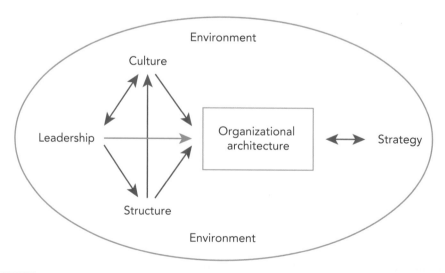

Figure 19.4 Influences on organizational architecture

Table 19.1   Handy's Gods of Management

Leadership style	Organizational culture	Organizational structure
Zeus The patriarch of all gods. Charismatic/visionary leader: visionary, independent, instinctive, persuasive, builder of relationships, power and networks. Excited by the challenge of uncertainty.	**Club culture** Individuals are independent but responsible, trusted (not controlled) to make right decisions, understanding the consequences of wrong decisions. Power relationships influence behaviour.	**Spider's web structures** Built upon relationships with the leader in the middle. Managers are professionals, free to follow instincts. They are also leaders.
Apollo The god of rules and order. Leader by appointment: authoritarian, logical, sequential, analytical, scientific, with everything in its place. Enjoys repetition.	**Role culture** Individuals are assigned tasks and organized and controlled through rules, regulations, job descriptions and direct supervision. People are cogs in the wheel, predictable, inflexible and unresponsive to change.	**Traditional hierarchical bureaucracies** Strong management control. Managers are administrators.
Athena The warrior goddess, problem-solver of craftsmen and a pioneering sea captain. Leader by expertise and experience: credible, convincing, focused, but unadventurous.	**Task culture** The problem is the task. Individuals are judged on how well they undertake the task/problem. Talent, creativity, initiative and intuition are all valued.	**Matrix structures** Project-based team-work. Managers define and solve problems by assigning staff and resources. They are valued for their expertise and experience. Teams form and reform to undertake different tasks/problems.
Dionysus The god of wine and song, individual and independent. Partner rather than leader. Professionally competent.	**Culture of individualism and independence** The organization is the servant of the individual. No boss. Individual talent is valued. Decision-making by consent and consensus.	**Organic structures** Supporting structures with loose coordination of independent individuals with talent. No boss.

Zeus is characterized as the charismatic and visionary entrepreneur, managing through interpersonal relationships and sitting in the middle of the spider's web. This contrasts with Apollo's traditional hierarchical bureaucracy and its rules and regulations. Athena is the team-working leader in a matrix organization, continually solving problems or addressing new tasks. Finally there is Dionysus, the partner rather than leader in an organic organization that supports people's independence without threatening it.

Of course no organization is exclusively dedicated to one god, they balance the gods. The task of leadership is getting that balance right. Handy sees this as influenced by four factors:

> Size – The larger the group of people (or organizations) that need to work together, the more likely Apollo is to rule. Small groups or teams prefer Athena.

> Work patterns – Where work is repetitive and routine, Apollo rules. Where work is continually changing, Zeus and Dionysus rule, but if it is undertaken in groups, Athena rules.

> Life cycle – If the life cycle is short and new product development is important, Athena rules. If the life cycle is long Apollo re-exerts his influence.

> People – Professionals, the young and better educated people prefer Dionysus. Countries with conformist cultures (using Hofstede's dimensions these are high collectivist and high power distance cultures such as Saudi Arabia – see Chapter 3) are more comfortable with Apollo, whereas countries that value individualism, such as the USA or UK, prefer Zeus or Dionysus.

Handy's typologies illustrate how combinations of different cultures and structures support or result from different leaders. The entrepreneurial leader we described in Chapter 18 is definitely not Apollo, but is a mix of Zeus, Athena and Dionysus and their related cultures and structures. This is not surprising since, while wanting to retain a strong entrepreneurial focus (Zeus), we have emphasized small group working (Athena), speed of competitive response (Athena) and continuous change (Zeus and Dionysus). And that is before we consider the people you might lead. It all goes to underline the point that effective leadership is an art rather than a science and, while we can isolate the main factors that influence it and point to good practice in particular contexts, there is no magic formula.

Building an entrepreneurial architecture

As we have seen throughout this book, there are three key characteristics in an entrepreneur's approach to managing an organization:

> Their ability to develop strong networks of relationships within and outside the organization;
> The way they develop strategy and make decisions;
> The way they mitigate risk through knowledge, partnerships and structures.

So, while there is no one-size-fits-all blueprint for an entrepreneurial architecture, it needs to reflect these key characteristics through its four pillars.

Leadership

Chapter 18 outlined a blueprint for effective entrepreneurial leadership – a leadership that will carry over into an entrepreneurial organization and is appropriate for a changing and unpredictable environment. It should be visionary, transformational but distributed (team based). Although effective leadership depends upon a range of contextual factors including group, task and situation, leaders need to have good emotional intelligence – self and social awareness and social skills. The 10 characteristics of a good leader for an entrepreneurial organization were set out in Table 18.2. The high-level leadership team in an entrepreneurial organization ideally comprises just half a dozen executives who trust each other, share information and cover for each other. They must behave like an effective partnership with high levels of cohesion and 'shared cognitions', built upon mutual trust. That model is replicated across the entire organization.

Culture

Chapter 18 also explained that establishing an appropriate corporate culture is vital if you want to develop an entrepreneurial organization. Entrepreneurs develop deep relationships and this is one of the characteristics of the culture of an entrepreneurial organization. Based on values, norms and beliefs, the organizational culture influences individual and social behavioural norms. The culture needed to form an entrepreneurial architecture should:

> See change as the norm, certainly not something to be feared and value creativity and innovation;
> Value strong personal and group relationships and generate a strong sense of group identity – Hofstede's 'in-group' (Chapter 3). This can be built around the vision for the organization as well as its recognizable values, norms and beliefs. It needs to be consistent with the leadership style within the organization. This cultural characteristic extends to the development of a wide partnership network;
> Encourage empowerment and motivation to make decisions for the good of the organization. This involves a balance between two elements from Hofstede's culture. Firstly, this implies that while individual initiative and achievement is valued (high 'individual' and 'masculine' culture), so too are cooperative relationships (high 'feminine' and 'collectivism' culture) through cooperation, networks and relationships. This generates a clear identity as an 'in-group' and a feeling of competition against 'out-groups'. This 'can-do' attitude should give confidence in an uncertain future;
> Encourage measured risk-taking through experimentation, tolerating mistakes but encouraging learning from them. In Hofstede's terms this is low 'uncertainty avoidance'. Indeed

decision-making will be delegated down, as far as possible, and information will be shared rather than hoarded;

> Be egalitarian but slightly anti-authoritarian – always daring to be different. In Hofstede's terms this means a low power distance with flat organizational structures, open and informal relationships and open, unrestricted information flows.

 Practice insight Measuring organizational culture

Measuring the dimensions of organizational culture is extremely difficult and there are alternatives to Hofstede's model outlined in Chapter 3. The Organizational Culture Assessment Instrument (OCAI) is a simple validated instrument developed by Professors Robert Quinn and Kim Cameron and free to use. Consequently, it is claimed to be used by over 10,000 companies worldwide. You are asked to distribute 100 points between statements that typify six dimensions of organizational culture: dominant organizational characteristics, organizational leadership style, management of employees, organization glue, strategic emphases and the criteria for success. The points can be distributed to represent how the organization is now and how you would prefer it to be. The dimensions are designed to measure an organization's position on the Competing Values Framework (Quinn and Rohrbaugh, 1983), which measures the conflict between the internal and external focus of the organization and its preference for stability and control or flexibility and discretion. The resulting analysis consists of four typologies:

> **Hierarchy culture** – the traditional organizational structure with hierarchical controls that respect position and power, emphasizing efficiency and stability;

> **Market culture** – controls through trying to minimize costs and moving towards market efficiency by looking outward at the cost of transactions, achievement and results orientated;

> **Clan culture** – less focused on structure and control through rules and regulations, with greater emphasis on flexibility, driving direction through vision, shared goals, a sense of family (Hofstede's 'in-group'), loyalty, mentoring and nurturing, often with flat structures using team working;

> **Adhocracy culture** – even more independence and flexibility with greatest speed of response to change, more entrepreneurial with greater risk-taking, using ad hoc teams to address new challenges.

The OCAI analysis gives you a map (below) showing where you are now (solid orange line) and where you might want to be on these typologies (dotted line).

An online version is available at www.ocai-online.com. Individuals can use the test for free, and the analysis includes a brief explanation.

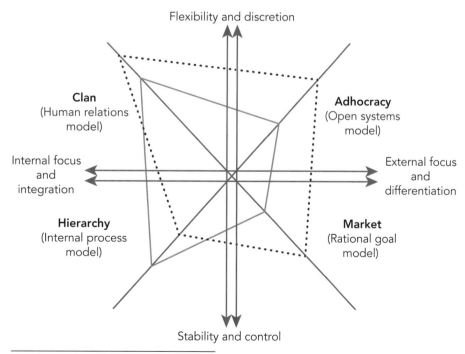

Reproduced with kind permission of Kim Cameron.

I believe in as flat a management structure as possible … in leading without title … I never put any emphasis on my title. I most certainly try to lead by example and I'm very much a big believer in making my mistakes public so that other people feel confident and comfortable to be able to air their own mistakes.

Shaa Wasmund, founder, Mykindaplace and Brightstone Ventures, *Management Today* (www.managementtoday.co.uk), 18 July 2008

Structure

Chapter 12 explained that structures create order in an organization but there is no single 'best' solution – there are too many variables. The most appropriate structure depends on the nature of the organization, the strategies it employs, the tasks it undertakes, the culture it wishes to encourage, the environment it operates in and its size. Entrepreneurial organizations typically face a high degree of environmental turbulence, and if the tasks they need to undertake are complex, they are best served by an organic organizational structure that may well change and evolve in different situations. Organic structures are not appropriate for all organizations and it is probable that a multi-business will need to have different operating divisions or subsidiaries with more traditional structures, reflecting their different capabilities. What will emerge is a hybrid-organic structure. Operating divisions or subsidiaries will be relatively autonomous but linked to the head office through an organic structure with entrepreneurial architecture (like the Virgin Group). Control should be loose, or at least balanced, but there needs to be tight accountability. The idea is to give people autonomy but hold them accountable for the outcomes of their actions. A strong organizational culture is particularly needed because of this informal organization structure and loose management control. Another characteristic of entrepreneurial architecture would be the range of partnerships developed by the organization.

Strategies

The strategies that an organization pursues are particular to its situation and the markets within which it operates. However, Chapter 12 outlined how an entrepreneur and therefore an entrepreneurial organization should approach strategy development. Strategy development might be a combination of emergent and deliberate, but it should be characterized by continuous strategizing at all levels in the organization, underpinned by a strong vision and sense of direction. This vision should be ambitious but rooted in reality, creating a tension sufficient to motivate the organization to change. The organization should be good at scanning the environment for opportunities and threats, developing strategic options. This will often be helped by the network of relationships and partnerships developed at all levels of the organization. As a result of an organization's culture, structures and approach to strategy development, decision-making will tend to be decentralized, incremental and adaptive, so as to maintain maximum flexibility. However, it will be underpinned by a strong vision and strategic intent. This should provide sufficient guidance for decision-making because staff will know enough about the organization and be motivated to do the best they can for it. Mistakes will be tolerated and learned from. In this way, the organization will be able to respond speedily to opportunities or threats.

Matching architecture and environment

An entrepreneurial architecture may not be appropriate for all organizations. It is not appropriate for a benign, unchanging environment in which simple tasks are undertaken with a view to achieving maximum efficiency. Entrepreneurial firms thrive in environments of change, chaos, complexity, competition, uncertainty and even contradiction, where innovation is essential – and this is what an entrepreneurial architecture is designed for. This is the sort of environment many organizations find themselves in today:

> The interconnectedness of markets and economies tends to amplify small initial changes – in customer needs or market trends – and this makes for instability and unpredictability and it means that traditional forms of strategic planning no longer work. Where rapid change is valued by customers – for example because of their need for knowledge and information – markets offer considerable 'first-mover advantage' and reinforce the importance of a rapid response to developments. These sorts of markets are often characterized by rapid technological change;

> Markets might be highly price sensitive, with low barriers to entry and high economies of scale. New competitors might be emerging all the time and these new competitors might be very price competitive and/or good at innovating;

> New markets could be emerging and the whole structure of the market might be changing, with many mergers or takeovers. In these circumstances customers might be seen as promiscuous as their 'needs' change rapidly and, as a result, the industry spends increasing amounts on advertising in order to get their attention;

> As product life cycles shorten, it can lead to unbalanced product/service portfolios that require rapid rebalancing through product/market innovation.

Adding to all these problems might be rapid economic and social change, pressures for greater corporate social responsibility, and problems in attracting suitable staff. These are the sorts of environment that an entrepreneurial architecture is designed to deal with.

Since there is no one-size-fits-all blueprint for an entrepreneurial architecture the exact form it takes also depends on the economic, technological and societal environment in which the organization operates. It can also be sectorally and geographically dependent. It can vary with the nature of the entrepreneurial intensity. This means structuring the organization so that each operating unit can be organized in such a way as to best deal with the environment it faces – possibly with structures within structures, subcultures within cultures and different approaches to leadership within an overall approach. Not all parts of a multi-business organization may exhibit the same characteristics because of differences in their operational needs (for example, the stage in the life cycle of products) and/or their contextual situations (for example, they do not operate in an entrepreneurial environment). We have characterized the entrepreneurial environment as one of rapid change and uncertainty where speed of response and innovation are vital and knowledge and learning are of paramount importance. Where a 'multi-business' like a conglomerate that operates across different sectors (e.g. Virgin Group) has different organizational needs in its various operating divisions or subsidiaries, what is important is that the overarching structure linking the divisions or subsidiaries has an entrepreneurial architecture. The divisions or subsidiaries may have a different architecture that is more appropriate to their operating needs.

 ## Case insight   Haier Group

Corporate entrepreneurship

Zhang Ruimin

Although little known in the West, Haier Group is one of the largest non-state-owned enterprises in China. With 14% of the global market, it is the largest manufacturer of 'white goods' in the world. It is also the world's fastest growing appliance manufacturer. Haier was hailed by *Strategy + Business* as a 'high-performing and truly entrepreneurial global business' (Issue 77, Winter 2014). Its CEO, Zhang Ruimin, was invited to give the keynote address at the 2013 annual meeting of the Academy of Management and was lauded by the journal for 'organizing the company around a conceptual framework that has guided its development for years – in Haier's case, practically since its founding'. That framework you will recognize has all the characteristics of corporate entrepreneurship.

'As soon as a company grows large, its employees learn to work in accordance with the company's rules. As regulations multiply and companies control their employees more tightly, everyone becomes really good at following orders. Their sensitivity to the market decreases accordingly ... Lack of entrepreneurial spirit is a major reason for the decreasing competitiveness – and

Continued...

Continued from previous page...

even the eventual collapse – of big enterprises. It is an extremely difficult problem for Chinese companies in particular ... An enterprise must evolve into a system that stands on its own, and does not depend on the whim and fancy of its current leader'.

Haier started its life as a manufacturing firm that was partly owned by the city of Qingdao, one of China's first enterprise zones. It was not successful. Many of their products had to be repaired before they could be used. Zhang, who was then an assistant administrator in the city, was instructed to find a managing director who could turn the business around. He failed and so in 1984, at the age of 25 and with little or no business experience, he took the job himself. It took time, but Zhang eventually succeeded.

Today Haier manufactures a wide range of appliances like refrigerators, washers, dryers, entertainment electronics and air and water conditioners. It has differentiated itself by targeting the needs of market niches. For example, it manufactures large washing machines for Pakistani robes, small ones for Chinese delicate fabrics and durable ones with large hoses for washing vegetables on Chinese farms. These have water purifiers that remove specific pollutants and are used by some 220,000 communities across China (Hair jointly holds some 20 water purification patents). Hair is also repositioning itself from being a manufacturer to being a 'provider of solutions to consumers' problems', selling both home appliances and services such as water safety information. Part of this repositioning involves dealing with customers more directly, online and through social media, involving them in product selection (for example by offering different configuration of products – colour and design), testing or reviews (sharing feedback) and even product development.

> *'We have a culture of self-questioning. Everyone is always challenging their own ideas and continuously surpassing themselves ... Those inside Haier, especially managers, understand that it's crucial that we adapt to the evolving needs of users and the changing environment.'*

Haier's success hinges on four key capabilities:

> **Customer responsive innovation** – the ability to tailor products or services to local needs;
> **Operational excellence** – the ability to produce high quality products at very low prices through a commitment to continuous improvement, a zero-defect policy and internal competition;
> **Management of local distribution networks** – an ability developed in China's decentralized value chain and applied to emerging markets;

> **On-demand production and delivery** – combining a customer-pull distribution chain and a zero-inventory logistics system to deliver high variety at very low cost.

Key to achieving this was the move towards decentralization, participative management and autonomous but accountable work teams and platforms. Every part of the company is an autonomous, platform-based profit centre. They can make their own decisions about target customers, employees and who they partner with – including other parts of the company. R&D projects involve collaborative working with outside designers, academics – even competitors. For example, the Air Box is a smartphone-controlled intelligent controller for monitoring and managing the climate in a building – linking heating, air conditioning and air filtration. The concept was developed with significant customer input but the product was also developed in partnership with Samsung and Apple so that it can control any climate control system, not just those manufactured by Haier.

> *'We used to have a pyramid style [organization] structure for our sales in China. The people in charge of sales had to manage business at the national, provincial, and city level. After the arrival of the internet age, we realized that under this triangular hierarchical structure, people had a difficult time adapting to the requirement of the times. So we reorganised ourselves as an entrepreneurial platform. We flattened everything out, taking out all the middle management. We decentralized the structure to one with more than 2,800 counties. Each county organization has seven people or fewer.'* (Zhang Ruimin, CEO, Haier Group, *Strategy + Business*, Issue 77, Winter 2014)

❑ Visit the website: http://www.haier.com

QUESTIONS:

1 Why is Haier an entrepreneurial organization?
2 How does it achieve this?

Using relationships to develop competitive advantage

One of the key characteristics of the way entrepreneurs approach business and management is the way they develop and use relationships. And organizational architecture enables them to build upon this defining strength. Kay (1993) observed that architecture is based upon 'relational contracts', with customers, suppliers and staff. These are long-term relationships, not necessarily just legal contracts, which are 'complex, subtle and hard to define precisely or to replicate'. They are only partly specified and only really enforced by the need of the parties to work together. They are often based on shared values, but like all relationships, they are primarily based upon trust, although underpinned by mutual self-interest. This self-interest discourages one party from acting in some way at the expense of others because it is important that they continue to work together. Individuals participate in these relationships voluntarily because of a strong personal feeling that it is in their interests because they are participating in a 'repeated game' in which they share the rewards of collective achievement. The relationships solve problems of cooperation, coordination and commitment. However, if the bond of trust is broken the relationship will break down.

Just as entrepreneurs use networks of relationships to help them operate in a way that allows them to seize opportunities quickly, architecture should allow the entrepreneurial firm to respond quickly and effectively to change and opportunity. Developing organizational architecture is a systematic exploitation of one of the main distinctive capabilities of entrepreneurs. It builds in dynamic capabilities that are difficult to copy. It does this by creating within the organization the knowledge and routines that enable this to happen smoothly and unhindered. Staff are somehow motivated in themselves to make this happen, knowing it is good for the organization – empowerment.

These relationships are characterized as having a high but structured degree of informality, something that can be mistaken as haphazard, chaotic or just lucky. But, as Kay points out, 'truly chaotic organizations rarely perform well' and, as we have seen, entrepreneurs create their own luck. Architecture is difficult to copy because individuals only know or understand a small part of the overall structure. It is not a legal contract and not written down anywhere, relying instead on the complex network of personal relationships throughout the organization. It can therefore create barriers to entry and competitive advantage. However, Kay observed that it was easier to sustain than to create, and even more difficult to create in an organization that does not have architecture in the first place.

With this description we start to glimpse reflections of the start-up entrepreneur in the middle of a spider's web of informal, personal relationships – recognizing opportunity everywhere, trying to innovate and trying to replicate success, using networks, and relying on personal relationships with customers, staff and suppliers. They prefer influence and informal relationships to formal contracts. They use these to secure repeat sales at the expense of competitors and to secure resources or competitive advantage that they might not otherwise have. For example, close partnerships with suppliers where information and knowledge are shared can lead to significant advantages in lowering costs, lead times and inventories.

Building a learning organization

There are many parallels between the entrepreneurial architecture we have described and the concept of a 'learning organization'. A learning organization has been defined as one that 'facilitates the learning of all its members and continuously transforms itself … adapting, changing, developing and transforming themselves in response to the needs, wishes and aspirations of people, inside and outside' (Pedler et al., 1991). Writings on the learning organization stress how it is flexible, adaptable and better equipped to thrive in a turbulent environment. A learning organization facilitates learning for all its members and continually transforms itself:

> Encouraging systematic problem-solving;
> Encouraging experimentation and new approaches;

> Learning from past experience and history;
> Learning from best practice and outside experience;
> Being skilled at transferring knowledge in the organization.

Senge (1992) observed that learning organizations can only be built by leaders with fire and passion: 'Learning organizations can be built only by individuals who put their life spirit into the task.' The similarity to the entrepreneur is striking. Indeed, the similarities can also be seen from the literature on entrepreneurs. For example, Timmons (1999) observed that successful entrepreneurs were 'patient leaders, capable of instilling tangible visions and managing for the long haul. The entrepreneur is at once a learner and a teacher, a doer and a visionary.' Being a learner and a teacher are two of the prime tasks for a leader in a learning organization. And the parallels go further. The literature says that a learning organization thrives in turbulent and changing environment because it is fast and responsive. Using Hofstede's terms, this requires a more collectivist culture – a belief that the interests of the organization and the individual are the same, with shared values and a sense of being part of a team or an 'in-group'. The atmosphere is cooperative within the 'in-group', although it may be uncharacteristically competitive with 'out-groups'. As a result, staff feel empowered to influence the direction of the organization and believe that continually developing, learning and acquiring new knowledge is the way to do this. Truly entrepreneurial organizations, therefore, are also learning organizations. This goes to the heart of their architecture.

Constant learning by organizations requires the acquisition of new knowledge and skill and the willingness to apply them to decision-making (Miller, 1996). It includes the unlearning of old routines (Markoczy, 1994) so that the range of potential behaviour is altered (Wilpert, 1995). This is at the heart of what a learning organization is about and there are some lessons to be learned from how it goes about doing so. Knowledge is about more than just information sharing. It is about learning from each other and from outside the organization. It is about getting a better understanding of inter-relationships, complexities and causalities – the causes rather than just the symptoms of a problem.

Kim (1993) suggested that effective learning can be considered to be a revolving wheel – the wheel of learning (Figure 19.5). During half the cycle, you form and then test existing concepts and

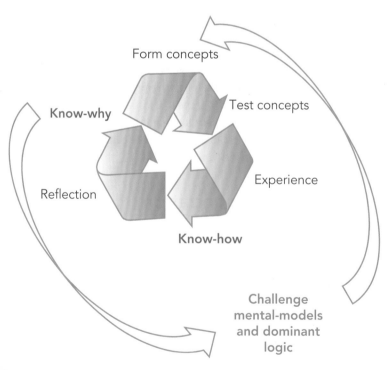

Figure 19.5 The wheel of learning

observe what happens through experience – learning 'know-how'. In the second half of the cycle, you are reflecting on the observations and forming new concepts – learning 'know-why' – often called '**double-loop learning**' (Argyris and Schön, 1978). It is this second sort of learning that is of particular value to the organization because it is at this point that root causes of problems are diagnosed and systematic solutions put in place. This is when you question your 'mental models' or 'dominant logic' – the assumptions and theories about the world upon which your learning (or the problem you seek to solve) is based. You start asking 'why?' and 'why not?' and start thinking more creatively (Chapter 4).

Real learning is about application, continuous problem-solving and understanding the root cause of problems rather than being distracted by the symptoms. It is about all those things we looked at in Chapter 4 – knowledge, awareness and connectivity. It is at the heart of practising those 'discovery skills'. Above all, it is about continually challenging our mental models and dominant logic and actively trying to be more creative. Dominant logic is the mindset with which an organization collectively sees itself and the world it inhabits – its position with customers, competitors and other stakeholders. It filters the information, subconsciously interpreting environmental data in a certain way and influences behaviour. Since dominant logic is a social construct, it can be influenced and changed by the organizational architecture, albeit over time. By embedding double-loop learning within the organization you can change the dominant logic of managers and get them to reframe the way they approach business to become more creative. It is a vital skill for an entrepreneurial organization.

The constant turning of the wheel of learning, sharing knowledge of know-how and know-why, embeds double-loop learning within an organization. Dominant logic is constantly challenged and constantly changing. Over the years this generates organizational learning, becoming part of the collective 'memory' of the organization. Although this accumulated knowledge is tacit (i.e. embedded in minds and activities, rather than written down) as well as being shadowy and fragile, it is unique to the organization and difficult to copy. It is therefore a valuable part of the architecture that underpins the organization's competitive advantage.

> There are countless successful companies that are thriving now despite the fact that they started with little more than passion and a good idea. There are also many that have failed, for the very same reason. The difference is that the thriving companies gathered the knowledge that gave them the substantial edge over their competition, which they then used to improve their execution.
>
> **Michael Dell**, founder, Dell Corporation (1999) *Direct from Dell: Strategies that Revolutionized an Industry*, New York: Harper Business

---

 ## Case insight   LEGO®

Entrepreneurial transformation

Jørgen Vig Knudstorp

LEGO, the well-known children's building system, has been around for a long time, and in an age when new toys come and go with astonishing rapidity and technology-based toys like computer games are reaching astonishing heights of sophistication, it might be difficult to understand the enduring market appeal of these basic building bricks. Now called LEGO Systems in Play, over 60 billion LEGO bricks and other elements are made every year; if all the LEGO bricks ever produced were divided among the world population each person would have at least 100 bricks. The name 'LEGO' is an abbreviation of two Danish words '*leg godt*', meaning 'play well'. The company was founded by Ole Kirk Kristiansen in 1932 and it still remains a privately owned fourth-generation family business. It is now one of the world's largest and most profitable manufacturers of toys, with its head office in Billund, Denmark, and branches throughout the world. The traditional interlocking LEGO brick has twice been named toy of the century by *Fortune* magazine, then by the British Association of Toy Retailers.

Photos courtesy of the LEGO Group. ©2015 The LEGO Group

The LEGO range

The brick was launched in its present form in 1958. However, the LEGO Group's product range is now far wider than just the world-famous LEGO Classic brick. It also includes LEGO DUPLO and LEGO Juniors which are targeted at younger children, extending the target market age from 1½ to 11 years. Since the late 1970s, LEGO products have been sold not just as building bricks but as a medium of creative expression for children to start stories around various themes. The company has developed numerous 'play

Continued...

Continued from previous page...

themes' for all their products, such as fire stations, police, airport, knights, castles and racing cars. Sets of bricks, together with mini-figures, can be used to build these themed scenes – LEGO City. Characters and scenes from movies or cartoons like LEGO Harry Potter, Spiderman, Bob the Builder, Star Wars and Batman – produced under licence – are also available. There are newer products like BIONICLE, which allows children to construct action figures like knights and to develop a detailed online world into which they can be placed to play through a story. The LEGO Group has also moved into different market segments. In 2012, LEGO Friends was introduced, aimed at young girls, allowing them to construct scenes from everyday life or from the world of fairy tales. LEGO Group now produces video games (e.g. LEGO Star Wars) and even makes its own movies. These developments have evolved through four 'eras':

1   The first was developing construction and building as the central elements in play, augmented in 1962 by the introduction of the LEGO wheel.
2   The second era evolved as LEGO products gained motion through wheels, small motors and gears through the introduction of LEGO Technic in 1972.
3   The third era, which evolved alongside the second in the 1970s, was role play, when LEGO mini-figures were born. This heralded the development of a new business model called 'System within the System' based upon play themes, the first being LEGOLAND® Town, LEGOLAND® Castle and LEGOLAND® Space.
4   The fourth era introduced intelligence and behaviour with such products as the LEGO MINDSTORMS (robot building sets).

The 2003 crisis

However, LEGO Group's current success has been hard won. In 2003 the company reported a record loss of $240 million, spawning rumours that it might be taken over. It had lost confidence in the brick as the core of its product offering, and many of its efforts to innovate with the aim of becoming a lifestyle brand for families with children – both within and outside its traditional business – had proved to be unprofitable or outright failures. What is more, costs were not being controlled effectively, with sales of individual components not being matched to production in the supply chain. CEO and owner Kjeld Kirk Kristiansen (grandson of the founder) decided to step down, appointing Jørgen Vig Knudstorp in his place in 2004. Jørgen Vig Knudstorp (known as JVK), a one-time management consultant, had joined the company as director of strategic development in 2001. He was given a clear mandate for radical change by the Kristiansen family, who injected additional funding of $178 million, giving the

company space for a turnaround. And although Kjeld Kirk Kristiansen stepped down as CEO, he worked closely with JVK and other members of the board and the leadership team to pinpoint the company's problems.

The turnaround involved a number of parallel initiatives to halt the decline in sales, cut costs and focus on improving cash flow. Cutting costs and improving cash flow was vital. Without this, it might not have survived. Competition from lower-priced, similar products was eating into sales. Based in the high-cost country of Denmark, LEGO Group's supply chains were long and expensive. They were also geared to supply small retailers rather than the big-box stores, resulting in high levels of stock-holding. To address this, the company had to eliminate inefficiencies and re-gear to compete in the new retail world. The team decided to approach this issue holistically, analysing the entire process from product development, sourcing, manufacturing and, finally, distribution. While the team believed the company was good at innovating, it also believed that there were just too many innovation projects and they were not being managed well. It discovered that each successive generation of innovation in established product lines seemed to deliver slimmer margins as product complexity increased. Designers were simply not factoring in the price of materials or costs of manufacture when they developed new products.

The first steps were to reduce the number of unique pieces manufactured, from over 13,000 to 6,000, and establish new manufacturing bases in the lower-cost countries of Hungary and Mexico (by 2014 this had been extended to Czech Republic, with a new factory planned for China to cover the growing Asian market). Individual products were cut as a review revealed that just 30% of products generated 80% of sales. A pirate kit included eight pirates with 10 different legs, developed without a thought of the cost of manufacture or stock-holding. Indeed, two-thirds of the

Inside the LEGO Factory production facility in Nyíregyháza, Hungary

Continued...

Continued from previous page...

company's stock turned out to be items that were no longer manufactured. With more than 11,000 suppliers, growing all the time as designers sought new materials to develop new products, there was plenty of scope to rationalize sourcing and leverage the buying power of the company. The Danish factory was one of the largest injection-moulding operations in the world and yet it operated a fragmented, batch production system, responding to frequent changes in production demands. This was inefficient and capacity utilization was only 70%. Although the 200 largest toy chains generated over two-thirds of sales, LEGO Group devoted as much effort to supplying the thousands of smaller shops that generated the balance, often supplying them with small orders at short notice.

A team approach to driving transformation

JVK adopted a twin-track approach to driving the transformation, each involving different multi-disciplinary teams. A leadership team developed the strategies, and a management team, consisting of managers from sales, IT, logistics and manufacturing, drove the changes at an operational level. The management team met daily in a 'war room' to prioritize and coordinate the changes, assigning responsibility for specific initiatives to individual managers. They tracked progress, anticipating resistance and dealing with obstacles as they arose. The room itself had white boards, and often these were covered in action lists and schedules. JVK himself would visit the war room regularly checking on the status of various initiatives, always pushing to get the changes through as quickly as possible. The teams worked in a very open way, debating how to change in the first place but, once agreed, only deviating from it should the approach prove ineffective.

The leadership team also operated in an open way, taking time for consensus building, between themselves and the management team. The workforce was also involved and the need for the changes – including redundancies – made clear. The policy was one of transparency, including debate around the realities of the situation. The workforce was involved in how redundancies would be implemented. The belief was that, although this process took time, the changes would be more effectively implemented and the benefits more lasting if they were understood and, as far as possible, staff 'bought into them'.

Early wins

The team piloting changes to sourcing was headed by LEGO Group's former chief financial officer, Jesper Ovesen, with the intention of signalling the importance of this initiative. The first task it tackled was the cost of the different coloured resins that went into the production of the bricks – the largest material cost the company faced. The team

included the head of product innovation and the manager of the company's supply chain. The team cut the number of coloured bricks by almost half, cut back on slow-moving lines and slashed the number of different suppliers by 80%. By leveraging its buying power LEGO Group was able to cut resin costs by a massive 50%. The speedy success of this initiative and its effect on the finances of the company led to an early sense of optimism – a 'quick win' for the change initiative that increased confidence that they would succeed.

Integrating cost into design

One management team took on the task of encouraging designers to consider costs in their new product decisions. They developed a cost matrix that allowed them to see the costs associated with making changes to established bricks. In this way, designers were encouraged to think about designing to price points, using existing bricks as far as possible and generally reducing complexity. Cutting the number of resins and bricks made the task of simplifying the production cycles easier. Specific moulds were assigned to specific machines and set production cycles established based upon monthly sales schedules. The leadership team assigned decision rights and protocols for changing production schedules so that accountability for changes was clear. Manufacturing of some of LEGO Group's simpler products was outsourced. At the same time, manufacturing was also moved to lower-cost countries. However, by selecting countries close to its main markets it cut its delivery lead times, resulting in a further net saving. Logistics was also rationalized, with providers reduced from 26 to 4, reducing costs by a further 10%.

Partnering with retailers

Finally the marketing team started working more closely with the large retailers. LEGO Group had previously failed to marry up sales forecasts of individual components with production in the supply chain, resulting in high levels of stock-holding. By working more closely with these large retailers and offering customized, big-box products, it was better able to match supply with demand. It was also better able to provide marketing support. There was the added advantage of this partnering providing a greater insight into buyer behaviour and market trends – helping with product development.

The various efficiency gains were forecast to yield savings of over $200 million. As a result, the LEGO Group returned to profitability in 2005 – a rapid turnaround by any standards. Restoring profitability and getting the core business right – product development, sourcing, manufacturing and distribution – allowed JVK and his team to focus once more on creativity and innovation, the elements that would give the company sustainable competitive advantage.

Continued...

Continued from previous page...

Embedding innovation in the organization

Perhaps the most interesting of the changes JVK introduced was the more focused approach to innovation – despite the fact that it was thought to be an inherent strength. Over the decades the LEGO Group has proved to be good at innovation. It was deep in the corporate culture. However, by 2003, customers and retailers felt it had wandered too far away from its original concept of a 'creative building experience' and had to get back to basics while continuing to innovate. As a result, it developed its Innovation Matrix to help identify, staff and coordinate the different types of innovation needed to develop new products over the crisis period. This acted as a guide for restructuring the company and clarifying the specific innovation responsibilities of each department. The company assigned responsibility for innovation to four groups or departments:

> The functional groups – such as sales or manufacturing;
> The Concept Lab – which developed fundamentally new products and play experiences;
> Product and Marketing Development (PMD) – which developed the next generation of existing products and innovated on existing play themes, packaging and marketing campaigns;
> Community, Education and Direction (CED) – which supported customer communities and tapped them for product ideas, managed the retail chain, the online store and educational market offerings and created online play experiences.

It also introduced a cross-functional Executive Innovation Governance Group to coordinate the process of innovation – to decide on the portfolio of innovation projects to be undertaken, delegate authority for each new development across the four groups, to allocate resources and monitor developments.

The four groups or departments influenced eight areas of innovation. The functional groups were given responsibility for innovation in areas where the degree of innovation could vary widely:

1 Core processes – sales, operations and financial planning, performance management.
2 Enabling processes – forecasting, marketing planning.

The Concept Lab (with its high degree of innovation) and PMD (with its medium degree of innovation) were given responsibility for innovation in:

3 Messaging – advertising campaigns, websites.
4 Offerings – products and packaging.
5 Platforms – toys' technology elements.

CED was given responsibility for wide-ranging innovation in:

6 Customer interaction – communities, customer services, including the Creativity Labs.
7 Sales channels – retailers, direct to customers.
8 Business models – revenue, pricing.

Current organization

The company is now organized into four strategic business areas, each represented on the Management Board: Operations (manufacturing, procurement, supply chain planning and distribution, engineering and quality etc.), Marketing Management and Development (organized by geographic areas plus shopper marketing and channel development), Product and Marketing Development (organized by product group plus innovation and consumer marketing) and finally Business Enabling (IT, finance, legal etc.).

Concept and product development now take place primarily within the Product and Marketing Development, based at the company's headquarters in Billund. Its creative core is made up of over 200 'set designers' recruited from around the world, most having trained at art school. Applicants attend a workshop at Billund where they go through a process that allows them to demonstrate their creative skills using LEGO bricks. The company plays great store on learning from the creativity of its customers – children – and how LEGO bricks can be used to play games. It has what it calls 'listening posts' in a number of cities around the world. These take children from different countries and encourage them to try out different combinations with the same LEGO pieces and create worlds of their own, which the company can incorporate into its 'play themes' – often then developed further on the company's website. The Labs try to spot trends in children's play, understand the motivations behind them and translate them into what it means for the company and new product development – effectively trying to systematically understand children's' creativity

Continued...

Continued from previous page...

by observing them at play – also drawing on inputs from customer communities.

Open innovation and crowdsourcing

The story of LEGO MINDSTORMS shows how LEGO Group's policies to encourage innovation have evolved. Strategic partnerships have played an important part in LEGO Group innovations over the years, but more recently the company has also relied on customer involvement to leverage innovation (area 6 in the Innovation Matrix) and has turned to policies of 'open innovation' and 'crowdsourcing'. The story of MINDSTORMS starts in 1984, before digital development really took off, when LEGO entered into a partnership with Media Laboratory at Massachusetts Institute of Technology. By blending physical and virtual worlds into an integrated play universe, the company came up with new products. LEGO Technic Computer Control was the first tangible product of the partnership, launched in 1986. These programmable bricks paved the way for the introduction in 1998 of LEGO MINDSTORMS, integrating robot technology, electric motors and sensors with LEGO bricks and LEGO Technic pieces such as gears, axles and beams. It enabled children to create and program intelligent LEGO models and rapidly became one of the company's best-selling lines.

The programmable brick at the heart of LEGO MINDSTORMS has undergone several updates. LEGO MINDSTORMS NXT, launched in 2006, includes sensors that detect touch, light, sound and ultrasonic waves. It allows children to build and program their own robot so that it can see, hear, speak, feel and move – in as little as just half an hour. The original brick was programmed using proprietary, copyrighted software that ran only on PCs, but in the early 1990s Chris Rogers, a professor at Tufts University in the USA who was using MINDSTORMS for teaching purposes, adapted it to run on Macs using a program produced by a company called National Instruments, later licensing this development back to the LEGO Group. The complexity of these original programs was a key limitation which, curiously, probably explained why over 70% of users were in fact adults. Simplification was a key objective for NXT.

Early in its development, the LEGO Group had decided to use an open innovation approach involving customers. It discovered early in the life of MINDSTORMS that adults like Chris were illegally hacking into their original software and changing it, but, rather than trying to control or restrict this, the LEGO Group decided to facilitate it by making source codes available and allowing hacking as part of the software licence. They decided that it would be impossible to predict how customers might use MINDSTORMS and decided instead to encourage experimentation and innovation. The LEGO Group also facilitated the development of online communities and organized robot competitions. For example, in partnership with a US non-profit organization called FIRST (For Inspiration and Recognition of Science and Technology), the LEGO Group established FIRST LEGO League, a worldwide tournament in which children compete by designing their own robots and participate in a series of scientific and mathematical or technical projects. These vibrant user communities comprised not just customers but also suppliers and partners who earn a living from the product, as well as professors, teachers, consultants and others who used MINDSTORMS as part of their day-to-day job. They acted as promoters and champions of MINDSTORMS. The LEGO Group identified this group as vital to the development of NXT and had a development team member whose sole responsibility was to manage this community and ensure they were listened and responded to. But the LEGO Group went further. It identified 'lead customers' and then involved them – without payment – in the development of NXT. Lead customers were among the most advanced users of MINDSTORMS – each inventing new ways to extend the functionality of the original product – and reflected the large customer base of adults. Chris Rogers was designated a lead customer and he reintroduced the LEGO Group to National Instruments, the company that eventually developed the software platform for NXT. Lead customers also helped develop complimentary products like sensors, software, books and educational programs. NXT has become the best ever selling LEGO product.

LEGO communities

As a result of the success of this open innovation approach, the LEGO Group now has some 40 LEGO Ambassadors in over 20 countries representing user communities. They provide dialogue and initiate activities between the LEGO Group and some 220 communities of adult LEGO users called AFOLs (Adult Fans of LEGO). There is also LEGO Club, with some five million members across 18 global markets. These communities have their own websites, blogs and discussion forums and organize face-to-face meetings on a regular basis. The LEGO Group also organizes events and exhibitions for them and encourages them to get directly involved in product development. It also has a crowdsourcing website to which these communities are encouraged to suggest ideas for new LEGO products. In 2014, four LEGO Ideas products were launched based on user-developed projects uploaded to the LEGO Ideas website.

LEGO philosophy and values

One of the reasons for LEGO Group's continuing popularity is that it has changed with the market. The company continues to invest large sums around the world to understand changes in children's tastes and to explore new product developments based around its mission 'to inspire children

Continued...

Continued from previous page...

to explore and challenge their own creative potential'. Central to the LEGO philosophy are its ideas about what play is about and its importance. It sees LEGO play both as a way of learning structure and something that can stimulate creative thinking. This effectively spells out how children use LEGO building experiences to build a model and play out an adventure with it.

LEGO Group's brand values can be summed up in six words, with explanations taken from the company's website:

Imagination – Curiosity asks 'Why?' and imagines explanations or possibilities (if... then). Playfulness asks 'what if?' and imagines how the ordinary becomes extraordinary, fantasy or fiction. Dreaming it is a first step towards doing it. Free play is how children develop their imagination – the foundation for creativity.

Creativity – Creativity is the ability to come up with ideas and things that are new, surprising and valuable. Systematic creativity is a particular form of creativity that combines logic and reasoning with playfulness and imagination.

Fun – Fun is the happiness we experience when we are fully engaged in something that requires mastery (hard fun), when our abilities are in balance with the challenge at hand and we are making progress towards a goal. Fun is both in the process, and in the completion. Fun is being active together, the thrill of an adventure, the joyful enthusiasm of children and the delight in surprising both yourself and others in what you can do or create.

Learning – Learning is about opportunities to experiment, improvise and discover – expanding our thinking and doing (hands-on, minds-on), helping us see and appreciate multiple perspectives.

Caring – Caring is about the desire to make a positive difference in the lives of children, for our partners, colleagues and the world we find ourselves in, and considering their perspective in everything we do. Going the extra mile for other people, not because we have to, but because it feels right and because we care. Caring is about humility – not thinking less of ourselves, but thinking of ourselves less.

Quality – From a reputation for manufacturing excellence to becoming trusted by all – we believe in quality that speaks for itself and earns us the recommendation of all. For us quality means the challenge of continuous improvement to be the best toy, the best for children and their development and the best to our community and partners.

The LEGO Group is adamant that the business is about a greater purpose than just making money, and that these values stem from its ownership as a privately owned family business. These values are in its DNA. Employees become part of the LEGO 'family' and the company is seen in Denmark almost as a religious group – secretive, with employees always 'on-message' and wary of the outside world (an 'in-group'). JVK has said that he tries to guide things in the company through role modelling and relationships rather than regulation and believes this allows the company to be more 'purposeful'.

Visit the company website at www.lego.com to see some of the features described in this case. The website is more than just a showcase for the company's products; it allows children to play games, enjoy stories and undertake activities, stimulating ideas and creativity. This is important because stories spur children to play games – and the website encourages those games to include LEGO.

Toy sales are heavily influenced by movies and TV series, and LEGO has been able to tie in many of its sets to successful ones like the Harry Potter or Star Wars movies. However, none of these movies or TV series included LEGO figures, so it was always the company that had to make the association – and pay licence fees. In 2013 the company broke new ground with *The LEGO Movie*. It was an instant success in cinemas and subsequently on DVD. With this, the LEGO Group took control of its future, becoming less dependent on other non-LEGO movies that might be popular with children. All at once, the LEGO figures took on a life of their own.

QUESTIONS:

1 Does LEGO have an entrepreneurial architecture? Explain.

2 How did LEGO transform itself?

3 How important was the commitment of top management? How did this show itself?

4 How has LEGO embedded innovation into its DNA?

5 What form does partnering with stakeholders take at LEGO?

6 What lessons do you learn from the development of MINDSTORMS?

7 LEGO is still owned by the Kristiansen family. Looking back to Chapter 17, what lessons has LEGO learned about how to run a family business?

All information in this case study is collected and interpreted by its author and does not represent the opinion of the LEGO Group.

Intrapreneurs and venture teams

Intrapreneurship may be an isolated activity, designed to see a new project into the marketplace, either as part of the existing organization or as a spin-off from it. On the other hand it may be part of a broader strategy to reposition or reinvigorate the whole organization or even reinvent an entire industry. It can be undertaken at many different levels – corporate, divisional, functional or project level. We looked at the character traits of an intrapreneur in Chapter 3. As an individual they will rarely have all the skills necessary to see the project through to completion and at some stage it is likely that they will work as part of a larger team – usually called a venture team. One advantage of using intrapreneurs and venture teams is that it helps organizations to compartmentalize the change agent(s) and reduce risk, while still pursuing commercial opportunities.

Because they might lack the authority of a certain level of senior management, intrapreneurs need a high-level sponsor to protect them when times are difficult or vested interests are upset and to help them unblock the blockages to change as they occur. The sponsor will help secure resources, provide advice and contacts. They will need to nurture and encourage the intrapreneur, particularly early on in the life of the project or when things go wrong, and will need to endorse and create visibility for the project at the appropriate time. Underpinning this must be a good relationship between the sponsor and the intrapreneur. But intrapreneurs still need to be managed. Although they need to have autonomy, since they will inevitably end up breaking the rules they also need to be controlled. We saw in Chapter 12 how this can be achieved using a 'light-touch' and a balance between autonomy and control.

Based on empirical analysis, Kuratko et al. (1990) found that the four most significant enablers of intrapreneurship were senior management support, organizational structure, resources (including time) and reward. To these a subsequent study added tolerance of risk-taking (Hornsby et al., 2002). Without these, intrapreneurship would not flourish. Christensen (1985) expanded on what these meant, saying that the most appropriate enabling organizational structures were corporate venturing, cross-functional new venture teams, internationalization and external networks; the best rewards (other than regular pay and job security) were promotion, expanded job responsibility, autonomy, recognition, free time to work on pet projects and bonuses.

Within this framework there also needs to be a clear vision and plan for a longer time horizon that is effectively communicated to employees and highlights the importance of intrapreneurship (Sathe, 2003). And all these factors should be nested in a supportive culture, which Hisrich (1990) defines as one that develops visions, goals and action plans; takes action and rewards action; encourages suggesting, trying and experimenting; encourages creating and developing regardless of the area; and encourages the taking of responsibility and ownership.

 Practice insight 13 commandments for intrapreneurs

Pinchot (1985) set out 'Ten Commandments' for how intrapreneurs should approach their role:

1   Come to work each day willing to be fired.
2   Get round any orders aimed at stopping their dream.
3   Be prepared to do anything needed to make their project work, regardless of their personal job description.
4   Build up a network of good people who are willing to help.
5   Build a highly motivated but flexible team. Choose the best.

6   Work 'underground' for as long as possible. Once they 'go public' barriers will emerge to restrain them.
7   Be loyal and truthful to their corporate sponsor. In this way they build a solid relationship.
8   Remember it is better to ask for forgiveness than permission.
9   Be true to their goals but realistic in how they can be achieved.
10 Be thoroughly engaged and take ownership of the project – and always persevere, no matter what.

Continued...

Continued from previous page...

To this list Morris and Kuratko (2002) added a further three:

11   Manage expectations and never over-promise – it is better to promise less and deliver more.
12   Show a few early wins with tangible deliverables in order to create confidence. Small wins can evolve into significant accomplishments and develop a momentum for the project that becomes difficult to stop.
13   Set the parameters of what you do and how they do it – in other words, change the rules of the game – so that you start to control as much of the project and how it is evaluated as you can.

Venture teams can take many forms. Their one characteristic is that they are ad hoc. They form and reform to tackle different projects. They may be led by an intrapreneur. However, they may become a group of intrapreneurs working together. Reich (1987) used the term '**collective entrepreneurship**' where individual skills are integrated into a group and the team's capacity to innovate then becomes greater than the sum of individuals. Whatever form a venture team takes, the 'rules' under which it operates are the same as for the intrapreneur.

Team working is commonplace now across most businesses and is particularly valuable in pushing through innovations, whether or not they eventually end up as standalone new ventures. For example, at Google, all staff are involved in product development work in some form. They work in small teams of three or four people. Larger teams get broken down into smaller sub-teams, each working on specific aspects of the bigger project. Each team has a leader that rotates depending on the changing project requirements and most staff work in more than one team.

To be successful the team as a whole needs to have the core competencies required for the project (Stopford and Baden-Fuller, 1994). This is likely to involve managers from a wide range of different disciplines such as engineering, marketing and finance. They will need to balance creativity with project execution. The team also needs to have compatible personal characteristics so that team roles are complementary (see Belbin's Team Roles on page 202), an ability to collaborate and resolve conflict (see Thomas-Kilmann Conflict Modes on page 479) and a strong sense of identity and cohesion (Hofstede's 'in-group' again). As with all teams, these things will take time to build.

 ## Case insight   Boeing

Encouraging intrapreneurship

Boeing, in the USA, has what it calls its Phantom Works project whose stated mission is: 'To be the catalyst of innovation for the Boeing Enterprise'. Within this are various programmes designed to encourage intrapreneurship.

The Chairman's Innovation Initiative (CII) was launched in 2000 to encourage employees to develop new business ideas from company-developed technologies and processes. Since then, hundreds of new ideas for businesses have been submitted, with some notable successes. The Autonomous Underwater Vehicle (AUV) is now a joint venture involving two other companies that undertake undersea surveying for the gas, oil and telecom industries; IntelliBus Network Systems has developed technology for automotive application and AVChem is a chemical management service provider to the aerospace industry.

Another, larger, programme is called CREATE. This focuses on commercializing military applications, perhaps trying to transform existing technologies that have had disappointing results into money spinners. It brings together intrapreneurial teams made up from both Boeing staff and outside staff – for example from suppliers or universities – to work on each project. These teams come together from far-flung locations to 'brainstorm in meetings punctuated by organic meals and hourly exercise like power walking, yoga and racquetball.' Sometimes projects emerge from the CII programme to be worked on further within the CREATE framework.

QUESTION:

1   How do these programmes encourage entrepreneurship within Boeing?

Organizing new venture developments

Once the flow of new venture ideas has started from intrapreneurs and venture teams, the question will arise as to what to do with them, in particular, whether they are kept 'in-house' or 'spun out' in some way. Burgelman (1984a, 1984b) uses the typology shown in Figure 19.6 which suggests that the answer depends on two factors:

> How strategically important the development is for the future of the company;
> How operationally related it is to the core technology and capabilities of the firm.

Generally, the more important the development and the more operationally related and therefore familiar it is, the more it is likely to be kept 'in-house' and ownership maintained. Familiarity is likely to involve innovation that is more incremental and therefore easier to absorb into existing structures. Strategic importance is likely to mean the organization retaining control of the development. Using Burgelman's typologies there are nine organizational options:

1. Direct integration

This is recommended where the development is both strategically important and operationally related, for example when a new product development is integrated into a product range. Changes in the product or process are likely to have an immediate impact on mainstream operations and staff involved are likely to be those involved in day-to-day operations.

2. New product or business department

These remain in-house because of their importance but for some operational reason a new department needs to be established to get the product to market. This might be the case with product extension. It is particularly useful where new products are likely to emerge from day-to-day operations fairly frequently but the product needs to be marketed differently in some way. The department therefore needs strong marketing skills, possibly linking with a number of different departments, divisions or subsidiaries dealing with different market segments.

3. Micro new business departments

Where the strategic importance is uncertain the situation needs to be clarified before a final decision is made. This option keeps the development 'in-house' within a department because of the strong operational relatedness, pending that final decision.

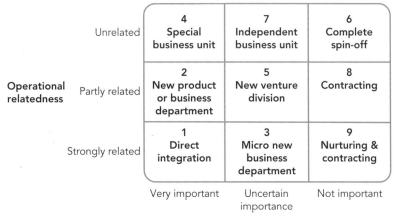

Figure 19.6 Organizing new venture developments

Source: Figure 2:" Organization Designs for Corporate Entrepreneurship" in Burgelman, Robert, 'Designs for Corporate Entrepreneurship in Established Firms', *California Management Review*, Vol. 26, no 3, Spring 1984, pp. 154-166 © 1984 by the Regents of the University of California. Published by the University of California Press.

4. Special business unit

Where operational relatedness is minimal, new staff with different skills may have to be recruited (or key staff identified and extracted from their day-to-day roles) and the unit given greater independence and operational freedom, while the company still retains ownership until decisions are made about its future. Because of its strategic importance it is likely to require strong top-management supervision.

5. New venture division

This should be used to deal with developments that require further investment before their final fate is decided. They could ultimately be spun out or integrated into the mainstream, depending on the final assessment. Because of the uncertainty of its strategic importance, it is also likely to require strong top-management supervision. This very popular organizational form is covered in more detail in the next section.

6. Spin-offs

If there is little or no operational relatedness and the development has little or no strategic importance to the existing business, then it should be completely spun off, with no ownership retained, reflecting the move away from being regarded as a conglomerate, for reasons dealt with in Chapter 16. The most important condition for a spin-off, according to Garvin (1983), is that the core competencies are embodied in skilled labour rather than physical assets because the individuals transfer the knowledge to new firms. He argues that when new market segments develop opportunities for industries in the mature stage of their life cycle these industries are most likely to generate spin-offs because of the information advantage of insiders:

> An industry whose technology is embodied in skilled human capital is a prime candidate for spin-offs, for techniques, designs, and ideas are readily appropriable by individuals and transferable to new firms ... Spin-offs in particular are encouraged by the existence of multiple market segments, information and start-up advantage accruing to members of established firms, readily transferable technologies, and environments in which skilled human capital is the critical factor of production.

There is some ambiguity in the literature about the ownership of spin-offs (e.g. Ito, 1995). Spin-off can be partial or complete, and ownership (or part of it) can be retained by the parent organization. So, for example, in 2006 McDonald's spun out its Chipotle chain of restaurants by making an initial purchase offering (IPO) whereby investors purchased 20% of the company and Chipotle became a public company. Later that same year, McDonald's eliminated its 80% stake by offering to exchange these shares with McDonald's shareholders, leaving Chipotle 100% independent.

Unless the spin-off is a complete sell-off or the result of a management buy-out or buy-in, it is likely that the management will come under some degree of control by the corporate parent. And, as you would expect, the degree of control they exercise is likely to affect the entrepreneurial behaviour of the spin-off. Too much formal control will diminish innovative behaviour and stifle creativity (MacMillan et al., 1986). However, most parent companies might like to at least influence and provide direction to that innovation – and herein lies the balancing act that is part of managing the entrepreneurial organization.

There are three further 'half-way houses':

7. Independent business units

These have greater independence than other formats. Often they are joint ventures with other strategic partners with different degrees of ownership ranging from subsidiary to minority interest and ultimately the unit being spun off completely as factors become more certain. This format allows the unit to focus exclusively on its own activities rather than those of the larger organization. It is also a convenient legal format for knowledge transfer, facilitating learning from external sources. Finally, separation allows associated risks to be mitigated and compartmentalized.

8. Contracting

This is appropriate where the core competencies are embodied in some physical assets or processes that are owned by the company but they are of little strategic importance. These can then be offered for use by other firms on a contract or licence basis.

9. Nurturing and contracting (also called nurtured divestment)

Where the development has commercial value but is not critical to the mainstream business, it might need to be nurtured prior to being offered to other firms under contract or licence. The development is likely to have evolved from mainstream operations.

New venture divisions

A new venture division is a permanent division set up for the purpose of developing innovations, when it is not clear whether the development might be integrated into the core business or spun out. Being part of an existing organization, they allow existing competencies to be leveraged at the same time as maintaining the potential to learn new ones. New venture divisions may operate at corporate or other operating levels within the organization. By separating out the development of innovation, the organization hopes that the division will be able to establish its own leadership, management, structures and culture that encourage and facilitate innovation as a continuous process. Mainstream activities can continue as 'business as usual' in the rest of the organization. Each and any innovation coming out of the division may take the organization in a new strategic direction and therefore how the innovation is integrated into the organization – or indeed sold off or separated out – depends entirely on the nature of the innovation.

Thus, the new venture division may be expected to produce a stream of innovations that include a greater number of bolder breakthroughs than the ad hoc venture team. The scale of each innovation is likely to be greater. Maletz and Nohria (2001) found that placing innovative projects in the organizational 'whitespace' – outside the formal organization with its usual rules and procedures – accelerated natural experimentation. By not imposing the traditional processes of planning, organizing and controlling, projects were nurtured until they were ready for moving over to the regular organization. Managers need to set the boundaries of this whitespace broadly. They need to provide organizational, moral and adequate (but not sufficient) financial support, build enthusiasm among those outside the project and then monitor the project's progress to decide upon the next steps.

This approach is based on the idea of product life cycles (see Chapter 13) and the need for different approaches at different stages in the life cycle. New product/market offerings may need entrepreneurial approaches to management, but those at the mature stage require the secure guiding hand of a strong financial director. The approach recognizes the strength of the portfolio of different product/market offerings, each with its different cash-flow profile, but equally the challenge of the very different management approaches. The new venture division is an attempt to institutionalize the continuous flow of innovations within a large and complex organization that has a diverse portfolio to manage. However, David (1994) speculated that having an intrapreneur involved in developing a new venture, rather than a new venture division, might be more likely to lead to commercial success because the intrapreneur is self-motivated, whereas a new venture manager has their role assigned.

Successful corporate venturing

Corporate venturing is essentially about regenerating an organization by giving it new competencies. Internally, it can manifest itself in various degrees through the structures outlined in this chapter. Not surprisingly, the success of internal corporate venturing does seem to vary from company to company, depending on the conditions encountered. However, it is difficult to assess, not least because of problems of financial measurement. Tidd and Bessant (2009) claim that on average around half of all new ventures survive to become operating divisions and that they will typically achieve profitability within two to three years, with almost half profitable within six years. They also suggest that internal corporate venturing is a less risky strategy for diversification than the acquisition or merger strategies discussed in Chapter 13. They go on to say that four factors characterize firms that are consistently successful at internal corporate venturing. These firms:

> View venturing as a learning process, learning from both success and failure;
> Distinguish between bad decisions and bad luck in failed ventures;
> Set agreed milestones in advance and check progress regularly, redirecting as necessary;
> Are willing to terminate the venture when necessary, rather than making further investments.

They claim that the two main reasons for failure are 'strategic reversal' – when the timescales for the new venture conflict with those of the existing business – and the 'emergency trap' – where internal politicking undermines the venture. To minimize the possibility of both, the venture needs to have a clear purpose and a clear time for delivering against agreed milestones, as well as the operational characteristics outlined in this chapter. The failure of the parent company to define and articulate the role of the venture in this way will just lead to conflict. Indeed, without it the appropriate organizational structure for the venture cannot be selected.

Internal corporate venturing is just one of a number of tools managers have to help in the task of corporate renewal. Strategic alliances/partnership and joint ventures (Chapter 9) and external corporate venturing through acquisitions (Chapter 13) are others. The appropriateness of each of these tools depends on how far the parent company is straying from its core competencies, and in particular how far it is straying from its existing products and markets. Figure 19.7 shows how these tools might be best used in connection to new products and markets. Strategic alliances/ partnership and joint ventures are particularly valuable when the partners have complementary

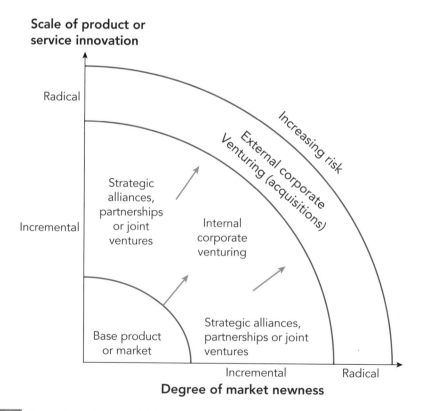

Figure 19.7 Corporate venturing and risk

capabilities to each other, facilitating the development of new products or markets. For the partnership to work, each partner must have strengths related either to the product or market development being undertaken. The degree of relatedness of new products or markets will often determine how far a company is able to move into new products and markets on its own through internal corporate venturing, causing it, in some instances, to have to resort to external corporate venturing. In reality these are not alternatives and many companies use all three tools to push out the envelope of innovation as far as possible.

Case insight   Google (3)

Entrepreneurial architecture

The ubiquitous Google, a US multinational, runs over one million servers in data centres around the world and processes over one billion data requests every day. With a turnover in excess of $30 billion, it employs over 25,000 people worldwide and has its headquarters in Mountain View, California, in a campus called Googleplex. Google's mission is 'to organize the world's information and make it universally accessible and useful'. Founded in 1996 by Larry Page and Sergey Brin when they were both PhD students at Stanford University, Google has moved beyond being a mere search engine. It now has numerous products and services including online productivity software such as Gmail, social networking tools such as Orkut and Google Buz, open source web browser Google Chrome, Picasa photo editing and organization software and Google Talk instant messaging. It also led the development of the Android mobile operating system and in 2010 released an Android phone under its own name called Nexus One. Its many subsidiaries include the equally ubiquitous YouTube. Advertising still generates 99% of Google's revenues.

Google is known for the power of its search engine algorithm and the elegance of its business model that matches text ads to searches. It is known for its innovative culture. Google's spectacular growth has come through organic growth combined with new product development (such as Gmail and Streetview), acquisitions (such as Google Maps and YouTube) and partnerships to take it beyond its core search engine business. It exhibits many of the internal architectural features of an entrepreneurial organization as well as following many widely used entrepreneurial growth strategies.

Culture

Google has an informal corporate culture and regularly features in *Fortune* magazine's list of best companies to work for. It likes to think of itself as still 'small' despite the fact it is anything but. Phrases used to illustrate the culture include 'you can be serious without a suit', 'work should be challenging and challenge should be fun' and 'you can make money without being evil'. It has a tradition of creating April

Fools' Day jokes. This started in 2000 when it 'launched' MentalPlex – Google's ability to read your mind and visualize the search result you want. It tries to add humour to its services. For example, if you ask the search engine for 'the answer to the ultimate question of life the universe and everything' it will actually give you the answer of '42' (Douglas Adams, *The Hitchhiker's Guide to the Galaxy*). Google supports philanthropy. The not-for-profit Google.org creates awareness about climate change, global public health and poverty. After a two-year search, in 2010 Google gave some $10 million to various community projects. In 2011 it gave €1 million to the International Mathematics Olympiad. Google is also a noted supporter of network neutrality.

Structures

Google has a flat, decentralized organization structure. It is highly democratic and tightly interconnected – like the internet itself. It has been said that this comes from the founders' own dislike of authority. All of the staff are involved in product development – almost half of Google's employees work in small teams of three or four people. Larger teams get broken down into smaller sub-teams, each working on specific aspects of the bigger project. Each team has a leader that rotates depending on the changing project requirements. Most staff work in more than one team.

Google encourages creativity in a number of ways. Many companies that work on building successful teams or encouraging creativity are known to facilitate playful environments. The lobby in Googleplex has a piano, lava lamps, old server clusters and a projection of search queries on the wall. The corridors have exercise balls and bicycles. Other playful elements include a slide and a fireman's pole. Recreational facilities – from video games and ping-pong tables to workout rooms – are scattered throughout the campus. It also has functional elements that aid idea generation and dissemination. For example it has enclosed, noise-free projectors that can be left on at all times and employees can automatically email meeting notes to attendees. As one newspaper commented:

'To visit Google's headquarters in Mountain View, California, is to travel to another planet. The natives

Continued...

Continued from previous page...

wander about in T-shirts and shorts, zipping past volley-ball courts and organic-vegetable gardens while holding their open laptops at shoulder height, like waiters' trays. Those laptops are gifts from the company, as is free food, Wi-Fi-enabled commuter buses, healthcare, dry cleaning, gyms, massages and car washes, all designed to keep its employees happy and on campus.' (Ken Auletta, *The Guardian*, 4 March 2010)

Pictures and videos of the campus can be seen on their website. For an alternative view go to http://www.youtube.com/watch?v=43wZNGzXjFg.

Strategies

Marissa Mayer was one of Google's earliest employees. She helped launch over 100 products and features including Gmail and Google Instant before being promoted to head up the newly formed Geographic and Local Services, as VP of Search Products. She developed Google's 9 Principles of Innovation (20 February 2008, www.fastcompany.com):

1   **Innovation, not instant perfection:** Google has a low-cost, try-it-out, experimental approach to new product development. Because of the mould-breaking nature of many of Google's innovations, it wants its products to be launched early and then developed and perfected as it learns what the market wants: 'The beauty of experimenting in this way is that you never get too far from what the market wants. The market pulls you back.' The problem has been that many of these products have been far from perfect when launched.

2   **Ideas come from everywhere:** The company has several technology-enabled solutions to foster creativity among employees. Google Ideas acts as a repository for innovative ideas. It enables employees to share new ideas on products and services and to comment on the ideas of others. The tool also has a feature to rate the ideas submitted on a scale of 0–5, 0 denoting 'Dangerous or harmful if implemented' and 5, 'Great idea! Make it so': 'We have this great internal list where people post new ideas and everyone can go on and see them. It's like a voting pool where you can say how good or bad you think an idea is. Those comments lead to new ideas.'

3   **A licence to pursue your dreams:** Google has built in slack to encourage creativity through its '70/20/10 Rule' – staff spend 70% of their time working on their core projects, 20% on ideas that are closely related to their projects, and 10% on any other ideas they would like to pursue. Half of Google's new product launches have originated from this scheme, including two of Google's best-known products, Gmail and Google News. Google

News was created by Krishna Bharat. After the 9/11 terrorist attacks, he found himself tracking information from several news sites. This caused him to come up with the idea of creating a tool that could trawl through different news sites to cluster the type of information he wanted to read. Google magnified this idea to form a complete news service on their site. Google also encourage rapid low-cost experimentation early in the life of projects so as to continually check feasibility.

4   **Morph projects, don't kill them:** Google believes every idea that makes it to its Labs must have the kernel of a good idea somewhere, even if the market does not respond to it, and the trick is to see how it can be used. And few innovators are able to succeed every time. Consider the case of Lars Rasmussen and Jens Rasmussen, who created Google Maps. The Rasmussen brothers also created Google Wave – billed as tool that would transform online communication and collaboration – which failed spectacularly to live up to its promise to be a social collaborative platform that would replace email and was closed down in 2009. However, Google was positive about learning from such failures, stressing that, while there may not be have been the user adoption they would have liked, the knowledge from the technological developments will not be lost. It viewed Wave almost as an experiment. Indeed the first of Google's Principles of Innovation is to launch early then develop the product into what the market really wants - only sometimes the market really does not want the product.

5   **Share as much information as you can:** Google has its own intranet called MOMMA that allows staff to share information. Every week staff jot down the five or six things they have been working on. These are indexed and made into a giant web page allowing anyone to search to find what staff are working on that week. Google also encourages employees to pay attention to what is happening in the outside world – new ideas from many different sources. For example, it hosts regular 'Tech Talks' with speakers including distinguished researchers from around the world and experts in other fields, such as artists, writers and chefs. Google shows that it values these talks by including the number an employee has hosted in staff performance reviews.

6   **Users, users, users:** Innovations need users. Users generate a marketplace. With a marketplace, a business model will emerge. This is Google's market focus.

7   **Data is apolitical:** Google believes design is a science, not an art, relying on data: 'Run a 1% test (on 1% of the audience) and whichever design does best against the user happiness metrics over a two-week period is the one we launch.'

Continued...

Continued from previous page...

8   **Creativity loves constraints:** Google engineers love a challenge – to be told something cannot be done and then prove you wrong. Google also recognizes the tension between staff freedom and control and the need to have a senior supporter for any project going forward for development. It believes staff need a sponsoring manager to be a 'guardrail' – setting reasonable boundaries within which they can be creative and experiment with ideas. The sponsor and employee must develop an experimentation plan that covers details such as expectations, timelines and resource commitments. Key milestones for the development of the idea are agreed and regular check-in points scheduled where the employee can update the sponsor on the experiment's progress. Sponsors build 'dashboards' to capture the key metrics of their programs. They take any opportunity to share these metrics with their peers and superiors so as to remind them about the value of their program.

9   **You're brilliant? We're hiring:** Google employs only people who it thinks are exceptionally talented. It believes you need to attract the right sort of people to build a successful innovating organization – people with ambition and a high regard for themselves. Then you need to build the team.

Corporate venturing

Google has pursued an aggressive policy of acquisition, focusing mainly on small venture capital backed start-up companies. Google Earth came out of the acquisition of Keyhole in 2004, Google Voice out of the acquisition of Grand Central in 2007. It also purchased YouTube in 2006, DoubleClick in 2007 (which developed technology that allows Google to determine user interests and target advertising), video software maker On2 Technologies and social network Aardvark in 2009 and, in 2010, hardware start-up Agnilux and web-based teleconferencing company Global IP Solutions.

Google also has its own venture capital arm, Google Ventures, which invested in some 30 firms between 2008 and 2010 in areas as diverse as educational software and biotechnology. Its annual budget of $100 million is invested in amounts of between $50,000 and $50 million, and companies are often sold off (for example, the gaming company, Ngmoco) or floated on the stock market (for example the holiday rentals and bed-and-breakfast portal Home Away). This is separate from Google's in-house projects, which in turn has projects as diverse as driver-less cars and new sources of alternative energy.

Google has also partnered with numerous organizations involved in anything from research to advertising. Examples include Sun Microsystems to share and distribute each other's technologies, AOL to enhance each other's video search services, Fox Interactive Media (part of News Corporation) to provide search and advertising on MySpace and GeoEye to provide satellite images for Google Earth.

Future growth

Now into its second decade of life, Google will need to stay nimble if it is not to come up against barriers to its growth. Its core search business is an enormous revenue generator. However, it has been said that, although it is not obvious from its financial results, Google's diversification policy has simply added costs and done little to boost revenues. There is a lack of coherence in Google's product development strategy and a lack of rigour and urgency in pushing through strategies:

'Google's problem has been in focus and execution of strategy. Despite having something like 90% search share in most markets, its fabled search algorithms are being exploited by spammers; despite the huge growth in sales of smartphones using its Android operating software, it hasn't been able to persuade mobile networks or handset makers to give customers the best deals by automatically upgrading their software; and more dangerously it faces an antitrust investigation in Europe over whether it cross-promotes its own services in its search results'. (Charles Arthur, *The Guardian*, 21 February 2011)

In contrast to Apple, which jealously guards its iPhone operating system (iOS), Google's Android system is open access and it is interesting to compare the success of these two very different strategies. Manufacturers can use the operating system free, thereby encouraging the development of a wide range of phones, compared to Apple's limited range. As a result, the Android system now accounts for some 78% of smartphone sales worldwide (mainly by Samsung) compared to Apple's 18% and Windows 3% (figures for first quarter 2015, source: http://www.idc.com/prodserv/smartphone-os-market-share.jsp). Anyone can write apps for Android, compared to Apple's strict control of its apps store. As a result, quality is variable. It has been estimated that Google Play sold $1.3 billion of apps worldwide in 2013 compared to $10 billion by Apple through its App store (http://www.techrepublic.com/article/google-play-v-apple-app-store-the-battle-for-the-mobile-app-market/). However, sales through Google Play do not tell the full story, as Google expects income to come from advertising, capitalizing on a user's location, and also from mobile music service. Unlike Apple's monopoly on apps, Android's open access means any company can set up an app store. Ironically, when Amazon opened what it called the 'Appstore' in 2011 (named despite the best efforts of Apple) it was a closed system, monitored and controlled by Amazon, just like Apple's own App Store.

Continued...

Continued from previous page...

The Android system is one of four main business opportunities facing Google. The second is YouTube, and the success of the business model for it. The third is the web browser Chrome, which has 15% of the market with more than 120 million users. This is being developed into a whole PC operating system that will compete with Microsoft Windows, and Google already has contracts with Acer and Samsung. The fourth opportunity is hosting office services 'in the cloud' – selling computer applications like email and word processing directly to business users.

But the virtual world is changing, and Google's lack of success in getting into the social networking market is an area of weakness often commented on in the press. Millions of Facebook users navigate from page to page according to friends' recommendations rather than the complicated algorithms underpinning the Google search engine. As one newspaper commented: 'Google looks positively ancient to the whiz-kids at Facebook and Twitter. … Google is the establishment now, plugged into government and Wall Street' (*The Sunday Times*, 3 April 2011). Google Buzz has not taken off and sparked a storm in 2010 when it revealed each Gmail user's list of contacts to others. Similarly, Wave, a Twitter-like message platform, has not proved popular.

Leadership

Just to add to these uncertainties, Eric Schmidt, the 10-year CEO of Google, resigned in January 2011 to become executive chair, focusing on 'deals, partnerships, customers and broader business relationships.' Replacing him was co-founder Larry Page, who, it was said, would be leading product development and technology strategy. Schmidt was seen as providing 'adult supervision' to the 'kids' who founded the company, being a key player in growing the business and presenting the company's public face, something Larry Page was not known for.

In a newspaper article it is claimed that media mogul Barry Diller believes the founders, Brin and Page, are 'more than most people … wildly self-possessed'. The same article continues: 'Brin, who is more sociable than Page, has his own quirks. He will often get lost in deep thought and forget about meetings. So focused is he on engineering and maths, he sometimes displays a fundamental innocence about how the world works. … Google's engineering culture brings great virtue, but also a vice. The company often lacks an antenna for sensing how governments, companies and people will react to its constant innovations. YouTube, for example, is brilliantly engineered and hosts around 40% of internet videos – yet it makes no money, because advertisers shy away from user-generated content that is unpredictable and might harm their "friendly" ads' (Ken Auletta, *The Guardian*, 4 March 2010).

Another of the challenges facing Google is how to continue innovating quickly – beating competitors to the market. Brin and Page see this as a battle against bureaucracy and they aim to speed up decision-making by pushing down responsibility for decision-making. Commentators also observed that the management structure needed to be overhauled: 'The solution to Google's growing size is devolution' (*The Sunday Times*, 3 April 2011).

Find the latest news about Google from its corporate website at www.google.com/corporate.

QUESTIONS:

1 In your opinion, has Google lacked focus in the past?

2 Has Google followed the right strategy in getting products to the market quickly at the expense of getting products right the first time?

3 What aspects of Google's architecture encourage corporate entrepreneurship?

4 Compare and contrast once more the culture at Google with that at Apple (Case insight, page 484). Why are there differences? Which do you think has greater sustainability?

5 What do you think of Google's four main business opportunities?

6 Do you think Google should decentralize? If so, suggest how this might be done.

 Practice insight Corporate entrepreneurship audit

The Corporate Entrepreneurship Audit (CEA) is a free interactive diagnostic tool that allows you to assess the organizational architecture of a business and the environment it operates in. Part 1 allows you to assess 100 characteristics of an entrepreneurial organization in the four dimensions of organizational architecture – leadership, culture, structure and strategies. Part 2 allows you to assess the commercial environment the organization faces using 25 criteria. The idea is that the entrepreneurial degree of the architecture can be benchmarked against the degree of competitiveness in the commercial environment.

The CEA can be applied to any level of organization – the organization overall, division, department and so on. It provides a means of analysing potential areas for improvement, rather than a crude pass/fail test. This involves making

Continued...

Continued from previous page...

informed judgements about certain criteria and, as such, is subjective rather than objective. It does not answer the question as to why things are the way they are. Scores are totalled and mapped onto a CEA Results Grid (an example shown below), allowing the company's footprint to be compared against best practice in the industry (if available) and the appropriateness in terms of its environment (which is shown by the red line).

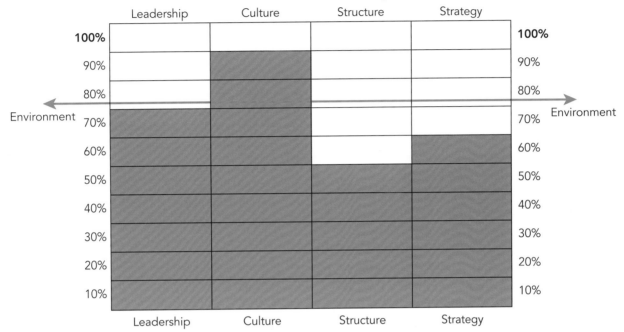

Architectural and environmental profile

An example of a CEA profile

The CEA is a snapshot at a point of time based upon your judgements, and possibly those of others within the organization. Combining it with an understanding of the strategic direction the organization is taking and in the context of its portfolio of operations it gives you the opportunity to really understand not only how entrepreneurial it is, but also how entrepreneurship might be further facilitated and encouraged. The tool should be used as a basis for a detailed discussion about the architecture of the organization – understanding what the underlying causes of the CEA results are and why they are important. It is not meant to be used as a crude good/bad or pass/fail measure. In looking at the detail it uncovers, never forget to also look at the commercial results generated by the organization – whether or not it is performing well in its industry.

The interactive version of CEA is available free of charge at http://www.palgrave.com/companion/Burns-Corporate-Entrepreneurship/student-zone/Corporate-entrepreneurship-audit/.

⊃ Summary

> Corporate entrepreneurship is the term used to describe entrepreneurial behaviour in an established, larger organization – encouraging entrepreneurial intensity. It includes terms such as entrepreneurial transformation, strategic renewal and strategic entrepreneurship. Organizations involved in these processes have been said to exhibit a sustained pattern of entrepreneurial behaviour over time, which in turn has been called an entrepreneurial orientation (EO). These patterns of behaviour are the result of an organizational architecture that is entrepreneurial.

> Corporate venturing (both internal and external) is a major tool for encouraging corporate entrepreneurship and part of an entrepreneurial architecture.

> The four pillars of organizational architecture are leadership, culture, structure and strategies. These can be crafted to make an entrepreneurial architecture which becomes a network of relational contracts within or around an organization – its employees, suppliers, customers and networks.

> Entrepreneurial architecture creates within the organization the knowledge and routines that allow it to respond flexibly to change and opportunity in the very way the entrepreneur does. It is not necessarily based on legal contracts and often only partly specified; therefore it is not easy to copy. It is based upon trust and mutual self-interest. Because it is complex, architecture can be a major source of sustainable competitive advantage.

> An entrepreneurial organization is also a learning organization. They thrive in environments of change, chaos, complexity, competition, uncertainty and even contradiction. Real knowledge means using the wheel of learning to understand the root cause of problems so as to put in place systematic solutions to problems – 'knowing how', 'knwoing why' and doing something about it. This double-loop learning also involves challenging mental models or dominant logic and can be a way of encouraging managers to become more entrepreneurial. The knowledge generated is also tacit and therefore more difficult to copy by competitors.

> There can be no prescriptive blueprint for entrepreneurial architecture. It depends on the environment. It can be sectorally and geographically dependent. It can also vary with the nature of the entrepreneurial intensity. For the organization to work effectively, the organization architecture and the style of management need to be in sync.

> Intrapreneurs and venture teams push through innovations within larger organizations in an entrepreneurial fashion. Intrapreneurship can be an isolated activity, designed to see a new project into the marketplace, either as part of the existing organization or as a spin-off from it, or it can be part of a broader strategy to reposition or reinvigorate the whole organization – or even reinvent an industry.

> The four most significant enablers of intrapreneurship are senior management support, organizational architecture, resources (including time) and tolerance of risk-taking. Without these, intrapreneurship will not flourish.

> Internal corporate venturing, strategic alliances/partnership, joint ventures and external corporate venturing through acquisitions are tools that allow companies to move into new products and new markets, ultimately extending their core competencies.

> What to do with a new development depends on how strategically important and how operationally related it is to the business. The more important the development and the more operationally related it is, the more likely it is to be kept in-house. If there is little or no operational relatedness and the development has little or no strategic importance to the existing business, then it should be completely spun off, with no ownership retained.

> New venture divisions are designed to deal with projects that require further investment before decisions about their future are taken.

✓ Activities

1 List the types of organizations and market sectors or environments that face high degrees of turbulence. Select a particularly turbulent sector and research how the organizations within it are organized and the success, or otherwise, they have in dealing with it.

2 Select two organizations, one that you would describe as entrepreneurial, and the other that you would describe as bureaucratic. Using the OCAI as your framework, write a brief report contrasting their cultures.

3 Select an industry where a hierarchical, bureaucratic structure should be the best way to organize. Select a company in this industry and investigate its organizational structure. Write a brief report outlining its structures and explain why it conforms or otherwise to your expectations, taking into account the success of the business.

4 Select a large company spin-out. Research and write a brief report outlining its history and describe its success or failure. Explain the lessons to be learned from this.

5 Find an example of external corporate venturing that has proved either successful or unsuccessful and analyse why. Write a brief report outlining the lessons to be learned from this.

6 Use the Corporate Entrepreneurship Audit (CEA) to assess the organizational architecture of a selected business and the environment it operates in. Write a report on the organization.

🗨 Group discussion topics

1 Can large firms also be entrepreneurial? Is it in their interests to be so? What pressures are there for them not to be entrepreneurial?

2 What is corporate entrepreneurship?

3 What do you understand by the term 'entrepreneurial architecture' and how can it be shaped?

4 Why are relationships rather than legal contracts important within architecture and how can architecture give a firm sustainable competitive advantage?

5 How do you spread learning and knowledge in an organization?

6 Should an entrepreneur find building an entrepreneurial architecture easier than other people?

7 Can a traditional manager become an intrapreneur? What are the blocks or barriers and how can they be overcome?

8 Will an entrepreneurial architecture succeed in all economic or geographic environments? Explain.

9 Are any national cultures likely to mitigate against establishing corporate entrepreneurship? Explain.

10 In what circumstances might a bureaucratic organization be more successful than an entrepreneurial organization?

11 What is corporate venturing?

12 Why are operational relatedness and strategic importance important determinants of what to do with new ventures?

13 Is external corporate venturing any more than an excuse for buying up successful small firms?

14 What needs to be in place for corporate venturing to work?

15 Why should a large company want to spin out a new venture with good opportunities?

16 The number of people leaving to set up their own business is a sign of a 'real' entrepreneurial organization. Discuss.

17 Does there always have to be at least one intrapreneur in a venture team?

18 What are the advantages of having a new venture division? What are the risks?

19 How does a new venture division differ from a R&D department?

20 Why should new product/service ideas not simply be integrated into an existing business?

21 Why should a large company want to spin out a new venture with good opportunities?

☛ References

Antoncic, B. (2006) 'Intrapreneurship: A Comparative Structural Equation Modelling Study', *Industrial Management and Data Systems*, 137(3).

Argyris, C., and Schön, D. (1978) Organizational Learning: A Theory of Action Perspective, Reading, Mass: Addison Wesley.

Birkinshaw, J.M. (2003) 'The Paradox of Corporate Entrepreneurship', *Strategy and Business*, 30, Spring.

Brizek, M.G. (2014) 'Explaining Corporate Entrepreneurship: A Contemporary Literature Investigation', *Journal of Management and Marketing Research*, 14.

Burgelman, R.A. (1983) 'A Process Model of Internal Corporate Venturing in the Diversified Major Firm', *Administrative Science Quarterly*, 28.

Burgelman, R.A. (1984a) 'Designs for Corporate Entrepreneurship in Established Firms', *California Management Review*, 26(3).

Burgelman, R.A. (1984b) 'Managing the Internal Corporate Venturing Process', *Sloan Management Review*, Winter.

Burns, P. (2005) *Corporate Entrepreneurship: Building an Entrepreneurial Organization*, Basingstoke: Palgrave Macmillan.

Chesbrough, H.W. (2002) 'Making Sense of Corporate Venture Capital', *Harvard Business Review*, March.

Christensen, C.M. (1997) *The Innovator's Dilemma: When New Technologies Cause Great Firms to Fail*, Boston: Harvard Business School Press.

Christensen, K.S. (1985) 'Enabling Intrapreneurship: The Case of a Knowledge-Intensive Industrial Company', *European Journal of Innovation Management*, 8(3).

Covin, J.G. and Slevin, D.P. (1989) 'Strategic Management of Small Firms in Hostile and Benign Environments', *Strategic Management Journal*, 10(1).

Covin, G.C. and Wales, W.J. (2012) 'The Measurement of Entrepreneurial Orientation', *Entrepreneurship Theory and Practice*, 36(4).

David, B.L. (1994) 'How Internal Venture Groups Innovate', *Research Technology Management*, March – April.

Dell, M. (1999) *Direct from Dell, Strategies that Revolutionized an Industry*, New York: Harper.

Dess, G.G., Lumpkin, G.T. and McGee, J.E. (1999) 'Linking Corporate Entrepreneurship to Strategy, Structure, and Process: Suggested Research Directions', *Entrepreneurship Theory and Practice*, 23(3).

Drucker, P.F. (1985) *Innovation and Entrepreneurship: Practice and Principles*, London: Heinemann.

Foster, R.N. and Kaplan, S. (2001) *Creative Destruction: Why Companies that are Built to Last Underperform the Market – and How to Successfully Transform Them*, New York: Currency Doubleday.

Galbraith, J. (1982) 'Designing the Innovating Organization', *Organizational Dynamics*, Winter.

Garvin, D.A. (1983) 'Spin-offs and New Firm Formation Process', *California Management Review*, 25(2).

Ghoshal, S. and Bartlett, C.A. (1997) *The Individualised Corporation: A Fundamentally New Approach to Management*, New York: Harper Business.

Grant, R.M. (2010) *Contemporary Strategic Analysis*, 7th edn, Chichester: Wiley.

Hamel, G. (1999) 'Bringing Silicon Valley Inside', *Harvard Business Review*, September.

Handy, C. (1995) *Gods of Management*, London: Souvenir Press.

Hisrich, R. D. (1990) 'Entrepreneurship/Intrapreneurship', *American Psychologist*, 45(2).

Hisrich, R.D. and Peters, M.P. (1992) *Entrepreneurship: Starting, Developing and Managing a New Enterprise*, Homewood, IL: Irwin.

Hornsby, J.S., Naffziger, D.W., Kuratko, D.F. and Montagno, R.V. (1993) 'An Interactive Model of the Corporate Entrepreneurship Process', *Entrepreneurship, Theory and Practice*, 17(2).

Ito, K. (1995) 'Japanese Spin-offs and New Firm Formation Process', *California Management Review*, 25(2).

Kanter, R.M. (1982) 'The Middle Manager as Innovator', *Harvard Business Review*, July.

Kanter, R.M. (1989) *When Giants Learn to Dance: Mastering the Challenge of Strategy, Management and Careers in the 1990s*, New York: Simon & Schuster.

Kay, J. (1993) *Foundations of Corporate Success*, Oxford: Oxford University Press.

Kim, D.H. (1993) 'The Link between Individual and Organizational Learning', *Sloan Management Review*, Fall.

Kuratko, D. and Audretsch, D. (2009) 'Strategic Entrepreneurship: Exploring Different Perspectives of an Emerging Concept', *Entrepreneurship Theory and Practice*, 33.

Kuratko, D.F. and Audretsch, D.B. (2013) 'Clarifying the Domains of Corporate Entrepreneurship', *International Entrepreneurship and Management Journal*, 9(3).

Kuratko, D.F., Montagno, R.V. and Hornsby, J.S. (1990) 'Developing an Intrapreneurial Assessment Instrument for an Effective Corporate Entrepreneurial Environment', *Strategic Management Journal*, 11(1).

Lumpkin, G.T. and Dess, G. (1996). 'Clarifying the Entrepreneurial Orientation Construct and Linking It to Performance', *Academy of Management Review*, 21(1).

MacMillan, I.C., Block, Z. and Narashima, P.N.S. (1986) 'Corporate Venturing: Alternatives, Obstacles Encountered, and Experience Effects', *Journal of Business Venturing*, 1(2).

Maletz, M.C. and Nohria, N. (2001) 'Managing in the Whitespace', *Harvard Business Review*, 2/01.

Markoczy, L. (1994) 'Modes of Organizational Learning: Institutional Change and Hungarian Joint Ventures', *International Studies of Management and Organizations*, 24, December.

Miller, A. (1996) *Strategic Management*, Maidenhead: Irwin/McGraw-Hill.

Morris, M., Kuratko, D. and Covin, J. (2008) *Corporate Entrepreneurship and Innovation*, Mason, OH: Thomson/South-Western.

Morris, M.H. and Kuratko, D.F. (2002) *Corporate Entrepreneurship: Entrepreneurial Development within Organizations*, Fort Worth: Harcourt College Publishers.

Morse, C.W. (1986) 'The Delusion of Intrapreneurship', *Long Range Planning*, 19(2).

Nadler, D., Gerstein, M.C. and Shaw, R.B. (1992) *Organizational Architecture: Designs for Changing Organizations*, San Francisco: Jossey-Bass.

Naisbitt, J. (1994) *Global Paradox: The Bigger the World Economy, the more Powerful its Smaller Players*, London: BCA.

Pedler, M., Burgoyne, J.G. and Boydell, T. (1991) *The Learning Company: A Strategy for Sustainable Development*, London: McGraw-Hill.

Peters, T. and Waterman, R. (1982) *In Search of Excellence: Lessons from America's Best-Run Companies*, New York: Harper Row.

Pinchot, G. (1985) *Intrapreneuring: Why You Don't Have to Leave the Company to Become an Entrepreneur*, New York: Harper Row.

Quinn, R.E. and Rohrbaugh, J. (1983) 'A Spatial Model of Effectiveness Criteria: Towards a Competing Values Approach to Organizational Analysis', *Management Science*, 29.

Rauch, A., Wiklund, J., Lumpkin, G.T. and Frese, M. (2009) 'Entrepreneurial Orientation and Business Performance: An Assessment of Past Research and Suggestions for the Future', *Entrepreneurship Theory & Practice*, 33(3).

Reich, R. (1987) 'Entrepreneurship Reconsidered: The Team As Hero', *Harvard Business Review*, 65(3), May/June.

Sathe, V. (2003) *Corporate Entrepreneurship: Top Managers and New Business Creation*, Cambridge: Cambridge University Press.

Senge, P. (1992) 'Mental Models', *Planning Review*, March–April.

Sharma, P, and Chrisman, J. (1999) 'Toward a Reconciliation of the Definitional Issues in the Field of Corporate Entrepreneurship', *Entrepreneurship Theory and Practice*, 23(3).

Stopford, J.M. and Baden-Fuller, C.W.F. (1994) 'Creating Corporate Entrepreneurship', *Strategic Management Journal*, 15(7).

Tidd, J. and Bessant, J. (2009) *Managing Innovation: Integrating Technological, Market and Organizational Change*, Chichester: John Wiley.

Timmons, J.A. (1999) *New Venture Creation: Entrepreneurship for the 21st Century*, Singapore: Irwin/McGraw Hill.

Tushman, M.L. and O'Reilly, C.A. (1996) 'Ambidextrous Organizations: Managing Evolutionary and Revolutionary Change', *California Management Review*, 38(4).

Wales, W. Gupta, V. and Mousa, F. (2013) 'Empirical Research on Entrepreneurial Orientation: An Assessment and Suggestions for Future Research', *International Small Business Journal*, 31(4).

Wilpert, B. (1995) 'Organizational Behaviour', *Annual Review of Psychology*, 46, January.

Zahra, S.A. (1996) 'Governance, Ownership, and Corporate Entrepreneurship: The Moderating Role of Industry Technological Opportunities', *Academy of Management Journal*, 39(6).

 www.palgrave.com/Burns-Entrepreneurship-And-Small-Business-4e

Go online to access additional teaching and learning resources for this chapter on the companion website. Click here in the ebook to complete a multiple choice revision quiz for this chapter.

MEET THE ENTREPRENEURS

Part 4: Maturity

The final video instalments focus on organizations as they enter maturity, and the lessons learned along the way. Selyn is an interesting case, as it is a family business. Learn here about how generational succession is being managed with Sandra's daughter, Selyna, joining the team. AJ and Ross talk about the atmosphere in larger and corporate businesses. All the interviewees reflect on the leadership responsibilities of the entrepreneur and offer advice to new prospective entrepreneurs.

AJ Asver

Cassandra Stavrou

John Loughton

Ross Beerman

Selyna Peiris

Scott Cupit

Stefan Botha

Questions

> What are the benefits that Selyna sees in joining the family business? How difficult has it been for her?
> Can larger and corporate organizations still be entrepreneurial? How is innovation encouraged?
> Are the entrepreneurs still entrepreneurs? Or are they entrepreneurial leaders? What is the difference?

The full videos of each entrepreneur's story are available on the companion website.

SUBJECT INDEX

Author index

Quotes Index